The Criminology of Deviant Women

Freda Adler *Rutgers, The State University of New Jersey*

Rita James Simon *University of Illinois*

Houghton Mifflin Company • Boston

Dallas   Geneva, Illinois   Hopewell, New Jersey   Palo Alto   London

For Jill, Mark, and Nancy FA
For Julian and for David, Judith, and Daniel RJS

Printed in the U.S.A.
Library of Congress Catalog Card Number: 78-069555
ISBN: 0-395-26719-6

Contents

Preface

This text-reader presents a collection of essays on women in crime. In some cases, original writings are included because our search of the literature did not turn up useful material. The aim of the editors has been to deal with significant contemporary issues in female criminality and their solution by the criminal justice system, with an historical and cross-cultural emphasis representing all the theoretical schools of thought.

The book is intended for use in a variety of courses in sociology, psychology, criminology, and criminal justice, as well as in the area of women's studies. Our purpose has been to assemble as exhaustive and representative a collection as the field permits. Of the five major sections into which the volume is divided, the first contains material of historical interest and the last contains essays that view the problem across different societies and cultures. In the three middle sections, we examine the types of crimes women commit, the treatment they receive in the courts, and their behavior and adjustment in prison. Some excerpts, such as the selections from Ward, Simon, and Nagel and Weitzman, emphasize rates and types of deviance. Others, such as the excerpts from Millett, Burkhart, and Singer, focus on individual characteristics, case histories, or legal issues.

We purposely tried to select pieces that had appeared in different types of publications and were likely to have reached different audiences. Law review articles are thus represented along with excerpts from social science and criminology journals and monographs with more clinical or practical perspectives.

Not all of the pieces contain empirical data. Some are speculative, perhaps raising more questions than providing answers. For example, the excerpts on property offenses tell us little about the types of women or the contexts in which they steal, defraud, or embezzle. On some topics, such as women in prison and prostitution, we were confronted with an abundance of riches, and the limitations of space determined the number of selections we could include. On others, we found a dearth of material—for example, empirical studies of how women are treated in the courts. This latter condition was more common than the former. To deal with it, we contacted scholars who have worked in some of the areas: white-collar crime and political terrorism are examples here. We asked these contributors to prepare essays that considered women's participation in those activities.

In the United States the decade of the seventies may be remembered as the decade of the women's movement and, perhaps, as the decade in which an amendment was added to the Constitution guaranteeing women equal rights. It is difficult to remember, writing today, that it was as recently as 15 years ago that Barbara Wootton called our attention to the fact that

> no serious attempt has yet been made to explain the remarkable facts of the sex ratio in detected criminality; for the scale of the sex differential far outranks all the other tracts (except that of age in the case of indictable offenses) which have been supposed to distinguish the delinquent from the nondelinquent population. It seems to be one of those facts which escapes notice by virtue of its very conspicuousness. It is surely, to say the least, very odd that half the population should be apparently immune to the criminogenic factors which lead to the downfall of so significant a proportion of the other half. Equally odd is it, too, that although the criminological experience of different countries varies considerably, nevertheless the sex differential remains.[1]

Certainly since at least the beginning of this decade the topic of women and crime has not been neglected. Some half dozen monographs have appeared, numerous conferences have been held, debates have been aired, all seeking to explain why more women are engaging in crime at this time than in any recent period, or in any period for which arrest statistics are available. In our view, interest in the topics, women in crime and how women fare in the criminal justice system, has not yet peaked. We expect much more research will be done on the subject over the next few years. As those studies and ideas appear, new collections will be needed to provide both teacher and student with a guide through the field. For now, we think this volume performs that function.

The authors and the publisher are grateful for the assistance of those who made professional reviews of the manuscript. Reviews at different stages of manuscript development provided valuable assistance in shaping the final form of the book. These reviewers, to whom we give thanks, were Sarah L. Boggs, University of Missouri; Lois B. DeFleur, Washington State University; Kenneth E. Magoon, Santa Rosa Junior College (California); Lynn T. Osborne, University of Nevada, Las Vegas; and Kenneth Polk, University of Oregon.

F. A.
R. J. S.

1. Lady Barbara Wootton, "A Magistrate in Search of the Causes of Crimes," *Crime and the Criminal Law,* 1963, pp. 6–8.

Part one
The female offender: a historical perspective

Female criminal offenders have traditionally been underrepresented in reports by the mass media and in studies by the scientific community. Both groups have chosen to view female crime as either nonexistent or individual aberration deserving little further study. Women have been a relatively insignificant subset of male research populations, viewed more often as an embarrassment than a threat to society.[1] This state of affairs has been changing, however. As women increasingly assume societal roles previously performed by men, their illegitimate as well as their legitimate activities are becoming subjects for study. The purpose of Part One is to provide some relatively recent historical views on female offenders. The selections are taken from studies done in the United States and Europe in the nineteenth and early and mid-twentieth centuries.

The first scientist of the nineteenth century to inquire into female criminality was the French mathematician and astronomer Quetelet. In studies of the numerical constancy of voluntary acts, including crime, Quetelet posited that the physical strength of women was half that of men and attempted to demonstrate that female violent criminality approximated male violent criminality also by half. His work stimulated debates about free will and determinism that had influence on criminal legislation.[2] In Italy in the mid-1800s, Lombroso began measuring the bones of human skeletons from Turin prisons, claiming to find that criminal women had certain physical abnormalities. He sought to categorize those abnormalities that would predestine women to be criminals from birth, asserting that females had innate propensities to certain types of crimes. A selection from Lombroso's work is included here.[3]

In the start of the twentieth century, researchers continued to measure physical characteristics, attempting to make connections between the basic motivations of female offenders and biologic disorders or peculiarities.[4] In 1916, however, there was a shift in orientation in the work of Bonger, a Dutchman influenced by Marx, who introduced arguments for the social and economic determination of female crime. The Bonger selection considers the lower incidence of female compared with male crime and proposes that women's "smaller criminality is like the health of a hothouse plant; it is due not to innate qualities, but to the hothouse which protects it from harmful influences. If the lives of women were like those of men their criminality would hardly differ at all as to quantity, though perhaps somewhat as to quality."[5] Also influential early in the twentieth century was Freudian thinking, which suggested that women might commit crimes out of a sense of deficiency.[6]

In 1934, in a landmark criminological study reflecting advances in

social science method, the Gluecks in the United States attempted to
see the female offender in light of a complex of biological and environmental determinants.[7] The Gluecks monitored a group of women
offenders in a Massachusetts prison, taking into account inmate behavior and attitudes before, during, and after incarceration. Their conclusions were distinctly sociological; among them was a proposition
that change in the social milieu from which female criminals came
would be necessary for change in the incidence of female crime. A
selection from the Gluecks' study is included.

In 1950, Pollak, sharing with the Gluecks a care for data, advanced
a thesis that viewed the female criminal in light of her total integration
as a human being in society. Pollak proposed there was a "masked
character" to female crime that kept it from being properly recorded
or otherwise taken into statistical account.[8] Although arguing that
women commit certain crimes as a result of their social conditioning,
Pollak continued to maintain that these crimes were limited by the
psychological and physiological characteristics inherent in female
anatomy. The influence of Freud on Pollak's conception is evidenced
in the selection included.

Although not reported in the studies here, it is worthy of note that
in the 1940s, when American women moved into the jobs and duties
vacated by men who had gone to war, they also moved into crime in
unprecedented numbers. Between 1940 and 1945, crimes by women
almost doubled. After the war, they declined. A similar trend was
experienced in Great Britain. Little attention was called to it.

In the 1960s, there was new interest in the issue of female criminality. One important attempt to review the situation in historical
and comparative perspective was made by Mannheim, who focused on
the discriminatory nature of much of the penal legislation in the
United States and Europe and attempted to assess the impact such
legislation was likely to have on female offenders.[9] A selection from
his more general study on the sociology of crime is included. Following
it is a review by Klein that, while also sociological, assumes a markedly different perspective and shows the influence of the women's
movement of the 1960s.[10]

One of the by-products of that movement was the attention paid to
women's criminal behavior, which led to fundamental questions about
how it had thus far been studied. Klein criticized criminologists for
their sexist, racist, and class biases, suggesting that future research
break with former assumptions and start with a new feminist orientation. In Klein's view, sexist oppression is one of the major causes of
women's participation in crime. In the selections included, Klein and
Kress address problems of contemporary studies and point out that

increases in arrest rates of women may reflect the politics of law enforcement, changing perceptions of female offenders by the criminal justice system, and changing realities of women's economic position.[11]

In the past, women were associated with and prosecuted for certain classes of crimes almost exclusively: witchcraft, poisoning, infanticide, adultery, incest. In more recent times, female criminality has been concentrated in shoplifting, prostitution, and "passion" murders of husbands and boyfriends. The kinds of crimes engaged in seem to reflect behavior appropriate to women's roles in society. In light of our work, selections from which open and close this part, it seems reasonable to expect that the participation of women in crime will increase and broaden with the increased and broadened opportunities afforded women in all ways in society. Yet the pattern of that participation is not clear. The studies of women offenders bequeathed by the past, involved as they were with concerns particular to the intellectual debates of their times, are not very helpful in predicting the future. Studies of the present are plagued by lack of data. There is a need at present for testable hypotheses relevant to the nature of contemporary society and for research designs that take into account some of the difficulties of data collection in this area.

If there is a lesson to be learned from past attempts to explain women's criminal behavior, it may be simply to guard against letting any one view of the nature of women or society determine what is studied and how. The study of women in crime offers a chance not only to study the behavior of women in the context of criminal justice but to probe some of the taken-for-granted workings of our systems of choice and opportunity, a task worthy of multiple assumptions and approaches.

Notes

1. We should, however, take note of Mannheim's admonition:

   [I]t is a distortion of the truth to maintain that the subject has been entirely ignored. Female scholars such as Pauline Tarnowsky, . . . Johanna C. Hudig, the American sociologist Mabel A. Elliott, and English psychiatrists Grace W. Pailthorpe, Hedwig Schwarz and Phyllis Epps, and the psychiatric social worker Moya Woodside—a list which is by no means complete—have made valuable contributions to it . . .

   Hermann Mannheim, *Comparative Criminology*, Vol. II, Boston: Houghton Mifflin, 1965, p. 691. Mannheim might have added Melanie Klein and her daughter Melitta Schmideberg to the list.
2. A. Quetelet, *Sur l'homme et le developpement de ses facultes; sa de physique sociale*, Paris: Bachelier, 1835.
3. Caesar Lombroso and William Ferrero, *The Female Offender*, New York, the Wisdom Library, 1958, pp. 2–3.
4. Edith R. Spaulding, "The Results of Mental and Physical Examinations of Four

Hundred Women Offenders—with Particular Reference to Their Treatment During Commitment, *Journal of the American Institute of Criminal Law and Criminology*, 5 (1914–1915): 704–717.

5. William A. Bonger, *Criminality and Economic Conditions*, Boston: Little, Brown, 1916, p. 478.

6. Frances Keller, "Psychological and Environmental Study of Women Criminals," *The American Journal of Sociology*, 5 (1900): 527–543, 671–682. W. I. Thomas, *The Unadjusted Girl*, New York: Harper & Row, 1967 (originally published in 1923). J. Weidensall, *The Mentality of the Criminal Woman*, Baltimore: Warwick & York, 1916. M. R. Fernald, M. H. S. Hayes, and A. Dawley, *A Study of Women Delinquents in New York State*, New York: Century, 1920.

7. Eleanor and Sheldon Glueck, *Five Hundred Delinquent Women*, New York, Alfred A. Knopf, 1934.

8. Otto Pollak, *The Criminality of Women*, University of Pennsylvania Press, 1950.

9. Mannheim, *Comparative Criminology*.

10. Dorie Klein, "The Etiology of Female Crime: A Review of the Literature," *Issues in Criminology*, 8 (Fall 1973): 3–30.

11. Dorie Klein and June Kress, "Any Woman's Blues," *Crime and Social Justice* (Spring-Summer 1976).

1 A Look to the Future

Rita James Simon

Traditionally people who have written about female criminality have usually adopted one of two positions, which they cling to with great tenacity. One group perceives women who commit crimes as poor, benighted creatures who are victims of male oppression and of society's indifference and disinterest. The other group perceives women offenders as being more cunning and more crafty than men; as having learned how to commit crimes that are more difficult to detect; and as counting on the chivalry of male law enforcement officials to avoid arrest, conviction, and imprisonment.

Those who have adopted the first position do not argue with what the official statistics show about the prevalence of women in crime; namely, that women account for only a small proportion of all crimes and that they are generally underrepresented considering their proportion in the population. But those who have adopted the second position assert in no uncertain terms that the statistics distort rather than describe the real picture of the amount of crime that women commit. Rather, they argue that if male victims, police, prosecutors, and judges would forego their chivalrous behavior, the proportion of women arrested and convicted would be vastly increased.

The position that leaders of the women's movement have taken on this issue seems to fall in between these two perspectives. The leaders of the women's movement claim that women are prepared to lose or to give up whatever preferential treatment the double standard has allowed them. Some of the women who are at the helm of the women's movement are prepared to trade protective labor laws for equal job opportunities and equal pay; just as they are prepared to trade preferential and paternalistic treatment at the hands of law enforcement officials for due process in civil and criminal procedures. The women's movement also claims that women are no more moral, or conforming, or law abiding than are men and that women should neither bask

From *The Contemporary Woman and Crime* by Rita James Simon. National Institute of Mental Health, Washington, D.C., 1975. Pp. 84–88.

in their superiority over men nor feel trapped into wearing a mask of morality and goodness.

If one of the consequences of sexual equality should turn out to be higher crime rates among women, the women's movement would not feel that its efforts have all been in vain. The contemporary leadership might then do what the leaderships of earlier women's movements have done after their immediate goals were realized—turn their efforts and energies to treating other important social ills that affect both men and women.

In the few years since the contemporary women's movement has crystallized as a social movement distinct and independent of either the civil rights or the new left movements, it has attracted a good deal of attention. It would be reasonable to assume, therefore, that it has had some effect on the psyche, the consciousness, and the self-perceptions of many women in American society. But the extent to which it has motivated those women to act outside the law in order to gain financial rewards, vengeance, or power is still too early to assess.

In reviewing demographic data, it was found that proportionally there are more women in the labor force today than there have ever been in American history (during periods of peace) and that married women with children are holding full-time jobs in higher proportions than ever before. More women are also attending college today than in the past.

But, when women's participation in the labor force was examined in more detail, it was found that there has not been a big increase in the proportion of women who are employed in the higher status occupations. Indeed, higher proportions of women today are represented in the traditionally female occupations than at any previous time. Before women's involvement in crime can be expected to match their representation in society, women must have the opportunities for committing those crimes. Those opportunities will come primarily through their positions in the labor force. It is not enough that almost one-half of all women work; they must also have those types of jobs that will provide them with the opportunities to commit offenses that are important enough to report. Even if we assume that women's psyche and motivations are no different from men's in their willingness to commit crimes, unless their opportunities expand, it is unlikely that women's crime rates will show a big increase.

Although some law enforcement officials may be moved, out of respect for the rhetoric of the women's movement, to give women the equality some say they want, it is much more likely that they will do so if police, prosecutors, and judges are confronted with much greater numbers of women who are accused of defrauding, embezzling, and stealing significant amounts of money and property.

What the statistics show about the proportion of women in crime in 1974 is that there are more women involved today than at any time since the end of World War II, and probably before that. But the increase has been in certain types of offenses—forgery, fraud, and embezzlement—not in crimes of violence or in the traditional female crimes, such as prostitution and child abuse.

As of 1974, 31 percent of all persons arrested for major larceny were women; 33 percent of all persons arrested for fraud and embezzlement were women;

and 29 percent of all persons arrested for forgery were women. These proportions are not 50 percent but they are much higher (by at least twice) than they are for any other offenses committed by women. If present trends continue, in 20 years women will probably be involved in white-collar crimes in a proportion commensurate with their representation in the society. The fact that female arrests have increased for these offenses and not for all offenses is consistent both with the opportunity theory and with the presence of a sizable women's movement.

Unfortunately, judicial statistics are not available in a form that permits long-range analysis. The Federal statistics show that there has been an increase in the proportion of women who have been convicted of white-collar offenses from 1963 to the present time. They are useful, at least, in that they are consistent with the arrest data.

But the California data on the proportion of women convicted between 1960 and 1972 do not show that the increase in convictions has followed the increase in arrests for the same types of offenses. Although there has been an increase of 31 percent in the proportion of women convicted for all types of crimes from 1962 to 1972, that increase has been due solely to the higher conviction rates for violent offenses. A comparison of the likelihood of a man's being convicted for a given offense over that of a woman's being convicted shows that for every 12 men who are convicted there will be 10 women convicted.

The prison statistics do not show a growing proportion of women being sentenced; rather a better case can be made for the opposite outcome. When decisions about whether to grant paroles are considered, women do not appear to have any great advantages. Once parole is granted, however, they are somewhat more likely than men to stay out of prison. The two types of exceptions are women with prior commitments and women with a history of drug usage.

Interviews were conducted recently with approximately 30 criminal trial court judges and prosecuting attorneys in four large cities in the midwest: Chicago, St. Louis, Milwaukee, and Indianapolis. These experts in law enforcement were asked to describe their experiences with female offenders and, more specifically, to characterize the types of offenses with which women are usually charged, the personal and socioeconomic characteristics of those women, and to explain whether they treat female defendants differently than they do male defendants. In addition, these judges and attorneys were asked whether they have observed changes in the number and types of women who appear in their courtroom today in contrast to those who appeared 5 or 6 years ago—differences in types of offenses with which women are charged, their roles in those offenses, their demeanor, and their personal and socioeconomic characteristics.

In the last part of the interview, the respondents were asked to think ahead several years and to tell us whether they expected any changes in the number and types of women who were likely to appear in their courtroom; changes in the types of offenses for which they would be charged; changes in the roles that they would be likely to perform during the criminal acts; changes in their demeanor, personal appearances, and social characteristics. Finally, they were asked whether they thought they would treat women defendants differently in the future than they have in the past or the present.

The profile that can be drawn of the women whom these officials see most often is that of black, lower class, poorly educated women with several children. The crimes with which they are charged most often are shoplifting and other forms of theft, drug use, and crimes of passion that involve killing a husband, a lover, or the "other woman." Both the judges and prosecutors emphasized that women tend not to be the managers, the organizers, or the planners of most of the crimes with which they are involved. They do not see, nor do they expect to see, any "Ma Barkers" in their courtrooms. Most often the women are accomplices who get involved because of their commitment to a boyfriend or a husband. In drugs, they tend to be the users, rarely the pushers, and not the organizers. The women, they claim, are not connected with organized crime.

When asked about their treatment of women, more than half of the judges said that they do treat women more leniently and more gently than they do men; that they are more inclined to recommend probation rather than imprisonment; and that if they sentence a woman, it is usually for a shorter time than for a man. Only a small proportion of the judges said that they were less likely to convict the women. The point at which they differentiate in favor of the women is at the time of passing sentence. The statistics describing the proportion of women at the arrest, conviction, and sentencing stages support the judges' observations.

Practically none of the respondents thought that they were seeing more women in the courtroom today, or that the women they were seeing were different from the women they had seen 5 or 6 years ago, with the exception that more women of all classes were coming in as drug users.

As far as the future is concerned, most of the respondents did not anticipate any real difference, either in the numbers or types of women they would see; in the types of offenses with which they would be charged; in the roles they would play; in their demeanor in the courtroom; or in the respondents' treatment of the women. Most of the respondents still expected that they would be easier on the women when it came to passing sentence. Of those few who did anticipate differences, all thought that more women would be involved in financial or white-collar crimes than in the past because more women would be in the labor force, and, therefore, would have more opportunities to embezzle and defraud. Only three of the respondents mentioned the women's movement as a possible source of influence. Those who did felt that the women's liberation movement gave women a greater sense of independence and a belief that they could do anything that a man could do: If men can commit all types of crimes, so can women.

2 Criminals and Prostitutes

Caesar Lombroso and William Ferrero

Among the most ridiculous of the prohibitions obtaining in Italy, or rather in the Italian bureaucracy, which is certainly not the first in Europe, is the absolute impossibility of measuring, studying, or photographing the worst criminals once they have been condemned.

So long as there is a presumption of innocence, so long as these persons are only suspected or accused, one can discredit them in every way, and hold them up to publicity by recording their answers to their judges.

But once it is admitted beyond question that they are reprobates, once the prison doors have closed for good upon them—oh, then they become sacred; and woe to him who touches, woe to him who studies them!

Consumptive patients, pregnant women, may be manipulated, even to their hurt, by thousands of students for the good of science; but criminals—Heaven forefend!

When one of the writers wished to publish photographs of male criminals in his "Uomo Delinquente," he was driven to the German prison "album"; and the difficulties thrown in his way by the Italian authorities were doubled in the case of female offenders and prostitutes, whose sense of shame it was considered necessary to respect in every way.

In Russian prisons Madame Tarnowsky was afforded every facility, and after making a complete study of the body and mind of the delinquents, she forwarded us their photographs.

1. Female criminals

We will first take 5 homicides, of whom the two first have the true type of their class.

From *The Female Offender* by Caesar Lombroso and William Ferrero. T. Fisher Unwin, London, 1895. Pp. 88–93.

The first, aged 40, killed her husband with reiterated blows of a hatchet, while he was skimming the milk, then threw his body into a recess under the stairs, and during the night fled with the family money and her own trinkets. She was arrested a week later and confessed her crime. This woman was remarkable for the asymmetry of her face; her nose was hollowed out, her ears projecting, her brows more fully developed than is usual in a woman, her jaw enormous with a lemurian appendix.

No. 2, aged 60. Was constantly ill-treated by her husband, whom she finally joined with her son in strangling, hanging him afterwards so as to favour the idea of suicide.

Here again we have asymmetry of the face, breadth of jaw, enormous frontal sinuses, numerous wrinkles, a hollowed-out nose, a very thin upper lip, with deep-set eyes wide apart, and wild in expression.

No. 3, aged 21. Was married against her will, ill-treated by her husband, whom she killed, after a night altercation, with a hatchet while he slept.

In her we find only a demi-type. Her ears stand out, she has big jaws and cheek-bones, and very black hair, besides other anomalies which do not show in the photograph, such as gigantic canine teeth and dwarf incisors.

No. 4, aged 44. Strangled her husband by agreement with her lover, and threw him into a ditch. She denied her crime. Hollowed-out nose, black hair, deep-set eyes, big jaw. Demi-type.

No. 5, aged 50. A peasant. She killed her brother at supper, so as to inherit from him. She denied her guilt persistently. Was condemned, together with her hired accomplices, to twenty years' penal servitude. She had black hair, grey eyes, diasthema of the teeth, a cleft palate, precocious and profound wrinkles, thin lips, and a crooked face. Demi-type.

Passing now to poisoners, we find the following to be the most remarkable out of twenty-three:—

No. 6, aged 36. Of a rich family, with an epileptic mother, and a father addicted to alcohol. She poisoned her husband with arsenic after sixteen years of married life. Nose hollowed out and club-shaped, large jaws and ears, squint eyes, weak reflex action of left patella. She confessed nothing. Character resolute and devout. Type.

No. 7, aged 34. Also poisoned her husband with arsenic; also denied her guilt. An enormous under jaw. On close examination displayed gigantic incisors, and down so long as to resemble a beard. Demi-type.

No. 8, aged 64. Poisoned her son's wife and the mother of the same. Deep wrinkles, ears much higher than the level of the brows. A singularity is the size of the neck-muscles, exaggerated as in oxen. Thin lips, and a cleft palate. Demi-type.

No. 9, a peasant, aged 47. Poisoned her daughter-in-law because of inability to work. Fluent in speech, never confessed the crime. Asymmetrical face, oblique eyes (a feature, however, which might be ethnological), huge, unequal jaws, small ears, nose club-shaped and hollowed out. On a near view she displayed big canine teeth, and a great parieto-occipital depression. Her children like her grandfather were epileptic. Type.

No. 10, aged 20. Attempted to poison her husband, an old man, who treated her ill. Darwin's lobule was enormously developed in her ear, as may be seen even from the photograph. Hydrocephalic forehead, nose hollowed out and club-shaped, large, unequal jaws, eyes and hair black. Type.

No. 11, aged 35. Poisoned her daughter-in-law, for an unknown reason, with some medicine. Fair hair, asymmetrical face, overlapping teeth. Guilt confessed.

Now we come to the incendiaries, of whom there are 10, four of a striking type.

No. 12. Set fire to the village palisades to revenge herself on some malignant gossips. A large nose, thin lips, lowering expression, with incisors replaced by molars. Type.

No. 13, aged 63. Set fire to a neighbour's house because of a quarrel about money. Denied the offence. Defective teeth, big, feline eyes, very large ears, asymmetry of eyebrows. Demi-type.

No. 14, aged 25. Set fire, in concert with her husband, to a neighbour's house out of revenge. She accused her husband and denied her own complicity. Many wrinkles, projecting parietal bones, big ears and jaws, low forehead. Demi-type.

No. 15, aged 41. A peasant. Set fire to nine houses out of revenge; pretended to have done it while drunk. Very ferocious countenance, asymmetrical, with enormous ears and jaws. Sullen, very black eyes, fair hair, diasthema of the incisors, narrow arch of palate. Type.

No. 16, aged 45. Convicted more than once as a receiver, who had twice hidden convicts in her house. Crooked face and teeth, hollowed-out nose, large, prognathous face, enormous superciliary arches.

Out of 9 infanticides, 3 presented the salient type.

No. 17, aged 60. Killed a newborn babe to save her daughter's reputation. Cut the infant into pieces and hid it. Confessed nothing. A strong character. Many wrinkles, enormous cheek-bones, ears, and frontal sinuses. Right side of face higher than the left. Forehead receding as in savages. Canine teeth gigantic and badly placed. Sunken eyes, brownish-green in colour.

No. 18, aged 60. Assisted her daughter to drown the latter's newborn child; then afterwards accused the daughter, in consequence of a quarrel about a lover whom the two women shared.

Physiognomy relatively good, in spite of the subject's licentious tendencies which age could not eradicate. Nothing anomalous beyond the hollowed-out nose and very wrinkled skin. The face, however, though it does not appear so in the photograph, was really asymmetrical, and the woman had the cleft palate and fleshy lips which betray a luxurious disposition.

No. 19, aged 19, the domestic servant of a priest, had a child, of which the father was a stable-boy. Driven out of every house, she killed her child by beating it on the frozen ground. Crooked face, a hollowed-out nose, big ears and jaws, incisors overlapping.

Finally comes a female brigand—No. 20, aged 25. Was the companion in arms of a band of brigands, one of whom was her lover. A hollowed-out nose, large jaws and ears, a virile physiognomy; and in her also there is congenital division of the palate.

Many may find that after all these faces are not horrible, and I agree, so far, that they appear infinitely less repulsive when compared with corresponding classes among the men whose portraits were reproduced by us from the "Atlas de L'Homme Criminel." Among some of the females there is even a ray of beauty, as in Nos. 19 and 20; but when this beauty exists it is much more virile than feminine.

3 The Criminality of Women

William A. Bonger

In order to give an idea of [the] extent and nature [of the criminality of women] we must begin with some statistics.

Germany, 1886–1895[1]

CRIMES	TO 100,000 PERSONS OVER 12 OF THE SAME SEX, THERE WAS AN AVERAGE NUMBER OF PERSONS SENTENCED OF:	
	Men	Women
Simple theft	352.49	132.25
Aggravated theft	57.95	7.19
Embezzlement	80.97	18.25
Robbery and extortion	2.44	0.10
Receiving stolen goods	28.21	16.33
Fraud	88.06	19.50
Forgery	18.78	3.75
Perjury	6.83	2.31
Threats	46.36	2.65
Procuration	5.21	7.23
Rape, etc.	20.63	0.15
Insults	204.32	69.52
Domiciliary trespass	90.38	12.25
Malicious mischief	80.37	4.85
Arson	2.43	0.54
Violence and threats against officials	77.45	5.90
Minor assaults	118.30	12.71
Serious assaults	256.86	25.99
Murder	0.56	0.13
Homicide	0.75	0.15
Crimes in general	1847.03	380.42

From *Criminality and Economic Conditions* by William A. Bonger. Little, Brown, Boston, 1916. Pp. 463–474, 478.

This table shows that women have a general criminality from 4 to 5 times less than that of men. The figure for women exceeds that for men in the case of one crime only, procuration; for the others it is smaller, and for some very small (*e.g.* assaults, assassination, etc.). The following table gives an idea still clearer and more detailed.

Germany, 1896[1]

	NUMBER OF PERSONS CONVICTED TO 100,000 OF SAME SEX.		NUMBER OF WOMEN CONVICTED TO EACH 100 MEN CONVICTED.
CRIMES	Men	Women	
Abandonment of children	0.02	0.1	800.0
Abortion	0.4	1.7	437.3
Procuration	6.0	9.2	167.7
Receiving stolen goods (repeated recidivism)	0.07	0.1	158.3
Receiving stolen goods (simple)	26.5	13.1	53.9
Simple theft	274.6	100.8	40.1
Perjury	3.1	1.2	38.7
Insults	223.7	76.5	34.2
Simple theft (repeated recidivism)	51.7	14.4	30.5
Homicide	0.5	0.1	22.0
Arson	2.2	0.5	21.8
Embezzlement	85.6	17.6	20.6
Fraud	101.7	20.4	20.1
Crimes in general	2177.07	388.9	17.9
Extortion	3.0	0.4	14.3
Aggravated theft	45.0	5.6	13.5
Domiciliary trespass	103.8	12.3	11.8
Minor assaults	138.3	15.4	11.1
Aggravated theft (repeated recidivism)	14.4	1.2	9.1
Serious assaults	448.4	32.8	7.3
Violence, etc. against officials	88.3	5.6	6.3
Violence and threats	60.7	3.6	5.9
Malicious mischief	93.6	5.4	5.8
Robbery	2.4	0.07	2.9
Crimes against morals upon children	25.3	0.2	0.7

.   .   .

England and Wales, 1893–1894[2]

	NUMBER OF WOMEN TO 100 PERSONS SENTENCED	
CRIMES	1893	1894
Abortion and failure to report birth	91	86
Kidnapping and cruelty to children	70	57
Counterfeiting, etc.	18	21
Malicious mischief	15	20
Crimes against property without violence	19	19
Other crimes	16	16
Crimes of violence against persons	11	13
Robbery and extortion	10	11
Forgery	9	8
Domiciliary trespass, etc.	3	4
Sexual crimes	4	3

These statistics show, then, that in England also the criminality of women is not as great as that of men. However there is great divergence in the crimes taken separately.

.   .   .

[We turn next to France, Italy, and the Netherlands.]

France, 1881–1900 (persons accused)[3]

	1881–1885		1886–1890		1891–1895		1896–1900	
	Average annual number	%	Average annual number	%	Average annual number	%	Average annual number	%
Before the assizes								
Men	3,767	86	3,589	85	3,389	84	2,900	85
Women	615	14	646	15	631	16	500	15
Before the correctional tribunals								
Men	162,573	86	172,162	86	179,194	86	165,586	86
Women	26,330	14	27,719	14	29,992	14	28,049	14

.   .   .

Italy, 1894–1895[4]

	NUMBER OF WOMEN CONVICTED							
	Justices of the peace		Correctional tribunals		Assizes		Total	
YEARS	Number	%	Number	%	Number	%	Number	%
1884	46,683	18.31	——	——	304	6.00	——	——
1885	48,063	17.58	——	——	304	5.91	——	——
1886	51,199	18.23	——	——	297	6.38	——	——
1887	45,598	17.58	4,690	9.30	265	5.11	50,553	16.05
1888	49,125	17.38	4,482	8.56	290	5.81	53,897	15.86
1889	53,690	18.38	4,910	9.08	272	5.68	58,872[5]	16.78
1890	——	——	——	——	——	——	23,984	18.29
1891							26,182	18.23
1892							25,638	17.21
1893							22,959	16.21
1894							26,274	17.34
1895							28,502	16.96

The following table shows us to what extent the women are guilty of the different crimes:

Italy, 1891–1895[6]

	To 100 sentenced for each offense there were:	
Offenses	Men	Women
Infanticide	7.70	92.30
Procuration	19.11	80.89
Abortion	21.65	78.35
Defamation	53.70	46.30
Insults	54.78	45.22
Offenses against morals and order of the family	58.27	41.73
Abandonment of children, abuse of means of correction	62.85	37.15
Simple theft	75.63	24.37
Fraud in commerce and industry	79.46	20.54
Offenses in general	82.81	17.19
Minor assaults	83.32	16.68
Corruption of minors and offenses against decency	84.80	15.20
Fraud, etc.	85.74	14.26
Aggravated theft	88.77	11.23
Threats	90.68	9.32
Rebellion and insults to public officials	90.95	9.05
Forgery	92.49	7.51
Serious assaults	93.61	6.39
Murder	93.91	6.09
Counterfeit money	95.02	4.98
Homicide	96.74	3.26
Offenses against public order	97.70	2.30
Robbery, etc.	97.77	2.23
Rape, etc.	99.04	0.96

.   .   .

Finally some figures for the Netherlands:

Netherlands, 1896–1900[7]

	Number sentenced			
	Men		Women	
Years	Number	%	Number	%
1896	13,964	89.6	1,625	10.4
1897	14,483	90.0	1,613	10.0
1898	14,018	89.5	1,646	10.5
1899	13,928	90.5	1,463	9.5
1900	13,234	91.3	1,254	8.7

Women participate in the different crimes in the following proportions:

Netherlands, 1901[8]

	To 100 sentenced there were:	
CRIMES	Men	Women
Debauch of a minor (as principal or accessory)	6.2	93.8
Simple insults	64.9	35.1
Simple theft	79.0	21.0
Fraud	80.0	20.0
Offenses against public decency	81.8	18.2
Homicide	89.5	10.5
Aggravated theft	90.5	9.5
Embezzlement	91.1	8.9
Receiving stolen goods	91.8	8.2
Forgery	92.1	7.9
Assault	93.5	6.5
Serious assault	94.7	5.3
Malicious mischief	95.5	4.5
Mendicity and vagrancy	96.5	3.5
Assaults upon officials	97.3	2.7
Domiciliary trespass	98.1	1.9
Rebellion	98.7	1.3

The whole population being divided in 1901 into 50.5% women and 49.5% men, the figures given above make the criminality of woman appear a little greater than it really is.

Here, then, are the facts, which may be reduced to this, that in all the countries named the criminality of women is much less than that of men. However, it is greater than we should suppose from the figures, since almost all the figures (except those for France) have to do with persons convicted, and acquittal is much more common in the case of women than in that of men. We have already given the figures for Germany in regard to this matter. In England the percentage of convictions is 82% for men and 79% for women.[9]

In France the differences are still greater:

France, 1881–1890 (assizes)[10]

	PERCENTAGE OF ACQUITTALS			
SEX	1881–1885	1886–1890	1891–1895	1896–1900
Men	25	25	26	28
Women	45	47	50	52

. . .

These figures lead to the presumption that in other countries also women are more apt to be acquitted than men.

Other reasons why the criminality of women seems smaller than it really is are the following: As is shown by the statistics cited, the offenses of which women are most often guilty are also those which it is most difficult to discover, namely those committed without violence. Then, those who have been injured are less likely to bring a complaint against a woman than against a man.[11] But even when we take account of all these things, the criminality of women remains much smaller than that of men. This may be explained as follows:

First. An examination of the tables shows that women participate less in the crimes which require strength or courage. The first cause is to be found in the fact, then, that the average woman of our time has less strength and courage than the average man, and consequently commits on the average fewer crimes than he.

Second. It is clear that women take small part in sexual crimes (for procuration is not a sexual crime but an economic one), which is to be explained by the fact that most sexual crimes cannot, from their nature, be committed by women. Another reason is that the rôle of women in the sexual life (and thus in the criminal sexual life) is rather passive than active.

Third. The small part played by women in economic crimes committed because of poverty or even of greed, is explained by prostitution, which generally yields greater and more certain returns than crime, and avoids the risk of prison.

Fourth. A comparison of the criminal statistics of different countries has not much value for the different reasons already given. . . . Only when the figures are very different may one draw a conclusion from them. A comparison of the tables brings out the fact that the criminality of women does not differ much in the countries named. However, when we fix our attention upon the crimes and misdemeanors more or less grave in the Italian statistics (assizes and correctional tribunals) we discover that there is a considerable difference between England, for example, on the one side, and Italy on the other. While the former country shows about 12% (offenses tried on indictment) and 23% (offenses tried summarily) of women among those convicted, the figures are 5 to 6% (assizes) and about 9% (corr. trib.) in the latter country. This difference shows that the direction in which the principal reason for woman's small part in crime must be sought is in her social position. This differs less from that of the man in England than in Italy. However, there are figures much more significant than those I have just cited. Between 1893 and 1899 the percentage of convicts in prison in Scotland was between 36 and 37.[12] In Denmark from 1876 to 1885 about 26% of the convicts were women.[13] It is an incontestable fact that Denmark and Scotland are countries where the social position of women approaches most closely that of men. Let us set in opposition to this now a country like Algeria where the life of woman is entirely different. It appears that there between 1881 and 1900 3% of those arraigned before the assizes were women, and 4% of those arraigned before the correctional tribunals.[14]

An examination of the criminality of women in the different parts of the same country, Germany for example, shows that the highest figures for female criminality are furnished by the great cities and the countries most developed economically.

Germany, 1897–1898[15]

	PERCENTAGE OF WOMEN AMONG THE CONVICTS	
CITIES OR COUNTRIES	1897	1898
Berlin	27.8	27.6
Hamburg	24.7	25.3
Saxony	22.0	21.7
Prussia	21.8	21.5
Germany as a whole	20.6	20.3
Bavaria	18.6	18.6
Alsace-Lorraine	17.3	18.1
Wurtemberg	16.7	15.8
Hesse	15.2	14.4
Baden	13.8	12.1

As regards England, Morrison says that of misdemeanors 25% are committed by women in London (Metropolitan Police District), and 33% in Manchester; while women commit only 10% of the misdemeanors in Surrey, and about 14% in Lancashire.[16] The high percentages come then in the places where the social position of woman is most nearly equal to that of man.

.   .   .

In looking the whole field over I see nothing to justify the opinion that the less criminal character of women indicates a higher morality, whether innate or acquired. The consequences of her manner of life, in so far as they are harmful to the formation of character, are probably counterbalanced by those which are favorable. Her smaller criminality is like the health of a hothouse plant; it is due not to innate qualities, but to the hothouse which protects it from harmful influences. If the life of women were like that of men their criminality would hardly differ at all as to quantity, though perhaps somewhat as to quality.

Notes

1. "Kriminalstatistik f. d. Jahr 1896", Erläuterungen, II, p. 33.
   [NOTE TO THE AMERICAN EDITION: The "Kriminalstatistik für das Jahr 1903" contains very important data bearing upon the period 1882–1902, with regard to feminine criminality in Germany.]
2. "Judicial Statistics, England and Wales, Criminal Statistics, 1894", p. 19.
3. "Rapport au président de la république française sur l'administration de la justice criminelle de 1881–1900", pp. xix, cxvi.
4. For the years 1884–1889 taken from the "Statistica giudiziaria penale per l'anno 1889", and for the years following from the "Notizie complementari alle statistiche giudiziarie penali degli anni 1890–95".
5. The fact that a new penal code went into effect in 1890 makes a noticeable change in the total figures.
6. *Op. cit.*, p. xxxvii.
7. Taken from "de Gerechtelijke Statistiek van het Koningrijk der Nederlanden", 1896–1899, and "de Crimineele Statistiek," 1900. For more detailed information upon the Netherlands see *Loosjes*, "Bijdrage tot de studie van de criminaliteit der vrouw", pp. 8–30.

8. Figured from "Krimineele statistiek over het jaar 1901".

9. "Criminal Statistics, 1899", p. 27. See in the same place the reason for thinking that the figures quoted for the number of women acquitted are too small. *Morrison* says that in England one woman in four is acquitted, and one man in six. ("Juvenile Offenders", p. 46.)

10. "Rapport", etc., p. xxxiv.

11. See *Colajanni*, "Sociologia criminale", II, p. 83; *Földes, op. cit.* 630, 631; and *Morrison, op. cit.*, p. 46.

12. "Criminal Statistics of England and Wales, 1899", p. 54.

13. *Loosjes, op. cit.*, p. 50.

14. Figured from Tables 23 and 24 of the "Rapport au président de la république française", etc.

    [NOTE TO THE AMERICAN EDITION: Wadler tells us that in Servia the percentage of feminine criminality is between 3.71 (1893) and 6.25 (1903); in Greece, about 2 (1899–1902); in Bulgaria, about 3.2 (1899–1906); in Bosnia and Herzegovina, between 5.07 (1899) and 6.69 (1902) (*op. cit.*, pp. 94, 102–104). In Rumania, Minovici tells us, the percentage is 2.42 (1874–1890).]

15. "Kriminalstatistik für das Jahr 1898", II, p. 73.

16. "Judicial Statistics, England and Wales, Criminal Statistics, 1894", p. 19.

4 Five Hundred Delinquent Women

Eleanor and Sheldon Glueck

When we consider the family background of our women, we should rather marvel that a sizable fraction of them, by one influence or another, abandoned their misbehaviour, than that so many of them continued their delinquencies. They were born and bred in households in which poverty or near-poverty and its attendant evils and miseries were the common lot. Their fathers were inefficient, irregular workers who, even when fortunate enough to be employed, could hardly support their abnormally large families. As often as not their mothers had to neglect their household duties and responsibilities in order to supplement a meagre family income. And the homes of many of the families were unattractive, crowded, and set in unwholesome neighbourhoods, where children could hardly be happy or develop healthily.

But more serious than the physical milieu in which these girls were reared was the unfortunate psychologic atmosphere of their homes. Their parents were on the whole of low mentality and in large measure illiterate. There was misunderstanding and friction arising from the conflict of cultures between foreign-born parents and native-born children. The moral standards of a great many of these families were low, and delinquency and criminality were frequent among them. The conjugal relations of the parents were in many instances inharmonious, thus rendering the homes unfit for the proper rearing of children. To this must be added the fact that the disciplinary practices of the parents were often unintelligent or worse. As if these evils were not yet sufficient, an abnormally high proportion of the homes were early broken by the death, desertion, or divorce of the parents.

The women are themselves on the whole a sorry lot. Burdened with feeblemindedness, psychopathic personality, and marked emotional instability, a large proportion of them found it difficult to survive by legitimate means.

From *Five Hundred Delinquent Women* by Eleanor and Sheldon Glueck. Alfred A. Knopf, New York, 1934. Pp. 299–303, 308–310, 317–324, 331–332. Reprinted by permission of Sheldon Glueck.

Many suffered from serious physical ailments or handicaps in childhood and adolescence, and the great majority were venereally diseased before they were twenty-one years old. In educational achievement they fell considerably below the average, as to both length of schooling and competence as students. Few had the advantage of vocational guidance or training. Too early in life most of them were thrown into the industrial maelstrom to sink or swim. Employed largely as factory hands or domestics, their competency as workers ranged as a rule from only fair to poor; their status was essentially that of irregular workers; their earnings were miserably low.

Most of them left their homes at an early age, and many had undesirable or abnormal environmental experiences: over a fourth of them had been in foster-homes, for example, and many had experienced commitment to institutions, often for long periods. Throughout childhood and adolescence their leisure time was largely frittered away or absorbed in harmful pursuits and endangered by companionships with the vicious and criminal with whom they frequented unwholesome places of recreation. During childhood half of our girls did not attend church regularly, and during adolescence three fourths of them were neglectful of their religious duties.

The great majority of them misbehaved in childhood or showed other evidences of abnormal development that should have been recognized as danger-signals of probable maladjustment in adult life. At least a fourth of them had "bunked out," run away from home, or truanted before they were fourteen; over a third were "stubborn children," a fourth had indulged in illicit sex practices, a seventh stole. During adolescence these misconduct trends became more widespread and marked, reaching a point where ninety-five per cent of the girls had vicious habits. Two fifths of them ran away from home or truanted from school, over four fifths indulged in illicit sex practices, a fourth had become excessive alcoholics.

Illicit sexual indulgence was the chief form of their adolescent and early-adult misbehaviour. All but two per cent of our women had been sexually irregular prior to their commitment to the Reformatory, and over seven tenths of those who were married had indulged in illicit sex acts previous to marriage. Sexual malpractices were of long duration. In fact, a fifth of the girls had their first unconventional sex experience before they were fifteen, and their average age at such time was but seventeen years. Illicit sexuality was practically simultaneous with the onset of other forms of delinquency and with unstabilizing environmental experiences (such as leaving the parental roof at an early age). Four fifths of the girls entered upon unconventional sexual practices voluntarily. In the vast majority of cases these erotic adventures were shared with casual acquaintances or "pick-ups." *Over half the entire group of five hundred women had illegitimate pregnancies, and a third gave birth to children out of wedlock.*

Over half of the women had been prostitutes before their admission to the Reformatory. Over a fifth of these were sixteen or younger when they began to commercialize themselves. Prostitution was usually of long duration, almost four years on the average, though a fourth of the women had been prostitutes for less than a year.

The high proportion of delinquency and criminality among our women prior to their arrest and conviction for the offence which sent them to the Reformatory is evidenced in the fact that only five of them had never previously come into conflict with the law or misconducted themselves in any way which might have resulted in arrest. The predominating offence of these women was unlawful sexuality in over half the cases, immorality and stealing in a tenth, illicit sexuality and drunkenness in a sixth, and stealing (uncomplicated by other forms of misconduct) in five per cent.

Sentence to the Reformatory was not, in the vast majority of the cases, the first experience which our women had with legal authorities and institutions. Two thirds of them had been previously arrested, the average number of arrests being three and two thirds, the average frequency of arrests one in every ten months. Over a fourth of the women were first taken into custody for sex offences, a fifth for "stubbornness," a tenth for crimes against property, a tenth for drunkenness. Considering *all* their prior arrests, a third of them were for drunkenness, a fourth for offences involving chastity, a seventh for property crimes, the remainder for various other offences.

Prior to admission to the Reformatory our women had already been subjected to the entire gamut of punitive and correctional devices. Thus, seven tenths of the three hundred and thirty-three women who had been previously arrested were at one time or another placed on probation, almost half had been committed to peno-correctional institutions, a sixth had been fined, a fourth had had the charges against them placed on file. A third of all their arrests had resulted in probation, over a fourth in imprisonment, six per cent in fines, a tenth in filing, and another tenth in a finding of "not guilty."

The poor calibre of our delinquent women is further reflected in other aspects of their careers. *Thus, the women who married prior to commitment (half the group) had done so with a casualness and irresponsibility which could only end in tragedy.* Most of them married "pick-ups"—often vicious and criminal wasters and irregular, inefficient workers—with whom they had scraped acquaintance. On an average the girls were between nineteen and twenty when they married—younger than girls of the general population—an eighth of them being under fifteen, and two fifths between sixteen and eighteen. *A third of the marriages were "forced"—that is, entered into because the girls were illicitly pregnant.*

Obviously such liaisons could not work out satisfactorily. In over four fifths of the cases, the young wives neglected their family responsibilities, and in three fourths the husbands were likewise irresponsible. *Conjugal relations were poor in four fifths of the marriages; and three fourths of the unions were broken by desertion, separation, or divorce*—a much higher proportion than is found in the general population. A fifth of the marriages were disrupted within six months after they had been contracted. By a reasonable standard, only two of the three hundred and one marriages could be deemed entirely successful. The reasons for the failure of the marital ventures of our women involved not only their own shortcomings but those of their husbands. In addition to the latter's incapacity as bread-winners, the majority of them were vicious and criminal. Another reason for the early wreck of the matrimonial ship lies in the fact that in over half the cases the newly-married couples did not set up independent households, but went to live with relatives.

That the unfortunate social heritage of these families will in large measure be handed down to subsequent generations may be inferred from the fact that in at least four fifths of the cases the attitude of our women toward their children was one of indifference if not of actual hostility.

Conduct within a year of commitment. When attention is focused on the year immediately preceding the sentence of our women to the Reformatory, *the conclusion is inevitable that in most of the aspects of their lives they had become progressively worse.* Thus, in not even a tenth of the cases were husband and wife actually living together when the women were committed, and less than half of these compatibly; and a seventh of the group were living with lovers when arrested. So also the moral atmosphere of the homes within a year of commitment of the offenders was poor in three fourths of the cases; the physical condition of their homes was unwholesome in two thirds; the neighbourhood conditions were vicious in seven tenths.

The economic status of the group, if not worse than previously, had certainly not improved within a year of their commitment. Thus, seven tenths of them were unemployed when arrested for the offence which resulted in sentence to the Reformatory, three fourths were in "marginal" economic circumstances (that is, unable to save anything or hanging on the ragged edge of poverty), and one seventh were entirely dependent for support on social agencies or on relatives.

Their use of leisure time and their habits had also become definitely worse as reflected in their activities during the year preceding commitment. All but two per cent of the women were indulging in harmful spare-time pursuits, all but ten per cent were habituées of unwholesome places of recreation, and all but three per cent consorted with immoral or criminalistic persons. The proportion of those failing to attend church had also grown greater. Only two of the entire group of five hundred women had no harmful habits or did not misconduct themselves in any way. All but three per cent were carrying on illicit sexual practices, two fifths drank to excess, a fourth were runaways or truants, a fifth stole, five per cent used drugs, others expressed themselves in still different forms of antisocial behaviour. All this spells a marked rise in unwholesome and socially harmful conduct and attitude as compared with the years preceding the last year before their commitment to the Reformatory.

This swarm of defective, diseased, antisocial misfits, then, comprises the human material which a reformatory and a parole system are required by society to transform into wholesome, decent, law-abiding citizens! Is it not a miracle that a proportion of them were actually rehabilitated?

.   .   .

The fundamental forces involved in the manifestations of human and social maladjustment that we call crime are the deeply anchored and pervasive socio-economic and biologic factors that condition all human enterprise.

Economic influences. In numerous researches it has been shown that economic insufficiency and insecurity and industrial inefficiency on the part of certain classes of the population, together with the evils they bring in their train, are among the most potent conditioning factors in the careers of offenders. True, this situation also characterizes many who never commit crimes; but the fact remains that it is exceedingly difficult to establish a milieu favourable to the prevention of delinquency and the rehabilitation of offenders so long as fundamental socio-economic forces are interfering with the process. To reduce the need of rehabilitation, we must have more wide-spread habilitation.

Such a conclusion is justified, as is shown by many findings in this research, some of which are particularly pertinent: that over half the mothers of our girls worked outside the home in order to supply or supplement the meagre family income; that over a fourth of the fathers were irregular workers; that three fourths of the families at one time or another during the childhood of our delinquents had to be aided by various social welfare agencies; that over two fifths of the homes were crowded and unattractive, and many were established in neighbourhoods inimical to wholesome child life; that half the girls had to leave school in order to earn a living—many of them at a tender age—only to enter upon occupations involving moral hazards. The degree of directness of the influence of poverty or near-poverty upon the misconduct of women offenders cannot be accurately determined except in certain individual instances. But that these conditions loom large in the complex of adverse factors in their careers is clear.

While such obvious reforms as slum-clearance and housing-projects can help to improve some of these adverse conditions, in the final analysis the situation calls for a more healthy and just economic planning of society as a whole.[1]

Biologic influences. Nor should we limit the deeper influences upon the delinquency problem to economic factors alone. The biologic handicaps of the parents and children involved in this study cannot be ignored, though their relative participation in the total crime-producing complex of factors is diffi-cult to determine. It cannot be proved by even the most ardent exponent of economic determinism that these biologic weaknesses are exclusively caused or conditioned by economic factors. No one can as yet say with precision which of the handicaps of mental defect, psychopathy, neuroticism, and poor physical health found among our women and their families are innate, and how many, or which, are acquired. But unquestionably they are obstacles to a legitimate struggle for survival. However perfectly society might be organ-ized from an economic point of view, not all crime would disappear. In the long run a fundamental attack upon the problems of antisociality depends not only on the raising of the status of the economically underprivileged, but on the elimination or better control of the biologically handicapped.

Partially in recognition of this fact, many states have enacted sterilization laws.[2] It is questionable whether the processes of human heredity are as yet sufficiently understood and prediction of the type of offspring to be expected is sufficiently reliable[3] to justify the basing of a social policy of compulsory sterilization on the ground of heredity alone.[4] On the other hand, the evidence is overwhelming that persons of the kind so largely represented in our group are unfit to care properly for children.[5] Nor can it be gainsaid that a large proportion of them are irresponsible and prolific breeders. As we have seen, they give birth to many illegitimate children, and their offspring are as a rule more numerous than in the population at large.

In determining upon a social policy to meet this serious problem, it must not be overlooked that while compulsory sterilization laws have on the whole not been abused in American jurisdictions, and while legal and administrative safeguards are thrown around such laws, they always present the danger of being transformed into instruments of oppression. Moreover, it is difficult to enforce compulsory sterilization laws.[6] Voluntary sterilization is a different matter.[7] In a field full of prejudices and queries concerning which mental abnormalities are hereditary and which acquired, what degree of mental defect or disease will be necessary in the individual case, and how and by whom the sterilization laws shall be administered, it is best to err on the side of caution. Practically, therefore, it would seem that at the present juncture voluntary sterilization laws are preferable to compulsory. Given wise social case work, in which the true implications of harmless sterilization measures will be interpreted to those who would probably benefit from such treatment, this instrumentality can be made to yield desirable societal and individual results. The adoption of voluntary sterilization measures in states which are as yet unequipped with such laws seems advisable, together with a campaign of education on the nature of sterilizing operations.[8] A less satisfactory alternative to such means of controlling irresponsible breeding by delinquents and others is to segregate them until they have passed the period of fertility.[9]

· · ·

Courts. In considering court organization and function as related to a more effective coping with delinquency and criminality we are faced with the alternative of a superficial patching of the existing structure or its fundamental redesign. Thus far, specialized courts dealing with female offenders have taken the form of "morals courts" or women's courts. Their creation was due largely to the fact that sexual offences, and particularly prostitution, are the ones that receive the most emphasis in the administration of criminal justice as it affects women. By centralizing the hearing of such cases in a specialized branch of a municipal court it was hoped, as was said of the Chicago Morals Court, "to reduce commercialized prostitution by a concentration of all prostitution and allied cases in one court, which would demonstrate the tremendous volume of the business of prostitution, and thereby result in arousing the public conscience; to check up the workings of the police in this particular field; to avoid waste of judicial power, save time, promote efficiency of administration, and lastly to deal more wisely with offenders and to marshal the social agencies organized for the assistance of such cases."[10] These are desirable ends and can be attained through a *fundamental reorganization* of court systems that promises, in addition, to yield even more valuable results. To stress the "morals" feature as a basis for specializing courts is, as the evidence of the make-up and background of offenders indicates, to run the danger of taking too superficial a view of the intricate issues involved. Courts must be redesigned to improve not only trial practices, but, perhaps more important, *sentencing* practices.

One way of doing this is to extend juvenile court procedure and philosophy to adults.[11] When a realistic view is taken of the etiology of misconduct, the arguments behind the constitutionality of juvenile procedure seem equally applicable to adult offenders.[12] To be sure, they hinge on the point that in juvenile courts it is a *child* that is involved. But if one turns from the legal conception of a "child" to that held by the psychologist, psychiatrist, and social worker and reviews the evidence of the irresponsibility of women of the type described in this work, one must conclude that they need just as much protection and "salvation" as children; that many of them are, in fact, psychologically children in their incapacity for assuming social responsibilities.

But juvenile-court informality introduced into the procedure of criminal courts for adults is not without danger of abuse.[13] Adult offenders are more likely to be in jeopardy of arbitrary treatment by courts which have informal procedure, few or no rules of evidence, no jury trial, than are juvenile delinquents whose youth in a measure protects them. Therefore, without ignoring the need of improving the trial aspect of adult-court procedure, the wisdom of extending juvenile-court practices to adult tribunals so far as the method of determining guilt is concerned is still open to question.[14] This does not mean, however, that adult criminal courts cannot be radically redesigned to effectuate desirable aims and yet retain wise constitutional safeguards.

The basic direction of reform lies not in the trial procedure but in the sentencing practices of the courts. The familiar complaint against existing methods of sentencing offenders is that there is little uniformity in the punishment of offenders committing the same crimes.[15] But this problem goes deeper than non-uniform sentences; it involves the fact of *too little scientific consideration of offenders* on the part of the judges. They do not devote sufficient time and study to each offender's situation in order to determine the type of sentence best suited to his needs. And it is a serious question whether most of the judges in criminal sessions are today qualified to do so. Regardless of the excellence of their legal education, they are as a rule unequipped in such disciplines as sociology and social case-work, psychology and psychiatry, education and penology, all of which must be drawn upon if the sentencing practices of our courts are to be radically improved.

That the sentencing practices of the courts do need basic transformation is shown by much evidence in this research. In the first place it is demonstrated by the poor work of *primary classification and distribution* of offenders done by the judges in sentencing our women. This inefficiency is illustrated by these cogent findings: (a) they sentenced to the Reformatory a substantial number of irreformable prostitutes, feeble-minded and psychopathic women, including many who had previously suffered deterioration in jails and houses of correction;[16] (b) they committed many promising women—those of our non-delinquent type—to an institution, when these women might just as well have been treated in the community under probation with less expense to the state and less chance of moral contagion to themselves; (c) they frequently resorted to sentences far too brief for the objectives to be achieved; (d) they often imposed fines.[17]

Secondly, the need of improving sentencing practices can be deduced from the fact that at present the type of crime committed evidently plays too weighty a part in determining the sentence imposed. That this is unsound is shown in the following proof that the type of crime committed is frequently not a safe peg upon which to hang the sentence: (a) in analysing "treatment types" the offence committed was found to be but one element—and not always the most significant—in a complex of interrelated factors; (b) the offence committed bears but a minor relationship to future behaviour of delinquents; (c) women of all three post-parole *behaviour* types (delinquents, non-delinquents, and up-grade delinquents) are to be found within each offence group.

That it is feasible to substitute a scientific system of sentencing offenders for the existing essentially haphazard one is indicated by the findings as to the reformability of different classes of offenders. We have shown, for example, that reformative efforts should be largely concentrated on persons of the type of the non-delinquents and up-grade delinquents. The latter group are most difficult for criminal courts to define and select from the stream of convicts to be sentenced, because they possess many of the good qualities of the non-delinquents, but also some of the characteristics of the women who continue their delinquencies unabated. They are, so to speak, "on the fence"; and the way they will jump depends on their intelligent selection by the sentencing tribunal and appropriate treatment of them thereafter.[18]

In the light of evidence like the foregoing,[19] a number of students of the sentencing practices of criminal courts have in recent years been insisting upon the importance of two elements that seem indispensable to a thorough overhauling of the existing system: (a) the sharp separation in function and personnel of the trial procedure and the sentencing procedure; (b) the establishment of one or more clearing-houses or "remand stations" in each state, to which convicted offenders would as a matter of course be committed for a period sufficient to permit of their thorough examination and study, the working-out of recommendations for sentence, and an individual plan of treatment.[20]

As to the first suggestion, it is urged that one or more sentencing bodies, staffed by trained and experienced psychiatrists, psychologists, sociologists, and educators, as well as lawyers, should be set up in each state as "treatment tribunals."[21] The second suggestion is an indispensable adjunct to the proposed division of judicial labour. Hasty judgments regarding the forces and situations involved in the criminality of the prisoner at the bar and the kind of sentence most likely to bring desired results do not usually afford a sound basis of peno-correctional treatment. This is one reason why so many of the wrong types of prisoners are sent to institutions and so many others are erroneously disposed of by probation, suspended sentence, or fine.[22] The casual impressionism of many criminal courts of today ought to give way to a more thoroughgoing procedure. Adequate study of each offender at a scientifically staffed and well-equipped clearing-house and remand station should greatly improve the work of original classification and distribution of offenders by the courts.[23] In addition, courts would thereby be in a position to contribute to the fund of knowledge of the social and psychologic conditions making for delinquency, and to experiment with new forms of correctional treatment.[24] A venereal clinic and educational and vocational services attached to the clearing-house and remand station might serve not only as a place of many-sided treatment of probationers but as an important research laboratory.

Indeterminate sentence. Various portions of this study have demonstrated the desirability of either a completely indeterminate sentence or one allowing an adequate zone of discretion to institutional and parole authorities in deciding when to return prisoners to the community.[25] It has been shown further that it is possible to determine with sufficient accuracy which types of offenders require only short periods of training in an institution like the Reformatory, which need longer custodial control, which require permanent segregation,[26] which are likely to do well under a brief period of parole supervision, which will probably relapse when parole oversight is removed. We have further seen that the biologic and psychologic changes that come with the passage of time play an important role in determining at least partially whether antisocial behaviour will be continued or abandoned.[27] It would seem wise, therefore, from the standpoint of protecting society as well as rehabilitating offenders, to substitute a completely indeterminate sentence, or at least one providing a wide zone between the minimal and maximal limits, for most of the varied existing statutory punishments.[28] In Massachusetts this suggestion is particularly directed against the "two-year indeterminate" and the "five-year indeterminate" sentences.[29] We are aware that there is one serious objection to a wholly indefinite sentence: the danger of arbitrariness in keeping imprisoned those no longer requiring incarceration. However, *periodic review* of each prisoner's record by the treatment tribunal, as a standard practice, should eliminate the possibility of any inmate being "forgotten" or dealt with unfairly by the institution authorities.[30]

It may be argued that offenders should not be subjected to the risk of protracted incarceration, perhaps lifelong imprisonment, for "a mere sex offence." Such a view ignores the true significance of the facts. We have seen that far more is involved in the careers of most of our women than an occasional lapse from moral conventions. We are dealing not only with a complicated network of biologic and socio-economic deficiencies, but with such socially dangerous consequences as the spread of venereal infection, the unrestricted birth of illegitimate, underprivileged children, and like tangible ill effects of unrestrained sexual indulgence. In effect, the majority of our women may truly be regarded as irresponsible members of society, requiring, in many cases, continuous control if not lifelong quarantine. Society has been forced to commit the mentally ill and feeble-minded to special institutions for wholly indefinite terms and to keep many of them under restraint throughout their lives; further, in a number of states, including Massachusetts, "defective delinquents" are committable to an institution for a completely indefinite period, and if need be they are kept in custody for life. From time to time numbers of the insane, feeble-minded, and defective delinquent are released from hospitals or other special institutions under conditions similar to parole. When shown to be dangerous to themselves or others, they are returned to the institutions without the expense of new trials. Persons who have violated criminal laws and who require long-time or continuous oversight ought sensibly to be dealt with likewise.

In this connection two basic principles need to be borne in mind: (a) "No one should ever be cast into [or retained within] prison so long as it is safe for himself and society that he be free." (b) "There is no rational excuse for the discharge of a criminal whom the State has at great expense once detected, arrested, tried, and convicted, so long as he continues a criminal in disposition and character, and may be expected to compel the State to incur the same expense again."[31]

As shown by the evidence in various parts of this book, the completely indeterminate or wide-zone sentence is so indispensable an adjunct to an effective administration of criminal justice that social statesmanship requires its adoption.

Releasing authority. This brings us to the important question whether prisoners should be released by a separate parole board, as (in Massachusetts and certain other states) at present; and if so, what relation such a board should bear to the courts on the one hand, and to the correctional institutions on the other. We have already shown that lack of integration between the courts and the institutions leads to undesirable commitments of many prisoners to places where they do not belong. This is but one illustration of the general imperfect coherence in society's "system" for coping with delinquency and criminality. In fact, there is little that is systematic about the processes considered as a whole; for each institution, beginning with the police and ending with the parole board, is inclined to move in its own narrow ambit with little regard for what the others are doing.[32] But the most marked lack of integration evidently exists between the courts and the peno-correctional establishments and between the latter and the parole board.

A rational system of criminal justice would consist of an integrated series of agencies, all having the same ultimate goals and all recognizing that for their efforts to be effective they must function in the closest interrelation. As between the courts and institutions, the establishment of one or more treatment tribunals and clearing-houses should in itself bring about increased consistency of aim and method. In addition it may be necessary for the tribunals to have inspective powers over the correctional institutions.[33] As between these latter and the releasing authorities we have come to the conclusion that, since, scientifically considered, the entire process ought to be continuous, it would seem wise to turn over the work of parole boards (or parole committees of institutions) to the proposed treatment tribunals. Thereby the same experts who originally studied the offender and determined upon the best disposition of her[34] case would keep in touch with her progress in the institution (or while under probation or some other form of treatment) and would review her case at stated periods to determine how the treatment program originally planned should be modified in the light of the offender's response. Release of a prisoner from a correctional institution on parole is just as much of a modification of the treatment originally prescribed by the court as is commitment of a probationer to an institution when he fails to respond to oversight; yet for historical reasons the first is under direction of a separate parole board while the second remains under authority of the court which originally sentenced the offender. This disconnectedness of what ought to be a unified system is partially responsible for so much of the inefficient and contradictory treatment reflected in the case histories of offenders. If the recommended treatment tribunal were charged not only with making the original disposition of cases but with following the progress of offenders and determining when and under what conditions they could be released, the entire procedure would become more effective. Not only would a good deal of working at cross-purposes thereby be eliminated, but offenders and their families might learn to regard correctional treatment as a continuous process which, from beginning to end, is, and for successful results needs to be, under single auspices and guidance.

In the proposed system, the treatment tribunal should also have authority to transfer offenders from one institution to another. This is closely related to both the sentencing work and the parole function. Errors in primary classification could thereby readily be remedied, provided, of course, that proper institutions existed for certain offenders, such as some of the feeble-minded and psychopathic.

Not only should such a unified process make for greater efficiency, but it would also be more economical than the existing jumble of disjointed agencies and authorities. Much duplication of effort in examining offenders, determining their social background, and supervising their conduct which is carried on more or less separately in at least three different places—the court, the institution, and the parole board—would thereby be avoided. It should also be remembered in this entire connection that many offenders (such as our non-delinquents and some up-grade delinquents) would under the new system be properly disposed of through probation and would not require a later commitment to some peno-correctional institution, to be followed by oversight on parole. Women merely unconventional in their sex life, who do not present other problems requiring treatment and are not dangerous as spreaders of venereal diseases or irresponsible breeders of illegitimate children, might be summarily disposed of without any officially prescribed special control, or, at most, with only reference of their cases to appropriate social agencies for treatment of special problems. On the other hand, professional prostitutes of long standing might be placed under more or less continuous control or be entirely segregated from the community. All this would mean far fewer trials for new offences committed by old offenders, and should in the long run be more economical than the existing practices.

The suggestion made in the preceding pages may carry forward a modest distance the attack of society upon delinquency and criminality. It ought to be stressed, however, that those who harbour too great expectations from any of the measures proposed for coping with these great evils are doomed to disappointment. In this enterprise, as in so much of human endeavour, understanding must precede control; but unfortunately the sciences and arts upon which depend a more successful, yet civilized, attack on delinquency and criminality are as yet in a very imperfect state. We still know little about the basic problem of the relative roles of hereditary and acquired qualities in the disposition and behaviour of human beings. Psychology, psychiatry, social case work, and educational practices have as yet not reached a very high degree of effectiveness, though happily they seem ever to be improving. Wise societal planning is still in embryo. Hence it is of the utmost importance that careful biologic and sociologic research and experimentation go hand in hand with "practical programs" designed to "produce immediate results." In the last analysis, our hope lies in the methods of the scientist; that is, in disciplined intelligence conscientiously and fearlessly applied to the search for the truth wherever it may lead.

Notes

1. Considering specifically commercialized vice, it is clearly the profit-making motive that is involved in its promotion. The "third party interest" exists because large sums of money are made in stimulating the demand for prostitutes and in supplying such demand. Here, then, is another potent economic factor making for delinquency.
2. The arguments in favour of sterilization and the progress of the movement in America are set forth in *Collected Papers on Eugenic Sterilization in California.* The Human Betterment Foundation (Pasadena, 1930). A more objective appraisal will be found in J. H. Landman: *Human Sterilization, the History of the Sexual Sterilization Movement* (New York, 1932)
3. "We assume that the Legislature would not feel justified in compelling any persons to submit to sterilisation, unless it could be shown beyond reasonable doubt that some at least of their offspring would either be mentally defective or would develop mental disorder. In the present state of knowledge no such proof can be produced. While the results of our enquiry and the other statistics we have collected may justify some prediction as to the average results in a large group of cases, it would be hazardous to attempt to forecast the genetic results of any particular union."— *Report of the Departmental Committee on Sterilisation Presented by the Minister of Health to Parliament by Command of His Majesty, December, 1933* (London: His Majesty's Stationery Office; 1934), p. 37. This English report is admirable for its objectivity and lucidity.
4. For a good critical analysis of the status of science in this field, see Landman, op. cit., particularly Part III. "These serious criticisms of the present status of eugenics show its great need for more science and less speculation. Any new program for social therapy must be held in abeyance until such time when an adequate scientific basis for it is established. Human sterilization, as a social program, requires more scientific evidence. In the meantime, if human sterilization must be employed, it should be employed cautiously."—Landman, op. cit., p. 197. See also the English report cited in the preceding note.
5. "Defectives make inefficient parents; if only for social reasons they should not have children."—*Report of the Departmental Committee, etc.,* p. 31.
6. Ibid., pp. 37–8. Other reasons advanced against compulsory sterilization laws by the English committee are: that they prevent hopeful cases from seeking hospitalization by creating the impression that forceful sterilization is a necessary condition to release from a mental hospital; that in the United States sterilization has been most practised in jurisdictions where it is administered on a voluntary rather than a compulsory basis; that it is not practicable to define the classes to which compulsory sterilization would apply in a way "to limit its use to exceptional cases only."
7. "By voluntary human sterilization we mean that the legal execution of the human sterilization law cannot be effected until the patient and or his legal guardian consents to the surgery."—Landman, op. cit., p. 279.
8. In the public mind sterilization is likely to mean castration.
9. Less satisfactory because many of them might well lead a harmless life in the community were it not for their weakness in the above respect. This is indicated

by our analysis of the factors entering into the determination of treatment types. However, certain women will have to be retained in institutions for considerable periods of time for other reasons than a tendency to unbridled and irresponsible sex expression.

10. See Worthington and Topping, op. cit., p. 6, summarizing statements of Judge Harry M. Fisher, *Tenth and Eleventh Annual Reports, Municipal Court of Chicago, 1915–1917*, pp. 85–6.

11. E. H. Sutherland: *Criminology* (Philadelphia, 1924), pp. 307 et seq.

12. The arguments supporting the constitutionality of juvenile courts are clearly put in the well-known case of Commonwealth v. Fisher, 213 Penn., 48 (1905): "In pressing the objection that the appellant was not taken into custody by due process of law, the assumption, running through the entire argument of the appellant, is continued, that the proceedings of the act of 1903 are of a criminal nature for the punishment of offenders for crimes committed, and that the appellant was so punished. But he was not. . . . To save a child from becoming a criminal, or from continuing in a career of crime, to end in maturer years in public punishment and disgrace, the legislature surely may provide for the salvation of such a child, if its parents or guardian be unable or unwilling to do so, by bringing it into one of the courts of the state without any process at all, for the purpose of subjecting it to the state's guardianship and protection. The natural parent needs no process to temporarily deprive his child of its liberty by confining it in his own home, to save it and to shield it from the consequences of persistence in a career of waywardness, nor is the state, when compelled, as *parens patriæ* to take the place of the father for the same purpose, required to adopt any process as a means of placing its hands upon the child to lead it into one of its courts. When the child gets there and the court, with the power to save it, determines on its salvation, and not its punishment, it is immaterial how it got there" (pp. 52–3).

As to denial of the right of trial by jury, "here again is the fallacy, that he was tried by the court for any offense. . . . There was no trial for any crime here, and the act is operative only when there is to be no trial. The very purpose of the act is to prevent a trial. . . . The act is not for the trial of a child charged with a crime, but is mercifully to save it from such an ordeal, with the prison or penitentiary in its wake, if the child's own good and the best interests of the state justify such salvation" (pp. 53–4). See also *Ex parte* Januszewski, 196 Fed. 123 (1911).

13. See Seabury, op. cit., pp. 247, 248, 251, which illustrates the ready opportunity for abuse of power that exists in adult courts where trial procedure is too informal. It is of course not a matter exclusively of procedure, but also, and perhaps most important, of personnel; but procedural safeguards are important curbs on possible arbitrariness or corruption.

14. As was pointed out, there is, however, a question whether certain sexual offences should be dealt with by the criminal law. See p. 98.

15. Comparing the disposal of cases in the district and municipal courts of the Boston area, a governmental commission arrived at the conclusion that "these courts . . . exercise within their several districts the same criminal jurisdiction . . . and although the social and economic conditions of their various districts do not differ essentially, there exists a radical and multiform variation and antagonism of practice in matters essential to the enforcement of the law."—The Commonwealth of Massachusetts, House No. 1638, *Report of the Commission on the Inferior Courts of the County of Suffolk*, 1912, p. 7. See also the annual report of the City Magistrates' Courts of the City of New York (First Division), 1914, and Waterman, op. cit., p. 63.

16. Of course not all the responsibility for this is on the judges; the fact of limited state facilities for commitment of such types is also involved.

17. Many modern authoritative writers condemn the use of fines, particularly in cases like prostitution. See, for example, Waterman, op. cit., pp. 66, 73, 152. Fines may serve as a means of income to the state, but not infrequently they are paid by others than the one who should suffer them. Thus, either an unjust burden falls on the wrong persons, or, as in the case of a "landlady" of a house of prostitution, fines enable exploiters to further enslave their victims. That fines have very little effect in preventing repetition of offences is shown by a follow-up investigation of any series of such cases.

18. See pp. 264, 272, 278.

19. To the above we may add two other evidences of the not altogether atypical outlook of judges of ordinary criminal courts: (1) The practice of automatic increase in punishments with repetition of crime (see Worthington and Topping, op. cit., pp. 9, 86). This simplistic solution of a complex problem rarely results as anticipated. (2) The practice of solving the problem presented by an unmarried mother, without regard to her own and her lover's make-up and background, by "blessing" the union with an enforced marriage as a condition of avoidance of punishment.

20. See, for example, S. Glueck: "Principles of a Rational Penal Code," *Harvard Law Review*, Vol. XLI (1928), pp. 453 et seq.

21. The implications of such a reform and the methods to be employed by the proposed sentencing tribunals are far more complex than appears. They will be fully gone into in forthcoming volumes of the Harvard Law School Crime Survey.

22. There are other reasons for this which have largely local significance, such as, for example, the appeal and double-trial system in vogue in Massachusetts. (See Worthington and Topping, op. cit., pp. 217–20; The Commonwealth of Massachusetts, Senate No. 125, *Report of the Special Crime Commission*, Boston, 1934, pp. 67, 69, 71.) But even if the local situation were remedied by the abolition of trials *de novo* in cases appealed from the Boston Municipal Court and the district courts, the major difficulty discussed above would not be obviated. In this chapter we are largely concerned with suggestions for improving a general situation that, with minor local differences, exists throughout the country.

23. See pp. 15 et seq. for Mrs. Hodder's views on this subject. We have not gone into the question whether, in Massachusetts, the proposed clearing-house and temporary detention place should be established at one of the existing penal or correctional institutions. That is a matter of local policy, and we are interested in the more general proposal described above. It may be recalled that Mrs. Hodder, the late superintendent of the Massachusetts Reformatory for Women, urged that her institution be used as the clearing-house for women offenders. A proposal has also been made that the Charlestown State Prison be utilized as a clearing-house for male offenders. Each state must decide for itself whether it can transform some existing structure into the laboratory and remand station proposed above.

24. See p. 296.

25. See pp. 292–3.

26. Why are helpless derelicts, incorrigible wrongdoers, spreaders of disease, and breeders of illegitimate offspring, like Grace (pp. 152 et seq.), Florence (pp. 157 et seq.), Fleur (pp. 162 et seq.), Angelina (pp. 168 et seq.), Minnie (pp. 172 et seq.), and Dora (pp. 177 et seq.), permitted to circulate in society like bad coins, in and out of jails, farms, almhouses, hospitals?

27. See Chapters XII to XVII inclusive, where various aspects of this important problem are analysed.

28. What to do with the death penalty is a question to be left to local differences of policy.

29. See p. 187. When the indefinite-sentence idea was first propounded, the wisdom in principle of a completely indeterminate sentence was recognized. But the idea was

abandoned because its proponents feared it would fail to receive legislative support. See S. and E. T. Glueck: *500 Criminal Careers* (New York, 1930), p. 150, note 4.

30. It will be recalled that Mrs. Hodder's plan to review each case at staff meetings every three months was not often enforced, owing to limitations of personnel and the pressure of other work (pp. 129 et seq.). But under the proposed system, review of each case at definite intervals would be an indispensable guaranty.

31. H. M. Boies: *The Science of Penology, the Defence of Society against Crime* (New York, 1901), p. 154.

32. See p. 294.

33. This, in turn, would probably necessitate that the commissioner of correction or other official in charge of the correctional institutions have some close connection with, perhaps membership on, the treatment tribunal. This entire question raises a number of complex issues that have been thoroughly canvassed by the members of the Harvard Law School Crime Survey, and a detailed exposition of the implications of some of the recommended reforms may be expected in some of the forthcoming reports of that survey.

34. These recommendations of course refer to both male and female offenders, since the issues involved are not "sex-linked."

5 The Masked Character of Female Crime

Otto Pollak

In our male-dominated culture, women have always been considered as strange, secretive, and sometimes as dangerous. Men have always tried to understand them and have generally failed in their efforts. Suppressing them and needing them at the same time, men have never been completely comfortable in their apparent state of social superiority and have always been apprehensive of the possibility of rebellion or revenge on the part of women. This mood of apprehension exists frequently on the part of oppressors. As between men and women, however, it has been accentuated by the fact that the early childhood experience of complete dependence upon the mother is hardly ever overcome entirely in its emotional consequences and that the latter contradict the social arrangement of male superiority. In this emotional discomfort, men have made many illogical and self-contradictory attempts to alleviate their fears resulting from this conflict. Basically they have attempted to deny women the ability to do things men do and have either idealized them into a sweetness and purity which made them appear docile and harmless, or they have maligned them in order to be able to condemn them. Both types of behavior help men to feel better about their denial of equality to women. Thus, many male attempts to understand women have actually been attempts to rationalize men's treatment of the other sex and have frequently been nothing but self-deceptions.

With regard to crime this male self-deception about women seems to have been excessive. It has been the traditional opinion of criminologists that women commit relatively few crimes and that when they do so they somehow betray their womanhood by venturing out into a reserve of men. In this parochial view they have overlooked all the basic tenets of our understanding of human behavior. They have also failed to use even the few valid insights which, in spite of their unconscious handicap, men have been able to gain

From *The Criminality of Women* by Otto Pollak. University of Pennsylvania Press, Philadelphia, 1950. Pp. 149–161. Reprinted by permission of Otto Pollak.

regarding the nature of female behavior. Therefore, it seemed important to collect and analyze the available information regarding female crime and to check the prevailing beliefs against this material. This was done particularly with regard to the following points of interest.

The quantity of female crime

Since crime is always a rebellion against established values and since men are basically afraid of women, most criminologists have been eager to rely on every bit of evidence, however shaky, that seems to support the belief that women do not participate in crime to any appreciable degree, and to disregard all observations which seem to contradict the validity of this belief. Their main weapons in this defensive type of scientific inquiry have been official criminal statistics which on their face value actually suggest that women are less criminal than men. However, criminal statistics are probably the least reliable of all statistics because they undertake to measure something which is designed to escape observation and thus to escape measurement. This deceptive nature of criminal statistics has been recognized as such, and considerable refinements in their interpretation have been developed. It has been particularly noted that various types of crime yield themselves with various degrees of reliability to statistical measurement. It is now accepted doctrine that a crime to be reliably reported in criminal statistics must fulfill at least three requirements: (1) it must be considered highly injurious by the members of society, (2) it must be of a public nature, and (3) it must induce the fullest possible coöperation of the victim, or of those interested in the victim, with the law.[1] Since it was the main purpose of this study to apply these requirements in statistical analysis to the available data about female crime, our scientific investigation had to start with an inquiry as to whether our existing knowledge of the ways in which women commit their crimes suggests that these three requirements are met. Actually it has been possible to show that all we know about female crime on the basis of case observation and cultural analysis contradicts this assumption. First of all, we have seen that her lack of physical and social strength has suggested, and at least by the force of tradition still suggests, to woman indirection and deceit as one of her most promising weapons for the achievement of her goals. We have further seen that woman's physiological make-up permits successful concealment of her true feeling in the important sphere of sex relations, while the male in this respect is biologically forced to show the true state of his feelings. It cannot be categorically denied that this differential experience may well result in a greater degree of confidence in successful misrepresentation on the part of woman. It has also been possible to show that our social mores give woman a different evaluation of deceit than they give man, because concealment of the truth in certain biological respects as well as in general social behavior is considered appropriate conduct for members of the female sex. Thus, for biological as well as for cultural reasons, woman seems to possess greater powers of concealment than does man. And for this group of our population which is therefore better equipped to achieve the supreme goal of most criminals, namely, to remain undetected, our culture furnishes almost ideal conditions for the perpetration of crime.

One of the outstanding concomitants of the existing inequality between the sexes is chivalry and the general protective attitude of man toward woman. This attitude exists on the part of the male victim of crime as well as on the part of the officers of the law, who are still largely male in our society. Men hate to accuse women and thus indirectly to send them to their punishment, police officers dislike to arrest them, district attorneys to prosecute them, judges and juries to find them guilty, and so on.

Furthermore, in studying the ways in which women commit their crimes, we have had occasion to see over and over again that our culture assigns them social roles which furnish them with opportunities for concealed criminal attacks and with types of victims who are, for one reason or other, least to be expected to coöperate with the police. The imposition of restrained behavior upon women in our culture often forces them into the role of the instigator rather than the direct perpetrator of the crime, and thus removes them from apparent connection with the offense. In our society the roles of women are still primarily those of the homemaker, of the preparer of meals, of the rearer of children, of the nurse of the sick, of the shopper, and of the domestic-service worker. Abundant temptations to commit crimes and opportunities to carry them out in a secretive fashion follow from these roles. Actually, woman's task of preparing food for the members of the family has made her the poisoner par excellence, and her function in nursing the sick has had a similar effect. The helplessness of children as victims of crime has brought within her realm a group of victims least equipped to put up any resistance against criminal attacks and practically unable to enlist the help of the law for purposes of prosecution. In the sphere of property crimes, our modern sales organization has developed into a formidable trap for the shopper with weak internal inhibitions, because the external obstacles to theft have been practically obliterated in the display of the merchandise. By the self-service system in department stores, five-and-tens, and food markets, the accessibility of objects for theft has reached a degree formerly unknown. The job of domestic-service workers puts many women within reach of a practically endless array of temptations and opportunities for theft as it leaves them unsupervised in close physical proximity to all the objects of the household in which they work.

. . .

Effects of social equalization of the sexes upon female crime

One of the characteristic phenomena of our time is women's progress toward reaching social equality with men. This raises the interesting question whether we may assume that, in consequence of this development, female crime will change its nature, become masculinized as it were, and lose its masked character. To be sure, the last half-century has opened to women many pursuits from which they were excluded and has thus given them new opportunities for crime which formerly did not come their way. In periods of pronounced social stress, such as war, in which women assume many roles which are otherwise open to men only, the experience in various countries seems to indicate that crimes of women against property increase. But if this were a true expression of social equalization, we should have to assume that simultaneously the amount of undiscovered female crime would decrease. Cultural analysis, however, contradicts the validity of this assumption, because their new roles have not freed women from their traditional ones. They may have become wage earners and household heads in increasing numbers, but they have not stopped being the homemakers, the rearers of children, the nurses of the sick, the domestic servants, the shoppers, or the prostitutes. In other words, they have retained all those social roles which account for the amount, the nature, and particularly the masked character of their traditional criminal behavior. Thus, we have to assume that, with the burden of their social functions increased, their opportunities for crime have not undergone a process of substitution so much as a process of increase.

Specificity of female crime

After the question of the probable extent of female crime, which, as we have seen, has been so largely misconceived in the past, we tried to investigate the question whether there are any specifically female crimes, i.e., crimes which play a much greater role in female criminality than in male criminality, or crimes which can be committed only by women. Our investigation has led us to the conclusion that there is only one offense, prostitution, which can be called a specific female crime in this sense. Except for this type of behavior, which only in the United States represents a criminal offense, there seems to exist no specifically female crime whatsoever. Only in the ways in which women commit their crimes, particularly the weapons which they employ and the victims whom they choose, the opportunities of which they can avail themselves, the persons with whom they coöperate, and finally the part which they play in the actual perpetration of the crime, in other words in cultural determinants, could we see differences characteristic of female criminality. The weapons which female offenders employ are characterized by subtlety rather than violence. The victims they choose in attacks against the person are mostly children, particularly infants, husbands, and lovers. In buying and receiving stolen goods they are usually the receivers of objects stolen by a family member, and in property crimes with violence they play more frequently the role of the instigator or of the decoy and watcher rather than of the actual perpetrator. In short, women commit all types of crime but their procedure is different from that used by men in their criminal pursuits.

The personal characteristics of female offenders

From the description and analysis of the amount and nature of female crime, we have then turned to the challenging search for causative factors. As an introduction to this part of our inquiry, we have been first concerned with the personal characteristics of female offenders such as age, marital status, occupation, intelligence, and race. Of course, all these descriptive characteristics in themselves could not explain questions of causation proper, but they proved of considerable value in guiding our research into meaningful channels. Biological as well as social determinants are indicated in these characteristics. Particularly, special age and special marital status liabilities of women offenders furnish a number of characteristic leads. With regard to age, we found that girls seem to start their delinquency later than do boys, that women reach the peak of their criminal activities at a later stage than do men, and that the criminality of women seems to decline more slowly with advancing age than the criminality of men. Since in our culture, with its premium on youth, women are apt to understate their age after they have passed the mid-twenties, this phenomenon of delay in female crime is even more pronounced than the available figures suggest. It seems, therefore, that women pay for maturity a significantly higher price in crime than do men. To the student of the causes of criminal behavior, this furnishes a very interesting guide for further investigation.

Proceeding to the study of the marital status of female offenders, we found another startling difference between women and men: the influence of marriage upon the criminal behavior of the two sexes. Marriage does not seem to be so conducive to law-abiding behavior on the part of women as it seems to be on the part of men. At least in the culture of Western civilization, the amount of crime committed by married women—independent of age—seems to be higher than the amount of crime committed by single women. The incidence of crime of unmarried men, however, seems to be in general larger than the frequency of crimes committed by married men. Therefore, we are forced to ask whether in our culture marriage may help men to settle down while it may cause women to become disturbed and on occasions violators of the law.

Causative factors in female crime

Thus alerted by the comparatively high criminal liabilities of women in the brackets of childbearing age and of married women independent of age, we turned to an investigation of the biological and social factors which seem to have a causative influence on female crime. Throughout the investigation of these two types of factors, we had to keep in mind that the human being is first a biological organism, but one who can never be studied outside a social environment. The individual being born into society cannot be thought of as separated from it.

The correlation between the incidence of female crime and the period of childbearing age indicated from the start that the biological phenomena which characterize this age period in women deserve our attention. Actually from this angle, menstruation, pregnancy, and the menopause have to be considered of central research interest in this respect. The student of female criminality cannot afford to overlook the generally known and recognized fact that these generative phases are frequently accompanied by psychological disturbances which may upset the need and satisfaction balance of the individual or weaken her internal inhibitions, and thus become causative factors in female crime. Particularly because of the social meaning attached to them in our culture, the generative phases of women are bound to present many stumbling blocks for the law-abiding behavior of women. Menstruation with its appearance of injury must confirm feelings of guilt which individuals may have about sex activities which they have learned to consider as forbidden. As a symbol of womanhood, it must also, because of its recurrent nature, aggravate any feeling of irritation and protest which women may have regarding their sex in a society in which women have had, and still have, to submit to social inequality with men. In both instances, it must lead to a disturbance of the emotional balance of the individual and thus become potentially crime-promoting. Pregnancy in a culture which frowns upon illegitimacy and fosters in large sectors of society limitation in the number of children or even childlessness must become a source of irritation, anxiety, and emotional upheaval in many instances. The menopause in a society which makes romance and emotional gratification the supreme value in a monogamous marriage system must be experienced, at least by married women, frequently as a threat to the basis of their emotional security if not to their general marital existence. In view of these cultural implications of the generative phases and their psychological consequences, it is difficult to understand why the existing literature contains so little discussion of their possible crime-promoting influence. Only the sex taboos which dominate our culture seem to furnish an explanation of this phenomenon. Still, we have been able to find some statistical corroboration which supports the foregoing analysis. Thefts, particularly shoplifting, arson, homicide, and resistance against public officials seem to show a significant correlation between the menstruation of the offender and the time of the offense. The turmoil of the onset of menstruation and the puberty of girls appears to express itself in the relatively high frequency of false accusations and—where cultural opportunities permit—of incendiarism. Pregnancy in its turn is a crime-promoting influence with regard to attacks against the life of the fetus and the newborn. The menopause finally seems to bring about a distinct increase in crime, especially in offenses resulting from irritability such as arson, breaches of the peace, perjury, and insults.

In the social sphere proper, we have found two groups of factors which seem to be of specific crime-promoting influence upon women. In the first group belong the double standard of our sex morality with its discrimination against women, our modern sales-promotion methods in the retail trades with their concentration on the female shopper, and the specific female occupation of domestic employment with its many irritations and frustrations. In the second group belong the special opportunities which the traditional cultural roles of women in our society offer for the commission of crimes.

The general sex repression which characterizes our culture is particularly strict with regard to women. Violations of sex morality meet with much stronger disapproval if they are committed by women than if they are committed by men. This double standard adds therefore to the burden of frustration of the sex urge, the burden of discrimination. It is only natural that women should protest against the situation, and they seem to do so in various ways. On the surface, they appear to demand only the equal enforcement of our sex morality for the members of both sexes. More deeply, however, they seek other expressions of this protest, which frequently seem to lead them into crime. The vicarious flights into fantasy through which unmarried women seek to compensate for their sex repression and sex discrimination are well known, but it is not sufficiently recognized how often these fantasy experiences may lead them into false accusation with sexual content. Only too seldom do our law-enforcement officers realize how often the accusation of an unmarried woman against a man may indicate an experience which she consciously fears and abhors but unconsciously desires, and how often the mental conflict between desire and social restraint may lead her into false accusations of a sexual character and thus to perjury. On the other hand, married women seem to resort more frequently to overt protests against the double standard by criminal attacks against errant husbands, or if they do not dare to do so, against scapegoats in the persons of their children or their neighbors. This seems to explain why women who have committed a crime against the person of their husband or lover do not feel morally guilty although they recognize that their behavior is technically a violation of the law. From their own point of view, they consider themselves as administrators of a higher justice, a mechanism which is always present in actions motivated by a desire for protest and revenge.

Next to the double standard, modern sales techniques with their exploitation of the female role of shopper create desires which may lead women into crime more frequently than they do men. With almost uncanny ingenuity the display of the merchandise is so organized that visual temptations are put in one's way before one can reach the objects originally intended for purchase. Of course, men are as much impressed and motivated into such unintended purchases as are women, but women shop more frequently and more regularly than do men. The former are, therefore, more exposed to this creation of desire for goods which may not be needed or at least may not be within their financial reach.

Revenge desires are created by the female occupation of domestic service. This occupation exposes many women to the frustration of a daily experience of difference between their own standard of living and the living standards of their employers. Such a situation exists in hardly any other line of work. To see what other people have, and what she herself does not have, can almost be called the essential job experience of the domestic servant. In our time of class antagonism and in our country of race antagonism in which domestic workers are frequently colored or at least members of another ethnic group than their employers, the situation is psychologically mined. Logically, it must lead to a tremendous amount of pent-up resentment which cannot help but create a desire for aggressive compensation.

Our culture, however, not only creates all these specific frustrations for women but also surrounds them with opportunities to respond to them by unlawful behavior. Each of the social roles which women perform in our culture furnishes such opportunities. Marriage in itself delivers a whole array of possible objects of attack for crimes against the person, practically defenseless, into the hands of the potential woman offender. Compared with the ease with which the preparer of meals, the child-rearer, and the nurse of the sick can direct an attack against physical well-being or life, the task of the male killer in our society is difficult indeed. Compared with the lack of economic restraint which the average housewife enjoys in our society, the pressures which force the wage earner into complying behavior are overwhelming. It need not surprise, therefore, that married women participate to a higher degree in crime, and particularly crimes against the person, than do single women.

Similarly, the accessibility of objects of theft to the woman offender who either is or poses as a shopper or domestic must appear almost as the criminal's dream to our male burglars and robbers who have to struggle with the formidable array of defense mechanisms which our technological advances have put in their way.

In summary, then, we are forced into the conclusion that the amount of female crime has been greatly underestimated by traditional opinion. At least in our culture, women are particularly protected against the detection of criminal behavior on the one hand and exposed to a wealth of irritations, temptations, and opportunities which may lead them to criminal behavior on the other. Therefore, meaningful differentials between male and female crime must be looked for, not in any appreciable and validly demonstrable difference in the crime volume, but in the ways in which women commit their crimes and in the causes of their criminal behavior. They must be looked for in the interplay between biological and cultural determinants which distinguishes this behavior from that of man. In short, the criminality of women reflects their biological nature in a given cultural setting.

Note

1. Sellin, *Research Memorandum on Crime in the Depression*, p. 70.

6 The Sex Factor: Female Delinquency
Hermann Mannheim

1. Introductory remarks[42]

Before going into the details of this fascinating subject, the following general points have to be made.

a. While there is no doubt that according to official statistics and our general impressions the total female crime rate is much lower everywhere than that of males we should avoid the frequent mistake of studying the subject solely under such comparative aspects. This one-sided approach inevitably induces the observer to search for nothing but plausible explanations of the differential crime rate and unwittingly to limit his attention to those factors which are likely to furnish good reasons why females should commit less crime than males. An objective and scientific approach should try to treat female crime as a topic in its own right, which does not, of course, make frequent comparisons with its male counterpart unnecessary. Nor does it mean that we should try to understand female criminality exclusively from the sexual angle.

b. Another mistake often found in statistical comparisons of the sex rates is to ignore the striking differences between the various categories of offences and between the various age groups. For the latter, reference can be made to [statistics] which show that the contrast between the overall male and female crime rates varies considerably according to age; while, for example, the 1962 ratio for the eight-year-old ones was 24 males to one female, for those 60 and over it was only two males to one female. The position when compared with pre-war figures has, on the whole, changed to the advantage of women, especially in the older age groups. A striking contrast between male and female crime rates . . . lies in the far smaller variations in the female rates, the male

From *Comparative Criminology* by Hermann Mannheim. Routledge and Kegan Paul Ltd., London, 1965. Pp. 690–707, 748–750. Reprinted by permission of Routledge and Kegan Paul Ltd. (The original footnote numbers of the source are retained.)

peak age figures being about 46 times higher than the lowest ones, whereas for females the peak age figures are only about 12 times higher than the lowest. In pre-war years the contrast was, as far as the male figures were concerned, less striking.[43]

The sex differences for individual offences will be discussed below.

c. Criminologists have occasionally been criticized for paying but scant attention to the subject of female crime. Lady Wootton in particular has accused them of being prejudiced and 'curiously blind to the obvious'; 'hardly anyone seems to have thought it worthwhile to try to find out' why there was such a difference in the respective crime rates.[44] If this were true we might well ask why this distinguished author, with her exceptionally favourable equipment both as a scholar and as a female protagonist, did not make use of her opportunities to fill the gap. In fact, the accusation is not altogether well-founded. It is certainly true that much less research has so far been done on the characteristics and possible explanations of female than on those of male crime, but this is largely due not to 'blindness' but to the comparative scarcity of case material and the greater difficulty of access to it; to the smaller numbers of female research workers who would be particularly interested in the subject and qualified to do research on it; and to the difficulties presented to statistical enquiries by the small numbers of cases. In any case, it is a distortion of the truth to maintain that the subject has been entirely ignored. Female scholars such as Pauline Tarnowsky, the Russian student of Lombroso, the Dutch lawyer Johanna C. Hudig, the American sociologist Mabel A. Elliott, the English psychiatrists Grace W. Pailthorpe, Hedwig Schwarz and Phyllis Epps, and the psychiatric social worker Moya Woodside—a list which is by no means complete—have made valuable contributions to it, and a not inconsiderable literature has also been produced by several male authors.

d. There is, however, another point of fundamental importance which has not often received in criminological literature the attention due to it, i.e. the fact that hitherto female crime has, for all practical purposes, been dealt with almost exclusively by men in their various capacities as legislators, judges, policemen; and at least up to the end of the last century the same was true of the theoretical treatment of the subject not only by scholars but also by poets and novelists. This could not fail to create a one-sided picture. It has been said, not without justification, that what human beings think of members of the opposite sex is usually the result of their personal disappointments and therefore distorted. This centuries-old male predominance in theory and practice and the consequent distortions have, however, not throughout worked in the expected direction, i.e. to the disadvantage of females, but may indeed rather have favoured them in various ways. Men seem to have made penal laws mainly to prevent and punish actions which they thought endangered their personal interests, whereas certain specifically female forms of misconduct were often regarded as not serious enough or too pleasant or indispensable to them to warrant penal measures. The legislators, being males, may unwittingly have moulded the whole system of criminal law in such a way as to turn a blind eye to some of those anti-social actions most frequently committed by women, such as prostitution—which, unless accompanied by certain other activities, is not an offence in most countries—or lesbianism, lying or quarreling. However, as the example of witchcraft shows, this hypothesis should not be stretched too far. Nevertheless, there have been occasional traces of what might be regarded as a guilty conscience in this man-made criminal law, showing that male legislators, aware of the under-privileged position of women in pre-twentieth-century society, have made special efforts to protect them against some of the consequences of that lack of equality. In this connection the English common law presumption has to be mentioned that a woman who committed a felony (except murder or treason) in the presence of her husband had committed it under compulsion and was therefore entitled to an acquittal, but this presumption was abolished by the Criminal Justice Act, 1925, s. 47, because of the improved social position and consequent greater independence of women.[45] A statutory provision in favour of women, but limited to one crime, infanticide, is contained in the Infanticide Act, 1938. On a far broader basis rests art. 37L of the Cuban Penal Code of 1936, which accords the benefit of mitigating circumstances to a woman who has committed a crime when under the influence of a mental disturbance due to climacterium, pregnancy, menstruation or the abnormal effect of child-birth.[46] On the other hand in a few countries adultery is a punishable offence only for women or at least punished more severely and in a more general fashion in the case of women than of men.[47]

.   .   .

In addition to such legal distinctions made in favour of the female sex there is further the inequality observed in detection and the practice of prosecution and sentencing. It has been argued by several investigators that women tend to commit mainly such offences which, by their very nature, can be detected only with special difficulties and are, even if detected, only rarely reported and prosecuted. Pollak mentions in particular non-professional shoplifting, thefts by prostitutes and domestic servants, abortions, perjury and indecent exposure.[49] To some extent this argument is probably correct, but exact proof is obviously impossible to obtain, and it can also be maintained that there are certain specifically male offences which show very low rates of detection too, such as burglary and housebreaking. While many of Pollak's points may be valid, one gets the impression that in his efforts to show that the sex difference in crime rates is actually much smaller than generally assumed he goes too much to the other extreme and tends to under-rate the size of the dark numbers in male criminality. As far as pilfering from employers is concerned, for example, male workers have probably the same opportunities as their female colleagues, and the proportion of those who use these opportunities is probably not lower than in the case of women, but all this is hardly more than mere conjecture. For blackmail v. Hentig offers some interesting observations to show that men are more vulnerable and open to exploitation by female secretaries, chambermaids or prostitutes, and that such acts of blackmail committed by women will very rarely reach the courts.[50] This, too, is very likely correct, but no exact proof is possible.

It is, however, not only the type of offence but also their manner of participating in it which reduces the official crime rate of women as they are more likely to play the role of instigator, aider and abetter than that of the actual doer, and it is usually more difficult to detect the former than the latter.[51]

Our criminal law and, we might add, our administration of criminal justice are 'almost exclusively doer-centred' (Reckless).[52] As criminal statistics do not distinguish according to differences in participation it cannot be proved statistically, however, that there is such a sex difference in the kind of participation, and we are mainly dependent on the observation of individual cases.

Closely connected with the form of participation is the sex difference concerning acquittal: as those who take part in crime in less direct ways than as actual doers are more difficult to track down they stand a better chance of being acquitted in case of prosecution. To take, for example, a few post-war years at random, in 1954 of 17,806 males and 930 females brought before Assizes and Quarter Sessions, which is a ratio of 19:1, 1,739 males and 141 females were acquitted, i.e. 12:1. In 1961, 33,040 males and 1,284 females were brought to trial before Assizes and Quarter Sessions, i.e. a ratio of 25:1, whereas acquittals numbered 2,784 males against 163 females, i.e. a ratio of 17:1.[53] That members of the public are far more reluctant to take action against girls than against boys is common knowledge and accounts, at least to some extent, for the disparity of cases brought before the juvenile courts. Where proceedings are taken they are more often for being in need of care and protection or beyond parental control than for criminal offences, even in cases where the latter have actually been committed.

Moreover, when charged and found guilty women are more leniently treated by the courts than men,[54] but this does not of course affect the crime rate with which we are here primarily concerned. In many cases this greater leniency is probably justified, but in some others it is entirely misplaced.

On the other hand, the treatment facilities available for female offenders are usually even less adequate and up-to-date than those for males, mainly because their smaller numbers make it more difficult to classify, staff and equip institutions. . . .

Actually, while the institutional treatment of delinquent women is, in some ways, even more difficult than that of men, there are also reasons why it could be made more progressive than the latter. The security aspect is less intricate as public opinion is less insistent here on maximum security than in the case of male prisoners, and the smaller numbers involved should make individual case work more easy to practise. On the other hand, the recruitment of suitable staff presents additional problems.

·   ·   ·

2. Historical sketch of female delinquency

Historically seen, the crimes in which women were mostly involved in former ages used to be adultery and incest, witchcraft, poisoning and infanticide. Penologists and legal historians have collected much material to show how in ancient society, before the coming into existence of a state penal system, women caught in adultery were punished by their husbands exercising their right as heads of the family.[58] Penologists have also studied the medieval differences in penal methods as applied to the two sexes; drowning, burning or burying alive were regarded as particularly appropriate forms of execution for women in the Middle Ages.[59] In the medieval witchcraft trials women had to bear the brunt of the prosecutions because they were believed to be more likely to enter into sexual relations with the devil.[60] A fascinating international history of the witchcraft trials has recently been published in German by Kurt Baschwitz. He shows that most of the accused were elderly women and poor specimens. Jeanne d'Arc was one of the exceptions, but according to Baschwitz she was tried not for witchcraft but for heresy; although the original indictment had been for witchcraft, too, this point was dropped in the course of the proceedings.[61] The great astronomer Johann Kepler succeeded in 1621, after a struggle lasting six years, to rescue his mother from the stake. In some cases, in Sweden, for example, the authorities used children as witnesses against women accused of witchcraft (p. 318), and the same happened in the famous trial at Salem, Massachusetts (Baschwitz). The last of these trials took place in the middle or towards the end of the eighteenth century.

According to Pike, women were continually mentioned in the fourteenth century not only as receivers of stolen property but also in connection with brigandage and other crimes of violence; they were, he writes, often 'almost as brutal as their husbands or paramours',[62] and among the masses of vagrants women, too, played a prominent part not only as companions of the males but often without them as prostitutes and beggars.[63] Later, in the eighteenth century, the type of female crime which attracted most of the attention of criminal law reformers and poets was infanticide; Radbruch and Gwinner call it 'the key offence of all eighteenth-century efforts to modernize the medieval criminal law'.[64] The tragic story of Gretchen in Goethe's *Faust* has, as these authors remind us, at least in part to be traced back to the execution of a Frankfurt woman for infanticide; and other great contemporary German poets, such as Schiller and Bürger, made effective propaganda in their works for the abolition of the death penalty for this crime. That the French Revolution should greatly stimulate such efforts was only natural, and it is not surprising that a prize-competition held in 1780 in Germany on the question 'Which are the most practicable means to prevent infanticide?' elicited nearly four hundred replies, among them Pestalozzi's book on the subject. Infanticide came to be regarded as one of the crimes symptomatic of the callous exploitation by the aristocracy of women belonging to the lower social classes.

At the same time, however, women who were themselves members of the French aristocracy took a prominent part in crimes of an entirely different kind. In the sensational 'Affair of the Queen's [i.e. Marie Antoinette's] Necklace', which was widely believed to bear some of the responsibility for the downfall of Louis XVI and his dynasty, the Comtesse de la Motte played the leading part, and the Marquise de Brinvilliers[65] had already made criminal history in the seventeenth century by using for the first time arsenic on a large scale to poison first some hospital patients, whom she used for experimental purposes, and afterwards several members of her own family.

There has been much less glamour in female crime since those romantic happenings, and the scene has been largely dominated by such more prosaic offences as drunkenness, prostitution, cruelty to children, shoplifting, and, of late, motoring offences.

·   ·   ·

4. Possible explanations of the differential sex rate

Notwithstanding the existence of many strong arguments which make it likely that the 'masked' sector of female crime is much larger proportionally than its male counterpart and that the actual difference between the male and female sex rates is therefore considerably smaller than shown in official statistics, it is nevertheless almost universally agreed that such a difference does in fact exist in favour of the female sex. The exact extent of this difference is likely to vary greatly between different countries and civilizations, offences, and age groups. We have now to ask for possible explanations of this phenomenon and also, as pointed out before, try to understand the factors behind female crime regardless of its numerical relations to the male crime rate.

Naturally, most of the attempts so far made follow the traditional pattern by dividing their explanations into physical, psychological, and sociological ones and trying to combine them in an eclectic manner. We are not in a position radically to break with this pattern which is, after all, in line with our general approach. Pollak's suggestion that on close analysis the tripartition could be replaced by a bipartition, omitting the psychological section . . . does not seem to be acceptable. As pointed out above, physical and social or economic factors can become operative only by going through the 'transformator' of a psychological or psychiatric factor.[69]

a. Physical factors. . . . [A] distinction has to be made between physical factors of whatever kind which might possibly affect criminal behaviour, on the one hand, and definite physical types, on the other. . . . In the case of girl delinquents, physical over-development is often blamed for sexual misbehaviour, and it is only natural that where their physical precocity greatly outstrips their intellectual and emotional maturity violations of the social and legal norms of conduct are likely to happen. The frequency of 'care and protection' cases coming before the juvenile courts, most of which are, in fact, cases of sexual irregularity, often coupled with petty criminal offences, bears witness to this.[70] While some American writers lay special stress on the physical over-development of such girls,[71] this point is less conspicuous in the scanty English material available.[72] Dr. Epps, in her survey of a sample of Borstal girls, made between 1948 and 1950, received the general impression of a 'group of well-developed and physically healthy girls'.[73] In any case, this factor seems to be less strongly related to crime than to sexual irregularity. For women who have passed the stage of adolescence the menstruation factor, pregnancy and later the menopause, play a more important part. . . .

Lack of physical strength has often been quoted as explaining the lower female rate of offences against the person, but Pollak argues against this that in the present age technological inventions enable the weaker sex to be physically aggressive without possessing manual strength, and if women are strong enough to do comparatively heavy work in factories, shops and households, why should they not be capable of physical aggression, too? . . . It is, he concludes, the 'cultural stereotype', the 'assignment of certain social roles' rather than their physique that reduces their use of violent methods. To some extent this is true, but one has to bear in mind that, as Pollak shows himself aware in other parts of his book, the average physical inferiority of women which can hardly be denied has inevitable psychological consequences favouring non-violent techniques. This in conjunction with their actual lack of physical strength explains why women prefer poisoning to other techniques of killing, or at least try to dope the victim before resorting to violence.

> Some years ago, two young London women described as 'housewives' were sentenced to 12 months' imprisonment each at the Old Bailey. Armed with a pad soaked in ether and a knife, they had tried to rob a chauffeur who had given them a lift, by pressing the pad over his face (*The Times*, 20.1.1959). As the knife shows, they were quite prepared to kill or at least seriously injure him after overcoming his resistance by means of ether.

Lombroso and, following him, Sighele[75] speak of the greater 'ferocity' of women criminals, the latter explaining it as a consequence of their weakness, whereas the former believes at least the 'born criminal' variety to be less sensitive to pain and therefore devoid of compassion.

.   .   .

b. Psychological and sociological factors. The material presented under (*a*) on the effect of physical factors has again clearly shown their close connection with the psychological and sociological side of the problem. Starting with biological characteristics Lombroso and his followers have inevitably been driven to the discussion of psychological traits and sociological differences. The list of such traits and differences used in the literature on female crime is impressive perhaps more through its length than its persuasiveness; nevertheless, a number of points have been made which are worth mentioning, if only to see whether a coherent picture emerges from them.

It is, generally speaking, easier to produce lists of personality differences allegedly existing between the sexes than to prove that such differences are responsible for a higher or lower crime rate. Nevertheless, as will be shown below, several such personality differences have been quoted in the literature as having some effect on crime.

Lombroso wrote of the greater, biologically conditioned, conservatism of women, which makes it easier for them to accept the existing social order even where it is to their disadvantage. On the other hand, he had to admit that their sense of property was not very strong; in Paris, he reports, lost property was almost invariably brought to the office by men, and shoplifting was already at that time regarded as a typically feminine occupation, a view confirmed by the figures for 1961 quoted above. It has to be borne in mind, however, that shopping, too, is a typically feminine occupation, and something is therefore to be said for the view of Gibbens and Prince that in proportion to the total numbers of shoppers there are even more male than female shoplifters.[78] A similar point was made by the present writer in *Social Aspects of Crime* with regard to larceny by servants, where it was pointed out that the official figures, apparently so unfavourable to women, should be interpreted in the light of the numbers of existing servants of either sex, which at the time showed a considerable predominance of females (p. 341). Roughly at the time when Lombroso made his point on the greater conservatism of women the fight for their emancipation and equal rights was already on. Alexandre Dumas junior had published his *Les femmes qui tuent et les femmes qui votent*,[79] where he tried to show that women, deprived of any legal opportunities to air their grievances, had to resort to crimes of violence, and Gunnar Myrdal draws a parallel between the Negro struggle for equal rights and that of women.[80] In both instances resort to violence proved to be unavoidable; for the English Suffragettes movement before the First World War a few figures have been given in *Social Aspects of Crime* (p. 347) to show its impact on criminal statistics. Another famous figure in the movement for women's emancipation, not less important than the real ones, Ibsen's Nora, committed no crime of violence but forgery in the interest of her family. 'It appears that a woman has no right to spare her dying father, or to save her husband's life! I do not believe that . . . I believe that before all else I am a human being.' Apparently, the conservatism of women allows for certain exceptions not only in favour of their struggle for equality but also for the sake of their families. Women can become rebels against established authority just as well as men and commit crimes for the sake of the values in which they believe.

> A married woman with eleven children living with her real and a biga-
> mous husband in the same house, was sentenced to four months' im-
> prisonment at Birmingham Assizes. When the Judge told her: 'You have
> set the marriage laws of the country at complete defiance, you have
> made a mockery of the whole thing,' the woman replied: 'Did I do wrong
> in doing this for my children? The children are happy.' (*The Times*,
> 8.7.1939.) Apparently, according to her interpretation of the marriage
> laws at least two husbands were required to help her to feed eleven
> children.

Similarly, Mary Stevenson Callcott[81] tells us that in the earlier days of the Soviet regime the male peasants, seeing that opposition was useless, did not resist collectivization as fiercely as was done by their womenfolk who used to poison their cows or pigs before they were taken from them; no vision of the perfect communist society of the future could compensate them for the immediate loss of their property. In short, political ideals, whether conservative or communist, have to take second place in the female mind; the immediate needs of her own family come first and have to be protected if necessary by criminal action. This more individualistic approach to life also colours the female selection of property offences: for example women prefer shoplifting to looting, where individual choice of the articles is difficult, or to stealing money. Their lack of respect for abstract ideas such as the state and its system of justice shows itself in the greater ease with which they commit perjury. Admittedly, this is difficult to prove statistically (sex ratio for 1961, 1:6· 8), but practical court experience leaves no doubt that it is true.[82]

Whether there is a wider variety in the male than in the female personality is a controversial issue;[83] men have probably produced more extreme types than women, i.e. more geniuses, saints and leaders, but possibly also more subnormal persons, although the latter is far from certain (see also below). For example Murphy and Newcomb report that as a rule sex differences in intelligence have not been found[84] and Cyril Burt does not even mention the matter as a general problem except for the statement that among his samples of girls, particularly the older ones inclined towards sex delinquency, the proportion of defectives was perceptibly higher than among the boys.[85] On the other hand, most writers agree that there are distinct sex differences in certain special aptitudes, attitudes and temperamental traits. . . .

Girls do not form gangs, although they may occasionally join them for the sake of sexual adventures, nor do they often commit their offences in company with other females. With regard to self-assertiveness—a trait which the Gluecks distinguish from self-assertion, whereas Burt makes no such distinction[87]—this appears as a (minor) factor in Burt's table far more frequently among delinquent boys than among delinquent girls and leads among the former to 'feats of rivalry, daring and defiance', among the girls, however, to 'vain and romantic lying' and at a later age to theft and immorality to obtain gay clothes, jewellery, etc. Lying and cheating in school were observed by Hartshorne more often in girls than in boys, but mainly because of their higher ambitions.[88] The greater deceitfulness of women is also used by Pollak to explain their greater success in 'masking' their crimes; his explanation of the prevalence of this trait is partly a biological, partly a sociological one. Women are forced by the sex mores of our society every four weeks to conceal their period of menstruation and to misrepresent the 'facts of life' to their children; they are also forced to suppress their natural aggressive instincts— all of which is bound to make them deceitful.[89]

William Healy, who also found among his cases more female than male liars, is inclined to blame largely the social environment for it.[90]

We might add that the male-dominated character of the criminal law, to which we referred before, has made women, except for the natural 'rebels', accustomed to get 'around' rather than act against the law; one might therefore even venture the paradox that in a female-dominated legal system their crime rate would increase. Closely connected with this, the greater capacity of women to adapt themselves to reality and their greater elasticity and resourcefulness have been stressed. Men trained for a specific calling find it more difficult to adapt themselves to another occupation than their wives who, mostly possessing no such training, are usually elastic enough to change their life pattern.[91] Johanna C. Hudig, too, speaks of the greater adaptability of women who resign themselves more readily to the inevitable, who possess 'greater pliancy and tact'.[92] Added to this, men are at a further disadvantage in having to bear heavier responsibilities towards their families and the sometimes excessive financial demands of their wives. East quotes in this connection the observation of a bank employee that in nine out of ten cases bank clerks went wrong because of such demands,[93] but figures of this kind have invariably to be treated with the greatest caution. Moreover, criminologists have been aware of the profound changes in the social and occupational status of women in the course of the present century. Reference has already been made to the criminological impact of the political movements which helped to produce these changes; now we have to consider the impact of these developments on the female crime rate. Since Bonger, nearly fifty years ago, expressed the view that women were like hothouse plants, sheltered from the icy blasts of life and therefore less criminal,[94] women have assumed new roles in the economic and occupational life of society. The present century is not the first period of upheaval in the occupational lives of women.[95] The Industrial Revolution, too, deprived many of them of their previous work in the home and forced them to enter the factory. In the twentieth century it was first the two world wars that not only added greatly to their domestic responsibilities but also turned millions of married women into industrial workers or shop assistants, etc., and some of them even into managers and company directors. In the United States, with its female labour force of over 21 million in 1957, the proportion of married women in employment increased from 30 per cent in 1940 to 54 per cent in 1957. In Britain, 'between 1946 and May 1955 the number of married women in gainful employment rose by two and a quarter million to three and three quarter million or 48 per cent of all women at work'.[96]

While the number of domestic servants has greatly declined, that of female factory workers, office employees, etc., has greatly increased. Has this led to a corresponding increase in the female crime rate for offences connected with their employment? English official figures again show no coherent picture. . . . There is, therefore, no uniform increase, and we should avoid hasty conclusions.

In certain other ways, however, the changed social and occupational position of women shows itself occasionally in the nature of the criminal situations in which they are caught. In former days it was one of the familiar patterns of spy trials to see more or less beautiful women being used as baits to extract military or political secrets from middle-aged men in high positions. Now we find a middle-aged woman holding an influential job in a government department, drawing a salary of £3,800, pleading guilty to eight counts of 'unlawfully communicating documents contrary to s. 2(1) of the Official Secrets Act, 1911' to an official of a foreign Embassy, to whom she had formed an attachment. She was sentenced to two years' imprisonment, and the Court of Criminal Appeal, stressing in particular the obligations of her high position, refused her application for permission to appeal against this sentence, in spite of the presence of a number of mitigating circumstances.[97] In another, less sensational, recent case a married woman bank clerk, again of middle age, was sentenced to 12 months' imprisonment for stealing foreign currency and obtaining money by forgery from her employers under pressure from her lover (*The Times*, 5.9.1963). Extra-marital associations may, criminologically speaking, cut both ways: women may be persuaded or even forced by their lovers to steal, embezzle, defraud, receive or kill, or they may use them to commit such offences or crimes of violence for them. Their fairly high rate for receiving is, as Pollak rightly says (p. 87), largely due to their traditional role in the family as being given money for house-keeping, but also as receivers of presents. Not surprisingly, some small sums of the money stolen in the great train robbery of August 1963 . . . were found in the possession of a few women who were however found not guilty of receiving.

Albert K. Cohen . . . has tried to explain the lower female crime rate by suggesting that women may have their own brand of subculture which approves or disapproves conduct in ways fundamentally different from their male counterparts, with ideals and solutions entirely their own.[98] Their social status is largely determined by that of their husbands, whereas the opposite is not true to the same degree (with some notable exceptions, we might add). Consequently, Cohen argues, their behaviour is also less determined by opposition to the middle-class norms, with all the criminogenic dangers which such opposition implies. He admits the so far rudimentary and over-simplified character of his arguments which may not do full justice to the fact that in our society women are actually among the worst victims of the 'status-seeking' mania. . . .

Attempts, occasionally made by older writers, to use the lower crime rate of women to prove their higher moral standards or greater religiosity, have now been abandoned. Already Quetelet was rather sceptical, and later on von Oettingen derided the view expressed by a French writer that because women went to church five times as often as men it was only natural that their crime rate should be only one-fifth of the male.[99]

Notes

42. On the Sex Factor: Cesare Lombroso and G. Ferrero, *La donna delinquente, la prostituta e la donna normale,* Torino, 1893, Eng. ed. *The Female Offender,* London, 1895; Pauline Tarnowsky, *Etude anthropometrique sur les prostituées et les voleuses,* Paris, 1889; also *Les femmes homicides,* Paris, 1908; Johanna C. Hudig, *De Criminaliteit der Vrouw,* Utrecht–Nijmegen, 1940; Hermann Mannheim, *Social Aspects of Crime in England between the Wars,* London, 1940, Ch. 11; Stephan Hurwitz, *Criminology,* pp. 269–79; Mabel E. Elliott, *Crime in Modern Society,* New York, 1952, Chs. 8, 9; Otto Pollak, *The Criminality of Women,* Philadelphia, 1950; Hans v. Hentig, *Crime: Its Causes and Condition,* New York, 1947, Ch. 5; J. M. van Bemmelen, *Kriminologie,* 3rd ed., Zwolle, 1952, Ch. 11; Wolf Middendorff, *Soziologie des Verbrechens,* Düsseldorf–Köln, 1959, pp. 248–256; 'The Female Offender', *N.P.P.A. Journal,* Vol. 3, No. 1, Jan. 1957; S. and E. Glueck, *Five Hundred Delinquent Women,* New York, 1934; Ernst Roesner and Max Hagemann in *Handwörterbuch der Kriminologie,* Vol. 1, 1933, pp. 574–95, and Vol. 2, 1936, pp. 1049–63; Jean Pinatel, *Criminologie,* Paris, 1963, pp. 154 ff.; Sebastian von Koppenfels, *Die Kriminalität der Frau im Kriege,* Leipzig, 1926; Leon Radzinowicz, 'Sex Rates of Criminality', *Sociol. Rev.,* Vol. 29, Jan. 1937 (Polish material); Grace W. Pailthorpe, *Studies in the Psychology of Delinquency,* Medical Research Council, H.M.S.O., London, 1932; Hedwig Schwarz, 'The Psycho-Analysis of a Case of Stealing, *Brit. J. Delinq.,* Vol. 1, No. 1, July 1950, pp. 29–44; Phyllis Epps, 'A Preliminary Survey of 300 Female Delinquents in Borstal Institutions', *Brit. J. Delinq.,* Vol. 1, No. 3, Jan. 1951, pp. 187–97; the same, 'A Further Survey of Female Delinquents Undergoing Borstal Training', *Brit. J. Delinq.,* Vol. 4, No. 4, April 1954, pp. 265–71; the same, 'Women Shoplifters in Holloway Prison', in T. C. N. Gibbens and Joyce Prince, *Shoplifting,* Ch. 14, London, 1962, I.S.T.D.; Moya Woodside, 'Women Drinkers in Holloway Prison', *Brit. J. Crim.,* Vol. 1, No. 3, Jan. 1961, pp. 221–35; Ann D. Smith, *Women in Prison,* London, 1962, Chs. 1, 2.
43. See *Social Aspects of Crime,* pp. 336–7.
44. Barbara Wootton, *op. cit.,* pp. 31–2, 318.
45. Freud, in *Totem and Taboo,* p. 21, quotes from Sir James Frazer an instance of the same presumption of coercion in a New South Wales tribe.

46. On this and similar provisions in other foreign codes see H. H. Heldmann, *Mschr. Kriminol. Strafrechtsreform*, Vol. 40, Nos. 3–4, June 1957, pp. 86–104.
47. See *Criminal Justice and Social Reconstruction*, p. 77.

•   •   •

49. Pollak, *op. cit.*, Ch. 1: 'The Masked Character of Female Crime'.
50. v. Hentig, *Zur Psychologie der Einzeldelikte*, Vol. 4: 'Die Erpressung', Tübingen, 1949, pp. 220 ff.
51. *Social Aspects of Crime*, p. 344.
52. Reckless in N.P.P.A. *Journal*, p. 1.
53. *Criminal Statistics for 1961*, p. 32.
54. See, e.g., *Social Aspects of Crime*, pp. 342–4; *Criminal Statistics for 1961*, pp. 40–1; Pollak, *op. cit.*, pp. 3–5.

•   •   •

58. See, e.g., H. von Hentig, *Die Strafe*, Vol. 1, Berlin, 1954, pp. 122 ff.
59. Ann D. Smith, *op. cit.*, p. 57.
60. Radbruch-Gwinner, *Geschichte des Verbrechens*, Ch. 15, esp. p. 158; Wallace Notestein, *A History of Witchcraft in England 1558–1718*, Washington, 1911.
61. Kurt Baschwitz, *Hexen und Hexenprozesse*, München, 1963.
62. L. O. Pike, *A History of Crime in England*, London, 1873–6, Vol. 1, pp. 255–6.
63. Radbruch-Gwinner, *op. cit.*, Ch. 9, esp. p. 94.
64. On this and the following text see Radbruch–Gwinner, *op. cit.*, Ch. 22.
65. See Frances Mossiker, *The Queen's Necklace*, London, 1961, and on this and the case of the Marquise de Brinvilliers Henri Robert, *Les grands procès d'histoire*, Paris, 1923–35.

•   •   •

69. See above, Preliminary Observations to Part 3.
70. Report of the Children's Department, Home Office, H.M.S.O., 1964.
71. E.g., Pollak, *op. cit.*, pp. 123–5.
72. E.g., Gibbens, *Brit. J. Delinq.*, Vol. 10, No. 2, Oct. 1959, pp. 81–103.
73. Epps, *Brit. J. Delinq.*, Vol. 1, p. 150.

•   •   •

75. Scipio Sighele, *La foule criminelle*, 2nd ed., Paris, 1901, pp. 97–8.

•   •   •

78. Gibbens and Prince, *op. cit.*, p. 126.
79. Alexandre Dumas, *op. cit.*
80. Gunnar Myrdal, *An American Dilemma*, New York-London, 1944, pp. 237–62.
81. Mary Stevenson Callcott (*op. cit.* at note 10), p. 62.
82. See also Middendorff, *op. cit.*, p. 251, who gives the sex ratio for perjury in Germany as 1:3.
83. See, e.g., F. H. Allport, *Institutional Behavior*, Ch. 18.
84. Murphy–Murphy–Newcomb, *Experimental Social Psychology*, New York-London, p. 71.
85. *The Young Delinquent*, pp. 299–300.

•   •   •

87. Burt, *op. cit.*, pp. 470, 491; S. and E. Glueck, *Family Environment and Delinquency*, p. 207.
88. Hugh Hartshorne and Mark A. May, *Studies in Deceit*, New York, 1930, Vol. 1, p. 177. On this study see also *Group Problems in Crime and Punishment*, p. 21.
89. Pollak, *op. cit.*, pp. 9–12.
90. W. and M. T. Healy, 'Pathological Lying, Accusation and Swindling', Crim. Sci. Monogr. No. 1 (Supplement to *J. Amer. Inst. Crim. Law Criminol.*), London, 1915.

91. Karl Mannheim, *Man and Society in an Age of Reconstruction*, London, 1940, p. 156.
92. Johanna C. Hudig (*op. cit.* at note 42), p. 257.
93. W. Norwood East, *The Adolescent Criminal*, London, 1942, p. 300.
94. Willem A. Bonger, *Criminality and Economic Conditions*, Boston, 1916.
95. For the following see Mabel A. Elliott and Francis E. Merrill, *Social Disorganization*, 4th ed., New York, 1961, Ch. 9.
96. Richard M. Titmuss, *Essays on 'The Welfare State'*, London, 1958, p. 102.
97. See *The Times*, 29.11, 8.12.1962, 22.1.1963 (Court of Criminal Appeal).
98. Albert K. Cohen, *Delinquent Boys*, pp. 44, 137 ff. In a small but useful piece of research Ruth R. Morris, *Brit. J. Crim.*, Vol. 5, 1965, has undertaken to prove that the differential sex rate is due to the 'different sex role objectives for boys and girls ... Society provides more cultural and sub-cultural support for male than female delinquency.' There is more tolerance for male than for female delinquency. It may be doubted whether this is generally true. One can often observe a greater reluctance on the part of representatives of society to charge girls before a juvenile court than there would be in the case of boys.
99. A. Quetelet, *Recherches sur le penchant au crime*, 1838, p. 38; A. v. Oettingen, *Die Moralstatistik in ihrer Bedeutung für eine Sozialethik*, 3rd ed., Erlangen, 1882, p. 526, fn. 2. Also Gabriel Tarde, *Philosophie pénale*, 4th ed., 1895, p. 379, fn. 1.

7 The Etiology of Female Crime
Dorie Klein

Introduction

The criminality of women has long been a neglected subject area of criminology. Many explanations have been advanced for this, such as women's low official rate of crime and delinquency and the preponderance of male theorists in the field. Female criminality has often ended up as a footnote to works on men that purport to be works on criminality in general.

There has been, however, a small group of writings specifically concerned with women and crime. This paper will explore those works concerned with the etiology of female crime and delinquency, beginning with the turn-of-the-century writing of Lombroso and extending to the present. Writers selected to be included have been chosen either for their influence on the field, such as Lombroso, Thomas, Freud, Davis and Pollak, or because they are representative of the kinds of work being published, such as Konopka, Vedder and Somerville, and Cowie, Cowie and Slater. The emphasis is on the continuity between these works, because it is clear that, despite recognizable differences in analytical approaches and specific theories, the authors represent a tradition to a great extent. It is important to understand, therefore, the shared assumptions made by the writers that are used in laying the groundwork for their theories.

The writers see criminality as the result of *individual* characteristics that are only peripherally affected by economic, social and political forces. These characteristics are of a *physiological* or *psychological* nature and are uniformly based on implicit or explicit assumptions about the *inherent nature of women.*

"The Etiology of Female Crime: A Review of the Literature" by Dorie Klein, in *Issues in Criminology,* vol. 8, no. 2, Fall 1973: 3–30. Permission to reprint this article has been granted by *Crime and Social Justice,* P.O. Box 4373, Berkeley, California, 94704.

[The author wishes] to acknowledge the major contributions made by the Women's Caucus of the School of Criminology, University of California, Berkeley.

This nature is *universal,* rather than existing within a specific historical framework.

Since criminality is seen as an individual activity, rather than as a condition built into existing structures, the focus is on biological, psychological and social factors that would turn a woman toward criminal activity. To do this, the writers create two distinct classes of women: good women who are "normal" noncriminals, and bad women who are criminals, thus taking a moral position that often masquerades as a scientific distinction. The writers, although they may be biological or social determinists to varying degrees, assume that individuals have *choices* between criminal and noncriminal activity. They see persons as atomistically moving about in a social and political vacuum; many writers use marketplace models for human interaction.

Although the theorists may differ on specific remedies for individual criminality, ranging from sterilization to psychoanalysis (but always stopping far short of social change), the basic thrust is toward *individual adjustment,* whether it be physical or mental, and the frequent model is rehabilitative therapy. Widespread environmental alterations are usually included as casual footnotes to specific plans for individual therapy. Most of the writers are concerned with *social harmony* and the welfare of the existing social structure rather than with the women involved or with women's position in general. None of the writers come from anything near a "feminist" or "radical" perspective.

In *The Female Offender,* originally published in 1903, Lombroso described female criminality as an inherent tendency produced in individuals that could be regarded as biological atavisms, similar to cranial and facial features, and one could expect a withering away of crime if the atavistic people were prohibited from breeding. At this time criminality was widely regarded as a physical ailment, like epilepsy. Today, Cowie, Cowie and Slater (1968) have identified physical traits in girls who have been classified as delinquent, and have concluded that certain traits, such as bigness, may lead to aggressiveness. This theme of physiological characteristics has been developed by a good number of writers in the last seventy years, such as the Gluecks (1934). One sees at the present time a new surge of "biological" theories of criminality; for example, a study involving "violence-prone" women and menstrual cycles has recently been proposed at UCLA.[1]

Thomas, to a certain degree, and Freud extend the physiological explanation of criminality to propose a psychological theory. However, it is critical to understand that these psychological notions are based on assumptions of universal *physiological* traits of women, such as their reproductive instinct and passivity, that are seen as invariably producing certain psychological reactions. Women may be viewed as turning to crime as a *perversion of* or *rebellion against* their *natural feminine roles.* Whether their problems are biological, psychological or social-environmental, the point is always to return them to their roles. Thomas (1907; 1923), for example, points out that poverty might prevent a woman from marrying, whereby she would turn to prostitution as an alternative to carry on her feminine service role. In fact, Davis (1961) discusses prostitution as a parallel illegal institution to marriage. Pollak (1950) discusses how women extend their service roles into criminal activity due to inherent tendencies such as deceitfulness. Freud (1933; Jones, 1961) sees any kind of rebellion as the result of a failure to develop healthy feminine attitudes, such as narcissism, and Konopka (1966) and Vedder and Somerville (1970) apply Freudian thought to the problem of female delinquency.

The specific characteristics ascribed to women's nature and those critical to theories of female criminality are uniformly *sexual* in their nature. Sexuality is seen as the root of female behavior and the problem of crime. Women are defined as sexual beings, as sexual capital in many cases, physiologically, psychologically and socially. This definition *reflects* and *reinforces* the economic position of women as reproductive and domestic workers. It is mirrored in the laws themselves and in their enforcement, which penalize sexual deviations for women and may be more lenient with economic offenses committed by them, in contrast to the treatment given men. The theorists accept the sexual double standard inherent in the law, often noting that "chivalry" protects women, and many of them build notions of the universality of *sex repression* into their explanations of women's position. Women are thus the sexual backbone of civilization.

In setting hegemonic standards of conduct for all women, the theorists define *femininity*, which they equate with healthy femaleness, in classist, racist and sexist terms, using their assumptions of women's nature, specifically their sexuality, to justify what is often in reality merely a defense of the existing order. Lombroso, Thomas and Freud consider the upper-class white woman to be the highest expression of femininity, although she is inferior to the upper-class white man. These standards are adopted by later writers in discussing femininity. To most theorists, women are inherently inferior to men at masculine tasks such as thought and production, and therefore it is logical that their sphere should be reproductive.

Specific characteristics are proposed to bolster this sexual ideology, expressed for example by Freud, such as passivity, emotionalism, narcissism and deceitfulness. In the discussions of criminality, certain theorists, such as Pollak, link female criminality to these traits. Others see criminality as an attempt away from femininity into masculinity, such as Lombroso, although the specifics are often confused. Contradictions can be clearly seen, which are explained by the dual nature of "good" and "bad" women and by the fact that this is a mythology attempting to explain real behavior. Many explanations of what are obviously economically motivated offenses, such as prostitution and shoplifting, are explained in sexual terms, such as prostitution being promiscuity, and shoplifting being "kleptomania" caused by women's inexplicable mental cycles tied to menstruation. Different explanations have to be made for "masculine" crimes, *e.g.*, burglary, and for "feminine" crimes, *e.g.*, shoplifting. Although this distinction crops up consistently, the specifics differ wildly.

The problem is complicated by the lack of knowledge of the epidemiology of female crime, which allows such ideas as "hidden crime," first expressed by Pollak (1950), to take root. The problem must be considered on two levels: women, having been confined to certain tasks and socialized in certain ways, are *in fact* more likely to commit crime related to their lives which are sexually oriented; yet even nonsexual offenses are *explained* in sexual terms by the theorists. The writers ignore the problems of poor and Third World women, concentrating on affluent white standards of femininity. The experiences of these overlooked women, who *in fact* constitute a good percentage of women caught up in the criminal justice system, negate the notions of sexually motivated crime. These women have real economic needs which are not being met, and in many cases engage in illegal activities as a viable economic alternative. Furthermore, chivalry has never been extended to them.

The writers largely ignore the problems of sexism, racism and class, thus their work is sexist, racist and classist in its implications. Their concern is adjustment of the woman to society, not social change. Hence, they represent a tradition in criminology and carry along a host of assumptions about women and humanity in general. It is important to explore these assumptions and traditions in depth in order to understand what kinds of myths have been propagated around women and crime. The discussions of each writer or writers will focus on these assumptions and their relevance to criminological theories. These assumptions of universal, biological/psychological characteristics, of individual responsibility for crime, of the necessity for maintaining social harmony, and of the benevolence of the state link different theories along a continuum, transcending political labels and minor divergences. The road from Lombroso to the present is surprisingly straight.

Lombroso: "there must be some anomaly . . ."

Lombroso's work on female criminality (1920) is important to consider today despite the fact that his methodology and conclusions have long been successfully discredited. Later writings on female crime by Thomas, Davis, Pollak and others use more sophisticated methodologies and may proffer more palatable liberal theories. However, to varying degrees they rely on those sexual ideologies based on *implicit* assumptions about the physiological and psychological nature of women that are *explicit* in Lombroso's work. Reading the work helps to achieve a better understanding of what kinds of myths have been developed for women in general and for female crime and deviance in particular.

One specific notion of women offered by Lombroso is women's physiological immobility and psychological passivity, later elaborated by Thomas, Freud and other writers. Another ascribed characteristic is the Lombrosian notion of women's adaptability to surroundings and their capacity for survival as being superior to that of men. A third idea discussed by Lombroso is women's amorality: they are cold and calculating. This is developed by Thomas (1923), who describes women's manipulation of the male sex urge for ulterior purposes; by Freud (1933), who sees women as avenging their lack of a penis on men; and by Pollak (1950), who depicts women as inherently deceitful.

When one looks at these specific traits, one sees contradictions. The myth of compassionate women clashes with their reputed coldness; their frailness belies their capacity to survive. One possible explanation for these contradictions is the duality of sexual ideology with regard to "good" and "bad" women.[2] Bad women are whores, driven by lust for money or for men, often essentially *"masculine"* in their orientation, and perhaps afflicted with a touch of penis envy. Good women are chaste, "feminine," and usually not prone to criminal activity. But when they are, they commit crime in a most *ladylike* way such as poisoning. In more sophisticated theory, all women are seen as having a bit of both tendencies in them. Therefore, women can be compassionate *and* cold, frail *and* sturdy, pious *and* amoral, depending on which path they choose to follow. They are seen as rational (although they are irrational, too!), atomistic individuals making choices in a vacuum, prompted only by personal, physiological/psychological factors. These choices relate only to the *sexual* sphere. Women have no place in any other sphere. Men, on the other hand, are not held sexually accountable, although, as Thomas notes (1907), they are held responsible in *economic* matters. Men's sexual freedom is justified by the myth of masculine, irresistible sex urges. This myth, still worshipped today, is frequently offered as a rationalization for the existence of prostitution and the double standard. As Davis maintains, this necessitates the parallel existence of classes of "good" and "bad" women.

These dual moralities for the sexes are outgrowths of the economic, political and social *realities* for men and women. Women are primarily workers within the family, a critical institution of reproduction and socialization that services such basic needs as food and shelter. Laws and codes of behavior for women thus attempt to maintain the smooth functioning of women in that role, which requires that women act as a conservative force in the continuation of the nuclear family. Women's main tasks are sexual, and the law embodies sexual limitations for women, which do not exist for men, such as the prohibition of promiscuity for girls. This explains why theorists of female criminality are not only concerned with sexual violations by female offenders, but attempt to account for even *nonsexual* offenses, such as prostitution, in sexual terms, *e.g.,* women enter prostitution for sex rather than for money. Such women are not only economic offenders but are sexual deviants, falling neatly into the category of "bad" women.

The works of Lombroso, particularly *The Female Offender* (1920), are a foremost example of the biological explanation of crime. Lombroso deals with crime as an atavism, or survival of "primitive" traits in individuals, particularly those of the female and nonwhite races. He theorizes that individuals develop differentially within sexual and racial limitations which differ hierarchically from the most highly developed, the white men, to the most primitive, the nonwhite women. Beginning with the assumption that criminals must be atavistic, he spends a good deal of time comparing the crania, moles, heights, etc. of convicted criminals and prostitutes with those of normal women. Any trait that he finds to be more common in the "criminal" group is pronounced an atavistic trait, such as moles, dark hair, etc., and women with a number of these telltale traits could be regarded as potentially criminal, since they are of the atavistic type. He specifically rejects the idea that some of these traits, for example obesity in prostitutes, could be the *result* of their activities rather than an indicator of their propensity to them. Many of the traits depicted as "anomalies," such as darkness and shortness, are characteristic of certain racial groups, such as the Sicilians, who undoubtedly comprise an oppressed group within Italy and form a large part of the imprisoned population.

Lombroso traces an overall pattern of evolution in the human species that accounts for the uneven development of groups: the white and nonwhite races, males and females, adults and children. Women, children and nonwhites share many traits in common. There are fewer variations in their mental capacities: "even the female criminal is monotonous and uniform compared with her male companion, just as in general woman is inferior to man." (*Ibid.*:122), due to her being "atavistically nearer to her origin than the male" (*Ibid.*:107). The notion of women's mediocrity, or limited range of mental possibilities, is a recurrent one in the writings of the twentieth century. Thomas and others note that women comprise "fewer geniuses, fewer lunatics and fewer morons" (Thomas, 1907:45); lacking the imagination to be at either end of the spectrum, they are conformist and dull . . . not due to social, political or economic constraints on their activities, but because of their innate physiological limitations as a sex. Lombroso attributes the lower female rate of criminality to their having fewer anomalies, which is one aspect of their closeness to the lower forms of less differentiated life.

Related characteristics of women are their passivity and conservatism. Lombroso admits that women's traditional sex roles in the family bind them to a more sedentary life. However, he insists that women's passivity can be directly traced to the "immobility of the ovule compared with the zoosperm" (1920:109), falling back on the sexual act in an interesting anticipation of Freud.

Women, like the lower races, have greater powers of endurance and resistance to mental and physical pain than men. Lombroso states: "denizens of female prisoners . . . have reached the age of 90, having lived within those walls since they were 29 without any grave injury to health" (*Ibid.*:125). Denying the humanity of women by denying their capability for suffering justifies exploitation of women's energies by arguing for their suitability to hardship. Lombroso remarks that "a duchess can adapt herself to new surroundings and become a washerwoman much more easily than a man can transform himself under analogous conditions" (*Ibid.*:272). The theme of women's adaptability to physical and social surroundings, which are male initiated, male controlled, and often expressed by saying that women are actually the "stronger" sex, is a persistent thread in writings on women.

Lombroso explains that because women are unable to feel pain, they are insensitive to the pain of others and lack moral refinement. His blunt denial of the age-old myth of women's compassion and sensitivity is modified, however, to take into account women's low crime rate:

> Women have many traits in common with children; that their moral sense is deficient; that they are revengeful, jealous . . . In ordinary cases these defects are neutralized by piety, maternity, want of passion, sexual coldness, weakness and an undeveloped intelligence (*Ibid.*:151).

Although women lack the higher sensibilities of men, they are thus restrained from criminal activity in most cases by lack of intelligence and passion, qualities which *criminal* women possess as well as all *men*. Within this framework of biological limits of women's nature, the female offender is characterized as *masculine* whereas the normal woman is *feminine*. The anomalies of skull, physiognomy and brain capacity of female criminals, according to Lombroso, more closely approximate that of the man, normal or criminal, than they do those of the normal woman; the female offender often has a "virile cranium" and considerable body hair. Masculinity in women is an anomaly itself, rather than a sign of development, however. A related notion is developed by Thomas, who notes that in "civilized" nations the sexes are more physically different.

> What we look for most in the female is femininity, and when we find the opposite in her, we must conclude as a rule that there must be some anomaly . . . Virility was one of the special features of the savage woman . . . In the portraits of Red Indian and Negro beauties, whom it is difficult to recognize for women, so huge are their jaws and cheekbones, so hard and coarse their features, and the same is often the case in their crania and brains (*Ibid.*:112).

The more highly developed races would therefore have the most feminized women with the requisite passivity, lack of passion, etc. This is a *racist* and *classist* definition of femininity—just as are almost all theories of *femininity* and as, indeed, is the thing itself. The ideal of the lady can only exist in a society built on the exploitation of labor to maintain the woman of leisure who can *be* that ideal lady.

Finally, Lombroso notes women's lack of *property sense,* which contributes to their criminality.

> In their eyes theft is . . . an audacity for which account compensation is due to the owner . . . as an individual rather than a social crime, just as it was regarded in the primitive periods of human evolution and is still regarded by many uncivilized nations (*Ibid.*:217).

One may question this statement on several levels. Can it be assumed to have any validity at all, or is it false that women have a different sense of property than men? If it is valid to a degree, is it related to women's lack of property ownership and nonparticipation in the accumulation of capitalist wealth? Indeed, as Thomas (1907) points out, women are considered property themselves. At any rate, it is an interesting point in Lombroso's book that has only been touched on by later writers, and always in a manner supportive of the institution of private property.

Thomas: "the stimulation she craves"

The works of W. I. Thomas are critical in that they mark a transition from purely physiological explanations such as Lombroso's to more sophisticated theories that embrace physiological, psychological and social-structural factors. However, even the most sophisticated explanations of female crime rely on implicit assumptions about the *biological* nature of women. In Thomas' *Sex and Society* (1907) and *The Unadjusted Girl* (1923), there are important contradictions in the two approaches that are representative of the movements during that period between publication dates: a departure from biological Social-Darwinian theories to complex analyses of the interaction between society and the individual, *i.e.*, societal repression and manipulation of the "natural" wishes of persons.

In *Sex and Society* (1907), Thomas poses basic biological differences between the sexes as his starting point. Maleness is "katabolic," the animal force which is destructive of energy and allows men the possibility of creative work through this outward flow. Femaleness is "anabolic," analogous to a plant which stores energy, and is motionless and conservative. Here Thomas is offering his own version of the age-old male/female dichotomy expressed by Lombroso and elaborated on in Freud's paradigm, in the structural-functionalist "instrumental-expressive" duality, and in other analyses of the status quo. According to Thomas, the dichotomy is most highly developed in the more civilized races, due to the greater differentiation of sex roles. This statement ignores the hard physical work done by poor *white* women at home and in the factories and offices in "civilized" countries, and accepts a *ruling-class* definition of femininity.

The cause of women's relative decline in stature in more "civilized" countries is a subject on which Thomas is ambivalent. At one point he attributes it to the lack of "a superior fitness on the motor side" in women (*Ibid.*:94); at another point, he regards her loss of *sexual freedom* as critical, with the coming of monogamy and her confinement to sexual tasks such as wifehood and motherhood. He perceptively notes:

> Women were still further degraded by the development of property and its control by man, together with the habit of treating her as a piece of property, whose value was enhanced if its purity was assured (*Ibid.*:297).

However, Thomas' underlying assumptions in his explanations of the inferior status of women are *physiological* ones. He attributes to men high amounts of sexual energy, which lead them to pursue women for their sex, and he attributes to women maternal feelings devoid of sexuality, which lead *them* to exchange sex for domesticity. Thus monogamy, with chastity for women, is the *accommodation* of these basic urges, and women are domesticated while men assume leadership, in a true market exchange.

Why, then, does Thomas see problems in the position of women? It is because modern women are plagued by "irregularity, pettiness, ill health and inserviceableness" (*Ibid.*:245). Change is required to maintain *social harmony*, apart from considerations of women's needs, and women must be educated to make them better wives, a theme reiterated throughout this century by "liberals" on the subject. Correctly anticipating a threat, Thomas urges that change be made to stabilize the family, and warns that "no civilization can remain the highest if another civilization adds to the intelligence of its men the intelligence of its women" (*Ibid.*:314). Thomas is motivated by considerations of social integration. Of course, one might question how women are to be able to contribute much if they are indeed anabolic. However, due to the transitional nature of Thomas' work, there are immense contradictions in his writing.

Many of Thomas' specific assertions about the nature of women are indistinguishable from Lombroso's; they both delineate a biological hierarchy along race and sex lines.

> Man has, in short, become more somatically specialized an animal than woman, and feels more keenly any disturbance of normal conditions with which he has not the same physiological surplus as woman with which to meet the disturbance . . . It is a logical fact, however, that the lower human races, the lower classes of society, women and children show something of the same quality in their superior tolerance of surgical disease (*Ibid.*:36).

Like Lombroso, Thomas is crediting women with superior capabilities of survival because they are further down the scale in terms of evolution. It is significant that Thomas includes the lower classes in his observation; is he implying that the lower classes are in their position *because* of their natural unfitness, or perhaps that their *situation* renders them less sensitive to pain? At different times, Thomas implies both. Furthermore, he agrees with Lombroso that women are more nearly uniform than men, and says that they have a smaller percentage of "genius, insanity and idiocy" (*Ibid.*:45) than men, as well as fewer creative outbursts of energy.

Dealing with female criminality in *Sex and Society* (1907), Thomas begins to address the issue of morality, which he closely links to legality from a standpoint of maintaining social order. He discriminates between male and female morality:

> Morality as applied to men has a larger element of the contractual, representing the adjustment of his activities to those of society at large, or more particularly to the activities of the male members of society; while the morality which we think of in connection with women shows less of the contractual and more of the personal, representing her adjustment to men, more particularly the adjustment of her person to men (*Ibid.*:172).

Whereas Lombroso barely observes women's lack of participation in the institution of private property, Thomas' perception is more profound. He points out that women *are* property of men and that their conduct is subject to different codes.

> Morality, in the most general sense, represents the code under which activities are best carried on and is worked out in the school of experience. It is preeminently an adult and male system, and men are intelligent enough to realize that neither women nor children have passed through this school. It is on this account that man is merciless to woman from the standpoint of personal behavior, yet he exempts her from anything in the way of contractual morality, or views her defections in this regard with allowance and even with amusement (*Ibid.*:234).

Disregarding his remarks about intelligence, one confronts the critical point about women with respect to the law: because they occupy a *marginal* position in the productive sphere of exchange commodities outside the home, they in turn occupy a marginal position in regard to "contractual" law which regulates relations of property and production. The argument of differential treatment of men and women by the law is developed in later works by Pollak and others, who attribute it to the "chivalry" of the system which is lenient to women committing offenses. As Thomas notes, however, women are simply not a serious *threat* to property, and are treated more "leniently" because of this. Certain women do become threats by transcending (or by being denied) their traditional role, particularly many Third World women and political rebels, and they are *not* afforded chivalrous treatment! In fact, chivalry is reserved for the women who are least likely to ever come in contact with the criminal justice system: the ladies, or white middle-class women. In matters of *sexual* conduct, however, which embody the double standard, women are rigorously prosecuted by the law. As Thomas understands, this is the sphere in which women's functions *are* critical. Thus it is not a matter of "chivalry" how one is handled, but of different forms and thrusts of social control applied to men and women. Men are engaged in productive tasks and their activities in this area *are* strictly curtailed.

In *The Unadjusted Girl* (1923), Thomas deals with female delinquency as a "normal" response under certain social conditions, using assumptions about the nature of women which he leaves unarticulated in this work. Driven by basic "wishes," an individual is controlled by society in her activities through institutional transmission of codes and mores. Depending on how they are manipulated, wishes can be made to serve social or antisocial ends. Thomas stresses the institutions that socialize, such as the family, giving people certain "definitions of the situation." He confidently—and defiantly—asserts:

> There is no individual energy, no unrest, no type of wish, which cannot be sublimated and made socially useful. From this standpoint, the problem is not the right of society to protect itself from the disorderly and antisocial person, but the right of the disorderly and antisocial person to be made orderly and socially valuable . . . The problem of society is to produce the right attitudes in its members (*Ibid.*:232–233).

This is an important shift in perspective, from the traditional libertarian view of protecting society by punishing transgressors, to the *rehabilitative* and *preventive* perspective of crime control that seeks to control *minds* through socialization rather than to merely control behavior through punishment. The autonomy of the individual to choose is seen as the product of his environment which the state can alter. This is an important refutation of the Lombrosian biological perspective, which maintains that there are crime-prone individuals who must be locked up, sterilized or otherwise incapacitated. Today, one can see an amalgamation of the two perspectives in new theories of "behavior control" that use tactics such as conditioning and brain surgery, combining biological and environmental viewpoints.[3]

Thomas proposes the manipulation of individuals through institutions to prevent antisocial attitudes, and maintains that there is no such person as the "crime prone" individual. A hegemonic system of belief can be imposed by sublimating natural urges and by correcting the poor socialization of slum families. In this perspective, the *definition* of the situation rather than the situation *itself* is what should be changed; a situation is what someone *thinks* it is. The response to a criminal woman who is dissatisfied with her conventional sexual roles is to change not the roles, which would mean widespread social transformations, but to change her attitudes. This concept of civilization as repressive and the need to adjust is later refined by Freud.

Middle-class women, according to Thomas, commit little crime because they are socialized to sublimate their natural desires and to behave well, treasuring their chastity as an investment. The poor woman, however, "is not immoral, because this implies a loss of morality, but amoral" (*Ibid.*:98). Poor women are not objectively driven to crime; they long for it. Delinquent girls are motivated by the desire for excitement or "new experience," and forget the repressive urge of "security." However, these desires are well within Thomas' conception of *femininity*: delinquents are not rebelling against womanhood, as Lombroso suggests, but merely acting it out illegally. Davis and Pollak agree with this notion that delinquent women are not "different" from nondelinquent women.

Thomas maintains that it is not sexual desire that motivates delinquent girls, for they are no more passionate than other women, but they are *manipulating* male desires for sex to achieve their own ulterior ends.

> The beginning of delinquency in girls is usually an impulse to get amusement, adventure, pretty clothes, favorable notice, distinction, freedom in the larger world . . . The girls have usually become 'wild' before the development of sexual desire, and their casual sex relations do not usually awaken sex feeling. Their sex is used as a condition of the realization of other wishes. It is their capital (*Ibid.*:109).

Here Thomas is expanding on the myth of the manipulative woman, who is cold and scheming and vain. To him, good female sexual behavior is a protective measure—"instinctive, of course" (1907:241), whereas male behavior is uncontrollable as men are caught by helpless desires. This is the common Victorian notion of the woman as seductress which in turn perpetuates the myth of a lack of real sexuality to justify her responsibility for upholding sexual mores. Thomas uses a market analogy to female virtue: good women *keep* their bodies as capital to sell in matrimony for marriage and security, whereas bad women *trade* their bodies for excitement. One notes, of course, the familiar dichotomy. It is difficult, in this framework, to see how Thomas can make *any* moral distinctions, since morality seems to be merely good business sense. In fact, Thomas' yardstick is social harmony, necessitating *control*.

Thomas shows an insensitivity to real human relationships and needs. He also shows ignorance of economic hardships in his denial of economic factors in delinquency.

> An unattached woman has a tendency to become an adventuress not so much on economic as on psychological grounds. Life is rarely so hard that a young woman cannot earn her bread; but she cannot always live and have the stimulation she craves (*Ibid.*:241).

This is an amazing statement in an era of mass starvation and illness! He rejects economic causes as a possibility at all, denying its importance in criminal activity with as much certainty as Lombroso, Freud, Davis, Pollak and most other writers.

Freud: "beauty, charm and sweetness"

The Freudian theory of the position of women is grounded in explicit biological assumptions about their nature, expressed by the famous "Anatomy is Destiny." Built upon this foundation is a construction incorporating psychological and social-structural factors.

Freud himself sees women as anatomically inferior; they are destined to be wives and mothers, and this is admittedly an inferior destiny as befits the inferior sex. The root of this inferiority is that women's *sex organs* are inferior to those of men, a fact *universally* recognized by children in the Freudian scheme. The girl assumes that she has lost a penis as punishment, is traumatized, and grows up envious and revengeful. The boy also sees the girl as having lost a penis, fears a similar punishment himself, and dreads the girl's envy and vengeance. Feminine traits can be traced to the inferior genitals themselves, or to women's inferiority complex arising from their response to them: women are exhibitionistic, narcissistic, and attempt to compensate for their lack of a penis by being well dressed and physically beautiful. Women become mothers trying to replace the lost penis with a baby. Women are also masochistic, as Lombroso and Thomas have noted, because their *sexual* role is one of receptor, and their sexual pleasure consists of pain. This woman, Freud notes, is the *healthy* woman. In the familiar dichotomy, the men are aggressive and pain inflicting. Freud comments:

> The male pursues the female for the purposes of sexual union, seizes hold of her, and penetrates into her . . . by this you have precisely reduced the characteristic of masculinity to the factor of aggressiveness (Millett, 1970:189).

Freud, like Lombroso and Thomas, takes the notion of men's activity and women's inactivity and *reduces* it to the sexual level, seeing the sexual union itself through Victorian eyes: ladies don't move.

Women are also inferior in the sense that they are concerned with personal matters and have little social sense. Freud sees civilization as based on repression of the sex drive, where it is the duty of men to repress their strong instincts in order to get on with the worldly business of civilization. Women, on the other hand,

> have little sense of justice, and this is no doubt connected with the preponderance of envy in their mental life; for the demands of justice are a modification of envy; they lay down the conditions under which one is willing to part with it. We also say of women that their social interests are weaker than those of men and that their capacity for the sublimation of their instincts is less (1933:183).

Men are capable of sublimating their individual needs because they rationally perceive the Hobbesian conflict between those urges and social needs. Women are emotional and incapable of such an adjustment because of their innate inability to make such rational judgments. It is only fair then that they should have a marginal relation to production and property.

In this framework, the deviant woman is one who is attempting to be a *man*. She is aggressively rebellious, and her drive to accomplishment is the expression of her longing for a penis; this is a hopeless pursuit, of course, and she will only end up "neurotic." Thus the deviant woman should be treated and helped to *adjust* to her sex role. Here again, as in Thomas' writing, is the notion of individual accommodation that repudiates the possibility of social change.

In a Victorian fashion, Freud rationalizes women's oppression by glorifying their duties as wives and mothers:

> It is really a stillborn thought to send women into the struggle for existence exactly the same as men. If, for instance, I imagined my sweet gentle girl as a competitor, it would only end in my telling her, as I did seventeen months ago, that I am fond of her, and I implore her to withdraw from the strife into the calm, uncompetitive activity of my home . . . Nature has determined woman's destiny through beauty, charm and sweetness . . . in youth an adored darling, in mature years a loved wife (Jones, 1961:117–118).

In speaking of femininity, Freud, like his forebearers, is speaking along racist and classist lines. Only upper and middle-class women could possibly enjoy lives as sheltered darlings. Freud sets hegemonic standards of femininity for poor and Third World women.

It is important to understand Freudianism because it reduces categories of sexual ideology to explicit sexuality and makes these categories *scientific*. For the last fifty years, Freudianism has been a mainstay of sexist social theory. Kate Millett notes that Freud himself saw his work as stemming the tide of feminist revolution, which he constantly ridiculed:

> Coming as it did, at the peak of the sexual revolution, Freud's doctrine of penis envy is in fact a superbly timed accusation, enabling masculine sentiment to take the offensive again as it had not since the disappearance of overt misogyny when the pose of chivalry became fashionable (Millett, 1970:189).

Freudian notions of the repression of sexual instincts, the sexual passivity of women, and the sanctity of the nuclear family are conservative not only in their contemporary context, but in the context of their own time. Hitler writes:

> For her [woman's] world is her husband, her family, her children and her home . . . The man upholds the nation as the woman upholds the family. The equal rights of women consist in the fact that in the realm

of life determined for her by nature, she experience the high esteem that is her due. Woman and man represent quite different types of being. Reason is dominant in man . . . Feeling, in contrast, is much more stable than reason, and woman is the feeling, and therefore the stable, element (*Ibid.*:170).

One can mark the decline in the position of women after the 1920's through the use of various indices: by noting the progressively earlier age of marriage of women in the United States and the steady rise in the number of children born to them, culminating in the birth explosion of the late forties and fifties; by looking at the relative decline in the number of women scholars; and by seeing the failure to liberate women in the Soviet Union and the rise of fascist sexual ideology. Freudianism has had an unparalleled influence in the United States (and came at a key point to help swing the tide against the women's movement) to facilitate the return of women during the depression and post-war years to the home, out of an economy which had no room for them. Freud affected such writers on female deviance as Davis, Pollak and Konopka, who turn to concepts of sexual maladjustment and neurosis to explain women's criminality. Healthy women would now be seen as masochistic, passive and sexually indifferent. Criminal women would be seen as *sexual* misfits. Most importantly, *psychological* factors would be used to explain criminal activity, and social, economic and political factors would be ignored. Explanations would seek to be *universal,* and historical possibilities of change would be refuted.

Davis: "the most convenient sexual outlet for armies . . ."

Kingsley Davis' work on prostitution (1961) is still considered a classical analysis on the subject with a structural-functionalist perspective. It employs assumptions about "the organic nature of man" and woman, many of which can be traced to ideas proffered by Thomas and Freud.

Davis sees prostitution as a structural necessity whose roots lie in the *sexual* nature of men and women; for example, female humans, unlike primates, are sexually available year-round. He asserts that prostitution is *universal* in time and place, eliminating the possibilities of historical change and ignoring critical differences in the quality and quantity of prostitution in different societies. He maintains that there will always be a class of women who will be prostitutes, the familiar class of "bad" women. The reason for the universality of prostitution is that sexual *repression,* a concept stressed by Thomas and Freud, is essential to the functioning of society. Once again there is the notion of sublimating "natural" sex urges to the overall needs of society, namely social order. Davis notes that in our society sexuality is permitted only within the structure of the nuclear family, which is an institution of stability. He does not, however, analyze in depth the economic and social functions of the family, other than to say it is a bulwark of morality.

The norms of every society tend to harness and control the sexual appetite, and one of the ways of doing this is to link the sexual act to

> some stable or potentially stable social relationship . . . Men dominate
> women in economic, sexual and familial relationships and consider
> them to some extent as sexual property, to be prohibited to other males.
> They therefore find promiscuity on the part of women repugnant
> (*Ibid.*:264).

Davis is linking the concept of prostitution to promiscuity, defining it as a
sexual crime, and calling prostitutes sexual transgressors. Its origins, he
claims, lie not in economic hardship, but in the marital restraints on sexuality.
As long as men seek women, prostitutes will be in demand. One wonders why
sex-seeking women have not created a class of male prostitutes.

Davis sees the only possibility of eliminating prostitution in the liberali-
zation of sexual mores, although he is pessimistic about the likelihood of
total elimination. In light of the contemporary American "sexual revolution"
of commercial sex, which has surely created more prostitutes and semi-pros-
titues rather than eliminating the phenomenon, and in considering the revolution in China where, despite a "puritanical" outlook on sexuality, prostitution has largely been eliminated through major economic and social change,
the superficiality of Davis' approach becomes evident. Without dealing with
root economic, social and political factors, one cannot analyze prostitution.

Davis shows Freudian pessimism about the nature of sexual repression:

> We can imagine a social system in which the motive for prostitution
> would be completely absent, but we cannot imagine that the system
> will ever come to pass. It would be a regime of absolute sexual freedom
> with intercourse practiced solely for pleasure by both parties. There
> would be no institutional control of sexual expression . . . All sexual
> desire would have to be mutually complementary . . . Since the basic
> causes of prostitution—the institutional control of sex, the unequal scale
> of attractiveness, and the presence of economic and social inequalities
> between classes and between males and females—are not likely to dis-
> appear, prostitution is not likely to disappear either (*Ibid.*:286).

By talking about "complementary desire," Davis is using a marketplace notion
of sex: two attractive or unattractive people are drawn to each other and
exchange sexual favors; people are placed on a scale of attractiveness and may
be rejected by people above them on the scale; hence they (*men*) become
frustrated and demand prostitutes. Women who become prostitutes do so for
good pay *and* sexual pleasure. Thus one has a neat little system in which
everyone benefits.

> Enabling a small number of women to take care of the needs of a large
> number of men, it is the most convenient sexual outlet for armies, for
> the legions of strangers, perverts and physically repulsive in our midst
> (*Ibid.*:288).

Prostitution "functions," therefore it must be good. Davis, like Thomas, is
motivated by concerns of social order rather than by concerns of what the

needs and desires of the women involved might be. He denies that the women involved are economically oppressed; they are on the streets through autonomous, *individual* choice.

> Some women physically enjoy the intercourse they sell. From a purely economic point of view, prostitution comes near the situation of getting something for nothing . . . Women's wages could scarcely be raised significantly without also raising men's. Men would then have more to spend on prostitution (*Ibid.*:277).

It is important to understand that, given a *sexual* interpretation of what is an *economic* crime, and given a refusal to consider widespread change (even equalization of wages, hardly a revolutionary act), Davis' conclusion is the logical technocratic solution.

In this framework, the deviant women are merely adjusting to their feminine role in an illegitimate fashion, as Thomas has theorized. They are *not* attempting to be rebels or to be "men," as Lombroso's and Freud's positions suggest. Although Davis sees the main difference between wives and prostitutes in a macrosocial sense as the difference merely between legal and illegal roles, in a personal sense he sees the women who *choose* prostitution as maladjusted and neurotic. However, given the universal necessity for prostitution, this analysis implies the necessity of having a perpetually ill and maladjusted class of women. Thus oppression is *built into* the system, and a healthy *system* makes for a sick *individual*. Here Davis is integrating Thomas' notions of social integration with Freudian perspectives on neurosis and maladjustment.

Pollak: "a different attitude toward veracity"

Otto Pollak's *The Criminality of Women* (1950) has had an outstanding influence on the field of women and crime, being the major work on the subject in the postwar years. Pollak advances the theory of "hidden" female crime to account for what he considers unreasonably low official rates for women.

A major reason for the existence of hidden crime, as he sees it, lies in the *nature* of women themselves. They are instigators rather than perpetrators of criminal activity. While Pollak admits that this role is partly a socially enforced one, he insists that women are inherently deceitful for *physiological* reasons.

> Man must achieve an erection in order to perform the sex act and will not be able to hide his failure. His lack of positive emotion in the sexual sphere must become overt to the partner, and pretense of sexual response is impossible for him, if it is lacking. Woman's body, however, permits such pretense to a certain degree and lack of orgasm does not prevent her ability to participate in the sex act (*Ibid.*:10).

Pollak *reduces* women's nature to the *sex act,* as Freud has done, and finds women inherently more capable of manipulation, accustomed to being sly, passive and passionless. As Thomas suggests, women can use sex for ulterior purposes. Furthermore, Pollak suggests that women are innately deceitful on yet another level:

> Our sex mores force women to conceal every four weeks the period of menstruation ... They thus make concealment and misrepresentation in the eyes of women socially required and must condition them to a different attitude toward veracity than men (*Ibid.*:11).

Women's abilities at concealment thus allow them to successfully commit crimes in stealth.

Women are also vengeful. Menstruation, in the classic Freudian sense, seals their doomed hopes to become men and arouses women's desire for vengeance, especially during that time of the month. Thus Pollak offers new rationalizations to bolster old myths.

A second factor in hidden crime is the roles played by women which furnish them with opportunities as domestics, nurses, teachers and housewives to commit undetectable crimes. The *kinds* of crimes women commit reflect their nature: false accusation, for example, is an outgrowth of women's treachery, spite or fear and is a sign of neurosis; shoplifting can be traced in many cases to a special mental disease—kleptomania. Economic factors play a minor role; *sexual-psychological* factors account for female criminality. Crime in women is *personalized* and often accounted for by mental illness.

Pollak notes:

> Robbery and burglary ... are considered specifically male offenses since they represent the pursuit of monetary gain by overt action ... Those cases of female robbery which seem to express a tendency toward masculinization come from ... [areas] where social conditions have favored the assumptions of male pursuits by women ... The female offenders usually retain some trace of femininity, however, and even so glaring an example of masculinization as the 'Michigan Babes,' an all woman gang of robbers in Chicago, shows a typically feminine trait in the modus operandi (*Ibid.*:29).

Pollak is defining crimes with economic motives that employ overt action as *masculine,* and defining as *feminine* those crimes for *sexual* activity, such as luring men as baits. Thus he is using circular reasoning by saying that feminine crime is feminine. To fit women into the scheme and justify the statistics, he must invent the notion of hidden crime.

It is important to recognize that, to some extent, women *do* adapt to their enforced sexual roles and may be more likely to instigate, to use sexual traps, and to conform to all the other feminine role expectations. However, it is not accidental that theorists label women as conforming even when they are *not*; for example, by inventing sexual motives for what are clearly crimes of economic necessity, or by invoking "mental illness" such as kleptomania for shoplifting. It is difficult to separate the *theory* from the *reality*, since the reality of female crime is largely unknown. But it is not difficult to see that

Pollak is using sexist terms and making sexist assumptions to advance theories of hidden female crime.

Pollak, then, sees criminal women as extending their sexual role, like Davis and Thomas, by using sexuality for ulterior purposes. He suggests that the condemnation of extramarital sex has "delivered men who engage in such conduct as practically helpless victims" (*Ibid.*:152) into the hands of women blackmailers, overlooking completely the possibility of men blackmailing women, which would seem more likely, given the greater taboo on sex for women and their greater risks of being punished.

The final factor that Pollak advances as a root cause of hidden crime is that of "chivalry" in the criminal justice system. Pollak uses Thomas' observation that women are differentially treated by the law, and carries it to a sweeping conclusion based on *cultural* analyses of men's feelings toward women.

> One of the outstanding concomitants of the existing inequality . . . is chivalry, and the general protective attitude of man toward woman . . . Men hate to accuse women and thus indirectly to send them to their punishment, police officers dislike to arrest them, district attorneys to prosecute them, judges and juries to find them guilty, and so on (*Ibid.*:151).

Pollak rejects the possibility of an actual discrepancy between crime rates for men and women; therefore, he must look for factors to expand the scope of female crime. He assumes that there is chivalry in the criminal justice system that is extended to the women who come in contact with it. Yet the women involved are likely to be poor and Third World women or white middle-class women who have stepped *outside* the definitions of femininity to become hippies or political rebels, and chivalry is *not* likely to be extended to them. Chivalry is a racist and classist concept founded on the notion of women as "ladies" which applies only to wealthy white women and ignores the double sexual standard. These "ladies," however, are the least likely women to ever come in contact with the criminal justice system in the first place.[4]

The legacy of sexism

A major purpose in tracing the development and interaction of ideas pertaining to sexual ideology based on implicit assumptions of the inherent nature of women throughout the works of Lombroso, Thomas, Freud, Davis and Pollak, is to clarify their positions in relation to writers in the field today. One can see the influence their ideas still have by looking at a number of contemporary theorists on female criminality. Illuminating examples can be found in Gisela Konopka's *Adolescent Girl in Conflict* (1966), Vedder and Somerville's *The Delinquent Girl* (1970) and Cowie, Cowie and Slater's *Delinquency in Girls* (1968). The ideas in these minor works have direct roots in those already traced in this paper.

Konopka justifies her decision to study delinquency in girls rather than in boys by noting girls' *influence* on boys in gang fights and on future generations as mothers. This is the notion of women as instigators of men and influencers on children.

Konopka's main point is that delinquency in girls can be traced to a specific emotional response: loneliness.

> What I found in the girl in conflict was . . . loneliness accompanied by despair. Adolescent boys too often feel lonely and search for understanding and friends. Yet in general this does not seem to be the central core of their problems, not their most outspoken ache. While these girls also strive for independence, their need for dependence is unusually great (1966:40).

In this perspective, girls are driven to delinquency by an emotional problem—loneliness and dependency. There are *inherent* emotional differences between the sexes.

> Almost invariably her [the girl's] problems are deeply personalized. Whatever her offense—whether shoplifting, truancy or running away from home—it is usually accompanied by some disturbance or unfavorable behavior in the sexual area (*Ibid.*:4).

Here is the familiar resurrection of female personalism, emotionalism, and above all, *sexuality*—characteristics already described by Lombroso, Thomas and Freud. Konopka maintains:

> The delinquent girl suffers, like many boys, from lack of success, lack of opportunity. But her drive to success is never separated from her need for people, for interpersonal involvement (*Ibid.*:41).

Boys are "instrumental" and become delinquent if they are deprived of the chance for creative success. However, girls are "expressive" and happiest dealing with people as wives, mothers, teachers, nurses or psychologists. This perspective is drawn from the theory of delinquency as a result of blocked opportunity and from the instrumental/expressive sexual dualism developed by structural-functionalists. Thus female delinquency must be dealt with on this *psychological* level, using therapy geared to their needs as future wives and mothers. They should be *adjusted* and given *opportunities* to be pretty, sociable women.

The important point is to understand how Konopka analyzes the roots of girls' feelings. It is very possible that, given women's position, girls may be in fact more concerned with dependence and sociability. One's understanding of this, however, is based on an understanding of the historical position of women and the nature of their oppression. Konopka says:

> What are the reasons for this essential loneliness in girls? Some will be found in the nature of being an adolescent girl, in her biological make-up and her particular position in her culture and time (*Ibid.*).

Coming from a Freudian perspective, Konopka's emphasis on female emotions as cause for delinquency, which ignores economic and social factors, is questionable. She employs assumptions about the *physiological* and *psychological* nature of women that very well may have led her to see only those feelings in the first place. For example, she cites menstruation as a significant event in a girl's development. Thus Konopka is rooted firmly in the tradition of Freud and, apart from sympathy, contributes little that is new to the field.[5]

Vedder and Somerville (1970) account for female delinquency in a manner similar to that of Konopka. They also feel the need to justify their attention to girls by remarking that (while female delinquency may not pose as much of a problem as that of boys) because women raise families and are critical agents of socialization, it is worth taking the time to study and control them. Vedder and Somerville also stress the dependence of girls on boys and the instigatory role girls play in boys' activities.

Like Freud and Konopka, the authors view delinquency as blocked access or maladjustment to the normal feminine role. In a blatant statement that ignores the economic and social factors that result from racism and poverty, they attribute the high rates of delinquency among black girls to their lack of "healthy" feminine narcissism, *reducing* racism to a psychological problem in totally sexist and racist terms.

> The black girl is, in fact, the antithesis of the American beauty. However loved she may be by her mother, family and community, she has no real basis of female attractiveness on which to build a sound feminine narcissism . . . Perhaps the 'black is beautiful' movement will help the Negro girl to increase her femininity and personal satisfaction as a black woman (*Ibid.*:159–160).

Again the focus is on a lack of *sexual* opportunities for women, *i.e.,* the black woman is not Miss America. *Economic* offenses such as shoplifting are explained as outlets for *sexual* frustration. Since healthy women conform, the individual delinquents should be helped to adjust; the emphasis is on the "definition of the situation" rather than on the situation.

The answer lies in *therapy,* and racism and sexism become merely psychological problems.

> Special attention should be given to girls, taking into consideration their constitutional biological and psychological differences, and their social position in our male dominated culture. The female offender's goal, as any woman's, is a happy and successful marriage; therefore her self-image is dependent on the establishment of satisfactory relationships with the opposite sex. The double standard for sexual behavior on the part of the male and female must be recognized (*Ibid.*:153).

Like Konopka, and to some extent drawing on Thomas, the authors see female delinquents as extending femininity in an illegitimate fashion rather than rebelling against it. The assumptions made about women's goals and needs, including *biological* assumptions, lock women into a system from which there is no escape, whereby any behavior will be sexually interpreted and dealt with.

The resurgence of biological or physiological explanations of criminality in general has been noteworthy in the last several years, exemplified by the XYY chromosome controversy and the interest in brain waves in "violent" individuals.[6] In the case of women, biological explanations have *always* been prevalent; every writer has made assumptions about anatomy as destiny. Women are prey, in the literature, to cycles of reproduction, including menstruation, pregnancy, maternity and menopause; they experience emotional responses to these cycles that make them inclined to irrationality and potentially violent activity.

Cowie, Cowie and Slater (1968) propose a *chromosomal* explanation of female delinquency that hearkens back to the works of Lombroso and others such as Healy (1926), Edith Spaulding (1923) and the Gluecks (1934). They write:

> The chromosomal difference between the sexes starts the individual on a divergent path, leading either in a masculine or feminine direction ... It is possible that the methods of upbringing, differing somewhat for the two sexes, may play some part in increasing the angle of this divergence (*Ibid.*:171).

This is the healthy, normal divergence for the sexes. The authors equate *masculinity* and *femininity* with *maleness* and *femaleness*, although contemporary feminists point out that the first categories are *social* and the latter ones *physical.*[7] What relationship exists between the two—how femaleness determines femininity—is dependent on the larger social stucture. There is no question that a wide range of possibilities exists historically, and in a non-sexist society it is possible that "masculinity" and "femininity" would disappear, and that the sexes would differ only biologically, specifically by their sex organs. The authors, however, lack this understanding and assume an ahistorical sexist view of women, stressing the *universality* of femininity in the Freudian tradition, and of women's inferior role in the nuclear family.[8]

In this perspective, the female offender is *different* physiologically and psychologically from the "normal" girl.

The authors conclude, in the tradition of Lombroso, that female delinquents are *masculine.* Examining girls for physical characteristics, they note:

> Markedly masculine traits in girl delinquents have been commented on ... [as well as] the frequency of homosexual tendencies ... Energy, aggressiveness, enterprise and the rebelliousness that drives the individual to break through conformist habits are thought of as being masculine ... We can be sure that they have some physical basis (*Ibid.*:172).

The authors see crime as a *rebellion* against sex roles rather than as a maladjusted expression of them. By defining rebellion as *masculine,* they are ascribing characteristics of masculinity to any female rebel. Like Lombroso, they spend time measuring heights, weights, and other *biological* features of female delinquents with other girls.

Crime defined as masculine seems to mean violent, overt crime, whereas "ladylike" crime usually refers to sexual violations and shoplifting. Women are neatly categorized no matter *which* kind of crime they commit: if they are violent, they are "masculine" and suffering from chromosomal deficiencies, penis envy, or atavisms. If they conform, they are manipulative, sexually maladjusted and promiscuous. The *economic* and *social* realities of crime—the fact that poor women commit crimes, and that most crimes for women are property offenses—are overlooked. Women's behavior must be *sexually* defined before it will be considered, for women count only in the sexual sphere. The theme of sexuality is a unifying thread in the various, often contradictory theories.

Conclusion

A good deal of the writing on women and crime being done at the present time is squarely in the tradition of the writers that have been discussed. The basic assumptions and technocratic concerns of these writers have produced work that is sexist, racist and classist; assumptions that have served to maintain a repressive ideology with its extensive apparatus of control. To do a new kind of research on women and crime—one that has feminist roots and a radical orientation—it is necessary to understand the assumptions made by the traditional writers and to break away from them. Work that focuses on human needs, rather than those of the state, will require new definitions of criminality, women, the individual and her/his relation to the state. It is beyond the scope of this paper to develop possible areas of study, but it is nonetheless imperative that this work be made a priority by women *and* men in the future.

Notes

1. Quoted from the 1973 proposal for the Center for the Study and Reduction of Violence prepared by Dr. Louis J. West, Director, Neuropsychiatric Institute, UCLA: "The question of violence in females will be examined from the point of view that females are more likely to commit acts of violence during the pre-menstrual and menstrual periods" (1973:43).
2. I am indebted to Marion Goldman for introducing me to the notion of the dual morality based on assumptions of different sexuality for men and women.
3. For a discussion of the possibilities of psychosurgery in behavior modification for "violence-prone" individuals, see Frank Ervin and Vernon Mark, *Violence and the Brain* (1970). For an eclectic view of this perspective on crime, see the proposal for the Center for the Study and Reduction of Violence (footnote #1).
4. The concept of hidden crime is reiterated in Reckless and Kay's report to the President's Commission on Law Enforcement and the Administration of Justice. They note:

   A large part of the infrequent officially acted upon involvement of women in crime can be traced to the masking effect of women's roles, effective practice on the part of women of deceit and indirection, their instigation of men to commit their crimes (the Lady Macbeth factor), and the unwillingness on the part of the public and law enforcement officials to hold women accountable for their deeds (the chivalry factor) (1967:13).

5. Bertha Payak in "Understanding the Female Offender" (1963) stresses that women offenders have poor self-concepts, feelings of insecurity and dependency, are emotionally selfish, and prey to irrationality during menstruation, pregnancy, and menopause (a good deal of their life!).

6. See Theodore R. Sarbin and Jeffrey E. Miller, "Demonism Revisited: The XYY Chromosomal Anomaly." *Issues in Criminology* 5(2)(Summer 1970).

7. Kate Millett (1970) notes that "sex is biological, gender psychological and therefore cultural . . . if the proper terms for sex are male and female, the corresponding terms for gender are masculine and feminine; these latter may be quite independent of biological sex" (*Ibid.*:30).

8. Zelditch (1960), a structural-functionalist, writes that the nuclear family is an inevitability and that within it, women, the "expressive" sex, will inevitably be the domestics.

References

Bishop, Cecil
>1931 *Women and Crime.* London: Chatto and Windus.

Cowie, John, Valerie Cowie and Eliot Slater
>1968 *Delinquency in Girls.* London: Heinemann.

Davis, Kingsley
>1961 "Prostitution." *Contemporary Social Problems.* Edited by Robert K. Merton and Robert A. Nisbet. New York: Harcourt Brace and Jovanovich. Originally published as "The Sociology of Prostitution." *American Sociological Review* 2(5)(October 1937).

Ervin, Frank and Vernon Mark
>1970 *Violence and the Brain.* New York: Harper and Row.

Fernald, Mabel, Mary Hayes and Almena Dawley
>1920 *A Study of Women Delinquents in New York State.* New York: Century Company.

Freud, Sigmund
>1933 *New Introductory Lectures on Psychoanalysis.* New York: W. W. Norton.

Glueck, Eleanor and Sheldon
>1934 *Five Hundred Delinquent Women.* New York: Alfred A. Knopf.

Healy, William and Augusta Bronner
>1926 *Delinquents and Criminals: Their Making and Unmaking.* New York: Macmillan and Company.

Hemming, James
>1960 *Problems of Adolescent Girls.* London: Heinemann.

Jones, Ernest
>1961 *The Life and Works of Sigmund Freud.* New York: Basic Books.

Konopka, Gisela
>1966 *The Adolescent Girl in Conflict.* Englewood Cliffs, New Jersey: Prentice-Hall.

Lombroso, Cesare
>1920 *The Female Offender.* (translation). New York: Appleton. Originally published in 1903.

Millett, Kate
    1970 *Sexual Politics.* New York: Doubleday and Company.
Monahan, Florence
    1941 *Women in Crime.* New York: I. Washburn.
Parsons, Talcott
    1942 "Age and Sex in the Social Structure." *American Sociological Review* 7 (October).
Parsons, Talcott and Renée Fox
    1960 "Illness, Therapy and the Modern 'Urban' American Family." *The Family.* Edited by Norman Bell and Ezra Vogel. Glencoe, Illinois: The Free Press.
Payak, Bertha
    1963 "Understanding the Female Offender." *Federal Probation* XXVII.
Pollak, Otto
    1950 *The Criminality of Women.* Philadelphia: University of Pennsylvania Press.
Reckless, Walter and Barbara Kay
    1967 *The Female Offender.* Report to the President's Commission on Law Enforcement and the Administration of Justice. Washington, D.C.: U.S. Government Printing Office.
Sarbin, Theodore R. and Jeffrey E. Miller
    1970 "Demonism Revisited: The XYY Chromosomal Anomaly." *Issues in Criminology* 5(2)(Summer).
Schwendinger, Herman and Julia
    1973 "The Founding Fathers: Sexists to a Man." *Sociologists of the Chair.* New York: Basic Books.
Spaulding, Edith
    1923 *An Experimental Study of Psychopathic Delinquent Women.* New York: Rand McNally.
Thomas, W. I.
    1907 *Sex and Society.* Boston: Little, Brown and Company.
    1923 *The Unadjusted Girl.* New York: Harper and Row.
Vedder, Clyde and Dora Somerville
    1970 *The Delinquent Girl.* Springfield, Illinois: Charles C. Thomas.
West, Dr. Louis J.
    1973 *Proposal for the Center for the Study and Reduction of Violence.* Neuropsychiatric Institute, UCLA (April 10).
Zelditch, Morris, Jr.
    1960 "Role Differentiation in the Nuclear Family: A Comparative Study." *The Family.* Edited by Norman Bell and Ezra Vogel. Glencoe, Illinois: The Free Press.

8 Any Woman's Blues

Dorie Klein and June Kress

The changing nature of women's position in the workforce and in the family has given rise to a new set of issues concerning women's participation in crime. Among these are increasing rates of and fluctuating patterns in women's offenses, and growing resistance both through the emergence of political movements and through rising militance in women's prisons. These developments, in turn, have stimulated not only the portrayal of a new "violent" woman by the media, but also a flurry of speculation among criminologists. However, the great majority of academic material has lacked serious consideration of the economic and social position of women, and consequently has been limited by a narrow correctionalist perspective.

. . .

Basing their work on the sexual theories of motivation, few traditional criminologists recognize sexist oppression itself as a causative factor or the need for its elimination. Their recommendations for rehabilitation impose standards of femininity, which are in fact ruling class standards. One example of this is the imposition of certain conditions for parole, which we discuss later in the paper. Thus, social control, not social justice, is the underlying thread of unity in this literature. And, more importantly, any attempts at reform have neither changed the balance of power within the criminal justice system, nor have they fundamentally altered the class-biased nature of that system.

. . .

One of the outcomes of popular struggles waged during the 1960's by women, students, Third World people and various political organizations has

From "Any Woman's Blues: A Critical Overview of Women, Crime, and the Criminal Justice System" by Dorie Klein and June Kress, in *Crime and Social Justice*, no. 5, Spring/Summer 1976:34–49. Permission to reprint part of this article has been granted by *Crime and Social Justice*, P.O. Box 4373, Berkeley, California 94704.

been an ongoing transformation of the field of criminology. Taking its early direction from the ideas and writings of prisoners themselves, a radical analysis of crime and criminal justice was in fact created outside of the academic community and adopted by students and a small number of faculty.

Theoretically, radical criminology utilizes a multidisciplinary approach to examine the issues of crime and justice, emphasizing the study of political economy. Representing a sharp break from the traditional field, radical criminology has begun to challenge the dominant assumptions long held by academic practitioners and by workers within the criminal justice system. One such challenge is to the legal definition of crime. In contrast to the traditional definition, radicals see as a starting point the notion of human rights to self-determination, dignity, food and shelter, and freedom from exploitation. This perspective defines crime as a violation of these rights, whereby the focus is on specific systems of exploitation, or criminogenic systems, such as imperialism, racism, capitalism and sexism, because they promote inherently repressive relationships and social injury. In this orientation, the solution to crime is predicated on a total transformation of society and its inequitable political and economic system. Thus, in its broadest theoretical sense, radical criminology involves a move towards a redefinition of crime and justice.

Coupled with this is an ongoing evaluation of the criminal justice system according to whether it meets people's needs. In challenging that system, we do not deny the existence of street crime such as rape or burglary, or consider that people who commit such crimes are totally victims of an unjust society. On the contrary, petty criminals do exploit working people, and street crime is a pressing problem that demands immediate attention. But a primary focus of our work is how the economic system *itself* promotes the conditions for typical criminal behavior (see Platt, 1974b). This requires an analysis of the material basis of criminality, the illegal marketplace of goods and services, e.g., drugs and prostitution,[1] and the connections between exploitative social relations and economic foundations.

In drawing its main attention away from individual offenders, radical criminology concentrates on the social structure through its recognition of the criminal justice system as a class phenomenon; that is, as an instrument of the ruling elite to maintain a social system that is class-biased, racist and sexist (see Balbus, 1973; Wolfe, 1973). Our work is guided by a perspective that views the state as serving certain segments of the population over others.[2] As one coercive arm of the state, the criminal justice system protects corporate and private property. While it brings full pressure to bear on petty property offenders from the poor sectors of the population, it virtually ignores major corporate crime and handles white-collar offenses through "wrist-slapping" civil procedures.[3] Thus, the legal apparatus is in effect a dual system of justice for the rich and against the poor.

In making the study of women and crime a priority, radical and progressive criminologists have begun to confront the economic, social and political conditions that have a direct bearing on the incidence of crime. The historical and contemporary role of women in society is analyzed in order to account for the kinds of crimes that women commit. By attempting to break down oppressive sexual attitudes that surround women, radical criminologists incorporate a political view of justice. While our theoretical work emphasizes the need to eliminate sexism and ruling class standards of femininity, our political practice concentrates on strategies of resistance to bring about fundamental change, for example anti-rape groups that are now growing on a national scale. This developing body of literature on women is characterized by a high degree of feminist consciousness. Moving well beyond mere critiques of traditional approaches, radicals and progressives have begun to develop their own political analyses of female criminality and the institutions of criminal justice that act as agents of control.

. . .

Man may work from sun to sun,
But woman's work is never done.
            —traditional verse

. . .

The family

An understanding of the relationship between women and criminal behavior requires a brief examination of women's unique economic and social position in modern capitalist society, which is rooted in the sexual and maternal aspect of female life.

The economic position of women hinges on their location in the institution of personal survival, life-support, and emotional refuge known as the family. Within it, women have historically been treated as the laboring property of their individual men—fathers and husbands—who themselves have mostly had to sell their labor to other men. Thus, women have been, in the words used to describe the double oppression of black women, the "slaves of slaves." In the shift from pre-industrialism to contemporary advanced capitalism, the economic role of the family in the U.S. has changed from being a center of production, for exchange as well as use value, to being essentially a center of consumption, as the goods required for life-support, e.g., food, clothing, are increasingly mass-produced. Thus, women's work has changed, too (Rowbotham, 1973:107–8). In that the family consumes the goods, reproduces the workers, keeps them alive, and helps to inculcate children and adults alike with the values required to maintain the legitimacy of present arrangements, women's work bolsters capitalism.

The structure of the family itself is legitimated by the ideology of sexism, which assures us that the roles filled by women are their "natural" ones. Women are meant above all to be wives and mothers, either because of their physiology (not only do women bear children, they are soft and weak as well) or their psychology (women are passive, gentle, irrational, personal, expressive). Or, if one is a liberal sociologist who scorns such superstition, women are meant to be wives and mothers above all because they do it so well, and women's work is necessary work.

Women's work

Below we shall briefly outline the separate, though interrelated, elements of women's work, and note the sexist ideology that reinforces the ensuing web of oppression.[4] First, women are unpaid houseworkers in the family, doing the vital chores that allow their husbands, fathers, sons and daughters to leave home and do a full week's work at a job.[5] And although it might appear that technological advances and mass production would free women from much housework, it has been estimated that the average housewife spends 99.6 hours a week performing these tasks (Rowbotham, 1973). The tyranny of housework partly stems from the fact that a woman's self-esteem is tied into it: a woman is judged by the appearance of her house, and the ideal of the good housekeeper is promoted by the mass media to sell products.

Secondly, women are nurturing agents. They raise children, emotionally care for men, do unpaid charity work, and generally act as softening agents in a harsh and competitive society.[6] Sexist notions that women should be gentle and passive keep women nurturing others at their own expense.

Thirdly, women are the "sexual backbone" of society.

·   ·   ·

Women arrested

The great majority of women arrested are petty offenders. Both in 1972 and in 1974, women and men were arrested in rank order for the offenses indicated in Table 1. For both years, the women's and men's lists are fairly similar. Women are apparently being arrested for proportionately fewer "violent" offenses than men: 6.1% in 1972 and 3.8% in 1974 of female arrests (aggravated assault and other assaults) vs. 8.5% and 7.1% in 1974 of male arrests (aggravated assault, robbery, and other assaults). A relatively greater percentage of women are arrested for larceny and fraud (22.6% in 1972 and 25.5% in 1974), and of course women constitute almost all of the arrests for prostitution (which can be masked as "disorderly conduct"). By and large, a good number of these women and men are not a dangerous lot. If certain "victimless" offenses (prostitution, drug use, drunkenness, and juvenile running away) were decriminalized, the number of women arrested could drop considerably.

Women and men showed percentage increases for arrests in certain categories from 1960–1973 and from 1973–1974, as illustrated in Tables 2 and 3 (p. 87). Along with rape, these seven offenses constitute the FBI Index for which national data are collected.

Despite the increase in arrests for women, we must remember that they still comprise a small percentage of all arrests, although it is still growing. This is shown below in Table 4.

In studying the figures, it is obvious that arrests for women are going up, relatively and absolutely. However (see Tables 2, 3, and 4), over the last decade women's rate of increase for the so-called "violent" crimes without obvious economic motive (murder, aggravated assault) has not been as great as men's or as great as their (women's) rate of increase for property and drug offenses.

Table 1 **Rank order of offenses and percent arrested out of all female and male arrests, 1972 and 1974**

		1972		
	WOMEN		**MEN**	
Rank	Offense	% Female arrests	Offense	% Male arrests
1	Larceny/theft	20.2	Drunkenness	22.9
2	Drunkenness	9.8	Drunken driving	9.0
3	Disorderly conduct	8.5	Disorderly conduct	8.5
4	Narcotic drug laws	6.0	Larceny/theft	8.2
5	Other assaults	4.1	Narcotic drug laws	5.8
6	Drunken driving	3.8	Burglary	4.7
7	Prostitution	3.4	Other assaults	4.5
8	Liquor laws	2.7	Liquor laws	2.9
9	Embezzlement/fraud	2.4	Aggravated assault	2.2
10	Aggravated assault	2.0	Robbery	1.8
11	All other offenses	37.1	All other offenses	29.5
	Total	100.0	Total	100.0

		1974		
	WOMEN		**MEN**	
Rank	Offense	% Female arrests	Offense	% Male arrests
1	Larceny/theft	22.5	Drunkenness	16.3
2	Disorderly conduct	11.2	Drunk driving	10.9
3	Juvenile runaways	8.8	Larceny/theft	9.8
4	Drunkenness	6.6	Disorderly conduct	8.3
5	Narcotic drug laws	6.5	Narcotic drug laws	7.5
6	Drunken driving	5.0	Burglary**	6.2
7	Prostitution	4.1	Other assaults	4.5
8	Other assaults	3.8	Liquor laws	3.1
9	Fraud*	3.0	Vandalism	2.6
10	Liquor laws	2.9	Aggravated assaults	2.6
11	All other offenses	25.6	All other offenses	28.2
	Total	100.0	Total	100.0

Sources: Simon, 1975:45; Federal Bureau of Investigation, 1975:189.

*Does not include embezzlement.

**Includes breaking and entering.

Over the past ten years, women's rate of increase *has* exceeded men's for robbery, burglary, auto theft and fraud, although it is still true that in these categories women's actual number of arrests barely approaches that of men (see Table 4). Fraud has been one of the traditional "women's offenses." Women have also always been arrested for drug offenses. This stands in contrast to media reports and sociologists' warnings (see Adler, 1975) that a new "violent" breed of female criminal is on the rise, and that women are becoming more aggressive. As Simon (1975:46) states:

> In sum, the arrest data tell us the following about women's participation in crime: the proportion of female arrests in 1972 was greater than the proportion arrested one or two decades earlier; the increase was greater for serious offenses than it was for all Type I and Type II offenses

Table 2 **Total arrests for men and women, 1960-73**

	PERCENTAGE INCREASE	
	Males	Females
Murder	141	103
Robbery	160	287
Aggravated assault	116	106
Burglary	76	193
Larceny	84	341
Auto theft	59	155
Fraud	50	281
Narcotic drug laws	995	1027

Source: *Newsweek*, 1975:35.

Table 3 **Total arrests for men and women, 1973-74**

	PERCENTAGE INCREASE	
	Males	Females
Murder*	5.6	1.2
Robbery	13.6	14.1
Aggravated assault	9.9	14.6
Burglary/breaking & entering	20.5	20.1
Larceny/theft**	25.6	23.0
Motor vehicle theft***	−2.9	3.8
Fraud	11.8	22.4
Narcotic drug laws	2.5	−.1

Source: Federal Bureau of Investigation, 1975:190.
*Includes non-negligent manslaughter.
**Includes larceny under $50.
***Includes all kinds of motor vehicles.

combined.[7] The increase in female arrest rates among the serious offenses was owing almost entirely to women's greater participation in property offenses, especially larceny. In 1953, roughly 1 out of 7 arrests for larceny involved a woman; in 1972, the proportion was approximately 1 out of 3. Contrary to impressions that might be gleaned from the mass media, the proportion of female arrests for violent crimes has changed hardly at all over the past two decades. Female arrest for homicide, for example, has been the most stable of all violent offenses.[8]

A rise or decline in arrest rates does not necessarily indicate a rise or decline in real illegal activity. It may reflect the political situation in or growth of law enforcement circles, different organization of the data, changes in arrest categories, and altered perceptions of women offenders by the police. (Not all offenders are equally vulnerable to capture. For example, rapists have often escaped being reported, and the high estimated rape rate is in contrast to the low arrest rate for charged rapists.) However, the arrest figures above do raise questions about women's participation in the illegal marketplace. As we have previously discussed, women are economically an underpaid group, and in a simplistic determinist view, we would expect very high rates of petty property offenses because of their economic situations. We do not agree with Pollak (1950) that women *do* commit as many offenses as men, but receive more lenient treatment and hence escape the law. There are other factors involved.

Due to women's historical position in the management of commodity production and distribution, including the competitive illegal marketplace of goods and services, e.g., drugs and prostitution, most women are not socially, psychologically or economically in a position at this time to aggressively steal, nor do those with male providers have such a need. Women are traditionally just as timid and just as limited by male constrictions on their roles and male leadership within the arena of crime as they are "above ground." They are no more big-time drug dealers than are they finance capitalists. They are, however, first, petty offenders in the area of "consumerism," which reflects their

Table 4 **Percentages of females among all arrests, 1953-74**

| Year | All crimes | Serious crimes* | |
		Violent**	Property***
1953	10.8	11.9	8.5
1954	11.0	11.6	8.2
1955	11.0	12.0	8.4
1956	10.9	13.5	8.0
1957	10.6	13.1	8.5
1958	10.6	12.0	9.3
1959	10.7	12.7	10.1
1960	11.0	11.8	10.8
1961	11.2	11.6	11.4
1962	11.5	11.5	12.6
1963	11.7	11.6	12.9
1964	11.9	11.6	13.9
1965	12.1	11.4	15.0
1966	12.3	11.3	15.6
1967	12.7	10.8	16.0
1968	13.1	10.3	16.1
1969	13.8	10.6	18.0
1970	14.6	10.5	19.7
1971	15.1	10.9	20.1
1972	15.3	11.0	21.4
1973	15.6	10.0	21.1
1974	16.1	10.2	21.2

Sources: Adapted from Simon, 1975:35, 38; 1973 and 1974 figures from Federal Bureau of Investigation, 1975:190.

*All those included in FBI Crime Index except rape.

**Homicide, robbery, aggravated assault.

***Burglary, larceny, motor vehicle theft.

position as houseworkers in "straight" society. They shoplift, use illicit drugs purchased from men—especially the less-threatening barbiturates and amphetamines, often over-prescribed—and pass bad checks. Second, they may act as accomplices to men in offenses such as robbery. Third, just as most women must sell themselves, in a sense, in marriage, so prostitution affords other women the opportunity to earn a living through their sexuality. To understand why women become prostitutes, then, one must look, not only at their personal histories, but at women's general condition. As surrogate wives and lovers, prostitutes serve the same functions of sexual work and nurturance that other women do. Fourth, women "on the streets" are harassed for vagrancy and drunkenness much as men in their situation are, chivalry notwithstanding. Fifth, juvenile females are apprehended for status offenses, such as running away. And finally, women commit "crimes of passion," primarily against husbands and lovers, and strike out sometimes at children as well, which may reflect emotional frustration created by sexist roles.

Women's lack of participation in "big time" crime highlights the larger class structure of sexism that is reproduced in the illegal marketplace. Also reproduced is the structure of racism: for example, black streetwalkers are the worst-paid and worst-treated group of prostitutes, and young white call girls are the most highly privileged. Of course, black prostitutes have disproportionately high arrest rates; in New York City in the late 1960's, blacks were arrested on that charge ten times more frequently than whites (Winick and Kinsie, 1971:43).

In the current economic crisis, with the likelihood that women—along with other non-favored groups such as Third World people and the young—will be the first fired, one may expect that women may begin to commit more "street offenses" as they are thrown out of work. Conversely, with the rise of job opportunities for certain classes of women, and the increased integration of women into the labor force partly due to the successes of the women's movement, women who *are* working may be more affluent and may also have more opportunities for the types of crimes once remote: white-collar offenses such as embezzlement. The change in the family structures and functions, such as women increasingly heading households, may also affect future patterns of illicit activity.

With these changes, does it mean that we will see a great change in women's crime rates? We do not have an answer to this question but we can pose some hypotheses. First, the incorporation of women into the labor force does not mean the end of sexism. Women continue to be trained for low paying "women's work" in roles that require submissiveness and compliancy; and sexist ideology continues, of course, to be legitimated and reproduced by the mass media and educational and cultural institutions. This may mean, then, that we can expect an increase in or at least a maintenance of the rate of traditional women's crime (accomplices to men, check writing, etc.). On the other hand, if the women's movement develops a class analysis of women's oppression and a program around which working class women can be organized, then we may witness a decrease in women's individualism, self-destructiveness, competitiveness and crime. Finally, what is the relationship between the deteriorating economic situation and women's crime rates? We can expect greater pressure on the wives and lovers of working class men who are laid off from their jobs and perhaps an increase in crime-related activities such as welfare fraud and prostitution.

Whatever the outcome of this process, we are certain that the women's movement is not criminogenic. Freda Adler's book owes its popularity, no doubt, to the fact that it reinforces sexist stereotyping and is written by a woman. In contrast to her simplistic analysis of the roots of women's crime, we must look more deeply into the social relations under capitalism and to the systematic and special oppression that women suffer. Clearly, these relationships require further study.

Notes

1. We are indebted to the Schwendingers for introducing us to this concept.
2. See Ralph Miliband (1969) for an analysis of the role of government in capitalist society and economic and state elites.
3. An excellent analysis of corporate crime may be found in David Gordon (1971).
4. For a fuller discussion of the elements of women's work, see Juliet Mitchell (1969), Margaret Benston (1969), and Paddy Quick (1972).
5. In discussing housework under capitalism, Paddy Quick (1972:67) notes:

If it admitted that the family is maintained at the expense of women, capitalism would have to devise some other way of getting the work done. Although this is not inconceivable, and housework could be socialized within capitalism, the political and social consequences as well as the economic cost would be considerable. At present it would seem to be more profitable for the capitalist system to continue to 'preserve the family.'

6. See Tony Platt (1969) for an historical analysis of women reformers.
7. Type I offenses are the FBI Index Crimes. Type II offenses are, for example, non-aggravated assault, fraud, forgery, narcotics laws, and prostitution.
8. In 1953, women comprised 14.1% of homicide arrests; by 1972, they were still only 15.6% (Simon, 1975:40).

References

Adler, Freda
    1975 *Sisters in Crime: The Rise of the New Female Criminal.* New York: McGraw-Hill.
Balbus, Isaac D.
    1973 *The Dialectics of Legal Repression.* New York: Russell Sage Foundation.
Platt, Tony
    1969 *The Child Savers.* Chicago: University of Chicago Press.
    1974b "Problems in the Development of Radical Criminology." Paper presented at the 69th Annual Meeting of the American Sociological Association, Montreal (August).
Pollak, Otto
    1950 *The Criminality of Women.* Philadelphia: University of Pennsylvania Press.
Rowbotham, Sheila
    1973 *Woman's Consciousness, Man's World.* London: Pelican Books.
Simon, Rita James
    1975 *Women and Crime.* Lexington: D. C. Heath and Company.
Winick, Charles and Paul Kinsie
    1971 *The Lively Commerce: Prostitution in the U.S.* New York: Signet Books.
Wolfe, Alan
    1973 *The Seamy Side of Democracy.* New York: David McKay.

9 Changing Patterns

Freda Adler

In the early sixties, civil-rights actions swirled across the country with the fervor of a revitalization movement, challenging Americans to reaffirm their commitment to equality before the law, and redefining that equality to include those previously alienated by color or age or sex. Man's characteristic tendency to assign other people—whether they were Asians, blacks, young, poor, or women—to a subhuman status which barred them from equal protection under law was the real issue of the civil-rights movement, and women were now ready to recognize their stake in it. Why this moment was propitious for recognition is difficult to say. The theme of women as a suppressed social class had been carefully documented in 1953 by Simone de Beauvoir in her book *The Second Sex*, but it failed to develop as a serious national concern until the mid-sixties. America of the mid-sixties was rife with disillusionment and ripe for change. We were fighting what Omar Bradley called "the wrong war at the wrong place at the wrong time, and with the wrong enemy"—liberals were adding, "for the wrong reason." In this climate of disillusionment with leadership that was white, male, and over thirty, change was inevitable, and the seeds of liberation rooted in fertile soil. By the decade's end, large numbers of American women in all walks of life had begun to see themselves as Betty Friedan had portrayed them in *The Feminine Mystique:* a systematically and subtly suppressed majority whose real security lay in the strength of their own right arm, and whose time of delivery had arrived.

Many of these believers gravitated to organizations such as NOW, the National Organization for Women, which has a current membership of 18,000 in 255 chapters in 48 states.[1] The women's liberation movement suffered several distortions in the press and, at the same time, added a few bruises to its own image via the actions of a few of its more outspoken members. Hence, "women's lib" came to designate—perhaps for the majority of Americans—organized groups of women who were primarily shrill-voiced witches with clenched fists and slovenly, unloosed breasts. Not so today.

There was, and is, more to women's lib. Much more. And the portrait is changing. The organization and its goals are becoming separated from its antiquated image. There is an ever-growing national awareness of women's rights which is perhaps best described as the "new feminism." The new feminism is not an organized movement, it does not hold meetings or press conferences. It is an all-pervasive consciousness which has permeated to virtually every level of womanhood in America.

The new feminism pertains to the women who may deny any sympathy for the formalized action, but who have recently secured their first job since marriage or decided to go back to school. It applies to the women who staunchly defend their "right to be feminine," and their right to define "feminine" as a variety of human rather than as a complement of masculine. They are standing up and speaking without apology at parent-teacher meetings, they are organizing demonstrations, walking picket lines, and influencing decisions at all levels of their community. It includes the nuns who are asking for rights more closely aligned with the rights which priests enjoy, and the housewives who have come to expect their husbands to share more of the duties of the home. It also means sexually honest women who expect the same orgastic satisfaction as men, and who are requiring that men do something about it. And most relevant to our subject, it describes the women who have concluded that prostitution and shoplifting are not their style: embezzlement, robbery, and assault are more congenial to their self-image.

"You wouldn't catch me doing no boosting," said one female inmate in New York who was somewhat offended by the inference that she might have been a shoplifter. The woman—in her late twenties—found the idea of shoplifting or "boosting" undignified. She did not like "small stuff." Records say she was involved in a robbery of a large movie-theater ticket office. Other inmates privately related that the same woman was nearly killed in recent underworld warfare which broke out when she was thought to have "ripped off" a local heroin dealer for a few thousand dollars' worth of his product. The others spoke of her escapades with envy and obvious admiration.

The entrance of women into the major leagues of crime underscores the point that the incidence and kinds of crime are more closely associated with social than sexual factors. This is so for at least three reasons. First, while cupidity may be universal, ability and opportunity are less evenly distributed. Housewives might pilfer from the supermarket while doing the grocery shopping, but could not embezzle from a corporation unless they work out of the executive office. Secondly, since a crime is a transgression as socially defined by the group in power, authorities are prone to overlook upper-class practices and lean a bit too heavily on the lower class. "The law," declared Anatole France, "forbids the rich as well as the poor from sleeping under bridges and stealing bread in the marketplace." Arrests for prostitution are a pertinent example. If sex on the open market is an illegal commodity, then penalties should fall on the buyer as well as the seller, particularly if it can be established that the buyer understood the nature of the transaction and was a material participant. But such is not the case. While prostitution continues to be a crime for which a significant number of women are arrested every year, the number of males arrested for consorting with prostitutes is so small that it does not even merit a special category in the Uniform Crime Reports. The third reason why kinds of crimes are more closely linked with social roles than sex has to do with mental sets. According to the group-system hypothesis,[2] behavior is directed by a largely conscious desire to please one's own significant groups, and by a predominantly unconscious tendency to conform to an early ingrained set of attitudes. So decisive is this set for the way we think and feel and act that few people breach its boundaries, even in imagination, even in deviance. We go crazy and we go criminal along the well-worn paths that our "mazeway" has constructed for us. Running amuck is not something that Bostonians do, nor do sex-kittens rob banks—they peddle their bodies as untold generations of sex-kittens before them have done. How else can we understand the female (or, for that matter, male) offender except in the context of her social role? The mother becomes the child-beater, the shopper the shoplifter, and the sex-object the prostitute. Adolescent girls have a particularly difficult task because they are attempting to negotiate puberty with nowhere near the spatial and sexual freedom of males. That they often deviate outside their narrow confines is understandable.

In the emergence of women as a socially rising group, we are witnessing an interesting phenomenon which has implications for other upwardly mobile groups. As they become more visible in positions of prestige and power, they receive more attention from the media, and are thus further bolstered in their rising achievement. Old mental sets of devaluation and self-contempt gradually yield to new ones of pride, and sometimes an overcompensating arrogance. Black shifts from denigration to beautiful. Sexually active bachelor women are no longer "ruined" but "free" or, at the very least, "the ruined Maid," as Thomas Hardy described her, exacts no small tribute of envy from her raw country sister. How quaint seem the fallen women of literature—the Charlotte Temples and Hester Prynnes and Catherine Barkleys—who earned red letters or died in childbirth to mark well for generations of women the evils of extramarital sex. They are quaint because women are increasingly imitating men's attitude toward sex rather than submitting to one he designed for her, and they are quaint because sex is no longer the best road out of the female ghetto. In her education, in her jobs, and in her crimes she has found much faster routes to travel. The journey, relatively speaking, has just begun. While the rate of increase of major crimes for women is surpassing that for males, the data[3] still provide some justification for the epithet "fair sex" in that men continue to commit the majority of crimes, and that the highest proportion of females are still arrested for larceny, primarily shoplifting.[4]

However, even here a comparison of figures for 1960 and 1972 shows an unmistakable across-the-board trend. Females are cutting themselves in for a bigger piece of the pie in every category but murder and, in a few—like the subtotal for major crimes, forgery and counterfeiting, and fraud and embezzlement—that piece is 80 to 100 per cent bigger than it had been twelve years before.

In summary, what we have described is a gradual but accelerating social revolution in which women are closing many of the gaps, social and criminal, that have separated them from men. The closer they get, the more alike they look and act. This is not to suggest that there are no inherent differences. Differences do exist and will be elaborated later in this book, but it seems clear that those differences are not of prime importance in understanding female criminality. The simplest and most accurate way to grasp the essence of women's changing patterns is to discard dated notions of femininity. That is a role that fewer and fewer women are willing to play. In the final analysis, women criminals are human beings who have basic needs and abilities and opportunities. Over the years these needs have not changed, nor will they. But women's abilities and opportunities have multiplied, resulting in a kaleidoscope of changing patterns whose final configuration will be fateful for all of us.

Notes

1. For a history of the National Organization for Women, see Jo Freeman, "The Origins of the Women's Liberation Movement," *American Journal of Sociology*, January 1973, 78:792–811.
2. Herbert M. Adler, M.D., and Van Buren O. Hammett, M.D., "Crisis, Conversion, and Cult Formation: An Examination of a Common Psychosocial Sequence," *American Journal of Psychiatry*, August 1973, 138:861–64; and Herbert M. Adler, M.D., and Van Buren O. Hammett, M.D., "The Doctor-Patient Relationship Revisited," *Annals of Internal Medicine*, April 1973, 78:595–98.
3. Figures calculated from data of Uniform Crime Reports, United States Department of Justice (Washington, D.C.: U.S. Government Printing Office, 1972), p. 124.
4. For a comprehensive discussion of shoplifting, see Mary Owen Cameron, *The Booster and the Snitch* (New York: The Free Press, 1964). See also, T. C. N. Gibbens and Joyce Prince, *Shoplifting* (London: The Institute for the Study and Treatment of Delinquency, 1962).

Part two
The crimes women commit

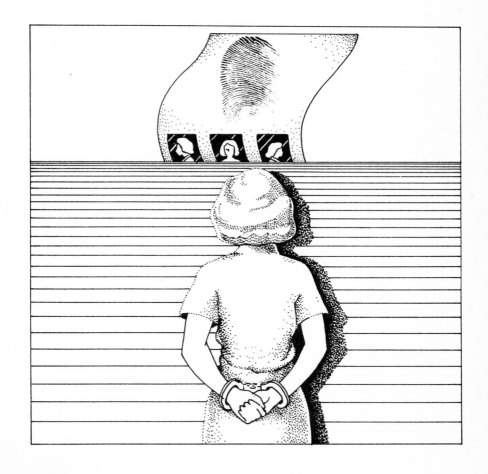

Recent interest in women's involvement in criminal activities has emphasized two major aspects. The first is that more women are committing serious criminal acts, as measured by the increase in the proportion of female arrests among the total number of persons arrested in the past decade. The second concerns the types of crimes women are committing. On that aspect, there are more differences of opinion than on the first.

The mass media have publicized the increase in crimes committed by women. They have carried news stories, sought out experts for "informed" interviews, prepared special features, and editorialized on the issue. When Sara Jane Moore and Lynette Fromme were charged with attempted assassination of President Ford, *Newsweek, Time,* and many of the country's leading newspapers saw in those events the possibility of an organized political terrorist movement "manned" by women. Several reporters and commentators connected the "Patty Hearst phenomenon" and the presence of women in the leadership of the Symbionese Liberation Army with the assassination attempts and feared that women had taken to political terrorism in large numbers. In addition to political terrorism, there were reports that women, especially girls in their late teens, were engaging in crimes of violence that had no direct political implication: Assaults, robberies, and muggings were becoming more common among young women than had been noticed at any prior time. The picture, then, that has been emerging is that more women are involved in crime in the United States than ever before, and the types of crimes women are committing are not those usually associated with female deviance: prostitution, sexual promiscuity, and other types of victimless offenses.

The accounts of the mass media, interesting and dramatic as they have been, provide a rather distorted image of the changes that are occurring in the roles women perform vis-à-vis criminal activities. The one aspect of media reporting that is consistent with the data is that there has been a recent significant increase in the proportion of women engaged in criminal activity, and indeed, that increase has been accounted for largely by female participation in serious crimes. As shown by the statistics in the first selection in this part, by Simon, the average rate of increase for all types of crimes committed by women from 1953 to 1974 is .25. The average rate for all Type I offenses (homicide, rape, aggravated assault, robbery, larceny, burglary, and auto theft) is .46. But—and this is the issue on which scholarly investigations and mass media reporting differ—the statistics also show that almost all of the increase in women's participation in serious crime has come about as a result of their increased involvement in property offenses.

Table I in the Simon selection shows that there has been practically no increase in women's participation in homicide and aggravated assault. The largest increase occurred in larceny, an activity in which women have always accounted for a high proportion of arrestees. Burglary and robbery have also increased, but not nearly as much as larceny. Additional figures, showing women's involvement in what are referred to by the FBI as Type II offenses (offenses that are not as common or as serious as those in the Type I category) are consistent with those given in Table I of the Simon selection. They show that there has been a marked increase in women's propensity to commit embezzlement, forgery, and fraud. These too are property and economic offenses in which women were well represented prior to 1967, the year that marked the beginning of the overall increase in women's participation in criminal activities.

This first selection contains statistics that describe women's participation in crime from 1953 through 1974. It shows the crimes with which women have been traditionally associated and the types of crimes in which women's participation has increased more markedly, and it draws several profiles of how women arrestees have distributed their activities over the past two decades. However one chooses to examine the data, it is evident that the major source of increase in women's criminal participation is in the property, economic, and white-collar offenses, and not in the violent offenses, such as assault and homicide, for which women have received recent notoriety.

The other excerpts in Part Two are organized around types of offenses: violent, property, and victimless crimes. The section on violent crime includes the Ward, Jackson, and Ward account of women who had been convicted of murder, assault, or robbery. It describes the types of women involved, the circumstances under which their acts occurred, and whether the women acted alone or in collaboration.

The excerpt from Wolfgang's *Patterns in Criminal Homicide* is based on a 1950 study of violent crime in Philadelphia. It emphasizes the relatively minor role that women performed in such crime, but also describes the characteristics (especially age and race) of the women who were involved. The data are more than two decades old, and if the arrest statistics in the first selection had not been available, it might be assumed that they were too old to be worth considering. But knowing as we do that women have not noticeably increased their participation in homicide, the descriptions available from the Wolfgang study are still useful, and probably accurate.

The essay "Woman as Terrorist" was written especially for this volume. In it, Cooper claims that women are joining terrorist political organizations and assuming positions of leadership. As examples he cites the recent activities of women in the Irish Republican Army, in the Baader-Meinhof group in West Germany, and in the Symbionese

Liberation Army. Cooper argues that terrorism occurs within the context of a bitterly intense struggle for power. It is a weapon of the weak, and women have been regarded—and regarded themselves—as the weaker sex. Terrorism, then, becomes one of the responses women make to the frustrations they feel about their relative weakness and powerlessness. Once involved in terrorism, according to Cooper, women exhibit more hostility than men and are less inclined to bargain or compromise. The essay does not consider such issues as the number of women, the types of women, or the political cultures that are likely to inspire the development of women as terrorists.

Despite the fact that arrest statistics indicate that more than one out of three arrests for larceny, embezzlement, fraud, and forgery are women, few empirical studies have analyzed these women. In almost all of the research on white-collar crimes and property offenses, the subjects are men. What empirical work there is on female property offenders tends to focus on women who engage in shoplifting. Cameron's *The Booster and the Snitch* details the distinctions between white-collar crime and property-offense behavior and describes the characteristics of women who engage in shoplifting regularly. A selection from that study is included here.

The pieces by Franklin on employee theft and by Sparks on "Crime as Business" were prepared especially for this volume. The earlier work from which Franklin prepared the piece included here did not focus on women but sought to explain the relationship between position in an organization and the amount of money and goods stolen by different types of employees. In the Sparks essay we are reminded once again of the paucity of data about women who engage in white-collar crime, which Sparks calls "crime as business." The issue of who perpetrates the act is not a salient question, according to him. Explanations about the important features of "crime as business" are not concerned with the attributes of individuals but rather with concepts of social and economic organization, commercial products, and technology.

The Block excerpt on women in the Mafia is a colorful account of the role women played in such notorious organizations as Murder Incorporated and other Mafia-type groups that were prominent in New York City prior to World War II. Women occupied positions of some importance then, as madams, as directors of loan-shark or policy operations, or as "bag men," or messengers. Block suggests that their counterparts do not exist in organized crime today.

Perhaps as the arrest statistics reported in the first excerpt receive wider dissemination, social researchers will be motivated to find out more about the characteristics and motivations of women who embezzle, defraud, and steal, and about the conditions under which they carry out such behavior. If they were so motivated, then later anthologies about women in crime might include more representative pieces under the heading of property offenses than those that appear in this edition.

The prostitution section suffered from an abundance of riches. The problem here was to filter out from a great many studies those that captured the essence of the changing demographic, occupational, and personality characteristics of prostitutes in the current period. The piece by Heyl was written especially for this volume. It analyzes the social organization of the prostitutes' world with special emphasis on the power differences that exist between the males and females who people that world and on the system of stratification that exists among the different types of prostitutes. Heyl makes the point that upward mobility is rare: The streetwalker or the house prostitute is not likely to move up to the level of call girl, and the economic class background of the woman is a strong indicator of the level at which she is likely to begin to work as a prostitute.

The excerpt from Millett's *Prostitution Papers* is a stream-of-consciousness piece by a young woman who describes the special indignity and humiliation of prostitution—feelings that are produced as a result of the man's perception of the situation. Because the man involved is likely to perceive sex as dirty, an activity to be enjoyed with someone who is not quite human, he degrades the prostitute. The excerpt from Adler's *Sisters in Crime* emphasizes the changes that are occurring in the types of women who engage in prostitution. More and more of them, Adler claims, are individual operators who occupy dual roles as housewives or secretaries or models, and they are better educated and more independent than their sisters were twenty years or so earlier.

What research has been done on females and drugs has been largely within the purview of the literature on prostitution. The issue most often studied is whether women become prostitutes in order to support their habit, or whether they become dependent on drugs in order to deaden their feelings about the type of work they do. There are no studies of women as "pushers" or managers or entrepreneurs in the illicit drug world. Perhaps there are no data because women do not play such roles and have not gained admittance into the criminal hierarchy of the buying and distribution of illicit drugs. The Cuskey piece is a description of the extent to which females were involved in illicit drug use in the United States from 1850 to 1970. It characterizes the backgrounds of the female addicts and their marital and family status.

We think it important to emphasize what Part Two does *not* contain because of the lack of research on certain topics. To date, there have been no major studies describing the socioeconomic characteristics of women who are involved in crime. Data on the socioeconomic status of women (men, too, for that matter) who have been arrested are sorely needed. The FBI reports, the data source most widely used by social researchers, list the race, age (under and over eighteen), and sex of the arrestees. Unfortunately, while it is possible to obtain frequencies on both race and age, and age and sex, data are not published in a form that allows the researcher to tabulate both the sex and race of the arrestee. But aside from these three characteristics, there are no data on the marital status, educational background, occupational status, or income level of the arrestee. Any analysis that a researcher wishes to make on the relationship between the social status of the arrestee and his or her propensity to commit various types of property or violent offenses must first involve the collection of original data—an enormously time-consuming and expensive endeavor.

In our own studies of the changing patterns of female crime, as well as in the analysis of other researchers, hypotheses are made about the potential relationships between the political and legal status of women, women's expanded employment opportunities, changes in the sociocultural characteristics of women's roles, changes women have experienced in their self-images, and the increase in women's involvement in crime, particularly in property and white-collar offenses. But only the availability of more detailed demographic information and socioeconomic status indicators will allow both those who hold those hypotheses and those who do not accept such interpretations to demonstrate the empirical validity of their positions. The willingness of researchers who are beginning to examine the extent of women's participation in a range of deviant activities to write proposals that call for the collection of such information, and the creation of budgets that allow such information to be collected, would be a significant benefit to all of us working on this topic.

A related issue on which more empirical work needs to be done is that of the female property offender. As revealed by the selections included in this volume, researchers have studied women who commit homicide and other forms of serious, violent offenses, women who engage in prostitution, women who use drugs, and women who shoplift. But approximately one out of three of all the people who commit larceny, embezzlement, and fraud are women. What types of women are they, under what circumstances do they steal or embezzle, and how much money is involved? These are questions for which there are practically no sound answers.

10 Arrest Statistics

Rita James Simon

The first opportunity for examining longitudinal national data about the number of women involved in crime and the types of crimes with which they are charged comes at the time of arrest. These statistics have been available since 1930, when the Federal Bureau of Investigation published its first *Uniform Crime Reports*. These reports, which are currently based on data obtained from approximately 10,000 law enforcement agencies all over the country, describe the number of arrests that have occurred in a given year, the offenses for which suspects have been arrested, and the age, sex, and racial backgrounds of those arrested. Arrest rates and trends are shown by cities, suburbs, and rural areas, as well as for the United States as a whole.

The specific crimes for which arrest data are available are divided by the FBI into two categories. Type I offenses include criminal homicide—murder and nonnegligent manslaughter, and manslaughter by negligence, forcible rape, robbery, aggravated assault, burglary, larceny, and auto theft. These offenses are used to establish an "Index in the Uniform Crime Reporting Program" to measure the trend and distribution of crime in the United States. These particular offenses are selected because as a group "they represent the most common local crime problem. They are all serious crimes either by their nature or due to the volume in which they occur" (*Uniform Crime Reports*, 1953–72, p.1).

Type II offenses include other assaults, arson, forgery and counterfeiting, fraud, embezzlement, stolen property (buying, receiving, possessing), vandalism, weapons (carrying, possessing, etc.), prostitution and commercialized vice, sex offenses (except forcible rape, prostitution, and commercialized vice), narcotic drug law violations, gambling, offenses against the family and children, driving under the influence, liquor law violations, drunkenness, disorderly conduct, vagrancy, all other offenses, and suspicion.

From *The Contemporary Woman and Crime* by Rita James Simon. National Institute of Mental Health, Washington, D.C., 1975. Pp. 34–48.

In this article, type I offenses are considered for the reasons previously stated: they are the most serious and the most common. (Rape will not be included because it is almost exclusively a male offense.) Some of the type II offenses are commented upon usually because there has been a change in the arrest pattern for women or because they are offenses for which arrest rates for women are consistently high.

It may appear that this discussion uses arrest statistics as proxies for describing crime rates among men and women without regard for the hazards of doing so. It is important to emphasize at this time the danger of using the terms "arrests" and "crimes committed" interchangeably and that arrest statistics may not be the most reliable source of data for determining actual crime rates. But, unfortunately, there are no other data prior to these statistics that provide information about the characteristics of the suspect as well as the offense he or she is believed to have committed. Criminologists usually prefer to use statistics for determining crime rates that are computed on the basis of crimes known to the police, but unfortunately those statistics do not identify the suspect in any way. The situation then is that arrest data are used in this monograph to describe crime rates of women and to compare rates between men and women for different types of offenses because they are the only data available. It is also recognized that the proportions of arrest vary considerably from one type of offense to another. For example, the proportion of crimes in the type I category that were cleared by arrest in 1972 are as follows: murder, 82 percent; forcible rape, 57 percent; aggravated assault, 60 percent; robbery, 30 percent; burglary, 19 percent; larceny, 20 percent; and auto theft, 17 percent. Arrest rates are obviously more accurate proxies for behavior in violent types of crimes than they are for crimes against property.

With these qualifications and precautions in mind, let us turn to the arrest data and note first the proportion of women who have been arrested for all types of crime as well as for those crimes that are included in the crime index from 1953 to 1974. The average rate of change in the proportion of women arrested in both categories for 1953–74, 1958–74, and for 1967 and 1974, is shown in table 4.1. The last period is particularly crucial because the expectation is that the rate of change would be marked by the greatest increase during this period.

In 1974, one out of 6 persons arrested was a woman. The average rate of change over the entire two decades was .25. For the serious crimes in 1953, 1 out of 10.6 persons arrested was a woman, and in 1974, the ratio had dropped to 1 out of 5.4. The average rate of increase was .46 for the entire period. The average increase in the proportion of women arrested for serious crimes is greater than the average increase in the proportion of women arrested for all crimes. In table 4.1, the data also show that the average rate of increase was greatest in the period from 1967 to 1974—.49 for all crimes and .57 for serious offenses. Note also that from 1961 onward the percentage of women arrested for serious crimes was greater than the percentage of women arrested for all offenses.

In table 4.2, the proportions of female and male arrests for serious crimes as a percentage of total male and female arrests for all crimes are reported. In 1953, 1 out of 12.8 women arrests was for serious crimes as opposed to slightly

Table 4.1 **Percentage of females among arrests, 1953–74**[1]

YEAR	ALL CRIMES	SERIOUS CRIMES[2]
1953	10.84	9.40
1954	10.97	8.89
1955	11.00	9.12
1956	10.91	9.06
1957	10.63	9.29
1958	10.61	9.73
1959	10.68	10.54
1960	11.04	10.95
1961	11.26	11.47
1962	11.47	12.38
1963	11.68	12.65
1964	11.93	13.54
1965	12.12	14.37
1966	12.33	14.80
1967	12.67	15.03
1968	13.08	15.04
1969	13.82	16.58
1970	14.58	18.04
1971	15.07	18.34
1972	15.27	19.25
1973	15.3	18.7
1974	16.1	19.0
Average rate of change, 1953–74	+0.25	+0.46
Average rate of change, 1958–74	+0.34	+0.58
Average rate of change, 1967–74	+0.49	+0.57

Source: Data for 1953–74 from *Uniform Crime Reports.* Washington, D.C.: U.S. Department of Justice, Federal Bureau of Investigation.

[1] Arrest data for cities with populations 2,500 and above.

[2] Serious crimes are all those included in the crime index, except rape.

less than 1 out of 10.9 male arrests. But two decades later, more women were arrested for serious offenses (about 1 out of 4) than were males (about 1 out of 5.2). The average rate of change among the women was greater during each of the three time periods than it was for the males. But the timespan from 1967 to 1974 does not show a greater increase when compared with time periods that extend farther back.

In table 4.3 is shown the proportion of women who have been arrested for those crimes of violence and property that are included in the index of serious offenses such as homicide, robbery, aggravated assault, burglary, larceny amounting to $50 or more, and auto theft.

A popular impression that in recent years women have been committing crimes of violence at a much higher rate than they have in the past is disputed by the facts shown in table 4.3. In fact, the increase in the proportion of arrests of women for serious crimes is due almost wholly to the fact that women seem to be committing more property offenses than they have in the past. Indeed, the percentage of women arrested for crimes of violence shows neither

Table 4.2 **Males and females arrested for serious crimes as percentages of their respective sex cohorts arrested for all crimes, 1953–74**

Year (1)	Females arrested for serious crimes as percent of all females arrested (2)	Males arrested for serious crimes as percent of all males arrested (3)	Difference column 2 and column 3
1953	7.8	9.2	−1.4
1954	8.2	10.3	−2.1
1955	8.5	10.4	−1.9
1956	8.2	10.3	−2.1
1957	9.3	10.8	−1.5
1958	9.9	10.9	−1.0
1959	10.6	10.8	−0.2
1960	12.4	12.6	−0.2
1961	13.4	13.2	+0.2
1962	14.6	13.3	+1.3
1963	15.9	14.4	+1.5
1964	18.0	15.6	+2.4
1965	18.9	15.5	+3.4
1966	20.1	16.1	+4.0
1967	20.8	16.9	+3.9
1968	20.7	17.8	+2.9
1969	22.2	17.9	+4.3
1970	23.8	18.4	+5.4
1971	24.2	19.2	+5.0
1972	25.2	19.2	+6.0
1973	25.8	20.3	+5.5
1974	28.2	23.9	+4.3
Average rate of change, 1953–74	+0.97	+0.70	
Average rate of change, 1958–74	+1.14	+0.81	
Average rate of change, 1967–74	+1.06	+1.00	

Source: Data for 1953–74 from *Uniform Crime Reports*. Washington, D.C.: U.S. Department of Justice, Federal Bureau of Investigation.

an upward nor a downward trend. Between 1953 and 1974, the percentages fluctuated from a high point in 1956 of 13.51 to a low in 1968 of 10.2.

But the picture for property offenses is markedly different. In 1953, about 1 in every 12 persons arrested was a woman. In 1974, 1 in 4.8 persons arrested was a woman. Not only has there been a consistent increase since 1953 in the percentage of women who have been arrested for property offenses, but the biggest increases have occurred in the period beginning in 1967. This last finding is most congruent with our major hypothesis: that woman's participation in selective crimes will increase as her employment opportunities expand and as her interests, desires, and definitions of self shift from a more traditional to a more liberated view. The crimes that are considered most salient for this hypothesis are various types of property, financial, and white-collar offenses.

Table 4.3 **Breakdown of serious crimes and percentage of females arrested among all arrests for violent and property crimes**

YEAR	VIOLENT CRIMES	PROPERTY CRIMES	SERIOUS CRIMES
1953	11.93	8.46	9.40
1954	11.60	8.18	8.89
1955	12.03	8.36	9.12
1956	13.51	8.04	9.06
1957	13.06	8.51	9.29
1958	11.96	9.26	9.73
1959	12.73	10.07	10.54
1960	11.77	10.76	10.95
1961	11.61	11.44	11.47
1962	11.51	12.57	12.38
1963	11.56	12.87	12.65
1964	11.64	13.92	13.54
1965	11.41	14.99	14.37
1966	11.32	15.58	14.80
1967	10.79	16.00	15.03
1968	10.33	16.11	15.04
1969	10.63	17.96	16.58
1970	10.50	19.71	18.04
1971	10.91	20.06	18.34
1972	11.01	21.35	19.25
1973	10.2	21.1	18.7
1974	10.2	21.2	19.0
Average rate of change, 1953–74	−0.08	+0.44	+0.45
Average rate of change, 1958–74	−0.08	+0.58	+0.58
Average rate of change, 1967–74	−0.08	+0.74	+0.57

Source: Data for 1953–74 from *Uniform Crime Reports.* Washington, D.C.: U.S. Department of Justice, Federal Bureau of Investigation.

In table 4.4, the same phenomenon is shown when the proportions of men and women who have been arrested for serious violent and property offenses between 1953 and 1974 are compared with all of the men and women who were arrested in that period. The percentage increase of men who have been arrested for violent offenses over the two decades is almost four times the percentage increase for women. For property offenses, it is the percentage of increase for women who have been arrested that is three times the percentage increase for men.

More details about the types of serious property and violent offenses for which women have been arrested are shown in table 4.5. Note that among all six offenses, only one shows a marked increase over time. From 1960 on, the proportion of women who have been charged with larceny or theft in any given year is much greater than is the proportion in any of the other offenses, property as well as violent. It is interesting to note that until about 1960 the proportions of women who were arrested for homicide and aggravated assault were similar to those arrested for larceny, but in 1974 the percentage in the larceny category had almost doubled the 1960 percentage; whereas from 1960

Table 4.4 **Females and males arrested for crimes of violence and property as percentage of all arrests in their respective sex cohorts, 1953–74**

	VIOLENT CRIMES		PROPERTY CRIMES	
YEAR	Female	Male	Female	Male
1953	2.2	2.0	5.6	7.2
1954	2.2	2.1	6.0	8.2
1955	2.3	2.1	6.2	8.3
1956	2.3	1.9	5.9	8.4
1957	2.2	1.8	7.1	9.0
1958	2.1	1.9	7.8	9.0
1959	2.3	1.9	8.3	8.9
1960	2.5	2.4	9.9	10.2
1961	2.5	2.4	10.9	10.8
1962	2.4	2.4	12.2	10.9
1963	2.5	2.4	13.4	12.0
1964	2.6	2.6	15.4	13.0
1965	2.6	2.7	16.3	12.8
1966	2.8	3.0	17.3	13.1
1967	2.8	3.2	18.0	13.7
1968	2.5	3.5	18.2	14.3
1969	2.6	3.6	19.6	14.3
1970	2.5	3.6	21.3	14.8
1971	2.7	3.2	21.5	15.3
1972	2.9	4.4	22.3	14.8
1973	3.0	4.7	22.8	15.5
1974	3.0	5.1	25.1	17.9
Average rate of change, 1953–74	+0.04	+0.13	+0.93	+0.51
Average rate of change, 1958–74	+0.06	+0.20	+1.08	+0.63
Average rate of change, 1967–74	+0.01	+0.27	+1.01	+0.60

Source: Data for 1953–74 from *Uniform Crime Reports.* Washington, D.C.: U.S. Department of Justice, Federal Bureau of Investigation.

on, the proportions have remained roughly the same for the homicide and aggravated assault offenses.

In table 4.6, the proportion of males and females arrested for those same type I offenses shown in table 4.5 are compared. These data show that within each of the violent crime categories, the differences in arrest rates between men and women are either nonexistent or slight. For criminal homicide the percentages of males and females have remained remarkably stable over the past 20 years and the average rate of change is practically nil. For the crimes of robbery and aggravated assault, males register an almost steady increase over females. Even within the last 5 years there has been no significant increase in the proportion of females who have been arrested for these crimes.

The most striking change is in the arrests for larceny. The average rate of increase during any of the timespans within the two decades shows that rates for women have increased between three and four times as much as they have for men. In 1953, about 1 in every 20 arrests of women was for larceny. In 1974, the ratio was down to 1 in 4.5. For males the proportion shifted from 1

Table 4.5 Females arrested as percentage of all arrests for type I offenses, 1953–74

YEAR	CRIMINAL HOMICIDE	ROBBERY	AGGRAVATED ASSAULT	BURGLARY	LARCENY-THEFT	AUTO THEFT
1953	14.1	4.3	15.9	2.0	13.9	2.6
1954	14.2	4.2	15.9	2.2	13.0	2.5
1955	14.2	4.2	16.0	2.3	13.3	2.6
1956	14.8	4.3	17.6	2.3	12.6	2.5
1957	14.7	3.9	17.5	2.0	13.2	2.7
1958	16.4	4.5	15.7	2.4	14.3	3.2
1959	16.8	4.6	16.4	2.7	15.4	3.2
1960	16.1	4.6	15.3	2.8	16.8	3.6
1961	15.9	4.9	15.2	3.2	18.0	3.7
1962	17.2	5.1	14.7	3.6	19.6	3.9
1963	15.9	4.9	14.9	3.3	20.1	3.7
1964	16.6	5.3	14.4	3.7	21.4	4.3
1965	16.3	5.3	14.4	3.8	23.2	4.2
1966	15.9	5.1	14.0	3.8	24.0	4.1
1967	15.4	5.2	13.6	4.1	24.8	4.3
1968	15.4	5.5	13.1	4.1	25.2	4.9
1969	14.8	6.3	13.2	4.3	27.2	5.1
1970	14.8	6.2	13.3	4.6	29.0	5.0
1971	16.0	6.4	13.9	4.8	29.1	6.0
1972	15.6	6.6	13.9	5.1	30.8	5.7
1973	15.1	6.8	13.2	5.4	31.5	6.0
1974	14.6	6.8	13.4	5.4	30.7	6.5
Average rate of change, 1953–74	+0.02	+0.12	−0.12	+0.16	+0.80	+0.19
Average rate of change, 1958–74	−0.11	+0.14	−0.14	+0.19	+1.02	+0.24
Average rate of change, 1967–74	−0.11	+0.23	−0.03	+0.19	+0.84	+0.31

Source: Data for 1953–74 from *Uniform Crime Reports*. Washington, D.C.: U.S. Department of Justice, Federal Bureau of Investigation.

Note: Rape has been omitted.

Table 4.6 Serious crimes: percentage of total arrests of females and males, 1953–74

YEAR	CRIMINAL HOMICIDE Female	CRIMINAL HOMICIDE Male	ROBBERY Female	ROBBERY Male	AGGRAVATED ASSAULT Female	AGGRAVATED ASSAULT Male	BURGLARY Female	BURGLARY Male	LARCENY-THEFT Female	LARCENY-THEFT Male	AUTO THEFT Female	AUTO THEFT Male
1953	0.2	0.2	0.3	0.7	1.7	1.1	0.4	2.3	4.9	3.7	0.3	1.2
1954	0.2	0.2	0.3	0.8	1.7	1.1	0.5	2.6	5.2	4.3	0.3	1.3
1955	0.2	0.2	0.3	0.7	1.8	1.2	0.5	2.6	5.4	4.3	0.3	1.4
1956	0.3	0.2	0.2	0.6	1.8	1.1	0.5	2.5	5.1	4.4	0.3	1.5
1957	0.2	0.2	0.2	0.6	1.6	1.0	0.5	2.7	6.2	4.8	0.4	1.5
1958	0.2	0.2	0.3	0.7	1.8	1.0	0.6	2.8	6.8	4.8	0.4	1.4
1959	0.2	0.2	0.3	0.6	2.0	1.1	0.6	2.7	7.3	4.8	0.4	1.4
1960	0.2	0.1	0.3	0.9	1.9	1.4	0.8	3.3	8.6	5.3	0.5	1.6
1961	0.2	0.1	0.4	0.9	1.8	1.4	0.9	3.6	9.5	5.5	0.5	1.7
1962	0.2	0.1	0.4	0.9	1.9	1.4	1.0	3.5	10.6	5.6	0.6	1.8
1963	0.2	0.1	0.4	0.9	2.0	1.6	1.0	3.8	11.8	6.2	0.6	2.0
1964	0.2	0.1	0.4	0.9	2.0	1.6	1.1	4.0	13.6	6.8	0.7	2.2
1965	0.2	0.1	0.4	1.0	2.2	1.9	1.1	4.0	14.5	6.6	0.7	2.2
1966	0.2	0.1	0.4	1.0	2.1	1.9	1.1	4.0	15.5	6.9	0.7	2.2
1967	0.2	0.1	0.5	1.2	1.8	1.9	1.3	4.4	16.0	7.0	0.7	2.3
1968	0.2	0.2	0.5	1.4	1.8	1.9	1.3	4.7	16.1	7.2	0.8	2.4
1969	0.2	0.2	0.6	1.5	1.7	1.9	1.3	4.5	17.5	7.5	0.8	2.3
1970	0.2	0.2	0.6	1.5	1.8	2.0	1.3	4.6	19.3	8.1	0.7	2.1
1971	0.2	0.2	0.7	1.7	2.0	2.2	1.4	4.8	19.4	8.4	0.7	2.1
1972	0.2	0.2	0.7	1.8	2.1	2.4	1.4	4.7	20.2	8.2	0.7	1.9
1973	0.2	0.2	0.7	1.7	2.1	2.6	1.7	5.4	20.4	8.0	0.7	2.0
1974	0.2	0.2	0.7	1.9	2.1	2.6	1.9	6.2	22.5	9.8	0.7	1.9
Average rate of change, 1953–74	—	—	+0.02	+0.06	+0.02	+0.07	+0.07	+0.19	+0.84	+0.29	+0.02	+0.04
Average rate of change, 1958–74	—	—	+0.02	+0.08	+0.03	+0.10	+0.08	+0.21	+0.98	+0.31	+0.02	+0.02
Average rate of change, 1967–74			+0.03	+0.10	—	+0.10	+0.09	+0.26	+0.93	+0.40	—	−0.06

Source: Data for 1953–74 from *Uniform Crime Reports*. Washington, D.C.: U.S. Department of Justice, Federal Bureau of Investigation.

in 27 to 1 in 10.2. Burglary and auto theft were male-dominated offenses in 1974 as they were in 1953. Burglary, perhaps more than any of the other offenses examined thus far, involves skills that are usually acquired within a criminal subculture and women have not been connected into such networks. Their opportunities for acquiring such skills are thus much more limited.

In tables 4.7 and 4.8, trends in the proportion of women arrested for selected offenses in the type II category are tested. The figures show that in 1974 approximately 1 in 3.5 persons arrested for forgery was a woman and 1 in 3.5 arrests for embezzlement and fraud involved a woman. If present trends in these crimes persist, approximately equal numbers of men and women will be arrested for fraud and embezzlement by the 1990s and for forgery and counterfeiting the proportions should be equal by the 2010s. (The prediction made for embezzlement and fraud can be extended to larceny as well.) On the other hand, if trends from 1958 to 1974 continue, fewer women will be arrested for criminal homicide and aggravated assault.

The proportions of men and women who were arrested in 1972 for the 10 most frequently cited type I and type II offenses are ranked in table 4.9. The data indicate the average rate of change between 1958 and 1972. These 10 offenses account for 71 percent of all men and 63 percent of all women arrested in 1972.

Among the women, there has been a big change in two categories: larceny, which has increased sharply, and drunkenness, which has decreased sharply. Disorderly conduct has declined by about half as much as the first two offenses, and the use of narcotics has increased. For all the other offenses, the pattern has remained stable from 1958 to the present time. Among men, the ordering has been even more stable. Except for a decline in the proportion arrested for drunkenness and disorderly conduct and an increase in arrests for narcotics, there have been no marked changes. Among both men and women the sharp decrease in arrests for drunkenness and disorderly conduct may be as much, or even more, an indication of a shift in police attitude than in the behavior of men and women.

In summary, the data on arrests indicate the following about women's participation in crime: The proportion of women arrested in 1974 was greater than the proportion arrested one or two decades earlier; and the increase was greater for serious offenses than it was for all type I and type II offenses combined. The increase in female arrest rates among the serious offenses was caused almost entirely by women's greater participation in property offenses, especially in larceny.

In 1953, roughly 1 in 7 arrests for larceny involved a woman; however, in 1974 the ratio was approximately 1 in 3. Contrary to impressions that might have been gleaned from the mass media, the proportion of females arrested for violent crimes has changed hardly at all over the past two decades. Female arrest rates for homicide, for example, have been the most stable of all violent offenses. Further probing of female arrest rates in the type II offenses revealed that the offenses that showed the greatest increases were embezzlement and fraud and forgery and counterfeiting. The increases were especially marked for the period from 1967 to 1974. None of the other offenses included in either type I or type II save larceny and theft showed as big a shift as did these two

Table 4.7 Other crimes: percentage of total arrests for various crimes of females

YEAR	EMBEZZLEMENT AND FRAUD	FORGERY AND COUNTERFEITING	OFFENSES AGAINST FAMILY AND CHILDREN	NARCOTIC DRUG LAWS	PROSTITUTION AND COMMERCIALIZED VICE
1953	18.3	14.0	9.3	15.7	73.1
1954	14.4	13.4	9.6	17.5	70.1
1955	15.6	15.2	9.8	17.1	68.8
1956	15.5	16.6	9.1	16.3	62.9
1957	14.4	14.8	9.0	15.6	69.2
1958	14.3	15.1	8.6	16.4	69.0
1959	14.9	16.2	8.9	16.2	65.2
1960	15.7	16.8	9.7	14.6	73.5
1961	15.7	17.5	11.2	15.4	71.8
1962	17.6	18.1	11.0	15.1	76.1
1963	18.3	18.7	11.5	14.2	77.0
1964	19.5	19.3	11.3	14.1	81.2
1965	20.7	19.2	11.0	13.4	77.6
1966	21.8	20.9	12.1	13.8	79.3
1967	23.4	21.4	11.4	13.7	77.2
1968	24.4	22.3	10.9	15.0	78.0
1969	26.3	23.2	11.4	15.5	79.5
1970	27.8	24.4	11.3	15.7	79.1
1971	27.4	24.8	11.6	16.3	77.4
1972	29.7	25.4	12.3	15.7	73.5
1973	31.2	26.7	9.2	14.5	75.5
1974	32.6	28.6	11.9	14.2	75.6
Average rate of change, 1953–74	+0.68	+0.70	+0.12	−0.07	+0.12
Average rate of change, 1958–74	+1.14	+0.84	+0.21	−0.14	+0.40
Average rate of change, 1967–74	+1.31	+1.03	+0.07	+0.07	−0.23

Source: Data for 1953–74 from *Uniform Crime Reports*. Washington, D.C.: U.S. Department of Justice, Federal Bureau of Investigation.

Table 4.8 Other crimes: females and males arrested for various crimes as percentage of total arrests in their respective sex cohorts, 1953–74

YEAR	EMBEZZLEMENT AND FRAUD		FORGERY AND COUNTERFEITING		OFFENSES AGAINST FAMILY AND CHILDREN		NARCOTIC DRUG LAWS		PROSTITUTION AND COMMERCIALIZED VICE	
	Female	Male	Female	Male	Female	Male	Female	Male	Female	Male
1953	1.1	0.6	0.5	0.4	0.9	1.1	0.5	0.3	7.7	0.3
1954	1.0	0.8	0.6	0.5	1.1	1.3	0.6	0.4	8.6	0.5
1955	1.0	0.7	0.6	0.4	1.1	1.3	0.6	0.3	8.3	0.5
1956	0.9	0.6	0.7	0.4	0.9	1.1	0.5	0.3	4.1	0.3
1957	1.1	0.7	0.6	0.4	0.9	1.1	0.5	0.3	4.0	0.2
1958	1.1	0.8	0.7	0.5	0.8	1.0	0.6	0.4	4.9	0.3
1959	1.1	0.8	0.7	0.4	0.8	1.0	0.6	0.4	4.3	0.3
1960	1.3	0.8	0.8	0.5	0.8	0.9	0.8	0.6	4.7	0.2
1961	1.3	0.8	0.9	0.5	0.9	0.9	0.9	0.6	4.4	0.2
1962	1.3	0.8	0.9	0.5	0.9	0.9	0.9	0.7	4.3	0.2
1963	1.5	0.9	0.9	0.5	1.0	1.0	0.8	0.7	4.2	0.2
1964	1.6	0.8	0.9	0.5	0.9	1.0	1.0	0.8	4.3	0.2
1965	1.6	0.8	0.8	0.5	0.8	0.9	1.1	1.0	4.7	0.2
1966	1.6	0.9	0.9	0.5	0.9	0.9	1.4	1.2	4.8	0.2
1967	1.7	0.9	0.9	0.5	0.7	0.8	2.0	1.8	4.9	0.2
1968	1.7	0.8	0.9	0.5	0.6	0.7	3.3	2.8	4.9	0.2
1969	1.8	0.9	1.0	0.5	0.6	0.7	4.4	3.8	5.0	0.2
1970	2.0	0.9	1.0	0.5	0.5	0.7	5.6	5.1	4.5	0.2
1971	2.3	1.0	1.0	0.5	0.4	0.6	5.9	5.4	4.4	0.2
1972	2.4	1.0	1.0	0.5	0.4	0.5	6.0	5.8	3.4	0.2
1973	2.7	1.1	1.1	0.6	0.4	0.7	7.0	7.5	0.4?	0.8
1974	3.0	1.2	1.1	0.5	0.4	0.6	6.5	7.5	4.1	0.3
Average rate of change, 1953–74	+0.09	+0.03	+0.03	—	−0.02	−0.02	+0.29	+0.34	−0.17	—
Average rate of change, 1958–74	+0.12	+0.02	+0.02	—	−0.02	−0.03	+0.38	+0.44	−0.05	—
Average rate of change, 1967–74	+0.19	+0.04	+0.03	—	−0.04	−0.03	+0.64	+0.81	−0.11	+0.01

Source: Data for 1953–74 from *Uniform Crime Reports.* Washington, D.C.: U.S. Department of Justice, Federal Bureau of Investigation.

Table 4.9 **Rank order of offenses for which females and males are most likely to be arrested, 1972**

RANK	OFFENSE	PERCENT OF ALL FEMALE ARRESTS	AVERAGE RATE OF CHANGE, 1958–72 (PERCENT PER YEAR)	OFFENSE	PERCENT OF ALL MALE ARRESTS	AVERAGE RATE OF CHANGE, 1958–72 (PERCENT PER YEAR)
1	Larceny-theft	20.2	+0.96	Drunkenness	22.9	−1.24
2	Drunkenness	9.8	−1.25	Drunken driving	9.0	+0.31
3	Disorderly conduct	8.5	−0.60	Disorderly conduct	9.0	−0.60
4	Narcotic drug laws	6.0	+0.40	Larceny-theft	8.2	+0.24
5	Other assaults	4.1	+0.06	Narcotic drug laws	5.8	+0.40
6	Drunken driving	3.8	+0.11	Burglary	4.7	+0.14
7	Prostitution	3.4	−0.11	Other assaults	4.5	+0.09
8	Liquor laws	2.7	−0.04	Liquor laws	2.9	−0.06
9	Embezzlement and fraud	2.4	+0.10	Aggravated assault	2.2	+0.09
10	Aggravated assault	2.0	+0.03	Robbery	1.8	+0.06

Source: Data for 1953–72 from *Uniform Crime Reports.* Washington, D.C.: U.S. Department of Justice, Federal Bureau of Investigation.

white-collar offenses. Should the average rate of change that occurred between 1967 and 1974 continue, female arrest rates for larceny/theft, embezzlement, and fraud will be commensurate to women's representation in the society, or, in other words, roughly equal to male arrest rates. There are no other offenses among those contained in the uniform crime reports, save prostitution, in which females are so highly represented.

These statistics describe arrests, not known or observed behavior at the scene of a crime. From the arrests, actual participation in the criminal act is inferred. But in discussing women and crime, this inference might be especially fanciful because of the discretion available to police and the way in which the police have been presumed to exercise that discretion.

Remember Pollak's argument that the differential rate of crime attributed to men and women was due in large measure to chivalry on the part of law enforcement officials. Indeed, Pollak and other authors might claim that the sharp increase in the percentage of women who have been arrested in the past 6 years is because the police have become less chivalrous, or less paternalistic and are treating women in the same way as male suspects. Indeed, in large measure, the phenomena we are witnessing are changes in the attitudes and behavior of the police rather than in the propensities of women to engage in crime. The fact, however, that the rates of female arrests have varied by the nature of the offense indicates that the hypothesized change in police behavior cannot account for all the shifts. There would be no reason to assume, for example, that police would respond to female property offenders differently than they would to women who were suspected of killing or assaulting their victims.

Two final observations: (1) It is plausible to assume that the police are becoming less "chivalrous" to women suspects and that women are beginning to receive more equal treatment; (2) Police behavior alone cannot account for the large increases in larceny, fraud, embezzlement, and forgery committed by women over the past 6 years, or the absence of increases in homicide, aggravated assaults, and other violent crimes.

The more parsimonious explanation is that as women increase their participation in the labor force their opportunity to commit certain types of crimes also increases. This explanation assumes that women have no greater store of morality than do men. Their propensities to commit crimes do not differ, but, in the past, their opportunities have been much more limited. As women's opportunities to commit crimes increase, so will their deviant behavior and the types of crimes they commit will much more closely resemble those committed by men.

11 Crimes of Violence by Women

David A. Ward, Maurice Jackson, and Renee E. Ward

There has been only one really detailed study of the character of criminal homicide in the United States—Marvin E. Wolfgang's *Patterns in Criminal Homicide.*[9] Using police reports of 588 cases of murder which occurred in the city of Philadelphia over a 5-year period, Wolfgang presents data pertaining to the race, age, and sex of persons charged with homicide, the time and place where the homicides occurred, the methods and weapons used to inflict death, and the relationship between victims and offenders. In our effort to focus upon critical elements of the roles played by women in committing violent crimes we used the findings of Wolfgang's study and Pollak's report as the basis for specific lines of inquiry.

After a preliminary search identified those aspects of criminal roles that could be reliably obtained from prison files, we abstracted this information for each inmate confined in the California Institution for Women (in 1963–64 and in 1968) and in the Minnesota Women's Reformatory (1964–66) for the following offenses:

Murder:

Murder, first
Murder, second
Voluntary manslaughter
Involuntary manslaughter

Robbery:

Robbery, first
Robbery, second
Attempted robbery
Kidnaping for purpose of robbery
Assault with intent to rob

From "Crimes of Violence by Women" by David A. Ward, Maurice Jackson, and Renee E. Ward. In *Crimes of Violence,* ed. Donald Mulvihill, et al. U.S. Government Printing Office, Washington, D.C., 1969. Pp. 864–889, 906–909. The original footnote numbers of the source are retained.

Assault: *Burglary:*

Assault with/without deadly weapon   Burglary, first
Assault with intent to kill; rob   Burglary, second
Attempted murder; assault   Attempted burglary
Assault with caustic acid
Wife, child beating; mayhem

The reasons for including homicide, assault, and robbery cases in a study of crimes of violence are self-evident. We have, however, included burglary, which is not in the "crimes against persons" category. We were interested in the involvement of women in this type of crime because it implies behavior that is atypical, given the stereotypical roles of women in our society. Burglary suggests force in terms of breaking and entering and a burglar runs the risk of personal confrontation with victims should he—or she—be discovered in the course of committing the burglary. Crimes such as forgery, bad-check writing, theft, and narcotics use do not involve behaviors that are particularly "unlady-like." Other crimes important in typologies of male criminals have so little relevance for women that we did not include them for sheer lack of number. The dozen or so women convicted of auto theft, for example, were generally companions to men who actually stole the vehicles. No women were committed to the California or Minnesota prisons for rape and the several "sex offenders" in the CIW population were involved in secondary roles in these crimes. (In one case the woman had obtained money as a "pimp" for a teenage prostitute and in another case the woman had encouraged the statutory rape of her daughter by her new husband.) Data on the cases of women who were convicted of kidnaping, arson, and criminal abortion were gathered, but the small number and the extremely unusual character of most of these crimes did not warrant their being included in our analysis.

The features of crimes of violence and burglary committed by women presented in this paper are by no means all of the items that a criminologist would want to have available if he wished to construct an adequate picture of the situational complex within which a particular form of criminal activity took place. We have mined from police, court, and prison records and from personal statements made by the offenders themselves those data we considered to be the most reliably and accurately reported in prison files. The best source of detailed data on the circumstances under which any crime occurred is where Wolfgang gathered his data—in the records of the homicide detail in a police department. This discussion is thus limited to aspects of criminal homicide which were related to the roles of the participants in the crime drama. Given these limits in the range of our data the reader should not expect to get a sense of the "character" of these types of criminal activity from reviewing only the tabular material. We have therefore included descriptions of some of the 444 crimes committed by our study population. These descriptions have been grouped into several categories to illustrate the findings of the statistical analysis, to point up some additional features of these crimes and, perhaps most importantly, to show how the features of the crimes that were quantitatively measured mesh together in one criminal action. The descriptions were taken verbatim from the prison records and our editing consists only of deletions of redundant or extraneous statements. In some cases we have used an inmate's statement, in other cases the statements of police officers or excerpts from the transcripts of criminal proceedings.

Findings

We present below a summary of the principal conclusions to be drawn from our effort to answer several very basic questions about the nature of violent criminal behavior by women. Case descriptions follow the summary and supporting tabular materials. The aspects of violent crimes examined include: whether the women acted alone or with others, who the victims were, where the crimes took place, whether the crimes were premeditated, what weapons were used, whether physical strength was required, what the condition of the victim was at the time of the assault, and what rationale, justification or explanation was given by the women for their crimes.

1. The criminal roles of women

The number of roles women can play in committing crimes of violence and burglary include that of the *conspirator,* who instigates or has knowledge of the crime but who does not participate in committing the criminal act itself; the *accessory,* who plays a secondary role in committing the crime—acting as lookout, driving a getaway car, carrying weapons, tools, or the proceeds of robberies and burglaries; the *partner,* who participates equally in all aspects of the crime; and finally, the woman who acts as the *sole perpetrator* of the crime. Data presented in [tables 18 and 19] indicate that most of the women

Table 18 **Offender's role: violent offenders, 1963 and 1968 groups combined [in percent of offense category]**

CRIMINAL ROLE	HOMICIDE	ASSAULT	ROBBERY	BURGLARY
Conspirator	3	5	4	10
Accessory	3	1	23	15
Partner	16	16	57	56
Sole perpetrator	77	75	14 .	15
No information	1	3	2	4
Total	100	100	100	100
N	(179)	(80)	(105)	(80)

Table 19 **Crime partner: violent offenders, 1963 and 1968 groups combined [in percent of offense category]**

PARTNER	HOMICIDE	ASSAULT	ROBBERY	BURGLARY
Husband/lover[1]	51	53	40	25
Friend/acquaintance	49	47	60	75
Total	100	100	100	100
N	(39)	(17)	(89)	(68)

[1] Includes female homosexual intimates.

in our study population who committed homicide or assault acted alone, but when they were involved in robberies and burglaries they accompanied someone else. When other persons were involved in homicide and assaults, they were husbands and lovers in about half the cases and friends or acquaintances in the others. In robbery and burglary cases women tended to accompany friends or acquaintances rather than persons intimately related to them.

2. The victims of female offenders

That murder tends to be a family affair has been documented in a number of studies and reports, including the *Uniform Crime Reports*: "The significant fact emerges that most murders are committed by relatives of the victim or persons acquainted with the victim."[10] In 1967 approximately 37 percent of all murders involved a spouse killing a spouse, a parent killing a child, and other family killings, romantic triangles, and lovers' quarrels. Our data on violent crime show that husbands, lovers, or children were the victims in over half of the cases of homicide and in over one-third of the assault cases.

Table 20 **Victim: violent offenders, 1963 and 1968 groups combined [in percent of offense category]**

VICTIM	HOMICIDE	ASSAULT	ROBBERY	BURGLARY
Adult female	16	23	6	5
Adult male	61	48	39	6
Husband/lover	35	19		
Friend/acquaintance	18	13	11	4
Stranger	8	16	28	2
Child	19	17		
Commercial personnel	2	5	47	5
Commercial establishment			6	83
Not known	2	7	2	1
Total	100	100	100	100
N	(179)	(80)	(105)	(80)

Table 21 **Locale of offense: violent offenders, 1963 and 1968 groups combined [in percent of offense category]**

LOCALE	HOMICIDE	ASSAULT	ROBBERY	BURGLARY
Residence of offender and victim	47	39	3	2
Offender's residence	13	11		
Residence of victim (same neighborhood as offender)	2	5	1	6
Offender's neighborhood	6	2	12	8
Nonlocal (i.e., away from offender's neighborhood)	32	43	84	84
Total	100	100	100	100
N	(179)	(80)	(105)	(80)

Male adults and female adults were victims in 61 percent and 16 percent, respectively, of the homicide cases; nearly all were friends or acquaintances of the murderer. Assault cases involved strangers and women somewhat more often than in cases of homicide.

Robbery victims were generally strangers to the offender. Commercial personnel were the victims in about half of these cases; unknown men (i.e., men not victimized in connection with their employment) constituted an additional 28 percent. Few women were victimized.

By definition burglary is not a crime against a person, hence the concept of "victim" was taken more broadly to include a person's property. Women committed to prison for this offense seldom victimized an individual, instead they stole from commercial establishments.

Given the relationship between female offenders and their victims, the finding that 60 percent of the homicides and 50 percent of the assaults took place in the offender's residence is not surprising. (In most of these cases, it was the victim's home also.) Robbery and burglary victims tended to be strangers, since the great majority of these offenses occurred away from the residence and neighborhood of the offender.

3. Premeditation

We were able to obtain from the prison files of about 70 percent of our study sample some evidence of the degree to which the women consciously and deliberately planned their crimes. Operationalizing the concept of premeditation is no easy task, for the amount of time between the point at which one begins to think about and plan for committing a crime and the time when the criminal act actually occurs, which is necessary to constitute premeditation, is subject to different interpretations by judicial authorities, legal experts, psychiatrists and sociologists. We have tried to avoid the intricacies of resolving such issues as how long a period can one's behavior be said to be the result of "hot blood" and how much activity is required to constitute a deliberately planned robbery or burglary. To do this we have categorized the crimes of our subjects as premeditated *only* when there was a definite statement about a definite plan of action made by the subject or her crime partners, when the crime was one of a series of similar crimes, or when the crime was first-degree murder. In the latter instance we, in effect, accepted the definition of premeditation used by prosecuting attorneys in determining the degree of murder with which the subject was charged. In the case of other offenses this was not a reliable method of establishing premeditation. File data indicated that in some cases the woman was with someone else who actually planned the crime without her knowledge, but she was charged with the offense in the first degree because once the criminal action began she participated actively; in other cases there was evidence in the file of prior planning but perhaps as the result of "plea bargaining" the subject was actually charged with a lesser degree of the crime. In about one-third of the homicide and assault cases in our sample there was not enough information in the prison files to permit us to designate the crime as premeditated or not. For the remaining cases of homicide 21 percent were classified as premeditated; 40 percent as not pre-

Table 22 **Premeditation: violent offenders, 1963 and 1968 groups combined [in percent of offense category]**

PREMEDITATION	HOMICIDE	ASSAULT	ROBBERY	BURGLARY
Yes	21	31	63	78
No	46	31	7	2
Unable to determine	33	38	30	20
Total	100	100	100	100
N	(179)	(80)	(105)	(80)

meditated. The classifiable assault cases were evenly divided in terms of whether or not premeditation was evident. Robbery and burglary cases gave greater evidence of planning, as might be expected.

4. The use of physical strength and agility by female offenders

Examining this aspect of criminal conduct posed a serious problem for operational definition. Some physical strength is required to engage in any activity and we chose to rely upon a definition that focused upon gross rather than subtle actions. In the cases of murder and assault, we looked for instances of physical combat in which the female fought or attacked the victim with her fists or with a knife or some other weapon. We thus excluded from the "physical-strength-required" category cases where the woman walked up to or came upon the victim and shot him; cases where death was caused by poison or neglect; robbery cases where the female *herself* did not participate in subduing, beating, tying up or otherwise physically acting against the victim; and burglary cases where the female did not physically force or assist in forcing entry into rooms or buildings. The data in table 23 indicate the use of some physical strength was required in about 4 of 10 murders and 6 of 10 assaults, but in only a small minority of the robbery and burglary cases. The physical strength aspect of female criminality is meaningful only when it is considered with two other classes of data: the use of weapons, and the "condition" of the victim at the time of the crime.

5. The use of weapons in assaultive crimes

The need for women to use physical strength, particularly in the assault cases, is more understandable in the light of the type of weapons that were at hand

Table 23 **Use of physical strength: violent offenders, 1963 and 1968 groups combined [in percent of offense category]**

WAS PHYSICAL STRENGTH USED	HOMICIDE	ASSAULT	ROBBERY	BURGLARY
Yes	43	59	22	12
No	51	39	71	74
Unable to determine	6	2	7	14
Total	100	100	100	100
N	(179)	(80)	(105)	(80)

Table 24 **Weapons used: violent offenders, 1963 and 1968 groups combined [in percent of offense category]**

WEAPON USED	HOMICIDE	ASSAULT	ROBBERY	BURGLARY
Knife or household implement	35	49	6	1
Gun	34	29	35	1
Other*	8	7	6	3
No weapon used by subject	23	15	53	95
Total	100	100	100	100
N	(179)	(80)	(105)	(80)

* *Other:* Clubbing instruments other than household articles—pipe, rocks, baseball bat; caustic chemicals not normally found in homes; special-purpose tools such as surgical instruments.

at the time of the crime. As can be seen in table 24, a knife or some household implement (e.g., kitchen utensils, hand tools, lye, gasoline, bottles, closet pole, steam iron, straight razor, garden hose, woman's shoes) was used in almost half of the assaults and about one-third of the murder cases. Guns were less frequently used than knives in the assault cases (it may be that since guns are more likely to produce lethal injuries some assaultive acts become homicides). The use of a gun—the great equalizer—by women in assaults, murder, and in about one-third of the robberies, helps to explain why the use of physical strength is not a necessary feature of these crimes. Since burglaries do not involve physical confrontations with victims the extremely limited use of weapons in the crimes is not surprising. Our data also indicate that there were very few cases in which women took weapons on burglaries "just in case" someone discovered the crime in progress. Guns were used in some of the robberies or available in some of the burglaries but the women did not personally carry them.[11]

Although one might assume that an unarmed woman is unable to physically harm a healthy, adult male, in our study population more than half the women's victims were adult males. And, in fact, an examination of the victim's "condition" at the time of assault substantiates this assumption. Victims were incapacitated in some way—either ill, drunk, off-guard, or asleep—in 42 percent of the homicides, 38 percent of the assaults, and 44 percent of the robberies. Furthermore, the female's role in cases of adult male robberies should be viewed in connection with the role played by male partners. Burglaries were not committed against persons in the sense of assaultive crimes and were excluded from analysis for this item.

Table 25 **Victim's condition at the time of the crime: violent offenders, 1963 and 1968 groups combined [in percent of offense category]**

"CONDITION" OF VICTIM	HOMICIDE	ASSAULT	ROBBERY
Helpless (child)	19	19	
Ill, drunk, off-guard, asleep, infirm (adult)	42	38	44
Not incapacitated (adult)	28	28	44
No information	11	17	12
Total	100	100	100
N	(179)	(80)	(105)

6. Offender's rationale

Twenty-two percent of the women who committed homicide and 19 percent of those who committed assault claimed self-defense or the defense of others as the rationale for their crimes. Of the homicide cases only 2 percent said the victim "deserved it" and 17 percent said that the crime was accidental compared with 13 percent and 8 percent in these categories for assault offenders. Drunkenness accounted for 5 percent of the rationale in homicide cases and 11 percent in cases of assault. Innocence (i.e., nonguilt) was asserted by 13 percent and by 10 percent of those women who committed homicide and assault. There was not enough information to determine how the offender characterized her action in 21 percent of the homicides and in 13 percent of the assault cases.

It was even more difficult to determine the rationale of robbery and burglary offenders; 31 percent and 44 percent, respectively, of these cases included no information pertaining to the offender's rationale. Such information as there was suggested that motives for robbery were seldom expressed in terms of personal assault; rather, economic and psychological reasons were cited in 28 percent of these cases. Sixteen percent claimed they had been "framed" and 11 percent blamed others for getting them involved in the robberies. Sixteen percent of the burglary offenders indicated that the rationale for their crime was based upon economic factors, while 10 percent claimed drunkenness. These findings should be regarded only as suggestive, due to the large "No-Response" category.

The data presented above deal with those aspects of violent crime by women which are amenable to quantitative analysis. At best, this is a beginning step to far more detailed statistical studies of the nature of criminal activity. Until

Table 26 **Rationale for commission of the crime: violent offenders, 1963 and 1968 groups combined [in percent of offense category]**

Offender's rationale	Homicide	Assault	Robbery	Burglary
Offender claims innocence—framed	13	10	16	9
Offender claims justifiable action	24	31	1	3
Victim deserved it	2	12	1	3
Self-defense, or defense of others	22	19	—	—
Offender claims extenuating circumstances	34	36	46	35
Drunk	5	11	7	10
Accidental	17	8	1	—
Others to blame	3	6	11	5
Psychological reasons	9	9	12	3
Economic reasons	—	2	15	17
Multiple reasons or other reasons	8	10	6	9
No information	21	13	31	44
Total	100	100	100	100
N	(179)	(80)	(105)	(80)

those additional steps are taken we feel that the reader can gain some sense of the nature of the violent criminal behavior of women by reading descriptions of their crimes. In the pages that follow we have provided a representative sample of the reports of robberies, burglaries, assaults, and homicides committed by women in our study group.

Descriptive accounts of robberies and burglaries by women

• Perhaps the most striking characteristic of the robberies and burglaries committed by or involving the women in our study group is that most of them were so badly planned. This seems to be because these crimes often resulted from a spur-of-the-moment suggestion made by one of a group of three or four persons that the group embark immediately to rob or burglarize some "easy touch." The risks taken were great and the possible financial rewards small. Our data clearly indicate that the women tended to play secondary roles in these hastily contrived schemes. The following robbery cases illustrate these points:

Offense: robbery, 1st degree

The defendant and two male accomplices robbed the victim (male stranger) of $350. They had been drinking all day, moving from bar to bar, and when they realized that the man they had met in a bar [the victim] was carrying a large sum of money with him, they got into the car, and drove out to a deserted country road. The two male co-defendants got out of the car, and the defendant enticed the victim to get out also. When the victim left the car, the two male defendants beat him up while the defendant stood by the car watching. The victim fell to the ground and one of the men took his billfold and gave it to the defendant. The three left him behind on the ground and drove off in his car. The defendant claimed that she met the two accomplices on the three or four days prior to the incident. They gave her a ride home and met her the next day at a bar. They spent the entire day drinking. She had intimate relations with one of the co-defendants and continued doing so for the next few days. They went to a bar and met the victim. She thought that one of the co-defendants had known him before. The defendant claims that there was absolutely no plan to rob the victim. However, one of the co-defendants said that they had discussed it while waiting for the victim as he bought some liquor in a store the day of the offense.

Offense: accessory after robbery

. . . four farm laborers were robbed and beaten in their bunkhouse on a range located in a remote area, far off main roads . . . the robbers wore masks and carried a shotgun and two pistols . . . within three hours after the crime, the three men were arrested [in a stolen car]. The car was

being driven [by subject] . . . In the trunk [was] a 12 gauge shotgun.
[Subject] had about half of the total (of money allegedly stolen).

Subject had prostituted in area of farm laborers and knew where the
men lived and that they were getting seasons-end wages. "The three
male robbers must have had a guide" [to find bunkhouse in isolated area
at 3 A.M.]. Robbers got victims to open bunkhouse door by saying, "open
the door, we have a woman for you guys." Subject helped plan the
robberies, made the masks and drove the getaway car.

Offense: attempt to commit robbery 1st and robbery 1st degree

In two separate cars, the defendant and her husband, and the defendant's
mother and father-in-law drove to a market. While the women waited
in the cars, the men entered the market, each being armed and disguised.
They announced their intention to rob the market . . . a policeman, on
duty in the store, fired at the men who returned his fire and fled. The
defendant's father-in-law collapsed at the car and died . . . the defendant
fled to Arizona where she was arrested.

Another robbery occurred previously . . . the defendant's husband held
up a gas station and ran to a waiting car, driven by the defendant's
father-in-law. The defendant and her mother were waiting in a car
nearby. "My father-in-law would just stop someplace and give mother
and I orders and we'd better do them or else . . . I was scared . . . I didn't
know what maybe he'd hurt mother, my son, or even my husband, his
own son . . ."

. . .

A wide variety of items were taken in the burglaries in which our study
subjects were involved. In one case the "take" consisted of $5–$6 in pennies,
25 packs of cigarettes, sandwiches, cookies, potato chips, four cigarette light-
ers, and lighter fluid. In another case the subject, a female companion and two
male companions took not only $9 in cash from a bakery but *also* some cakes
and rolls. The casual basis under which these criminal activities proceeded
and the pathetic rewards are underscored in the following:

Offense: burglary, 3d degree

In the early morning the defendant, with three accomplices, all male,
entered a country club and took liquor, cigarettes, and an electric razor.
Entry was made by removing a screen and breaking a window through
which one of the male accomplices crawled to open the front door,
thereby enabling the others to enter.

"I met one of the male defendants in his home Monday night (day
prior to the burglary), and we started walking toward the bridge. We had
been dating for some time. While walking we encountered . . . who
talked with the one accompanying the subject. Not until then was I
informed of their plan to burglarize the club. We all decided to walk out
to the club and look the situation over, and hid in the nearby bushes
until the club members left. At about 1:00 A.M. . . . tore off the screen,

another crawled in the broken window, which he smashed with an empty pop case, and opened the front door for us. I went in and stood by the door as a lookout. While I saw the others carry out the cases of liquor and look for money, I know I didn't. I know something about the law and have read up on it. Therefore, I knew that if I did not touch any of the stolen goods, it was unlikely that I would be charged with felony. Then . . . hid the liquor in the bushes, gave . . . some money, and they split up. I'm not sure if the money given to my boyfriend was stolen. My boyfriend and I then went back to town and slept in a used car lot because my folks had locked me out of the house. I was arrested that same afternoon and questioned by the police. I didn't expect to get by with it, but I didn't worry about it either because I figured out just how much I could get away with.''

· · ·

Offense: burglary, 1st degree

Probation was revoked because the defendant made little effort to make restitution for her offense. Also, the defendant has been extremely lax in reporting to the Probation Officer.

The defendant and co-defendant, a 14-year-old male, gained entry to a private home by breaking a rear bedroom window. Clothing, jewelry and toys were taken, a pan of roast beef was partially eaten and left inside the house and a partially consumed ham salad was left outside. . . .

· · ·

Offense: burglary, 3d degree

. . . Subject stated that on the night of the offense, she and two male friends, Frank and Bill, had been drinking in the . . . Bar . . . She said they had left there at closing time, and while walking down the street, the man she calls "Bill" pointed out a liquor store and said he would like to have some more whiskey. She claims that when she asked how he would get it, he replied, "Here is a brick." The subject and Frank tried to talk her out of it, but when unable to do so, left her and walked down the street. She then took the brick, threw it at the window, crawled into the store, and took two or three bottles of whiskey, in addition to some money from an unlocked cash register. She then crawled back out of the window and went to the back of the building where Bill was. She gave him some whiskey, and while walking down the street, came upon Frank and gave him a bottle of whiskey. Bill then reappeared and suggested they go back for more, so the two of them again crawled through the window and removed more liquor. Subject says that when she crawled out of the window she saw a taxi cab standing in front of the building. The driver told her to get in. She refused, and instead walked down the street with Bill. All of a sudden he disappeared into an empty lot, so she kept on walking. Within minutes after that she was stopped by the police officers.

· · ·

These descriptions of burglaries are neither atypical in terms of the roles women played, nor in the amount or variety of "loot." Simply stated, there is very little evidence that female burglars qualify as "master criminals." It may well be, of course, that the women who plan crimes carefully are not caught. A prison sample of criminals—male and female—is by definition more likely to include the foolish, inept, careless burglar than the careful, professional racketeer, or white-collar criminal. We do not mean to suggest that we found no reports of systematically planned robberies or burglaries, nor do we mean to suggest that none of the women played aggressive roles in the robberies or burglaries in which they were involved, but these cases were rare. The following, for example, represent the most sophisticated burglaries involving our study subjects:

Offense: burglary, 2d degree

Defendant burglarized two houses, getting a mink coat worth $3,000 and some jewelry in one house and $5,100 worth of jewelry from the second. She knew both homes would be unoccupied when the burglaries occurred as both victims were friends of her employer [subject worked as a domestic]. Defendant admits drinking prior to both offenses: "The liquor took over on me." Unable to explain her motivation as she did not need the items. "Loneliness," she explains, "could have been a possible factor in that when I was alone too much, I just got all balled up." Subject had babysat at homes of both victims.

·   ·   ·

Offense: burglary

Subject and female partner caught by police. One in car—another approaching car—both picked up as result of a call reporting a suspicious person at door.

In gutter under passenger door, officers found flashlight and pair of black ladies gloves. In car, they found black and red journal containing numerous names and addresses, including one from which report was made. Defendants [stated that] in July 1966 they began burglarizing. Picked victims from death and society columns of local newspapers. Entered through unlocked windows and sometimes by prying doors open. Police went to defendants' home and found [enough] stolen items [to fill four police cars].

Victim one: not a planned burglary. Defendants intended to burglarize residence next door. They had walked to rear of address with intention of going over wall and entering residence. They observed car, found revolver, food, tool box, and $60.

Victim two: had left home on weekend trip. Defendants entered through unlocked rear window, removed jewelry, clothing, antiques.

Victim three: out of state. Through unlocked rear door [defendants] removed jewelry, furs, silver and auto key.

Victim four: on vacation. [Defendants] pushed open sliding glass window, safe was removed [along with] over $130,000 in stocks and securities and jewelry. [Defendants] transported safe to home. Took all items home and sold two or three small silver candle holders and pawned some jewelry in Las Vegas.

[Defendants] would check obituary columns and society pages that listed funerals or vacations then record the names in book. Telephone book would be checked and telephone call made. If there was an answer, residence would not be burglarized. Code was used after each name: "V" for vacant, "Dec." for deceased, "No ans." for no answer, "A" for answer. If no answer was received location was checked out. Burglary usually occurred between midnight and 4 A.M.

[Defendants] admitted committing approximately 30 to 40 burglaries and maybe more. Thirty-one victims were able to claim property that was returned.

Even in several of these cases where some planning and "professional" skill was involved and where the proceeds of the burglaries were more substantial, the general points about the character of female property crimes—carelessness and participation that was consistent with a "feminine" role—still apply.

.   .   .

Robbery involving physical assaults on victims

Fewer than five percent of the cases of robberies we examined involved a physical assault upon the victim. One case involved three homosexual women, with the leader of the trio a "butch" (a label given to a woman who plays the masculine homosexual role). In this case the aggressive behavior of the leader may be seen as an effort to emulate the role of a male robber. The other two cases of assaultive robberies should be regarded as exceptions to our general propositions about the roles played by female robbers.

Offense: robbery, 1st degree

The victim stated the following: the defendant and co-defendant, No. 1 and co-defendant No. 2 came to the victim's home and requested the use of the telephone saying that their vehicle had broken down . . . once inside co-defendant No. 1 pulled a gun and told one of the victims to sit in a chair . . . the victim was told to call her sister from the kitchen . . . when the latter entered the room, the defendant and co-defendant No. 1 and No. 2 threatened to choke both of the victims and kicked one of the sisters on the leg and in the stomach . . . co-defendant No. 1 then ordered the defendant to tie both of the victims up and to go through the house to see what she could get. Both victims had their wrists bound by a woman's silk hose, arms placed behind their backs . . . one of the victims stated that she and her sister had been threatened with a knife at their throats. . . . The defendant and the co-defendants left after ransacking the house. The victims, aged 68 and 65, are sisters. Money and a watch were taken. The defendant and her two female co-defendants met in a bar, and knew each other less than a month prior to the offense. All three are admitted homosexuals and were living together.

In addition to the above offense, the defendant and co-defendant No. 2 committed two motel robberies and the defendant and co-defendants stole a car on the way to the above victims' house.

Defendant stated: "I was with the co-defendants on the night preceding the robbery. We were out drinking at a bar and decided to do something exciting . . . we decided to ride to . . . to see if we could pick up some money . . . we took a friend's car but it wasn't running well so we got off the freeway and stole a car, switched license plates with another car and proceeded . . . we drove to the home of the victims (the defendant stated it was she who pointed out the house as she had noticed while attending school that there seemed to be only women around the place)."

.   .   .

Offense: kidnaping with intent of committing robbery and bodily harm—2 counts

Subject, her husband and a friend in a borrowed car, bought beer and had guns in their possession. They picked up a hitchhiker. Subject, the driver. Victim (A) hit on head by gun by friend of subject. Victim, at direction of friend and subject was forced to strip off his clothes. His money, 15 cents, was taken from him. Subject and friend wielded guns, which were both loaded. Victim was told to make a break for it. As he did so, jumping off a 43 foot cliff, he was shot in the back. The bullet lodged in his spine and caused permanent paralysis. The three, with subject's husband driving, then drove off until they met a car wherein a man was sleeping. Friend and subject approached victim (B)'s car. Subject stuck her gun in his neck and friend hit victim over the head with his gun. Victim forced to strip, robbed of $41. He was then told to make a break for it and started to run for a clump of trees. Husband fired a shot but missed. Subject fired a shot which struck victim . . . then she went up to victim and fired three more shots into his body. His watch was taken.

Subject referred to by prosecuting attorney as "one of the most depraved, cruel, cold-hearted females that ever existed. From the evidence . . . it is very apparent that [subject] was the instigator and leader of this entire escapade . . ." *It was due to her being a young woman that she was not actually sentenced to death.* [Italic ours]

Descriptive account of assaults and homicides by women[12]

Unlike the robberies and burglaries in which women acted in the company of others, most of the homicides and assaults were the actions of a solitary offender. Also, as indicated earlier, slightly more than half of the homicide victims were husbands or lovers (35 percent) and children (19 percent); only 10 percent did not know the victim prior to the crime. Assaults also involved intimates, but to a lesser degree. Strangers accounted for somewhat more than one-fourth of the assault victims, and women were somewhat more likely to have been the victim of an assault than a homicide. The similarities, as well as the differences, between groups of women committed for homicide and assault may be seen in the following cases, but it should be emphasized that the distinction between homicide and assault is often a fine one: whether the victim lives or dies. Wolfgang points out in *Studies in Criminal Homicides* that victims of assaults have a greater chance of survival today than they had a generation ago due to technological achievements such as improved communications to report injuries, rapid transportation to medical facilities, and advances in medical science.

Subcultural violence

These cases fall into a category that Wolfgang and others have called "subcultural violence." Wolfgang has noted that studies of homicide and assault in this country and abroad consistently report that these offenses are committed by persons in the lowest socioeconomic class whose values allow, or at least tolerate, interpersonal violence.

> When homicide is committed by members of the middle and upper social classes, there appears to be a high likelihood of major psychopathology or of planned, more "rational" (or rationalized) behavior. This, the fact that they commit an act of willful murder, which is in diametric opposition to the set of values embraced by the dominant social class establishment of which they are a part, often means that these persons are suffering severely from an emotional crisis of profound proportions. Or they have been able . . . to meditate and mediate with their own internalized value system until they can conceive of the murder act without the consequence of an overburdening guilt and thereby justify their performing the deed. This self-justificatory behavior undoubtedly requires of the actor considerable time and much introspective wrestling in order to remain within, yet contradict his supportive value system . . .
> . . . our thesis contains principally the notion that the man from a culture value system that denounces the use of interpersonal violence will be restrained from using violence because of his positive perspective that conforms to his value system, not because of a negation of it.
> The absence of that kind of value system is hardly likely to be a vacuous neutrality regarding violence. Instead, it is replaced by a value system that views violence as tolerable, expected, or required. As we approach that part of the cultural continuum where violence is a requisite response, we also enter a subculture where physically aggressive action quickly and readily can bleed into aggressive crime. The man from this culture area is more likely to use violence, similarly because of a positive perspective that requires conforming to his value system. Restraint from using violence may be a frustrating, ego-deflating, even guilt-ridden experience. Questions of the risks of being apprehended and the distant, abstract notion of the threat of punishment are almost

irrelevant to he who acts with quick, yet socially ingrained aggressivity, neither reasoning nor time for it are at his disposal.[13]

The first account below represents the kind of subcultural violence in which assaults are provoked by a barroom or heavy drinking situation. Also in this group are altercations between prostitutes, between prostitutes and pimps, or between prostitutes and customers. Often the precipitating incident is a disparaging remark or an "offensive" gesture.

Of particular note in these assaults is the number of cases in which the woman carried a weapon such as a knife or razor blade for "protection." The availability of weapons suggests something about problems the women encountered in their work as "hustlers," or waitresses, or in their drinking experiences with men—friends or strangers.

Offense: assault with deadly weapon with intent to commit mayhem

Following drinking and a cafe argument with the victim [male], during which he allegedly slapped her, defendant slashed victim across genitals and thigh. Victim testified he did not know defendant's name, that she slapped him and invited him outside to fight. He remained drinking coffee. Defendant went outside, returned and said, "I will cut your balls off," and then she hit him, cutting him with the razor. Defendant immediately left scene and victim was hospitalized for four days.

Defendant claims victim called her dirty names and attempted to drink her whisky. She snatched glass out of his hand; he slapped her and they fought; she claims he knocked her down so she cut him in self-defense. Subject says she ran after cutting victim because she was afraid of him as he was an ex-prize fighter. Subject carried the razor in her bra. Usually carried a penknife for her own protection. Frequents bars where fights occur regularly.

Subject has many drunk arrests and ADW charges on *separate* occasions for use of ice pick, penknife, broken beer bottle, snap-blade knife, twin-blade-knife, knife, razor, gun, knife, butcher knife, knife. [Subject has record of] 48 arrests, including 11 assaults.

Offense: mayhem

Victim, his wife, subject and her husband and a male friend were all drinking in victim's home. All parties knew each other. A fight ensued during which time subject's husband took $20 from victim's pocket and defendant [subject] took out a straight-edge razor and cut off the tip of victim's nose. Subject says she was drunk, denied carrying razor or cutting victim. [Subject had a record of] 61 arrests for drunkenness [and] prostitution.

·   ·   ·

Offense: manslaughter

The female victim was fatally stabbed to death by defendant. . . . Both the defendant and the victim were in a bar where they exchanged some words, apparently about a mutual male acquaintance. Defendant then left the bar and shortly thereafter re-entered, having changed her clothes. Subsequently the defendant stabbed the victim. At the time of her arrest defendant claimed that the victim had struck her first with a beer bottle and that after this attack, defendant removed a paring knife from her brassiere and struck the victim an unknown number of times.

Defendant states she went to the bar to avoid a quarrel with her husband. While at the bar she had a couple of beers and saw a male friend who in turn told her that his lady friend [referring to the victim] was there so he could not talk to her. When she got up to leave, the victim met her in the middle of the floor of the place and called her a "bitch." Defendant called the victim a smart "bitch." . . . Defendant left the bar, changed to her working clothing and returned to the bar to get a ride from a friend up to her girl friend's house. As defendant walked through the bar, the victim was sitting on a bar stool . . . as defendant walked by, the victim hit her on the head with a beer bottle. This stunned defendant, then she claims the victim continued hitting her and this is when defendant tried to defend herself, bringing out the knife and stabbing victim. She [defendant] went outside to wait for the police.

Defendant's arrest record shows four previous arrests for violent attacks. Two arrests involved fights with her husband; once she threw an ash tray and cut him; another time she chased him with an ice pick. The other arrests involved attacks on bar patrons; one time she cut a man with a beer bottle and the second time she stabbed a man with a knife.

. . .

Domestic violence I

This group of violent crimes relates to deteriorated marriages, threatened divorces, infidelity, love triangles, and to assaults upon children. In Part II of "Domestic Violence" we shall deal with cases involving *repeated* acts of violence directed toward child victims. In both groups some violent crimes occurred on a spur-of-the-moment basis and others were deliberately planned. The violence we are discussing here is often what Conrad calls "situational" violence.[14]

Almost always when violence is used to settle a personal problem, the problem has been large enough to distort the individual's judgment. He has been enraged by frustration, humiliated by his inability to arrive at a reasonable understanding with everybody else concerned or his very livelihood has been put in jeopardy. Most such situations involve interpersonal relationships of a very close quality in which passions are engaged and the tolerance of the individual to rejection or humiliation has been reduced.

It is worth pointing out again that in some of these cases the difference between a prison sentence for assault and a prison sentence for murder was a fortuitous circumstance such as the woman's poor aim, the fact that medical attention was quickly given to the victim or that others intervened before further injury could be done to the victim. The case below is such an instance.

Offense: assault, 1st degree

The defendant is charged with assaulting her husband by shooting him seven times with a .22 caliber pistol which she had purchased that day. Her husband was divorcing her, and claiming in the divorce papers that he would get all of the property they owned. She was very upset, and went to a hardware store to buy a pistol. After her husband came home, she said she wanted to talk to him about the divorce. He said she should talk to his attorney about it. She reached for the gun and started shooting. Nine bullets were discharged from the gun. He ran to the back steps and yelled for help. They had struggled for the gun; he was able to take it away from her. She was not able to get it back in order to shoot herself. She said that she wanted to kill him first, and then shoot herself, but it just didn't work out that way.

·   ·   ·   ·

Offense: murder, 2d degree

The defendant killed her husband by stabbing him in the heart with a paring knife. . . . After dinner they watched television with the victim saying he wanted to see the Kennedy programs. Defendant objected to political programs and after some bickering the victim called his mother and complained that defendant was a Republican and that all Republicans should be killed. The mother told him to forget it and leave the house. Defendant then unsuccessfully attempted to call the mother, noticed the victim sitting on a stool in the kitchen and had words with him, the nature of which she did not recall . . . her next recollection was the striking of him in the shoulder area, with the victim [crying] "You've killed me." She then called her son, and through him police were called. The victim was dead on arrival at the hospital.

The landlady informed the police that the defendant had repeatedly, at least fifteen times, stated that "some day I'm going to kill that son-of-a-bitch," meaning the victim. The defendant's mother-in-law reported that the couple argued constantly during their six months of marriage. The victim's sister and the victim's friend both stated that they heard previous deadly threats by the defendant and against the victim.

The defendant said the victim would slam her around, and that they argued often, especially after they'd been drinking . . . she claimed she knew enough not to argue with the victim when he was drunk, as he was at that time. She thought he was picking an argument with her so she tried to get out of the way. . . . She denied making threats against him as stated by witnesses.

Offense: murder, 1st degree[15]

After years of fighting, separations and alleged abuse by her husband, the subject "had enough" and when he returned home after a row, she shot and killed him.

Statement of son 12 years old: "On this date I got up at about 7 A.M. . . . and my father left for work soon afterwards. [A man] came to the house and he had a quart of whiskey. My mother and he had several drinks together. . . . In the afternoon two men came to the house. I do not know who they were, but one of the men limped, and they had a gallon of wine. They came back with some groceries and some more wine; and then my dad came home. I was watching television and the program was "My Friend Flicka" and I think that program comes on about 6 P.M. My mother and dad were arguing and he slapped her. He told her to get her things together, and get the hell out by tomorrow morning. Dad then told me that there was plenty to eat in the house and that he would come back to get me. I thought he was going to walk to [town]. Mother then got very mad, cursing him and kicking the TV set. She knocked books and things that were on top of it on the floor. Dad came around to hit her with his fists. I had asked Mother not to kick the television as I had a program on. Dad then went out the side door of the front room, and mother went to the bedroom and got the rifle. I took all the shells away from her except the one that she had in the chamber. I asked her to give it to me and she told me not to do that. I thought that she would go to sleep and I know that she would have to go to sleep sometime and then I would get the rifle. I hid 18 shells. Mother said that she was going to sit there if she had to wait for a month and that when he came in she was going to shoot him—in the guts. About half-an-hour passed and Dad came back. Mother was sitting in the dining room off of the kitchen in a chair and as he came in the door, she pointed the rifle at him and pulled the trigger. Dad had reached for the rifle, and he nearly grabbed ahold of it. The [male visitor] fell down on his knees, for he was afraid of being hit by a bullet and when Dad fell he fell over the top of the man that was kneeling. Mother then laid the gun down and she hunted for a shoe that was missing off her foot. I went into the bedroom and tried to wake up the man that had gone to sleep. I shook him, told him that my father had just been shot and to please take me to [town]—as I didn't want to stay there anymore."

Most homicides and assaults involving women assailants occur suddenly, in the context of marital squabbles, street or barroom altercations, or interpersonal conflicts associated with the consumption of large amounts of alcohol.

The woman who kills deliberately, after carefully planning her crime, is rare, although the newscopy these crimes generate when they do occur may contribute to the stereotype of the female murderer as more diabolical than her male counterpart. There were only ten cases in our study population of a planned and deliberate killing of an adult in which the female offender was *not* described by one or more psychiatrists as insane or suffering from severe psychological disability. The accounts that follow are examples of premeditated murder arising out of domestic situations.

Offense: murder, 1st degree

M. worked as a hired man on the P.S. farm about two months during the summer. At that time, there commenced an illicit love affair between M. and Mr S.'s wife, the defendant, continuing until the spring. The two discussed the possibility of marriage, and in that connection, there evolved a plan for eliminating her husband by the use of poison. M. purchased a vial of strychnine poison at the drugstore. Subject accompanied M. for that purpose. She took the strychnine, mixed it in a partially filled bottle of whiskey which she kept in the closet in their home. She became angered at her husband because of his drinking, and she transferred a portion of the poisoned whiskey into an empty whiskey bottle, placing the bottle under the front seat of his car, within easy sight and reach. By a quirk of fate, he also on that day placed a nearly empty bottle under the seat. One morning her husband drank the remaining contents of the bottle he had placed there, and later in the day, he took out the other bottle and offered a drink to two acquaintances. One drank a portion, and became violently ill, and was later saved from death by his doctor. Unfortunately, the other man consumed the remainder of the contents and died within 15 minutes of strychnine convulsions. The defendant admits committing the crime but doesn't feel she's guilty of murder in the first degree. On the Saturday before the commission of the crime, her husband began drinking, and continued for several days. He left and said that he would be back, but failed to show up. She and the children did the chores, and when he came home he was staggering drunk. Her son drove the car into the garage. She poured a small amount of the strychnine crystals into the bottle of whiskey and put them on the floor of the car near his seat. She says that she put the poison into the whiskey to sicken her husband so that he would stop drinking. When questioned about threats she made against her husband's life, namely from M.'s testimony, she stated that there had been some joking remarks between herself and M. as to putting poisoned wheat in her husband's coffee. They kept poisoned wheat in the attic to destroy the mice. M. had cleaned the attic and knew where it was. When questioned about M.'s testimony that she had asked him to run over her husband with a tractor, she stated some laughing remark between her and M. had been made when they watched her husband in the fields. When questioned about shooting her husband, she said that M. had jokingly remarked of "clipping her husband off the tractor with a rifle, saying he would only get five years for it."

Offense: murder, 1st degree

Subject and victim [husband] met through a lonely hearts club. Subject hid the fact that she was an alcoholic from him and they were married.

In July the victim got violently ill in a restaurant, he was hospitalized in October; in November a doctor went to his home and advised hospitalization, victim refused. Next day the subject asked a neighbor to come over as husband was dying and then called a doctor. The husband was taken to hospital where he died. The subject asked the doctor not to have an autopsy but one was held and arsenic poisoning was determined. It had been administered orally over a period of several months.

Subject had been married five times and lived with a number of other men. She was told by the victim to stop drinking or leave. A week after her husband's death subject contacted an old boy friend and arranged to go to Nevada with him. She also applied to several lonely hearts clubs.

After the death of her husband, the subject visited her son and his wife. She disliked the latter and gave her a box of arsenic-poisoned chocolates.

· · ·

Domestic violence II: systematic abuse of children

Some 75 years ago, Lombroso wrote about the female violent offender: "The culminating examples of . . . barbarity are offered by mothers in whom maternal affection, the most intense of human sentiments, is transformed into hatred."[16] In this section we focus attention upon the most brutal crimes and the most pathetic victims encountered in this study—examples of "maternal hatred."

Among female murderers and assaulters confined in California and Minnesota prisons during our study, 34 were convicted of having killed a child and 14 for assaulting a child. The victim, although not always the woman's own child, was nearly always a child (or children) with whom she lived—stepchild, foster child, or the son or daughter of her common-law husband. (In only three cases was the child victim not related in one of these ways to the assailant.) All but three of the victims were under 8 years of age.

The salient feature of the accounts that follow is the fact of repeated abuse. Cases that involve the death of minor children through repeated physical abuse do not fall into the "premeditated" category because it is not clear that the women intended to kill the child; rather their expressed intent was to inflict physical harm as "punishment."

· · ·

Offense: murder, 2d degree

The victim was a three-year-old who was the daughter of defendant's boyfriend. . . . Defendant admitted and neighbors verified there had been a long course of brutal conduct toward the child. The child was severely beaten on numerous occasions. . . . On day of the offense, a glass of milk was spilled in the kitchen of defendant's home. Defendant summoned the child into the bathroom and asked whether she had knocked the milk over. Defendant picked up a broom handle and struck the child several times over the top of the head. About one-half hour after this the child collapsed and was taken to the hospital by the defendant. She was subsequently arrested and charged.

Subject stated: "Although the crime I committed was not intentional, I am guilty in many ways. I did lose my temper which is bad."

Offense: manslaughter, 2d degree

The Police Department received a call from physician at a hospital, reporting the presence of an infant suffering from severe bruises who was not expected to live. Two men from homicide division went to the hospital. After questioning the defendant and her husband, they learned the baby had been hurt at home. The baby died at noon that day, and had suffered from severe head bruises and abrasions with possible brain damage, fracture on the upper left arm, broken wrist bones, fractures on both knees. There were also teeth marks on the right wrist. The doctor stated that some of the injuries were sustained approximately three weeks ago. The defendant was originally charged with murder in the third degree but this was reduced to manslaughter, second degree, and she pled guilty. The facts leading up to the offense are vague; the defendant states she does not really remember the weeks prior to her offense. Her husband was working long hours, and when he returned home the baby was usually sleeping, so he did not notice anything unusual about her. He did notice that the defendant was somewhat on edge, but it was nothing he could put his finger on. On one occasion just prior to the baby's death, the defendant's husband states that they had company, and the wife brought the baby down for the company to see. In looking back, he thought it was rather unusual that she would not let anyone hold the child. After a minute or two she returned the child to the bedroom. In describing the offense, the defendant states she cannot remember the occurrence—only that she knows she hurt her child and took her to the hospital. She appears not to realize that she had killed her child. She refers to the incident as when she hurt her baby. She says she does not remember the actual events leading up to the offense, but if what people tell her is true regarding the offense, it must have been terrible.

·   ·   ·

Offense: involuntary manslaughter

The victim, the 22-month-old son of the defendant, died from malnutrition. The body, which weighed only 11 pounds, was discovered in a lot wrapped in a curtain with a sock stuffed in its mouth. A neighbor of the defendant informed the police that the body recovered could be the body of the defendant's child . . . upon questioning, the defendant said the child was in good health and with relatives of hers . . . the relatives could not be found. . . . Upon further investigation the defendant admitted the child found was hers and that it was dead when she put it there.

Husband not involved apparently. Another child [of subject] died "under very mysterious circumstances."

. . .

Offense: corporal (traumatic) injury to child

Subject admitted slapping, hitting and punching her infant daughter almost since the date of her birth. She stated she dropped the child at the approximate age of one month, which resulted in cranial hemorrhage and hospitalization. . . . She admitted hitting the child on the jaw three months later and further stated that two months after that, when the child began crying she picked her up, shook her and hit her because she, the defendant, was tired and nervous. On another occasion she admitted losing her temper and hitting the child with her fist which may have caused the child's broken ribs.

Child suffered permanent brain damage and will eventually necessarily be committed to a state institution. . . . Police were informed of the child's injuries by suspicious hospital personnel.

. . .

Extent and trends of robberies by women—

in 1967, 5 out of every 1,000 women (0.5 percent) arrested in the United States was arrested in connection with robbery charges. (There has been a steady increase since 1960 when 0.3 percent were arrested for robbery.)
robbery is the least "female" violent offense: of the 60,000 persons arrested in 1967 for robbery, 5.2 percent were women; while the percentage is small, it has been increasing during this decade.
of prison commitments for robbery the ratio of men to women was 98 to 2.
female arrests for robbery have shown the greatest percentage increase since 1960 of the three violent crimes.

Some general comments on crimes of violence by women

One of the interesting aspects of crimes of violence and burglary by women is that these actions seem to directly contradict the role women in our society are supposed to play. The notion of the female as an aggressive, fist-swinging, gun-carrying criminal ready to take on any potential victim—healthy, adult males included—is difficult to reconcile with the stereotype of the female as the relatively passive, dependent, physically weaker partner to the male. It was thus our task to examine instances in which women violated not only the criminal law, but also the norms that define behavior appropriate for "ladies." What we found was that the participation of women in robbery and burglary was not consistent with the criminal role males play in these crimes but that their behavior was consistent with their role as women. Our female offenders robbed few healthy adult males by themselves. In burglaries too they acted as supporting players to men who played the leading criminal role. In short, we found that very few females are arrested for serious crimes, that only a very small portion of the women who were arrested for felonies were involved in robberies and burglaries and that the women who were involved in these crimes did not, in most cases, act in a very unladylike manner.

In the case of homicides and assaults the salience of the sex role was also apparent. The objects of violent attacks by women were most often persons with whom they had affectional relationships such as husbands, lovers, and children. Unlike male violent offenders, the victims of women rarely included store keepers, service station attendants, or others slain or assaulted in the course of committing robberies and burglaries (some 21 percent of the homicides reported to *Uniform Crime Reports* in 1967 were "felony or suspected felony type" murders). When adult males were the victims of assaults by women, the usual case was not that they were beaten up by women tougher or stronger than they, but that a weapon was used by the woman, that the victim was drunk, asleep, or off-guard, or that the woman had help from other persons.

The most obvious conclusion to be drawn from this study is that female criminality is a separate and distinct order of criminal behavior in which cultural factors relating to sex roles in our society are of critical importance. Those who study the etiology of criminal behavior should be prepared to find that most of the current theories of crime causation are inappropriate when applied to female offenders.

Those persons charged with the responsibility of doing something about the problem of violence in our society will find it difficult to draw policy implications from this study. The problem is based in part perhaps upon the primitive level of knowledge we can provide about female violence, but such data as we have indicate that in order to prevent a major portion of the criminal violence in which women engage, one would have to do something about unhappy marriages and love affairs, drunken brawls, and in some cases, stupidity or bad judgment. Intervention might be possible however in the area of crimes against children, because the assaults occur over time. A major difficulty here is that our data indicate that in many cases other persons did know or have reason to suspect that children were being brutalized but they still did not attempt to intervene or call the situation to the attention of medical, welfare or police agencies. Laws pertaining to protection against libel charges for physicians, the handling of child abuse cases by agencies other than police departments and more public awareness of the child abuse problem may be helpful in encouraging the reporting of these cases. One other category of violence cases where intervention, that is, prevention of further violence, may be feasible are the cases in which the presence of severe psychological disabilities gives warning of future trouble. The problem here again is in encouraging those most likely to detect the onset of psychological problems, namely family members and friends, to bring cases to the attention of physicians, clergymen, or social agencies which can initiate remedial action. For women overwhelmed by disappointments, crises, and life experiences the availability of community mental health centers would provide valuable orthopsychiatric assistance. Finally we want to remind those who point to the small contribution women make to the overall population of violent offenders that the trend in violence by women is upward, and that the rate may be accelerated as women become emancipated from traditional female role requirements.

Notes

9. Marvin E. Wolfgang, *Patterns in Criminal Homicide, op. cit.* Brief comments or discussions about crimes of violence by women not cited elsewhere in this report may be found in Evelyn Gibson and S. Klein, *Murder,* Home Office Research Unit Report No. 4, London: Her Majesty's Stationery Office, 1961; John M. Macdonald, *The Murderer and His Victim,* Springfield, Ill.: Charles C. Thomas, 1961, pp. 31–32; Nancy Barton Wise, "Juvenile Delinquency Among Middle-Class Girls," in Edmund W. Vaz (ed.), *Middle-Class Juvenile Delinquency,* New York: Harper & Row, 1968, pp. 179–188; James S. Wallerstein and Clement J. Wyle, "Our Law-abiding Law-breakers," *Probation,* 225, Mar.-Apr. 1947, p. 110; Lester Adelson, "Slaughter of the Innocents," *The New England Journal of Medicine,* 264, No. 26, June 1961, pp. 1345–1349. See also the articles by Wolfgang, Mooris, and Blom-Cooper, Verkko, and Bohannan in Marvin Wolfgang, *Studies in Homicide,* New York: Harper & Row, 1967.
10. *Crime in the United States 1967, op. cit.,* p. 8.
11. It should be noted that our "No weapons used" category included those cases in which the subject was an accessory or partner in a crime where a weapon was used by others and those cases where death or injury was the result of beatings, strangulation, or other types of physical attack where the "weapon" was hands, arms, feet, etc.
12. Our groupings of homicide and assault cases are analogous to four of the types of violent offenders described by John Conrad in a paper entitled "The Nature and Treatment of the Violent Offender: A Typology of Violence." Conrad's paper and the report of an effort to implement his typology for purposes of classifying men committed to the California Department of Corrections may be found in Carol Spencer, *A Typology of Violent Offenders,* Research Report No. 23, Research Division, California Department of Corrections, Sacramento, September, 1966. Our use of these categories is intended only to help organize the descriptive materials, and the reader should be aware that some kinds of "domestic" or "economic" violence may also be classified as "sub-cultural" in character and that "domestic" violence may be committed by "borderline psychotic" or "pathological" women.
13. Marvin E. Wolfgang, "Criminal Homicide and the Subculture of Violence," in Marvin E. Wolfgang (ed.), *Studies in Homicide,* New York: Harper and Row, 1967, pp. 6–7. See also in the same volume, Marvin E. Wolfgang and Franco Ferracuti, "Subculture of Violence—A Socio-Psychological Theory," pp. 271–280, and the discussion of the "culturally violent" offender by Spencer and Conrad in Spencer, *op. cit.,* pp. 9–12 and 61–63.
14. Conrad in Spencer, *op. cit.,* p. 68; also Spencer, pp. 20–23.
15. This case is particularly interesting because of the dispassionate manner in which the boy described the murder of his father by his mother. His account of the crime suggests not only that he had grown accustomed to domestic warfare, but also is a reminder that while some studies have focused on the murderer and his or her victim, none that we know of has systematically examined the impact upon the child of criminal homicide involving his own parents.
16. Caesar Lombroso, *The Female Offender,* originally published 1893; Philosophical Library Edition, published 1958, pp. 147–49.

12 Race and Sex Differences
Marvin Wolfgang

National criminal and mortality statistics attest to the greater amount of recorded criminal homicide committed by males. Of 6,336 arrests for this offense in 1950, 5,482 were males and 854 were females—a ratio of six to one. This ratio is less than the nine-to-one ratio for all offenses in 1950. However, of all male arrests, criminal homicide accounted for .8 per cent, and of all female arrests, 1.1 per cent were for criminal homicide.[1]

Although not precisely comparable to the Philadelphia data, national prison statistics reveal higher sex ratios than those for criminal homicide arrests in Philadelphia. In 1950 the sex ratio of all persons received from the courts and imprisoned in state and federal institutions was about twenty-four to one. The ratio for persons who had committed criminal homicide was only nine to one. There was a relatively greater preponderance of institutional commitments for criminal homicide among females. About 5 per cent of all male prisoners and nearly 14 per cent of all female prisoners were incarcerated for criminal homicide.[2] General mortality *rates* of victims in specific race and sex groups for 1950 show a white male rate (3.6) approximately three times larger than the white female rate (1.3). The non-white male rate (42.8) was nearly four times larger than the non-white female rate (11.2).[3]

Comparison to other homicide studies discloses sex distributions in some that are similar, and in others that are dissimilar to the Philadelphia distribution.[4]

Homicide victims during 1926–1927 classified by sex and race in Cook County, Illinois, were distributed as follows: 56 per cent white males; 16 per cent white females; 22 per cent colored males; and 6 per cent colored females. For both races, male victims constituted a group over three times greater than females, a sex distribution corresponding closely to that in Philadelphia.[5]

In Harlan's Birmingham study, 78 per cent of the 500 victims and 76 per cent of the 492 offenders were male.[6] This sex ratio of about three to one is similar to the Philadelphia victim data, but is not similar to the offender ratio of five males to every female. Part of this difference lies in the fact that there were only 12 cases during the eight years in Birmingham in which two or more agents were charged with the same crime. In Philadelphia, there were 44 such cases with a total of 71 offenders over the five years, and 95 per cent of the multiple offenders or defendants were male. In both Philadelphia in 1950 and in Birmingham in 1940, males comprised 48 per cent of each of the respective populations. Thus, in both cities, male homicide victims and offenders exceeded their expected proportions to about the same degree.

Similarly, the Meyers report in St. Louis revealed that 77 per cent of the 212 victims and 74 per cent of the 207 offenders were male during the three years studied.[7] Information given regarding multiple agents of homicide indicated there were nine cases of two assailants each who were charged with the same crime. Dublin and Bunzel found a still higher male proportion among offenders:

> Since reliable information regarding the murderer is extremely rare, we undertook a few years ago to analyze over 600 records of homicides committed in 1922–1924. In the cases where sex was specified, 93 per cent of the assailants were males. In the vast majority of cases, both the slayer and his victim were men. Among the males, 36 per cent were white and 64 per cent Negro.[8]

This race distribution among males shows a slightly higher white proportion than was true of Philadelphia homicides, where only 27 per cent of the victims and 25 per cent of the offenders were white.

In a highly select group of 200 murderers, Cassidy[9] found males nine times more frequent than females. Calvin Schmid's[10] analysis of homicides, taken from the death records of the coroner's office in Seattle between 1914 and 1924, resulted in a sex ratio similar to that of Philadelphia. In Seattle, 74 per cent of the victims were males. But the homicide death rate per 100,000 in Seattle in 1920 was over twice as high for males (8.9) as for females (3.7), whereas in Philadelphia the male rate was over three times as high as the female rate.

Of the 1,606 homicides taken from death certificates recorded in 37 counties in New York State, 1921–1930, DePorte and Parkhurst[11] found that 77 per cent were male, and 23 per cent female. In addition they pointed out that "the risk of a woman being killed was relatively greater among the native-born white than among either the foreign-born or the Negroes. Among the former, one in three of the victims was a woman as compared with one in four among the Negroes and one in seven among the foreign-born."[12] An unbalanced sex ratio of more males among the foreign-born during those years was affected by the age distribution among victims.

In an earlier and more elementary analysis of Birmingham homicides than that by Harlan, Frederick Hoffman referred to the sex distribution of homicide victims recorded on death certificates for the five-year period 1920–1925.

Having used the term "murder" within a context indicating that he meant "homicide," the author claimed:

> During that period there were 567 deaths due to murder. . . . The number of deaths of males was 457 . . . while the number of deaths of females was 110. . . . In addition to the foregoing, there occurred 303 deaths from murder in the county of Jefferson, outside the city of Birmingham. . . . In the whole county of Jefferson during the five years under observation there were 870 deaths from murder, of which 701 were deaths of males and 169 were deaths of females.[13]

Computing from Hoffman's figures, 81 per cent of the victims in both Birmingham and in the whole of Jefferson County were male. In a similar treatment of data from New Orleans over a five-year period ending in 1924, the same author reported that of 475 homicide deaths, 83 per cent were male.[14] It should be remembered that these figures refer to mortality data and therefore include non-criminal as well as criminal homicides.

The Growdon study of 54 juvenile homicide offenders reported a distribution of 46 males and only 6 females. The 9–18 year age group in the Ohio population in 1940 from which the juveniles came had only 50 per cent male, compared to 89 per cent in the homicide group.[15]

In an analysis of national mortality statistics for the period 1924–1926, Brearley found that females made up a smaller proportion of Negro homicides than of white homicides:

> For these years there was one female slain among the Negroes for every 4.5 males, while among the whites there was one to every 3.86 males. The ratio of Negro males to white males slain was one to 1.31, while for females it was one Negro to every 1.53 whites. This indicates that a Negro woman is less likely to be slain, considering the high homicide rate for this race, than is a white woman. In other words, provided the three years studied are typical, if the relative rates for the two races be taken into consideration, a woman is somewhat less likely to be numbered among the Negro homicide victims than among the white victims.[16]

Elsewhere he raises the same question regarding offenders:

> Little evidence is available to show whether white or Negro women are more liable to become slayers. Of 407 persons who committed homicide in South Carolina, where the two races were at the time of the study approximately equal in numbers, 20 were Negro and 13 were white females, while there were 141 Negro and 220 white males and 13 unknown offenders included in the total. Since most of these cases were secured from the files of newspapers, the ratio between the sexes of each race should be approximately the same. Since the Negro women exceeded the white women while the Negro males did not equal the white males in number it might be correctly assumed that Negro women, in

South Carolina at least, are more likely to slay an adversary than are white women. This conclusion is rather credible in view of the Negro woman's greater freedom of life, physical vigor, and familiarity with weapons. Nevertheless, this inference may, like so many other "common sense observations" concerning racial differences, prove upon further investigation to be erroneous.[17]

Relative to these earlier comments by Brearley, a set of interesting hypotheses have recently been tested by Henry and Short[18] regarding suicide and homicide in the United States. Among other assumptions, these authors assume that males as a gross category rank higher in the American status hierarchy than females. They then tested the hypothesis that homicide rates are higher in the low status category and lower in the high status category. Data collected by the authors on the relation between homicide and sex contradicted their hypothesis, which predicted that homicide rates would be higher for females, the lower status category, than for males. Our Philadelphia material and abundant data from the literature also reject the sex hypothesis. However, because Negroes generally make up a disproportionate share of the total number of homicides, Henry and Short claim that the status differentiation between males and females within this racial group would be worth examining. They suggest that perhaps the Negro female in American society has a status higher than the male. Thus,

> If it is true that the prestige position of the Negro female is higher, on the average, than the prestige position of the Negro male, we would predict from our hypothesis that the Negro female would have a lower homicide *rate* than the Negro male.
>
> Data are not available adequately to test this formulation. If it is correct, however, further research should show that the ratio of male to female *homicide* among Negroes is higher than the *ratio* of male to female homicide among whites.[19]
>
> This hypothesis may be tested by research comparing the ratios of male to female homicide among the white and Negro categories. If our interpretation is correct, we would expect the *ratio* of male to female *murderers* among Negroes to exceed the ratio of male to female murderers among whites. Further research on the status position of the female in the Negro family is also needed.[20]

No measurement of the status of the Negro female in American life is intended in the present Philadelphia study. However, when a Negro was killed, a female was less frequently numbered among the victims than when a white was killed. In the five-year period examined, 43 white females made up 27 per cent of all white victims; whereas, 96 Negro females comprised 22 per cent of all Negro victims. This means that, relatively, females made up a proportion of white victims nearly 19 per cent greater than females among Negro victims. The ratio of males to females among whites was 2.7 to 1.0 while among Negroes it was 3.4 to 1.0. Using rates per 100,000 instead of percentage distributions, we have noted that the Negro male had a rate (36.9) about four times greater than the Negro female (9.6), while the white male had a rate (2.9) only three times that of the white female (1.0). Hence, among *victims*, the Henry and Short assumption regarding the relative position of the Negro female is correct.

However, among *offenders* the prediction of these authors is contradicted. Negro females numbered 93, or approximately 20 per cent of all Negro offenders; white females numbered only 16, or less than 12 per cent of all white offenders. A relative percentage difference indicates that Negro females comprised a proportion 66 per cent greater among Negro offenders than did white females among white offenders. Expressed differently, the sex ratio of males to females among white offenders was 8.6 to 1.0, but among Negroes was only 4.0 to 1.0. Using rates per 100,000, the Negro male had a rate (41.7) that was over four times that of the Negro female (9.3), while the white male had a rate (3.4) that was eight times that of the white female (.4).

If the Henry and Short prediction was meant to apply to offenders rather than victims, it is obvious that the hypothesis is not supported by the Philadelphia data.

It should be clear that *among female homicides*, whether victims or offenders, or both, a Negro was much more likely to be involved than a white. Proportionately, Negro females were twice as frequent as white females among victims, and about six times as frequent among offenders. Rates per 100,000 indicate that a Negro female was ten times more likely to be numbered among the slain and twenty-three times more likely to be a slayer than a white female. Finally, there were 12 cases in which a Negro female was killed by a Negro female, and only 5 cases in which a white female was killed by a white female.

Again it is necessary to point to the striking differences that may exist between victims and offenders. Henry and Short, like many other students of homicide, do not always make clear to which of these two groups, or to both, they intend their hypotheses to apply. Unfortunately, lack of clarity involving such terms as "homicides," "victims," "murderers," "rates," "ratios," etc., prevails even in the most recent literature. Examination of the Philadelphia data relative to the Henry and Short sex hypothesis reaffirms the contention that valid inferences regarding characteristics of offenders cannot be drawn from victim data, or vice versa.

Drawing attention to European literature which discusses the relationship between women and homicide, Pollak[21] shows that:

1. Austrian statistics for 1899 reveal that while 14 women appeared in every 100 convictions, female participation in murder was reflected by 30 women in each 100 convictions for that offense.
2. In 1896 in Germany there were 18 female convictions for each 100 male convictions, but that in homicide there were 22 women for each 100 men convicted.
3. Italian statistics (contrary to the U.S., England, Austria, and Germany) list poisoning as a special offense, and reveal a specific sex ratio of 123 females per 100 male offenders convicted; and when poisonings are added to other types of criminal homicide except infanticide, the sex ratio was still 63 women per 100 men for the three years 1885–1889.

Basing his conclusions on both American and Continental material, Pollak suggests that female homicides make up a larger proportion of all female offenses than is true for males, and "that if all types of victims and all methods of killings are included, the relative liability of women for homicide is greater than that of men."[22]

A study of suicide and homicide in Ceylon by Jacqueline and Murray Straus,[23] using data taken from the registrar-general's report for 1946, shows rates of homicide victims similar to those in Philadelphia. In Ceylon, the rates were 9.7 per 100,000 for males and 2.1 for females. This is a male rate between four and five times higher than the female rate, and is a slightly greater differential than that in Philadelphia where the male rate was about three times higher than that for females. It is interesting to note that in a number of ways, other than that of sex ratios, the pattern of homicide in Ceylon is in striking agreement with what is known of this phenomenon in the West.

An exceptionally high male proportion among homicide offenders was found in Ching-yueh Yen's *A Study of Crime in Peiping,*[24] covering the period from 1919 to 1927. Unfortunately, data for this study were collected from the Peiping prisons and result, as the author has pointed out, in a highly select group, especially in view of his reference to much police inefficiency, differential treatment in the courts, etc. Comparisons with American data, and with Philadelphia police records in particular, must be made cautiously. Keeping in mind these differential sources, computation from the author's basic statistics shows that of the 14,309 male criminals incarcerated during the nine years studied, 3 per cent had been imprisoned for homicide, and that of the 1,286 females, 1.7 per cent had been committed for homicide.[25] Of the 459 persons imprisoned for criminal homicide, therefore, approximately 95 per cent were male and only 5 per cent female. The proportion incarcerated for homicide within each sex appears to be different from the general proportions usually found in the United States. This much higher proportion of male homicide offenders in Peiping suggests the correctness of Sutherland's statement that

> the sex ratio in crime varies widely from one nation to another, with the female rate showing some tendency to approach closest to the male rate in countries in which females have the greatest freedom and equality with males, such as Western Europe and the United States, and being most remote from the male rate in countries in which females are very closely supervised. . . .[26]

Criminal homicide appears to be an offense detectably committed more often by males regardless of time or space. Ethnological descriptions of primitive societies seem to support this contention although a general review of anthropological literature on homicide yet remains to be written.[27] Cultural rather than biological reasons are invariably given to explain these sex differentials, however varied the social environments may be. One example might be used merely to show that a like phenomenon (officially recorded high proportion of males committing homicide) may have unlike causes. In an especially enlightening summary of homicides and suicides in a primitive Asiatic Indian society, Elwin says:

The reason for the low incidence of homicide among Maria women is possibly connected with the strong aboriginal belief that it is supernaturally dangerous for a woman to take life. This is the ultimate reason why there are no women priests, for the priest has to offer sacrifice. Maria women are not supposed to kill goats or even chickens. They are not permitted to join in hunting. The only pursuit of the kind which is not taboo to them is fishing—but fish are cold-blooded creatures.[28]

Criminal statistics in the United States for 1950 indicate that the number of male offenders was six times higher than that of females, and mortality rates show that males were counted among victims approximately four times more frequently than females. However, sex ratios in England disclose a higher proportion of females than in the United States. Basing some of his speculative remarks on Calvert's article on "Murder and the Death Penalty,"[29] and incorrectly comparing homicide with murder, Brearley says:

> ... the slaying of women is much less frequent in the United States than in England. During the period 1924–1926, there were in the United States registration area states 24,949 *homicides*. In 4,874 of these, females were the victims, 19.5 per cent of the total. Slightly more than four times more males than females were homicide victims. In England, however, women are more often slain than are men. Although nine out of every ten *murders* are committed by men, "two out of every three persons murdered are women."[30]

Referring to this statement by Brearley, von Hentig says:

> In discussing the sex of his homicide victims Brearley has wondered why in the United States more than four times as many males as females were homicide victims, whereas in England "two out of every three persons murdered are women".
>
> This apparent discrepancy can easily be explained. The legal concept of murder differs widely in England, Germany, France and all of Europe from the American notion. It corresponds somewhat to the first degree murder of our statutes and is even more restricted than that. We erroneously, therefore, try to draw a parallel between two incomparable magnitudes.[31]

As the latter author points out, however, where legal notions coincide, similar results occur, for 56 per cent of 135 murder victims who were slain during 1928, 1929, and 1930 in Germany were females.[32]

Computation from data in the recent report of the Royal Commission on Capital Punishment discloses that the percentage of female *victims* in Germany coincides with that in England and Wales. During a twenty-year period ending in 1905, 313 or 57 per cent were female victims from a total of 551 criminal homicides for which the offenders were convicted.[33] With respect to *offenders*, tables of "persons arrested for murder," supplied by Templewood in *The Shadow of the Gallows*, reveal a grand total between 1900 and 1948 of 4,077, of whom 1,318, or 32 per cent, were women.[34] This is a sex ratio among offenders of approximately two males to each female, as compared to a five-to-one ratio in Philadelphia. However, it is most important to segregate clearly Negroes from whites when making this type of international comparison. In Philadelphia, *among white victims*, 27 per cent were female, a ratio just short of three males for each female and considerably different from the reversed ratio of victims in England and Wales, where there was only one male for each 1.3 females. *Among white offenders* in Philadelphia, 10 per cent were female, but in England 32 per cent of all "persons arrested for murder" were female. This means that more women were counted among both victims and offenders in England than in Philadelphia when like races are compared. No striking differences in comparative results occur, however, when Negroes are included, for 24 per cent of the total victims and 18 per cent of all offenders in Philadelphia were female. Finally, it may be that the proportion of females arrested for murder in England is approaching the American proportion. In the 1910–1919 period, 39 per cent of all persons arrested for the offense in England were female; in 1920–1929, 36 per cent; in the 1930–1939 decade, 30 per cent, and in the nine years from 1940 to 1948, 22 per cent were women.[35] This last period shows a female proportion among offenders similar to those in the United States and in Philadelphia.

Veli Verkko has discovered some interesting historical changes in the sex ratio of victims in Finland. During the last period included in his analysis, which is somewhat comparable to the Philadelphia material, he says that between 1939 and 1944, 23 women were killed in Finland for every 100 men, and that the rates per 100,000 of the population were 7.1 for men and 1.6 for women.[36] Swedish data by sex of victims of crimes against life are available from 1881 and reveal that from this time up to 1940 the ratio of women killed per 100 men has increased considerably. In the twenty-year period from 1881–1900 only 25 per 100 males were female victims, between 1901–1920 the ratio was 37 to 100, and in 1921–1940, their ratio climbed to 63 per 100 males.[37]

This brief review of some of the homicide literature related to sex cannot fail to report Verkko's "laws" regarding regular sex sequences in crimes against life. He claims that fluctuations in crimes against life have been mainly in the numbers of male victims, and he has established the following rule: "Distribution by sexes of victims of crimes against life in any country is always dependent on the frequency level of the crime concerned."[38] This general rule is illustrated in greater detail by two laws, he contends, one of which is static and the other dynamic. The static law is: "In countries of high frequency of crimes against life the female proportion of those killed is small; and vice versa: in countries of low frequency of crimes against life the percentage of female victims is perceptibly greater than in countries of high frequency of crimes against life."[39] He includes Finland, Serbia, Bulgaria, Italy, Chile, and the United States in his first group of high frequency of homicides where female victims are below 10 per cent of the total. It is interesting to note that because the United States provides "an erroneous picture of the distribution of the victims of crimes by sexes,"[40] he excludes this country from his presentation of ratios. In countries of low frequency of homicides, including Sweden, Norway, Denmark, Prussia, England and Wales, and Switzerland, the proportions of female victims fluctuate between 18 and 48 per cent. His dynamic law of victims is: "If frequency of crimes against life in a country is on the increase, the increase affects mainly the number of male victims of crimes against life, and vice versa: if the statistics of crimes against life in a country reveal a declining trend, the reduction affects primarily the number of men killed."[41] Using the historical method, abundant evidence is presented by the author to help prove his contentions. For example, he says, "The figures for Sweden indicate an even decline during the period 1881–1940. The total killed per 100,000 inhabitants declined from 0.90 to 0.49. The ratio for men was reduced from 1.46 to 0.60 while that for women was at the beginning 0.37 and at the end 0.38."[42]

Verkko establishes a static and a dynamic law for *offenders* as well, and treats them similarly:

> The static law reads as follows: In countries of high frequency of crimes against life the participation of women in these crimes is small; and vice versa: in countries of low frequency of crimes against life the participation of women in these crimes is perceptibly larger than in countries of high frequency of crimes against life. . . .
>
> The dynamic law reads: If the frequency of crimes against life in a country tends to increase, the increase primarily affects the number of male criminals, and vice versa: if the frequency of crimes against life in a certain country is on the decline, the decline primarily affects the number of male criminals.[43]

Data on men and women prosecuted for, and found guilty of, crimes against life collected from an earlier investigation by the author tend to support his hypotheses.

Five years may be too short a period to test Verkko's hypotheses, although in some of his own data as few as three years are used. We have already noted the relatively higher proportion of female victims and offenders in England and Wales (a low frequency area) compared to the proportion of that sex in Philadelphia (a high frequency area), thus indicating support for his two "static laws." However, the various United States urban studies included in this review show no consistent relationship between the general victim and offender rates and proportions of females in either group. Special tabulations and computations were made for the Philadelphia data to test his "dynamic laws." For example, the distribution of 139 female victims throughout the five years under review is as follows:

YEAR	NUMBER OF VICTIMS	NUMBER OF FEMALE VICTIMS	PER CENT FEMALES OF TOTAL
1948	113	23	20.4
1949	117	32	27.4
1950	117	23	19.7
1951	110	28	25.5
1952	131	33	25.2

Inspection of female percentages shows an inconsistent fluctuation, with little or no apparent relationship to the total number of homicides. It might also be mentioned that these annual female percentages correspond very closely to the percentage distributions Verkko lists among the countries of *low* frequency of homicide rather than to the countries of *high* frequency to which he claims the United States belongs. Similarly the Philadelphia data lend no support to his "dynamic law" with respect to 109 females among the 621 total offenders when examined for each of the five years. A longer time period, however, may produce different results.

Despite the fact that the regularities which Verkko discusses are based on relatively reliable criminal statistics for the various countries, national differentials of conduct norms, of legal definitions, and of judicial treatment of the sexes are not given cognizance in his analysis. Perhaps even if these difficult impediments to valid international comparisons were removed, conclusions would be virtually the same. At any rate, Verkko's explanation for his "static and dynamic laws," namely that "it is obvious that the different biological qualities of men and women are the fundamental cause of this phenomenon,"[44] is hardly palatable to the socio-psychological emphases in American criminology.

Notes

1. *Uniform Crime Reports*, 1950, p. 106.
2. *National Prisoner Statistics, Prisoners in State and Federal Institutions, 1950*, Washington, D.C.: U.S. Government Printing Office, Federal Bureau of Prisons, p. 63.
3. Vital Statistics—Special Reports, *op. cit.*, p. 148.
4. Because primary source material used in other studies was not available to the present author, and because other studies have not always used comparable data, it was impossible to compute various statistical facts that would be relative to the Philadelphia findings. May it suffice, in most cases, to present the documented studies as they were reported by the authors.
5. *The Illinois Crime Survey*, pp. 607–608.
6. Harlan, *op. cit.*, pp. 739–740.
7. Meyers, Jr., *op. cit.*, p. 26.
8. Dublin and Bunzel, *op. cit.*, p. 130. Presumably the authors mean "offender" where they have used the term "murderer."
9. J. H. Cassidy, "Personality Study of 200 Murderers," *Journal of Criminal Psychopathology* (January, 1941), 2:297.
10. Calvin F. Schmid, "A Study of Homicides in Seattle, 1914 to 1924," *Social Forces* (September, 1925–June, 1926), 4:745–756.
11. DePorte and Parkhurst, *op. cit.*, pp. 56–57.
12. *Ibid.*
13. F. L. Hoffman, "The Increase in Murder," *op. cit.*, pp. 23–24.
14. *Ibid.*, p. 26.
15. C. H. Growdon, *op. cit.*, p. 4.
16. H. C. Brearley, "The Negro and Homicide," *Social Forces* (1930), 9:251.
17. *Ibid.* See also, H. C. Brearley, *Homicide in the U.S.*, pp. 107–108.
18. Andrew F. Henry and James F. Short, Jr., *Suicide and Homicide*, Glencoe, Illinois: The Free Press, 1954.

19. *Ibid.*, p. 88. Emphasis is that of the present author.
20. *Ibid.*, p. 124. Emphasis is that of the present author. It should be noted, relative to our earlier discussion of the confusion of terminology, that in the previous reference, authors used the term "homicide" and in the immediate reference the term "murderers." Context again suggests—but does not confirm—that "criminal homicide" was intended in both references. Likewise, in the previous reference both "rate" and "ratio" were used; and in the present reference only "ratio" is found.
21. Pollak, *op. cit.*, pp. 80–82.
22. *Ibid.*, p. 82.
23. Jacqueline and Murray Straus, "Suicide, Homicide, and Social Structure in Ceylon," *American Journal of Sociology*, Vol. 58 (March, 1953), pp. 461–469.
24. Cheng-yueh Yen, *A Study of Crime in Peiping*, Peiping, China: Yenching University, Department of Sociology and Social Work, Series C, No. 20, December, 1929.
25. Based on *ibid.*, pp. 7–9. The author uses the term "murder," but context suggests he means "criminal homicide," as these terms are defined in this research.
26. E. H. Sutherland, *Principles of Criminology*, p. 100.
27. A review and comparative analysis of the law of homicide and of whatever statistics might be available from non-literate societies, similar to the review of law in general by E. Adamson Hoebel in *The Law of Primitive Man* (Cambridge, Mass.: Harvard Univ. Press, 1954), would be highly desirable and might add much to our understanding of the variables associated with homicide.
28. V. Elwin, *Maria Murder and Suicide*, London: Oxford University Press, 1943, p. 162.
29. E. Roy Calvert, "Murder and the Death Penalty," *Nation*, 129:405–407, quoted by Brearley, *Homicide in the U.S.*, p. 81.
30. H. C. Brearley, *Homicide in the U.S.*, p. 81. Emphasis is that of the present author.
31. Hans von Hentig, "Remarks on the Interaction of Perpetrator and Victim," *Journal of Criminal Law and Criminology* (1940–1941), 31:305.
32. *Ibid.*
33. Computed from *Royal Commission on Capital Punishment, 1949–1953 Report*, Table 1, Appendix 6, p. 329.
34. Viscount Templewood, *The Shadow of the Gallows*, London: Victor Gollancz, Ltd., 1951, pp. 132–137.
35. Computed from *ibid.*
36. Veli Verkko, *Homicides and Suicides in Finland and Their Dependence on National Character*, p. 42. "Finland is the only country in the world able to present a curve of nearly 200 years showing the development in the number of male and female victims of crimes against life" (*ibid.*, p. 44).
37. *Ibid.*, p. 47.
38. *Ibid.*, p. 51. Brearley must be given credit for pointing out this same relationship. He says: "There is the possibility that the relative danger to women increases when the homicide rate is low. In England, for example, where very few persons are killed, two out of every three victims are women, but in the United States with a much higher homicide rate the proportion is one female to approximately four male victims" (*Homicide in the United States*, p. 108).
39. *Ibid.*
40. *Ibid.*
41. *Ibid.*, p. 52.
42. *Ibid.*, p. 54.
43. *Ibid.*, pp. 55–56.
44. *Ibid.*, p. 57.

13 Woman as Terrorist

H. H. A. Cooper

> *I understand, now, how deceiving appearances are. When I later became a leader in Seattle, other women feared and resented me as I feared and resented Kathy. To women and men who didn't know me, I was arrogant, impetuously strong and egotistical. Strange that I have never been able to see myself as others see me. Maybe it was the same with Kathy.*[1]

Terrorism is an extraordinarily difficult concept to encapsulate in a few words.[2] Over the years, it has come to mean a variety of things to many different people. Expatiating sagely upon the problem of conceptualization, one of the more authoritative commentators has observed:

> No one had a definition of terrorism. In academia, the various concerned disciplines could not even define "terror," or the basic causes of the phenomenon, or the best means of approach to analyze it. The lawyers sought recourse in law, the psychologists in the personality, the historians in the slow unwinding of the past. Some applied the frustration-aggression thesis, and others the tools of quantitative social science.[3]

Few, if any, seem to have captured in words the essence of terrorism. It has a Zen-like quality; it is to be comprehended through the senses rather than by way of erudite debate. It is truly propaganda of the deed.[4]

Yet it may be noted that this evident lack of agreement on definition, or even on how to arrive at one, has not greatly deterred those who would write about terrorism, for the literature on the subject, whatever its scope and limits, has expanded enormously during the last few years, and the flow shows little sign of abatement.[5] These writings encompass every facet of the subject

Original contribution.

and range from the journalistic to the most scholarly, from the most concrete to the extremes of abstraction. There is, nevertheless, one significant area where the literature still remains sparse, where little of a profound nature has yet been committed to paper. Women terrorists have but recently begun to lay serious claim to the attention of scholars and practitioners. With dramatic suddenness, it seems, woman as terrorist has been discovered, and the floodgate holding back the analyses, investigations, explanations, and the like is about to be opened with a vengeance. Through the actions of a few extremely vicious examples, the world has come to the shocking, and almost certainly correct, realization that, after all, the female of the species may well be deadlier than the male.

It may be that the present lack of understanding of woman as terrorist springs from viewing this problem through masculine eyes. Perhaps we are handicapped because so few women commentators have, as yet, turned their attention to this aspect of terrorism. Terrorism is the ugly side of man and woman alike. Yet men are still conditioned to look for beauty in women, whether it be physical or spiritual. This romantic notion has persisted despite the brutal surgery it has undergone during the course of the twentieth century, but it now exists in starkest contrast to woman terrorist, capable of ugly violence.

Our attitudes toward this new brand of female terrorist are, in the main, quite notably sexist. The words and deeds of those achieving this brief, unsavory notoriety would be truly horrifying whether attributable to men or women. Yet somehow, even to the most case-hardened, they seem to take on a new dimension in horror when associated with women, and mostly young, attractive women at that. This reaction is the product of a classically masculine mold of thought; terrorism is simply not women's work. Even if women do participate in this business, their role is traditionally regarded as fetcher and carrier, giver of aid and comfort to the masculine mastermind behind the scenes, and stout helpmeet—but nothing more—to the male operative in the field. The shattering of these role images is almost as much a shock for some as the terroristic crimes themselves.

The female terrorist has not been content just to praise the Lord and pass the ammunition; hers has been, as often as not, the finger on the trigger of some of the most powerful weaponry in the arsenal of the modern-day terrorist. This new woman revolutionary is no Madame Defarge patiently, if ghoulishly, knitting beside the guillotine while waiting for heads to roll. The new breed of female terrorist not only must have its hands firmly on the lever but must be instrumental in the capture of the victim and in the process of judgment, as well as in dragging the unfortunate to the death instrument. Women terrorists have consistently proved themselves more ferocious and more intractable in these acts than their male counterparts. There is a cold rage about some of them that even the most alienated of men seem quite incapable of emulating. This intractability is exemplified in the behavior of a young female hostage taker of the Irish Republican Army, Marion Coyle, age nineteen. Together with Eddie Gallagher, accounted one of the most ruthless men in the IRA, she kidnaped Dr. Tiede Herrema, a Dutch businessman. In October 1975, she was cornered by the Irish police with her companion and the victim in a small house in Monasteverin, near Dublin. The siege lasted twelve days, and had Coyle not been fortuitously struck by illness toward the end of it, she might well have killed both Gallagher and Herrema rather than surrender. Describing her, Dr. Richard Clutterbuck wrote: "Marion Coyle was said by Dr. Herrema to have spoken no single word to him for the whole time they were together."[6] This single-minded, fanatically inhuman behavior contrasted neatly with that of Gallagher, who displayed no such hostility or contempt for his victim's humanity—even, with a touch of gallow's humor, offering Herrema the bullet from the gun with which he had been terrorized during the long siege. Certainly, Coyle's self-imposed isolation insured that no sympathy that might have affected the outcome could develop between captor and captive.[7] Her behavior on this occasion is typical of the pitiless attitude many women terrorists are capable of assuming. It is one that men find curiously hard to match.

Not only have women proved themselves excellent terrorist material, but they are also tending more and more to take dominant roles, both quantitatively and qualitatively, in many of the more formidable extremist groups operating throughout the world today. It has been estimated that approximately one-half of the active terrorists in West Germany are women, while in other countries women terrorists have even come to preponderate. Women have done much more than take over the dominant role in terroristic operations; they have become organizers and leaders of their own groups. And these groups include male terrorists, who have shown themselves more than willing to operate under the command of the opposite sex. The fearsome, nihilistic Rengo Sekigun, the Japanese United Red Army, seems to have been largely the creation of a woman, Fusako Shigenobu, who organized its members, orchestrated its activities, and offered it for hire among the disaffected of the world.[8] Although the final evaluation of the place and importance of the original Baader-Meinhof group in the terrorism of West Germany has yet to be made, it is evident that the moving force and guiding spirit was not Andreas Baader, who should, as one commentator suggested, be "dismissed as a particularly nasty German lover boy."[9] In providing an ideological basis for the group's activities, Ulrike Meinhof was incomparably more influential than any of the male members, while Gudrun Ensslin seems to have supplied the initial thrust and much of the momentum thereafter. Nor is this entry on the terrorism scene a case of women taking up the cudgels left upon the battlefield by their dead kinfolk, husbands, and lovers. In the main, women have been inspired to enter into terrorism for its own sake, moving rapidly to positions of responsibility for these heinous activities by using their own fatal proclivities and ability. In some cases, they have been actively sought after, while in others, women themselves seem to have been the seekers. What is painfully evident in consequence is that woman as terrorist is now a deadly force to be reckoned with, and her activities have altered many preconceptions, prejudices, and patterns of response. The double standard in the ugly world of terrorism is fast disappearing. Chivalry has no place or meaning in this deadly struggle. Experience has shown that woman as terrorist must be dealt with after the fashion of the Gorgon if those responding would survive.

This assertive new role of women in terrorist organizations is worthy of the closest examination, for it is often a key to an organization's aims and objectives. The short, spectacular life of the Symbionese Liberation Army is most instructive in this regard.[10] Although its titular leader was a black man, a majority of its active members were women. Its theoretical underpinnings, derived from a variety of disparate sources, were the creation of women, and its operations were executed by a majority of female participants. Indeed, this deadly bunch of amateurs seems to have had its own affirmative action program, with the real power and policy-making functions deliberately consigned to women and the few minority members who could be persuaded to join the desperate venture. Everything about this pathetic, self-styled army had a strange, fantasylike quality, utterly divorced from any social or political reality. Its actions, such as the tragic murder of Marcus Foster, the brilliant black school superintendent of Oakland, betrayed a shallow impetuosity devoid of real significance even in terroristic terms. Only the alienation, the bitter hatred, and inability to confess error come through with sincerity. The Symbionese Liberation Army was rage and frustration personified. Tania Hearst, that curious, artificial creation, had her genesis in this medium of angry, alienated, questing women.[11] What were they seeking through this terrible violence that only the flames of the Los Angeles house that was their funeral pyre could destroy? We shall never know, for those who might have told us have passed forever from the scene. Yet there is little evidence that *they* knew their true aim and direction, and their untimely deaths lent no meaning to their cause. However misguided or inept the endeavors of this bizarre band, what remains as an abiding impression is the fanaticism of its female members. Their words and actions ring with an unreasoning, demented, religious zeal. They find strange echo and emphasis in the taped declarations of their copyist and eulogist, Tania Hearst. Yet whatever it was that they were seeking by way of this terrorist enterprise—power, respect, sexual liberation—they clearly did not find it. Had the army not perished in the flames of the fire it might well have drowned, ultimately, in the sea of doubt.

It may be questioned whether it is ever possible for a woman to find fulfillment through the pursuit of terrorism in collaboration with men. The short history of women's involvement in this way with terrorist movements shows a consistent pattern of creeping disillusionment.[12] Even the elevation of women over men in terroristic enterprises does not, it seems, produce the revolution or eradicate sexism. In the initial, euphoric moments of commitment, preparation, and organization, women, particularly those who have never engaged in such pursuits, are eager to learn from men all that they can about the skills and techniques of the violent terrorist. They show an almost childish delight in aping the mannerisms and behavior of soldiers, both regular and irregular, even to the details of dress; the Symbionese Liberation Army had, as befitted its self-image, a near uniform for operational purposes. They literally glory in their newfound profession, displaying a naive eagerness to experiment with all they have learned from their supposedly more experienced menfolk. Such well-motivated pupils all too readily surpass their masters in both violence and rhetoric. At the start, there seems to be a general expectation on the part of the women that their entry into terrorism on equal terms, their sharing of the risks in this dangerous undertaking, carries with it an automatic entitlement to a sharing of the profits. Disillusionment comes when this process does not go far or fast enough. The practical consequences are predictable. The women move away to form their own collective, excluding the men on the ground that they are superfluous or expendable.[13] For the narrow purposes of terrorism, that may very well be the case. Women have certainly proved, in Annie Oakley fashion, that anything the male terrorist can do, they can do at least as well if not better.

Yet despite the rejection, real or apparent, of men, the female terrorist seems unable to escape male influence in this sphere, either in a personal sense or through involvement with men's movements or objectives. It has been suggested elsewhere that there is a strong connection between terrorism and sex worthy of the closest investigation.[14] This nexus is strikingly apparent from even the most superficial study of women as terrorists. The emotional involvement of women terrorists is unusually intense and invariably very personal. It has an obsessive, pathological quality. It is useless to inquire why women become terrorists. It is only productive to ask why this woman or that sought fulfillment through these means. The lines of inquiry invariably lead back to men in general or to some man in particular. In some cases, terrorism has a clear connection with some basic sexual need or drive, and the horrifying story of the Manson women offers instructive material for study.[15] Indeed, it has been advanced that a primary cause of female terrorism is erotomania.[16] While the evidence is too slight to support this premature conclusion, there are grounds for more penetrating research here. The Symbionese Liberation Army, as one example, had its genesis in a debasing kind of sexual involvement on the part of the women who later took dominant roles in it.[17] Clearly, the sexual relationships of women terrorists have considerable influence on what they do and why they do it.[18] The key to female terrorism undoubtedly lies hidden somewhere in woman's complex sexual nature. That the task of finding it is daunting can be no excuse for its postponement. There can be no effective response to this novel phenomenon until a satisfactory basis for understanding its nature can be established.

The present lack of comprehension of woman as terrorist is a severe handicap to those responsible for designing appropriate countermeasures. Hitherto, the responses to female terrorism have been little more than adaptations or modifications of those employed against men. A failure to perceive the distinctive psychology of women in this role can be disastrous, for the effectiveness of the response is determined by the extent to which it is matched to the peculiarities of the individual or individuals at whom it is directed. Terrorism is, fundamentally, part of a bitterly intense struggle for power. It has long been recognized as the weapon of the weak or, more properly, of those who perceive themselves to be weak.[19] Classically, women have been regarded as the weaker sex and, whatever the truth of the label with which they have been saddled, it has certainly left a mark upon women's psychology that is painfully apparent when they resort to terrorism. Insecurity precludes any concession. What cannot be effectively brought under control—particularly in the emotional sphere—must be utterly prohibited.[20]

The whole matter is too complex for any in-depth examination here, but there is one facet of it deserving of special mention. Terrorism in its purposeful phase seeks to create a bargaining situation designed to alter in some way the balance of power. This strategy is seen at its clearest and most dramatic in the kidnaping or hostage-taking situation. The successful resolution of such incidents, from society's perspective, depends upon a subtle chemistry designed to produce compromise and agreement.[21] Consensus is produced, in large measure, through the formation of bonds or relationships between those negotiating the settlement. Mutual respect is essential, even though it is apparent that one side or the other, for the moment, holds all the master cards. Such respect is difficult to attain when one party, as in the case of many women terrorists, has a low self-image.[22] The unreasonableness and alienation of the woman terrorist seemingly inhibits the formation of such relationships. Her fixation with what she is doing and the nature of her personal relationships lead to a strategic and tactical blindness, the consequences of which extend to all who must deal with her. The woman terrorist does not seek to strike a hard bargain. She may well be quite uninterested in bargaining at all. In multiple hostage situations where a woman or women are among the hostage takers, special attention must be paid by the responding authorities to such persons, for, at the crucial moment, even their leaders may be unable to place constraints on their hostility.[23] The prevalence of such attitudes must radically alter the premises upon which responses rest.

The overall picture presented by woman as terrorist is one of confusion of both identity and objectives. The strongest impression conveyed is that women are playing a male game using thinly disguised and poorly adapted male roles. There is no real, underlying female terrorist philosophy of a distinctive kind—or, if there is, it has yet to be articulated with clarity. It is axiomatic to raise the inquiry with regard to terrorists: Who are they and what do they want? These questions, in general terms, are never easy to answer. When they are applied to women as terrorists, an answer is all but impossible, unless we content ourselves with the superficial. Like men, women are identified with causes and often share, ostensibly, the same political objectives as male terrorists. Yet there are observable if subtle differences, particularly where women rather than men are the guiding lights of the terrorist movement. They seem to be linked not only by their sense of themselves as women but also by a frightening bitterness and alienation, and by a nihilism that is pathetic and saddening. Woman as terrorist has yet to find herself, just as she has yet to find a cause worthy of such a perversion of herself as a woman. There is, moreover, no real joy in the voyage of discovery by this route, only pain and eventual disillusionment.[24] Woman as terrorist remains a riddle enveloped in an enigma even to herself. Perhaps the only cause worthy of such a struggle as the resort to terrorism must demand is woman herself. And that cause simply cannot be won by such crude means. The story of woman as terrorist spells out more clearly than any other the failure of terrorism as a tactic or technique of revolution and its tragedy for those seduced by it. For terrorism is not the ultimate aphrodisiac but, rather, a somewhat ineffective analgesic for tortured souls. The terrorist has not come among us solely to destroy others—that is terrible but incidental. The terrorist's ultimate victim is the self.

Notes

1. Susan Stern, *With the Weathermen*, New York: Doubleday, 1975, pp. 51–52.
2. Brooks McClure, an eminent authority in this field, has written: "Early in 1976, experts from the United States and Europe met in Washington for two days to discuss terrorism. When their conference ended, they found they had done little more than try to define the problem; the matter of concrete counter measures had to be left for another time. Law enforcement officials, who had attended the meeting in hopes of getting some new insight for handling terrorist incidents, came away disappointed and frustrated. This experience illustrates the first essential difficulty with the kind of violence which can be called terrorism: it has so many forms, motivations, intensities and effects that it defies simple definition." *The Dynamics of Terrorism*, Gaithersburg, Md.: International Association of Chiefs of Police, Clandestine Tactics and Technology (CTT) Series, 1977, p. 1.
3. J. Bowyer Bell, "Trends in Terror: The Analysis of Political Violence," *World Politics*, 24 (April 1977): 476–488 at 481–482.
4. On this, see Barbara W. Tuchman, *The Proud Tower*, New York: Bantam Books, 1972, pp. 72–132.
5. The *Annotated Bibliography on Transnational and International Terrorism*, published in December 1976 by the Central Intelligence Agency (PR76 10073U), contains 1,277 entries. The literature written since that bibliography was prepared is enormous.
6. *Guerrillas and Terrorists*, London: Faber & Faber, 1977, p. 103.
7. It is a well-attested belief of law enforcement that protracted association of the terrorist and the victim during which an empathy develops between them is likely to inhibit any violent action on the part of the terrorist. A conscious effort to preserve distance on the part of the terrorist is necessary if this inconvenient effect is to be avoided. Terrorists who have not observed this axiom have found themselves, at the crucial moment, unable to kill their victims, as witness Wilfried Böse at Entebbe.
8. On the organization and activities of the Japanese Red Army and Fusako Shigenobu, see the testimony of Brooks McClure, *Terroristic Activity: Hostage Defense Measures*, Hearings before the Senate Internal Security Subcommittee of the Committee on the Judiciary, Washington, D.C.: U.S. Government Printing Office, 1975.
9. *The Economist*, September 10, 1977, p. 130.
10. On this, generally, see Vin McLellan and Paul Avery, *The Voices of Guns*, New York: G. P. Putnam's Sons, 1977.
11. See, for example, David Boulton, *The Making of Tania Hearst*, London: New English Library, 1975.
12. Of particular interest are some of the documents constructed by the remnants of the Symbionese Liberation Army, in which the influence of Emily Harris is notably strong. "[We] still weren't moving as a collective as fast as we should have been. The men were dragging their feet. Their sexism made them afraid of our strength in spite of the fact that they could intellectualize about how great it was objectively, subjectively they felt threatened. . . . We realize, however, how much we can accomplish as a group of strong, unified revolutionary women struggling against sexism in a cell situation." Cited in McLellan and Avery, p. 421.
13. This seems to have been the experience of the Weather Underground as well as that of the remnants of the Symbionese Liberation Army. The growing proportion of women terrorists in countries such as West Germany suggests similar developments there.
14. H. H. A. Cooper, The Terrorist and His Victim, testimony before the Subcommittee on Internal Security, Committee on the Judiciary, United States Senate, Washington, D.C.: U.S. Government Printing Office, 1977.

15. See, for example, the series of articles by Susan Atkins entitled "A Manson Slave," published in the *San Francisco Chronicle*, August 29, 30, 31, and September 1, 2, 3, 1977.
16. "The Female Terrorist and Her Impact on Policing," Top Security Project No. 2, Part IV, *Top Security* (November 1976): 242–245 at 245.
17. Much has been written on this subject and, in particular, the involvement with black inmates at the Vacaville facility, but of more than passing interest is John Bryant, *This Soldier Still at War*, New York: Harcourt Brace Jovanovich, 1975, especially pp. 115–170.
18. A lengthy catalogue could readily be compiled for study: Rose Dugdale and Eddie Gallagher; Jane Alpert and Sam Melville; Wendy Yoshimura and William Brandt; Gudrun Ensslin and Andreas Baader; Evelyn Barge and Mohamed Boudia; Carlos Ramirez Sanchez and a host of women. Each and every one of these relationships could form the subject of an important study to shed light on the make-up and motivation of the woman terrorist.
19. On this see H. H. A. Cooper, "Whiter Now? Terrorism on the Brink," 25 *Chitty's Law Journal*, 6 (1977): 181–190 at 185.
20. Even the toughest women terrorists seem, at times, close to emotional breakdown. Sheikh Yamani, one of the OPEC ministers taken hostage by Carlos, relates of his ordeal on the plane that "the girl went forward and burst into tears" during the frustrating stopover at Tripoli, Libya. This "girl" was the formidable Gabrielle Kröcher-Tiedemann. An exaggerated self-control seems necessary to prevent such consequences.
21. For a more extended discussion, see H. H. A. Cooper, *Hostage Negotiations: Options and Alternatives*, Gaithersburg, Md.: International Association of Chiefs of Police, CTT Series, 1977.
22. Biographical materials are particularly suggestive on this point. The autobiography of Susan Stern, cited in note 1, is especially revealing. Of one companion she writes, "Apparently Georgia made a complete turnabout in personality when, at the age of twenty-three, she joined Weatherman. Lonely, neurotic, and in terrible need of love and understanding, she threw herself into Weatherman totally. With tremendous effort she repressed her fears and timidity, and became a study of the tough, masculine woman that characterized so many Weatherwomen. Wearing heavy men's boots, jeans, and an army jacket, her hair uncombed, no make-up, chain-smoking with trembling hands and drinking either tea or wine constantly, she learned the Weatherman line and stuck to it. By the time I entered the collective she was a drawn, thin nervous wreck. Through sheer force of will she managed to function under the tremendous pressure of the collective. Her mind was kept together with safety pins; I always expected them to come open at any moment." Stern, p. 96.
23. The female West German terrorist killed at Entebbe is a case in point. She was universally feared and hated by the hostages for her attitude, and was clearly the most dangerous of the group. Gabrielle Kröcher-Tiedemann, apprehended in Switzerland at the end of 1977, cold-bloodedly, on her own initiative, killed a police officer in Vienna during the kidnaping of the OPEC ministers. See Christopher Dobson and Ronald Payne, *The Carlos Complex*, New York: G. P. Putnam's Sons, 1977, p. 106.
24. See, for example, "Nightmares over La Bianca Killings/Still Haunted, Miss Van Houten Says," *Los Angeles Times*, September 17, 1977. "I'm embarrassed to say it now, but back then I really believed in Charlie's 'Helter Skelter' plan to start a race war. Now, the hardest thing is to realize the crimes were so senseless."

14 An Interpretation of Shoplifting

Mary Owen Cameron

Most shoplifting, including pilfering, appears to be chronic, habitual or systematic behavior. In substantiating this generalization, it may be well to summarize the evidence.

Sixty-one per cent of women in the store sample had more than one stolen object in their possession when arrested.

Only about 5–10 per cent of women detected in shoplifting are reported to have, when arrested, merchandise in their possession for which they had purchase receipts. It seems probable that a considerable section of the other 90–95 per cent were in the store intending to shoplift rather than to buy.

Most pilferers are reported by store detectives to have developed techniques for getting rid of price tags and other incriminating evidence; to have planned ways of evading detection; to have come to the store equipped with receptacles for stolen merchandise; to be alert to potential followers. With these evidences of sophistication in technique it appears impossible to think of these pilferers as impulsive, accidental, or adventitious thieves.

There may or may not exist in any considerable number a third group of shoplifters consisting of impulsive persons who are overcome either by an unexpected urge to steal or an unpremeditated desire for a particular object. Occasional souvenir hunters are arrested by store police, but store protection personnel do not believe that these people represent any important section of shoplifters either in numbers or certainly in their contribution to inventory shrinkage. Economically and residentially the data show that people who steal one object before being apprehended are not different from other shoplifters.

Another generalization arising from the data presented is that most pilferers appear to have no present or sustained contact with a criminal subculture. Evidence on this point takes five forms.

1. Ratios for the small selection sample of prosecuted shoplifters for whom prior records were obtained from the Police Department showed, when extrapolated to apply to the Court sample of adult women, that about 90 per cent of women who were officially charged with shoplifting had probably never before been convicted of any offense. Store data show that a maximum of two per cent of all women and 12 per cent of all men who were apprehended for shoplifting had a prior criminal record with either private or public police in Chicago.

2. Socioeconomic data on pilferers showed them to be mainly "respectable" employed persons or equally "respectable" housewives.

3. The residences of the Lakeside Co. pilferers in the city were not concentrated in slum areas, and neither were the residences of a sample of 407 white women whose addresses were obtained from the Court records and who had received "token" sentences or probation. Of this group, about 90 per cent (see No. 1 above) were persons who had probably never before been convicted of crime. Their residential distribution in Chicago was approximately that of the Lost and Found claimants of Lakeside Co., a measure presumed to be representative of typical shoppers in that store.

4. The small value of the merchandise taken by pilferers implies that it could hardly have been stolen for sale to "fences" through recognized criminal channels. About 50 per cent of the women charged with shoplifting in the Court sample had been charged with stealing merchandise worth less than $14.95, and 15 per cent of the total had stolen less than $5.00 worth of merchandise. The actual median price tag values of merchandise stolen by persons arrested in the Store were $6.74 for adult women and $8.30 for adult men.

5. Finally, the attitude of pilferers toward arrest may be cited as evidence of absence of contact with criminal subculture. In witnessing unobserved by the accused person, as the writer did, interrogations of arrested shoplifters, ignorance on the part of arrested pilferers of both criminal folkways and the actions of law enforcing agencies was only too obvious. Pilferers had no knowledge of arrest procedures, and they had clearly given little or no forethought to the consequences of their arrest. They appeared to have thought about being "caught," but not about being *arrested*. Not understanding that they would be searched, for example, many attempted to give fictitious names (for a woman, usually her maiden name) while at the same time carrying a billfold or pocketbook with complete identification papers. (They did not realize that arrest implied search.) They consistently offered to pay for the stolen merchandise, failing to understand that they had been arrested and that the merchandise stolen had been impounded as evidence of theft and could not be bought by the thief. They frequently signed a waiver against suit of the store immediately after arrest—tantamount to a confession of guilt—but having signed the waiver, they talked threateningly about suit. (The waiver is simple in appearance, saying that there has been no damage, physical or

otherwise, at the hands of store personnel, and detailing possible physical damage. The "otherwise," of course, is the waiver against all suit.) Not infrequently pilferers confessed some of their past thefts to store detectives, detailing the time, place, and objects stolen. Some of these past thefts had been memorable events arousing and continuing to arouse strong feelings of guilt.

These data seem to establish the fact that there exists a substantial number of persons who systematically steal merchandise usually for their own use and who are not in contact with a specific criminal subculture.

Although these persons were not, then, in association with law-violating groups, it is, however, possible and even probable that they had such associations in the past. Adult pilferers who work alone may have begun their careers as group juvenile delinquents, although not necessarily lower-class delinquents. It is apparent from the data that a large number of young people in Chicago practice shoplifting and presumably learn attitudes and rationalizations favorable to shoplifting and techniques for shoplifting in contact with other adolescents. There is a steady and marked relationship between increasing chronological age and the proportions of shoplifters arrested without companions or accomplices. For women, especially, the number of cases is sufficient to establish a trend, namely a steady and increasing proportion of persons arrested "alone" for each 5-year period between the ages of 15 and 65. The increase of those alone when arrested is most marked between the ages of 15 and 25. Year by year, there is an increase from the ages of 9 to 19 of the proportion of shoplifters alone when arrested. In five-year intervals, the range in the proportion "with others" when arrested runs from 100 per cent for those less than nine years to 0 per cent for those above 65 years of age. If indeed shoplifting is a form of criminal behavior in which the techniques and supporting attitudes are learned in the companionship of others, one would expect to find decreasing evidence of companionship as age increases, for at the younger age levels more people would be in the initial stages of the learning process. This is found, and found regularly and strikingly, in the proportion in which it would be expected. But the evidence on the question is certainly incomplete. As far as the data show, it is theoretically possible that the "group shoplifters" who are mainly juvenile may have ceased shoplifting on reaching maturity and a wholly different segment of people began shoplifting in their mature years. It seems more reasonable, however, to suppose that at least an important proportion of the juvenile pilferers either continued to shoplift or later restarted shoplifting.

Adult systematic or habitual pilferers, then, appear to be mainly "respectable" people not in contact with criminal subculture and showing no special knowledge of the adult criminal world. Although of adult age, pilferers' behavior when apprehended and their excuses for theft appear to be similar to the excuses of the juvenile group. The writer's impression was that in attempting to explain away their thefts, adult pilferers were using the lies, rationalizations, and alibis characteristic of children caught in acts considered reprehensible by adults. They were not realistically facing the different problem of being an arrested adult.

A further generalization from the data on shoplifting is that adult pilferers do not appear to be compulsive, neurotic personalities. Material bearing on the relationship of personality structure to shoplifting is as follows:

1. Shoplifting is not frequently associated with psychoses of sufficient intensity to warrant commitment to a mental hopsital. Only 12 of 873 or 1.4 per cent of women charged in the Court were committed to mental institutions; of the 1153 people in the Store sample, only four were committed, a rather smaller proportion, it would seem, than would be found in an unselected cross section of the population.

2. Shoplifters were not found in psychiatric examination to have any consistent psychoneurotic patterns. Of the 873 women in the Court sample, 57 were recommended by the judges for psychiatric examination. Positive findings were recorded for 55. Of these, 12 (noted above) were committed to mental institutions. Of the remaining 43, eight were found to be suffering from involutional disturbances and this was the most frequent finding. No other single diagnosis was made for more than six cases. Thus we can say that no particular trend of personality aberration was recorded as characteristic of any considerable number of women shoplifters.

3. Neither store arrests nor official charges indicate a tendency for shoplifting rates of women to increase during the ages (45–50) when menopause most frequently occurs.

4. Among pilferers who are apprehended and interrogated by the store police but set free without formal charge, there is *very little or no recidivism*. This point, to be discussed later, is important in several respects and is relatively well established by the data of this study. The figures presented here on recidivism are in most respects more complete than "official" figures which are usually used. They include: 1) official figures of arrest by the Chicago Police Department for some cases; 2) the outcome of trial for a larger number of cases—an outcome, it has been established, based largely on known prior arrests; 3) the private arrest records cooperatively kept by the association for store protection maintained by ten downtown department stores in Chicago.

If shoplifting were a form of compulsive, neurotic, or irrational behavior (kleptomania), a very high rate of recidivism among pilferers would have been found. Few persons arrested for shoplifting ever receive the psychiatric attention necessary to alleviate deep-rooted personality disturbances. Yet, once arrested, interrogated, and in their own perspective, perhaps humiliated, pilferers apparently stop pilfering. The rate of recidivism is amazingly low. The reward of shoplifting, whatever it is, is not worth the cost to reputation and self-esteem. Pilfering is *not* for all, or almost all, shoplifters a basic neurotic manifestation in the sense that alcoholism or other compulsive behaviors seem to be. Even at great cost to their status and apparent comfort, alcoholics continue drinking. No compulsive neurotic ceases his neurotic behavior merely because he is told to do so no matter how forcibly he is told, but apparently shoplifting is a form of behavior which the person can govern apart from the general control of whatever psychoneurotic tendencies he may have.

It can be argued, and it may be a valid argument, that having been blocked from theft, emotionally disturbed persons merely find other ways of expressing hostile, antisocial, or compulsive behavior. Nevertheless if the focus of attention is on shoplifting specifically or even on criminality in general, the concrete direction taken by pathological impulses and the apparent modifiability of these directions is a matter of considerable practical importance. The housewife who has (hypothetically) had shoplifting as an outlet for hostility and finds after arrest that this outlet is now possible only at a greater risk to her reputation, self-esteem, and personal freedom than she is prepared to take, may turn to nagging her husband or she may develop an ulcer. To the psychotherapist whose goal is general personality adjustment, perhaps no essential change has been made. In the eyes of the law, the sociologist, or the store owner, however, the change has been very important, and the mechanism through which this change has been made needs to be understood as completely as possible.

. . .

Explanation of pilfering

It seems probable that most adult pilferers start their careers as children or adolescents in groups where the techniques of successful pilfering are learned from other more experienced children. Later as group activity is abandoned some of the group members continue the practices they learned as adolescents. The lavish displays of merchandise which department stores exhibit to encourage "impulse buying" are, for the experienced pilferer, there for the taking.

Adult women pilferers, generally belonging to families of rather modest income, enter department stores with a strong sense of the limitations of their household budgets. They do not steal merchandise which they can rationalize purchasing: household supplies, husband's clothes, children's wear. But beautiful and luxury goods for their personal use can be purchased legitimately only if some other member of the family is deprived. Although pilferers often have guilt feelings about their thefts, it still seems to them less wrong to steal from a rich store than to take from the family budget. Pilferers seem to be, thus, narcissistic individuals in that they steal for their own personal use, but, on the other hand, they do not use the limited family income for their own luxury goods.

Pilferers differ in one outstanding respect, at least, from other thieves: They generally do not think of themselves as thieves. In fact, even when arrested, they resist strongly being pushed to admit their behavior is theft. This became very clear as I observed a number of interrogations of shoplifters by the Store detective staff, and it was supported in conversations with the detectives who drew on their own wider experience. It is quite often difficult for the store staff to convince the arrested person that he has actually been arrested, even when the detectives show their licenses and badges. Again and again store police explain to pilferers that they are under arrest as thieves, that they will, in the normal course of events, be taken in a police van to jail, held in jail until bond is raised, and tried in a court before a judge and sentenced. Much of the interview time of store detectives is devoted to establishing this point; in making the pilferer understand that what happens to him from the time of his arrest is a legal question, but it is still a question for decision, first of all, by the store staff.

Store detectives use the naivete of pilferers as an assistance in arrest procedures while the pilferer is in the presence of legitimate customers on the floor of the store. The most tactful approach possible is used. The store detective will say, for example, "I represent the store office, and I'm afraid the office will have to see what's in your shopping bag. Would you care to come with me, please?" If the pilferer protests, the detective adds, "You wouldn't want to be embarrassed in front of all these people, would you? In the office we can talk things over in private."

Edwards states that the method of making an arrest is important in preventing excitement and even disorder.

> A gentle approach will usually disarm any shoplifter, amateur or professional, while a rough seizure or loud accusation may immediately put him on the defensive. At other times it may result in a nervous or hysterical condition accompanied by an involuntary discharge which may be embarrassing to both the arrestor and the arrested.[1]

Inbau adds the thought that the gentle approach is helpful too in forestalling suits for false arrest.

> The finesse with which defendant accosts plaintiff is a definite factor also affecting the temper with which the court approaches a case. The defendant acting in good faith with probable cause, whose attitude is quiet, non-threatening, and deferential to the plaintiff's feelings can weather an honest mistake much more cheaply than otherwise. At the most it may induce a court to find there was no imprisonment at all. At the least, it will relieve defendant of punitive damages and reduce the amount of actual damages.[2]

The "deference" of the arresting detective combined with the already existing rationalizations of the pilferer sustain in him the belief that whereas his behavior might be reprehensible, the objects taken were, after all, not of great value; he would be glad to pay for them and be on his way. "Yes, I took the dress," one woman sobbed as she was being closely interrogated, "but that doesn't mean I'm a thief."

Arrest forces the pilferer to think of himself as a thief. The interrogation procedure of the Store is specifically and consciously aimed at breaking down any illusions the shoplifter may have that his behavior is regarded as merely "naughty" or "bad." The breakdown of illusions is, to the store detective staff, both a goal in itself and a means of establishing the fact that each innocent-appearing pilferer is not in fact, a professional thief "putting on an act." In the interrogation the shoplifter is searched for other stolen merchandise and for identification papers. Pockets and pocketbooks are thoroughly examined. All papers, letters, tickets, bills, etc., are read in detail in spite of considerable protest from the arrested person. Each person is made to explain everything he has with him. If suspect items such as public locker keys, pawn tickets, etc., are found, he will have to explain very thoroughly indeed and agree to have the locker examined and the pawned merchandise seen to avoid formal charge. In any event, once name, address, and occupation have been established (and for women, the maiden name and names in other marriages), the file of names and identifying material of all persons who have, in the past years, been arrested in any of the State Street department stores is consulted. The shoplifter is questioned at length if similarities of names or other identifying data are encountered.

While identification and prior record are being checked, store detectives, persons in charge of refunds, and even experienced sales clerks may be summoned to look at the arrested person to determine if he has been previously suspected of stealing merchandise or has been noted as behaving suspiciously.

In the course of all this investigation, it becomes increasingly clear to the pilferer that he is considered a thief and is in imminent danger of being hauled into court and publicly exhibited as such. This realization is often accompanied by a dramatic change in attitudes and by severe emotional disturbance. Occasionally even hysterical semi-attempts at suicide result.

The professional shoplifter who has been arrested and knows he is recognized, on the other hand, behaves quite differently. He does, of course, make every effort possible to talk his way out of the situation. But once he finds that this is impossible, he accepts jail and its inconveniences as a normal hazard of his trade.

"This is a nightmare," said one woman pilferer who had been formally charged with stealing an expensive handbag. "It can't be happening to me! Why, oh why can't I wake up and find that it isn't so," she cried later as she waited at a store exit, accompanied by a city and a store policeman, for the city police van to arrive. "Whatever will I do? Please make it go away," she pleaded with the officer. "I'll be disgraced forever. I can never look anyone in the face again."

Pilferers expect no "in-group" support for their behavior. As they become aware of the possible serious consequences of their arrest (trial, jail, etc.), pilferers obviously feel isolated from all supporting relationships. Store detectives report that the most frequent question women ask is, "Will my husband have to know about this?" Men, they say, express immediate fear that their employers will be informed of their arrest when questions about employment are raised. Children are apprehensive of parental reaction. Edwards says,

> The composure of juveniles being detained has never ceased to amaze me, that is, until notified that they must tell a parent of their misdemeanor. Then the tears flow and pleadings begin. The interviewer must be firm in his denial that notification will "kill" the parent, and he must sell the child on the idea that any deviation from accepted practice must be discussed with the person most interested in his welfare.[3]

Pilferers feel that if their family or friends learn about their arrest they will be thoroughly disgraced. The fear, shame, and remorse expressed by arrested pilferers could not be other than genuine and a reflection of their appraisal of the attitudes they believe others will take toward them. One woman was observed who, thoroughly shaken as the realization of her predicament began to appear to her, interrupted her protestations of innocence from time to time, overwhelmed at the thought of how some particular person in her "in-group" would react to her arrest. Her conversation with the interrogator ran somewhat as follows: "I didn't intend to take the dress. I just wanted to see it in daylight. [She had stuffed in into a shopping bag and carried it out of the store.] Oh, what will my husband do? I *did* intend to pay for it. It's all a mistake. Oh, my God, what will my mother say! I'll be glad to pay for it. See, I've got the money with me. Oh, my children! They can't find out I've been *arrested!* I'd never be able to face them again."

Pilferers not only expect no in-group support, but they feel that they have literally *no* one to turn to. The problem of being embroiled in a wholly unfamiliar legal situation is obviously not only frightening but unexpected. Apparently they had anticipated being reprimanded; they had not anticipated being searched by a licensed detective, identified, etc., and on the whole, placed in a position in which the burden of argument for keeping out of jail is theirs.

The contrast in behavior between the pilferer and the recognized and self-admitted thief is striking. The experienced thief either already knows what to do or knows precisely where and how to find out. His emotional reactions may involve anger directed at himself or at features in the situation around him, but he is not at a loss for reactions. He follows the prescribed modes of behavior, and knows, either because of prior experience or through the vicarious experiences of acquaintances, what arrest involves by way of obligations and rights. He has some familiarity with bonding practice and either already has or knows how to find a lawyer who will act for him.

Because the adult pilferer does not think of himself, prior to his arrest, as a thief and can conceive of no in-group support for himself in that role, his arrest forces him to reject the role (at least insofar as department store shoplifting is concerned). The arrest procedure, even though not followed by prosecution, is in itself sufficient to cause him to redefine his situation. He is, of course, informed that subsequent arrest by any store will be followed by immediate prosecution and probably by a considerable jail sentence. But since this does not act as a deterrent to the self-admitted thief nor could this kind of admonition deter the compulsive neurotic, neither the fear of punishment nor the objective severity of the punishment in itself is the crucial point in relation to the change from criminal to law abiding behavior. Rather the threat to the person's system of values and prestige relationships is involved. Social scientists who have investigated criminal activities which have subcultural support are unanimous in pointing out the persistence of criminal activity, the high rate of recidivism and the resistance to reform shown by law violators. Pilfering seems to be the other side of the coin. Not having the support of a criminal subculture, pilferers are very "reformable" individuals. If the findings of this study are substantiated by studies of other offenses in which the offenders are similarly without support of a criminal subculture, there would be a strong argument in favor of keeping pilferers out of jail lest they receive there the kinds of knowledge and emotional support they need to become "successful" commercial thieves. Crime prevention would seem best achieved by helping the law violators retain their self-image of respectability while making it clear to them that a second offense will really mean disgrace.

Notes

1. Edwards, Loren. *Shoplifting and Shrinkage Protection for Stores* (Springfield, Ill., 1958), p. 134.
2. Inbau, Fred E. "Protection and Recapture of Merchandise from Shoplifters," *Illinois Law Review.* Vol. 46, No. 6, 1952.
3. Edwards, *op. cit.*, pp. 135–136.

15 Criminality in the Work Place: A Comparison of Male and Female Offenders

Alice Franklin

The purpose of this selection is to describe the differences between male and female employees who committed theft during the course of their employment in a large retail organization. Data were obtained from personnel records, security apprehension books, and interviews with key personnel in the organization. The study population included all of the 447 "known" dishonest employees (prosecuted/nonprosecuted) who were involved in theft of cash and/or merchandise or misuse of organizational equipment during a two-year period from 1973 to 1975.[1]

Our first finding is that male employees committed more thefts against the organization than did female employees. Although males were a minority in the work force (40 percent males, 60 percent females), they committed over one-third more thefts: 56 percent of the violators were men. Females, on the other hand, committed 27 percent less theft than their representation in the work force: 44 percent of the violators were women.

Although the employees most prone to steal were those in the youngest age group (18 to 22), older female employees (41+) were more likely to steal than were older male employees. Female employees comprised 43 percent of the low age group (18 to 22), 43 percent of the moderate age group (23 to 40), and 72 percent of the high age group (41+). Of all the employees who committed theft, only 3 percent of the males were in the 41+ age group, compared to 10 percent of the females.

The male employees who committed theft were more likely to be single than were the female employees involved in theft (73 percent versus 57 percent). Among all the employees, 66 percent were single, 29 percent were married, and 5 percent were divorced. Sixty-one percent of the male employees were single, compared to 39 percent of the females.

In general, our data showed that there was a relationship between sex role in the organization and theft. The more stereotypical the role relative to the

---

Original contribution.

traditional functioning of males and females, the higher the rate of theft committed by that particular sex. For example, managerial, stock, and positions defined as "others" (including maintenance, technicians, garage operators, and so on) are those in which men typically have the highest representation, while clerical and sales positions are more typically occupied by women. We found that men represented 100 percent of the personnel committing theft in managerial positions, 87 percent in stock, and 74 percent in "others." Women who committed theft were represented most heavily in the clerical and sales positions, 64 percent and 53 percent, respectively. The data also show that irrespective of sex, theft tends to be committed mostly by persons in sales, and "other" positions: 20 percent. (See Table 1.)

Not surprisingly, we also found a relationship between the sex of the violator and the value of the theft. The greater the value of the theft, the greater the likelihood it was committed by a male rather than a female employee. While 74.7 percent of all the theft committed was valued at between $1 and $150, male violators committed 51 percent of the low thefts ($1 to $150), 64 percent of the moderate thefts ($151–$1,000), and 70 percent of the thefts in the high category (above $1,000).

When asked to explain why they committed the acts they did, only 175 of the 447 discharged employees were willing or able to answer the question. The reasons given by those who answered are shown in Table 2. Note that women are somewhat more likely than men to say that they were influenced by others.

Table 1 Organizational position, sex, and theft

ORGANIZATIONAL POSITION	MALE Number	MALE Percent	FEMALE Number	FEMALE Percent	TOTAL Number	TOTAL Percent
Managerial	7	100.0 3.2 1.8	0	0.0	7	1.8
Clerical	5	35.7 2.3 1.3	9	64.3 5.4 2.3	14	3.6
Sales	119	46.9 55.1 31.0	135	53.1 80.4 35.0	254	66.1
Stock	27	87.1 12.5 7.0	4	12.9 2.4 1.0	31	8.1
Others	58	74.4 26.9 15.1	20	25.6 11.9 5.2	78	20.3
Total	216	56.3	168	43.8	384	100.0

Chi Square = 39.34

$P < .01$

Gamma = .43

D.F. = 4

Table 2 **Reason for theft by sex of violator**

REASON	MALE		FEMALE		TOTAL	
	Number	Percent	Number	Percent	Number	Percent
Needed money	41	64.1	23	35.9	64	36.6
		39.0		32.9		
Influenced by others	5	33.3	10	66.6	15	8.6
		4.8		14.3		
Didn't know it was wrong	9	56.3	7	43.8	16	9.1
		8.6		10.0		
Didn't know why—sorry	20	57.1	15	42.9	35	30.0
		19.0		21.4		
Was going to put it back	9	75.0	3	25.0	12	6.9
		8.6		4.3		
Temptation	14	63.6	8	36.4	22	12.6
		13.3		11.4		
Deserved more	3	60.0	2	40.0	5	2.9
		2.9		2.9		
Didn't feel he/she would get caught	4	66.7	2	33.3	6	3.4
		3.8		2.9		
Total	105	60.0	70	40.0	175	100.0

Chi Square = 6.45

P > .49

D.F. = 7

Gamma = −0.02

Missing Observations: 272

In sum, our data show that the sex of the violator was related to the rate of theft, the position in the organization, and the amount of theft involved. We also found that the men who committed theft were more likely to be young and single, while the women tended to be older and married.[2] Females work primarily in sales and clerical positions; males are represented throughout the store. By and large, the women employees are located in the "mainstream" of the store. Their work is more visible, and the crimes they are likely to commit are more vulnerable to detection. Stock positions and positions defined as "others" are in the organization's back region and are characterized by a lower level of supervision and monitoring. The same is true for managerial positions, which are subject to the least amount of supervision and control. The higher theft rates on the part of the male employees may be explained in part by the different opportunities afforded by their positions in the organization.

Most thefts of high value were committed by male employees. The female thefts were relatively petty: 81 percent of all the thefts committed by females were valued at between $1 and $150. Embezzlement, which accounted for the greatest value in theft loss, and which requires sophistication in accounting and financial manipulation, was most closely associated with upper-level positions that were occupied by men. Thus, the petty nature of the female theft not only reflects a lack of opportunity but may also reflect a lack of skill in certain types of record keeping and financial manipulations.

Notes

1. The order of the sex variable is an extension of the assumption that males will commit theft more frequently than females and are given a ranking of 1 relative to a 2 ranking for females. See Robert M. Terry, "The Screening of Juvenile Offenders," where this approach is used. *The Journal of Criminal Law, Criminology and Police Science*, 58, No. 2 (1967).
2. The amount of time the employee worked for the organization, his or her educational status, race, and the type of theft committed were not related in any significant manner to the sex of the discharged employee.

16 "Crime as Business" and the Female Offender
Richard F. Sparks

When Edwin H. Sutherland first used the term "white-collar crime" to refer to "crimes by businessmen and other persons of respectability and high social status"[1] he was not, in my opinion, intending to offer a logically rigorous definition, in terms of necessary and sufficient conditions. Instead, his aim was to point, in a rather general way, at a number of criminal and quasi-criminal forms of behavior that had been virtually ignored until he wrote (and that have received far too little attention since then). His reasons for doing this seem to have been of two kinds. On the one hand, his concern was scientific: he saw "white-collar crimes" as a counterexample that would decisively rebut theories of crime causation based on individual "pathologies" such as poverty, mental illness, or the "broken" home. On the other hand, it seems to me that he also had an ideological or political concern: In all of his writings on the subject, there is a strong sense of the *unfairness* of definitions of "crime" that focus almost exclusively on the misbehavior of the poor and the powerless, and as a result legitimate a criminal justice system that ignores the misbehavior of business enterprises and their middle-class managers.

Whatever its animus, Sutherland's concept has been a source of much confusion and sterile debate. As has often been pointed out, his shorthand definition contains two different, and theoretically disparate, elements. First, it refers to crimes committed by "persons of high social status," which could include *individual* acts of, for example, embezzlement or income tax fraud, even though those had nothing to do with the offender's business or profesional activities. Second, it refers to crimes committed "in the course of" an occupation—though it would exclude occupational theft by lower-class persons, such as pilfering from factories, as well as union racketeering and bribe taking by policemen.

Edwin Lemert has stated that he once asked Sutherland whether he meant by "while-collar crime" a type of crime or crime committed by a special class

Original contribution.

of people, and that Sutherland replied that he was not sure.[2] Most of the examples he discussed involved offenses by corporations, under the antitrust laws or regulatory statutes such as the Food and Drug acts. Others have used the concept, however, to refer to offenses committed by individuals; an example is Cressey's study of "criminal violation of financial trust."[3] As we shall see, this distinction is crucial for explanatory purposes; its relevance will be seen when we consider the involvement of women in these types of offenses.

In an effort to clarify some of the conceptual issues surrounding so-called "white-collar crime," I recently proposed an alternative conception of "crime as business."[4] By this expression I mean those crimes (or, more generally, deviant[5] acts) possessing all or most of the following features:

1. They are carried out primarily for economic gain, and involve some form of commerce, industry, or trade. Thus, the category of "crime as business" would exclude such acts as kidnaping for ransom and the skyjacking of aircraft for ransom; it would also exclude most art thefts, though the marketing of stolen art works is probably a borderline case.

2. They necessarily involve some form of organization, in the sense of a set or system of more or less formal relationships between the parties involved in committing the criminal acts. This organization is either based on, or adapted to, the commission of the crimes. Thus, "crime as business" would include most of what is usually called "organized" (or "syndicated") crime; it would also include price-fixing conspiracies, most types of company frauds, and the "laundering" of money through illegal banking or other financial transactions. But individual illegal acts—such as cheating on one's income tax, or the solitary embezzlement of a bank teller or union treasurer—would be excluded.

3. They necessarily involve either the use or the misuse, or both, of legitimate forms and techniques of business, trade, or industry. What distinguishes such things as price-fixing conspiracies, invoice faking, and bankruptcy fraud from robbery, burglary, and shoplifting is that the former do, but the latter typically do not, involve methods and techniques that are also used for legitimate business purposes.

I do not intend, any more than Sutherland did, to offer with these three conditions a precise definition, in terms of logically necessary and sufficient conditions. At this stage it does not seem desirable—*a fortiori* it does not seem necessary—to do this. What can be claimed, I think, is that the features just mentioned mark off a number of types of criminal and quasi-criminal behavior that, in sociological terms, have significant similarities. These similarities have often been obscured in the past in discussions of "white-collar crime."

Any attempt to understand what is here called "crime as business" must begin with the truism that the pattern of economic crime displayed by any society necessarily depends on that society's pattern of legitimate economic development and that changes in the form and frequency of economic crime are in large measure a consequence of changes in the patterns of legitimate economic enterprise. This is so, in part, because of the crucial role of *opportunity* in the explanation of criminal behavior. Opportunity is generally important in shaping crime and deviant behavior, of course; it is not relevant only to "crime as business." But it is of special importance there, because of the scale and complexity of the new forms of business and industry that are characteristic of the twentieth century, and in particular of the last fifty years.

Of special importance here are developments in the world of banking and finance. As corporate and governmental investment has grown, in the post–World War II years, new and increasingly complex forms of funding have been developed, which in turn have permitted new forms of fraud. Financial service conglomerates like Equity Funding; "offshore" mutual funds; multinational corporations—all have made possible new forms of fraud and have multiplied opportunities for the violation of regulatory statutes, of a kind which could not have been carried out in the simpler financial world of fifty years ago. What Mary McIntosh[6] has called "picaresque," "craft," and "project" crime organizations have been supplemented, especially over the past half-century, by "crime as business"; this could not have happened until the requisite forms of business had first been developed.

To some extent, my conception of "crime as business" has some affinities with the "theory of illicit enterprise" recently sketched by Dwight Smith.[7] Smith points out that conventional definitions of enterprise "tend to assume that the marketplace ends at the edge of legitimacy."[8] He notes, however, that legal boundaries can shift sharply, shutting off some segments of the legitimate marketplace or opening up new market areas; Prohibition is the obvious example. He then goes on to note that "entrepreneurial transactions can be ranked on a scale that reflects levels of legitimacy within a specific marketplace";[9] there is, for example, a market spectrum in the banking industry that ranges from trust companies and commercial banks at one end, through commercial credit companies to usurers at the other. Once we conceive of the subject in this fashion, we can ask many important and illuminating questions—about the technology of the enterprise, the extent of legitimacy for a given market, the protection of core technology, and so forth.[10]

Smith's theory comes at the end of a book about what has come to be called "organized" crime; in that book he is mainly concerned to rebut some of the wilder speculations lately current, about the Mafia, Cosa Nostra and similar phantasmagoria. But I believe that his approach—and my concept of "crime as business"—are capable of much wider application; they include some of what Sutherland called "white-collar crimes," and also many activities of so-called "organized crime." Indeed, it may be doubted that it is often useful to distinguish between persons who are (or regard themselves as) "racketeers"[11] and persons who purport to be legitimate businessmen or financiers: given comparable market or financial circumstances, the behavior of each group is often strikingly similar. (The "Mafia" is often *alleged* to launder money through banks in the Bahamas; the Gulf Oil Company has *admitted* laundering money through a bank in the Bahamas.[12])

Several students of so-called organized crime have alleged that the focus of such criminals' activities in recent years has turned away from such things as gambling, narcotics, and prostitution, and into the "infiltration" of banks, manufacturing and retailing companies, and other forms of legitimate business.[13] It remains to be ascertained how frequent this kind of "infiltration" is and whether it leads to any more crime than is committed by otherwise respectable businessmen in comparable circumstances. But it is undoubtedly true that there has been an increasing use, in recent years, of legitimate forms of business for dishonest purposes. Bankruptcy fraud (known as a "bust-out" or "scam" in the United States and as "long firm fraud" in England) is an example. In this type of fraud, a company or group of companies is set up, ostensibly for the purpose of trading (either retail or wholesale); credit is established, often through cross-references between one fraudulent company and another; large amounts of goods are bought on credit and then disposed of for a fraction of their value, either through legitimate channels or through receivers of stolen property; and the fraudulent companies are then dissolved either in bankruptcy or by the simpler expedient of the principals' absconding. The losses to the firms supplying the goods on credit are usually tax-deductible as bad debts; they are seldom reported to the police as involving fraud, and indeed the whole operation may look like nothing more than a law-abiding wholesaler or retailer who has imprudently overstretched his operations and gone bankrupt. Whether committed by a "racketeer" or by an otherwise reputable businessman, this type of crime involves a whole range of legitimate financial and commercial practices (such as incorporation, commercial credit); it is those practices, and the economic and social relations they involve, that are crucial to understanding long firm fraud.

At this point, the reader may well ask: What has all of this to do with female offenders? The answer is, *absolutely nothing*; and that is precisely the point. At an *individual* level, "sex of offender" is probably the variable with the strongest (zero-order) associations with crime and deviance. But that variable has no place whatever in explanations of the most important features of "crime as business," since those explanations are not individual-level explanations. Explanations of the frequency, distribution, patterning, or nature of "crime as business" would involve the concepts of economic and social organization, organizational roles, commercial practices, industrial or commercial technology, and so on. They would not be concerned with the attributes of the individual members of those organizations, of the incumbents of those roles.

Two further examples, of transnational crime, may make this clear. In many of the less developed countries, smuggling is a major economic and social problem: in Afghanistan, for example, it has been estimated that smuggling accounts for between 20 and 25 percent of total foreign trade.[14] The falsifying of invoices relating to exports or imports—in order to avoid exchange controls or make an illicit profit through *ad valorem* tariffs or export subsidies—is in many places as serious as smuggling in the traditional sense of that term.[15] The modus operandi of either type of crime can be very complicated. Three things, however, are clear. First, smuggling on a commercial scale requires a high degree of organization—just as does the legal importing or exporting of goods on a commercial scale. It must also involve corruption, such as the bribery of customs officials so that they misdescribe or do not record illegal shipments, and there must be collusive relations between importer and exporter. Second, the parties to such illegal transactions must either be, or be regarded as, legitimate businesspersons (to be able, for example, to dispose of goods known to have been smuggled). Third, the patterning of these crimes—indeed, whether they take place or not—will depend in large part on the provisions of different countries' criminal and commercial laws, tariff structures, export subsidies, and so on, which while intended to regulate international trade also control the profit structure of illegal trade. Explanations of smuggling and invoice faking will be in terms of features of this kind, and "sex of exporter" will obviously be irrelevant.

The same thing is true for the improprieties lately associated with large international and multinational companies—"transfer pricing,"[16] for example, and the mélange of "improper" or "unusual" payments admitted to have been made by companies such as Lockheed and Exxon corporations.[17] To begin to understand transfer pricing, we must first understand the relations between a company and its foreign subsidiary, and the legal and/or commercial barriers countries place on the activities of businesses; to begin to grasp the significance of the "unusual" payments, we need to consider such things as finder's fees, commissions, gratuities (in the case of facilitative payments or "grease money"), and the restrictions on political contributions or government purchasing systems (in the case of corruption and bribery). In neither type of case would it matter if the branch manager, importer, cabinet minister, or company treasurer were female.

An even stronger example concerns the relations between "crime as business" and the normative system of social control. As Aubert pointed out many years ago,[18] what is important is not whether or not a certain form of behavior is or is not properly *called* "white-collar crime"; what matters is why some forms of economic behavior are prohibited in some places but are permitted or even encouraged in others. Now, it is true that (1) there is great variation in the *scope* of laws relating to the regulation of business activity and to the *techniques* used to deal with particular forms of illicit activity (for example, price fixing[19]); and (2) it is an important feature of "crime as business" that those who perpetrate these forms of behavior tend to have an unusual amount of power to influence the legal and social definitions of their behavior, so as—to put it crudely—to get the law written to their own advantage. It is also true that persons involved in "crime as business" tend to have relatively high social status, or political power, or both. It would be a mistake, however, to treat these personal attributes as being important to the explanation of the law relating to the crime (or deviance) of businesses. To do so would be to overlook the importance of *organizational* factors—the institution of lobbying, the practice of consultation with powerful parties likely to be affected by quality-control legislation, the history of restrictions on overt politicking by corporations (or trade unions), the structural location of lawyers within the modern corporation, and so on. In short, individuals' social status is irrelevant here—and so is their gender.

I conclude, therefore, that for those types of behavior that fall within my vaguely sketched concept of "crime as business," questions about female criminality—such as whether women are more likely to be involved than men in such crimes, and if so why—are just irrelevant. Are there any other questions about "white-collar crime" as Sutherland or others conceived it, to which "sex of offender" might be relevant? I believe that there are two kinds of questions where this may be true.

The first class of questions concerns the behavior of females (as opposed to males) as *role incumbents* in organizations involved in what I have referred to as "crime as business." Given, say, a price-fixing conspiracy, an invoice-faking scheme aimed at fraudulent obtaining of export subsidies, or a bankruptcy fraud, I have argued that the most important elements of an explanation will involve concepts like *commercial practice, business organization,* and *organizational role.* Still, these roles—for example, of a negotiator in a price-fixing agreement, or of a company's agent negotiating with a bank to obtain fraudulent credit—have to be carried out by people: and it surely makes sense to ask whether female incumbents of such roles are more or less likely than male incumbents to engage in the rule-breaking behavior required for the crime or deviance in question.

To this question, Adler has given a forceful negative answer:

> As women invade the business world, there is no reason to expect them to be any more honest than men, and to the extent that crime is related to motivation and opportunity, the incidence of such white-collar offenses as embezzlement and fraud should achieve par with men.[20]

This statement is, of course, a hypothesis; but it seems to me to be a reasonable one. Unfortunately, data that would allow us to test it are now virtually nonexistent. This is scarcely surprising, given that data on "crime as business" in general are not available; in addition, we have now only fragmentary and inadequate data on women's participation in business at the levels at which "crime as business" takes place. Even though their participation in the labor force, in the United States and elsewhere, has greatly increased over recent years, it is clear that women are still grossly underrepresented at the boardroom or top management levels of the business world; and so long as they are denied access to these structural requirements for participation in "crime as business," it will be necessarily true that that participation in it will be severely limited.

The second class of questions that may be asked about female offenders and "white-collar crime" (in Sutherland's use of that term) relates to that group of crimes that do not involve any organizational factors: that is, roughly, to *individual* crimes committed by "persons of high social status." There are many types of crime that are only or characteristically committed by middle-class persons, that do not involve organizations based on or adapted to the commission of crimes, the use or misuse of complicated techniques of business, and so on, and that thus do not fall within the concept of what I have called "crime as business." Examples include individual income tax fraud, check forgery, credit card fraud, and individual acts of embezzlement by bank tellers, salespersons or secretaries.

It is important to note that the explanation of these crimes is never a *purely* individual matter. Check forgery, embezzlement, and so on have their own technologies, and thus participation in them is necessarily determined, in part, by technological factors. But those techniques are often very simple— forging a name on a check, faking receipts in a cash register—and they typically require no organization of the kind or degree that must enter into such things as price fixing or corporate bribery. (Thus, the *physiological* abilities required by these crimes' technologies—often claimed to limit females' participation in crimes such as burglary or armed robbery—are not relevant here.)

These "individual" crimes are also, of course, determined by opportunity structures; thus, credit card fraud requires the use of credit cards, embezzlement requires a job that involves physical access to money, just as shoplifting of food is facilitated by supermarkets and cheating on welfare greatly helped by being on welfare in the first place. But the opportunities for individual middle-class crimes, while probably not yet equally distributed between males and females in most Western societies, are much more widely available to women, at the present day, than are positions giving opportunities for participation in "crime as business." Casual observation suggests, for instance, that it is relatively easy for a woman to become a bank teller, though still uncommon for a woman to become a bank lending officer. Thus, the opportunity structure permitting embezzlement is relatively open; structural access to fraudulent lending schemes is less so.

Unfortunately, sex-specific data on participation in these crimes are also very limited at the moment: While it should be possible to get estimates of the numbers of males and females employed in jobs giving access to specific forms of embezzlement, no data are now available on the numbers of males and females committing such crimes. One research approach that I am at present investigating concerns the proportions of males and females covered by fidelity bonds—the "honesty insurance" companies take out in order to protect themselves against the consequences of employee theft—and the relative proportions of males and females involved in defalcations covered by such bonds. It is clear that only a small fraction of all employees who could engage in embezzlement or kindred forms of employee dishonesty are covered by such bonds; the companies involved are almost certainly not representative of American commercial, industrial, or financial organizations, and not all employee offenders covered by such bonds would be "persons of high social status." But employees covered by fidelity bonds are presumably those whom their employers think to be in positions where serious dishonesty is a realistic possibility; the numbers of females covered by such bonds is almost certainly increasing; and many well-known problems surrounding the nonreporting of such offenses presumably do not apply where recovery of fidelity insurance is concerned. Unfortunately, it appears that this segment of the insurance industry does not now collect statistics that would directly yield the desired information (such as numbers of males and females insured, numbers of males and females involved in defalcations). Investigation of case files from particular companies, however, may provide the necessary information. My own bet is that these data, if they can be obtained, will fully support Adler's hypothesis that "As women invade the business world, there is no reason to expect them to be any more honest than men."

In summary, I have argued that Sutherland's original concept of "white-collar crime" embraced two distinct categories of criminal and/or deviant behavior, to which different forms of explanation are appropriate. The first, which I have called "crime as business," includes a large and important variety of acts that take place within business organizations and the social, economic, and political institutions that surround them (such as prohibitions on price fixing and political contributions, product-quality legislation, foreign trade regulation). There are some subsidiary questions that may be asked, with reference to these types of crime, about the participation of women; but those questions are not of very much theoretical or practical importance.

The second class of crimes encompassed by Sutherland's original formulation—"crimes committed by middle-class persons"—essentially involves *individual* behavior, albeit within (usually) an organizational context of some sort. The explanation of these "crimes committed by a special class of people" (in Lemert's phrase[21]) should not be much different, in terms of its logical structure, from the explanation of other crimes; in particular, the same hypotheses about the participation of women in them should apply. For the moment, the (apparently) low rates of participation of women in these offenses, and their virtual nonparticipation in what I have called "crime as business," are a clear indication of the continued exclusion of women from the social and economic roles that would make that participation possible.

Notes

1. See E. H. Sutherland, *White Collar Crime* (New York: Dryden Press, 1949); E. H. Sutherland, "Crimes of Corporations," in A. Cohen, et al. (eds.) *The Sutherland Papers* (Bloomington, Ind.: Indiana University Press, 1956), pp. 78–96.
2. Edwin Lemert, "Human Deviance," *Social Problems and Social Control* 2nd ed. (Englewood Cliffs, N.J.: Prentice-Hall, 1972), pp. 43–44.
3. Donald R. Cressey, *Other People's Money* (Glencoe, Ill.: Free Press, 1953).
4. Richard F. Sparks, "Crime as Business: Organized Crime, White-Collar Crime and Corruption." Working paper on *Changes in Forms and Dimensions of Criminality— National and Transnational,* prepared for the fifth United Nations Congress on the Prevention of Crime and Treatment of Offenders, Geneva, September 1975.
5. I use the expression "deviant" here to mean "rule-breaking"; *not* to refer to acts that have been *labeled* as deviant.
6. See Mary McIntosh, *The Organization of Crime* (British Sociological Association Studies in Sociology; London: Macmillan, 1975), chaps. 3, 4.
7. Dwight C. Smith, Jr., *The Mafia Mystique* (New York: Basic Books, 1975), pp. 335–342.
8. *Ibid.,* p. 335.
9. *Ibid.,* p. 336.
10. *Ibid.,* pp. 337–342; Smith also considers ways in which legal boundaries can be expanded so as to limit illicit activities.
11. The term is Mary McIntosh's: see *The Organization of Crime,* p. 50. It seems as good a term as any.

12. On the Gulf Oil transactions see the report of the subcommittee headed by Mr. John J. McCloy, to the Board of Directors of Gulf Oil Company under an agreement with the Securities and Exchange Commission (Washington, D.C.: U.S. Government Printing Office, 1976).

13. Cf. Donald R. Cressey, *Theft of the Nation: The Structure and Operations of Organized Crime in America.* (New York: Harper & Row, 1969), esp. pp. 99–108.

14. Jagdish N. Bhagwati and Bent Hansen, "A Theoretical Analysis of Smuggling," in J. N. Bhagwati (ed.), *Illegal Transactions in International Trade* (Amsterdam: North Holland Publishing Company, 1974), p. 9.

15. Gordon C. Winston, "Overinvoicing, Underutilization and Distorted Industrial Growth," and J. N. Bhagwati, "Fiscal Policies, the Faking of Foreign Trade Declarations and the Balance of Payments," both in J. N. Bhagwati, *Illegal Transactions in International Trade,* pp. 49, 67.

16. For a discussion of "transfer pricing"—that is, pricing of transactions between a parent company and its subsidiary at other than "arm's length" or market prices—see Richard J. Barnet and Ronald E. Muller, *Global Reach: The Power of the Multinational Corporations* (New York: Simon & Schuster, 1974), pp. 164–65, 206.

17. See the Report of the Subcommittee on Multinational Corporations, Foreign Affairs Committee, United States Senate, vol. 13 (Washington, D.C.: U.S. Government Printing Office, 1976), for accounts of the Lockheed and Exxon payments.

18. V. Aubert, "White Collar Crime and Social Structure" *American Journal of Sociology*, 58 (1952): 263.

19. This example of different control techniques—exemplified in the provisions of antitrust legislation that make possible criminal penalties, punitive damages, and injunction for the same illegal acts—has probably been responsible for most of the confusion surrounding Sutherland's early work: see, in particular, Paul Tappan, "Who Is the Criminal?" *American Sociological Review*, 12 (1947): 96–103.

20. Freda Adler, *Sisters in Crime* (New York: McGraw-Hill, 1975), p. 252.

21. Edwin Lemert, "Human Deviance," p. 43.

17 Aw! Your Mother's in the Mafia: Women Criminals in Progressive New York

Alan Block

The criminal justice system in New York during the 1930s was an ethnic meeting ground: Irish, Jew and Italian were all part of a "social system held together by friendships and favors" and marked by a vision of the whole world as a racket and of themselves as "the smart guys who recognized how the world operated." Significantly, among the Jewish "smart guys" who functioned as more-or-less corrupt intermediaries within the system, were a number of women.[1] The examples were unique and suggestive enough to signal an area within the generally neglected topic of kinship patterns in organized crime that needed attention. This paper will deal, therefore, with women in organized crime. More specifically, it will focus on female criminals who operated primarily in the Jewish underworld in New York's Lower East Side during part of the Progressive Era. There are several reasons to center an inquiry on female criminals during the heyday of Progressivism. The most important one is that it was the period in which public attention was most intensely centered on female criminality and during which a particular and long-lasting image of the female criminal reached its malign apotheosis.

The only female criminal role discussed during the Progressive period is that of prostitute. And that literature, whether a study of the reformers who moved to eradicate the social evil, or the enterprise itself, depicted women as passive victims of social disequilibrium and the venality and brutality of men. Equally as striking, the image of the prostitute, especially as developed by Progressive-Era reformers, was of a lonely, detached and confused female. Nowhere was it suggested that prostitutes or madams consciously and aggressively chose their activities as a positive adaptation to urban life, their class position in society or as an escape from male oppression and economic exploitation.[2]

"Aw! Your Mother's in the Mafia: Women Criminals in Progressive New York" by Alan Block. *Contemporary Crises*, 1 (1977): 5–22. Reprinted by permission of the author and Elsevier Scientific Publishing Company, Amsterdam, The Netherlands.

Along with this particular view of the "dynamics" of prostitution, Progressive reformers concentrated their energies upon female deviance in the burgeoning immigrant neighborhoods of selected American cities. The controlling metaphor for prostitution during this period was "white slavery" and while there was compassion and concern for the rootless, uneducated immigrant prostitute, there was only hatred and contempt for the white slavers. It was a Progressive discovery or invention that the slavers were also members of the immigrant communities—in New York, especially, it was claimed that the leaders of supposedly vast vice operations were Russian and Polish Jews. It was undoubtedly of some solace to Progressive moralists that sexual slavery was an alien phenomenon.[3]

Perhaps the classic example of this vision of prostitution was broadcast by *McClure's Magazine* in a famous series of articles published in 1909. One of the essays, written by the editor of the magazine, S. S. McClure, begins with praise for the "Germanic races" as the architects of Western civilization. In contrast to this achievement, McClure holds that the

> great masses of primitive peoples from the farms of Europe, transported to this country as laborers, together with a considerable proportion of Negro slaves liberated by the Civil War, have struggled to degrade the standards and guaranties of civilization in America.

For proof, McClure turns to a description of the white slave traffic in New York linking it to Tammany Hall and the East Side immigrant Jews. McClure writes: "There has grown up, as an adjunct of this herd of female wretchedness, a fraternity of fetid male vermin (nearly all of them being Russian or Polish Jews), who are unmatchable for impudence and bestiality."[4]

Another of the essays was George Kibbe Turner's "The Daughters of the Poor". Turner's concern was the "transfer of a vast empire of prostitution from its European base to the East Side of New York". He notes that around 25 years before, during the "third great flush of immigration," which consisted of Hungarian, Austrian and Russian Jews, "a large number of criminals settled in New York". In fact, Turner writes, it was the "Jewish district" which opened "the eyes of the minor politician of the slums to the tremendous enterprise, the business of procuring and the traffic in women offered him". It is also stated that the largest number of prostitutes come from immigrant Jewish families. Turner adds, finally, that the East Side Jewish pimps, along with Jewish prostitutes, were transferring their activities to other American cities.[5]

Clearly enough, as Arthur A. Goren points out, these writers "played upon the widely shared anxieties of the times: the fear of organized conspiracy by amoral business and political interests," and the degradation of the immigrants who now appeared to control a number of American cities.[6] Actually, Egal Feldman reports in his excellent essay "Prostitution, the Alien Woman and the Progressive Imagination, 1910–1915," there were a couple of distinct campaigns or approaches to the issue of immigrants and crime during those years. First was "a nativistic attack on prostitution with all its ugly xenophobic overtones"; this was "paralleled by an anti-nativist outburst". The nativist simply blamed the immigrant communities for prostitution, while the anti-nativist not only attempted to uncover the causes and devise cures for the problem of prostitution, but also tried "at the same time to disassociate the reputation of the immigrant from commercialized vice."[7] For all its decency of purpose, however, the anti-nativist position was weak. Obviously, it was logically unsound as the premise of immigrant innocence precluded discussion of immigrant venality. More importantly, it subsumed female crime under the single heading of prostitution. And concomitantly it undermined any consideration of female criminality outside the Progressive formula of weak women and brutal, exploitative men. The somewhat remarkable staying power of this sort of imagery can be seen in the following passage from Moses Rischin's *The Promised City*, one of the finest historical studies of New York Jewry and published in 1962:

> The Bowery, way-station of derelicts, transients, and unsuspecting immigrants, attracted the less stable and wary of the immigrant girls. The dancing academies that sprang to popularity in the first decade of the twentieth century snared impetuous, friendless young women. Lured by promises of marriage, they soon were trapped by procurers for the notorious Max Hochstim Association and other white slavers who preyed upon the innocent and unsuspecting.[8]

But surely, it is past time to question the adequacy of the description of Progressive-Era prostitution in the Lower East Side as represented by innocent, unsuspecting, impetuous and friendless young women being lured, snared and trapped by white slavers. Unsettling as it may be, women could have rationally and consciously chosen criminal careers (even prostitution) as a path of upward mobility. Indeed, there is no necessary and obvious correlation between female criminality, including prostitution, and female weakness compounded by the brutal domination of men. Simply put, just as other Progressive formulations have been junked, it is time to cast off these early notions about female criminality.

The analysis of women in organized crime (organized crime in this essay covers those women who were career criminals, as well as those connected to bands, rings, syndicates, and combinations formed to conduct and/or aid illegal enterprises) which follows is based on information contained in the reports of a unique organization known as the Bureau of Social Morals which was part of a Jewish "self-defense" association called the Kehillah.[9] The New York Kehillah's considerable influence was routed through its annual conventions and scientific bureaus which by the late summer of 1912 included the Bureau of Social Morals formed in the aftermath of the infamous Rosenthal murder. More generally, the Kehillah and the Bureau were part of the Jewish community's response to accusations of Jewish criminality—that aspect of the nativist outburst discussed above. The Kehillah maintained the anti-crime Bureau of Social Morals for five years. Staffed by a number of private investigators, the Bureau focused on the First Inspection District, the 6 police precincts of the Lower East Side. The Bureau's most important communal contribution was the supplying of "detailed information that led to gambling raids, revocation of licenses, and the arraignment of individual criminals."[10] For the historian of crime the significance of this information is obvious.

Unfortunately, there is no summary or final comprehensive report on organized crime, and there is no particular organizational scheme to the material. The investigators' function was to document Jewish involvement in crime and then presumably to turn their evidence over to law enforcement agencies. But within the mass of material there are some data concerning ethnicity, criminal occupations, kinship, past criminal records, the geography of illegal enterprises, membership in particular gangs or vice rings, and so on for some of the 311 female criminals identified by the Bureau. There are several things to be said about the data, however. They are much more complete when discussing male criminals; for example, the investigators were more careful to include ethnicity when discussing male drug dealers than in their reports on female thieves. Even more significant is the nature of the evidence—all of it is positive. For almost every variable the value is either yes or unknown. This reflects the fact that while we positively know that a certain number of prostitutes in the sample were married, it cannot be assumed that all the others were not. In certain cases, of course, the absence of evidence has a special meaning. Given what is known about the Progressive imagination and the purposes of the New York Kehillah—the defense of the immigrant Jewish community from accusations of criminality—it is meaningful to note the virtual lack of information on either white slavery or the coercion of female criminals.

There were 5 fairly distinct groups of female criminals haphazardly described in the hundreds of Bureau reports: those involved solely in prostitution (prostitute); those who achieved a management position usually in a vice operation or displayed special business skills such as fencing stolen goods or corrupt bail bonding (entrepreneur); those whose criminality was exclusively some form of stealing (thief); an exceptionally small group who were both whores and thieves (whore-thief); and those who worked a combination of vice, gambling and drug dealing (narc). After careful scrutiny, the 311 women criminals have been distributed in the five categories in the following numbers: Prostitute (149); Entrepreneur (78); Thief (56); Whore-Thief (4); Narc (24). The data have then been analyzed to determine the differences and similarities of the various groups according to such variables as age and recruitment patterns. Another part of the investigation focuses on the issue of organization in the illegal enterprises and the influence such variables as kinship had on structure. Most importantly, however, this paper will suggest new parameters for female roles in organized crime during the Progressive Era in which willfulness, independence, and assertiveness (stereotypically masculine not feminine qualities) are central to an understanding of women in crime.

The married ladies

The first area to be discussed is personal background, and it begins with an admission of partial failure. It is impossible to determine with any degree of accuracy the question of ethnicity. Out of over 300 criminals in the sample, the Bureau's investigators only positively identified four as members of a particular ethnic group (the four were Jewish prostitutes). Clearly though, there is a strong likelihood that a substantial number of the sample were Jewish given the preponderance of Jewish surnames and Yiddish aliases. But for all the Cohens, Solomons and Yettas, Beckies and Minnies, there are also Ryans, Kellys and Martins along with such aliases as Spanish Mary, Toothpick Mollie and Sadie Africaner which cloud the ethnic picture. Ethnic variability seems to hold for all groups with a majority having Jewish names and the remainder Irish, German and Anglo names.

The information concerning age is more substantial as the investigators reported on the age of 82 of the women. The topic of age is of some importance because of its role as one of the implicit postulates in the stereotype of prostitution. Whores were "girls" whose youthfulness, impetuousness and inexperience with the world betrayed them. A natural corollary to this was the belief that prostitutes were quickly burned-out, becoming diseased "hags" at an exceptionally early age. That this was shown to be false as early as 1913 does not seem to have shaken the belief. George J. Kneeland's masterful study, *Commercialized Prostitution in New York City*, published under the auspices of the Bureau of Social Hygiene in 1913, notes that "the life of the professional prostitute has been [erroneously] estimated at 5 years, on the ground that she dies, withdraws, or is incapacitated" in that time. Kneeland goes on to state that according to his study of more than a thousand prostitutes the view is wrong. He writes: "The majority of these girls, though entering the life before 18 are at 24 still active and aggressive in seeking trade." Kneeland computes the average age of prostitutes at 25 years.[11] The Kehillah's figures are somewhat higher than Kneeland's, although the sample is much smaller, and, therefore, probably not as reliable when dealing only with prostitutes.

The average age for the 82 women in the Bureau of Social Morals reports is almost 31 years. The sample is composed of 60 prostitutes, thirteen entrepreneurs, four thieves, and five narcs. Figuring the groups separately the averages are 28.6 for prostitutes, almost 41 years old for the entrepreneurs, almost 31 for the four thieves, and 22 for the narcs. The most pronounced age cluster for the entire group is in the 24 through 30 year old bracket with 41 women represented. Between the ages of 40 and 50 years, the Bureau notes that 16 women are still active. For the same age group Kneeland counts 17 women, although in his study they only comprised 1.5% of the women investigated. In the Bureau of Social Morals reports this elderly group is almost 20% of the total. The extremes in age range from a 17 year old prostitute to four 50 year old criminals made up of three entrepreneurs and one prostitute. Unlike the Kneeland study, the Kehillah's investigators give no starting point for the criminal careers and, therefore, the duration of the illicit activities cannot be computed. But it does seem that most of the women had been criminals for a substantial number of years except for the narcs. Certainly there is no indication of any rapid deterioration or early termination of activities for the women.

One of the significant and unappreciated topics in female criminality is marital status. As noted earlier, it is part of the Progressive litany that prostitutes were lonely, detached and friendless. When marriages of prostitutes or

Table 1 Female criminals known to be married

CRIMINAL CLASS	NUMBER MARRIED	PERCENT OF KNOWN MARRIED IN EACH CLASS
Prostitute	20	13.4
Entrepreneur	22	28.2
Thief	35	62.5
Whore-thief	2	50.0
Narc	8	33.3

madams were discussed, the context typically has been, "Strange as it may seem, some men marry these women and find them devoted wives." Even stranger still, commentators have written, "year after year, through adversity and prosperity they have followed their masters and obeyed their will. Beaten, exploited, infected, jailed, they still remain steadfast."[12] The language of these accounts, obviously, implies that these are marriages in name only—legalized equivalents of master-slave, pimp-whore relationships.

With this viewpoint in mind, consider the data of marriage furnished by the Bureau of Social Morals. The reports contain information on 87 married women criminals distributed as shown in Table 1.

The percentages for each group are naturally the minimum possible, but even these exceptionally conservative figures indicate the importance of marriage and female criminality. What needs to be explored, of course, is the nature of these marriages—do they fit the Progressive model or not? To begin an answer Table 2 was constructed.

There are several things that could be said about these rather minimal figures. First, they may suggest that marriage for prostitutes and whore-thieves approximates the Progressive formula. On the other hand, the lack of information for 3 of the groups coupled with the 10 thieves who were partners with their husbands may indicate the opposite. Clearly, the Bureau's descriptions of the married criminals must be scrutinized for a more definitive answer.

Concerning the married entrepreneurs, the reports are extremely telling. For example, Sadie Chink, whose husband was Sam Schimil, was co-owner with Jennie Morris (Jennie the Factory), wife of Harry Morris, of a disorderly house that employed at the very least 3 prostitutes. Sadie and Jennie also employed Freda Martin, whose husband was Harry Martin, as a manager. Mrs. Martin was also a cocaine dealer. Ray Treibetz, married to Abe Treibetz,

Table 2 Business relationships among married criminals

CRIMINAL CLASS	WORK FOR SPOUSE	PARTNERS WITH SPOUSE
Prostitute	12	——
Entrepreneur	——	1
Thief	1	10
Whore-thief	2	——
Narc	1	——

owned a hairdressing parlor frequented by prostitutes which was additionally a gambling and opium parlor. Her husband was a professional fence and bail bondsman. Another of the married entrepreneurs was Rosie Barth who, like Ray Treibetz, ran a hairdressing parlor which catered to prostitutes. Her husband, Bernard Barth, was a bail bondsman, fixer and steerer (corrupt intermediary between criminals and members of the criminal justice bureaucracies), and loanshark. The Barths (who had 5 daughters) invested their money in real estate and reportedly owned several tenements.

Several of the other married entrepreneurs included one whose husband started her in the disorderly-house trade, another whose husband was an ex-policeman (Hannah Bernstein), one who was both an owner and madam in several whore houses employing a fairly large number of prostitutes, and a Mrs. Cooper who owned a building used or rented by drug dealers. One of the more interesting cases concerns a Mrs. Bowles who leased various properties and then moved in with a crew of both prostitutes and panhandlers. Also living with Mrs. Bowles were her daughter Freda and a grandson. Mr. Bowles, the investigators found, held a respectable position with the Zimmerman Provision Company.

The final example in this particular category was gathered from a series of reports filed by the Bureau in August 1912. This extensive investigation centered on a disorderly house owned by the Hertz family and located at 7 East First Street. The building was known as the Columbia Hotel and was owned by Rose Hertz, her husband Jacob Hertz and Max and David Rosenbach, brothers to Rosie Hertz. Also working there were two of Rosie Hertz's cousins, Hyman and Morris Goldman, the latter being the manager. The family were Hungarian Jews and supposedly ran some of the most famous whore houses in New York City. The Bureau notes that Rosie Hertz had made a great deal of money and owned "a few tenement houses on 5th Street, and also the house she occupies in Borough Park, Brooklyn." Concerning her past, the Bureau states "from an authentic source . . . that Rosie's mother Gittel was the first Jewish madam in New York, if not in the entire United States." Rosie's career began when she went from "one coal cellar to another—from one shoe-making basement to another." By living modestly, the Hertz's had succeeded in becoming "bosses in the disorderly house graft"; to protect their interests they "contributed $1,000 every year to both the Democratic and Republican organizations." Other interests that the Hertz family included were the fencing of stolen goods and a small bail bond business: Rosie would "very often sign bonds for gambling houses," although in those cases she supposedly never charged anything. The Bureau also notes that Rosie broke in such other female criminals as Hannah Bernstein, Slavish Anna, and Rosie Cheesecake among others.

Again, it is important to consider the implications in marital relationships between those who are married and either work independently of their husbands or are partners with them, and those who are employed by their spouses. In the cases of the entrepreneurs discussed above, all our examples with the exception of Rosie Hertz appear to have worked independently of their husbands. And the Hertz family, while technically a partnership, was run by Rosie not Jacob, according to the Bureau's investigators. Independence in the other examples does not, of course, mean that the husbands were either criminally innocent or of minimal importance in the lives of the female entrepreneurs. Except for Mrs. Bowles' arrangement, these seem to be complementary criminal enterprises some under the leadership of wives, others led by husbands.

These points are further developed by an examination of the category "thief". As was noted earlier out of 35 married thieves, 10 were partners with their husbands while only 1 was employed by hers. The terms partnership and employee, however, are not always clear and definitive. For instance, the one thief described by the Bureau as working for her husband is Rosie Stahl. But a careful reading of the investigators' reports suggests little substantive difference between working for, or with, in this case. The strong probability is of a series of criminal partnerships with no indication of either overt or covert coercion on the part of husbands. Of equal interest is the appearance of not only husband and wife criminal equality, but of a number of partnerships linked together by a variety of marital styles.

One of these confederations is composed of four of the married thieves including Rosie Stahl. The apparent leader or center of this group is Bessie London (Bessie Solomon) the wife of Meyer Solomon alias Meyer Boston. Bessie was reportedly a master thief and pickpocket responsible for training such other female criminals as Tillie Finkelstein the wife of Candy Kid Phil, Rosie Stahl and Skinny Mollie the wife of a thief known as Itschky. Another Bureau report also notes that Bessie Solomon trained her brother-in-law's wife and that the two women were so successful as thieves that their husbands (who were also brothers) were able to abandon stealing in order to specialize in gambling, loan sharking and the fencing of stolen goods. Other stealing combinations dominated by kinship relations involve a Mrs. Lubitz whose husband was "Lubitz the Pickpocket" and whose sister, Mrs. Greene Zindel worked with her husband. Dave Hoffman, Little Carl, and the husband and wife team of Harry and Toothless Kitty Davis also were members of this combination.

It is apparent that sexually-integrated teams far removed from the master-slave model of the Progressive imagination abounded among thieves. Consider Spanish Mary and her husband Earle Williams known as the "King of the Panhandlers" who worked ferry boats, elevated trains and subways. In the same category are Sarah and Jacob Glucksman, May and Joe Hess and the pickpocket team of Taube and Aaron Goldsbard. Another interesting case is that of Katt Schoenberg the wife of Joe Feldman alias Joe English. The Schoenberg family along with the already discussed Hertz and Solomon groups furnish one of the best examples of the familial dimensions of organized crime and the importance of aggressive female participation. The Schoenbergs' criminality began in the "old country" when Katt's mother and father started their illegal careers. Following in their parents' footsteps were two of their sons (one from a previous marriage), one of Katt's brothers-in-law and her first husband. At the time of the investigation, the Schoenberg-Feldman entourage seem to have concentrated their stealing in the fish markets under the Williamsburg Bridge. One final perhaps revealing instance of the nature of the marriage relationships among our thieves deals with Mrs. Rose Segal and her husband Louie Segal. The Bureau reports that Mrs. Segal was a thief and also co-owner of a restaurant with a pimp named Joe Bernstein. There is no evidence that Mr. Segal was involved in any criminal activities.

Information about the marital styles of the smallest group "whore-thief" is insufficient for any generalizations. There are, however, some things to be noted about those women in the category "narc". Eight out of 24 women in this group are known to have been married. For one of them the information about both her career and marriage is hopelessly confused. Another, Mary Lesser, was reportedly married to Hymie Lesser a "dope fiend and pimp" and a relative of some minor East Side politician. For unknown reasons Mary left her husband first to live with a pimp known as "Jack the Wop" and then finally to move in with another pimp, Edward Land. The Bureau adds that Mary not only solicits, but also smokes opium and plays poker in Ray Treibetz's hairdressing parlor. Another married prostitute and gambler the Bureau reports on is Annie Sullivan (Sloppy Annie) who lives with her "Irish pimp husband." The remaining five married women in this group also present a complicated picture. For three of them there is the decided possibility that they are another extended criminal family. The women are: Rose Newburger a prostitute and narcotic dealer married to Fred Newburger; Annie Newburger a co-owner of a cocaine joint with her husband, Joe Newburger; and Dolly Newburger who kept narcotics for Annie's husband, Joe. The last two married women in this classification might more accurately be placed in the entrepreneurial group. One owned and managed apartments used by prostitutes and drug dealers, the other was a prostitute, cocaine and opium user, and landlady who probably ran various vice and drug establishments. Aside from noting that they were married, the Bureau gives no information about their husbands.

The last criminal class tabulated in Table 2 to be discussed is that of "prostitute". According to the breakdowns, 20 of the 149 prostitutes were known to have been married and 12 of the 20 worked for their husbands. Based on the Bureau's all too meager reports there are some indicators that the relationships of 7 of them could fit the traditional model. Of the 5 remaining women there is no evidence on the marital/working relationships of 3 of them. For the fourth member of this group there is solid information that her husband (Andy Collins) was a pickpocket. It is possible, therefore, that Mrs. Collins' whoring was an independent venture (presumably encouraged by her husband) while at the same time the 2 of them were pickpocket partners. The last example is difficult to interpret although intriguing. The prostitute's name was Elsie Sonnenschein and although married and the mother of a child she lived with her mother. Apparently, Elsie's husband had attempted to make her a prostitute which so enraged her that she had him arrested and committed to jail. Subsequently, however, Elsie became a prostitute.

For the small group of 8 prostitutes known to have been married, but who were not employed by their husbands, there are a number of intriguing relationships. Sadie Gluck, the wife of Maxie Gluck, and the mother of 2 children, worked for one of the Lower East Side's most famous all-round criminals, "Dollar John." Then, there is Mrs. Friend, who had 3 children and both lived with and worked for a succession of men named Spinetti, Fisher and Louis Boston. The next woman is known only as Martha. She allegedly had several husbands, was rather elderly and appears to have been independently employed. The last prostitute in this category for whom there is much information is a Mrs. Greenberg who worked with another prostitute known only as Carrie who was employed by a Mrs. Klein. The most plausible explanation is that Mrs. Greenberg's marriage had little to do with her professional life, at least in a managerial sense.

The questions about marital relationships and styles is exceptionally complex and perhaps ultimately insoluble given the kinds of evidence needed. With this clearly in mind, however, certain speculations and tentative conclusions are warranted. For instance, given what is known about the nearly 28% of the 311 female criminals who were married, there is simply no reason to retain the Progressive notions of masters and slaves. The evidence on this particular point is especially persuasive when discussing the neglected areas of female criminality—stealing and management. Even for the relatively small group of known married prostitutes there is enough variability to call for a search for more accurate terms.

Sidelines and diversions

Other evidence pointing to the same conclusion—the need for new terms and concepts in dealing with the history of female crime—are the findings of collateral criminal occupations. These are illegal activities engaged in by members of the sample besides or in addition to their primary criminal occupations. We have already discussed a number of women whose primary occupations were in stealing or in prostitution, and who also were engaged in various other criminal sidelines. The total of women involved in one or more collateral criminal occupations is 269 out of 311. However, there is some confusion on this point in both the investigators' reports and in the open-minded nature of the criminal class designated entrepreneur to make the total questionable. Nevertheless, it is evident that female criminals were not only members of stealing rings, prostitutes, entrepreneurs, and narcotic dealers, but were involved in a multiplicity of illegal enterprises at the same time. The ability to create and take advantage of changing criminal opportunities seems to demand individuals who were aggressive, willful and adaptive. Quite the opposite of the dominated and helpless creatures traditionally portrayed.

Does marriage pay?

So far the analysis has dealt primarily with the known married criminals leaving virtually undiscussed the bulk of the sample (72%) whose marital status is unknown. There is nothing to add on the topics of age distribution, ethnicity and collateral criminal occupations as these examples were not cross-tabulated with marital status. The first area to examine is methods of recruitment concentrating on those women who were recruited by pimps and

Table 3 **Roles in illegal enterprises**

CRIMINAL CLASS	INDEPENDENT	PARTNER	BOSS	MEMBER OF A RING
Prostitute	6	7	—	7
Entrepreneur	—	3	18	—
Thief	3	—	—	—
Whore-thief	—	—	—	—
Narc	1	—	—	1

what the Bureau calls "boyfriends." As with ethnicity, however, the evidence on this point is meager. Out of 224 women only 13 are positively stated to have been recruited by pimps. As might be expected, all but 1 of the 13 was a prostitute. The exception was Jennie Feldman, a prostitute and opium dealer—"narc"—recruited by a pimp named Meyer the Special. The number of women recruited by boyfriends was only 16—they were all prostitutes. A more telling indication of the quality of relationships among male and female criminals might have come from the variable indicating employers' position, part of which, at an earlier stage, was displayed in Table 3. The values for employers' position are pimp, boyfriend, and spouse. Leaving out the value spouse, the frequency distribution shows that 28 women worked for pimps and 14 for boyfriends. But the sample consulted in this case includes all 311 women. The reason for not dropping the known married women is, as we have seen, that married female criminals were at times employed by both spouses and pimps or, while married, worked for pimps who were not their husbands, etc. Another difficulty in drawing conclusions between pimps and boyfriends is that the Bureau's investigators often used both terms in different reports concerning the same criminals. Rae the Muskateer a gambler and prostitute lived with an Italian pimp in some reports and an Italian boyfriend in others. In such cases it is impossible to know whether Rae's consort was her pimp in the traditional sense or whether they were lovers who shared in some equitable fashion Rae's illegal earnings as a prostitute and gambler.

A more fruitful comparison in determining female roles than the above is one related to female independence and female-male equality in organized crime, as reported by the Bureau's investigators. The criminal classes to be discussed are "prostitute" and "entrepreneur". Out of the 6 whores who work independently, there are 2 who are reportedly married. Of the 7 prostitutes who have partners none are reportedly married. Two of them are sisters (Sarah and Bessie Winters), and 2 others are partners with unrelated women. But, while partners in some instances, it also appears that 4 of these women are employees of pimps and madams at the same time. The unanswerable question is whether this complex group represents women who were basically partners and occasionally worked for others or the converse. More definitive answers can be made about the last category of prostitutes—those who were members of rings. None of them were reportedly married. The 7 women appear to have formed 14 separate rings. One was composed of Lizzie Articles, Mary the Bum and Hungarian Mary; another was formed by Lena, Jennie and Susie. Interestingly, it appears that Jennie and Susie joined a different ring with a whore known as Dutch Lilly which excluded Lena. It is unclear whether these last 2 combinations were contemporaneous. One other ring alluded to in the Bureau's reports includes 4 women 2 of whom are identified as Miss Marshall and Miss Wilson. (Obviously there are more than 7 women mentioned: those who were not identified by some type of name were not counted.)

Turning from the prostitutes to the "entrepreneurs" the meaning of female independence and equality becomes clearer. There are 18 women reliably described by the Bureau as both entrepreneurs and employers. As might be expected this is the only group found to contain bosses. The first thing to note about them is that 6 were married. While insignificant in itself, a comparison between the married entrepreneurs and the 12 others is revealing. With only 1 exception the married ones are property owners: 4 of them owned whore houses, 1 leased a series of disorderly houses, owning 1 of them. It is also important that these owners were involved in a multitude of criminal activities outside of owning and renting rooms in their establishments to criminals. When comparing this group with the 12 women entrepreneurs left in the boss category not identified as married, the difference in property-ownership is striking. Only 3 out of the 12 owned property described by the Bureau. And these 3 women either had male partners or were involved in several different criminal activities at the same time. One conclusion concerning ownership for this particular class—"entrepreneur"—seems inescapable: marriage and involvement in a variety of criminal enterprises probably meant the accumulation of enough capital to transform these criminals into property owners—surely some sort of ideal for members of the underworld.

If one thing should by now be clear, it is that women were as interested as men in extending their expertise, influence, power, and capital in the underworld, at least New York's Jewish underworld in the Lower East Side. There is certainly enough evidence to establish aggressive, purposeful, willful behavior on the part of female organized criminals. But perhaps the most startling of all the evidence is that which points to marriage as a primary building block for successful criminal careers for both men and women. Attention, therefore, might best be focused on criminal families, characterized by husband and wife partnerships and by the effects of capital accumulation gathered by husbands and wives pursuing related but often semi-independent criminal careers.

In order to devise a meaningful correlation about property ownership and marriage patterns, a list of those women known to have been either managers or owners of criminal establishments was compiled and then compared with two variables: (1) those women from this list known to have been married, and (2) the number of establishments owned or managed by them. It is important to remember that all these women were part of the "entrepreneurial" class. As Table 4 shows 57 individuals controlled 83 establishments. Significantly, the married female criminals in this group while comprising only 30% of the group controlled over 45% of the places. And it is crucial to remember that these are the minimum figures: undoubtedly some of the women whose marital status was unknown were married.

While it seems clear from Table 4 that marriage and the control of criminal establishments are significantly related it is important to differentiate between ownership and management which up until now have been included in the

Table 4 **Distribution of property control by female criminals**

	NUMBER OF ESTABLISHMENTS[a]						
MARITAL STATUS	1	2	3	4	5	6	7
Married	7	6	2	——	——	1	1
Unknown	35	5	——	——	——	——	——

a Criminal establishments refer to places where the female criminals lived, met and congregated, worked, managed, and owned. From the Bureau's reports 233 different places were identified including hotels, restaurants, saloons, disorderly houses, gambling places, hairdressing parlors, candy stores, etc. But, only 102 of the 233 addresses given by the investigators could be specifically identified as one of the above. Out of the 102 places there were 47 disorderly houses, 12 restaurants, 9 hotels, 9 saloons, 5 gambling places, and so on in descending order. The number of women identified as users of the different types of places is also interesting. For instance, although there were 5 gambling places only 5 women were reported as users: however, 45 women were found to meet and congregate, etc., at the 3 hairdressing parlors identified by the Bureau. It should also be pointed out that the places had multiple criminal and non-criminal uses and that their ultimate designation is somewhat arbitrary. Saloons were found in hotels, restaurants were also gambling dens, and hairdressing parlors were used to distribute narcotics.

notion of control. Unfortunately, there are not enough hard data to compute these differences, or the monetary value of the properties described. Nevertheless, the Bureau's reports do contain descriptive material relative to these points and the 4 married women who controlled 3 or more places. Sadie Chink owned outright 5 disorderly houses and was a partial owner of another along with Jennie Morris. Bertha Hitz owned 3 disorderly houses 1 of which was located in Baltimore, Maryland. And Rosie Hertz owned 2 disorderly houses, managed 4 other ones, and was also the manager of a gambling house. The last example is Freda Martin who spent her professional career managing 3 of Sadie Chink's houses.

In compiling the above figures it also seems pertinent to discuss those establishments with the largest reported clientele, to see if their owners or managers were likely to have been married. There are 13 places where the reported number of habitués was 4 or more (the highest figure was 29 for a hairdressing parlor frequented by almost the whole range of female criminals). Out of the 13 places, 3 were owned by women, 2 of whom were married, 3 were managed by married women, 4 were owned by men, and 3 are unclassifiable. The 1 unmarried woman in this group is Lena Hoberg whose apparent criminal affluence was probably based on her "romantic" relationship with an unidentified Police Captain.

Conclusion

The subject of female involvement in organized crime is, as we have seen, dominated by a series of sentimental conceptions dealing especially with prostitution and cast principally by Progressive reformers and their immediate forebearers as they grappled with the enormity of urban culture. Once firmly established, these notions left little room for any understanding of female criminality, including prostitution, as a rational method of adaptation to class structure and urban institutions. Indeed, the sentimentality of the approach fixed concern upon the single question of cause—what could have led girls to so degrade themselves, ultimately destroy themselves—was the reigning issue. This meant that female criminality would really become a part of the general field of juvenile delinquency, that area of criminology devoted to seeking reasons for the transformation of young people from potential citizens to criminals. Adult female criminality had seemingly been settled as a separate topic by that part of the Progressive formula which went inexorably from juvenile female crime to degradation, disease and death. Under this formulation, mobility in organized crime for females was an explicit one-way street, leading rapidly downward. As long as this is maintained, there is little sense in considering adult female criminals as more than the victims of brutal male criminals; used by them until they reach some disgusting level of disease which renders them criminally useless and then abandoned. The marriage of female criminals is, therefore, only another aspect of male domination confirming the gullibility of female criminals by tying them to their masters in a kind of masochistic frenzy.

Naturally, within this traditional litany of causes and concerns there is no room for female independence and equality in the world of adult crime. Women such as Rosie Hertz, Bessie Solomon, Sadie Chink, Katt Schoenberg, Sarah and Bessie Winters, etc., make little sense. Indeed, the criminal class called entrepreneurs is either a gross misinterpretation or, at best, a historical oddity with no general significance. Without some serious re-thinking, therefore, the indisputable facts that female criminals pumped money into local real estate and legitimate businesses, as well as providing often unique goods and services to a variety of urban consumers, lie dormant. Also unappreciated is the importance of female support (and sometimes ownership) of saloons, candy stores, hotels, disorderly houses, hairdressing parlors, pool rooms and gambling dens which materially contributed to the quality of urban life that such writers as Henry Miller found so interesting and valuable.[13] Once female criminality is taken seriously, of course, the list of important topics is only limited by the researchers' imagination. For instance, a searching look into female roles and their changes over time as intermediaries between the underworld and upperworld of the criminal justice systems in municipal America is needed.[14] Finally, while the subject of mobility in organized crime has long been posited,[15] the relationship between criminal mobility and marriage among criminals demands recognition and study.

Organized crime has been a functional part of urban America providing goods and services for a variety of patrons and clients and potential money and power for criminals both male and female. Contrary to many popular accounts organized crime is not the unique creation of any particular immigrant community, but flourished in a variety of urban ethnic communities. And as it was not ethnically unique, neither was it sexually segregated.

Notes

1. Alan Block (1975). "Lepke, Kid Twist and the Combination: Organized Crime in New York City, 1930–1944," (unpublished Ph.D. dissertation, UCLA). Especially chapter five.
2. See Howard B. Woolston (1969). *Prostitution in the United States: Prior to the Entrance of the United States into the World War.* Montclair, New Jersey: Patterson Smith; Edwin R. A. Seligman (ed.) (1912). *The Social Evil: With Special Reference to Conditions Existing in the City of New York.* New York: G. P. Putnam's Sons, chapters 1 and 6; Harry Benjamin and R. E. L. Masters (1964). *Prostitution and Morality: A Definitive Report on the Prostitute in Contemporary Society and an Analysis of the Causes and Effects of the Suppression of Prostitution,* New York: The Julian Press, Inc., chapters 3 and 4; Willoughby Cyrus Waterman (1932). *Prostitution and its Repression in New York City, 1900–1931.* New York: Columbia University Press; Helene Feldman King (1956). "The Banishment of Prudery: A Study of the Issue of Prostitution in the Progressive Era," unpublished Ph.D. dissertation, Columbia University; David J. Pivar (1973). *Purity Crusade: Sexual Morality and Social Control, 1868–1900.* Westport, Conn.: Greenwood Press, Inc., chapter 5; Roy Lubove (1963). *The Progressives and the Slums: Tenement House Reform in New York City, 1890–1917.* Pittsburgh: University of Pittsburgh Press, pp. 49–80, 132–149, and 187–215; Egal Feldman (1967). "Prostitution, the Alien Woman and the Progressive Imagination, 1910–1915," *American Quarterly,* XI (Summer). For some of the legislation dealing with prostitution including tenement house prostitution see *Digest of State and Federal Laws Dealing with Prostitution and other Sex Offenses, with Notes on the Control of the Sale of Alcoholic Beverages as it Relates to Prostitution Activities* (1942). New York: The American Social Hygiene Association, Inc., pp. 263–275.
3. In addition to the works cited above, one should also consult U.S. Congress, House, *White Slave Traffic,* H.R. 47, 61st Cong. 2d sess., where it is noted that "there are few who really understand the true significance of the term 'white-slave trade' . . . the inmates of many houses of ill fame are made up largely of women and girls whose original entry into a life of immorality was brought about by men . . . who by means of force and restraint, compel their victims to practice prostitution," p. 10. Much the same view is found in U.S. Congress, Senate, *Importing Women for Immoral Purposes,* S.D. 196, 61st Cong. 2d sess.

   The reported connections between New York's immigrant Jewish population and prostitution moved several residents of New York's Lower East Side to petition President William H. Taft protesting communal innocence. See U.S. Congress, Senate, *Petition of Citizens of Orchard, Rivington, and East Houston Streets, New York City, Relative to the Reports of Officials and the Conditions of Immigrants,* S.D. 785, 62nd Cong., 2d sess.

   A brilliant discussion of the whole issue of Jewish criminality during the Progressive Era is Arthur A. Goren's (1970). *New York Jews and the Quest for Community: The Kehillah Experiment, 1908–1922.* New York: Columbia University Press.
4. S. S. McClure (1909). "The Tammanyizing of a Civilization," *McClure's Magazine,* XXXIV (November). (1909), pp. 117–118.
5. George Kibbe Turner, "The Daughters of the Poor," Ibid., pp. 47, 49–52.
6. Goren, op. cit., pp. 138–144.
7. Feldman, op. cit. p. 197.
8. Moses Rischin (1962). *The Promised City: New York's Jews, 1870–1914.* New York: Harper & Row, pp. 77–78.
9. Information on the New York Kehillah was obtained from the Judah L. Magnes

Archives, The Central Archives for the History of the Jewish People, Jerusalem, Israel. I first became acquainted with the material in the Magnes Archives through Goren's study noted above. In Goren's note on sources he states that the Magnes Archives in Jerusalem "contain an outstanding collection of sources for the study of Jewish life in New York and Jewish communal politics in America from 1908 to 1922. . . . The largest part of this material consists of the Kehillah's records which contain a wealth of sources on Jewish education, religious life, philanthropic organization, industrial conditions, and crime". Using Goren's citation for the specific material on crime—MA (SP/125–SP/139)—I wrote to the Central Archives for the History of the Jewish People, Jerusalem, Israel, and requested a microfilm copy of the almost 2,000 "case histories of Jewish criminals prepared by the Kehillah's chief investigator and based on information supplied by his informers and agents." Ms. Hadassah Assouline of the Central Archives was kind enough to fulfill my request.

In his book on the Kehillah, Goren notes that the "first meeting of the executive committee" of the Kehillah set up "standing committees on religious organization, on Jewish education, on finance, on social and philanthropic work, and on propaganda and organization". It was the job of the committees to establish "permanent bureaus in their fields". The first bureau which dealt with Jewish education was formed in 1910. This was followed by the Bureau of Social Morals in 1912, and so on. Goren, op. cit., pp. 59–63.

10. Ibid., pp. 159–170.
11. George J. Kneeland (1913). *Commercialized Prostitution in New York City.* New York: The Century Co., p. 107. Kneeland's study is the definitive effort to investigate prostitution during the Progressive period. While extraordinarily inclusive and insightful, it suffers from a complete emphasis on prostitution, a system of documentation designed to protect identities, and a style that is characteristically male chauvinist.
12. Ibid., pp. 92–93.
13. Henry Miller (1955). *Nights of Love and Laughter.* New York: New American Library.
14. One might profitably consider the historical evidence gathered by Paul Blanshard head of the New York City Department of Investigations and Accounts in an investigation of bail-bond rackets in the mid-1930s. Blanshard identified 53 bail-bond racketeers 21 of whom were women. A breakdown of the ethnicity of the identified women racketeers reveals that 7 were Jewish, 7 Italian, 2 Hispanic, and 5 unidentifiable. See Department of Investigation and Accounts, *Investigating City Government in the La Guardia Administration: A Report of the Activities of the Department of Investigation and Accounts, 1934–1937.* Another important source for female involvement in bail-bonding rackets and loan sharking in the 1930s and 1940s is John Harlan Amen, *Report of the Kings County Investigation, 1938–1942.*
15. Daniel Bell (1962). "Crime as an American Way of Life: A Queer Ladder of Social Mobility," *The End of Ideology: On the Exhaustion of Political Ideas in the Fifties.* New York: Free Press, pp. 127–150.

18 Prostitution: An Extreme Case of Sex Stratification

Barbara Heyl

The basic idea of this selection is that sex-based inequalities exist at every level of social stratification in contemporary prostitution. There has been little attempt in the extensive literature on prostitution to analyze the occupation and the social world that surrounds it in social stratification terms, even though its different economic and prestige levels are usually acknowledged by authors dealing with the subject. In addition, with the exception of feminist writings on prostitution, no attempt has been made to relate male-female power differences to the social organization of the occupation.

Strong pressures stemming from the normative and structural characteristics of both the conventional and the prostitution worlds result in the dominance of prostitution by males. The control is exerted primarily by police, pimps, and legitimate businessmen (who employ prostitutes to service their customers). (The power of the prostitute's own clients will also be briefly discussed.) These three male groups—police, pimps, and businessmen—are differentially powerful at the three main levels of the occupation (streetwalking, the middle- or house-level of the business, and "call girl" operations). But males dominate at all levels by controlling the conditions under which the prostitute will work in her occupation. It may well be that the oldest profession is the most sexist of them all.

Presented to the Southwestern Sociological Association Meetings, Dallas, 9 April 1976, at the session on the Sociology of Sex Roles and Status, Mary Z. Ferrell, Chairperson.

The author wishes to acknowledge both the early support for this analysis and the helpful criticism of Joan Huber, University of Illinois at Urbana-Champaign, and the later substantive and editorial suggestions from Joseph L. Grabill, Illinois State University, Normal.

Social stratification of the prostitution world

Before beginning the analysis in sex stratification terms, I would like to describe briefly the *social* stratification of the prostitution world. In any serious discussion of prostitution it is necessary to distinguish among the various social-structural levels of the profession. (Thus, statements made about prostitution at the streetwalker level are frequently inaccurate when applied to call girls.) The various forms of prostitution can be grouped into three major levels, and these levels can be ranked roughly along both economic and prestige dimensions. The economic variable reflects the cost to client (rather than total profits, on which very little data are available—even to those within the business); the cost is always lowest at the bottom two levels of the hierarchy. The three main categories of professional prostitutes are: (1) streetwalkers; (2) prostitutes who work away from the street and charge middle-range prices; and (3) high-class call girls and convention or "party girls" associated with the business world. Prostitutes in the second category may work in hotels, bars, houses of prostitution, or for other small service businesses (such as massage parlors). Also in this category are some less expensive call girls. Madams, too, can be ranked on the same scale. That is, madams running "high-class" houses, with high costs to the clients, would be in a position comparable to the third category of prostitutes; all other madams would be in a position comparable to the second category. This paper, however, will deal with working prostitutes.

The prestige awarded these levels by those within the business usually parallels the cost-to-client hierarchy. Such a phenomenon is comparable to the tendency in conventional society to award greater prestige to those in sales or service who deal in expensive products whose price is to some extent negotiable and to award less prestige to those who sell relatively inexpensive products at fixed prices. Greenwald found the call girls he interviewed even identified themselves by the amount of money they charged. He writes that

> none of the girls included in this study would dream of charging less than fifty dollars. To do so would make them feel like "common prostitutes." Girls who charge above this minimum consider themselves on a higher status and one assured me . . . that she was "strictly a seventy-five dollar girl" (Greenwald, 1970:26–27).

Some prostitutes who work in houses, especially those in nonurban areas, may charge less than streetwalkers in urban areas. Nevertheless, streetwalkers are uniformly considered by all other prostitutes to be the lowest in the business. Streetwalkers, in retaliation, belittle the women who work in "cheap whorehouses"; they refer with disdain to such women as "flatbackers" (Sheehy, 1973:215; Milner and Milner, 1972:22, 247, 299).

One major characteristic of the stratified nature of the prostitution business is that there is little vertical mobility. A women who begins in the business as a streetwalker rarely becomes an independent call girl, and seldom does a call girl start walking the streets. The woman who has worked as a call girl has such a high professional opinion of her work and such a low one of streetwalkers—an attitude supported by all those in the business at the higher levels—that she could not "stoop so low" as to walk the streets. This attitude on the part of call girls also means that the streetwalker will be unlikely to find a call girl willing to train her in working at that level. Bryan (1965:296–297) found that being an apprentice to a working call girl was an effective way of gaining access to a list of clients—the key to beginning work at the call girl level. The streetwalker is also likely to have a pimp, as will be discussed later. Pimps who manage prostitutes at the streetwalker level have trained the women to work the "stroll." Pimps could encourage their women to obtain phone numbers from their street clients, gradually build up a book of such numbers, and then work out of their apartments as call girls. But although many pimps talk about developing "higher levels of the game," their actions seldom reflect such long-range planning for their prostitutes' careers (Milner and Milner, 1972:245–246).

The possibilities for movement into or out of the middle level of the prostitution world are somewhat greater than movement between the two extreme levels. A woman working for a madam may be able to steal clients from the house and set herself up in an independent call operation. The call girl may find a madam she feels is "high class" and decide to let the madam handle the problems with clients and the police, rather than have to handle them herself as an "independent call girl." The streetwalker, on the other hand, may find a madam who will accept her. But for the most part, the level at which the woman begins work in the prostitution world determines her general position in the occupation for much of her career as a prostitute. Changing levels requires contacts and a new set of work techniques and attitudes. The social networks within each level help maintain negative stereotypes of women working at the other levels and help prohibit vertical mobility in the structure of the occupation.

There is some evidence that the woman's economic background is an important predictor of the level of prostitution at which she will work. Greenwald's sample of call girls is one of the largest samples of professionals at that level for which economic background data are available.

> The facts about the socio-economic background of these girls were a surprising revelation. Many people think that all prostitutes come from extreme poverty. Three of the girls came from upper-class parents, fourteen from middle-class parents, and only three came from lower-class parents (Greenwald, 1970:163).

Bryan's 1965 study of call girls did not report class background for his sample. One can roughly infer class origin from Hall's 1973 extensive interview data. Of the four women at the top levels in the business, three—Foxy, the call girl for the garment manufacturer, and two of the three independent call girls— came from middle- or upper-class backgrounds (1973:102, 210, 220–221). (There was no background material on the third call girl or for the two madams interviewed by Hall.) It appears that Sherry, the masseuse, came from a middle-class black family, and the two streetwalkers from lower-class families

(1973:68, 18, 58). Thus, the economic backgrounds of Hall's sample seem to parallel their levels in the prostitution business. That the streetwalker usually comes from the lower classes is considered well known both in and out of the business. After a jail experience that brought streetwalkers and "house girls" together, one house prostitute was impressed with how much more calmly the streetwalker endured the experience than did the madam's middle-class women.

> The streetwalker is the toughest kind of prostitute in the world. She's made of another thing. . . . She has stamina and fortitude above and beyond middle-class America. Maybe because she's from the lower class. Higher-class chicks don't walk the street, because it's a whole different existence (Hall, 1973:194).

But that the call girls come primarily from middle- and upper-class backgrounds was, as Greenwald notes, a surprise. The stratification system of conventional society does not lose its impact, even during the complex process of moving into an illegal occupation.

Sex stratification

Acker (1973:936–941) argues that sex status is a much-neglected factor in stratification theory and research that, when taken into account, can help explain differentials in wealth, prestige, and power among individuals. To utilize sex as an explanatory variable in structural analyses, Acker recommends making the basic unit of study the individual, rather than the family, and accepting the following assumptions:

1. Sex is an enduring ascribed characteristic which (a) has an effect upon the evaluation of persons and positions, and (b) is the basis of the persisting sexual division of labor and sex-based inequalities.
2. The sex dichotomy cuts across all class and strata (Acker, 1973:940).

Sex stratification, then, refers to the economic, status, and power differences existing between males and females in any given social system. This selection attempts to apply these concepts to the prostitution world and explicate the relationship between the three main social structural levels of the occupation and the male-female power difference that exists at each level. For just as sex-based inequalities have been slighted in stratification literature on conventional society, so are they seldom systematically analyzed in the studies of deviant worlds.

To assert that prostitution in America is dominated by males at all levels is scarcely to distinguish it from the great variety of American professional and business enterprises—both legal and illegal. It can be distinguished from all others, however, in that only in heterosexual prostitution is woman the sole product line of the business—a product that, precisely because of her physiological characteristics as woman, makes the enterprise possible in the first place.

Table 1 **Some types of male power in the prostitution world**

MALE GROUP	TYPE OF POWER AVAILABLE
Police	Political power
Pimps	Physical power, psychological power
Businessmen (employers of prostitutes)	Economic power
Clients	Consumer power

The power of males over the working prostitute is defined as their ability to control the conditions under which she will work in her occupation.[1] Such control includes the men's ability to arrest the prostitute, to take a systematic "cut" (or even all) of her earnings, or to provide her with a necessary set of business arrangements (a setting, a "front," or a steady well-paying clientele). The table above indicates a tentative labeling of the type of power utilized by the different male groups with whom the prostitute has contact.[2]

The data presented in the central sections of the paper will illuminate the ways in which these types of power operate in the prostitution world. The power of the police rests in the laws making prostitution illegal and charging the police with enforcing the law. The pimps, as the only males in residence in the prostitution world, find power in their physical presence as the prostitutes' companions, lovers, and "protectors" from other male power. Pimps can and do use their superior physical strength against the prostitute, but most also use psychology—socializing the prostitute into accepting pimp control over her life. The woman's dependent position in a pimp-dominated sector of the prostitution world is expected and reinforced by both pimps and prostitutes. The woman's acceptance of that position reflects primarily the social pressures of living in that world more than it reveals some "need" in the woman's personality to be "dominated."

The businessmen who hire prostitutes to serve clients of their own, in order to increase the profits of their particular enterprise, can provide prostitutes with a chance to make steady money in a setting relatively safe from police harassment. To the extent that the prostitute wants such advantages, she must also conform to her employers' conditions. The prostitute's own clients exert control over her in much the same way as do customers of other small service businesses. They may deliberately boycott a particular establishment or simply be uninterested in what that business has to offer. In either case, the clients can exercise power over the prostitute by withholding the source of her income. Clients of a prostitute may also use physical power, by refusing to pay the prostitute or by harming her. But because the clients' power can be exercised over prostitutes working at any level of the occupation, this selection will emphasize the power of other male groups.

The power of police, pimps, and businessmen is differentially prevalent at the various levels of the occupation. The remainder of the selection is devoted to analyzing how the lifestyle associated with a particular level of the prostitution world is related to the type of male control over the women who work at that level. The major relationships are shown in Table 2.

Table 2 **Strata of the prostitution world and powerful male groups**

LEVEL OF PROSTITUTION	MALES WITH POWER AT THAT LEVEL
Streetwalkers	Police, pimps
Middle-range prostitutes (houses, hotels, massage parlors)	"Fringe" businessmen, pimps
	Legitimate, even top-level,
Independent call girls, party girls	businessmen

The streetwalker level—police and pimps

Streetwalkers are usually the least expensive prostitutes in cost to clients, have the least prestige within the business, and are the most vulnerable to male domination—primarily from police and pimps. The laws that prohibit prostitution should make all prostitutes subject to arrest, but due to the streetwalker's visibility in public places and the policeman's greater freedom to make arrests in public places (see Stinchcombe, 1963), the arrests for prostitution are overwhelmingly at the streetwalker level. New York lawyer Robert Sherwin, Director of the Society for the Scientific Study of Sex, notes: "We in the legal profession see the seamy side of the administration of prostitution laws and are amazed at the discrepancy in enforcement toward a $15 streetwalker as opposed to a $500 call girl" (1972:66). Some urban police departments set quotas for members of the vice squad. To fill such quotas— that is, to "do their job"—these policemen must make a certain number of prostitution arrests in a given time period. One way of meeting these requirements is to determine who the streetwalkers are in their area and then arrest the same women on a regular basis. One streetwalker describes this process:

> The cops have to turn in a certain number of girls every night. . . . The cops know me personally. They see me out there every night and automatically know what I'm doing—whether I be doing it or not. I can just walk down the street and they pick me up and take me to jail.
> If the cop picked me up for a "discon" [disorderly conduct charge] when he saw me talking to a guy . . . that would be okay. But I resent going into a restaurant and having a cop come in and take me out (Hall, 1973:60–61).

Liz Schneider, who has worked in the New York court system, notes that police arrest of prostitutes is a form of harassment, since the women seldom spend any time in prison. "Since I've been in court I've seen cases of women who have been arrested for years and years for nothing but prostitution— thirty-five, forty arrests in a year, maybe. Just back and forth, coming in and out" (Millett, 1973:148).

Repeated arrests result in repeated fines for streetwalkers. The more serious charges require bond money, and to meet these costs the streetwalker must rely on someone who has a stake in her trade but who is not subject to arrest. Schneider observes that in the New York City Criminal Court, where prostitutes are arraigned, "Every woman I've seen who comes in to pay bail, comes

in with a man, so one may be sure there is still a very active pimp trade"
(Millett, 1973:151). To rely on another prostitute to get her out of jail would
be risky. For, although prostitutes appear to treat one another cordially, there
is little real solidarity among them (Millett, 1973:152–153; Milner and Milner,
1972:56). Prostitutes know that the world around them is dominated by males;
they feel they need a man beside them to make their way in that world. As
one former streetwalker puts it: "If you're gonna whore you need protection:
a man's protection from other men. All men are in the protection business"
(Millett, 1973:130).

Pimps are quick to remind the prostitutes of their need for protection against
law enforcement on the street. Thus they are able to use police harassment
to heighten the woman's sense of her own vulnerability and the consequent
need for help. But the basis for prostitutes' feelings of vulnerability are real
enough. Police arrest streetwalkers in large numbers, and time in jail—even
if brief—is always a distressing experience. Kitty, a New York streetwalker,
describes the impact on the prostitute:

> I hate jail. It takes part of my mind away everytime I go. In jail, I'm
> losing. I'm caught. There ain't nothing I can do about it. I can't use my
> head. I can't trick my way out. I'm locked up in a little room. The cops
> have more on me than I have on them. I'm trapped (Hall, 1973:47).

A good pimp can keep his women out of jail by having the fine or bail money
available at all times. The lone streetwalker may not have such funds at hand.
The streetwalker with a pimp, however, has this important financial pillar;
he is her protection against the jail experience (Hall, 1973:50–51). To be sure,
whether the pimp is there with the money when she needs him may be
another matter. As Kitty notes, the pimp may have to choose between getting
his El Dorado out of the shop or his "lady" out of jail; the car—critical to his
social status in the prostitution world—may come first (Hall, 1973:50–51).
Lacking any connection with a pimp, however, the streetwalker finds her
position especially precarious.

The streetwalker's dilemma between the police and her pimp is clear: Not
only does police harassment encourage her liaison with a pimp, but that very
liaison may increase her harassment by the police. As Cindy, a New York
streetwalker, notes:

> Cops anywhere resent players and their ladies. They hurt us and harass
> us and figure that's money out of our pockets. One time my man got
> arrested. The first thing the cop said was, "I hate pimps and junkies."
> Cops don't make much money so they can't stand to see someone else
> doing good (Hall, 1973:62).

Some streetwalkers feel that police hostility toward pimps is related not only
to their illegal source of income but frequently has racial overtones as well.
A majority of pimps in Northern cities are black, while many of their prostitutes are white[3]—a fact that bothers white policemen (see Hall, 1973:46). In
any case, because arresting a pimp is usually difficult, police may try to get

at the pimp by repeatedly arresting one or more of his "ladies." Kitty, a white woman with a black pimp, describes the policeman's attitude:

> The pross cop [whose task is to make prostitution arrests], Pete, arrests me every time he sees me. . . . He does it 'cause I'm with Daddy. He likes me as a person, but he wants me to go straight and be without a pimp. Whenever I leave Daddy, Pete don't arrest me. As soon as he finds out I've gone back [to Daddy], he puts me in jail (Hall, 1973:45–46).

One cannot assume, of course, that if Kitty left "Daddy" she would no longer be subject to arrest. As a streetwalker she may still be arrested by a policeman with less knowledge of, or interest in, Kitty's personal freedom as a prostitute. Police arrests are an indirect form of pressure on working prostitutes to establish a connection with a pimp. But pimps can use direct pressure of their own, especially at the streetwalker level. For just as police are free to patrol public areas where prostitutes are known to stand, so are the pimps. To be successful, a streetwalker must be visible in an area where she is likely to encounter potential clients—an area known as a streetwalker's "stroll." A woman without a pimp who decides to walk the "stroll" to make money for herself as a prostitute finds herself in a very difficult situation. One call girl describes the situation on Lexington Avenue in New York City:

> Every girl [there] has a pimp. If you tried to work the street on your own, you'd get caught by a pimp after two or three days out. Pimps drive around and watch *their* territory. If they think you're working alone and won't join up, they'll think nothing of just breaking a couple of your arms. The street is dangerous and rough for an individual entrepreneur. As a matter of fact, it's impossible (Hall, 1973:57).

To be sure, if a would-be streetwalker wants to go into business for herself and walks in areas where no interested clients would find her, her actions will raise no objections from any pimp. But in areas where a streetwalker can make money, the pimps enforce the rule that she must have a pimp if she wishes to be left alone by other pimps. The question is: How do pimps manage to know the street situation well enough to control it so completely? For example, could not the independent streetwalker simply announce, in answer to queries from pimps and other women on the "stroll," that she has an "old man"? At this point we encounter the grapevine of the prostitution world as a form of social control and the norm of male solidarity among pimps. Pimps know which men are in "the life" and can readily verify a prostitute's claim about already being with a pimp. But most importantly, pimps will cooperate in intimidating any woman who attempts to undermine their control of their particular sector of the prostitution world. This male solidarity among pimps was documented by the Milners in their five-year study of black pimps in San Francisco. Using anthropological techniques to study the culture of the pimps' social world, the Milners analyzed the rules of the game—the norms devised by the pimps to insure that they maintain control over their working prostitutes, who are their main source of income. The first rule is simply that the man is dominant over the woman. His control over her must be made obvious to others by her behavior toward him in public.

> When in the company of others, she must take special pains to treat him with absolute deference and respect. She must light his cigarettes, respond to his every whim immediately, and never, never contradict him. In fact, a ho is strictly not supposed to speak in the company of pimps unless spoken to (Milner and Milner, 1972:53).

The novice prostitute is taught that the slightest failure to show deference to her pimp in public will result in his losing status in the eyes of his peers (Milner and Milner, 1972:55; Heyl, 1974:74–75). Other pimps are quick to note and act on any evidence that a fellow pimp is not in complete control of his woman. Their actions, verbal or gestural, always support the pimp against the woman. As the Milners explain:

> This support of another pimp by his peers is both a signal that he is in danger of losing respect, and a show of male solidarity which the ho is not strong enough to withstand. Her loyalty to her man and her fear of his joining with other pimps against her are both evoked. Male dominance is therefore reinforced by every pimp backing up every other pimp (Milner and Milner, 1972:55).

The norm of male solidarity, then, is the second rule in the game. Under this rule, the pimps help one another out of financial difficulties whenever possible and prevent the women from ever playing one pimp off against another.

The pimps' rules of the game are meant to insure pimp control of their part of the prostitution business. Any independent prostitute who encounters that world—for example, by entering the street territory, bar, hotel, or house circuit controlled by a group of pimps—will meet the combined resistance of the pimps involved. Greenwald also found cooperation among pimps of call girls (1970:214). A woman who wishes to work as a prostitute without a pimp or to enjoy the company of a pimp without paying him for it will be criticized, belittled, and even threatened by the pimps she encounters (Milner and Milner, 1972:41; Hall, 1973:57). This social pressure is especially strong at the street and middle levels of prostitution. It is a genuinely sociological reason for the prostitute's liaison with a pimp. It is clear that, especially at the streetwalker level, the woman is caught between combined pimp and police power. Her decision to link up with a pimp may be necessary if she is to have "space" to work; it can be seen, therefore, as rational in economic and social terms, rather than requiring explanation in terms of her personality "needs."

Middle-range prostitutes—"fringe" businessmen and pimps

Prostitutes who work away from the streets—in houses, out of hotels that cater to prostitution, or in other small businesses, such as massage parlors—are freer from police power because their contacts with clients are made on private property. Thus, the police must be admitted to the premises before they can make a legal arrest. But to work indoors requires that the prostitute gain access as well. Madams always screen their potential employees, hoping to find "trustworthy" and congenial women who will be good moneymakers; but many will not hire a woman without a pimp (Heyl, 1974:67–69), feeling that if they have problems with a woman working in the house, they can simply call the woman's pimp and he will "straighten her out." Thus, access to house prostitution can be difficult for the individual entrepreneur.

In addition to screening out independent prostitutes, those madams who "turn out" women for pimps, that is, train novice prostitutes to become "professionals," teach them the pimps' rules of showing deference, turning over all earnings, and exhibiting complete honesty and fidelity to the pimp (Heyl, 1977). The pimps' power to see that their new women are trained in the proper attitudes extends to all levels of the prostitution world. Gray found that at the streetwalker level pimps soon took over the socialization of the new prostitutes, even those who initially began working as independents; the pimps' training consisted primarily of instilling a "proper attitude toward work" rather than teaching sexual or social skills (1973:413). Bryan found that even at the call girl level pimps were able to exercise power over the socialization of their new recruits: "Although the data are limited, it appears that the pimp retains his dominance over the trainee even when the latter is being trained by a call girl. The girl trainer remains deferential to the pimp's wishes regarding the novice" (Bryan, 1965:290). These training patterns tend to perpetuate pimp control even into the middle and upper levels of the prostitution business, although the training described pertains to women who enter those levels already committed to a pimp. Independents, if they can find an establishment that will accept them, may find training free of pimp indoctrination. There are some indications that at the house level of the occupation, increasing numbers of women are entering prostitution without pimps (Heyl, 1977:546). Thus, women entering prostitution at the middle level must combat the same types of obstacles women in the straight world do when they seek access to higher education and top jobs: first, the structural barriers of access, and second, the socialization patterns designed to keep them in their "place" (see, for example, Roby, 1972).

An example of a woman who moved into the middle level of prostitution, finding a space to work off the streets in a massage parlor and freeing herself from pimp control is Sherry, who tells her story in Hall's (1973) collection of autobiographical statements from working prostitutes in New York. Sherry states that she is from a middle-class black family, turned out with a pimp for three years, and then "began to see the pimp's game—he gets all the goodies and you have nothing substantial" (1973:68–70). When she left her pimp, she asserts that he did not give her a difficult time: "He was smart and knew that I'd just outgrown the pimp-whore thing" (Hall, 1973:70). She worked in bars and from her apartment by way of the telephone, before taking the job as a masseuse. Sherry cites not only her freedom from pimp exploitation but the security from the police that working for a business provides her: "I'm actually protected in the massage salon. [When I was on the street] . . . I spent all my time running away from the cops and playing hide and seek. Here, the boss can look out for me" (Hall, 1973:75). The problem is that the woman may not have as much protection as she thinks she does. The manager of the massage salon may claim ignorance of what takes place in the rooms, so that if a policeman arrests the masseuse for illegal procedures, she goes to jail but the manager does not (Sterba, 1974). The same illusions of security plague the house prostitute. Hall notes such a case:

> Every girl who worked for the madam thought she was protected. The madam had told me she paid the cops in her precinct. Part of the fifty-percent cut she takes from the girls covers police protection. When the house was raided, everyone had a different version of the mistake or mismanagement (Hall, 1973:190).

Male power is certainly diminished at the middle level of prostitution when compared with the streetwalker level. Pimps and police have somewhat less control over the women working indoors. Yet at this level, the madams (often with males in the background) and "fringe" businessmen, such as owners and managers of "prostitution hotels" and massage salons, take a cut of the prostitute's earnings while "protecting" her. The protection may or may not be there when she needs it, but in the meantime she has steadily satisfied the clientele of whatever business establishment she works for, so that the owners can make a profit.

The call girl level—legitimate businessmen

At the call girl level the prostitute is not subjected to the major pressures toward pimp dependence discussed earlier and should—given the hypothesis that such factors make a difference—be correspondingly freer of pimps. When compared to that practiced on streetwalkers and bar hustlers, police harassment of call girls is virtually nonexistent. The call girl frequently works from her private apartment, making appointments with clients by phone, and thus never appears in any public place as a prostitute. The pimps, too, have less power over her because she is not working on the streets or in business establishments, where their group social pressure can be brought to bear. Nonetheless, many call girls still have pimps. One madam has tried to explain why this is so: "It's very difficult for a call girl to have a social life. Her hours are hectic. The only people who go along with those hours are men who don't work—like pimps" (Hall, 1973:168). She notes, however, that mere congruity of working hours can scarcely account for this particular liaison; after all, other men are on the same schedule—bartenders, actors, musicians. But she adds what may well be the decisive reason for the call girl's tie with a pimp—the factor of prestige.

> Status is important to every girl in the business—the minks, the Lincoln Continental—those she must have. A girl with a pimp is particularly conscious of the show. He must have a brand new Cadillac every year, two-hundred-dollar suits, and she, sharp clothes and a mink. That is status (Hall, 1973:168-169).

Since respectability from the rest of society is denied even the call girl (if her occupation is known), she may seek prestige within the prostitution world. And the pimp, with his flashy style, can add to the impression she makes on her peers.

There are, however, many call girls who do not have pimps. In Greenwald's study of twenty call girls, only six had pimps—and two of those six may not have been professional pimps: one was a struggling artist and the other was more involved in dope pushing than pimping (1970:247–293). In Bryan's sample of thirty-three call girls, approximately two-thirds had no pimp at the time they were interviewed (1973:268). These two extensive investigations at the call girl level lend substantial support to the hypothesis that the sociological characteristics at this level facilitate greater freedom from pimp domination.

Henriques (1968), in the final pages of his three-volume historical study of prostitution in Western societies, concludes that the call girl form of prostitution is increasing rapidly due to the advanced economic development in these countries. He notes, too, that the hiring of call girls by business firms (frequently into their public relations departments) is described by businessmen as "the fastest way" for a firm to establish "an intimate relationship" with a buyer (1968:315). This modern response by business to an old demand confirms Henriques' basic thesis: "The type of prostitution which occurs is dependent upon the structure of the society in question. The call-girl constellation has arisen in response to social and economic changes in our society—legislation against street soliciting combined with economic expansion" (1968:315). In 1952, C. Wright Mills (1963) was perhaps the first sociologist to analyze the rise of the call girl career in response to new styles of conducting American business. Based on her own experience, an independent call girl describes the use of prostitution by modern businessmen:

> Prostitution may not be legal, but it is certainly legitimate. . . . Every industry in the world—manufacturing, import, export—every business would collapse if businessmen didn't use prostitution as a manipulating means of entertaining, a method of increasing sales and pacifying clients . . . our backs are the bridges which link business deals (Hall, 1973:204).

In the garment industry, for example, a buyer expects the merchandiser to provide him with a prostitute, compliments of the firm. The merchandiser may utilize a list of call girls when buyers are in town, or he may have a call girl on salary with the firm whom he may call at any time. Foxy has the latter arrangement with a garment manufacturer; she is white and apparently from an upper-class family (Hall, 1973:102).

> Foxy: I am a businesswoman. I happen to work as a hooker in the garment center. I am employed by a manufacturer, who pays me, and *well*, for my work. There's no baloney with cuts. I don't give my money to anyone. I do my work professionally and keep the profits for me! Working for a business protects me—I'm out of sight of the law and my employer knows each man I see. That's the advantage of my position (Hall, 1973:84).

Although she had had a good deal of sexual experience, Foxy was just sixteen when she first took a job with this company. She fell in love with her boss. The boss and his partner talked her into working for them as a prostitute and trained her to be a professional. Her original commitment is stated in terms strikingly similar to those of women who go to work for pimps: "I was in love with the boss. The boss's first love was his business. I knew I could help his business if I decided to work. So I did" (Hall, 1973:87).

In one sense, the call girl with strong business ties has traded her pimp for the businessman. It is an improvement: Her money is her own. But he provides the clients and is thus a pimp in the older, "procurer" meaning of the term. He can cut her off when she no longer pleases him; and for each client she sees for him, he gains, perhaps in vast sums of money for his business, while she earns her salary or is simply paid for seeing the one man. The legitimate businessman benefits from prostitution but avoids its stigma, while the prostitute is vulnerable to the penalties—socially and legally—for what she does.

Conclusion

Pimps, police, and businessmen—the male groups discussed here as having power over the prostitute—are only a few of the male-dominated groups that limit the prostitute's freedom while benefiting financially from her work. Sheehy notes: "Landlords are the one aspect of prostitution which has been almost totally ignored" (1973:12). She researched the names of owners of New York City property being used for prostitution, massage parlors, and pornography businesses and published the results, which were "all very embarrassing." It was a list of some of the most prestigious and wealthy men in the city, including politicians, bankers, and a relative of former President Nixon (1973:12). Efforts have been made recently to apply to these cases the law that makes the landlord responsible for the illegal use of his properties. But Sheehy adds: "Every city has these money-insulated real estate moguls. And every city to a greater or lesser degree guards them" (1973:13).

Numerous other male groups benefit from prostitution. Sheehy notes that politicians and police win public approval and support with each of their highly publicized "cleanup" campaigns (1973:11–12). The men on prostitution squads earn their living because prostitution is a thriving business that society has made illegal. Some policemen gain in payoffs from prostitutes and madams seeking to avoid arrest. The courts make fine and bond money from the steady processing of prostitutes in and out of the judicial system (Millett, 1973:160). Doctors and lawyers who cater to prostitutes are overpaid on a regular basis (Laner, 1973:415–416). Even taxi drivers and bellhops demand a cut of the woman's profits in return for sending her business or as a form of blackmail of a call girl. Sheehy notes the unfairness of a situation in which we exact "penalties for our moral hypocrisy" from the prostitutes, while all these other groups (including pimps and clients) benefit and go free (1973:200). The analysis developed here reveals prostitution as an extreme case of sex stratification—all the males win, and only the women pay the costs.

Finally, the penalties of prostitution do not fall evenly on all women in the business. The combined police and pimp power at the lower levels of the occupation places the prostitute in a more dependent position than does the economically based power of the businessmen at the upper levels. At the lower levels, the prostitute's very survival could be dependent on her male connection. Moreover, analysis of the stratified nature of the prostitution world shows that upward mobility in the occupation is rare. The woman's chances for working at the call girl level, where she has some degree of autonomy, are contingent on where she enters the profession in the first place. And the economic/class background of the woman appears to be a strong indicator of the level at which she will begin work as a prostitute. Thus, women working at the lower levels of the prostitution world are the most dominated by male power and the most vulnerable; we find here, once again, the perpetual victims—the women of the lower classes.

Notes

1. This definition falls within Weber's broader definition of power: "the chance of a man or of a number of men to realize their own will in a communal action even against the resistance of others who are not participating in the action" (Gerth and Mills, 1958:180).
2. This is a tentative identification of power dimensions at work in the prostitution world. There are, of course, other male groups with power to take a cut of the prostitute's earnings, such as landlords, doctors, lawyers, and bellhops and taxi drivers who "refer" clients to the prostitute.
3. In Southern cities the situation is often reversed—many pimps are white with black prostitutes.

References

Acker, Joan. 1973. "Women and Social Stratification: A Case of Intellectual Sexism." *American Journal of Sociology*, 78:936–945.

Benjamin, Harry, and R. E. L. Masters. 1964. *Prostitution and Morality*. New York: Julian Press.

Bryan, James H. 1965. "Apprenticeships in Prostitution." *Social Problems*, 12:287–297.

Gerth, H. H., and C. Wright Mills. 1958. *From Max Weber: Essays in Sociology*. New York: Oxford University Press. Originally published in 1946.

Gray, Diana. 1973. "Turning-out: A Study of Teenage Prostitution." *Urban Life and Culture*, 1:401–425.

Greenwald, Harold. 1970. *The Elegant Prostitute: A Social and Psychological Study*. New York: Walker & Company.

Hall, Susan. 1973. *Ladies of the Night*. New York: Trident Press.

Henriques, Fernando. 1968. *Modern Sexuality: Volume III of Prostitution and Society*. London: MacGibbon & Kee.

Heyl, Barbara Sherman. 1974. "The Madam as Entrepreneur." *Sociological Symposium*, 11:61–82.

———. 1977. "The Madam as Teacher: The Training of House Prostitutes." *Social Problems*, 24 (June): 545–555.

Laner, Mary Riege. 1974. "Prostitution as an Illegal Vocation: A Sociological Overview." *Deviant Behavior: Occupational and Organizational Bases*, edited by Clifton D. Bryant. Chicago: Rand McNally. Pp. 406–418.

Millett, Kate. 1973. *The Prostitution Papers: A Candid Dialogue.* New York: Avon Books.

Mills, C. Wright. 1963. "Plain Talk on Fancy Sex." *Power Politics and People: The Collected Essays of C. Wright Mills,* edited by I. L. Horowitz. New York: Ballantine Books. Pp. 324–329. Originally published as "Girls Using Vice to Help Careers," *New York Journal American International,* August 31, 1952.

Milner, Christina, and Richard Milner. 1972. *Black Players: The Secret World of Black Pimps.* Boston: Little, Brown.

Roby, Pamela. 1972. "Structural and Internalized Barriers to Women in Higher Education." In *Toward a Sociology of Women,* edited by Constantina Safilios-Rothschild. Lexington, Mass.: Xerox College Publishing. Pp. 121–140.

Sheehy, Gail. 1973. *Hustling: Prostitution in Our Wide-Open Society.* New York: Delacorte Press.

Sherwin, Robert Veit, and Charles Winick. 1972. "Debate: Should Prostitution be Legalized?" *Sexual Behavior* (January):66–73.

Sterba, James P. 1974. "Prostitution Is Flourishing in Rich Exurban Market." *New York Times,* June 9, 1974, Section 1, p. 55.

Stinchcombe, Arthur L. 1963. "Institutions of Privacy in the Determination of Police Administrative Practice." *American Journal of Sociology,* 69:150–160.

19 The Prostitution Papers

Kate Millett

I don't think you can ever eliminate the economic factor motivating women to prostitution. Even a call girl could never make as much in a straight job as she could at prostitution. All prostitutes are in it for the money. With most uptown call girls, the choice is not between starvation and life, but it is a choice between $5,000 and $25,000 or between $10,000 and $50,000. That's a pretty big choice: a pretty big difference. You can say that they're in this business because of the difference of $40,000 a year. A businessman would say so. Businessmen do things because of the difference of $40,000 a year. Call girls do go into capitalism and think like capitalists. But you can't say, even of the call girl, that she has so many other ways to earn an adequate living. Even with an undergraduate degree, chances are that she couldn't do better than earn $5,000 or $6,000 a year, outside of prostitution. Because it's very *hard* for women to earn an adequate living and so we do not have much economic choice—even the call girl. And the minority woman on the street— the poor woman—she has no choice at all.

For white women you usually can't say that there's no choice but prostitution. There is. But the choice itself is a choice between working for somebody else and going into business for yourself. Going into business for yourself and hoping to make a lot of money. There's that choice. Prostitution on those terms is a kind of laissez-faire capitalism. But it's also slavery, psychologically. And it's also feudalism, where the protection of a pimp is offered in return for services. Unless you're starving so bad you literally have no choice—as some women do—the choice is between a lower-middle income and a really good one, lots of money. Lots of whores are on junk: it's expensive. A junkie has very little choice. For the junkie the only choice is getting off junk, a tough thing to do. Then too, a junkie off junk wouldn't be a junkie anymore. Prostitution is a kind of addiction too. It's an addiction to money. I felt that.

The worst part about prostitution is that you're obliged not to sell sex only, but your humanity. That's the worst part of it: that what you're selling is your human dignity. Not really so much in bed, but in accepting the agreement—in becoming a bought person. When I really felt like a whore was when I had to talk to them, fucking up to them really while only talking. That's why I don't like to go out to dinner and why I don't like to spend the night. Because when they talk about "niggers," you've just got to go "uh-huh, uh-huh" and agree with them. That's what I really couldn't stand. It was that kind of thing. That's when I really felt I was kissing their ass—*more* than when I was literally kissing their ass. That's when I really felt that I was a whore. That's the most humiliating thing—having to agree with them all the time because you're bought.

That's why it's not as easy as just saying "prostitution is selling a service." That's why it's selling your soul and not selling a service. In business people sell their souls too, and that's why business destroys people—how would you feel about selling encyclopedias to poor people? But there's a special indignity in prostitution, as if sex were dirty and men can only enjoy it with someone *low*. It involves a type of contempt, a kind of disdain, and a kind of triumph over another human being. Guys who can't get it up with their wives can do it with whores. They have to pay for it. For some of them, *paying* for it is very important.

20 The Oldest and Newest Profession
Freda Adler

While it may be, as the experience of history suggests, that prostitution will remain with us indefinitely, it is also true that so long as it remains illicit, reliable data on its prevalence will be difficult to obtain. The only hard figures available come from the number of arrests, but we do not have a formula for estimating the ratio of number of offenses to number of arrests. Even if we did, however, victimless crimes such as prostitution generate such an uneven response from the public and law-enforcement agencies that they are subject to considerable variation in criteria for arrest. For example, many are arrested for vagrancy or disorderly conduct instead of the more severe charge of prostitution. Furthermore, arrest rates may reflect fluctuations in the activity of law-enforcement groups as well as fluctuations in offenses. An additional source of error in the arrest figures is the fact that those figures include multiple arrests of the same individual.[1]

According to speculative estimates, there are approximately one hundred thousand full-time prostitutes who work six days a week and service an average of three clients per day.[2] At an assumed average fee of $10, a prostitute grosses about $9300. There is thought to be an even larger but undetermined number of part-time prostitutes. The Americal Social Health Association has developed an index of commercialized prostitution which makes chronological comparisons possible. Pegging the categories of no commercialized prostitution at "0" and flagrant prostitution at "100," they have compiled the following figures:

From *Sisters in Crime: The Rise of the New Female Criminal* by Freda Adler. Pp. 64–74, 82–83, 263–264. Copyright © 1975 by Freda Adler. Used with permission of Mc-Graw-Hill Book Company.

Years	Average national score
1920–1929	99
1930–1938	92
1940–1946	49
1947–1949	74
1950–1959	35
1967	37

It would appear from these figures that, except for a post–World War II flare-up (which was not paralleled by a similar rise after the Korean war), commercial prostitution has shown the steady decline characteristic of a dying business. That is not to say that prostitution is a declining activity—it has, as we have said, attracted a large influx of part-timers—but simply that as an organized business enterprise it is languishing.

The patronage has shifted steadily to the "daytimers"—white, haughty, and businesslike—whose ranks include ex-models, jobless actresses, and bored housewives, who add upward of $60 per contact to their household budget. Police estimate that as many as 10 per cent of the prostitutes cruising Times Square on weekends are housewives from Long Island and New Jersey. There is also a younger set—the long-haired, high-booted, miniskirted amateurs from the suburbs or exurbs—whose carelessness and lack of experience make them easy prey for bulls (plainclothes policemen) and meat salesmen (pimps) alike, both of whom are interested in them but for different reasons. The independent call girls, unattached to pimps or madams, cluster around conventions, seeking the lucrative white-collar end of the business which might net them $1000 a week.

Aside from their common activity, there is little that distinguishes these women as a group. Here great change has occurred. They have not retained the solidarity of the pimp-run stables and madam-hosted brothels, nor have they developed an extensive and identifying argot. They are essentially individual operators unsupported by a social structure within which they can or would necessarily wish to advance. They may be the object of a recruiting campaign by pimps and they may be aware of the advantages of having a man around, but most will opt for individual ownership of their bodies.

The days of the colorful pimps and flamboyant madams, like Detroit's Silver-Tongue Jean and New York's Jennie the Factory, have for the most part passed into history, victims of their high visibility to the vice squad and changing social styles. In the heyday of the brothel, during the decades of the twenties and thirties, the madam served as entrepreneur, talent scout, public-relations agent, liaison officer to the police department, and housemother to her girls and their customers alike.[3] Within the madam's house (which Polly Adler wittily described as not the least bit homely) were "wives," who belonged to or were in the stable of a pimp.

The pimp not only helped prostitutes with the police and posted their bail, but he would also strong-arm obstreperous customers and prostitutes as he deemed appropriate. In 1935 it was estimated that there were sixty-three hundred pimps in Chicago alone.[4] Their ethnic background has tended to be similar to that of their stables, Italian and Jewish in the 1920s and 1930s, and more recently black and Puerto Rican. Sociologically, it would appear that these populations represented immigrant or otherwise disadvantaged groups which were nevertheless rising in social acceptance. Sex, like money, is a medium of exchange which often transcends social barriers, and for many of these girls it was their first contact with the American Establishment. But prostitution, like other labor-intense, service-oriented industries, could not enjoy the economies which ordinarily come with increases in size and concentration. On the contrary, the size of the brothel or stable was a double liability, exposing them to the depredations of both dishonest and honest police work through payoffs and raids, respectively. It was partly because size became counterproductive that the trend since the 1940s has been toward dispersion and individual entrepreneurships, making the role of the pimp largely but not entirely anachronistic.

The place is Sunset Strip, not far from the famed intersection of Hollywood and Vine, and the last bit of daylight is fading behind the mountains. It is just about "git-down time," the hour when the street-walkers "hit the bricks" in downtown Los Angeles to begin their nocturnal trolling for customers. On one corner, propped jauntily against a bus-stop bench, is Willie. Around the corner is Willie's car. It is a Cadillac, lime-green with large diamond-shaped cutouts in the rear window. Willie is wearing a suede hat with a large green plume. His shoes, which have four-inch heels, are the same color as his car, as well as his pants, which are held in place by a richly rhinestoned belt. Willie likes to talk about his profession, even boast about it. He is a pimp, he says, and has "girls all over the city."

Willie obviously enjoys playing the pimp, the gentleman of leisure who has become such a literary hero in recent years. Willie's talk, however, starts to sound a bit too exaggerated after a while, his claims just a bit too way out. "Got maybe hundred girls all over. Maybe hundred and fifty. I just blink my eyes, man, and I got three chicks going down on me if I want."

"That dude is way out," says another character who has been circulating in the underworld of the Strip for half a dozen years.

The man, also black like Willie, makes a disdainful face as he speaks of the pimp. "He's jiving. He's got maybe four girls. Two split from him last week. Right now he's dealing in dope to keep up the payments on his car and the clothes. It's like that a lot now. You know, the pimp has finally made it in the movies, but on the street, he's going down. You got a lot of chicks coming into town who aren't into dope. They're not putting out for dope. They're strictly into the bread. They want the money. They work their thing free-lance—no pimps, no connections. Some of them get roughed up for cutting into someone's action, but now you have so many of them floating around it's hard to fight it. There are a lot of pimps still going strong, but not like before. It's changing. A lot of dudes have gotten into something else, mostly working drugs or small ripoffs out of town. A couple I know who have made big money are getting into night clubs and stuff like that."

Although he may no longer be their legal and political protector (he may disappear at the first sign of trouble), the pimp may still play an important role in the lives of many prostitutes. For many there is still loneliness, isolation, and need for emotional support, which may make them seek out such a man to fill the aching emptiness of their existence. It is for this reason, some writers feel, that in spite of the diminution of his fiscal and organizational contribution, the pimp will continue to play a significant role in the life of the prostitute. The quality of that life was poignantly portrayed many years ago by Will Levington Comfort, a novelist and reporter, who recorded his impressions of a night-long conversation with a prostitute in police court.

The most tragic sentence I ever heard was from the lips of one of these women. . . . I talked with her through the night. She called it her work; she had an ideal about her work. Every turning in her life had been man-directed. She confessed that she had begun with an unabatable passion; that men had found her sensuousness very attractive when it was fresh. She had preserved a certain sweetness; through such stresses that the upper world would never credit. Thousands of men had come to her; all perversions, all obsessions, all madness, and drunkenness, to her alone in this little room. She told of nights when twenty came. Yet there was something inextinguishable about her—something patient and optimistic. In the midst of it all, it was like a little girl speaking:
"I wake up in the morning, and find a man beside me. I am always frightened, even yet—until I remember. I remember who I am and what I am . . . then I try to think what he is like—what his companions called him—what he said to me. I try to remember how he looked—because you know in the morning, his face is always turned away."[5]

In view of such experiences, which are neither unusual nor exaggerated, the question naturally arises as to how and why women become involved in what has euphemistically, if ironically, been designated as "the life." The reasons are as varied as the personalities of the women themselves and as their goals. It would be a mistake to simply conceptualize prostitution as pathological and search for its etiology or to emphasize its antisocial aspects and attempt to uncover its criminal roots. These may be valid assessments, but they are too limited for such a wide-ranging subject. The most useful approach to understanding this complex behavior might best begin with its definition: "the granting of sexual access on a relatively indiscriminate basis for payment."[6] Some theorists find in prostitution a Marxist example of economic exploitation,[7] while others emphasize its ecologic aspects,[8] social utilitarianism,[9] and disorganization associated with mobility.[10] Addressing themselves to the oft-reported frigidity and homosexuality[11] among prostitutes as well as to antisocial aspects, psychological theorists have understood prostitution primarily in terms of sexual "acting out" of underlying psychopathology.[12] Psychoanalysts have contended that the psychological defense mechanism of isolation which separates tender from sensual feelings is an important factor for both the prostitute and her client.[13] Of a certain group of people it can be said, "they cannot desire where they love, and they cannot love where they desire."[14] For them, prostitution plays an essential role in stabilizing their life because it permits them to isolate this objectionable sensuality from either their marital relationship or any other important interpersonal transactions. Were it not for such outlets, these impulses would have to be either repressed, resulting in psychoneurosis, or expressed, resulting in the disruption of important social institutions.

Apart from the psychosocial, economic interpretations contend that women "resort to sex as a means of redressing the status differential,"[15] this being the most accessible route to power and material rewards available to them within our culture. In other words, each gender utilizes whatever biological and social possibilities are available to satisfy either socially disallowed drives or to attain socially approved goals. Philosophically, at least, prostitutes may be only contractually removed from the sexual ploys an alluring and designing wife might use to seduce financial favors from her husband. These approaches are at best partial truths providing only a limited understanding of prostitution. To begin with, women are attracted to or drawn into it for many and conflicting reasons. Furthermore, the forces which sustain them in "the life" may be different from those which facilitated their initial entrance. Like Aesop's six blind men and the elephant, our theorists are describing different segments of a complex body of data. Psychoanalysts deal primarily with psychoneurotics who characteristically repress their impulses and inhibit their actions so that "prostitution fantasies" are as close as most of them ever get to such behavior. In addition, these patients are drawn from a middle and upper socioeconomic group which ordinarily has ample socially approved outlets for both sexual and aggressive drives, as well as financial access to material rewards. When executives steal they do not pilfer apples from fruit stands, nor do upper-class women proffer their sexual favors to strangers for money. Each finds means appropriate to his or her status to satisfy the ends.

Motivations may not differ between classes, but means certainly do. Those investigators who emphasize the masochistic[16] elements in prostitution may be failing to appreciate the financial incentive it offers to women who would otherwise be engaged as waitresses, factory workers, or domestics. As Shaw allowed in *Mrs. Warren's Profession,* society was "underpaying, undervaluing, and overworking women so shamefully that the poorest of them are forced to resort to prostitution to keep body and soul together." What they lose socially may in their view be more than compensated for in terms of both money and freedom from rigid job restrictions. If prostitution is, as one women's liberation placard declared, "men's crime against women," it must be acknowledged that prostitutes are very willing victims who are as eager as their male clients to be partners in crime. Such rebukes against society suggest that these women might be happier as file clerks or domestics, occupations which many of them have voluntarily relinquished for both psychological and financial reasons.

"I didn't get along with my family. I left home after high school. I came down to D.C. [Washington, D.C.] just to get away," said a twenty-four-year-old prostitute who grew up in western Pennsylvania. "I made friends here and I liked the city. I got a job as a typist and I was making $110 before deductions. So I was in with three other girls on this apartment because none of us could really afford a place of our own. I wasn't crazy about the work. I mean, I liked office work, but the sort of thing I wanted to do was work in the Library of Congress or something. That sounds silly, right? But for some reason that idea has always struck me. I was having a hard time with the money I was making. There was this guy in the office—he was married—he was always dropping hints to me. He was very nice. We went out to dinner one night and we walked around for a while and in the conversation I mentioned that I adored cashmere sweaters. It was an innocent remark. Later, we had more drinks and ended up in a motel. That was a Friday. On Monday there was a box on my desk. It was a cashmere sweater. At first I was going to give it right back, but later I thought, What the hell. I kept it.

"We went out a few more times after that. He always gave me something. I began to think about the things I needed. We picked things out together sometimes. It just happened after that. I didn't sleep with just anybody; only people who appealed to me. I got overconfident about it all and I quit my job. I expected to make a million as a high-society call girl, I guess. It's not as easy as you think. The secret between a streetwalker and a successful call girl is connections. I was lucky I ran into Jerry. He's not a 'pimp' in the usual sense of the word. He and I have a straight business arrangement. It's a commission on clients.

"I don't like the hustle of it all at times, but I do like the money and there is a lot of freedom. I read a lot, which I like to do. I mean, Jerry has good connections and the johns are nice guys, not just bums off the sidewalk. What can I say? Where else could I make as much money? How could I ever go back to being a typist after having what I have now? How could I afford this apartment? or the clothes? I don't know . . . one day you wake up and realize that you can't get out of it. The money and everything has you surrounded and maybe, deep down you really don't want to get out of it, because part of you really likes it."

But this is not true of all females, especially the large number of emotionally insecure and socially disoriented runaways who flock to the cities each year. These fragments of social disorganization which precipitate in heaps on the sidewalks of center-city business districts have few of the vocational or human resources which would provide them with viable alternatives to prostitution. "It used to be it was boys running away from home—and they were poor ones leaving the inner city headed outward," explained Sergeant Edward Smith, head of the Washington, D.C., Missing Persons Bureau. "That has changed a lot in the last few years. Now it's the girls who are running away more, and they're running away from the affluent suburbs to the inner city, where they end up as prostitutes or drug addicts or both."

Like Washington, cities across the country have been swamped with runaways. Virtually all major urban areas now tabulate that females comprise more than 50 per cent of the runaways on record. These girls are frequently depressed, have poor school records, and few, if any, family ties. They are quick to gravitate to any group or person who offers some measure of security or identity in an alien city. These are the emotionally vulnerable girls on whom pimps prey.

Explaining how such young girls are initially attracted and "turned out" into prostitutes, a New York pimp declared, "You've got to find out if they've got problems, if they're smart enough to say they are 18 when the cops make a bust . . . you've got to stomp her ass a few times to let her know where you're coming from. You've got to set the rules. . . . Maybe use a coat hanger—depends on what she needs. . . . You watch her close, maybe send another girl out with her. If she turns her first trick and comes back smiling, you've got her."[17]

A highly successful urban pimp who apparently prided himself on keeping abreast of scientific progress boasted that turning a young girl out is "a brainwashing process. The whole thing is creativity," he said. "When you turn a chick out you take away every set of values and morality she previously had and create a different environment."[18] His approach, while successful, is not nearly so impressive as he believes, because his subjects are as different from those of the Chinese interrogators as fish in a barrel are from fish in the open sea. He is not, as he boasts, cutting their previous ties, for if the ties were at all viable he would have few attractive inducements to tempt them into his stable. It is the very absence of those ties and the vulnerability inherent to the nonadapted state[19] that ensure his success. The usual process of brainwashing—crisis, conversion, and cult formation[20]—is already fully in progress at the time of initial encounter between the pimp and his prospective "wife." She is not agonized by a decision to switch from one set of group solidarities to another, but rather she is alienated from the "square society"[21] and eager to barter nothing for almost anything.

Prostitution, like all other complex social behaviors, is determined by a varied set of conditions. Its four component aspects—sexual, economic, psychological, and social—each influence the kinds of people who are attracted to it, and prostitution in turn is influenced by the caliber of its practitioners. Attracting and catering to different social classes, it may more easily be understood in terms of social class behavior than as a particular type of activity. At the upper level, among the full-time call girls and part-time housewives who appear to lead economically secure, stable, arrest-free lives, there is no evidence of special pathology. At the lower levels, inhabited by streetwalkers, drug addicts, juvenile runaways, and deviants of many different stripes, the population is so prone to psychosocial pathology that it is difficult to know what part, if any, prostitution contributes to their many difficulties. There is even some evidence that prostitution may help by improving their financial condition and providing essential though minimal stabilizing relationships. The alternative to prostitution for this population could be victim-oriented crimes. It appears that prostitution is not inherently pathological, but many prostitutes do exhibit psychopathology. Furthermore, given society's restrictions on sexual behavior and the willingness of a certain (sometimes disadvantaged) segment of the population to engage in sexual deviancy, it serves the social function of allowing relatively limited and therefore safe outlets which in toto preserve the social structure.

It is timely to wonder what society's attitude toward prostitutes would be if they were men and therefore were not violating a sexual taboo or, to put it another way, if the liberation movement succeeded in gaining for women the same sexual freedoms enjoyed by men. To judge from the influx of middle-class married women into the field, we would most likely see a shift toward more part-time and more socially stable practitioners who would look on their sexual activity as they would on any other job whose income furthered the interests of themselves and their families. If history is any guide, prostitution would seek its own level in the socioeconomic hierarchy based on the attributes of its practitioners, the social value of its services, and the financial return it could command.

As for the present practitioners, role distinctions have been blurring in both directions between "proper" women and prostitutes. If the former are acting more like prostitutes, the prostitutes have, for the most part, modified their conduct in the direction of conventionality. The flashy and distinctive styles of dress have either disappeared altogether or have faded into the commonplace as they have been adopted as fashion by the rest of society. It is often no longer possible to distinguish the prostitute from the matrons, college girls, or debutantes who might congregate at any public gathering. This is especially true of the impeccably groomed call girls who make individual appointments with their clients and hail them with such seemingly innocent suggestions as "How about a date?" The long-haired, clean-faced amateurs from the suburbs and the "occasional" or "part-time" prostitutes making their appearance in the majority of Western countries are the vanguard of a more mobile, less regimented group of female entrepreneurs who are beginning to dominate the field. These women are less dependent on pimps and less dependent on madams and brothels than their predecessors in the 1930s, not only because women are more independent in general but also because most of them have a solid base of emotional support in the larger society.

The stages through which many of these women have passed in their metamorphosis from promiscuous housewife through amateur prostitute and then on to semiprofessional standing are at each level extensions of socially tolerated (although not quite accepted) behavior. Under a variety of euphemistic names, each one emphasizing a different aspect of exhibitionistic promiscuity, group sex has been spreading throughout the middle class. "Partying," "freaking," "scening," and "swinging," as these orgies are called, have added a new and unanticipated meaning to the designation "bedroom community" for the suburban ring surrounding urban population centers.

• • •

Throughout the centuries, attitudes toward prostitution have ranged the spectrum from the esteem in which hetaerae were held to the contempt which greeted the medieval harlot. Characteristically, these changes in attitude pivoted around feelings toward women and feelings about sex, with many interesting variations. For example, women were at times glorified but only as chaste and empty vessels; at times, sex was glorified but women were demeaned. Historically, prostitutes have been praised, tolerated, or vilified, depending on the period, and it is tempting to conclude that current changes are cyclic repetitions of the past. But this would be misleading. What has been characteristic of the past was that women in general and prostitutes in particular were primarily the objects of male attitudinal changes. What is significant about the present is that women have become the subjects as well as objects, and prostitutes are being viewed in a perspective that is broader than their mere utility to men. Like other modern women, today's prostitute is better educated, better accepted, and more independent of men. She may be a housewife, bachelor woman, or graduate student. She may even become a professional in the allied health field. Although the prostitute is not a member in good social standing, it is less because she is a promiscuous woman than because she may be an antisocial person with unsavory connections. But legalization of prostitution, along with social acceptance of female sexuality, is taking it out of the nether world of vice to which it has been traditionally consigned. The changing role of women has brought them into the mainstream of society where they can interact as principals in their own destiny. In its scope and immensity, this upward movement is freeing women of their vices as well as their virtues, and is destigmatizing sex for both sexes.

Notes

1. Charles Winick and Paul M. Kinsie, *The Lively Commerce* (Chicago: Quadrangle Books, 1971), p. 4.
2. *Ibid.*, p. 5.
3. *Ibid.*, p. 97.
4. *Ibid.*, p. 109.
5. Will Levington Comfort, "The Police—Court Reporter" from *Midstream*, reprinted in Upton Sinclair, *The Cry for Justice* (Philadelphia: The John C. Winston Co., 1915), pp. 165–66.
6. John H. Gagnon, "Prostitution," *International Encyclopedia of the Social Sciences*, ed. David L. Sills (New York: The Macmillan Co. and the Free Press, 1968), 12:592–598.
7. W. A. Bonger, *Criminality and Economic Conditions* (Boston: Little, Brown and Co., 1916), pp. 321–56.
8. Robert E. Park and Ernest W. Burgess, *Introduction to the Science of Sociology* (Chicago: University of Chicago Press, 1921).
9. Kingsley Davis, "The Sociology of Prostitution," *American Sociological Review*, October 1937, 2:744–55.
10. Lemert, *op. cit.*, p. 233.
11. Frank S. Caprio, *Female Homo-Sexuality* (New York: Grove Press, 1954).
12. See for example, Edward Glover, *The Psychopathology of Prostitution* (London: Institute for the Study and Treatment of Delinquency, 1957). See also, Harold Greenwald, *The Elegant Prostitute* (New York: Walker & Co., 1970 [originally published in 1958]).
13. Otto Fenichel, *The Psychoanalytic Theory of Neurosis* (New York: W. W. Norton & Co., 1945).
14. Sigmund Freud, "Contributions to the Psychology of Love," *Collected Papers* v. 4 (New York: Basic Books Inc., 1959, originally published in 1924).
15. Lemert, *op. cit.* p. 247.

16. Winick and Kinsie, *op. cit.*, p. 86.
17. *Time,* June 5, 1972.
18. Christina Milner and Richard Milner, *Black Players, The Secret World of Black Pimps* (Boston: Little, Brown and Co., 1972).
19. L. F. Chapman and H. G. Wolff, "The Cerebral Hemispheres and the Highest Integrative Functions of Man," *A.M.A. Archives of Neurology,* 1959, 1:357.
20. Herbert M. Adler and Van Buren O. Hammett, "Crisis, Conversion, and Cult Formation: An Examination of a Common Psychosocial Sequence," *American Journal of Psychiatry,* August 1973, 130:861–64.
21. James H. Bryan, "Apprenticeships in Prostitution," *Social Problems,* Winter 1965, 12:287–97.

21 Survey of Opiate Addiction Among Females in the United States Between 1850 and 1970

Walter R. Cuskey, T. Premkumar, and Lois Sigel

Historical overview

America had more addicts during the last half of the nineteenth century than it has today, despite the tremendous and frightening increases since World War II, and the skyrocketing rises in the past few years. This is true even though the total population before World War I was less than half of that today, and despite the even more significant fact that the U.S. was much less urbanized then, and drug addiction has a high correlation with urbanization. No other western nation has such a history of drug abuse.

Female addiction, 1850–1921

In Britain, until 1926 at least, a drug addict was "a rather rare and even exotic creature, confined almost entirely to medical professionals with a fringe of bohemians."[2] Not so in America. Since 1850 at least, the use of opiates in America has been greater than our officials could cope with, understand, or record accurately. At the beginning of the century, as today, authorities assumed that they had not approached the true figure by half. This history has had a great and often determining influence on the control methods and philosophy our nation has employed against drugs; and the differences in histories between America and such countries as Britain and France have made it difficult to exchange information, or to profit from the solutions they put forth.

In 1867 a writer could say:

From "Survey of Opiate Addiction Among Females in the United States Between 1850 and 1970" by Walter R. Cuskey, T. Premkumar, and Lois Sigel. *Public Health Reviews* (1972). Pp. 8–13, 16–39. Reprinted by permission of International Health Publications, Tel Aviv, Israel. The original footnote numbers of the source are retained.

The habit is gaining fearful ground among our professional men, the operatives in our mills, our weary serving women, our fagged clerks, our former liquor drunkards, our everyday laborers, who a generation ago took gin. All our classes from the highest to the lowest are yearly increasing their consumption of the drug.[2]

A druggist in 1870, describing the increased use in his New England town of 10,000 said that, though the population had not increased in 20 years, his sales of opium had gone up from 50 pounds to 300, and sales of laudanum, a solution of opium in alcohol, had quadrupled. His experience was typical.

All authorities who collected data on addiction, or observed it, remarked on the large number of women addicts. *The fact is that during this entire period, from before the Civil War until immediately following the First World War, female drug addicts outnumbered male addicts two to one!* In view of our present situation and our present illusions, this fact is so astonishing that it should be repeated: from about 1850 until 1920, when the restrictions of the Harrison Act of 1914 became firmly established, twice as many women as men were addicted to narcotics. (The Harrison Act did make some technical provision for medical control and treatment of addicts, but the overall effect, from the way it was enforced and interpreted by the Federal Bureau of Narcotics, was to make narcotics illegal, and to shift the control of addiction from a medical to a law enforcement problem and responsibility.[3])

During the Civil War the widespread use of morphine as a pain-killer for the wounded administered with the newly-developed hypodermic syringe created a mass of opiate-addicts greater than at any time in our history.

There was a parallel development among women. In 1868 Horace Day spoke sympathetically, if perhaps too romantically, of the "anguished and hopeless wives and mothers, made so by the slaughter of those who were dearest to them, [who] have found, many of them, temporary relief from their sufferings in opium."[2]

In 1913 Tennessee passed an Anti-Narcotic Law which included provisions for providing maintenance dosages to the addicted, and for the filing of data. Reporting on the operation of this law in 1915, L. P. Brown, State Food and Drugs Commissioner, said that there had been 2370 persons registered during the preceding year—784 men and 1586 women. (He projected these figures to indicate a total of about 270,000 addicts for the entire United States "by no means so many as sensational writers appear to want us to believe [but] . . . bad enough."[2])

Throughout the studies and surveys made of addicts from pre-Civil War days to about 1920, the high ratio of women to men is constantly emphasized. In 1877, Marshall presented a study to the Michigan State Board of Health. He found that "the total number of opium eaters reported in the places given is 1313; of these 803 are females and 510 are males."[2] In a survey of druggists in 1885, Hull reported that he found 215 users of opium in various forms, including multiple use (morphine 129, gum opium 73, laudanum 12, paregoric 6, McMunn's Elixir 4 and Dover's Powder 3). Of these, 86 were men, and 129 women.[2] In 1913 Jacksonville, Florida had a law requiring druggists to report sizeable sales of opiates (three grains of morphine or equivalent) to the health office; sales were recorded to 228 men and 313 women. Projecting the same percentages for the entire nation (estimated population in 1913 of 97,163,330), Terry and Pellens gave the incidence as 782,118.[2] Current estimates (1972), on addiction with a national population well over twice as large, are 250,000.[4]

In many ways the period from pre Civil War to immediate post World War I was like a film negative of the present. In 1913 Negroes made up a small majority of the population of Jacksonville—34,200 blacks to about 33,000 whites; yet male addicts were 133 white to 40 black, and females 219 white to 94 black.[2] We do not have comparable figures from Jacksonville today but authorities agree that the racial percentages have shifted radically towards the darker minority groups.

According to figures from the hospital at Lexington, Kentucky, in the last thirty-odd years we have moved from the 11.6% of non-white admissions reported by Pescor[5] in 1936 to the 56% non-white reported by Ball and Chambers[80] in 1966, with the trend continuing. A study of female addicts between 1961 and 1967 by Cuskey *et al.* shows similar effects.[6]

In other respects also the old pictures were reversed. Different kinds of addicts came on the scene. In the post Civil War years a number of druggists pointed to the high incidence of use among physicians themselves; and most authorities blamed much addiction, even the "vast majority", on "the unpardonable carelessness of physicians, who are often too fond . . . of relieving every ache and pain by the administration of an opiate."[2]

In short, most of the addicted (and this must include the wounded of the Civil War who became hooked), were helped and recruited to this condition by the medical profession. They were either medical personnel themselves, or were addicted during treatment by prescription. The highest percentage of female addicts started by taking opiates to relieve pain, rather than for euphoria or escape. They were started by ignorant, frightened or harassed physicians taking the easy way, or through opium-laden home-remedies and patent medicines. (In Eugene O'Neill's autobiographical *Long Day's Journey Into Night,* the mother's addiction to morphine is blamed on an incompetent doctor.[7])

Before regulation, the availability of opium (then widely grown in the United States) must have seemed a godsend to patent-medicine makers. How else could they so confidently predict and secure pleasurable relief for so many complaints and ensure a continuing and growing demand? It appeared widely (as did alcohol) in such commonplace remedies as cough medicines, liniments, and the various cure-alls sold from the wagons of the medicine-shows. Terry and Pellens report that there was even a good deal of opium in "the dangerous so-called 'cures' of relief for opium-eaters' preparations designed to stop addiction."[2]

So, finally, most of those addicted were a good cross-section of respectable and health-conscious America, particularly among women. According to Hull's[2] report from Iowa, "the majority of them [addicts] are to be found among the educated and most honored and useful members of society; and as to sex, we may count out the prostitutes so much given to this vice, and still find females far ahead so far as numbers are concerned."[2] How can we account for this apparent wide acceptance of opium? But why not? Opium was legal;

it did kill pain; it did provide intoxication. And, strangely enough by present concepts, it was generally viewed as a relatively respectable substitute for alcohol. Opium was common among those "who crave the effect of a stimulant, but will not risk their reputation for temperance by taking alcoholic beverages."[2]

The descriptions in popular legend of "average" women during the Victorian and post-Victorian periods tend to be somewhat contradictory. On one hand they are often depicted as warm, strong, omnipresent and long-suffering earth mothers, enduring frequent births with little anesthetic, working hard with little help, caring for and feeding large broods. On the other hand they may be portrayed as delicate, ignorant and rather unworldly, given to frequent and mysterious female distempers and "vapours". Both kinds of women would need frequent relief from pain, tedium, and nervous tension. Our grandmothers used many home remedies and patent medicines whose ingredients would shock us today. Nor is that picture of frequent recourse by women to drugs really so alien to us today—they simply substituted the use of various pain killers, barbiturates and amphetamines for opium.

The Harrison Act of 1914

In 1914 the Harrison Act was passed. From 1919 to 1923 there were clinics dispensing low-cost narcotics in over 40 cities.[3] They are generally believed to have failed. What was more important, the federal narcotics officials felt they were bad, and moved to discredit and end them. This decision has since caused some controversy, renewed, since the opening in 1968, of clinics in Britain.[1]

However, passage of the Harrison Act was the watershed event that started the change that was to affect the entire complexion of American drug control and the pattern and extent of female drug abuse. The closing of American clinics within the decade or so effectively put an end to legal distribution of drugs to addicts, and pretty well destroyed medical influence over control. The strong decline of female addiction from two-thirds of the total before 1920 to the present one-fifth represents a radical change, however gradually it came about.

"In 1915" Terry and Pellens report "two things occurred simultaneously— the importations decreased, and the illicit traffic began to develop. This doubtless was due chiefly to the fact that chronic users, because of the restrictions placed upon physicians and pharmacists in the handling of these drugs, sought their supplies from underworld sources."[2]

The typical female addicts before 1920 had bought most opiates openly across the drug counter. When opium became illegal and disreputable, they were not likely to follow the prostitutes into that dark and expensive world of the pusher and the black marketeer, if they could avoid it. Certainly they were not likely to supply many new recruits.

The period between the world wars saw a general decline in opiate addiction, slight among men, significant among women. Heroin was the primary drug of addiction for both males and females. As Ball points out, the Harrison Act not only put strictures on the almost unlimited licit and legal distribution of narcotics, but made the illicit market profitable, so that a new pattern of illegal, black-market drug distribution came to be superimposed on the older, legal one.[2]

Establishment of federal drug addiction hospitals: 1935

Major bench marks in the drug history of the United States occurred in 1935, when the federal drug hospitals at Lexington and Fort Worth were established. These were important events, because they more firmly established the federal government's predominant role in drug control and treatment efforts. They also reflected the prevailing law-enforcement emphasis—prevention and control through custodial and punitive means rather than treatment. The hospitals became centers for the study of drug problems in the United States, and the primary sources for reliable statistics. Much of what we know of the demographic characteristics, personalities and histories of American opiate abuse comes from Lexington and Fort Worth records.

Female addiction, like female alcoholism, tends to be either hidden or tied in with male addiction. Robinson listed a number of representative reasons why the female addicts in Lexington had started on drugs. Of the seven sources listed five were male; one was a peer group which might have included males; and only one (older women friends) was female.[8] In each case, male or female, the source was someone already addicted. Modern drug abuse has been called the new plague.[9] Certainly it spreads by contagion.

The first female opiate addicts were accepted for treatment at Lexington in July, 1941, and are still being accepted there. Females of all races, registered at Lexington, admitted voluntarily or not, constitute about 18% of the total, coming close to the best estimates of the ratio of female to male addicts in the nation at large.

Post World War II developments

Another major event in the history of American drug addiction occurred during and immediately after World War II. In wartime it is the males who, in cohorts, suffer the pain and wounds, and who are willing to pay the price to continue the good times they had learned abroad, or to kill the pain and achieve the euphoria they first found in the hospital. The increase in addiction was not as profound in women. Women did achieve a form of emancipation— war work, and more going around without husbands or boyfriends. But they were not as directly affected. Nevertheless, the greatest predisposing factor for female addiction—at least in an illicit opiate market—was the addicted male associate.

·   ·   ·

Behavior and social characteristics

Who is the female addict, and what is she, that so many people with so little knowledge so widely condemn her?

Investigators do not speak of "typical" addicts. There are many different types. Some may be defined by the kinds of drugs used, by the kinds of life styles they have, by region, by special circumstances; some are also daughters of female addicts of the past.

When, in this article, we describe a "typical" or even "representative" addict, we are in fact considering the average of the largest, or most widely detected, sub-group today—the female opiate abuser. Even within this group there are varieties. Undoubtedly, in time, as more data on other sub-groups of women become available, they will be categorized; and they may contrast sharply with the heroin addict.

General characteristics

Age

In a study of 120 women addicts published in 1929, Magid found that the preponderance of them (102) were between 20 and 40 years of age, with slightly more than half over 30.[13] Pescor found the average age of the first 100 female admissions into Lexington to be 43.[5] In a study of female addicts in the Illinois Reformatory for Women in 1960, Robinson found that the average addict age was 27.5 years, the average inmate age 30 years, and the average of all females in Illinois at the time almost 33 years.[8] This is skimpy evidence, but it seems to support the general impression that female addicts are becoming slightly younger. Black female addicts have consistently been younger than their white cohorts, and their life styles and other factors also show distinctive differences.

During the 1960's the situation described in the literature becomes cloudy. In a study of 168 subjects at Lexington in 1965, Chambers found a mean of 30.4 years for black women and 37 years for white (overall average, 33.5).[14] But those populations outside Lexington seem to run fairly consistently younger averages according to Wiesen,[15] Blum,[16] Weiland,[17] and Hall.[18] However, Lexington always includes a sizeable percentage of repeaters (almost 60% of Chambers' sample), previously treated and released in the fond hope of remission or cure; so the expectation that the Lexington population should be older than that on the street (which includes some who have never been caught or treated at all) seems justified, and the data support this conclusion of Williams[19] and Cuskey.[6] In most respects the admissions to Ft. Worth and Lexington are good indicators of admissions throughout the nation, as Ball notes, but not for age. The female addicts are not only older than those in the street, but are older than the men admitted, 31.9 years.[20] Officers are more reluctant to arrest women, perhaps women are engaged in less serious crimes, or they avoid capture and detection. When admitted, they are older.

As noted, black female addicts are generally younger than whites; all studies reviewed confirm this. Between 1961 and 1967 Cuskey found that the median ages for white females dropped from 35–39 to 30–34; but black median ages remained the same, at a considerably lower level—25–29.[6] In 1965 Cuskey and Williams found the average age for white women to be 37.1 years, and for blacks 30.3. Mexican-American female admissions to Lexington were even younger—19–20.[21] One factor might be, of course, the greater willingness of police to arrest blacks; but it cannot be the determining factor.

On the basis of admissions records, the "typical" female addict is not much younger in the 1960's than her sister in 1929, and she may be older than her other sister of 1944. But blacks and other minority groups are much younger—and with more data, this trend should be confirmed.

Region

The south and southwest, the more conservative parts of the country, are still strongly influenced by the old pre–Harrison Act pattern (except for what might be called a heroin band along the Mexican border). Writing in 1965, Ball could still define *Two Patterns of Opiate Addiction*. The more modern, illicit pattern centers around the use of heroin, alone or in combination; it is characteristically urban, slum, male and minority. It is the typical pattern in the large cities and in New York, Puerto Rico, the District of Columbia, Illinois, New Jersey, Arizona and New Mexico. The older pattern might, "for want of a better name . . . be termed a southern pattern . . . exemplified by Alabama, Georgia and Kentucky". Less than 5% of addicts admitted to federal drug hospitals from these states use heroin; they still follow the older prescriptions of paregoric, morphine, codeine and dilaudid. Many (or most) were semi-legally or legally acquired through physicians or drug stores, for relief of pain and tension. The typical "southern" addicts are white, generally from small towns; addiction started at a later age, marihuana use is uncommon, and less than 20% earned their living by illegal means, with over 50% employed.[22]

Pescor reported in 1944 that the pre-war female addicts probably came from small towns or rural areas, very likely from the South, at most from a small city of less than 50,000 people.[5] Since then the drug problem has concentrated in the big cities, particularly New York, Chicago and Los Angeles. Half of all the approximate 50,000 female addicts live in New York. By 1966 83% of female addicts came from large metropolitan areas, and only 17% from the south.[23]

Race

It is impossible to discuss regional distribution or religion—or for that matter patterns and delinquency—without running into the question of race. Race is in many ways the prime variable for analysis—intimately associated with differences in region, life styles and patterns of use. Association, of course, is not the same thing as cause. America's drug history, social problems and law-enforcement philosophy are as much "causes" as individual weaknesses, or genetic differences.

The study of Chambers *et al.* noted many race-associated differences between white and black addicts. Over 91% of the female addicts they studied came from the South, North Central, and Middle Atlantic regions. But that bare statistic told only a small part of the tale. The South contributed 50% of whites, but only 14% of blacks; the North Central region (predominantly the urban areas of Chicago, Detroit, and other cities) contributed almost 51% of the black addicts but only about 21% of the white; and the Middle Atlantic provided about 17% of the white and close to 32% of the black addicts. The rest of the blacks came from the Pacific coast (3.5%), while the rest of the whites were scattered, including 3.6% from Puerto Rico. In short, the white women came typically from the South, while the blacks came mainly from the North Central regions. Further, while 78.4% of the white women reported that they came from urban areas, all of the black women did.[14]

All researchers agree that there has been a large shift in racial composition and geographical origin among addicts starting from before World War II. In 1929 Magid reported that the typical female addict was white and Protestant.[13] In 1935 and 1936 about 11% of all admissions to Lexington were non-white. By 1964 the Federal Bureau of Narcotics estimated that only about 28% of the narcotic addicts were minority group members, and in 1966 it was found that this applied to 56% of those in Lexington.[5] Nevertheless, examining only the 168 female addicts admitted to Lexington in the last half of 1965, Chambers found that white women outnumbered blacks by about two to one.[14] In other words, though minority group members made up the majority of all addicts, whites still predominated among women. Cuskey reported somewhat similar findings in a continuing trend, comparing female admissions during 1961 with those of 1967. However, though there were still more white women, the gap was rapidly narrowing. In 1961, 150 white women compared to 134 black were admitted voluntarily and in 1967 the count was 89 to 84. In 1967 Cuskey reported that almost half, 48.7%, of his female population was black. What may be significant is that a higher percentage of black admissions were of repeaters: 6.5% more white women were admitted for the first time in 1967 than in 1961; but black female first-timers decreased by 1.4%. Facilities that serve urban areas exclusively, or prisons, report even higher percentages of blacks and other non-whites, according to studies by Royfe,[24] Jaffe,[25] and Bates.[26]

Religion

In Ellinwood's study 47% of the women were found to be Protestant, 30% Catholic, and 17% had no clear religious preference.[23] Investigators reporting on exclusively urban population find fewer Protestants. About 55% of Willis' sample from New York were Catholic, reflecting the huge Puerto Rican barrio population.[10] As time passes, and the increased shift to urban patterns continues, along with an increased rate of addiction, it is safe to predict that the female addicts will become increasingly Negro, Puerto Rican and Mexican-American, with a higher national percentage of Catholics and non-believers.

The patterns

Many of the disabilities that blacks or other urban poor or minority groups suffer are specific to their situations, and cannot be simply and directly applied to middle-class whites, even after a time lag. Ghettoization of cities is a social and economic phenomenon more than a racial one, though it affects blacks and other minorities more profoundly than it does whites. And the involvement of big money and organized crime in drugs is not directly related to race or sex either. Nevertheless, in a rough way, it is correct to say that the developing patterns of opiate addiction, particularly heroin, become manifest and intense in blacks before whites, in the poor before the well-to-do, and in males before females. It is also true that, in addition to other new developments in drug use, the whites and females have been catching up more rapidly in the past decade than ever before.

Cuskey reported that by 1967, more than three-fourths of his black subjects lived either in the North Central (52.4%), or Middle Atlantic states (26.2%)— mostly urban areas.[6] Nearly 64% of all Negro women patients in Williams' sample came from New York, Washington and Chicago, while less than 30% of white patients came from these cities.[19] On the other hand, Cuskey found that 42.7% of his whites came from the South in 1961, and 52.4% in 1967.[6] Chambers found that about 30% of Mexican-Americans have migrated to the cities in recent years.[21] All these figures confirm the change toward the urban, minority, non-Protestant, heroin pattern.

The progression from marihuana to heroin or other hard drugs, deemed invariable by some law-enforcement people, is also race and region related, being associated predominantly with the urban pattern. In Chambers' study, 68.4% of the black female addicts had used marihuana.[14] But Mizener, in a study of college drug abusers, found that three-fourths of the medium to heavy marihuana smokers not only had not moved on to heavy drugs, but had discontinued all drugs by their senior years.[27] It might be noted that many of these reformed pot smokers had come from metropolitan areas, but few were ghetto blacks. Most inner-city populations, especially deviants, do have a high rate of progression from pot to heroin. Glaser *et al.*, comparing drug-using offenders in New York with drug-free offenders, found that about 40% of the marihuana-smoking offenders had heroin records five to ten years later.[28]

Recent studies indicate to what extent the white women of the Southern pattern still follow the pre-war tradition. Of the white women in Chambers' 1965 study, almost half (45.4%) got their drugs from medical sources, and even at the time of treatment got them from physicians (one-third) or druggists (about one-fifth). Only about 37% preferred heroin, the drugs of choice remaining the legal or quasi-legal codeine, morphine and paregoric.[14]

Almost 90% of Negroes, on the other hand, were introduced to drugs by their peers, who do not include physicians. Invariably they chose heroin (93%), and listed pushers (91.2%) as their source. Williams reports that in his study only one patient from the entire Chicago, Washington and New York grouping had a legal source of drugs—while two-thirds of the Southern patients got their drugs from physicians or pharmacies.

Chambers *et al.* also found rather surprising differences between the races in the drug they chose, preferred, and were primarily addicted to. "Among the Negroes, heroin was overwhelmingly the first opiate used, the opiate which was currently being used, the drug the addicts preferred to use, the drug which they used most frequently." About 81% preferred heroin, 93% used it most frequently. By contrast, only one-third of the white women used heroin most frequently, and only 36.9% preferred it. The whites most frequently gave medical or quasi-medical reasons for beginning their addictions; the black women (who averaged six years younger) spoke of "kicks" or "curiosity" and addiction through the pressure of peers, or in social situations.[29]

One of the better studies of the sources of female addiction is that conducted in Wisconsin. They found that in the reasons cited for initial drug abuse, curiosity (43%) was highest, with social pressure and pleasure also cited frequently. Why did they keep on? Most claim they did so for gratification or kicks, though almost as many admitted that they were hooked and could not quit. In the case histories quoted in *Drug-Trip Abroad*, it was generally agreed that long-time addicts got little positive kick out of opiates. They became necessities, "like insulin for diabetics", to achieve relief and ward off the pain of withdrawal. Those case histories were predominantly of men; but the physical response of women to opiates seems little different. To the long-time female addict, as to the male, "curiosity" and "kicks" are part of a legendary golden age of the past.[1]

Deviancy and personality

Deviancy

"The practical effect of American narcotics laws is to define the addict as a criminal offender", Schur[3] states in *Crimes Without Victims*. Further, as noted, in the United States, most addicts have to take to crime to pay for their drugs. Strictly speaking, therefore, to speak of deviancy of addicts is in a large part to speak of addiction itself.

But even without the legal aspects, who can say that addiction is not a deviant method of behavior and social adjustment? There is a great deal of evidence of deviance among addicts, and much of it precedes drug use. There is some evidence, in addition, that we are dealing with a psychological and social maladjustment that expresses itself in a form considered deviant. Addiction may be a form of adjustment to intolerable stress for maladjusted people. And in a pathological environment it may seem desirable compared to alternatives. Chein notes that addiction often serves, for the addict, "a humanizing function, by offering an identity, a place in society where one belongs, and a vocation around which to build one's life."[30] Descriptions of the addicts who stay in treatment in Britain according to Schur[3] and Cuskey[1] seem to show inadequate persons who have trouble relating or finding communion, except through drugs.

Some views of the personalities of addicts conflict. Most agree, however, that the majority of addicts are of average intelligence, and many are higher. Schuster says: "He [the addict] generally is an insecure, easily bored, unstable individual who, too often, is above average intelligence and unable to follow long-term goals".[31] In contrast, Preble and Casey find the adolescent addict involved in a meaningful existence pursuing challenging and demanding jobs and other interests.[32] But Ausubel states that his subjects appeared to have lost interest in life and are not motivated to achieve.[33] Analyzing teenage abuse, Levy states that during the turbulent teenage years certain individuals turn to narcotics and other drugs for "magical solutions" to problems.[34] Rado[35] and Fenichel[36] also point out the naive willingness of many users to accept drugs as "magical" instruments. Merton, in his "anomie" theory, hypothesizes that the addict is a "retreatist" from society, withdrawing from all aspects of competitive life.[37] Cloward[38] and Chein *et al.*[30] have, in a sense,

Table 1 Female addict demographic characteristics

Year	Author	Type of sample if other than general population	Mean age of sample	Predominant race in sample	Predominant influence on initiation into drug use
1929	Magid		30	*	Medical treatment
1936	Pescor		43	Mostly white	Medical treatment
1961	Cuskey		82% over 25	*	*
1961	Chambers	Mexican-Americans	26.4	*	*
1961	Robinson	Prison	27.5	Mostly Negroes	*
1966	Ellinwood		31	60% white 40% Negroes	*
1967	Cuskey		69% over 25	*	*
1967	Chambers	Mexican-Americans	26.2	*	*
1968	Hall	Prison	33	Mostly white	Peer group
1968	Glaser		32.8	50% white 40% Negroes 10% other	
1969	Poplar	Nurses	41.7	Mostly white	Medical treatment
1970	Chambers		*	*	Peer group
1970	Chambers	Negroes	33.7	67% white 33% Negroes	Peer group

* Information not reported.

all elaborated upon Merton's findings, suggesting that the adolescent addict cannot find a legitimate role in society, and often not even a successful criminal one.

As addiction becomes more widespread, and the ghettos worse, much of the blame for deviancy must be shifted from the imperfections in the addicts to the imperfections in the environments. To some children, addiction may be a reasonable option to a seriously abnormal environment. All these considerations indicate that the kinds of personalities who do or can become addicted may be becoming almost as numerous as the authorities who have opinions on the subject. Kolb describes five different types of addict personalities, and stresses that the borderlines between them are vague, with possible borrowing of traits back and forth.[39]

Deviant behavior cited in female sample populations is certainly broad and inclusive enough. Magid, in 1929, said that the female addict was much like other women, which was certainly true then.[13] Now, heroin addicts do have a high incidence of personality disorders. Addiction may be becoming a catch-all for misfits.

The theory that addiction is caused by, or is aided by, a pre-existing character or personality defect has existed for over a century.[40] Many modern investigators agree.[41, 42, 43] In a comparative study of adult and adolescent addicts, Willis finds that deviancy must be present early in life, before drug abuse, or at least that it must develop very soon after onset.[10] This character defect need not necessarily be genetic, but could develop from the interaction with poverty and ghetto conditions in early childhood.[44]

Some authorities criticize this theory of predisposition, pointing out that these conclusions are reached concerning persons already deviant; that the emotional problems are described at the time of admission to prison or treatment, usually a time of maximum disturbance.[45] O'Donnell points out that we cannot know the condition of addicts before or apart from addiction, unless we can somehow separate the effects of the deviancy and addiction.[46]

Personality

No doubt great deviancy is consistently found in heroin addicts. In the sample at Lexington, Chambers *et al.* found that all of the 91 women who remained in treatment for seven or more weeks had some kind of mental problem or deficiency: over 32% had personality trait disorders, 21% were sociopaths, about 32% had personality pattern disorders, 8.8% psychiatric disorders, 2.2% were neurotics, and 1% had brain damage.[14] Compared to other studies, Chambers' findings of disorders were rather high, but all findings were higher than the general population. All but one of Hall's addict-prisoners were found to be disturbed,[18] and Ellinwood's study finds about 80% disturbed.[23] How much is independent of the addiction itself, of course, is impossible to determine.

Willis found that about one-half of his female subjects exhibited psychological disturbances even during childhood. Another one-third had had severe tantrums in childhood, and about 45% were persistent truants from school. Most had been picked up as delinquents during adolescence.[10]

Committing crimes to get money for opiates is an almost inevitable concomitant of addiction. But the crimes female addicts commit tell a good deal about their particular problems.

In a study of female addict-prisoners by Ellinwood, 13 had been jailed for stealing, 37 for sexual offenses (prostitution), and only 7 for assault. Thirty-three were jailed for narcotic offenses.[23]

Female addicts commit fewer crimes of violence than male addicts, and are convicted and jailed less often and for shorter sentences; yet they also are employed less frequently and for shorter periods, and undergo fewer voluntary withdrawals. Prostitution and dependency give them surer, and perhaps safer, forms of getting money when legal methods fail.

Chambers *et al.* also found that over 90% of female Mexican-American addicts were unemployed, or involved in crime.[21] The two areas of crime in which women exceed men are prostitution and shoplifting—a form of non-violent theft. Of a sample of 89 female addicts in Wisconsin in 1969, 11 depended on prostitution to support their opiate habits, 25 depended on theft, while only 16 worked or borrowed the money.[15]

In studies of women's prisons such researchers as Ward and Kassabaum have demonstrated that lesbianism is a common female adjustment to prison.[48] But the amount of this homosexuality and frigidity, particularly their increase, along with the increase in attempts at marriage, must also involve other factors. Authorities claim a direct link between drug abuse and sexual deviancy. It is taken for granted by most addicts and those who work with them, that opiates have a definitely inhibiting effect on the sex drive. (See *Drug-Trip Abroad* for first person accounts.[1]) Some addicts find little difference, but most do.

Burke says that adolescent addicts of both sexes have real fear of homosexuality.[48] (This is a common factor, of course, in many weak personalities who have trouble establishing strong identities.) Hague points out that adolescent homosexuals turn to drugs because of their rejection by society.[49] Almost one-half of Willis' sample admitted to homosexual orientation.[10] Ellinwood found 34% of his female subjects, many of whom were married, admitted to occasional or heavy homosexual activity. In fact, only 33% said that they had not experienced frigidity with men.[23] Isbell established that narcotics suppress the libido, and thus reduce the frequency of intercourse.[50]

Burke concluded, too, that the understanding of love is generally distorted among adolescent addicts. There is little question of their need, but it "has a very infantile quality to it". For instance, their idea of true love often calls for no limit to giving by the other person. "Any imposition of limits upon behavior, however slight that imposition may be, is reacted to as a negation of love or as a proof that the love in question never existed."[48]

Family life

Youth and early sorrow

There is a great deal of evidence that female addicts, like males, come from "malignant familial environments". Since urban ghettos are concentrations of poverty, minority groups, broken families, psychopathology and lawlessness, who really knows what causes what? If an addict doesn't come from a broken home he can certainly create one.

Still, the associations are there. In 1944 Pescor reported that the female addicts at Lexington would typically have some family history of alcoholism, and that the parents would be in "marginal economic circumstances."[5] The poor lived in a state of permanent crisis, often only a step from disaster. The home life of the typical addict of 1944 would therefore be disturbed, and sometimes abruptly shattered by death, separation and divorce. Chambers *et al.* found that the majority of their 1965 addicts had been reared in homes broken before they were 16. Race differences could be summarized by adding, "with the blacks, more so."[14]

Chein *et al.* report that the parents of female addicts have more discord than most parents, that fathers are gone for long periods of time or are generally ineffectual, and that mothers are dominant in the homes and in their children's lives.[30] This is practically the definition—at least a dominant description—of the slum family. Female addicts' childhoods are often tormented and bad; they are usually either denied the gratification they need or are overindulged and given excessive mothering.

While most female addicts came from disturbed homes, with parents who worked with their hands, this was by no means true of all. All sections of society were represented among female addicts. Chambers *et al.*, for instance, found that about 21% of the addicts had fathers in professional or managerial occupations, and 5% in clerical sales. All told, about 26% were white collar, 74% blue collar.[14] The real pinch seems to come not from poverty, but from unstable homes, and from emotional thwarting and deprivation.[30] They found that the differences between races in this matter, too, was significant. Two-thirds of the fathers of white female addicts were blue collar, compared to 86.4% of black.[14]

There seems to be a significant relationship between mental disturbance, alcoholism, and drug dependence within families, for at least the last three decades. Pescor reported that female addicts almost always had some history of alcoholism in the family (if not parents, then a close relative).[5] This confluence of problems, problem families and drug dependency, has increased. About 40% of Ellinwood's sample had a close relative who had abused drugs, usually a parent or sibling. Nearly 30% had a parent who had served time in prison.[23] Willis reported that in his sample 30% had one or two alcoholic parents, about 13% had a parent who had been hospitalized for mental disorder, and half had one or both parents who were known to be mentally disturbed.[10] Guze *et al.* could definitely link social pathology, alcoholism and emotional disorder with the family.[51, 52, 53, 54]

In such malignant family structures the contagion within the family can rule: the non-addicts are frequently introduced to drugs and alcohol by other members of the family, and encouraged in abuse by them. Chambers found that 11% of his patients at Lexington reported that they were introduced to narcotics by an addicted family member. Moreover, the infected family usually is part of an infected environment.[14] Robinson says, "Junk is pushed where the population is least protected and where people are most avidly seeking a

Table 2 Female addict abuse characteristics

Year	Author	Predominant drug of choice	Mean age at onset of addiction	Source of drugs	Proportion legally employed %	Proportion with criminal record %
1929	Magid	Morphine	25	legal	*	*
1936	Pescor	Morphine	29	legal	*	0
1961	Cuskey	*		*	39.4%	22.5%
1961	Chambers	*	25	legal	*	100.0%
1966	Robinson	Heroin	18		30.0%	70.0%
1966	Ellinwood	Heroin	25.8			
1967	Ball	Heroin		illegal		48.6%
1967	Cuskey	Heroin	19.9	illegal	15.0%	100.0%
1967	Chambers	Heroin	24.8	illegal	10.0%	100.0%
1968	Hall	Heroin	25.4			80.0%
1968	Glaser	Morphine		illegal	30.0%	60.0%
1969	Willis	Demerol		legal	40.0%	
1969	Poplar	Heroin		illegal		91.2%
1970	Chambers	*	25.9	illegal	15.8%	69.6%
1970	Chambers				20.5%	

* Information not reported.

way out."[8] Cuskey *et al.* speak of "the sick environments" with their "psychological forces and environmental reinforcements that condition addicts to return to habits even when they receive so little heroin that physiological forces must be minimal."[1] In such environments physical health and proper nourishment have low priorities, and mental health is under constant siege. From childhood on it is very likely that the addict will have poor physical and mental health. Hall[18] and Stoffer[55] note that upon admission to treatment or prison, addicts are usually underweight and suffering from a number of physical and nutritional troubles of long standing. Ellinwood found, in his sample, that 13% had a history of asthma, 10% of thyroid disease, 13% of hypertension, and 10% of hepatitis. Even before they began using drugs 43% reported suffering painful menstruation and 23% miscarriages.[23]

The addict couple

It is scarcely surprising therefore that female addicts have great marital difficulties. They almost seem to seek out trouble. Like seeks out like: addicts (and potential addicts) marry one another. This is not only because they are thrown together and are hardly attractive to persons who do not take drugs, but also through a sort of magnetism of like traits and characteristics, inborn and acquired. Perhaps losers must seek solace where they can find it. Kraus[56] and Stein[57] have established this preference of like for like, and Guze *et al.* in a series of studies,[51, 52, 53, 54] demonstrated that children from multi-problem families marry more frequently than chance can account for. Eisenstein,[58] O'Donnell,[59] and Cuskey *et al.*[60] have shown, more specifically, that alcoholics and addicts quite often find spouses with the same addiction. A good place to start the study of marriage problems among female addicts, therefore, is to study addict couples. Almost all of the addiction-associated problems appear among addict couples. In 1966–67, 85 couples from all parts of the United States were treated at Lexington for addiction. Three-quarters were on heroin, the rest on diverse opiates; about three-fifths white (principally WASP), 28% black, 5% Puerto Rican, and the rest racially mixed. Of those reporting, 20% of the men and 23% of the women had had no previous marriage, and the majority of the rest had had no more than one. Present marriages had lasted four years among the heroin addicts, nine years among the others.

At time of hospitalization, the husbands averaged 35 years, the wives 31; both had been on drugs since about 20. Two-thirds of all had dropped out before finishing high school. Almost half the women had started using drugs only within the present marriages.[60]

Deviance, apart from and usually preceding addiction, had been strong in both husbands and wives while still adolescents. About half the boys had been arrested before 18, and before drug involvement; about half the girls had been married before 18, with four out of five marriages failing.

Early school dropout and arrest for the boys, and early pregnancy and marriage for the girls, indicate poor family lives and poor training in social and sexual control.

These patterns persisted throughout adulthood, marriage and hospitalization. Few of the adults were able to pursue reasonably normal personal and work lives. Most found partners in their own subculture: 54% of men and

60% of women married partners already addicted. Almost half of both men and women were married to partners diagnosed at Lexington as psychotic. Findings by Chein *et al.*[30] and Vaillant[61] were similar. O'Donnell,[59] in like fashion, found that his subjects tended to marry partners already deviant, and to become deviant themselves, if they had not already been so.

Marriage and the female addict

In spite of marital difficulties, female addicts do get married, and at a higher rate than formerly. To match, an increasing number per year fail. In Cuskey's comparative study, 25% of the 1961 sample were single when they entered Lexington, but only 17.3% of the 1967 patients were. In 1961 there were more intact than broken marriages—41.2% to 33.4%; in 1967 the reverse was true—36.4% to 46.2%.[6] Ellinwood found that only 30% of his female addicts, compared to 41% of his males, were single.[23] O'Donnell, too, has noted the trend toward more marriages among female addicts.

Divorce and separation

More marriages accompanied by more divorces must result in a kind of revolving-door situation. Back in 1944 Pescor[5] had predicted that many women addicts would ultimately be divorced or separated. The trend is confirmed not only by Cuskey's figures[6], but also by Weiland.[17] Chambers *et al.* found even higher rates of increase of divorce and separation for Mexican-American female addicts, despite their Catholic background—from 35.7 in 1961 to 50% in 1967. Some studies, particularly of Negro addicts, do show a higher percentage of intact marriages than these figures might indicate.[14] But these "intact" marriages include many common-law relationships of one year duration or more that are not considered marriages at all in many reckonings.

A more persuasive objection to making much of increased rates of marriage, separation and divorce among female addicts comes from the fact that there are similar, if not necessarily parallel, increases in all separations and divorces.[62] Interestingly, the divorce rate for male addicts is still significantly lower than for females, though it did rise from 10% in 1961 to 25.2% in 1967.[6] Female addicts tend to be more sympathetic to their addicted spouses than the reverse. It often works out to their disadvantage. (O'Donnell[59] and Eisenstein[58] document a similar phenomenon among alcoholics, indicating that this tendency lies in the nature of women, rather than of the drug.) Women will wait, often until they and their children have become social outcasts and they have suffered considerable damage, before they divorce, and then they are quite apt to go out and marry another addict or alcoholic.[58] Men are generally apt to shake loose much more quickly.

In sum, addicted women tend to marry addicted men, or at least men with severe problems. Into these homes children are born, often in poverty, in disturbance, in pathology, seldom with adequate care and food, and must then learn to live and build up adequate personality structures and identities. Hereditary factors, seriously disturbed parents, a malignant social environment, and all the distorted learning and conditioning experiences of such a background, interact in ways we cannot foresee. We do know some of the results. And what about the long-term consequences of successive generations of such matings?

Complications in pregnancy

Maternity

What happens to pregnancies and babies? In 1944 the typical female addict had one child. Ellinwood reports that female opiate addicts with families had, on the average, three children.[23] Figures are now more reliable because the increase of pregnant addicts coming into hospitals in the last decade has spurred research. In 1960, only one out of 164 admissions to the New York College–Metropolitan Hospital Center was a female addict. By 1969 the ratio was 1 to 47. Moreover, physicians have come to realize that many of the symptoms that they had ascribed to other causes were actually caused by, or associated with, the effects of drugs and addiction.

Maintaining good health in order to have healthy babies is, in most cases, low in the order of priorities for addict mothers. Blinick[63] and Perlmutter[64] note that hepatitis and some liver diseases are frequent among pregnant addicts. Howard found that 27% of the hepatitic subjects in his sample shared needles despite firm knowledge, or belief, that the needlesharer had hepatitis.[65]

Since prostitution is common, there is much VD—little of it treated or reported until the victim comes in for medical care. Stone et al.[66] report 17% positive serologies in their sample; in Perlmutter's,[64] 40%, previously untreated. Stern[68] found that the average patient had made less than one visit to the clinic prior to delivery. A great number appeared already in active labor.

Stone et al.[66] found that 30% of the sample was anemic; at least 90% of Stoffer's population had some abnormality in menstrual function[55]. Stone[66] found from a study of over 300 patients that more than 90% had had little or no prenatal care; 41% had some complication. There are high percentages of breech birth, pre-eclamptic toxemia and of hemorrhaging. Ignorance, poor health habits, unsterile needles, malnutrition and prostitution take their toll among babies as well as mothers.[66]

Obviously the typical addict, being unable to concentrate on anything beyond the necessity of the next fix, would have great difficulty being a good mother. Many are saved the trouble, because the rates of prematurity, of stillbirths, and of other neonatal deaths are a good deal higher than in the nonaddict population.

Precipitate labor

Reviewing histories from a number of admission groups over the past decade, Stone found that 62% of addicts went into labor before completing the 38th week.[66] Zelson found that 60% did not go to full term.[67] Of course in these matters, the memories and reported physical symptoms (like time of last menstrual period) of addicts are untrustworthy, so precise figures are difficult. Still, in 1967 only 6.2% of all live births in the United States were born prior to 37 weeks (Trends in Prematurity, United States, 1950, 1967); and ten times the normal rate of prematurity is significant. Addicts also suffer long labor both in total length and in the length of various stages.[64, 68]

The babies

Prematurity and low birth weight

The babies from addicted mothers are not only born earlier, but weigh less.[68, 69, 70, 71] In a study of 22 heroin-addicted women in the Obstetrics Service of the Brooklyn–Cumberland Medical Center, Perlmutter found that almost 57% of infants weighed less than 2,500 grams and averaged 2,296 grams.[64] Cobrink,[72] Semoff,[73] and others found a somewhat higher mean rate of 2,600 grams in the general population. Many experts have assumed that the rate of prematurity explained the light weights; but others have pointed out that they are light even for their own stage of development, and even full-term babies average lighter weights, indicating the possibility, as suggested by Snyder,[74] of retarded intrauterine growth. Undoubtedly the poor living and nutritional habits contribute to this.

The high incidence of breech presentations is related, apparently, to the light weight. Stern found 12% breeches in his addict sample, compared to 4.8% in the general admissions to the Metropolitan Obstetrical Service.[68] About 10% of Perlmutter's sample were breeches.[64]

Hooked babies

Sussman says that between 1875 and 1963, 286 cases of neonatal addiction were recorded. Since then there has been a sharp rise; the New York Hospital Committee found 300 cases in 1966 alone.[70] Several other studies since 1960 reported that from 60% to 90% of infants born to female addicts show symptoms. Nevertheless, many babies still pass through the system undiagnosed. Mothers often deny addiction. Some do not show obvious symptoms.[55] Sussman states that physicians need to be attuned to addiction signs in the babies themselves and that urine and blood studies must be made within 24 hours of delivery, since narcotic metabolites disappear rapidly.[70]

Most addict babies show symptoms severe enough to justify medication. Zelson found almost 78% of his baby sample needed treatment[67]; Cobrink found 60% in his.[72] If the mother took a fix a week or less before delivery, the baby would generally show symptoms; if more than a week, generally not.[75] Other investigators report that dosages of 12 milligrams or more daily would probably bring moderate to severe disturbances in newborns.[76]

Babies usually show symptoms within 24 hours, and they may last from a few days to two months. These may include rapid respiration, grunting, rib retraction, intermittent cyanosis, apnea, excess activity and trembling, twitching, convulsions, shrill crying, suckling of fingers as though hungry, vomiting, diarrhea, excess weight loss, sneezing and sweating. Since many newborns have one or more of these symptoms anyway, it is hardly surprising that before 1960 many of the withdrawal symptoms went undetected. Infants generally require no special treatment beyond swaddling, demand feeding schedules and limited handling. Paregoric and chlorpromazine have proven to be quite effective in treatment.

Dead babies

Fitting in with the rest of the pattern of complication and pathology, many addict babies are miscarried, born dead or die soon after birth. In a study of 66 addict mothers, Stern reported that about 7% of infants were stillborn.[68] In his study Perlmutter found a rate of 17.4% of perinatal deaths, compared to 2.2% among non-addicted mothers.[64] Stoffer found that of the 40 infants in his sample who survived pregnancy, about 10% died soon after, and about one quarter were critically ill but survived after therapy.[55] In the past, the death rate for infants with symptoms who were untreated ran as high as 93%. But Hill reports that as of 1963 the death rate for those who showed symptoms and were treated was 9%.[77] Other reports show a total mortality rate in the infant addict population of 7%–20%. Life or death may depend on quickness of diagnosis and treatment.

Most authorities place much or most of the blame on prematurity.[69] But a few are finding evidence of toxicity from the drugs themselves. Courville found distinct evidence of the feasibility of the direct action of narcotics on the nerve cell, or from indirect vasomotor action through the blood vessels.[78] Obviously such babies are extremely vulnerable, and need diagnosis and immediate and thorough help.

Special sub-groups

There are some sub-groups of female addicts that have distinct identities and characteristics. Perhaps most distinct are the female medical professionals, primarily nurses, who, like physicians, have access to opiates in their work, use legal and medical sources, and whose age, motivation and distribution are generally different from the rest of the addicts. From 1962 to 1967, 90 registered nurses were admitted to the Lexington Hospital for treatment of opiate addiction. Two-thirds had obtained drugs from physicians' or hospital supplies, while the remainder got theirs from drugstores, family, fraudulent prescription (which they were in a good position to forge) and, only lastly, pushers. At time of hospitalization they averaged 42 years of age and came from 30 states. By far, the most common drug used was Demerol, followed in turn by morphine, paregoric, codeine, Darvon and the barbiturates—the medicine cabinet choices. Far down the list was heroin. The average age of these ladies was 41.7—much older than the female addicts at Lexington.[79]

The future

The history of female drug involvement and treatment is, therefore, closely associated with society's attitudes towards drug use as reflected in the laws and law-enforcement practices. When opiates were provided legally by

Table 3 Female addict maternity characteristics

Year	Author	Mean age of mother	Proportion of premature birth	Proportion with breech presentations	Proportion with obstetrical complications	Proportion of cases with V.D. at admission	Proportion of perinatal mortality	Proportion of neonatal addiction	Proportion of congenital anomalies
1956	Cobrink		45.0%				0	91.0%	0
1963	Sussman		53.0%	21%			10.0%	79.0%	5%
1966	Stern		18.5%	12%	40.9%	20%	7.1%		
1967	Perlmutter	27.3	56.5%	10%		24%	17.4%	54.5%	13%
1968	Stoffer	28.9				68%	17.5%	57.5%	
1969	Blinick		34.0%	9%	11.0%	18%	3.0%		
1971	Stone	26.7	50.0%	9%	26.0%	17%	3.6%	67.4%	1%

physicians and druggists, female addicts were created and treated accordingly. When drug control fell into the hands of law-enforcement agencies, addiction fell, and treatment was administered in reformatories. However, since the early 1960's, important changes in patterns of female drug abuse and addiction have been taking place. These are concurrent changes, not all related.

First, many new self-help and drug-free treatment facilities have sprung into being and into popularity, including Synanon and Daytop Village. Increasing numbers of women are accepting help from these sources and from similar therapeutic groups.

Second, synthetic narcotics have been developed, notably methadone, which has provided addicts with maintenance support that allows them to give up opiates and lead relatively crime-free and trouble-free lives, without prostitution or theft. Clinics and treatment centers, many attached to hospitals, most admitting female patients, have risen in most major cities and enjoy widespread community support. They use methadone, psychotherapy, or other treatments in various combinations. The general public, alarmed by rising drug-crime statistics, has changed old attitudes toward addiction and addicts. All these developments presage a turning toward medical and social forms of control.

Other developments in the last decade have not been so encouraging. The gaps between men and women, whites and blacks, are narrowing. More women are getting involved in violence. The prostitute and her pimp, operating as a team of muggers, are reported to be significant in Times Square if not yet in the statistics. The increase in the number of addicts seems out of control. Writing in 1969, Ball and Chambers could compute that there were 108,424 known addicts in the United States of whom almost 31,000 had just been reported that year.[80] Since then, addiction has more than doubled and 50,000 or more are women.

A matter of great concern is the emerging pattern of sedative-hypnotic and stimulant abuse among middle-class women. Many of these are synthetics and are abused in combination. As Chambers and Moldestad have observed, "among contemporary opiate abusers, concurrent sedative abuse is the prevalent drug pattern regardless of which opiates are being abused".[14] It is impossible to watch this ominous development and not be stirred by the inevitable echoes of an old and sad song, becoming a trifle scratchy from the years but all too recognizable: legal drugs and respectable people, a majority of whom are housewives and working women, searching for something to combat the stress, pain and fatigue of life—something that is not illegal, or widely condemned, or even very noticeable. Little pills in little packages, with little attention paid to the addiction or psychosis that might come with that package. Predominantly middle-class, predominantly white . . . .

History may not repeat itself in detail, but events do tend to respond in similar fashion to similar pressures, similar needs, and similar mistakes.

Notes

1. Cuskey, W. R., A. W. Klein and W. Krasner (1972) *Drug-Trip Abroad.* The University of Pennsylvania Press, Philadelphia.

2. Terry and Pellens (1970) The extent of chronic opiate use in the United States prior to 1921. In: *The Epidemiology of Opiate Addiction in the United States.* Ball, J. C. and C. D. Chambers, eds. C. C. Thomas, Springfield, Illinois.

3. Schur, E. (1965) *Crimes Without Victims.* Prentice-Hall, Inc., Englewood Cliffs.

4. Meyerstein, A. N. (1964) Drug addiction: A review. *J. of Sch. Health.* 34:77.

5. Pescor, M. J. (1944) A comparative statistical study of male and female drug addicts. *Amer. J. of Psych.* 100:771.

6. Cuskey, W. R., H. Clifford and A. Moffett (1971) A comparison of female opiate addicts admitted to Lexington Hospital in 1961 and 1967. *HSMHA Rep.* 86:332.

7. O'Neill, E. (1956) *Long Day's Journey into Night.* Yale University Press, New Haven.

8. Robinson, B. F. (1961) Criminality among narcotic addicts in the Illinois State Reformatory for Women. *Ill. Med. J.* 119:320.

9. de Alarcon, R. (1969) The spread of heroin abuse in a community. *Bull. on Narc.* 21.

10. Willis, J. H. (1970) Drug dependence: some demographic and psychological characteristics in United Kingdom and United States subjects. *Br. J. Add.* 64:135.

11. Chambers, C. and D. Schultz (1971) *Ladies Home Journal,* Nov. p. 190.

12. Cockett, R. (1971) *Drug Abuse and Personality in Young Offenders.* Appleton Century Crofts, New York.

13. Magid, M. D. (1971) Narcotic addiction in the female. *Med. J. and Rec.* 129:306.

14. Chambers, C., L. Hinesley and M. Moldestad (1970) Narcotic addiction in females: a race comparison. *Int. J. of the Add.*

15. Weisen, R. L., R. Wang and T. J. Stemper. The drug abuse program at Milwaukee County Institutions—a six month report. *Wisc. Med. J.* 69:141.

16. Blum, R. H. *et al.* (1970) *Society and Drugs.* Jossey-Bass, Inc. San Francisco.

17. Weiland, W. and C. Chambers (1970) Two methods of utilizing methadone in the outpatient treatment of narcotic addicts. *Int. J. of Add.* 5:332.

18. Hall, M. E. (1968) Mental and physical efficiency of women drug addicts. *J. Ab. Soc. Psych.* 5.

19. Williams, J. E. and W. M. Bates (1970) Some characteristics of female narcotic addicts. *Int. J. of Add.* 5:245.

20. Ball, J. C., W. M. Bates and J. A. O'Donnell (1966) Characteristics of hospitalized narcotic addicts. *Health Education Welfare Indicators.* March.

21. Chambers, C., W. R. Cuskey and A. D. Moffett (1970) Mexican opiate addicts. In: *The Epidemiology of Opiate Addiction in the United States.* Ball, J. C. and C. D. Chambers, eds. C. C. Thomas, Springfield, Illinois.

22. Ball, J. C. (1965) Two patterns of narcotic addiction in the U.S. *J. Criminal Law, Criminology and Police Science,* 56:210.

23. Ellinwood, E. H., W. A. Smith and G. E. Vaillant (1966) Narcotic addiction in males and females: a comparison. *Int. J. of Add.* 1:33.

24. Royfe, E. H. (1966) Social and psychological characteristics of 100 patient drug addicts. *Penn. Psych. Quart.* 5:38.

25. Jaffe, J. H., M. S. Zaks and E. N. Washington. Experience with the use of methadone in a multi-modality program for the treatment of narcotic users. *Int. J. of Add.*

26. Bates, W. (1968) Occupational characteristics of Negro addicts. *Int. J. of Add.* 1:2.

27. Mizener, G. L., J. F. Barter and P. H. Werme (1970) Patterns of drug use among college students: a preliminary report. *Amer. J. Psych.* 127:15.

28. Glaser, D., J. T. Incardi and D. V. Babst (1969) Later heroin use by marihuana-using and non-drug adolescent offenders in N.Y.C. *Int. J. of Add.* 4:1.

29. Chambers, C. and A. D. Moffett (1970) Negro opiate addiction. *The Epidemiology of Opiate Addiction in the United States.* Ball, J. C. and C. D. Chambers, eds. C. C. Thomas, Springfield, Illinois.

30. Chein, I., D. L. Gerald, R. S. Lee and E. Rosenfeld (1964) *The Road to H: Narcotics, Delinquency and Social Policy.* Basic Books, Inc., New York.
31. Schuster, D. U. (1971) Drug treatment: avenues open to physicians. *Ind. J. State Med. Assn.* May, p. 417.
32. Preble, E. and J. Casey (1969) Taking care of business. *Int. J. of Add.* 4:1.
33. Ausubel, D. P. (1958) *Drug Addiction.* Random House, New York.
34. Levy, N. J. (1968) The use of drugs by teenagers for sanctuary and illusion. *Amer. J. of Psych.* 28:48.
35. Rado, S. (1963) Fighting narcotic bondage and other forms of narcotic disorders. *Comp. Psych.* 4:160.
36. Fencichel, O. (1945) *The Psychoanalytical Theory of Neurosis.* W. W. Norton Co., New York.
37. Merton, R. K. (1957) *Social Theory and Social Structure.* Free Press of Glencoe, New York.
38. Cloward, R. A. and L. E. Ohlin (1960) *Delinquency and Opportunity.* Free Press of Glencoe, New York.
39. Kolb, L. (1962) *Drug Addiction: A Medical Problem.* C. C. Thomas, Springfield, Illinois.
40. Dole, V. and M. E. Nyswander (1966) Rehabilitating heroin addicts after blockade with methadone. *N.Y. State J. Med.* August, p. 2011.
41. Hill, H. E., C. A. Haertzen and R. Glaser (1960) Personality characteristics of narcotic addicts as indicated by the MMPI. *J. Gen. Psych.* 62:127.
42. Glaser, F. B. (1970) Misinformation about drugs: a problem for drug abuse education. *Int. J. of Add.* 5:595.
43. Winick, C. and S. M. Finch (1962) The psychiatrist and juvenile delinquent. *J. Amer. Acad. Child Psych.* 1:619.
44. Robins, L., H. Gyman and P. O'Neal (1962) The interaction of social class and deviant behavior. *Amer. Soc. Rev.* 27:4.
45. Dole, V. and M. E. Nyswander (1967) Heroin addiction—a metabolic disease. *Arch. Int. Med.* 120:19.
46. O'Donnell, J. A. (1968) Social factors and follow-up studies in opiate addiction. *Res. Pub. Ass. Res. Nerv. Mental Dis.* 46:333.
47. Ward, D. A. and G. G. Kassebaum (1964) Lesbian Liaisons. *Trans-Action* 1:28.
48. Burke, E. L. (1968) Patient values in an adolescent drug unit. *Amer. J. Psych.*
49. Hague, B. (1969) In San Francisco's tenderloin. *Amer. J. Nurs.* 69:2180.
50. Isbell, H. and W. M. White (1953) Clinical characteristics of addiction. *Amer. J. Med.*
51. Guze, S. B., D. W. Goodwin and J. C. Crane (1960) A psychiatric study of the wives of convicted felons: an example of assortive mating. *Amer. J. Psychiat.* 126:12.
52. Guze, S. B., E. D. Wolfgram, J. K. McKinney and D. P. Cantwell (1967) Psychiatric illness in the families of convicted criminals, a study of 519 first-degree relatives. *Dis. Nerv. Syst.* 28:651.
53. Guze, S. B., V. B. Tuason, P. D. Gatfield, Stewart and B. Picken (1972) Psychiatric illness and crime with particular reference to alcoholism: a study of 223 criminals. *J. Ner. Ment. Dis.* 134:512.
54. Guze, S. B., D. W. Goodwin and J. B. Crane (1969) Criminality and psychiatric disorders. *Arch. Gen. Psychiat.* 20:583.
55. Stoffer, S. S. (1968) A gynecological study of drug addicts. *Amer. J. Obs. and Gyn.* 101:779.
56. Kraus, A. S. and A. M. Lilienfeld (1959) Some epidemiologic aspects of the high mortality rate in the young widowed group. *J. Chron. Dis.* 10:207.
57. Stein, Z. M. A. and M. Susser (1969) Widowhood and mental illness. *Br. J. Rev. Soc. Med.* 23:106.

58. Eisenstein, V. (1956) *Neurotic Interaction in Marriage*. Basic Books, Inc., New York.
59. O'Donnell, J. (1969) Narcotic addicts in Kentucky. *Public Health Service Publication*, No. 1881.
60. Cuskey, W. R., H. Clifford, A. D. Moffett and T. Premkumar (1972) Drug addiction among married couples at the Lexington Hospital, 1966 and 1967. Unpublished manuscript.
61. Vaillant, G. E. (1966) A 12-year follow-up of N.Y. narcotic addicts. *Arch. Gen. Psychiat.* 15.
62. Divorce Statistics Analysis, United States, 1964 and 1965. *Public Health Service, Vital and Health Statistics*, Series 21, No. 17, U.S. Department of Health Education and Welfare.
63. Blinick, G., C. Wallach and E. M. Jerez (1969) Pregnancy in narcotic addicts treated by medical withdrawal. *Amer. J. Obs. and Gyn.* 105:997.
64. Perlmutter, J. F. (1967) Drug addiction in pregnant women. *Am. J. Obs. and Gyn.* Oct. 15, p. 569.
65. Howard, J. and P. Borges (1970) Needle sharing. *Health Soc. Behav.* Sept. 11, p. 220.
66. Stone, M. L., L. J. Salerna, Green and C. Zeison (1971) Narcotic addiction in pregnancy. *Am. J. Obs. and Gyn.*
67. Zelson, R. E. and E. Wasserman (1971) Neonatal narcotic addiction: 10 years observation. *Ped.* 48:178.
68. Stern, R. (1966) The pregnant addict: a study of 66 case histories, 1950–1959. *Am. J. Obs. and Gyn.*
69. Rosenthal, T., S. W. Patrick and D. C. Krug (1964) Congenital neonatal narcotics addiction: a natural history. *Am. J. Pub. Health* 54:1252.
70. Sussman, S. (1963) Narcotic and methamphetamine use during pregnancy. *Am. J. Dis. of Child.* 106:325.
71. Claman, A. D. and R. I. Strong (1962) Obstetric and Gynecologic aspects of heroin addiction. *Amer. J. Obs. and Gyn.* Jan. 15.
72. Cobrink, R. W., T. Hood, Jr., E. Churid and L. B. Slobody (1956) The effects of natural narcotic addiction on the newborn infant. *Amer. J. Dis. Child.* 92:504.
73. Semoff, M. C. F. (1967) Narcotic addiction of the newborn. *Arizona Med.* 24:933.
74. Synder, F. F. (1949) *Obstetrical Analgesic and Anesthesia: Their Effects Upon Labour and the Child*. W. B. Saunders and Co., Philadelphia.
75. Neuberg, R. (1970) Drug dependence and pregnancy: a review of the problems and their management. *J. Obs. and Gyn.* 77:1117.
76. Nesbitt, R. E. L., Jr. (1957) *Perinatal Loss in Modern Obstetrics*. F. A. Davis Co., Philadelphia, p. 159.
77. Hill, R. M. and M. H. Desmond (1963) Management of narcotic withdrawal syndrome. *Ped. Clinics of N. Amer.* 10:67.
78. Courville, Cited in Nesbitt, R. E. L., Jr. (1957) *Perinatal Loss in Modern Obstetrics*. F. A. Davis Co., Philadelphia, p. 159.
79. Poplar, J. F. (1969) Characteristics of nurse addicts. *Am. J. Nur.* 69:117.
80. Ball, J. C. and C. D. Chambers (1970) Overview of the problem. In: *The Epidemiology of Opiate Addiction in the United States*. Ball, J. C. and C. D. Chambers, eds. C. C. Thomas, Springfield, Illinois.

Part three
Women in court

A major theme in works on women in crime and the criminal justice system is that male law enforcement officials treat women more generously, more permissively, and more courteously than they treat men. Translated into day-to-day behavior, this means people believe that the police are less likely to pick up, book, and arrest a female than a male engaged in the same sort of suspicious behavior, and that, if arrested, a female will be treated more gently by male police officers. These beliefs also extend into the courtroom, where, rather than being blind, justice is expected to be more understanding of the female's plight than of the male's. Indeed, when male judges are confronted by a female defendant (so the argument has been stated) it is difficult for them not to imagine their own mothers, sisters, or wives in the same circumstances, and act accordingly. This idea that women get a better shake from the criminal justice system than men in the same circumstances pervaded much of the literature on women and crime until the 1970s. The excerpt from Pollak in Part One is representative of this viewpoint.

A theme that has been heard less clearly and less frequently is that male law enforcement officials are *more* punitive toward women who are convicted than toward men. According to this view, for example, judges are more likely to throw the book at a female than a male defendant, because they see in her behavior a greater discrepancy between the behavior expected of a woman and her actual behavior than they do between the behavior expected of a man and the actual behavior of a male defendant. Women defendants thus pay for judges' beliefs that it is more in man's nature to commit crimes than it is in woman's. When a male judge is convinced that the woman before him has committed a crime, he is more likely to convict and punish her, not only for the specific offense but also for transgressing his expectations of womanly behavior in general.

All of the selections in this part examine the issue of whether women are the recipients of special treatment, be it of a positive or negative nature, by the courts. In the tables based on California judicial statistics found in the Simon selection, it may be noted that as recently as 1972, women seemed to be receiving some preferential treatment by the courts. The author concludes on the basis of those data "that the eyes of justice are neither blinded nor fully opened; rather, they seem to be open just enough to be able to discern the sex of the defendant and to allow that characteristic to influence the decisions to some extent."

The selection by Nagel and Weitzman compares verdicts and sentences that male and female defendants received for larceny and felonious assault. Nagel and Weitzman observe that a particular manifestation of the preferential treatment toward women that many attribute to trial court judges takes the form of paternalism, which has favorable as well as unfavorable consequences. Favorable consequences for women include decreased likelihood of remaining in custody during the pretrial period compared to men; decreased likelihood of being convicted once tried; and greater likelihood of receiving milder sentences if convicted. Unfavorable consequences are that women are less likely to have attorneys, preliminary hearings, or jury trials. Nagel and Weitzman note that women are more likely to be jailed in assault than in larceny cases and attribute the stricter treatment of women in assault cases to the fact that assault is a more "manly" crime. Women who commit it pay a price for their behavior by being treated more like men. The California judicial data in the Simon selection fail to support this thesis, however. In California, women who were accused of such typically male offenses as robbery, burglary, and auto theft were treated at least as preferentially as women who were accused of larceny, an offense that is more typically associated with women.

The Temin selection argues in favor of the passage of the Equal Rights Amendment on the grounds that passage would make null and void all existing statutes that prescribe longer sentences for female offenders and that permit only women to receive indeterminate sentences. The existence of such statutes as the indeterminate sentence for women is cited by Temin as evidence of the unfair, more punitive treatment accorded to women by the courts. Temin also cites the sanctioning of a procedure whereby only convicted male defendants have their minimum sentences determined by a judge in an open court hearing and in the presence of counsel, while the minimum sentence for female defendants is decided by a parole board in a closed session without representation by counsel. Upon review of the *Daniel* case in Pennsylvania and other cases in New Jersey, Maryland, Maine, Ohio, Iowa, and Massachusetts, Temin concludes that the courts are not the most appropriate or effective means for achieving equality of rights for women under the Fifth and Fourteenth Amendments, and that ratification of the Equal Rights Amendment is the most efficient way of bringing about an end to discrimination on the basis of sex.

Frankel's selection reviews the disparate treatment men and women receive in the criminal justice system and provides examples of the ways current state statutes and decisions will have to be changed and reinterpreted to bring them into compliance with the Equal Rights Amendment. As Frankel points out, under the ERA, sex is a prohibited classification. The examples she provides of statutes that will have to be changed to comply with the ERA are: (1) the doctrine of presumed coercion, which states that a married woman is not criminally responsible for acts done as a result of her husband's coercion; (2) the rule that a husband and wife cannot conspire together; (3) "female only" crimes, of which prostitution is the best example. Those states that have prostitution statutes that make a distinction on the basis of sex would have to change them in order to comply with the ERA; (4) statutes that offer special protection for female offenders; (5) laws that make distinctions based upon sex plus some other factor—that make an age distinction between males and females, for example; (6) laws that punish men and women differently for committing the same crimes. These include laws penalizing a married woman for having sexual intercourse with a man not her husband but not penalizing a married man who has intercourse with a woman not his wife. Frankel concludes that "much of the criminal law today reflects attitudes which are sex biased and outdated. The Equal Rights Amendment presents legislatures with the motivation and the opportunity to revise their criminal codes and eliminate antiquated laws as well as revise necessary laws which fail to treat men and women equally."

We made a plea for more data in the closing paragraphs of our introduction to Part Two. Such a plea is also appropriate to this section on the courts. The dearth of judicial statistics makes it difficult to conduct research in this area. At least at the arrest stage, we have national statistics collected annually that describe the number of people arrested, the offense with which they are charged, and some minimal demographic information, such as race, sex, and minor and adult status. Judicial statistics at the level of state trial courts are almost nonexistent, with California the rare exception. A mail survey of all state court systems conducted a few years ago by Simon failed to turn up any system save California that compiled judicial statistics on a regular basis.

Unlike Great Britain and most of the countries of Western Europe, the United States lacks a centralized data bank for judicial statistics that describe convictions and sentences for offenses such as those contained in the FBI compiled arrest reports. It would be extremely useful for persons concerned with public policy on matters pertaining to criminal justice, as well as for social researchers, to be able to follow offenders from the time of arrest through the trial and sentencing stages. Some needed evidence might be obtained if, for example, the office of Law Enforcement Assistance Administration were to make its financial allocations to states for the purpose of establishing criminal justice commissions contingent upon each state's compiling and making publicly available reports on numbers of defendants processed through trial courts, along with accounts of charges, verdicts, and sentences. If the states could also be prevailed upon to collect basic demographic and social status indicators, opportunities for carrying out meaningful research would be considerably enhanced. In addition to sex, race, and age breakdowns, social indicators of occupation, education, and marital status would be extremely useful. Of all the industrialized, technologically advanced countries, the United States stands almost alone in the absence of routinely compiled basic judicial statistics.

22 Women in Court

Rita James Simon

Two schools of thought prevail on how women defendants are treated in the courts of justice. The view held by most observers is that women receive preferential treatment which in operational terms means that they are less likely to be convicted than men for the same type of offense, that if convicted they are less likely to be sentenced, and that if sentenced they are likely to receive milder or shorter sentences. The factors that are thought to motivate judges toward leniency to women are chivalry, naivete (for example, judges often say that they cannot help but compare women defendants with other women they know well—namely, their mothers and wives, whom they cannot imagine behaving in the manner attributed to the defendant), and practicality (most of the women defendants have young children, and sending them to prison places too much of a burden on the rest of the society).

A particular manifestation of the preferential treatment toward women that many attribute to trial court judges takes the form of paternalism. Nagel and Weitzman (1971) assert that paternalistic behavior has favorable as well as unfavorable consequences for women defendants. The favorable consequences are that women are less likely to remain in custody during the pretrial period than are men. Once tried they are less likely to be convicted; if convicted, they are likely to receive milder sentences. The unfavorable consequences are that women are less likely to have an attorney, a preliminary hearing, or a jury trial.

Using data originally collected by Silverstein in a national survey of the defense of the poor, Nagel and Weitzman compared the treatment that men and women charged with assault and larceny received in the trial courts (Silverstein 1965).

Using these data, Nagel and Weitzman concluded that paternalism prevails almost equally for both types of offenses, save that women are more likely to

From *The Contemporary Woman and Crime* by Rita James Simon. National Institute of Mental Health, Washington, D.C., 1975. Pp. 49–60.

be jailed in assault than in larceny cases. Nagel and Weitzman attribute the stricter treatment of women in assault cases to the fact that assault is a more manly type of crime, and women who commit it pay the price for their behavior by being treated more like men.

Others believe that judges are more punitive toward women. They are more likely to throw the book at the female defendant because they believe there is a greater discrepancy between her behavior and the behavior expected of women than there is between the behavior of the male defendant and the behavior expected of men. In other words, women defendants pay for the judges' belief that it is more in man's nature to commit crimes than it is in woman's. Thus, when a judge is convinced that the woman before him has committed a crime, he is more likely to overact and punish her, not only for the specific offense but also for transgressing against his expectations of womanly behavior.

The existence of such statutes as the indeterminate sentence for women, or the sanctioning of a procedure whereby only convicted male defendants have their minimum sentences determined by a judge at an open hearing and in the presence of counsel, while the woman's minimum sentence is decided by a parole board in a closed session in which she is not represented by counsel, are cited as evidence of the unfair, punitive treatment that is accorded to women in the court.

•   •   •

Unlike the statistics that describe male and female arrest rates that are available in the *Uniform Crime Reports,* there are no comprehensive statistics that describe the relative conviction rates for men and women within each of the State court systems. California provides the best data on convictions and sentencing of any of the States; and we draw heavily on the California data for our information. Ohio also maintains some statistics by sex and those also are considered. But a mail survey of the 48 other State court systems failed to turn up any other judicial statistics for which it was possible to compare conviction rates between men and women.

Since 1963, the Administrative Office of the United States Courts has published an annual report that describes how defendants are disposed of in the 89 United States District Courts. These reports contain statistics that describe the proportion of men and women convicted by category of offense. The defense categories included in these reports are defined as follows:

Class I: *Fraud* includes frauds occurring against lending and credit institutions, the Veterans Administration, Railroad Retirement Act, and Social Security Act. *Embezzlement* includes embezzlement of bank or postal funds; public money or property; lending, credit, and insurance institutions; by officers of a carrier in interstate commerce and by officers of labor organizations. *Obscene mail* covers transmitting obscene matter in interstate commerce.

Class II: *Income tax fraud* covers evasion, failure to file income tax. *Other fraud* includes frauds connected with bankruptcy, excise tax, impersonation, nationality laws, passports, commodity credit, Security and Exchange Commission, claims, or statements and conspiracies not otherwise classified.

Class III: *Liquor, Internal Revenue* covers violations of Internal Revenue Liquor Law, U.S.C. title 26.

Class IV: *Theft* includes larceny and theft from banks which are federally insured, and from post offices, mail, U.S. property, and theft occurring on Government reservations, etc. *Postal fraud* includes fraud involving the use of the mails, wire, radio, etc. *Forgery* includes postal forgery and forgery of obligations and securities of the United States.

Class V: *Border registration of addicts and narcotics violators, assault and homicide* includes simple or aggravated assault. *Homicide* covers first and second degree murder and manslaughter. *Miscellaneous general offenses* includes all offenses not otherwise classified, such as bribery, traffic offenses, extortion, and racketeering, gambling and lottery, kidnapping, perjury, and laws dealing with firearms and weapons; also includes arson, abortions, bigamy, disorderly conduct, and malicious destruction of property.

Class VI: *Counterfeiting* and *burglary* include all offenses connected with the burglary or breaking and entering of federally insured banks, or of post offices in interstate commerce and on Government reservations; *interstate transportation of stolen property; marihuana* offenses involving violations of the Marihuana Tax Act; *Selective Service Act* violations of the Universal Military Training and Service Act of 1948; *other National defense laws;* and *Sex offenses* including rape, white slave traffic, and importing alien females for prostitution or immoral purposes.

Class VII: *Auto theft* includes transportation, etc., of stolen motor vehicles or aircraft, and sale or receipt of such vehicles.

Class VIII: *Narcotics* covers all violations of the Narcotic Control Act of 1956 and the Narcotic Drugs Import and Export Act. *Robbery* covers all offenses connected with federally insured lending and credit institutions, banks, and postal facilities. It also includes robberies carried out in the maritime and territorial jurisdiction of the United States and robbery of Government property from an officer or employee of the United States.

The limitations of these data should be obvious, especially after reading the descriptions of the offense categories upon which the statistics are based. Most defendants, male and female, in the United States are tried in State courts because they have broken a State law. The offenses listed in the annual report of 89 United States District Courts represent only a small proportion of all criminal trials in the United States. For example, in 1 year, 1968, about 26,000 defendants were convicted in all the Federal district courts compared to more than 47,000 defendants who were convicted in the California State courts alone.

Another factor that limits the generalizability of the Federal statistics for the purposes of this monograph is that some of the offenses are acts that pertain specifically to men—for example, violations of the Selective Service Act. Other offenses that are included in the Federal categories are ones in which organized crime must be heavily involved; and thus far, women seem to have been effectively barred from entry into organized crime.

But one use to which these Federal statistics may be put is simply to compare longitudinal trends; that is, the proportions of females who have been convicted in the Federal courts from 1963 through 1971. Even in this atypical context, the expectation is that women's visibility should have increased during the latter part of the 1960s. The number and proportion of

Table 5.1 **Number of males and females convicted and percentage of females among convictions in 89 U.S. District Courts, 1963–71**

YEAR	MALES CONVICTED (NUMBER)	FEMALES CONVICTED (NUMBER)	FEMALE (PERCENT)
1963	26,914	2,086	7.0
1964	26,228	2,080	7.1
1965	25,975	1,957	6.8
1966	24,528	1,975	7.2
1967	23,766	1,805	6.7
1968	23,069	2,033	7.9
1969	24,060	2,109	7.9
1970	25,203	2,382	8.5
1971	28,581	2,931	9.1
Increase	Percent	Percent	Percent
1963–71	6.2	40.5	30
Increase			
1967–71	20.3	62.4	35

Source: Data for 1963–71 from *Federal Offenders in the U.S. District Courts.* Table 17. Washington, D.C.: Administrative Office of the U.S. Courts.

female defendants who were convicted each year for all of the offense categories combined are given in table 5.1.

From 1967 through 1971 there was an increase of 62 percent in the overall number of women who were convicted in United States District Courts, compared to an increase of only 20.3 percent for males. Unfortunately, the information available from the Federal courts does not provide a separate breakdown for men and women by type and length of sentence, among those who have been convicted.

The proportion of convictions of women in selective offense categories between 1964 and 1971 is given in table 5.2. Three observations may be made about these data: (1) The offenses for which the highest proportion of women have been convicted during the entire 8-year timespan are fraud, embezzlement, and forgery. They are the same offenses for which the highest proportion of women are arrested and subsequently brought to trial in the State courts. (2) Those same offenses also show the greatest increase in the proportion of females convicted from 1964 through 1971. (3) These offenses are the types that are most congruent with the hypothesis that as the women's movement gains greater visibility and has more impact on its potential constituency, female crime rates will increase, and they will increase especially in these offense categories.

The proportion of men and women who were convicted and sentenced in the State of California over the past decade or so and over a shorter period of time in Ohio is also given. As indicated earlier, statistics for California constituted the major portion of the statistics available for examining how women fare in the State courts. It may not be unsound to generalize conviction rates from California to the rest of the country, because California arrest rates approximate those for the country as a whole (Ward 1968).

The proportion of females who have been convicted by offense categories in California superior courts from 1960 through 1972 is described in table 5.3.

Table 5.2 Percentage of females among convictions by specific offense categories, 89 U.S. District Courts, 1964–71[1]

	1964		1965		1966		1967		1968		1969		1970		1971		Average rate change	
Offense category	No.[1]	Percent	No.[1]	Percent	No.[1]	Percent	No.[1]	Percent	No.[1]	Percent	No.[1]	Percent	No.[1]	Percent	No.[1]	Percent	1964–71	1967–71
Class I:																		
Fraud	666	12.4	515	16.7	555	18.9	300	18.7	250	26.4	257	21.8	236	33.1	235	28.1	+2.24	+2.35
Embezzlement	1,231	20.7	1,207	19.7	1,148	21.0	1,220	24.5	1,231	24.6	1,421	26.4	1,602	27.3	1,940	26.7	+ .86	+ .55
Class II:																		
Income tax fraud	597	6.7	574	7.3	593	5.2	542	5.7	498	6.8	502	5.2	483	7.7	693	7.9	+ .17	+ .55
Other fraud	581	7.1	489	4.7	404	4.7	357	7.3	287	4.9	271	8.5	282	8.2	455	7.3	+ .03	0
Class IV:																		
Theft	2,418	10.5	2,256	10.8	2,223	9.7	2,137	8.9	2,282	10.6	2,281	9.8	2,488	10.5	3,088	11.8	+ .19	+ .73
Postal fraud	413	12.1	418	14.4	385	11.2	341	14.7	359	15.0	405	9.9	387	13.7	496	14.9	+ .40	+ .05
Forgery	2,517	22.4	2,117	21.9	1,958	23.5	1,642	24.1	1,787	24.5	1,441	25.3	1,741	26.3	2,042	27.1	+ .67	+ .75
Class V:																		
Assault, homicide	233	8.6	214	8.4	254	2.8	249	3.6	268	6.3	354	7.1	390	7.4	364	6.0	− .37	+ .60
Class VIII:																		
Narcotics	919	10.6	1,116	10.0	1,052	11.7	914	12.9	953	9.4	1,007	11.9	919	10.9	1,158	11.3	+ .10	− .40
Robbery	524	3.4	660	2.0	577	5.5	703	2.6	862	3.8	961	4.0	1,002	3.4	1,359	5.3	+ .27	+ .68

Source: Data for 1963–71 from *Federal Offenders in the U.S. District Courts*. Table 17. Washington, D.C.: Administrative Office of the U.S. Courts.
[1] Total number of persons, male and female, convicted.

Table 5.3 California: percentage of females among convictions in superior courts, 1960–64 and 1966–72[1]

	1960–64		1966		1967		1968		1969		1970		1971		1972	
Offense	Number[1]	Per-cent	Number[1]	Per-cent	Number[1]	Per-cent	Number[1]	Per-cent	Number[1]	Per-cent	Number[1]	Per-cent	Number[1]	Per-cent	Number[1]	Per-cent
Homicide and manslaughter	2,557	12.4	656	12.7	764	14.5	851	14.7	731	12.3	850	12.2	940	13.2	1,047	13.8
Robbery	8,756	2.6	1,666	3.2	2,721	5.0	3,050	4.7	2,106	3.9	2,207	3.1	2,719	3.6	2,753	3.7
Assault	7,860	8.2	2,553	8.6	2,650	10.4	3,284	11.0	3,495	10.1	3,373	9.2	3,654	10.3	3,681	9.6
Burglary	24,650	2.4	5,704	3.2	7,691	4.1	8,026	4.4	6,362	3.6	6,499	3.4	7,913	3.4	7,315	3.7
Larceny-theft	16,450	12.2	3,685	16.4	3,563	14.8	3,675	16.7	2,102	13.2	2,410	11.7	2,676	11.1	2,645	9.9
Auto theft	9,596	1.8	2,569	2.2	2,639	2.2	2,950	3.1	3,018	2.8	2,485	2.9	2,529	3.2	2,132	2.4
Forgery and checks	23,375	16.6	4,810	20.4	4,432	22.5	4,818	24.8	4,476	27.0	4,118	26.9	4,107	28.4	3,493	27.7
Drug law violations	14,439	10.3	5,334	9.6	9,877	11.3	12,889	12.0	18,367	12.3	18,672	13.9	20,808	14.4	15,954	14.5
Violent crimes	19,173	6.2	4,875	7.3	6,135	8.5	7,185	8.8	6,332	8.3	6,430	7.5	7,313	8.2	7,481	8.0
Property crimes	50,696	5.5	11,958	7.1	13,893	6.5	15,451	6.9	11,482	5.2	11,394	5.1	13,118	4.9	12,092	4.8
All crimes	136,083	8.3	36,844	8.9	41,027	9.7	47,277	10.5	50,123	10.9	49,679	11.1	55,734	11.2	48,730	10.9

Source: Data for 1960–64, 1966–72 from *Crime and Delinquency in California*. Sacramento, Calif.: State of California, Department of Justice, Bureau of Criminal Statistics.
Note: Data for 1965 missing.
[1] Total number of persons, male and female, convicted.

Note in table 5.3 that for all crimes combined, there has been a 31 percent increase in the proportion of women convicted between 1960 and 1972. There has been an increase of 29 percent in the proportion of women who were convicted of the violent offenses included in the Index of Serious Crimes (homicide, robbery, and assault), but a decline of 13 percent in the proportion of women who were convicted of the property offenses included in the index (burglary, larceny, and auto theft).

Thus, even though the proportion of women arrested has increased for the property offenses contained in the index and declined for the violent offenses, those women who have been arrested in the past few years for violent offenses are more likely to be convicted today than in the earlier part of the 1960s. But the increase in female arrest rates for type I property offenses has not been followed by an increase in female conviction rates for those offenses.

In the type II offenses, the level of women convicted has increased sharply for drug law violations. Indeed, if one looks at the distribution of convictions by offense category among the cohort of women who were convicted in any given year, one sees that drug law violations in 1972 accounted for almost half of all female convictions (43.5) (see table 5.4).

We can compare the California statistics with those obtained from Ohio for a 3-year-period, 1969–71. Among the eight offense categories for which there are comparable data, the rank order from highest to lowest conviction rates in each year is the same for both States. Forgery has the highest proportion of female conviction rates followed by homicide, narcotics, and theft, although not always in that order (see table 5.5).

In both States, when one examines the types of offenses for which females have the highest rates of conviction in a given year, drug violations and forgery occupy the highest positions (see table 5.6).

The proportions of men and women who pleaded guilty, and who were found guilty, by type of offense between 1969 and 1972 in California are compared in table 5.7. Note that for all offenses combined, there is no greater likelihood that men will plead guilty than women; and, indeed, the proportion of men convicted is not significantly higher than the proportion of women convicted. For example, for every 11 men who are convicted of violent offenses, there are also 10 women, and for property offenses the ratios are equal (see table 5.7).

The ratio of male to female convictions in Ohio and California for approximately the same time periods was also compared (the California data included 1972 and Ohio's data ended with 1971) for most of the same offense categories. For comparable offenses, California appears to be more evenhanded than Ohio. The biggest differences occur in the categories of homicide and manslaughter, burglary, and drug law violations. But, note also that women in California who plead not guilty are more likely to be acquitted than are men. Women who are accused of such typically male offenses as robbery, burglary, and auto theft are treated at least as preferentially as women who are accused of larceny, an offense that is more typically associated with women. These data, then, fail to support the Nagel-Weitzman theory that women who commit more manly type offenses pay the price for their behavior by being treated more like men.

Table 5.4 California: distribution of convictions among specific offenses, females convicted in superior courts, 1960–64, 1966–72

OFFENSE CATEGORY	1960–64	1966	1967	1968	1969	1970	1971	1972
Homicide & manslaughter	2.8	2.6	2.8	2.5	1.7	1.9	2.0	2.7
Robbery	2.0	1.8	3.5	2.9	1.5	1.3	1.6	1.9
Assault	5.7	7.1	7.0	7.2	6.5	5.6	6.0	6.6
Burglary	5.2	6.2	8.0	7.4	4.2	4.1	4.3	5.1
Larceny-theft	17.7	18.3	13.3	12.3	5.1	5.1	4.7	5.0
Auto theft	1.5	2.0	1.5	1.8	1.5	1.3	1.3	1.0
Forgery & checks	34.3	28.7	25.1	24.0	22.2	20.0	18.6	18.2
Drug law violations	13.2	16.4	28.1	30.9	41.6	35.3	47.8	43.5
Violent crimes[1]	10.5	11.5	13.3	12.6	9.7	8.8	9.6	11.2
Property crimes[2]	24.4	26.5	22.8	21.5	10.8	10.5	10.3	11.1
All crimes	100	100	100	100	100	100	100	100

Source: Data for 1960–72 from *Crime and Delinquency in California.* Sacramento, Calif.: State of California, Department of Justice, Bureau of Criminal Statistics.

Note: Numbers in columns do not add up to 100 because some crimes are omitted. Data for 1965 missing.

[1]Homicide, robbery, and assault.

[2]Burglary, larceny, and auto theft.

Table 5.5 **California and Ohio: percentage of females convicted, 1969–71**

OFFENSE	1969		1970		1971	
	California	Ohio	California	Ohio	California	Ohio
Homicide & manslaughter	12.3	14.9	12.2	10.5	13.2	12.7
Robbery	3.9	4.6	3.1	4.2	3.6	4.1
Assault	10.1	7.1	9.2	5.9	10.3	7.4
Burglary	3.6	1.9	3.4	2.0	3.4	1.7
Larceny-theft	13.2	9.3	11.7	10.6	11.1	8.8
Forgery & checks	27.0	19.4	26.9	19.1	28.4	21.2
Narcotic laws violations	12.3	12.8	13.9	12.6	14.4	12.8
All crimes	10.9	8.2	11.1	8.1	11.2	8.4

Source: Data from *Ohio Judicial Criminal Statistics*. Columbus, Ohio: Department of Mental Health and Mental Retardation, Bureau of Statistics. 1969—table 4, p. 14; 1970—table 3, p. 12; 1971—table 3, p. 12. Data for 1969–71 from *Crime and Delinquency in California*. Sacramento, Calif.: State of California, Department of Justice, Bureau of Criminal Statistics.

Table 5.6 **California and Ohio: distribution of convictions in percentages among specific crime categories for females, 1969–71**

OFFENSE	1969		1970		1971	
	California	Ohio	California	Ohio	California	Ohio
Homicide & manslaughter	1.7	4.3	1.9	2.7	2.0	2.8
Robbery	1.5	5.8	1.3	4.6	1.6	4.6
Assault	6.5	5.0	5.6	3.7	6.0	4.4
Burglary	4.2	6.4	4.1	6.9	4.3	5.4
Larceny-theft	5.1	11.7	5.1	14.4	4.7	11.0
Forgery & checks	22.2	23.1	20.0	22.7	18.6	26.3
Narcotic laws violations	41.6	12.7	35.3	17.9	47.8	22.3

Source: Data from *Ohio Judicial Criminal Statistics*. Columbus, Ohio: Department of Mental Health and Mental Retardation, Bureau of Statistics. 1969—table 4, p. 14; 1970—table 3, p. 12; 1971—table 3, p. 12. Data for 1969–71 from *Crime and Delinquency in California*. Sacramento, Calif.: State of California, Department of Justice, Bureau of Criminal Statistics.

Table 5.7 California: percentage of persons charged who plead guilty, and are convicted, 1969–72

OFFENSE CHARGED		1969			1970			1971			1972		
		Persons charged (number)	Guilty pleas (percent)	Convictions (percent)	Persons charged (number)	Guilty pleas (percent)	Convictions (percent)	Persons charged (number)	Guilty pleas (percent)	Convictions (percent)	Persons charged (number)	Guilty pleas (percent)	Convictions (percent)
Murder	Female	123	17.7	60.2	113	44.4	75.2	143	46.9	78.3	170	48.2	77.6
	Male	609	47.1	83.6	710	46.5	85.4	796	44.2	84.2	906	42.5	86.3
Manslaughter	Female	18	50.0	72.2	15	66.7	80.0	12	83.3	83.3	19	47.4	68.4
	Male	67	61.2	80.6	68	63.2	80.9	65	75.4	83.1	69	56.5	73.9
Robbery	Female	211	53.6	79.6	191	48.7	79.6	234	60.7	79.9	193	66.1	80.0
	Male	3,094	59.4	87.1	3,494	58.5	87.3	4,302	64.4	87.5	4,184	67.1	88.9
Assault	Female	430	50.9	82.3	372	50.5	79.3	427	55.0	82.2	415	61.4	82.4
	Male	3,163	54.6	86.2	3,026	56.7	83.7	3,253	58.4	83.5	3,603	64.7	85.2
Burglary	Female	440	64.5	84.5	478	58.8	87.2	541	70.8	82.4	513	72.7	85.0
	Male	8,651	68.8	91.3	8,938	67.0	90.3	10,515	75.3	91.8	9,478	79.4	91.7
Theft	Female	346	65.6	80.1	354	49.4	68.9	301	69.1	79.1	257	68.1	82.5
	Male	1,778	65.0	84.2	2,284	60.6	82.5	2,389	67.9	83.8	2,007	72.5	86.2
Embezzlement	Female	5	100.0	100.0	2	50.0	100.0	3	100.0	100.0	5	60.0	100.0
	Male	15	73.3	86.7	14	85.7	100.0	15	86.7	100.0	11	72.7	81.8
Petty theft	Female	39	82.0	97.4	39	69.2	94.9	42	81.0	95.2	46	87.0	97.8
	Male	226	67.7	94.2	215	73.5	95.3	269	79.9	93.7	272	82.7	95.2
Fraud	Female	16	43.8	75.0	24	41.7	62.5	9	66.7	88.9	61	77.0	86.9
	Male	23	73.9	95.7	41	73.2	80.5	48	68.8	83.3	91	70.3	84.6
Auto theft	Female	115	49.6	72.2	81	51.9	72.8	87	69.0	82.8	63	58.7	68.3
	Male	3,129	64.3	86.7	2,500	62.4	86.0	2,507	72.0	88.1	1,947	76.6	89.3
Forgery and checks	Female	1,335	80.0	94.0	1,236	78.0	92.4	1,285	84.7	93.0	1,058	87.2	94.6
	Male	3,590	80.8	93.4	3,303	77.6	93.0	3,223	83.6	93.3	2,808	86.4	93.1
Drug law violations	Female	3,016	56.7	76.4	3,389	55.1	77.8	3,850	61.4	79.2	2,931	64.5	79.9
	Male	19,519	60.7	66.0	19,776	57.9	82.3	21,406	66.2	84.3	16,136	70.3	85.3
Drunken driving	Female	57	72.0	89.5	48	79.2	95.8	58	82.8	94.8	71	81.7	100.0
	Male	581	75.9	94.3	663	74.7	95.8	735	77.0	94.7	645	76.9	92.7
All crimes	Female	6,689	62.5	81.4	6,850	58.9	80.8	7,616	66.2	82.2	6,394	69.2	83.2
	Male	51,713	63.9	86.4	51,721	61.7	85.3	56,966	68.8	86.8	49,567	72.1	87.6
Violent crimes[1]	Female	782	46.3	77.9	691	49.3	78.7	816	55.6	80.9	797	59.3	80.7
	Male	6,933	56.2	86.4	7,298	56.7	85.6	8,416	60.2	85.6	8,762	63.5	87.0
Property crimes[2]	Female	2,296	73.2	88.9	2,214	67.8	86.5	2,268	78.6	88.3	2,003	79.8	89.6
	Male	17,412	70.1	90.2	17,295	67.6	89.2	18,966	75.4	90.6	16,614	79.4	91.0

Source: Data for 1969–72 from Crime and Delinquency in California. Sacramento, Calif.: State of California, Department of Justice, Bureau of Criminal Statistics.

Note: Convictions include guilty pleas.

[1] Murder, manslaughter, robbery and assault.

[2] Burglary, theft, embezzlement, petty theft, fraud, auto theft, forgery and checks.

Table 5.8 **California and Ohio: comparison of average ratios of male to female conviction rates, 1969–71**

OFFENSE CHARGED	RATIO, MALE TO FEMALE OF % CONVICTED (INCLUDES GUILTY PLEAS)		RATIO, MALE TO FEMALE OF % CONVICTED WHO PLEAD NOT GUILTY
	Ohio	California	California
Murder & manslaughter	1.35	1.18	1.25
Robbery	1.08	1.10	1.32
Assault	1.23	1.04	1.06
Burglary	1.29	1.08	1.32
Larceny-theft	1.13	1.10	1.35
Petty theft		0.99	0.93
Auto theft		1.15	1.62
Embezzlement & fraud	0.94	1.04	0.96
Forgery	0.98	1.00	1.27
Drug law violations	1.12	1.00	1.19
Drunken driving		1.00	1.01
All crimes	1.08	1.11	1.21
Violent crimes[1]	1.22	1.11	1.16
Property crimes[2]	1.08	1.13	1.29

Source: Data from *Ohio Judicial Criminal Statistics.* Columbus, Ohio: Department of Mental Health and Mental Retardation, Bureau of Statistics. 1969—table 4, p. 14; 1970—table 3, p. 12; 1971—table 3, p. 20. Data for 1969–71 from *Crime and Delinquency in California.* Sacramento, Calif.: State of California, Department of Justice, Bureau of Criminal Statistics.

Note: There are some differences in crime classifications; Ohio specifies aggravated assault, whereas California specifies assault. Ohio specifies forgery and counterfeiting, in California we use the category forgery and checks.

[1]Murder, manslaughter, robbery, and assault.

[2]Burglary, theft, embezzlement and fraud, petty theft, auto theft, forgery (in Ohio, petty theft is not included).

Unfortunately, statistics such as those shown in tables 5.7 and 5.8 are not available for earlier years, so it cannot be said that the disparity in preferential treatment for women is on the wane, or that it has remained unchanged. These data indicate only that women as recently as 1972 seemed to be receiving some preferential treatment at the bar of justice. Available data indicate that the eyes of justice are neither blinded nor fully opened; rather, they seem to be open just enough to be able to discern the sex of the defendant and to allow that characteristic to influence the decisions to some extent.

References

Nagel, S. S. and L. J. Weitzman. "Women as Litigants." *The Hastings Law Journal* 23, no. 1 (November 1971): 171–98.

Silverstein, L. *Defense of the Poor in Criminal Cases.* American Bar Foundation, 1965.

Ward, D., M. Jackson, and E. Ward. "Crime and Violence by Women." *Crimes of Violence* 13, appendix 17. President's Commission on Law Enforcement and Administration of Justice, 1968.

23 Women as Litigants

Stuart S. Nagel and Lenore J. Weitzman

Women as criminal defendants

In the literature dealing with women's rights, researchers have indicated that "in several states higher penalties are imposed on a woman who commits a crime than on a man who commits the same crime."[1] These statements, however, have been based on those few state statutes and appellate test cases which describe the law on the books rather than the law in action. Empirical data has been needed to show how much time the average woman spends in prison as compared to the time spent by the average man, or at least showing the length of sentences given on conviction for various crimes to the average woman as compared to the average man.

Likewise, the literature dealing with discrimination against women has often drawn analogies between American society's treatment of women and of blacks.[2] These analogies may be valid in some fields like employment discrimination where one can sometimes explain both racial and sexual discrimination in terms of the desire of workers to limit competition and the desire of employers to have cheap labor, but the similarities between racism and sexism do not necessarily apply to all fields. Empirical data have also been needed to test the analogy's applicability to the treatment of blacks and women as criminal defendants by comparing black-white sentencing practices with male-female sentencing practices. Additionally, data on presentencing treatment (e.g., being released on bail or receiving a jury trial) might provide valuable comparative insights.

"Women as Litigants" by Stuart S. Nagel and Lenore J. Weitzman. *The Hastings Law Journal*, 23 (November 1971): 171–181. Reprinted by permission of *The Hastings Law Journal*.

This research is one of a series of policy science studies on measuring and achieving effects of alternative legal policies partly financed by the National Science Foundation grant GS-2875. The NSF is not responsible for the results.

In 1962 Lee Silverstein of the American Bar Foundation (ABF) arranged for attorneys and court personnel in a scientifically determined sample of 194 counties located in all 50 states to systematically compile data on 11,258 criminal cases.[3] The data were primarily designed to study procedures for providing attorneys to indigent defendants. Silverstein, however, included many other variables in his data such as the race, sex, and age of the defendants and the treatment they received at all stages of the criminal justice process from the preliminary hearing through the sentencing stage.

Two basic patterns of discrimination emerge when one uses the ABF data to correlate the background characteristics of criminal defendants with their criminal procedure treatment while holding constant the crime charged.[4] One pattern, which might be called the disadvantaged or disfavored pattern, applies to indigent, black, or elementary-educated defendants. This pattern involves unfavorable treatment at virtually all stages of the criminal justice process including (1) receiving a preliminary hearing, (2) being released on bail, (3) having a hired attorney rather than assigned counsel or no attorney, (4) being subjected to relatively long delay while in jail if not released on bail, (5) receiving a jury trial, (6) being dismissed or being acquitted, (7) receiving probation or a suspended sentence if convicted, and (8) receiving a relatively short sentence if jailed. One could generalize the disadvantaged or disfavored pattern to include personal injury and divorce cases by defining it as a pattern of court behavior in which there is harshness or relative deprivation in both the decisional outcomes and judicial processing of those groups which a society considers to be socially inferior.

The second discriminatory pattern or syndrome might be called the paternalistic pattern. It particularly applies to juveniles under age 21 as contrasted to adults. In criminal proceedings, it involves unfavorable treatment with regard to such safeguards for the innocent as having an attorney or having a jury trial. It involves favorable treatment, however, with regard to being kept out of jail pending trial, not being convicted, and not being sentenced to jail if convicted. One could generalize the paternalism pattern to include personal injury and divorce cases by defining it as a pattern of court behavior in which there is favoritism for the weak in the reluctance to impose negative sanctions, and disfavoritism in the awarding or enforcing of monetary awards and in the informality of judicial processing.

When female criminal defendants are compared with male criminal defendants, the treatment pattern fits the paternalistic mold much more closely than the disadvantaged mold as is indicated in table 1. The table separates the cases into those in which the single charge against the defendant was grand larceny (the most common felony against property) and those in which the charge was felonious assault (the most common felony against persons). This property-persons breakdown was made because it was important in understanding the differential treatment found between urban courts (which tend to be relatively more sensitive to crimes against persons) and rural courts (which tend to be more sensitive to crimes against property).[5] The property-persons breakdown was also important in understanding the differential sentencing of blacks who commit larceny (which tends to be a crime between races) and blacks who commit assault (which tends to be a crime within races).[6]

The paternalistic discrimination against and for women (like juveniles), however, applied almost equally in grand larceny and felonious assault cases. Relative to men though, women were somewhat more likely to be jailed in assault cases than in larceny cases. This may be due to the fact that assault is a more manly crime than larceny (as shown by the ratio of male to female defendants in the top and bottom halves of table 1), and women are therefore treated more like men when they commit assault than when they commit larceny.

Within the larceny cases (section I) and the assault cases (section II), the data are broken down between the chronological stages that relate to being jailed before or after conviction (rows 1 through 5) and the stages which emphasize formal safeguards for the innocent (rows 6 through 8).[7] Blacks and indigents are particularly discriminated against when it comes to being released on bail. Just the opposite discrimination is evident for women. Of the 63 female larceny defendants, 76 percent were released on bail; whereas of the 771 male larceny defendants, only 50 percent were released on bail, giving a difference of 26 percentage points (section I, row 1). This difference is in conformity with the paternalism pattern which shuns keeping juveniles and women in jail pending trial or after conviction. The same jail avoidance phenomenon pending trial can be observed for assault cases where a 19 percentage points difference is present (section II, row 1).

Likewise, women are given more lenient treatment than men if they are convicted. In grand larceny cases, 64 percent of the women received a suspended sentence or probation, whereas only 43 percent of the men did so (section I, row 4). A related although weaker difference is shown for the felonious assault cases (section II, row 4). Of those defendants who actually spent time in jail, there were too few women (20 or less)[8] in the sample to make meaningful comparisons with men as to the length of the pretrial jailing (rows 2) or the length of postconviction imprisonment (rows 5).[9] Possibly as a means of avoiding the imprisonment of women and avoiding the stigma of a criminal record, a lesser percentage of them are convicted than their male counterparts. Thus, it is indicated that 24 percent of the women were acquitted or had their larceny cases dismissed, whereas only 13 percent of the men did (section I, row 3). A similar difference is present for assault cases (section II, row 3).

When it comes to formal safeguards for the innocent, namely having a lawyer and having a jury trial, the favorable balance toward juveniles and women tends to tip in the other direction. Indeed until the case of *In re Gault*, juveniles in many states did not have a right to court-provided counsel.[10] They still do not have a constitutional right to a jury trial.[11] Since *In re Gault*, although the law has changed, empirical studies have shown that juveniles are still more easily persuaded against exercising and are more reluctant to exercise their right to counsel than are adults.[12]

Table 1, however, does not show a discriminatory pattern with regard to having a lawyer when women defendants are compared with men defendants in either larceny cases or assault cases (rows 7). The percentage differences are 3 and 1, respectively, and are too small to explain.[13] Likewise, no discrimination is observed with regard to receiving preliminary hearings (rows 6) although they are probably not as important a safeguard for the innocent as having counsel or a jury trial.[14]

Women, however, in conformity with the paternalism hypothesis, are less likely to receive the formal treatment of a jury trial than are men, at least in assault cases where the difference was 26 percent (section II, row 8). This disparity is contrary to the interests of women since juries are generally less likely to convict than are judges.[15] Conviction by a jury normally requires the unanimous agreement of twelve persons which is usually more difficult for a prosecutor to achieve than convincing a single judge. One disadvantage of jury trial is that a time-conscious prosecutor may have greater desire to recommend a longer sentence for a jury-convicted defendant than for one who pleaded guilty or took a relatively quick bench trial. The University of Chicago Jury Project research shows that both juries and judges tend to favor women in criminal verdicts, but juries do so to a greater degree.[16]

If juveniles and females are treated paternally in criminal cases (meaning favoritism on jailing and discrimination on jury trial and counsel), then female juveniles are probably treated the most paternally and male adults the least paternally. That is the finding when one uses the American Bar Foundation data to correlate sex and treatment of persons under 21 (while controlling for felonious larceny or assault) although few female juveniles were included in the data.[17] Between these two outer categories of paternalism, the categories of male juveniles and female adults are treated about equally, although male juveniles are less likely to have an attorney, jury trial, or preliminary hearing; whereas the female adults are more likely to be kept out of jail before and after conviction.

When the American Bar Foundation data are used to correlate race and treatment of women defendants, it appears that white women are less likely to be jailed before or after conviction than black women, but they are also less likely to have a lawyer. White women thereby better fit the paternalistic mold. With respect to having a lawyer, however, the data may reflect the greater likelihood of whites being nonindigent and thereby ineligible for court-appointed counsel.[18] Black women (unlike black men) do receive more favorable treatment than white men with regard to being jailed before or after conviction, when controlling for felonious larceny or assault. When sexual paternalism and racial discrimination are mixed, the results as to receiving a jury trial follow no consistent pattern.

Looking at table 1 from an overall perspective and integrating all of the data, there seems to be a pattern—women are substantially less likely than men to be subjected to jail before or after trial, but are less likely to have a jury trial. The differences discussed were of enough magnitude and based on sufficiently large samples that they could not readily be attributed to chance. However, some of the differences may have arisen from the fact that grand larcenies and felonious assaults committed by women may be generally less severe than those committed by men. Therefore, there may be generally less to merit a jury trial and less to merit a severe sentence when women are involved.

To the extent that the male and female larceny cases are comparable, and likewise with the assault cases, differences can possibly be explained by

Table 1 **How the treatment of females differs from males as defendants in criminal cases***

CASE TYPE AND TREATMENT STAGE	Number of defendants with available information		Percent receiving the treatment		Difference in percentage points	Does paternalism hypothesis seem to be confirmed?
	Females	Males	Females	Males		
I. GRAND LARCENY CASES						
A. Being jailed						
1. Released on bail	63	771	76%	50%	26	Yes
2. Had less than 2 months delay of those awaiting trial in jail	10	231	60	67	X	Too few women not released on bail
3. Case dismissed or acquitted	71	841	24	13	11	Yes
4. Received suspended sentence or probation of those convicted	47	656	64	43	21	Yes
5. Received less than one year imprisonment of those imprisoned	9	241	33	45	X	Too few women
B. Formal safeguards						
6. Received preliminary hearing	42	606	57	55	2	Difference too small
7. Had or given a lawyer	61	781	90	87	3	Difference too small
8. Received a jury trial of those tried	18	283	47	31	X	Too few women

II. FELONIOUS ASSAULT CASES

A. Being jailed						
1. Released on bail	43	615	77%	58%	19	Yes
2. Had less than 2 months delay of those awaiting trial in jail	6	152	17	49	X	Too few women released on bail
3. Case dismissed or acquitted	45	638	36	23	13	Yes
4. Received suspended sentence or probation of those convicted	25	415	44	36	8	Yes
5. Received less than one year imprisonment of those imprisoned	9	172	89	57	X	Too few women imprisoned
B. Formal safeguards						
6. Received preliminary hearing	31	451	74	73	1	Difference too small
7. Had or given a lawyer	42	620	88	89	1	Difference too small
8. Received a jury trial of those tried	24	262	19	45	26	Yes

* Based on 1103 grand larceny cases and 846 felonious assault cases from all 50 states for 1962

judicial attitudes which assume that women and juveniles are weaker and would therefore be more harmed by pretrial and postconviction jailing than would men.[19] The empirical data do show that women and juveniles are less likely to be hardened criminals in the sense that they are somewhat less likely to have prior records.[20] Likewise, judges may feel that both juveniles and women should be treated in a more informal, more fatherly, less legalistic way, and that jury trials and defense counsel interfere with such paternalistic informality. To supplement the behavioral case data of table 1, perhaps future psychological questionnaire studies of judicial attitudes will throw more light on how judges subjectively view jailing and jury trials for women defendants.[21]

The few statutes which provide different sentences for women and men generally provide for more indeterminate sentences for women,[22] just as juvenile statutes provide more indeterminate sentences for juveniles.[23] Legislators probably think that both women and juveniles are more susceptible to rehabilitation than are males and adults, and that indeterminate sentences contingent on prison progress facilitate rehabilitation. Testing that hypothesis would require determining legislators' attitudes, although it is probable that the more important attitudes concerning increasing or decreasing sexual discrimination are held by the judges who apply criminal statutes that allow for discretion.[24]

Notes

1. Seidenberg, *The Submissive Majority: Modern Trends in the Law Concerning Women's Rights,* 55 CORNELL L. REV. 262 (1970). *See also* L. KANOWITZ, WOMEN AND THE LAW 167–72 (1969) [hereinafter cited as KANOWITZ]; Schulder, *Does the Law Oppress Women?* in SISTERHOOD IS POWERFUL, 139, 153 (R. Morgan ed. 1970).
2. *E.g.,* C. BIRD, BORN FEMALE 110–25 (Pocket Book rev. ed., 1971); K. MILLETT, SEXUAL POLITICS 23–58 (1970).
3. Some of the data was the basis for L. SILVERSTEIN, DEFENSE OF THE POOR IN CRIMINAL CASES IN AMERICAN STATE COURTS (1965) in which the data compilation methods are described at pages 175–79, 183–86, and 207–12. The data can now be obtained on magnetic tape or punched cards from the Inter-University Consortium for Political Research at Ann Arbor, Michigan.
4. For further details on these and other disparities in criminal procedure see S. NAGEL, THE LEGAL PROCESS FROM A BEHAVIORAL PERSPECTIVE 81–112 (1969) [hereinafter cited as NAGEL]. Those pages also provide some reinforcing data from the federal courts, but the sample of women in the federal criminal cases used is too small to be meaningful.
5. *Id.* at 98–101.
6. *Id.* at 94. *See also* M. WOLFGANG, CRIME AND RACE: CONCEPTIONS AND MISCONCEPTIONS (1964).
7. No data were compiled on the arrest stage prior to the preliminary hearing. Women, however, may be arrested for some crimes that equally guilty men are not arrested for (*e.g.,* prostitution), and men may be arrested for some crimes that equally guilty women are not (*e.g.,* statutory rape). KANOWITZ, *supra* note 1, at 15–25. Likewise no data were compiled on the parole stage subsequent to sentencing. Women, however, may be more readily paroled than men for similar crimes (as indicated by their more readily receiving pretrial release and postconviction probation), although imprisoned women may represent a subsample of women who are particularly high recidivists. While in prison, women may also be treated differently than men. *See*

D. WARD & G. KASSENBAUM, WOMEN'S PRISON (1965); Tittle, *Inmate Organization: Sex Differentiation and the Influence of Criminal Subcultures,* 34 AM. SOC. REV. 492 (1969).

8. Twenty was used as a cut-off partly to make theoretical sense out of the data presented and partly because Guilford says: "If one asks, How small is N before we have a small sample? . . . Some place it is as low as 20." J. GUILFORD, FUNDAMENTAL STATISTICS IN PSYCHOLOGY AND EDUCATION 217 (4th ed. 1956). Guilford also says that special statistics should be used when any frequency is expected by chance to be less than 10. *Id.* at 234–35. If the number of females on a row is 20 or less, then by chance 10 or less should receive favorable treatment, and 10 or less unfavorable.

9. There would have been more imprisoned men and women on row 5 if convicted defendants ordered to serve indeterminate sentences had been included. Indeterminate sentences were excluded because they lack preciseness for making comparisons, unless one obtains data on time actually served, or unless one somewhat arbitrarily translates indeterminate sentences into determinate ones by averaging the minimum and maximum when those two figures are available. Of the 363 women in the total sample of 11,258 cases who received sentences, 27 percent received indeterminate sentences; while 35 percent of the 5,898 men who received sentences received indeterminate ones. Such sentences are associated with more serious crimes (*e.g.,* murder and arson) which men are more likely to commit relative to women than the less serious crimes (*e.g.,* bad checks). Even when the crime is held constant, however, the above data show men usually receive a slightly higher percentage of indeterminate sentences. Such sentences generally have higher maximums and sometimes even higher minimums than the fixed sentences for the same crimes and probably result in longer prison stays. These indeterminate-sentence findings are thus consistent with the fixed-sentence findings in that under both types of sentences, women tend to receive shorter sentences than men.

10. *In re* Gault, 387 U.S. 1 (1967).

11. McKeiver v. Pennsylvania, 403 U.S. 528 (1971).

12. Lefstein, Stapleton & Teitelbaum, *In Search of Juvenile Justice: Gault and Its Implementation,* 3 L. & SOC. REV. 491 (1969).

13. The cut-off level in this article is between differences that are too small to explain (7 percent and under) and differences that merit an explanation (9 percent and over). A percentage difference of 8 is the gray area in terms of making theoretical sense out of the empirical data presented.

    A difference of approximately 8 percent is attributable to chance less than 5 times out of 100 if the total sample size on which it is based (males plus females) is about 150. GUILFORD, *supra* note 8, at 178–82, 190–92, and 538–39. The smallest total samples in tables 1, 2, and 4 tend to be as large as or larger than 150. Such a probability calculation assumes one has hypothesized the direction of the difference between males and females as has been done in the tables in light of the paternalism hypothesis. *Id.* at 207–08.

14. Of these three safeguards, only preliminary hearings have not been made a due process right for adults by the Supreme Court. *See* Duncan v. Louisiana, 391 U.S. 145 (1968) (jury trial), and Gideon v. Wainwright, 372 U.S. 335 (1963) (right to counsel). For a discussion of the functions of preliminary hearings, defense counsel and jury trials see D. FELLMANN, THE DEFENDANT'S RIGHTS (1958); L. ORFIELD, CRIMINAL PROCEDURE FROM ARREST TO APPEAL (1947).

15. H. KALVEN & H. ZEISEL, THE AMERICAN JURY 55–65 (1966).

16. *Id.* at 191–218. Juries relative to judges may be especially sympathetic to women relative to men in more serious crimes and also in less manly crimes. This might explain why the lawyers of women defendants asked for jury trials more in grand larceny cases than in felonious assault cases. Larceny is generally a more serious

crime bringing a more severe sentence, as indicated by comparing the percentages on row 5 (length of sentence) of the larceny section with row 5 of the assault section. Larceny is also a less manly crime, as indicated by the female to male ratio in the larceny and assault sections of table 1.

17. Where the sample sizes are large enough to compare length of postconviction incarceration of female and male juveniles, female juveniles on the average are confined about two months longer when the nature of the crime is not held constant between females and males. CHILDREN'S BUREAU, U.S. DEP'T OF HEALTH, EDUCA-TION AND WELFARE, STATISTICS ON PUBLIC INSTITUTIONS FOR DELINQUENTS (1970). The longer confinement is generally justified on the grounds that young girls are more in need of protection, especially sexually, from the outside world than young boys are. See K. Olson, For Her Own Protection: A Case Study of the Conditions of Incarceration for Female Juvenile Offenders in the State of Connecticut, 1971 (unpublished paper, Yale Law School). In the Connecticut juvenile data, the main commitment reasons for boys were breaking and entering (33 percent), theft (22 percent), and car theft (20 percent); whereas for girls the main reasons were runaway (30 percent), pregnancy (16 percent), and sexual misconduct (15 percent). There were too few boys and girls committed for the same reason to be able to hold the "crime" constant.

18. The correlation coefficient is +.16 being white and being nonindigent in the 1,949 state criminal cases on which table 1 is based, and the correlation is +.20 between being nonindigent and lacking an attorney. The correlation is +1.00 between being classified as nonindigent and not having a court-appointed attorney in the federal data. These correlation coefficients are numbers similar in meaning to those in the "Difference" column of table 1 although the differences in table 1 are not stated as decimals, and the plus and minus signs are eliminated.

19. Judges may also give shorter sentences to women than to men convicted of the same crimes because judges think the weaker nature of women also makes them (1) less dangerous to society, (2) more deterred from repeating their crime, and (3) more easily rehabilitated. These points are in conformity with the custodial, deterrence, and rehabilitation goals of imprisonment.

20. NAGEL, supra note 4, at 111. The correlation between being a man and having a prior record, however, was only +.08 in the federal data, and prior record was unavailable for the defendants in the state data.

21. A questionnaire answered by 118 state and federal supreme court judges who were serving in 1955, contained the statement that "women are not the equals of men in intelligence and organizing ability." Seventeen percent of the judges agreed, and 73 percent disagreed. Nagel, Off-the-Bench Judicial Attitudes, in JUDICIAL DECI-SION-MAKING 29, 32, 53 (G. Schubert ed. 1963). No questions were asked, however, which specifically dealt with judicial attitudes toward the jailing of women and jury trials for women defendants. Only 12 percent of a nationwide sample of state legislators agreed with the same questionnaire item. NAGEL, supra note 4, at 199, 205.

22. See note 1 supra and the statutes discussed in Commonwealth v. Daniels, 430 Pa. 642, 243 A.2d 400 (1968); United States ex rel. Robinson v. York, 281 F. Supp. 8.

23. D. TAFT, CRIMINOLOGY 618 (1950).

24. After this article was written, a New York Times study headlined: "Crime Rate of Women up Sharply Over Men's." N.Y. Times, June 13, 1971, at 1, col. 1. The article quotes Phil Levin, a social work consultant to the Dallas police, as saying, "We in the criminal justice system are becoming less tolerant of women. They are becom-ing apprehended more frequently and not sheltered as in the past." Id. at 72, col. 5. This may portend decreased paternalism toward women criminal defendants in the future.

24 Discriminatory Sentencing of Women Offenders

Carolyn Engel Temin

It is one of the often encountered ironies of history that statutes imposing longer sentences on women than on men convicted of the same offense grew out of an effort to improve the lot of the female prisoner. The movement dedicated to this purpose had its origins somewhere around 1869 when Indiana became the first state to establish a separate reformatory for women. Prior to this, women prisoners had been incarcerated in the same county jails and penitentiaries housing male convicts.[14] By 1917, fourteen states had established similar institutions.[15] They were usually referred to as "reformatories" or "industrial homes" to distinguish them from penitentiaries.[16]

The reformatory ideal embodied much more than a physical plant. It embraced the notion—then revolutionary—that women criminals should be "rehabilitated" rather than "punished." It therefore followed, according to the correctional thinking of that period, that women should be detained in the institution for as long a time as necessary to achieve the desired level of "rehabilitation." In order to accomplish this, the statutes which established these "rehabilitative homes" also contained special sentencing provisions which applied only to the women sentenced to the particular institution.[17] Since most of these statutes required the courts to sentence to the "reformatories" all women over sixteen years of age who had been convicted of any crime,[18] the practical result was sex-based differential sentencing.

"Discriminatory Sentencing of Women Offenders: The Argument for ERA in a Nutshell" by Carolyn Engel Temin. *American Criminal Law Review*, II (Winter, 1973): 358–372. Permission to reprint has been obtained from the American Bar Association which holds the copyright privileges for the *Review* published quarterly by the Association's Section of Criminal Justice. (The original footnote numbers of the source are retained.)

Pennsylvania's Muncy Act

If the sentencing statutes had merely been different they might not have been such a problem. The difficulty arose from the fact that either on their faces or in practical application, they resulted in women getting longer sentences than men. In fact, in the early twentieth century it was thought that the ideal sentence to a women's reformatory should be "indeterminate" with no limits at all on the minimum and maximum terms that an inmate could be forced to serve. Fortunately, most states put some limit on the maximum sentence— usually the maximum term prescribed by law for the particular offence.[19]

Pennsylvania created the State Industrial Home for Women by the Act of July 25, 1913, P.L. 1311,[20] known colloquially as the "Muncy Act" (after the geographical location of the institution). The sentencing provision of this Act is an excellent example of the type of statute being discussed here.[21] It required that all women over the age of sixteen years who had been convicted of an offense punishable by more than one year imprisonment be given a general sentence to Muncy. If the offense was punishable by a term of three years or less, they could be confined for three years. If the crime called for a term longer than three years, then the maximum punishment prescribed by law for the offense was the maximum sentence.[22] The judge possessed neither the discretion to impose a shorter maximum sentence than the maximum provided by law nor the power to fix a minimum sentence at which the woman would be eligible for parole.

By contrast, the Pennsylvania statute for sentencing male offenders to a penitentiary permits the judge in his discretion to impose a shorter maximum sentence than the maximum prescribed by law. In addition the judge is required to set a minimum sentence which can be no longer than one-half of the maximum sentence actually imposed.[23] Where the statute prescribes "simple imprisonment," the judge may impose a flat sentence (stating the maximum term only), but may not exceed the maximum term provided by law for the offense.[24]

The sentencing laws of Pennsylvania discriminated against women in five ways:

1. They permitted a court to send a woman to Muncy for three years even if the maximum for the offense was less than three years, whereas a man could not be sentenced to more than the maximum punishment prescribed by law;
2. They mandated that women receive the maximum legal penalty if convicted of a crime punishable by more than three years, whereas a man could be sentenced to less than the maximum prescribed by law;
3. A woman was not to receive any minimum sentence, whereas a man was to have a minimum sentence not to exceed one-half of the maximum sentence imposed except in those cases where the judge in his discretion could impose a flat sentence stating a maximum only.[25]
4. Under Pennsylvania law, where a sentence is imposed for less than two years, the jurisdiction to parole is in the sentencing judge; whereas, if the sentence imposed is two years or more, jurisdiction to parole lies exclu-

sively with the parole board.[26] Since all sentences to Muncy were for more than two years, they came under the jurisdiction of the parole board. A person sentenced to less than two years may engage a lawyer to present and argue a petition for parole on his behalf. The prisoner may also present witnesses and enjoy the full panoply of due process rights. The Pennsylvania Board of Probation and Parole, on the other hand, makes its decisions in closed sessions and does not permit representation by counsel at its hearings.[27]

5. Under Pennsylvania law, where a statute prescribes "simple imprisonment" the sentence must be served in the county jail rather than in a state correctional institution.[28] Under the Muncy Act only women sentenced for offenses punishable by one year or less were eligible to serve their sentences in the county jail. There are very few such offenses in the Pennsylvania criminal code. Therefore, many women ended up in a penitentiary (i.e. Muncy) for offenses which would have merely sent a man to the county jail.[29]

Statutes similar to the Muncy Act are still in effect in Massachusetts,[30] New Jersey[31] and Connecticut.[32] Iowa law permits women to be confined up to five years for a misdemeanor,[33] whereas men can only be imprisoned for a maximum of one year unless otherwise stated in the statute defining the offense.[34] In Maine, women between the ages of 17 and 40 can be sentenced to reformatories for up to three years even if the maximum punishment for the offense is less.[35] Men, on the other hand, can only receive such treatment between the ages of 17 and 26.[36] Maryland permits judges to sentence women convicted of crimes punishable by three months imprisonment to the state women's reformatory for an indeterminate period not to exceed the maximum term of imprisonment provided by law.[37] Men are subject to such sentences only between the ages of 16 and 25.[38] Men over the age of 25 who are sentenced to the penitentiary receive a term stating both minimum and maximum limits.[39]

Some state legislatures have seen fit to change previously discriminatory sentencing provisions. Arkansas originally permitted women misdemeanants to be sentenced to confinement in the women's penitentiary,[40] whereas only male felons could be so confined. This was changed in 1971 specifically because it discriminated against women.[41] The discriminatory statutes which were upheld in *Dunkerton*,[42] *Heitman*[43] and *Brady*[44] have been repealed by the legislatures of Kansas and Ohio respectively and replaced by nondiscriminatory measures.[45]

The Case of *Commonwealth v. Daniel*

On May 3, 1966 Jane Daniel was convicted of simple robbery[46]—an offense carrying a maximum penalty of ten years under Pennsylvania law.[47] The trial judge sentenced her to serve one to four years in the County Prison. Thirty-one days later[48] her sentence was vacated on the grounds that it was illegal and she was given the required ten-year sentence to Muncy. The opinion of the trial court makes it clear that there were no other reasons for the change in sentence.[49] An appeal was taken to the Superior Court of Pennsylvania on the sole ground that the Muncy Act constituted a denial of equal protection of the laws under the fourteenth amendment of the United States Constitution by arbitrarily discriminating against women as a class.

This case was the first attack ever launched against the Muncy Act. The facts of the case were particularly helpful since they presented a situation where the defendant would clearly have received a much shorter sentence if she had been eligible for sentencing under the statute for men. If the judge had been permitted to exercise his discretion, Ms. Daniel would have served a minimum of one and a maximum of four years, but under the Muncy Act she was required to serve a minimum of three and one-half and a maximum of ten years.[50]

The main obstacle to the appeal was the fact that all previous attacks on similar sentencing statutes in other jurisdictions had failed,[51] for the courts which had faced this question had uniformly held that differential sentencing was constitutional on the ground that women constituted a reasonable class for discriminatory treatment in sentencing statutes. The following language illustrates the "legal" reasoning which produced this doctrine:

> It required no anatomist or physiologist or psychologist or psychiatrist to tell the Legislature that women are different from men. In structure and function human beings are still as they were in the beginning "Male and female created He them." It is a patent and deep-lying fact that these fundamental anatomical and physiological differences affect the whole psychic organization. They create the differences in personality between men and women and personality is the predominating factor in delinquent careers. . . .
>
> *   *   *
>
> . . . [T]he female offender not merely requires, but deserves, on account of matters touching the perpetuation and virility of the species, correctional treatment different from the male offender, both in kind and degree; . . . . Let it be conceded that the industrial farm for women may fail to accomplish the results hoped for; the statute represents a serious effort on the part of the Legislature to deal justly with a subject of great public concern, . . . and this Court is not authorized to declare that the classification . . . is either arbitrary or unreasonable.[52]

The Superior Court of Pennsylvania denied the relief requested and adopted the reasoning of the earlier cases. It held that the legislative distinction which imposed longer sentences on women than men was reasonable in view of the state's purpose of providing more effective rehabilitation for women. The opinion relied on the same factors which the prior decisions had found persuasive: the inherent physical and psychological differences between men and women.[53] The decision was particularly disappointing because of its complete disregard of any of the legal reasoning presented by the appellant's brief and oral argument. The case presented one of the earliest opportunities for a practical application of the arguments outlined in the seminal article, *Jane*

Crow and the Law by Pauli Murray and Mary Eastwood.[54] It was a dismal failure.

The only ray of hope was the opinion of Judge J. Sydney Hoffman, the lone dissenter.[55] He argued that the majority was wrong in merely applying the traditional rational basis equal protection test to legislation which impinged on the fundamental right to personal liberty.[56] He contended that where basic civil rights are involved, it should be incumbent upon the state to show a compelling state interest which justifies the legislative classification. Judge Hoffman recognized that there could be no overriding justification for a statute which, "under the guise of special rehabilitative treatment for women, . . . accomplishes little more than the imposition of a harsher punishment for women offenders."[57]

Daisy Douglas

Although this opinion could not become the law of the commonwealth, it was extremely helpful in convincing the Supreme Court of Pennsylvania to allow an appeal from the decision of the superior court. While the appeal was pending, a second attack on the Muncy Act was begun in the case of Daisy Douglas.

Daisy Douglas and her paramour, Richard Johnson, were tried together and convicted of robbery. Ms. Douglas, whose past record consisted of a number of arrests for prostitution, was duly sentenced to Muncy for the maximum term allowed by law for the offense of aggravated robbery—twenty years. Her co-defendant, whose past record consisted of six prior convictions for burglary, received a sentence of not less than three nor more than ten years in the men's penitentiary. A petition under Pennsylvania's Post-Conviction Hearing Act was filed on behalf of Ms. Douglas on the ground that her sentence constituted a denial of her fourteenth amendment rights. Her petition was dismissed on the sole ground that the judge was "constrained" to follow the decision of the superior court in the *Daniel* case.[58] An appeal was taken and the case was consolidated with the *Daniel* case for argument before the Supreme Court of Pennsylvania.[59]

For some reason, the *Douglas* case is never mentioned in articles which discuss *Daniel*, but it played an extremely important role in obtaining the successful result in the supreme court. The superior court in *Daniel* had said that a major flaw in the appellant's attack on the Muncy Act was her failure to substantiate the claim that if she were a man she would have received a maximum sentence of four years. Actually the court misunderstood the appellant's claim. Her argument was that if Jane Daniel could have been sentenced under the statute which applied to male offenders, she would have received a lesser sentence. Nevertheless the appellant's failure to produce data which supported this assertion prevented the court from overturning the Muncy Act on the basis that it discriminated against women.[60]

The facts of *Douglas* presented the unequivocal proof of the discriminatory effect of the Muncy Act which had been found lacking in the superior court. Male and female co-defendants were jointly tried and convicted of the same offense. The male, with a serious past criminal record, was sentenced to ten years. The female was required by statute to be sentenced to twenty years even though her past criminal involvement was extremely minimal. The male was eligible for parole after three years; the female was technically eligible for parole at any time but in practice was not considered eligible for three and one-half years.[61] Further proof of sex-based disparity in sentencing was provided by statistics kept by the Pennsylvania Board of Probation and Parole.[62] These showed that men on parole, convicted of a second similar offense, were rarely, even under these circumstances, sentenced to the maximum punishment permitted by law for the offense.

The consolidated appeals were argued on January 5, 1968 and on July 1, 1968 the supreme court reversed the judgments below and remanded the cases for resentencing. The court held that, while legislative classification on the basis of sex alone did not violate the equal protection clause, it could find no reasonable justification for a statute which imposed longer sentences on women than men convicted of the same crime. Acknowledging that

> ... there are undoubtedly significant biological, natural and practical differences between men and women which would justify, under certain circumstances, the establishment of different employment qualification standards[63]

the court specifically found that

> ... the considerations and factors which would justify a difference between men and women in matters of employment, as well as in a number of other matters, *do not govern* or justify the imposition of a longer or greater sentence on women than is imposed upon men for the commission of the same crime.[64]

With these words, the Supreme Court of Pennsylvania emphatically stated that the Constitution of the United States does not embody equal rights for women, although it does prevent the imposition of longer sentences on women than on men convicted of the same offense. A similar result was reached by the United States District Court for Connecticut in the case of *United States ex rel. Robinson v. York*[65] decided on February 28, 1968. That case struck down a Connecticut statute relating to the sentencing of women misdemeanants which was exactly the same as the Muncy Act Provision.[66] Since both courts reached the same conclusion independent of each other, it appeared, at the time, that the issue of the constitutionality of disparate sentencing statutes had been laid to rest forever. In the words of Leo Kanowitz, the *Robinson* and *Daniel* decisions appeared to be the "early heralds of a new day."[67]

Muncy Act amendment

But then came the backlash. On July 16, 1968, just a little more than two weeks after the Supreme Court of Pennsylvania handed down the decision in *Daniel*, the legislature passed a new version of the Muncy Act. The amendment provided that in sentencing a women for a crime punishable by more than one year, the court "shall not fix a minimum sentence, but shall fix such maximum sentence as the court shall deem appropriate, so long as such maximum sentence does not exceed the maximum term specified by law for the crime for which the prisoner is being sentenced."[68] Thus the small victory achieved by *Daniel* was narrowed still further. Although women would not have to receive a longer maximum sentence than men, they were still to be denied the right to have their minimum sentence set by a judge. By retaining this type of so-called "indeterminate" sentence at Muncy, women were still being denied equal treatment.[69]

The 1968 amendment to the Muncy Act has been challenged in Pennsylvania courts on two occasions. Immediately after its passage, in the case of *Commonwealth v. Blum*,[70] the superior court was asked to find that the new statute discriminated merely because it was different than the statute which applied to men and because it had been shown in the *Daniel* case that women serving indeterminate sentences were held in prison for longer periods of time before being released on parole than men who had been given minimum sentences.[71] The superior court affirmed the judgment of the trial court per curiam.[72] Subsequently the Supreme Court of Pennsylvania denied allocatur[73] and the Supreme Court of the United States denied certiorari.[74] Actually this issue would appear to have been disposed of in the *Daniel* case where as part of its discussion the court indicated that the only part of a sentence which has any legal validity is the maximum sentence and that the minimum sentence is only an administrative notice that the person is eligible for parole consideration.[75]

In the more recent case of *Commonwealth v. Piper*[76] the superior court once again avoided facing the issue by rendering a per curiam opinion. Judge Hoffman, however, wrote a dissenting opinion in which he stated that the 1968 Muncy Act is unconstitutional because the minimum sentence significantly affects parole eligibility and therefore the act results in discrimination between men and women in terms of consideration for parole.[77] The case is now pending on appeal to the Supreme Court of Pennsylvania.

It should also be noted that due process constitutes another basis for arguing that the 1968 Muncy Act is discriminatory. In Pennsylvania a man is entitled by law to have his minimum sentence set by a judge, at a hearing where representation by counsel is constitutionally mandated,[78] in open court and with the full panoply of due process rights; whereas a woman's minimum sentence is decided by the parole board, at a closed session, where she has no representation, or any other procedural rights.[79] Arguably, this constitutes as much a denial of equal protection as the imposition of mandatory maximum sentences.

New Jersey and *State v. Costello*

An even more devastating blow to the *Daniel* doctrine was dealt by the Supreme Court of New Jersey in the recent case of *State v. Costello*.[80] This case, the first since *Daniel* and *Robinson* to treat the issue of differential sentencing, involved a constitutional attack on a New Jersey statute similar to the Muncy Act.[81] The law requires that women convicted of crimes punishable by five years or less be sentenced to the Women's Correctional Institution for the maximum prescribed by law. If the offense is punishable by more than five years, then the judge may either sentence them to five years imprisonment, or to anything over five years but not to exceed the maximum prescribed by law. Men, on the other hand, receive a sentence stating a minimum and maximum within the limits prescribed by law.[82]

The court dismissed the *Robinson* case as inapplicable to this situation because it involved a statute which sentenced women to a longer maximum term than a man *could* have been sentenced for. Technically, this distinction is correct, since the New Jersey statute, unlike the Connecticut law, does not actually increase the maximum provided by law for the offense. It does, however, force judges to impose the maximum in all cases where they are sentencing a woman for an offense punishable by five years or less, and the result, as it was in *Daniel*, is that women receive longer sentences than men convicted of the same offense. *Robinson*, like *Daniel*, dealt with the issue of the constitutionality of the result of such statutes (i.e., longer sentences for women) and not with the method by which this result was obtained. The New Jersey court's reading of *Robinson* appears far too narrow.

The court refused to follow the ruling in *Daniel* that there could be no rational basis for a legislative classification which imposed longer sentences on women than on men for the same criminal conduct. Instead it remanded the case to the Appellate Division to give the state the opportunity to show a substantial justification for the sentencing scheme.[83] The opinion relied to a large extent on the reasoning of a recent case comment in the *Harvard Law Review*.[84] This article criticized the *Daniel* court's holding that statutory provisions like the Muncy Act would be arbitrary under all circumstances and suggested that such statutes could be sustained upon a showing of a "substantial empirical basis" for the classification. The author argued that social and psychological differences between men and women which rendered the latter more susceptible to rehabilitation might be a substantial justification for differential sentencing.[85]

If this reasoning sounds familiar, then it should come as no surprise that the court dredged up *Heitman, Platt, Brady* and *Gosselin*[86] as precedent for the proposition that sex-based discriminatory sentencing is not constitutionally prohibited.[87] The fact that most of the statutes vindicated in those cases are no longer on the books either never came to the court's attention or was not deemed significant.

A fifth case cited by the court in favor of this proposition was *Wark v. State*.[88] This 1970 decision from the Supreme Judicial Court of Maine upheld a statutory scheme whereby men could receive an unlimited sentence for jail break, whereas women could receive no more than eleven months for the same offense.[89] The Maine Court indicated that even if its previous decision in *Gosselin*[90] would have to be reexamined in the light of *Daniel* and *Robinson*, these cases were not controlling.[91] The court held that the legislature could reasonably have concluded that since men are stronger, more aggressive and more disposed toward violent action than women, they constituted a greater risk of harm upon their escape and required a longer sentence to deter them from such conduct. The Supreme Court of the United States denied certiorari.[92]

The *Costello* case was remanded and the defendant was given a chance to have her sentence reconsidered.[93] Ultimately, the defendant received a sentence which did not involve the issues raised here and the case was not appealed further.[94]

Slightly less than a month after the *Costello* decision, the United States Supreme Court decided in *Reed v. Reed*[95] that the states may classify on the basis of sex if the criteria for the classification bear a reasonable relation to the objective of the statute whose constitutionality is in question. Nothing in that decision is helpful in predicting the outcome of an appeal on the *Daniel-Costello* issue. It merely reaffirms the standard used by both the Pennsylvania and New Jersey courts to reach their disparate conclusions.

Conclusion

The inconsistent positions taken by the courts on the issue of differential sentencing demonstrate the need for the equal rights amendment. As one commentator put it:

> . . . one cannot say that the possibility of achieving substantial equality of rights for women under the Fourteenth and Fifth Amendments is permanently foreclosed. But the present trend of judicial decisions . . . indicates that any present hope for large-scale change can hardly be deemed realistic.[96]

Any case by case attack is subject to the same pitfalls as the one described here. A favorable decision in one jurisdiction is not binding on any other. Courts may interpret precedents too narrowly, thus diminishing the effect of an important decision. And a victory in the courts can be undone by the legislature. The fight must then begin again for territory already won.[97]

Only by ratification of the Equal Rights Amendment can we assure that statutory schemes such as discriminatory sentencing acts will cease to exist. The question remains as to the effect that the ERA will have on such statutes. It has been suggested that under ERA, special sentencing statutes relating to women would fall, leaving them subject to the "standard laws."[98] Another analyst states that where there are conflicting laws, one for men and one for women, the one containing the most beneficial provisions will survive.[99] The question will then be which type of sentencing scheme is preferable.[100]

Regardless of the result, the Equal Rights Amendment will bury for all time, the useless, chauvinistic discussions in the cases concerning the "unique" physiological, psychological and sociological aspects of women. These learned, intellectual acrobatics which have been used for so long to justify the demeaning, condescending and crass treatment of humans who are female by humans who are male have no place in a society seeking equality of treatment for all its members.

Notes

14. Rogers, *A Digest of Laws Establishing Reformatories for Women in the United States,* 8 J. CRIM. L.C. & P.S. 518 (1917).

15. *Id.* at 520. In addition to Indiana these included Massachusetts (1874), New York (1881), Iowa (1900), New Jersey (1910), Ohio (1911), Pennsylvania (1913), Wisconsin (1913), Maine (1915), Minnesota (1915), Connecticut (1917), Kansas (1917), Michigan (1917), and Rhode Island (1917).

16. *Id.* It is interesting to note that in most cases the names of these institutions have been changed and today most of them bear the designation "state correctional institution for women." In these cases the name change reflects the true state of affairs. These are no more nor less than penitentiaries for women. *See* Commonwealth v. Stauffer, 214 Pa. Super. 113, 117, 251 A.2d 718, 722 (1969).

17. *Compare* CONN. GEN. STAT. ANN. § 18–65 (Supp. 1972) *with* § 53a-35 (Supp. 1972) *Compare* MASS. GEN. LAWS ANN. ch. 279, § 18 (Supp. 1972) *with* ch. 279, § 24 (Supp. 1972).

18. *See, e.g.,* CONN. GEN. STAT. ANN. § 18–65 (Supp. 1972).

19. Rogers, *supra* note 14, at 526, 535. But Minnesota law originally provided that women could be sentenced to the reformatory for a term which would be "without limit as to time." MINN. LAWS 1915, ch. 324, § 1, *as amended* MINN. STAT. ANN. § 243.90 (1972).

20. PA. STAT. ANN. tit. 61, ch. 7 (1964). A 1959 amendment changed the name of the institution to the State Correctional Institution at Muncy. Act of October 22, 1959, P.L. 1356.

21. PA. STAT. ANN. tit. 61, § 566 (1964). *See also* CONN. GEN. STAT. ANN. § 18-65 (Supp. 1972); MASS. GEN. LAWS ANN. ch. 279, § 18 (1972); N.J. STAT. ANN. § 30:4–155 (1964).

22. These were the sentencing provisions in force at the time the *Daniel* case was brought in 1966. They were later changed by case law and statutory amendment as will be discussed *infra.*

23. The statutory language refers to this as an "indefinite" sentence. In this article I have refrained from describing sentences as indefinite, indeterminate, definite or otherwise since these terms are not used uniformly throughout the states.

24. PA. STAT. ANN. tit. 19, § 1057 (1964). Note that although the statutory language states "any person," prior to the *Daniel* case it only applied to men.

25. Under Pennsylvania law a minimum sentence is the time a person must serve before becoming eligible for parole. Flat sentences are only available for a small number of minor crimes. Since the repeal of the "good time" statute in Pennsylvania on July 22, 1965, flat sentences have fallen into disuse. (Before its repeal, Pennsylvania's good-time statute only applied to flat sentences and enhanced their appeal in the eyes of criminal defendants who often requested them at the time of sentencing.) Since women have no minimum sentence under the Muncy Act they are theoretically eligible for parole at any time after sentencing. On its face this appears to discriminate in favor of women. The actual effect of this provision will be discussed *infra.*

26. *See* PA. STAT. ANN. tit. 61, § 331.1 *et seq.* (1964).

27. The hearings referred to here are those where the decision to parole from a sentence is made. Pennsylvania does permit representation of counsel at hearings which consider technical violations of parole. *See* Commonwealth v. Tinson, 433 Pa. 328, 249 A.2d 549 (1969).

28. PA. STAT. ANN. tit. 19, § 891 (1964).

29. This effect of the Muncy Act was declared unconstitutional in Commonwealth v. Stauffer, 214 Pa. Super, 113, 251 A.2d 718 (1969). In Pennsylvania the county jail

is preferable to Muncy because of its location and other less tangible reasons which make "county time" less onerous to serve. A person incarcerated at Muncy is almost always cut off from her relatives and friends.

30. MASS. GEN. LAWS ANN. ch. 125, § 16 (1958).
31. N.J. STAT. ANN. § 30:4–155 (1964).
32. CONN. GEN. STAT. ANN. § 18–65 (Supp. 1972). Although the *Robinson* case declared the provision relating to misdemeanants to be unconstitutional, the felony sentencing provision has never been attacked. It is exactly the same as that provided under Pennsylvania's Muncy Act.
33. IOWA CODE ANN. § 245.7 (1969).
34. *Id.* at § 687.7 (1950).
35. ME. REV. STAT. ANN. tit. 34, § 853–54 (Supp. 1972).
36. *Id.* § 802. This provision is similar to the provision complained of as being discriminatory in *Ex parte* Gosselin, 141 Me. 412, 44 A.2d 882 (1945), but discrimination still exists based on the different age eligibility limits for the sexes.
37. MD. ANN. CODE art. 27, § 689(e) (1957).
38. *Id.* § 689(d).
39. *Id.* § 690.
40. Ark. Acts 1939, No. 117, § 1, at 270.
41. ARK. STAT. ANN. § 46–804 (Supp. 1971).
42. *See* note 2 *supra.*
43. *Id.*
44. *Id.*
45. KAN. STAT. ANN. § 21–4601 *et seq.* (Supp. 1970); OHIO REV. CODE ANN. §§ 5145.01, 5143.23 (Anderson 1970).
46. Brief for Appellant, Commonwealth v. Daniel, 430 Pa. 642, 243 A.2d 400 (1968) [hereinafter cited as Brief for Appellant].
47. PA. STAT. ANN. tit. 18, § 4704 (1963).
48. If the sentence had not been illegal, it would have become final after 30 days. PA. STAT. ANN. tit. 12, § 1032 (Supp. 1972); Commonwealth *ex rel.* Perotta v. Myers, 203 Pa. Super. 287, 201 A.2d 292 (1966).
49. Brief for Appellant, *supra* note 46, at apps. 1, 2.
50. Although theoretically a woman sentenced under the Muncy Act was eligible for parole at any time, in actuality the authorities at Muncy required that a certain amount of time be served before parole was considered depending on the offense for which the woman was convicted. *See* Commonwealth v. Daniel, 210 Pa. Super. 156, 167, 232 A.2d 247, 253 (1967) (Hoffman, J., dissenting).
51. See cases cited *supra* note 2.
52. State v. Heitman, 105 Kan. 139, 146–48, 181 P. 630, 633–34 (1919).
53. This court is of the opinion that the legislature reasonably could have concluded that indeterminate sentences should be imposed on women as a class, allowing the time of incarceration to be matched to the necessary treatment in order to provide more effective rehabilitation. Such a conclusion could be based on the physiological and psychological make-up of women, the type of crime committed by women, the relation to the criminal world, their role in society, their unique vocational skills and pursuits and their reaction as a class to imprisonment, as well as the number and type of women who are sentenced to imprisonment rather than given suspended sentences. Commonwealth v. Daniel, 210 Pa. Super. 156, 164, 232 A.2d 247, 251–52 (1967). It should be noted that the defendant's name was Jane Daniel. The superior court opinion incorrectly spelled her name as Daniels. It appears correctly in the opinion of the supreme court.
54. Although blacks have successfully invoked the protection of the Constitution, women have been unable to do so. The difficulty in asserting women's rights lies

not in the limited reach of the fourteenth amendment, but in the failure of the courts to isolate and analyze the discriminatory aspect of differential treatment based on sex. Laws discriminate by defining crimes to the acts of one sex but not the other and by differentiating in the punishment of criminals of different sexes. The Civil Rights Act of 1964, Title VII prohibits employment discrimination based on sex, however the Act does not totally preempt state laws which discriminate by sex (*e.g.*, laws prohibiting women from working at night in certain industries, weight lifting limitations for women, and maximum hour laws). The recent increase in activity concerning the status of women indicates a gradual trend in the law not to protect women by restriction and confinement, but to protect both sexes from discrimination. Murray & Eastwood, *Jane Crow and the Law: Sex Discrimination and Title VII,* 34 Geo. Wash. L. Rev. 232 (1965).

55. 210 Pa. Super. at 167, 232 A.2d at 253.

56. "In my view, the 'any rational basis' formula is inadequate to test the validity of the Muncy Act against the present challenge. That doctrine derives from a number of cases upholding economic regulatory measures or statutes not directly impinging on personal liberties or fundamental rights. . . . Surely, the proper inquiry here . . . is whether there clearly appears in the relevant materials some 'overriding statutory purpose' requiring the imposition of more severe penalties on women than on men and requiring the delegation of the sentencing power to a nonjudicial agency in whose hands it is manifestly susceptible to abuse." 210 Pa. Super. at 169–70, 232 A.2d at 254 (Hoffman, J., dissenting).

57. ". . . [U]nder the guise of special rehabilitative treatment for women, the legislature, in the Muncy statute, has adopted a system which accomplishes little more than the imposition of a harsher punishment for women offenders. As such it denies them the equal protection of the laws guaranteed by the Constitution of the United States." 210 Pa. Super. at 172, 232 A.2d at 255 (Hoffman, J., dissenting).

58. Brief for Appellants at app. 8, Commonwealth v. Daniel and Douglas, 430 Pa. 642, 243 A.2d 400 (1968).

59. Since Daniel was already pending before the supreme court it was possible for Douglas to skip the usual necessary stop at the superior court and proceed directly to the supreme court.

60. ". . . [A]ppellant argues that because she is a woman she has received a maximum sentence of ten years; . . . that if she were a man she would have received a maximum term of four years. . . . This argument rests on an invalid assumption, viz., that a man committing this crime would have received a maximum term of four years. Judge Stern's prior sentence of one to four years was imposed upon Jane Daniels, a female, and we cannot speculate as to what the sentence would have been had the person robbing the bar in question been a male." 210 Pa. Super. at 165, 232 A.2d at 252.

61. *See* Brief for Appellants, *supra* note 58.

62. *Id.,* at app. C.

63. 430 Pa. at 649, 243 A.2d at 403.

64. 430 Pa. at 650, 243 A.2d at 404.

65. 281 F. Supp. 8 (D. Conn. 1968). Apparently this decision had no influence on the ruling of the Pennsylvania Supreme Court as it was not cited in its opinion.

66. Conn. Gen. Stat. Ann. § 17–360 (1958).

67. L. Kanowitz, *supra* note 11, at 172.

68. Pa. Stat. Ann. tit. 71, § 566 (Supp. 1972).

69. For a general discussion of the effect of the indeterminate sentence at Muncy *see* Temin, *The Indeterminate Sentence: The Muncy Experience,* Prison Journal (1972). In Commonwealth v. Stauffer, 214 Pa. Super. 113, 251 A.2d 718 (1969), the court, relying on Daniel, held that women could not be sentenced to Muncy for

crime that was punishable by simple imprisonment since a man in that case could only be sent to the county jail. *See* Commonwealth *ex rel.* Monaghan v. Burke, 169 Pa. Super. 256, 82 A.2d 337 (1951). The effect of Stauffer is that women can get a minimum-maximum sentence for crimes punishable by "simple imprisonment" since the indeterminate sentence is only for sentences served at Muncy.

70. 220 Pa. Super. 703, —— A.2d —— (1972).
71. See Commonwealth v. Blum, Brief for Appellant, Superior Court of Pennsylvania, October Term, 1969 Nos. 208, 209.
72. 220 Pa. Super. 703, —— A.2d —— (1972).
73. 221 Pa. 691, —— A.2d —— (1972).
74. 408 U.S. 516 (1972).
75. 430 Pa. at 647–48, 243 A.2d at 403.
76. 221 Pa. Super. 187, 289 A.2d 193 (1972).
77. 221 Pa. Super. at 290, 289 A.2d at 196–97.
78. Mempa v. Rhay, 389 U.S. 128 (1967); Gideon v. Wainwright, 372 U.S. 335 (1963).
79. *See* Temin, *supra* note 69.
80. 59 N.J. 334, 282 A.2d 748 (1971).
81. N.J. STAT. ANN. § 30:4-155 (1964).
82. *Id.*
83. 59 N.J. at 345, 282 A.2d at 755. The equal protection challenge was first raised on appeal in the Supreme Court and thus there was no record on this issue.
84. 82 HARV. L. REV. 921 (1969).
85. "Under the regimen of a 'substantial empirical basis' test, the state would be required to show affirmatively that there are significant social and psychological differences between male and female offenders such that the latter are particularly susceptible to rehabilitative treatment under the 'flexible' indeterminate sentence. The Daniels [sic] court stated that there are no differences which would justify the penal effect of the legislature's classification. However, there is considerable evidence that women who perform criminal acts possess as a group a number of distinct qualities and characteristics and a plausible argument can be made that the rehabilitative possibilities are greater for a class which, for example, demonstrates a noticeably lower frequency of recidivism and parole violations than the class of male offenders." 82 HARV. L. REV. at 923–24.
86. *See* cases cited *supra* note 2.
87. 59 N.J. at 344, 282 A.2d at 754.
88. 266 A.2d 62 (Me. 1970).
89. *Id.* at 64. Maine is not alone in prescribing longer sentences for men convicted of prison breach than for women. *See, e.g.*, CONN. GEN. STAT. ANN. § 18-66 (Supp. 1972) and § 53a-169-70 (1958).
90. *See* note 2 *supra.*
91. 266 A.2d at 64.
92. 400 U.S. 952 (1970).
93. 59 N.J. at 347, 282 A.2d at 755.
94. Citizen's Advisory Council on the Status of Women, Item No. 24-N, February 1972.
95. 401 U.S. 71 (1971).
96. Brown, Emerson, Falk & Freedman, *The Equal Rights Amendment: A Constitutional Basis for Equal Rights for Women,* 80 YALE L.J. 871, 882 (1971) [hereinafter cited as Brown].
97. As in the case of the "new" Muncy Act. *See* notes 71 & 72 *supra* and accompanying text.
98. Brown, *supra* note 96, at 966. The authors of that article were evidently not aware that the legislature passed a new Muncy Act and that in Pennsylvania, at present,

women are still given special sentences. (A new sentencing code presently pending in the legislature would apply equally to men and women and would give the sentencing judge the option of imposing a minimum-maximum sentence on a Muncy-type sentence. S.B. 440.)

99. Eastwood, *The Double Standard of Justice: Women's Rights Under the Constitution,* 5 VALPARAISO L. REV. 281, 298 (1971).

100. The author of this article has discussed her preference in Temin, *The Indeterminate Sentence: The Muncy Experience,* PRISON JOURNAL (Spring 1972).

25 Sex Discrimination in Criminal Law

Lois J. Frankel

What are little boys made of?
Snips and snails, and puppy-dog tails;
That's what little boys are made of.
What are little girls made of?
Sugar and spice, and everything nice;
That's what little girls are made of.

Anonymous

Introduction

This simple rhyme eloquently summarizes the disparate attitudes towards males and females which are too often incorporated into our criminal laws. Males are expected to be aggressive and tough; females are supposed to be sweet and nice. And so, the criminal law chauvinistically protects nice sweet girls from bad aggressive boys, while punishing the naughty and sinful women who fail to conform to a sugary image for behavior which men are often praised for. Furthermore, besides imposing disparate behavior standards on men and women, the criminal law also tends to classify women with the infirm, weak, or helpless.[1]

Congress has finally recognized and condemned the double standard treatment of males and females. On March 22, 1972, it passed[2] a constitutional

From "Sex Discrimination in the Criminal Law: The Effect of the Equal Rights Amendment" by Lois J. Frankel. *American Criminal Law Review*, II (Winter, 1973): 469–473, 489–503, 509–510. Permission to reprint has been obtained from the American Bar Association which holds the copyright privileges for the *Review* published quarterly by the Association's Section of Criminal Justice. (The original footnote numbers of the source are retained.)

amendment proclaiming the right of equal treatment under the law for men and for women. This proposed twenty-seventh amendment reads:

> Section 1. Equality of rights under the law shall not be denied or abridged by the United States or by any State on account of sex.
> Section 2. The Congress shall have the power to enforce, by appropriate legislation, the provisions of this article.
> Section 3. This amendment shall take effect two years after the date of ratification.

As provided in the amendment itself, the United States Congress and the legislatures of the several states will have two years from the date of ratification to change or eliminate all statutes which conflict with the new amendment.[3] This *Note* reviews the present disparate treatment men and women are afforded in the criminal justice system in this country and discusses changes in criminal laws which will have to be made to bring them into compliance with the command of the Equal Rights Amendment. No attempt has been made to predict how courts will interpret the new amendment[4] or how the judiciary will deal with criminal laws which have an unequal impact on the sexes.[5] Instead, it is designed to aid and give possible direction to the legislative task which must be accomplished during a comparatively short two year period.

Impact of the Equal Rights Amendment

Under the Equal Rights Amendment, sex is a prohibited classification. That is, the existence of a characteristic or trait to a greater degree in one sex does not justify classification by sex rather than by the particular characteristic or trait. Laws must deal with particular attributes of individuals, not with a classification based on the broad and impermissible attribute of sex.[6]

According to some writers,[7] the twenty-seventh amendment will not preclude legislation which regulates, takes into account, or otherwise deals with a physical characteristic unique to one sex. For example, a law prohibiting castration[8] should be valid under the Equal Rights Amendment even though only a man can be the victim of castration. Only a ridiculous interpretation of the Equal Rights Amendment would suggest that a man's penis could not be protected just because a woman does not have one. Under the unique physical characteristics doctrine, laws regulating or prohibiting abortion should also remain unaffected by the Equal Rights Amendment.[9]

However, this principle should be applied with caution and reserve. It is limited to unique *physical* attributes and does not include characteristics which are dominant in one sex due to social training. Laws which do not rely solely on unique physical characteristics, such as laws relating to adultery, prostitution, incest, obscenity, slander, assault and battery, seduction, abduction, pandering, and support, will have to treat men and women equally or fall for unconstitutional discrimination.

On the other hand, the fact that men are more likely than women to commit a specific crime,[10] or vice versa, should not necessarily invalidate a criminal law. Although men commit the overwhelming number of violent crimes in this country, the Equal Rights Amendment will be no defense to a man charged with murder. His plea that he, a man, is unfairly discriminated against by the law prohibiting murder because it punishes more men will be unavailing as long as the prosecution can show a substantial non-sex discriminatory reason for the law. The law applies the same onus on everyone who commits murder—be they male or female. More importantly, both sexes are capable of committing the crime *and* do commit it. The same reasoning may defeat a woman challenging an anti-prostitution statute which applied to both men and women. As long as the criminal statute is applied equally to both sexes it should be valid.[11] A person should, however, have a valid constitutional argument if he or she could show that, although a law apparently applied to both sexes, only one sex was actually being prosecuted under it.

During the two-year hiatus between ratification and implementation of the Equal Rights Amendment, legislatures will be faced with a three pronged question:

1. Does a particular law make a distinction between men and women? Such a distinction can occur in several different ways. A law may make specified activity criminal for only one sex.[12] Or it may make the activity criminal for both sexes, but in some respect treat them differently.[13] Possibly a law may define the victim of a criminal act in terms of one sex only.[14] Or it may define the victim of criminal activity in terms of both sexes, but in some respect treat the victims differently.[15] Finally, a law may provide special treatment for one sex, but not the other.[16]

2. Is the distinction permissible? In most cases it will not be. If the difference is based on a unique physical characteristic which is closely related to the prohibited act or acts, the law can stand as is,[17] otherwise it would be improper.

3. Should the statute be rewritten to apply equally to both sexes or should it be stricken from the books? Certain laws, such as jury statutes which give women special treatment,[18] will have to be rewritten since it is necessary to have juries, preferably with women members. Certain other laws, or particular provisions of those laws, should probably be dropped altogether.[19] For example, laws which make it a crime to use obscene language in the presence of a female[20] should be erased from the criminal codes rather than expanding the protected class to include men, too.

In most cases, the changes necessary to make a criminal law constitutional under the Equal Rights Amendment will be simple, and the actual effect of the changes will be slight. For example, while prostitution statutes can easily be reworded to apply to both men and women, few men will be prosecuted as prostitutes, since there just are not very many male prostitutes.[21] Furthermore, most criminal laws which will have to be changed or eliminated are based on such outdated stereotypes that they simply are not relevant to today's behavior problems.[22]

Modifications to insure compliance with the Equal Rights Amendment will also have to conform to all other constitutional restrictions. For example, the right to privacy should permit segregation of the sexes in sleeping quarters in prisons.[23] It should also permit a statute or regulation which requires females to be searched by women police officers only.[24]

. . .

The list is not as long, but just as there are acts which are only unlawful if committed by a male, there are acts which are unlawful only if committed by a female, although the difference in treatment of male and female criminals does not stop with such laws. In some jurisdictions the criminal responsibility for the commission of unlawful acts differs for males and females, sentencing is often varied for males and females,[160] and the correctional system for males differs from the correctional system for females.[161]

Criminal responsibility of women: doctrine of presumed coercion

Unmarried women as well as men, whether married or single, are able to commit an offense and are held criminally responsible for it. The same rule does not always apply to a married woman.

At common law marriage does not affect the woman's capacity to commit a crime. Her coverture ordinarily is no defense.[162] However, at common law, a married woman is not criminally responsible for acts done as a result of her husband's coercion.[163] And crimes committed by a married woman in the presence of her husband are presumed to be committed due to his coercion.[164] This doctrine is a few thousand years old.[165] According to one writer[166] it arose, not under the old common fiction that husband and wife are one,[167] but due to a series of complex legal fictions during early English legal history.[168]

Today, however, regardless whether it developed from one fiction or a complex series, the reasons for the doctrine of presumed coercion no longer exist. Yet the doctrine hangs on, by case law in some states[169] and by statute in others.[170] However, it has in fact been repudiated as antiquated by a number of courts[171] and as no longer applicable because of the Married Women's Property Acts by still others.[172] Some states have extinguished the presumption by legislation.[173] In those states where the coercion defense is statutory, exceptions have been engrafted in the case of more serious offenses.[174]

It seems evident that the reason for the creation of the doctrine did not remain the reason for its continued place in the criminal law. Women were and are often presumed to be weak willed and subservient to their husbands. The doctrine presumes that if a husband orders his wife to commit a criminal act, she automatically complies. She is presumed to have no conscience and no control over her own behavior.

In People v. Statley[175] the California Appellate Court refuted the common law doctrine stating the following:

> We conclude then, that the reign of the thousand-year-old presumption
> has come to an end. In our society, where almost no bride promises to
> obey her husband, and where it is not accepted as the usual that a wife
> does what her husband wishes by way of yielding obedience to a dom-
> inant will, the basis for the presumption has disappeared. A presumption

that has lost its reason must be confined to a museum; it has no place in the administration of justice.[176]

The California court was not able to entirely reject the principle since it was part of the California criminal code.[177] But under the Equal Rights Amendment, such statutes will become invalid. The common law principle of presumed coercion must also fall as unconstitutional. Constitutionally, women can no longer be presumed to be the weaker sex. Legislatures will, of course, have the option of extending the principle to acts committed by men in the presence of their wives, instead of invalidating the existing statutes. This option should not be exercised.

Conspiracy

A married woman's exemption from criminal responsibility does not stop with the doctrine of presumed coercion. She can sometimes escape criminal prosecution under the law of conspiracy. "The broad definition or description everywhere accepted is that conspiracy is a combination between two or more persons to do or accomplish a criminal or unlawful act, or to do a lawful act by criminal or unlawful means."[178] Under the common law fiction that husband and wife lack separate identity, it logically follows that a husband and wife cannot conspire together. This principle has operated in the United States since 1889 when a California court held that a husband and wife could not be convicted of criminal conspiracy.[179] It has been rejected in at least three states[180] and expressly accepted in two others.[181] At least one state, Hawaii,[182] has a statute which explicitly says that a husband and wife cannot conspire together.

In an opinion written by Mr. Justice Frankfurter[183] the United States Supreme Court banned the principle from the federal courts. Justice Frankfurter suggested that the rule could proceed under one of two theories:

> . . . either that responsibility of husband and wife for joint participation
> in a criminal enterprise would make for marital disharmony, or that
> a wife must be presumed to act under the coercive influence of her
> husband and, therefore cannot be a willing participant.[184]

He concluded, "the former assumption is unnourished by sense; the latter implies a view of American womanhood offensive to the ethos of our society."[185]

The Equal Rights Amendment commands that each person must be treated as an individual. As with the doctrine of presumed coercion, the rule that husband and wife cannot conspire together must fail. Although the rule applies equally to both men and women, it is based on a theory which is in complete contradiction to the spirit and letter of the twenty-seventh amendment.

Female crimes only

The most obvious crimes, and perhaps the only crimes, which can be committed by women only are procuring an abortion for oneself or giving an abortion to oneself.[186] Since it is physically impossible for a man to undergo an abortion, these laws should not be affected by the Equal Rights Amendment under the unique physical characteristics doctrine.[187] Some abortion laws do apply to both men and women. Generally, these laws are aimed at persons who perform abortion,[188] procure abortion for others,[189] and advertise abortion.[190] Since men or women may be prosecuted under all these laws, they also should not be affected by the Equal Rights Amendment.

Some acts which men are as capable as women of performing are only unlawful if committed by a female. One example, found in at least seventeen states, is the unlawful concealment of the death of a child by a woman.[191]

Most "female only" crimes deal not with the husband-wife or the mother-child relationship, but with the prevention of sexual activity. For example, a Florida statute makes it unlawful for a female to entice a seaman from his vessel.[192] In North Carolina,[193] it is illegal for a lewd female to go within three miles of a college or boarding school. In Maryland, it is unlawful for a female to use a musical instrument to solicit funds for purposes other than charity.[194] In these states, no similar laws are applicable to men. However, the most common and best known "female only" crime is prostitution.

Prostitution

The common definition of prostitution is the practice of a female offering her body for indiscriminate sexual intercourse with men[195] usually for commercial gain.[196] Today, in only a few jurisdictions,[197] the prostitution statute itself or judicial gloss make the statute applicable to men as well as women.[198]

In several jurisdictions[199] the prostitution statute specifically indicates that it applies only to female prostitutes.[200] These laws have not gone unchallenged.[201] In Indiana, a woman was convicted of violation of the Indiana prostitution statute which applied only to females.[202] The woman, who had offered to commit sexual intercourse with an undercover vice squad officer for ten dollars, was sentenced to the Women's Prison in Indiana for a term of not less than two nor more than five years. She appealed her conviction on the ground that the statute was unconstitutional and void in that it violated a provision of the Indiana Constitution which forbade the General Assembly from passing any special laws for the punishment of crimes and misdemeanors.[203] Appellant argued that the statute was a special criminal law prohibited by the Constitution since it applied only to the class of all female persons and did not apply to male persons. The Supreme Court of Indiana rejected the appellant's contention and affirmed her conviction. In a dissenting opinion, Judge DeBruler wrote:

> It is obvious to me that the class of women was chosen arbitrarily for the application of this criminal sanction, and that there is no substantial ground upon which to justify singling women out for this treatment. The contrary position must maintain that a rational reason exists to punish a woman who makes such an offer without punishing a man who makes the same offer. But what such reason could possibly be put

forward? I believe there are none. In my judgment, the prostitute statute, wherein it makes it unlawful for any female to commit or offer to commit one or more acts of sexual intercourse or sodomy for hire, is void as special legislation.[204]

In most jurisdictions,[205] the prostitution statute itself makes no sex distinction. However males are not prosecuted under these statutes.[206] In some jurisdictions[207] male "prostitutes" are prosecuted for lewdness[208] or for soliciting for lewd and immoral purposes[209] while female prostitutes are simply prosecuted for prostitution.[210] In one such jurisdiction, the District of Columbia, a higher burden of production is put on the government regarding the conviction for "male" prostitution than is required where women are charged.[211] Although the penalty for prostitution is often light,[212] this is not always true. For example, in Missouri, only a female may be prosecuted for prostitution and, if convicted, she loses all her rights as a citizen, including the rights to vote and hold public office.

Under the Equal Rights Amendment, legislators will have to change those prostitution statutes which make a sex distinction. However the twenty-seventh amendment will not necessitate making the prostitute's customer criminally responsible as long as the government can show a non-sex-discriminatory reason. Whether this is possible is debatable.[213]

Special protection for female offenders

Once a female is convicted and sentenced for a crime, she may still be affected by a number of laws which are evidently designed for her protection. For instance, in several states[214] the criminal code commands that a woman put on probation for prostitution must be assigned a female probation officer. Under the Equal Rights Amendment, these laws are impermissible, unless a valid privacy argument can be made for sustaining them.[215] Another law which must fall, or be extended to include men, is a North Carolina statute which makes it unlawful to require women to work in chain gangs.[216] A New Jersey statute[217] which makes it unlawful to aid a girl's escape from a state home and a Texas law[218] which punishes a person for interfering with the training and custody of a female at a girls training school, must also be eliminated unless similar provisions are made for the interference with custody of a boy under similar circumstances.

Same law—different treatment

Numerous laws apply to males and females as offenders, victims, or impartial citizens, but do not apply to both equally. These laws can be divided into three categories: (1) laws which make distinctions based upon sex plus some other factor; (2) laws which punish men and women offenders differently for committing the same crime; and, (3) laws which treat impartial male and female citizens differently.

Sex-plus distinctions

The first category, laws which make a sex-plus distinction, can be separated into two groups: those which make a distinction based upon sex plus the age of the victim or offender; and those which differentiate based upon the sex plus the marital or parental status of a person.

Laws which make an age distinction between males and females are apparently based upon the assumption that males and females mature at different ages or that one sex needs protection under the law for more years than the other sex. A unique Arkansas law presents a good example.[219] It criminalizes tatooing a minor without the consent of his or her parents. However the law protects a female under eighteen years of age, while it protects a male under twenty-one years. In New York endangering the welfare of a male under sixteen years of age or a female child under seventeen years of age is a crime.[220]

Similar discrimination is applied to young offenders. A New York Family Court Act[221] defines a person "in need of supervision" as any male under sixteen or female under eighteen who is habitually "incorrigible, ungovernable, disobedient, or truant."[222] A Rhode Island bigamy statute excuses male offenders who had previously married when they were under fourteen years of age or female offenders who had married when they were under twelve.[223] These laws and others like them[224] are based on generalizations which do not comply with the Equal Rights Amendment. Assuming that some or even most girls mature faster than boys, this does not mean that every girl is more mature than every boy of her same age. Therefore unless age discrimination between sexes can be shown to be based on unique physical characteristics, and that seems highly unlikely, then these statutes must be modified.

Laws which make a marital or parental distinction between men and women are apparently based upon the same stereotyped sex roles that underline the desertion laws.[225] For example, in Mississippi it is illegal for a public agent or *his wife* to accept a bribe,[226] and in Montana it is illegal for a *wife* to make campaign expenditures above certain limits.[227] Assuming that Mississippi would not condone husbands of female public agents taking bribes and that Montana would not condone exorbitant campaign spending on the part of a husband, these laws reflect the sexist assumption that women will never be public officials or public candidates. Mothers and fathers are also distinguished from each other under criminal laws.[228] North Carolina[229] makes it a crime to separate a child under six months from his or her mother, but says nothing about separation from the father. However, best illustrating sex-plus discrimination are the adultery and paramour homicide statutes.

Adultery

Throughout history adultery has always been treated in a manner which discriminates on the basis of sex.[230] At English common law, adultery was not a criminal offense but merely a private wrong for which the aggrieved husband had a right of action for damages.[231] It was defined as sexual intercourse by a man, married or single, with a married woman not his wife.[232] Both parties were regarded as adulterers. Adultery was a wrong because it might introduce spurious issue into a family, thereby turning a man's inheritance away from his own blood to that of a stranger.[233] English ecclesiastical courts,[234] however, viewed adultery as a sin against the marriage vows and regarded the offense as equally serious whether the offender was a husband or a wife.[235] The ecclesiastical courts punished the unfaithful spouse for adultery, while punishing the other party for fornication.[236]

Today four states[237] apply the common law definition of adultery and provide penalties for sexual intercourse between a married woman and a man not her husband. In these states there is no similar penalty for intercourse between a married man and a woman not his wife.

In at least eight jurisdictions[238] elements of the common law and ecclesiastical law are combined to define the offense. In these jurisdictions, an unmarried female cannot be guilty of adultery for performing coitus with a married man, although an unmarried male can be punished for having intercourse with a married woman. A typical statute provides: "A married man who has sexual intercourse with a woman not his wife, an unmarried man who has sexual intercourse with a married woman or a married woman who has sexual intercourse with a man not her husband shall be guilty of adultery."[239] Under the Equal Rights Amendment, those states which do not provide equal treatment of men and women in terms of the adultery laws will either have to eliminate the statutes[240] or adopt a new statute which treats men and women equally.[241]

Paramour homicide

Perhaps the most outrageous of all discriminatory criminal statutes are those which condone the act of a husband who kills his wife's paramour if committed during the act of adultery.[242] These statutes are considered to be atrocious not merely because they do not apply to women who kill their husband's paramour but because the "state is in effect delegating the right of public execution to a private citizen."[243]

At least two states presently allow husbands to assert this defense.[244] A number of states consider adultery by a spouse committed in the presence of the other spouse sufficient provocation[245] to reduce a killing of the spouse, paramour, or mistress from murder to manslaughter.[246]

Obviously, the Equal Rights Amendment will demand changes in these statutes which discriminate between men and women. It is suggested that they be eliminated rather than extended to justify wives killing their husband's paramour. Other, more civilized alternatives, such as suing for divorce or alienation of affections or charging criminal adultery, would still be available,[247] and should be much preferred over homicide.

The fact that the discrimination is made on the basis of sex plus the age, or marital, or parental status of a person should not render the twenty-seventh amendment inapplicable. Although, under the Equal Rights Amendment,[248] a distinction can be made between the old and the young, the married and the unmarried, or the parent and the nonparent, there can be no distinction made between a male and female of the same age, or a married woman and a married man, or an unmarried woman and an unmarried man, or a mother and father, unless it is due to a unique physical characteristic. The sex-plus theory of discrimination has been offered, unsuccessfully, by a number of defendants[249] in Title VII cases.[250] The argument proffers that the discrimination is not based entirely on sex, but on sex, plus some other factor. The Fifth Circuit erroneously agreed with this reasoning in *Phillips v. Martin Marietta Corp.*[251] in which Ms. Phillips was denied a job because she was a woman with a pre-school age child. The court reasoned that a violation of Title VII

> . . . can only be discrimination based solely on one of the categories *i.e.*, in the case of sex; women vis-a-vis men. When *another* criterion of employment *is added* to one of the classifications listed in the Act, there is no longer apparent discrimination based solely on race, color, religion, sex, or national origin. . . . Ida Phillips was not refused employment because she was a woman nor because she had pre-school age children. It is the *coalescence* of those *two elements* that denied her the position she desired.[252]

The Supreme Court rejected the "sex-plus" theory[253] and remanded the case.[254] If this philosophy were permitted to stand, then anytime law makers wish to make a law applicable to men but not to women, or women but not men, they could merely add an unnecessary qualification to sex. For instance, law makers in states following the common law definition of adultery could argue that the law does not discriminate against women *per se*, but only against women who are married. This should be impermissible.

Differing penalties

The second category of laws, those which provide different criminal penalties for men and women committing the same crime, apparently are based on one of two theories. The first theory posits that all women offenders can be reformed and therefore correctional authorities should be able to subject the female offender to the rehabilitation process as long as necessary to rehabilitate her. This philosophy has been incorporated into sentencing statutes which provide longer sentences for women than for men who commit the same crime.[255] Pennsylvania[256] and Connecticut[257] courts have struck down such statutes under the equal protection clause. However, a New Jersey court,[258] rejecting the reasoning of the Pennsylvania and Connecticut courts, has recently upheld a discriminatory sentencing law. A number of other jurisdictions also still have such laws.[259]

The second theory underlying discriminatory sentencing is the familiar double standard which suggests men be penalized more heavily than women when the victim of the crime is a woman. For instance, Arizona defines aggravated assault as an assault made by a male upon a female or by a person over eighteen upon a child under fifteen.[260] If a female spits in the face of another female above the age of fifteen, she may be charged only with simple assault, and she may be penalized by a fine up to $300 or imprisonment up to three months.[261] However, a male who spits in the face of the same female victim may be charged with aggravated assault, and he may be penalized by a fine not less than $100 nor more than $2,000 and/or imprisonment for not less than one year nor more than five years.[262] Similar assault statutes exist in at least two other states.[263] These statutes which authorize different standards should fall under the Equal Rights Amendment. Men and women must not only be punished for the same crimes; they must be punished equally.

· · ·

Summary

Much of the criminal law today reflects attitudes which are sex biased and outdated. The Equal Rights Amendment presents legislatures with the motivation and the opportunity to revise their criminal codes and eliminate antiquated laws as well as revise necessary laws which fail to treat men and women equally.

The task ahead of the states in revising their criminal codes is relatively easy.[317] When legislators find a discriminatory provision they will simply have to decide whether the statute is worth saving and, if it is, make the appropriate changes. In most cases the legislature will only have to substitute the word "person" each time the words "male" or "female" are used. It will then be up to law enforcement officers and the courts to see that the criminal laws are enforced equally for both sexes.

Is it possible to erase all sexist laws from the criminal code? One only has to look at the recently revised criminal code of the State of Kansas to find that the answer is yes. It did so, with the exception of its rape statute which still applies to men only.

While it is not possible to predict just how the Equal Rights Amendment will actually affect life in the United States, one should be safe in predicting that the twenty-seventh amendment will not have an impact on the commission of criminal acts. While the amendment will require the modification of laws, it cannot possibly resocialize persons overnight. That is, one should not suddenly expect to see women raping men or men running around the streets of Alabama cursing at women. The Equal Rights Amendment will only require that men and women be protected equally and punished equally.

Notes

1. *See, e.g.*, Neb. Rev. Stat. § 28-1115 (1943), which defines a tramp to include whoever asks or subsists on charity, except minors, females, and the blind.
2. The Equal Rights resolution has been introduced in every session of Congress and has been reported on by the Judiciary Committee seventeen times between 1923 and 1972. Martin, *Equal Rights Amendment: Legislative Background,* 11 J. Family L. 363 (1971).
3. *See* U.S. Const. art. VI, § 2.
4. However, for purposes of this discussion, some initial assumptions will be made.
5. *See* Brown, Emerson, Falk & Freedman, *The Equal Rights Amendment: A Constitutional Basis for Equal Rights for Women,* 80 Yale L. J. 871, 915 (1971) [hereinafter cited as Emerson], for discussion of the courts' strict construction of penal laws.

6. Emerson, *supra* note 5, at 893.
7. *Id.*
8. *See* TEX. PEN. CODE art. 1-1168 (1961). Other examples of statutes which should not be invalidated under this doctrine are laws which stay the execution of a pregnant woman condemned to death, *e.g.*, ARIZ. REV. STAT. ANN. § 13-1695 (1958); MD. ANN. CODE art. 27, § 27-75(c) (1971 Repl. Vol.); OHIO REV. CODE § 2949.31 (1953); S.D. COMP. LAWS ANN. § 22-49-16 (1967), or laws which allow the pregnant wife of a convict to receive state aid. *E.g.*, OHIO REV. CODE § 2903.09 (1967).
9. *See* Emerson, *supra* note 5, at 894.
10. In 1971, law enforcement agencies reported that 8,858 men and 1,645 women were arrested for murder and that 75,023 men and 5,174 women were arrested for robbery. FBI, UNIFORM CRIME REPORTS Table 27, at 120 (1971) [hereinafter cited as UNIFORM CRIME REPORTS].
11. If, however, customers were not prosecuted and the government could not show a non-sex-discriminatory reason then the prostitution law should fall in violation of the Equal Rights Amendment. *See* Emerson, *supra* note 5, at 964.
12. *See* notes 99-106, 160-218 *infra* and accompanying text.
13. *See* notes 219-254 *infra* and accompanying text.
14. *See* notes 107-159 *infra* and accompanying text.
   As a result of the research for this note, only one statute was found which referred to male victims only and did not have a sister statute which applied to females only. See TEX. PEN. CODE art. 1-1168 (1961) (forbidding castration). Therefore, the notes and accompanying text cited above apply to female victims only.
15. *See* notes 25-106, 186-215 *infra* and accompanying text.
16. *See* notes 257-65 *infra* and accompanying text.
17. *See* notes 6-9 *supra* and accompanying text.
18. *See* notes 267-318 *infra* and accompanying text.
19. Courts have already invalidated state laws authorizing greater maximum penalties for women than for men, rather than extending the more severe penalties to men. United States *ex rel.* Robinson v. York, 281 F. Supp. 8 (D. Conn. 1968); Commonwealth v. Daniel 430 Pa. 642, 243 A.2d 400 (1968).
20. *See* notes 112-120 *infra* and accompanying text.
21. Arrests of women for prostitution and commercialized vice outnumber those of men by a factor of 3.6. UNIFORM CRIME REPORTS, *supra* note 10. Of course, this proportion will raise a question whether there is a non-sex-discriminatory purpose for penalizing the prostitute and not the customer as is the case in most states. *See* note 11 *supra*.
22. Arrests for crimes such as adultery, abduction, seduction, etc. are so rarely made that the Federal Bureau of Investigation does not even keep statistics on them. *See* UNIFORM CRIME REPORTS, *supra* note 10.
23. Emerson, *supra* note 5, at 901. *But see* Eastwood, *The Double Standard of Justice: Women's Rights Under the Constitution,* 5 VAL. U.L. REV. 279, 315-17 (1971). Eastwood asserts that the rule should be that the government has an obligation to construct its facilities so that integration of the sexes does not cause invasion of individual privacy, not that the government can segregate the sexes if necessary to avoid invasion of privacy.
   A number of states, besides having sentencing laws which provide for men and women to be sent to different correctional institutions, also have a specific law which makes it unlawful to keep prisoners of the opposite sex together unless they are married. *See, e.g.,* MASS. GEN. LAWS ANN. ch. 268, § 29 (1970); N.M. STAT. ANN. § 40A-22-14 (1953); S.D. COMP. LAWS ANN. § 24-11-20 (1967); OR. REV. STAT. § 169.140.

24. *See, e.g.,* FLA. STAT. ANN. § 944.22 (Supp. 1972) (providing that all employees coming into contact with female prisoners must be female).

· · ·

160. *See* in this *Symposium,* Temin, *Discriminatory Sentencing of Women Offenders: The Argument for ERA in a Nutshell.*
161. *See* in this *Symposium,* Singer, *Women and the Correctional Process.*
162. *See* State v. Renslow, 211 Iowa 642, 230 N.W. 316 (1930); State v. Cleaves, 59 Me. 298, 8 Am. R. 472 (W.D.Ct. 1871); Commonwealth v. Hopkins, 133 Mass. 381, 43 Am. R. 527 (1882); People v. Wright, 38 Mich. 744, 31 Am. R. 331 (1878); State v. Miller, 162 Mo. 253, 62 S.W. 692 (1901); State v. Cauley, 244 N.C. 701, 94 S.E.2d 915 (1956); Sentell v. State, 61 Okla. Crim. 229, 67 P.2d 466 (1937); State v. McDonie, 96 W. Va. 219, 123 S.E. 405 (1924).
163. Mulvey v. State, 43 Ala. 316, 94 Am. Dec. 684 (1896); Conner v. State, 95 Fla. 765, 117 So. 852 (1928); State v. Renslow, 211 Iowa 642, 230 N.W. 316 (1930); Anderson v. Commonwealth, 211 Ky. 726, 277 S.W. 1008 (Ct. App. 1925); Commonwealth v. Neal, 10 Mass. 152, 6 Am. Dec. 105 (Co. Ct. 1813); Davis v. State, 15 Ohio St. 72 (1846).
164. State v. Renslow, 211 Iowa 642, 230 N.W. 316 (1930); Cothron v. State, 138 Md. 101, 113 A. 62 (1921); State v. Ready, 251 S.E.2d (Mo. 1952); State v. Asper, 35 N.M. 203; 292 P. 225 (1930); Sentell v. State, 61 Okla. Crim. 229, 67 P.2d 466 (1937); Morton v. State, 141 Tenn. 357, 209 S.W. 644 (1919); State v. Buchannan 111 W.Va. 142, 160 S.E. 920 (1931).
165. *See* 4 BLACKSTONE COMMENTARIES 28.
166. *See* L. KANOWITZ, WOMEN AND THE LAW 89 (1969), *citing* R. PERKINS, CRIMINAL LAW 796–805 (1957).
167. *Id.*
168. At one time, hundreds of offenses were punishable by death. In order to spare members of the clergy from the death penalty, courts allowed them to raise their religious affiliation as a mitigation. This was known as "benefit of clergy." At a later date, this privilege was extended to every man who could read, whether or not he was a member of the clergy. The theory assumes that since married women could not become nuns, the common law courts hesitated to extend the privilege to them. Therefore, if a husband and wife committed a crime together, she might be put to death while he completely escaped punishment. Due to this unfair difference in treatment, Professor Perkins suggests, the doctrine of presumed coercion was developed. A married woman committing a crime in the presence of her husband could claim as her defense that her husband had forced her to commit the act. The husband in turn could claim "benefit of clergy" and he also could escape punishment. Note 166 *Supra.*
169. State v. Ready, 251 S.W.2d 680 (Mo. 1952); Doyle v. State, 317 P.2d 289 (Okla. Crim. App. 1957).
170. *See, e.g.,* ARK. STAT. ANN. § 41-114 (1964); ARIZ. REV. STAT. ANN. § 13-134 (1956); CAL. PENAL CODE ANN. § 26 (1970); DEL. CODE ANN. tit. 11, § 105 (1953); NEV. REV. STAT. § 194.010 (1968); OKLA. STAT. tit. 21, § 157 (1951); S.D. COMP. LAWS ANN. § 22-3-1 (1967); UTAH CODE ANN. § 76-1-41(8) (1953).
171. People v. Stately, 91 Cal. App. 2d Supp. 943, 206 P.2d 76, (1949); State v. Renslow, 211 Iowa 642, 230 N.W. 316 (1930); King v. City of Owensboro, 187 Ky. 21, 218 S.W. 297 (Ct. App. 1920); Morton v. State, 141 Tenn. 357, 209 S.W. 644 (1919).
172. State v. Renslow, 211 Iowa 642, 230 N.W. 316 (1930); King v. City of Owensboro, 187 Ky. 21, 218 S.W. 297 (Ct. App. 1920); Morton v. State, 141 Tenn. 357,209 S.W. 644 (1919). *Contra,* Braxton v. State, 17 Ala. App. 167, 82 So. 657 (1919).

173. *See, e.g.,* ORE. REV. STAT. § 161.270 (1971); WIS. STAT. ANN. § 939.46 (1958).

174. Murder: Bibb v. State, 94 Ala. 31, 10 So. 506 (1892); Conner v. State, 95 Fla. 765, 117 So. 852 (1928); Cothron v. State, 138 Md. 101, 113 A. 620 (1921); Martin v. Commonwealth, 143 Va. 479, 129 S.E. 348 (1925). Treason: McGregor v. State, 200 Ind. 496, 163 N.E. 596 (1928). Assault and Battery: State v. Cauley, 244 N.C. 701, 94 S.E. 2d 915 (1956); State v. McDonie, 96 W.Va. 219, 123 S.E. 405 (1924). *Contra,* State v. Baker, 110 Mo. 7, 19 S.W. 222 (1892) (mayhem); Davis v. State, 15 Ohio St. 72 (1846) (arson). These statutes and cases are somewhat in contradiction to the suggestion that the reason the presumed coercion doctrine came into effect was to save women from capital punishment. *See* note 168 *supra.*

175. 91 Cal. App. 2d Supp. 943, 206 P.2d 76 (1949).

176. *Id.* at 951, 206 P.2d at 81.

177. CAL. PENAL CODE ANN. § 26 (1970).

178. Commonwealth v. Donoghue, 250 Ky. 343, 347, 63 S.W.2d 3, 5 (Ct. App. 1933).

179. People v. Miller, 61 Cal. 107, 22 P. 934, 5 (1889). This principle was not overruled by the California Supreme Court until 1964. People v. Pierce, 40 Cal. Rptr. 845, 61 Cal. App. 2d 879, 395 P.2d 893 (1964).

180. Colorado: Dalton v. People, 68 Colo. 44, 189 P. 37 (1920). Illinois: People v. Martin, 4 Ill. 2d 105, 122 N.E.2d 245 (1954). Texas: Marks v. State, 144 Tex. Crim. 509, 164 S.W. 2d (1942).

181. New Jersey: State v. Struck, 44 N.J. Super. 274, 129 A.2d 910 (Co. Ct. 1957); Pennsylvania: Commonwealth v. Allen, 24 Pa. 65 (Bucks Co. Ct. 1900).

182. HAWAII REV. STAT. § 728-5 (1968). *Accord,* HAWAII REV. STAT. § 750-12 (1968) providing there can be no larceny between husband and wife. *But see* ALASKA STAT. § 11.20.040 (1970); HAWAII REV. STAT. § 723-11 (1968); ME. REV. STAT. ANN. tit. 17 § 165 (1967); R.I. GEN. LAWS ANN. § 11-4-7 (1956), which make a wife criminally responsible for burning or harming property which in whole or part belongs to her husband.

183. United States v. Dege, 364 U.S. 51 (1960).

184. *Id.* at 53.

185. *Id.*

186. *E.g.,* ARIZ. REV. STAT. ANN. § 13-212 (1956); CAL. PENAL CODE ANN. § 275 (1970); IND. ANN. STAT. § 10-106 (1956).

187. *See* notes 7–11 *supra* and accompanying text.

188. *E.g.,* ARK. STAT. ANN. § 41-301 (1964); CAL. PENAL CODE ANN. § 274 (1970); IDAHO CODE § 18-601 (1947); N.J. STAT. ANN. § 2A:87-1 (1969).

189. *E.g.,* CAL. PENAL CODE ANN. § 276 (1970); R.I. GEN. LAWS ANN. § 11-3-1 (1969).

190. *E.g.,* ARK. STAT. ANN. § 41-302 (1964); IDAHO CODE § 18-603 (1947); IND. ANN. STAT. § 10-2806 (1956).

191. Seven of these states make it unlawful to conceal the death of any child. ALASKA STAT. § 11.40.090 (1970); ARK. STAT. ANN. § 41-2225 (1964); MASS. GEN. LAWS ANN. ch. 272, § 22 (1970); MO. ANN. STAT. § 559.170 (1949); N.D. CENT. CODE § 12-25-06 (1960); OKLA. STAT. ANN. tit. 21 § 863 (1951); WIS. STAT. ANN. § 946.63 (1958). Ten of these states make it unlawful to conceal the death of an illegitimate child: COLO. REV. STAT. ANN. § 40-2-4 (1963); FLA. STAT. ANN. § 782.16 (1971); HAWAII REV. STAT. § 768-8 (1968); KY. REV. STAT. ANN. § 436.030 (1968); ME. REV. STAT. ANN. § 17-52 (1964); MICH. COMP. LAWS ANN. § 750.150 (1968); N.H. REV. STAT. ANN. § 585:15 (1955) (statute will be eliminated in November, 1973); N.J. STAT. ANN. § 2A:96-1 (1969); S.D. COMP. LAWS ANN. § 22-17-3, -4 (1967).

192. FLA. STAT. ANN. § 862.02 (1963).

193. N.C. GEN. STAT. § 14-198 (Supp. 1971).

194. MD. ANN. CODE art. 27, § 415 (1971).

195. State v. Stoyell, 54 Me. 24, 27 (1866).
196. *Id.* at 27.
197. *E.g.*, Illinois, ILL. ANN. STAT. ch. 38, § 11-14 (1971); New York, N.Y. PENAL CODE § 230.00 (Supp. 1971); Oregon, ORE. REV. STAT. § 167.002 (1971). For a complete list, *see* in this *Symposium,* Rosenbleet & Pariente, *The Prostitution of the Criminal Law.*
198. Males have not, however, always been included in order to bring about equality of the sexes under the law. In Illinois, for instance, the legislature recently revised their prostitution statute so that males could be prosecuted under it. But a reading of the legislative history reveals that this was done only so that male homosexuals could be held criminally responsible for their acts of prostitution. The Illinois government was still solely interested in protecting the public from lewd women and their female impersonators. *See* ILL. ANN. STAT. ch. 38, § 11-14 (1971) and accompanying notes. *Contra,* CONN. GEN. STAT. ANN. § 53a-84 (1972).
199. *See, e.g.,* ALASKA STAT. § 11.40.210 (1970); MO. ANN. STAT. § 563.010 (1949); WYO. STAT. ANN. § 6-94 (1957). For a complete summary of statutes which define prostitution as a female crime *see* in this *Symposium,* Rosenbleet & Pariente, *The Prostitution of the Criminal Law.*
200. In several jurisdictions, female prostitutes have been prosecuted under vagrancy statutes. *See, e.g.,* WIS. STAT. ANN. § 947.02(3) (1958) (held void for vagueness in State v. Starks, 186 N.W.2d 245 (1971)).
201. *See* in this *Symposium,* Rosenbleet & Pariente, *The Prostitution of the Criminal Law.*
202. "Prostitute.—Any female who frequents or lives in a house or houses of ill fame, knowing the same to be a house of ill fame, or who commits or offers to commit one or more acts of sexual intercourse or sodomy for hire, shall be deemed guilty of prostitution. . . ." IND. ANN. STAT. § 10-4220 (1956).
203. Wilson v. State, 11 CrL 2017 (Ind. Sup. Ct., March 1971).
204. *Id.*
205. *See, e.g.,* GA. CODE ANN. § 26-2016 (1971); TENN. CODE ANN. § 39-3501 (1955).
206. *See* in this *Symposium,* Rosenbleet & Pariente, *The Prostitution of the Criminal Law.*
207. *E.g.,* District of Columbia, Iowa.
208. IOWA CODE ANN. § 724.2 (1946).
209. D.C. CODE ANN. § 22-2701 (1961).
210. *See* State v. Gardner, 174 Iowa 748, 156 N.W. 747 (1916).
211. *See* Wajer v. United States, 222 A.2d 68 (D.C. App. 1966).
212. *E.g.,* D.C. CODE ANN. § 22-2701 (1967) (up to $250 and/or 90 days); IND. ANN. STAT. § 10-4219 (1956) ($10 to $100 fine and 10 to 60 days).
213. As pointed out by a number of writers, there is a difference between receiving payment for sexual services and giving payment for such services. *See* Eastwood, *supra* note 23, at 315; Emerson, *supra* note 5, at 964. Today a number of states punish the customer of a prostitute, *e.g.,* N.M. STAT. ANN. § 40A-9-12 (1953). However, the penalty imposed on the customer is not necessarily the same as the punishment for the prostitute. For example, in Wisconsin a prostitute may be sentenced to a fine of $500 and/or a year's imprisonment, while a male customer may only be sentenced to a $100 fine and/or three months' imprisonment. WIS. STAT. ANN. § 944.30.31 (1958).
214. *See, e.g.,* MD. ANN. CODE art. 27, § 17 (1957); N.D. CENT. CODE § 12-22-20 (1960); *accord,* VT. STAT. ANN. tit. 13, § 2633 (1959).
215. *See* notes 23 and 24 *supra* and accompanying text. If a privacy argument is unsuccessful legislators *cannot* make these laws constitutional simply by having

similar laws applicable to men. That is, a law which required male probation officers for male offenders would not validate a law which required female probation officers for females.

216. N.C. Gen. Stat. § 14-262 (1969).
217. N.J. Stat. Ann. § 2A:104-10 (1969).
218. Tex. Penal Code Ann. art. 333 (1952).
219. Ark. Stat. Ann. § 41-1130 to -1131 (1964).
220. N.Y. Penal Law § 260.10 (McKinney 1970).
221. N.Y. Family Ct. Act § 712(b) (McKinney 1970).
222. For discussion on the differential treatment of male and female juvenile offenders, *see* Gold, *Equal Protection for Juvenile Girls in Need of Supervision in New York State,* 17 N.Y.L.F. 570 (1971).
223. R.I. Gen. Laws Ann. § 11-6-1 (1956).
224. *E.g.,* Miss. Code Ann. § 2053 (1942) (unlawful to entice males under 21 and females under 18 residing with parents away from home for purposes of employment); Neb. Rev. Stat. § 28-931 (1943) (unlawful to harbor males under 21 and females under 18 in house of ill fame). *See also* discussion of statutory rape. Notes 86–92 *supra* and accompanying text.
225. *See* notes 47–57 *supra* and accompanying text.
226. Miss. Code Ann. § 2028 (1942).
227. Mont. Rev. Codes Ann. § 94-1428 (1947).
228. They are also often treated differently under civil law. *See* Stanley v. Illinois, 92 S. Ct. 1208 (1972), where the Court struck down an Illinois law requiring fathers of illegitimate children to go through adoption proceedings in order to gain custody of their children but having no similar requirements for unmarried mothers.
229. N.C. Gen. Stat. § 14-320 (1969). *See also* Ariz. Stat. Ann. § 13-821 (1956) (defines dependent persons as being under 18 and whose father is dead or has abandoned the family); Md. Ann. Code art. 27, § 2-18 (1971) (where husband is convicted of bigamy wife is entitled to same share of estate as if he had died intestate, although there is no comparable provision where the wife was guilty of bigamy); Minn. Stat. Ann. § 609.34 (Supp. 1967) (defining fornication as intercourse between any male and a single female); Mont. Rev. Codes Ann. § 94-4603 (1947) (burial statute putting heavier burden on unmarried female's relatives); Neb. Rev. Stat. § 28-944 (1943) (allows wife or guardian to recover money lost by husband or ward while gambling); Nev. Rev. Stat. § 202.100 (1967) (unlawful for bartender to sell or give intoxicating liquor to any person who is drunk or known to be an habitual drunkard, after being notified by the *wife,* father or mother, son or daughter; and also unlawful to sell liquor to *husband* or *father* whose wife is in destitute circumstances and not supplied with the common necessities of life by the husband or father, after notice from wife or child); N.C. Gen. Stat. §§ 14-326, -332 (1969) (father of minor has civil cause of action against person unlawfully selling liquor to minor while mother only has a cause of action if the father is dead); N.C. Gen. Stat. § 14-332 (1969) (not unlawful for female to abandon her child if she supports it, but is unlawful for father to abandon child).
230. In Babylonia, adultery was sexual intercourse between a married woman and a man, not her husband, but only the woman was guilty of the offense. A married man who had intercourse with a woman, not his wife, was not punished criminally. In Ptolemaic Egypt, the definition of adultery was broadened to include unfaithful sexual acts on the part of a married man. Women, however, were punished more harshly than men. Greek law was also stricter with women. A married man was guilty of adultery only if he had intercourse with the wife, sister,

or mother of another citizen. Conversely, a married woman was guilty if she had coitus with anyone other than her husband. Rome was also less tolerant with an unfaithful wife. A husband was punished only for having sexual relations with another man's wife, while a wife could not legally have coitus with anyone except her husband. Moore, *The Diverse Definitions of Criminal Adultery*, 30 U. KAN. CITY L. REV. 219 (1962).

231. 1 AM. JUR. *Adultery* § 2 (1936).

232. Warner v. State, 202 Ind. 479, 175 N.E. 661 (1931); Bashford v. Wells, 78 Kan. 295, 96 P. 663 (1908); State v. Weatherby, 43 Me. 258 (1857); Commonwealth v. Call, 38 Mass. (21 Pick.) 509 (1839); State v. Lash, 16 N.J.L. 330 (1838).

233. *See* Bashford v. Wells, 78 Kan. 295, 96 P. 663 (1908); State v. Roberts, 169 Wis. 570, 173 N.W. 310 (1919).

234. From prior to the Middle Ages until the 18th century, with the exception of the period between 1640 and 1661. Moore, *supra* note 230, at 220.

235. *See* Bashford v. Wells, 78 Kan. 295, 96 P. 663 (1908); State v. Bigelow, 88 Vt. 464, 92 A. 978 (1915).

236. Ohlson, *Adultery: A Review*, 17 B.U.L. REV. 328, 331 (1937). At common law, fornication was an act of illicit intercourse by a man, married or single, with an unmarried woman. Pollard v. Lyon, 91 U.S. 225 (1875). The distinction, at common law, between adultery and fornication depended on the marital status of the woman. *See* State v. Philipe, 26 N.D. 206, 144 N.W. 94 (1913).

237. Indiana, IND. ANN. STAT. § 10-4207 (1971); Maryland, MD. ANN. STAT. art. 27, § 4 (1957) (given common law meaning in Evans v. Murff, 135 F. Supp. 907 (1955)); New Jersey, N.J. REV. STAT. § 2A:88-1 (1952) (*see In re* Smith, 71 F. Supp. 968 (D.N.J. 1947); State v. Lash, 16 N.J.L. 380 (1838)); and Wyoming, WYO. STAT. ANN. § 6-86 (1957) (*see* Hood v. State, 56 Ind. 263 (1877) holding Indiana law applies because Indiana is law of origin).

238. Alaska, ALASKA STAT. §§ 11.40.010, 030 (1962); Massachusetts, MASS. GEN. LAWS ANN. ch. 272, § 14 (1970); Michigan, MICH. COMP. LAW ANN. § 750.30 (1968); Minnesota, MINN. STAT. ANN. § 609.36 (1964); New Hampshire, N.H. REV. STAT. ANN. § 579-2 (1955); North Dakota, N.D. CENT. CODE § 12-22-09 (1960); Utah, UTAH CODE ANN. § 76-53-3 (1953); and the District of Columbia, D.C. CODE ANN. § 22-301 (1961).

239. MASS. GEN. LAWS ANN. ch. 272, § 14 (1970).

240. Whether or not adultery should continue to be a crime is a collateral issue which shall not be discussed in this *Note*. According to Moore, *supra* note 232, at 227, n. 80, adultery laws are frequently violated and infrequently enforced. *See also* A. KINSEY, SEXUAL BEHAVIOR IN THE HUMAN FEMALE 416 (1953); A. KINSEY, SEXUAL BEHAVIOR IN THE HUMAN MALE 585 (1949).

241. *See, e.g.,* COLO. REV. STAT. ANN. § 40-9-3 (1963); MICH. COMP. LAWS § 750.29 (1968); N.Y. PENAL LAW § 255.17 (McKinney 1967); TEX. PENAL CODE ANN. art. 499 (1952).

242. Generally, a homicide under such circumstances is labelled "justifiable." "Justifiable homicide is the necessary killing of another in the performance of a legal duty, or where the slayer, without fault on his part, has a legal right so to kill." 40 C.J.S. *Homicide* § 97 (1944).

243. *See* Kanowitz, *supra* note 166, at 93.

244. Texas and Utah. Homicide is justifiable when committed by the husband upon one caught in the act of adultery with the wife. TEX. PENAL CODE art. 1219 (1971). A wife, however, who killed a woman committing adultery with her husband was held not justified by this article. Reed v. State, 59 S.W.2d 122 (Tex. Crim. App. 1933). "Homicide is also justifiable when committed by any person in either of the

following cases. . . . When committed in a sudden heat of passion caused by the attempt of the deceased to commit a rape upon or defile the wife, or when the defilement has actually been committed." UTAH CODE ANN. § 76-30-10(4) (1953). The husband, however, is not justified in killing his wife discovered committing adultery. Billings v. State, 277 S.W. 687 (Tex. Crim. App. 1926).

Georgia replaced such a statute in 1972. GA. CODE ANN. §§ 26-1101 *et seq.* (1972), *replacing* GA. CODE ANN. § 26-1016 (1935). In 1964 New Mexico repealed a similar statute. N.M. STAT. ANN. § 40A-2-4 (1964).

245. M. HALE, PLEAS OF THE CROWN (5th ed. 1716).
246. *See* Garcia v. People, 64 Colo. 172, 171 P. 1068 (1918); State v. Peffers, 80 Iowa 580, 46 N.W. 662 (1890); Sanchez v. People, 22 N.Y. 147 (1860); State v. Young, 52 Ore. 277, 96 P. 1067 (1908). *See also* W. VA. CODE ANN. § 61-2-1 (1972) (wife's confession of adultery affects degree of homicide in husband's killing of her paramour). Delaware just recently repealed a statute which read: "Whoever, being a husband, commits the crime of manslaughter on a person found in the act of adultery with his wife, and it is so found by the verdict, shall be fined not less than $100 nor more than $1,000, and imprisoned not more than 1 year." DEL. CODE ANN. tit. 11, § 575(b) (1953) (repealed 1972).
247. Whether these alternatives should be available is beyond the scope of this discussion.
248. There may be exceptions to this statement. If, for example, it could be shown that a law discriminating between married and unmarried persons affected one sex significantly more than the other it could be struck down under the 27th Amendment.
249. *E.g.,* Phillips v. Martin Marietta Corp., 400 U.S. 542 (1971); Sprogis v. United Air Lines, Inc., 308 F. Supp. 959 (N.D. Ill., 1970); Gerstle v. Continental Airlines, Inc. 50 F.R.D. 213 (D. Colo. 1970).
250. 42 U.S.C. §§ 2000 *et seq.* (1964).
251. 411 F.2d 1 (5th Cir. 1969), *rev'd,* 400 U.S. 542 (1971).
252. 416 F.2d 1260 (1969).
253. 400 U.S. 542 (1971). This illogical theory has also been rejected in Sprogis v. United Air Lines, Inc., 308 F. Supp. 959 (N.D. Ill. 1970) and Gerstle v. Continental Airlines, Inc., 50 F.R.D. 213 (D. Colo. 1970). Both cases involved claims by airlines that their policy of discharging stewardesses who married was not sex discrimination.
254. The court remanded for a determination of whether a bona fide occupational qualification existed.
255. *See* in this *Symposium,* Temin, *Discriminatory Sentencing of Women Offenders: The Argument for ERA in a Nutshell.*
256. Commonwealth v. Daniel, 430 Pa. 642, 243 A.2d 400 (1968).
257. United States *ex rel.* Robinson v. York, 281 F. Supp. 8 (D. Conn. 1968).
258. State v. Costello, 59 N.J. 334, 282 A.2d 748 (1971).
259. Massachusetts, Iowa, Maine, Maryland, and New York. *See* in this *Symposium,* Temin, *Discriminatory Sentencing of Women Offenders: The Argument for ERA in a Nutshell,* at notes 30, 31, 33 & 37.
260. ARIZ. REV. STAT. ANN. § 13-245 (1972).
261. ARIZ. REV. STAT. ANN. § 13-243 (1972).
262. ARIZ. REV. STAT. ANN. § 13-245 (1972).
263. North Carolina, N.C. GEN. STAT. § 14-33 (1969); and Texas, TEX. PENAL CODE ANN. art. 1147 (1971). Illinois treats incest in a similar fashion. A mother who has sexual relations with her son is punished for incest and a father who has sexual relations with his daughter is punished for aggravated incest. *See* ILL. ANN. STAT.

ch. 38, § 11-10 (Smith-Hurd 1972). *See also* Neb. Rev. Stat. § 28-906 (1964) (incest law applying only to father-daughter relations).

317. A number of states have recently revised and modernized their criminal codes. *E.g.,* Connecticut, Illinois, New Hampshire, and New York. For these states only a few changes will be necessary.

Part four
Women in prison and on parole

A long with other aspects of women's involvement in crime and criminal justice, the inmates of women's prisons have attracted a good deal of attention in the last five years. The label "forgotten offender," which had been used appropriately in the past to describe female inmates, does not fit quite as well today as it did as recently as a few years ago. The new interest in women inmates derives, we think, more from a general interest in the roles women occupy in society, from the greater visibility of female offenders, and from the movement for adoption of the Equal Rights Amendment than from any changes that have occurred in the characteristics or behavior of inmates. Further, arrest statistics indicate there has been an increase in the proportion of women committing serious crimes. If the numbers continue to increase (and there are reasons to believe they will), then the number of women who pass through the criminal justice system will increase. With this greater increase, judges are likely to become less reluctant to sentence women to prison. Thus, while it is still too early to observe a large increase in the number of female inmates, such an increase may occur in the next few years.

The selections in Part Four divide into two groups: women as inmates and women as parolees. The pieces by Arditi and Singer consider legal issues and discuss possible changes in statutes that would result in significant alterations in the conditions under which women serve prison terms. The selections from Giallombardo and Burkhart offer vivid and detailed accounts of women's lives in prison obtained by the authors' direct observations of women's prisons and by their interviews with inmates. Spencer and Berocochea's study examines the theory that women return to prison more frequently than men because the criminal justice system, which is more lenient toward women, sends to prison only those heavily committed to criminal behavior. The excerpt from Simon's monograph shows that studies concerned with recidivism rates indicate women parolees hold a small but consistent advantage over men parolees.

The major thrust of the Arditi selection is that although the Supreme Court has not yet made the same determination concerning segregation on the basis of sex that it made for segregation on the basis of color, the Equal Rights Amendment would compel such a determination. The practice of separate prisons for women, which started out in the 1880s as a reform intended to give women the same benefit of rehabilitation then being sought for young men and boys in reformatories, has in the current period become one of the targets of the equal rights movement. Advocates of the ERA who have directed their efforts at female offenders have claimed that the same reasoning that was persuasive to the Supreme Court in *Brown* v. *Board of Education*—that segregation denies equal opportunity and equality—applies to women when separate prison systems are maintained. Schools that segregate by race and prisons that segregate by sex are basically discriminatory.

Arditi recognizes some of the negative effects passage of the ERA is likely to have on female prisoners if the "separate cannot be equal" argument is extended to the prison system:

> In terms of physical facilities and the general prison environment, most women now receive better treatment than their male counterparts. The ERA would eliminate this differential by subjecting both men and women to the same physical surrounding in sexually integrated institutions. Ideally, the equalization would be up to the level presently enjoyed by the women. But in most States this would require either renovation of all or almost all existing male institutions or the construction of all new facilities designed to meet the high standards now found in most female prisons. Again, if the State faces an economic roadblock to equalizing up, the ERA would tolerate equalization down to a low, more economically feasible level (Arditi, 1973).

Singer challenges the observation that physical conditions in women's prisons are better than in men's prisons and that day-to-day living is easier and more pleasant for female inmates than for males. She describes the special restrictions and hardships that women inmates experience; for example, although more than 70 percent of female inmates are mothers, none of the prisons have special provisions for pregnant women or for women with children. Singer also cites the inferior vocational and educational programs available to female inmates. She sees in Title VII of the Civil Rights Act of 1964, which prohibits employment discrimination on the basis of race, religion, national origin, or sex, a possible remedy for the lack of equal rights women inmates currently experience. The reasoning behind her position is that female prisoners are not given access to the same employment or training opportunities as male prisoners and that the high pay and statutory good time associated with working in prison industries are denied to women because there are generally no industries in women's prisons, clear instances of employment discrimination as defined under Title VII. For example, a survey reported in the longer version of the Arditi selection claims that the average number of vocational programs in prisons for men is 10; in institutions for women it is 2.7. Whereas male prisoners have a choice of some fifty different vocational programs, the choices of female prisoners are limited to cosmetology (and in some states convicted felons are forbidden by law to work in this field), clerical training, food service, serving, IBM key punching, and nurse's aide. The industries available at men's and women's institutions that can provide a source of livelihood for the inmates show much the same picture. There is an average of 3.2 industries among the men's prisons compared to an average of 1.2 industries in women's prisons.

The 1966 Giallombardo study excerpted here is considered a landmark study of women's experiences in prison. It not only describes the day-to-day routine of the female inmates but provides socioeconomic and demographic data that help dispel some of the myths about female inmates being subnormal, unintelligent, incompetent, and immoral. Such a picture was derived largely from studies done in the 1930s by the Gluecks and others. Giallombardo's study shows, for example, that 85 percent of the women had been employed at legitimate occupations before their imprisonment. Among those tested, 70 percent were average in IQ. In most instances the crimes for which they were committed were property and economic offenses, not offenses against morality such as drunkenness, sexual promiscuity, or personal violence.

Giallombardo's description of the physical conditions under which women live in prison are consistent with the views most often expressed. Women's prisons are found to be more comfortable and more attractive than those provided for men. But there are special psychological deprivations that women inmates experience more keenly than men, the major ones being separation from babies, children, and personal contacts with family and friends. The difficulties are more severe for female inmates because women's prisons are usually farther away from the inmates' home communities than are the institutions to which men are sent.

Perhaps because she conducted her studies in the late 1950s and early 1960s, Giallombardo reports nothing to support the feminist beliefs about collective identities and loyalties that exist (or that feminists hope exist) among women. Quite to the contrary, she observes:

> It is not the constant fear of violence or sexual exploitation which creates a hardship for the Alderson prison inmates, as is so often the case with the male prisoner, but rather it is the adjustment that living in close proximity with other women in general engenders, the strain involved in being in the forced company of others who are believed to be untrustworthy and capable of predatory tactics.

Burkhart observed women inmates some seven or eight years after Giallombardo, when the women's liberation movement was highly visible and had attracted followers and considerable attention in the media. Because the movement had influenced how women felt about each other and induced a sense of solidarity among many of them, Burkhart's study of women in prison has as one of its major themes a sense of shared destiny and collective identity not found in

Giallombardo's work. How much of these feelings are real—that is, actually to be found among female inmates—and how much are the product of the author's own definition of how women should relate to each other is difficult to determine.

Many of the physical conditions and daily routines reported by Giallombardo are also found in Burkhart's later study. But the descriptions of the women's esprit de corps and their concern about the lack of educational and vocational opportunities, as well as the briefer discussion of homosexual activities are strikingly different. Burkhart's inmates are more independent, tougher, more politically aware, and more sophisticated than Giallombardo's. They are more conscious of the need to organize themselves than are the inmates Giallombardo describes. Part of this difference may be due to the real changes that have occurred in the female inmates' definitions of who they are and understanding what they can demand. But some of the differences are likely due to changes in the perceptions of the researchers, in what they were looking for and hoping to find. More studies need to be done on female prisoners to find out whether, and to what extent, they have internalized the changes in social roles, in self-definitions, and in rhetoric that have occurred among women in the larger society.

For a small proportion of those who have been caught in the maze of the criminal justice system, parole represents the last station before the doors close from behind and former inmates are free—free not only from the confinement of prison but from the supervision of the parole officer and from having to report one's whereabouts and activities. The remaining selections in Part Four are concerned with women parolees.

The available statistics (from the National Council on Crime and Delinquency Research for 1968–1970) show that the percentages of women who are paroled are only slightly larger than the percentages of inmates who are women in federal and state prisons—about 7 percent. At the parole stage of the criminal justice system, then, women do not appear to be the recipients of preferential treatment.

Once an inmate is selected for parole, the issue becomes: Will the inmate prove successful or will he or she be sent back to prison before the period of parole is over? The excerpt from Simon indicates that there is only a small difference between the way men and women fare once they are paroled. Spencer and Berocochea's hypothesis that women are expected to return to prison for parole violations more frequently than men is not supported by data examined in the course of their research. Except for California, the national TFT (return for parole rule violations) rates show little difference between men and women parolees. Men, however, are more likely than women to be returned to prison because they committed crimes when on parole.

We conclude here, as we have in introductions to earlier sections, with a plea for the systematic collection, on a continuing basis, of demographic and social indicator data. Reports of number of persons imprisoned on a state by state and federal basis, along with some basic demographic data such as sex, and minor and adult status, have been available for many years. What would be useful, and is not regularly available, is information concerning the occupational, educational, marital, and racial status of persons at the time of imprisonment. Collecting and reporting this kind of information routinely would be much less expensive than individual researcher collection for particular studies.

26 The Forgotten Offender: The Woman in Prison
Rita James Simon

The woman in prison has been referred to as "the forgotten offender" by those who want to call attention to her plight and to bring about changes in her situation. Part of the reason for the lack of interest in female inmates stems from the fact that there are so few of them. In 1971, about 18 in 100 persons arrested for a serious crime were women. In the same year about 9 in 100 persons convicted for a serious crime were women; but only about 3 in every 100 persons sentenced to a Federal or State prison were women. As of December 1970, of the approximately 196,000 inmates in State and Federal prisons, 5,600 were women. At the present time there are 3 Federal institutions for women and 23 for men. There are 40 State institutions for women and 250 for men.

Another reason for the lack of interest is that the women inmates themselves have called so little attention to their situation. Prison reforms, and indeed public and official interest in prisoners, are strongly influenced by the amount of disruption and violence that occurs inside the prisons. Prisoners may need to riot, to destroy property, to endanger the lives of guards and fellow inmates, or to submit a list of demands for reforming the institution, before they are likely to receive much attention.

Following such activities, the public demands an investigation, the Governor appoints a "blue-ribbon factfinding commission," and prison officials acknowledge that reforms are needed and will be made. Together with many other forms of social unrest, the 1960s and the early 1970s witnessed a number of serious prison riots in many large Federal and State institutions in which inmates and guards were killed. But throughout this period the number of riots in institutions for women was practically nil, and the amount of publicity and interest that such institutions received was proportionate to their failure to call attention to themselves.

From *The Contemporary Woman and Crime* by Rita James Simon. National Institute of Mental Health, Washington, D.C., 1975. Pp. 64–69.

Still a third reason for the lack of interest in women prisoners is that the crimes women commit are usually ones that inconvenience society less than the crimes men commit. The overwhelming majority of women offenders have not been involved with organized crime, with crime involving high losses of property, or with crimes that have endangered large numbers of people.

Despite this relative lack of interest extending back well into the 19th century, social reformers, clinicians, and law enforcement officers have been concerned about the physical conditions and facilities under which women inmates must live, the types of educational and vocational training programs that are available to them, the quality and background of the personnel who supervise them, and the social organization within the prison.

The social organization has attracted particular attention in the last two or three decades with the publication of two books (Giallombardo 1967, and Ward and Kassenbaum 1965). Both of these books place great emphasis on the informal organization that develops among the inmates and the types of obligations and responsibilities, especially of a sexual nature, that prisoners develop with one another. But much of this literature on female inmates, although interesting in itself, is not directly relevant to this discussion.

One of the anticipated byproducts of the contemporary women's movement is that it will make the woman more equal before the bar of justice and that, in effect, more women will be sentenced to prison than have been in the past. Carolyn Handy, of the U.S. Commission on Civil Rights, claims that there is a visible trend toward equal penalties for equal crimes with more and larger prison terms for women resulting (Wicker 1973).

The proportions of women and of men who were sentenced to all of the Federal and State institutions for selected years from 1950 to 1970 are given in table 6.1.

Note that what increase there has been in the proportion of women sentenced to prison has come solely from the three Federal institutions where only a small minority of all the women are sent. But the trend for the State institutions is in the opposite direction; there has been a decline in the proportion of women sentenced to State institutions over the past 2 decades.

These results do not support the "more equal treatment" hypothesis. There is no consistent trend that indicates that the courts have been committing a higher proportion of women to prisons in the past few years than they did one or two decades ago. Female commitments to State institutions dropped in 1967, rose in 1968 and 1969, but then dropped again in 1970 by about the same percentage that they dropped between 1965 and 1967. There may have been an increase in the proportion of women committed to Federal institutions from 1965 through 1970, but the numbers are too small to assume that they reflect a change in policy.

Commitment data by sex over some periods of time are available for New York and California, the two most populous States. In examining the New York data (see table 6.2), which are based on the number and proportions of women committed to New York State correctional institutions for each year from 1963 to 1971, one notes that the overall proportion of females who are committed has declined during this period. The highest proportion of female

Table 6.1 **Population of sentenced prisoners by type of institution and sex with relative percentages of male and female prisoners**

	MALE		FEMALE		FEDERAL INSTITUTIONS		STATE INSTITUTIONS	
YEAR	Number	Percent	Number	Percent	Male (percent)	Female (percent)	Male (percent)	Female (percent)
1950	66,161	95.2	3,312	4.8	96.7	3.3	94.9	5.1
1955	74,368	94.8	4,046	5.2	96.3	3.7	94.5	5.5
1960	84,264	95.1	4,311	4.9	95.9	4.1	95.0	5.0
1965	83,241	95.1	4,264	4.9	95.8	4.2	95.0	5.0
1967	74,400	95.6	3,450	4.4	95.8	4.2	95.5	4.5
1968	68,426	95.0	3,632	5.0	95.5	4.5	94.9	5.1
1969	71,479	95.0	3,798	5.0	95.6	4.4	94.8	5.2
1970	75,692	95.4	3,659	4.6	95.4	4.6	95.3	4.7
Percent change in proportions, 1950–70		0		−0.05	−0.01	+39.40	+0.40	−7.80

Source: Data from *National Prisoner Statistics Bulletin*. Washington, D.C.: U.S. Department of Justice, Bureau of Prisons, April 1972. Table 5, p. 8.

Table 6.2 **New York State: percentage of females among new commitments to correctional institutions, by type of offense, 1963–71**

REASON FOR COMMITMENT	1963		1964		1965		1966		1967		1968		1969		1970		1971	
	No.[1]	Per-cent	No.[1]	Per-cent	No.[1]	Per-cent	No.[1]	Per-cent	No.[1]	Per-cent	No.[1]	Per-cent	No.[1]	Per-cent	No.[1]	Per-cent	No.[1]	Per-cent
Murder	74	2.7	69	0	64	3.1	70	1.4	40	2.5	48	0	45	4.4	68	2.9	101	3.0
Homicide, negligent, nonnegligent	262	13.4	300	10.7	280	12.1	334	12.0	320	9.4	378	10.0	472	7.8	515	7.0	602	6.0
Robbery	760	1.3	757	.7	820	1.7	647	.9	751	.9	944	1.0	1,277	1.4	1,190	1.0	1,553	1.4
Burglary	538	1.1	465	.9	455	.4	353	1.7	360	.3	413	1.5	445	.9	414	.2	431	1.6
Felonious assault	476	4.4	400	3.3	415	5.5	392	5.3	377	2.7	311	5.1	274	3.3	246	3.3	272	2.6
Grand larceny	572	5.2	582	4.8	681	3.4	492	4.5	491	4.3	290	2.0	229	5.2	183	6.0	199	9.0
Auto theft	169	0	167	0	135	0	105	.9	106	0	53	3.8	28	0	28	0	22	0
Dangerous drugs	514	13.0	427	7.7	379	9.5	474	10.5	589	5.0	385	3.1	431	3.5	470	6.4	690	5.5
Forgery	123	9.8	91	9.9	92	7.6	58	17.2	77	10.4	55	20.0	71	11.3	56	5.4	73	9.6
All felonies	3,839	5.1	3,558	3.7	3,585	4.3	3,193	5.3	3,357	3.4	3,118	3.3	3,610	3.1	3,522	3.1	4,353	3.4

Source: Data for 1963–71 from *Characteristics of New Commitments*. Albany, N.Y.: State of New York, Department of Corrections.

1. Total number of persons, male and female, convicted.

Table 6.3 **California: prisoners by sex and year, 1945–72**

YEAR	Total (number)	Men (number)	Women (number)	Women (percent)
1945	6,628	6,436	192	2.9
1946	7,839	7,592	247	3.2
1947	9,041	8,759	282	3.1
1948	10,084	9,776	308	2.5
1949	10,899	10,581	318	2.9
1950	11,598	11,273	325	2.8
1951	11,939	11,551	388	3.2
1952	13,169	12,754	415	3.2
1953	14,149	13,699	450	3.2
1954	15,376	14,832	544	3.5
1955	15,230	14,673	557	3.7
1956	15,532	14,922	610	3.9
1957	16,918	16,249	669	4.0
1958	19,202	18,472	730	3.8
1959	19,299	18,490	809	4.2
1960	21,660	20,831	829	3.8
1961	23,927	23,058	869	3.6
1962	24,032	23,136	896	3.7
1963	26,133	25,272	861	3.3
1964	26,483	25,513	970	3.7
1965	26,325	25,143	1,182	4.5
1966	27,467	26,248	1,219	4.4
1967	27,741	26,658	1,083	3.9
1968	28,462	27,396	1,066	3.7
1969	27,535	26,494	1,041	3.8
1970	25,033	24,105	928	3.7
1971	20,294	19,403	891	4.4
1972	19,773	18,994	779	3.9

Source: Data for 1945–72 from *Crime and Delinquency in California.* Sacramento, Calif.: State of California, Department of Justice, Bureau of Criminal Statistics.

commitments in a given year occurred in 1966, after that the proportion declined to its current level, 3.4. The numbers for each year for specific offenses are so small (for example, in 1971 3 women were committed for murder, 7 for burglary, and 18 for grand larceny) as to make it foolhardy to project trends from these data. But when one examines the proportion of women who were committed for all felony offenses in a given year, it is clear that there has been no dramatic increase since the women's movement or the equal rights movement has surfaced (about 1969).

The California data, which denote the number of men and women prisoners in all California correctional institutions from 1945 through 1972 (see table 6.3), do not show a marked increase in the percentage of women prisoners from the late 1960s to 1972.

For 1967–69, we can compare the proportion of men and women who were committed to California correctional institutions based on the number convicted for specific offenses (see table 6.4). Note first that of the men and women convicted for all serious offenses, more than twice the percentage of men as of women are committed to prison.

Women are somewhat more likely to receive equal treatment for violent

Table 6.4 **California: percentage of convicted persons sentenced to prison, by crime and sex, 1967–69**

OFFENSE CATEGORY		1967 Persons convicted (number)	1967 Committed to prison (percent)	1968 Persons convicted (number)	1968 Committed to prison (percent)	1969 Persons convicted (number)	1969 Committed to prison (percent)	AVERAGE RATIO OF MALE TO FEMALE IMPRISONMENT RATE
Homicide:	Female	111	27.0	125	36.8	90	34.4	1.5
	Male	653	44.9	726	45.0	641	59.1	
Robbery:	Female	137	16.1	144	16.7	82	28.0	1.9
	Male	2,584	36.0	2,906	31.2	2,024	42.1	
Assault:	Female	276	7.6	361	5.3	352	6.0	1.9
	Male	2,374	13.4	2,923	11.5	3,143	11.3	
Burglary:	Female	319	7.5	370	3.5	231	7.4	1.6
	Male	7,372	11.4	8,156	9.5	6,131	11.8	
Theft:	Female	526	8.0	612	7.8	277	16.6	3.6
	Male	3,037	21.1	1,196	50.6	1,825	28.8	
Forgery & checks:	Female	996	8.3	1,196	5.7	1,209	3.6	2.3
	Male	3,436	15.7	3,622	12.8	3,267	10.0	
Narcotics:	Female	1,115	0.9	1,542	3.3	2,263	2.1	4.1
	Male	8,762	7.6	11,347	5.6	16,104	4.6	
All above crimes:	Female	3,480	7.4	4,350	6.2	4,504	5.1	2.2
	Male	28,218	15.0	30,876	13.1	33,135	11.8	
Violent crimes[1]	Female	524	13.9	630	14.1	524	14.3	1.9
	Male	5,611	27.4	6,555	23.9	5,808	27.3	
Property crimes[2]	Female	1,841	8.1	2,178	5.9	1,717	6.2	2.2
	Male	13,845	14.6	12,974	14.1	11,223	14.0	

Source: Data for 1967–69 from *Crime and Delinquency in California*. Sacramento, Calif.: State of California, Department of Justice, Bureau of Criminal Statistics.

[1] Homicide, robbery and assault.

[2] Burglary, theft, and forgery and checks.

offenses than for property offenses. Theft and narcotics are offenses for which women seem to receive the most preferential treatment. Unfortunately, statistics such as these are not available over longer periods of time so we cannot see whether the preferential status that women enjoyed in the late 1960s remained relatively stable or whether these ratios in fact represent a decline in their preferential status. But the years shown in table 6.4 are worth careful attention because they are part of that era that should have reflected the shift toward more equal treatment that the women's movement was supposed to influence. There is no indication in those data as there is none in the data based on percentages of women in correctional institutions that women are being treated more equally by the courts, when commitment to prison is the issue.

References

Giallombardo, R. *Society of Women: A Study of a Women's Prison.* New York: John Wiley and Sons, Inc., 1966.

Ward, D. and G. Kassenbaum. *Women's Prison.* Chicago: Aldine Publishing Co., 1965.

Wicker, T. *New York Times,* October 19, 1973, 43:5.

27 The Sexual Segregation of American Prisons

R. R. Arditi, F. Goldberg, Jr., M. M. Hartle, J. H. Peters, and W. R. Phelps

The Equal Rights Amendment: elimination of the dual system

Although there is . . . some possibility of reform under the Fourteenth Amendment, any substantial movement towards the equal treatment of men and women in correctional institutions must await ratification of the proposed "Equal Rights" Amendment, which requires that:

> Equality of rights under the law shall be denied or abridged by the United States or by any State on account of sex.[132]

The import of this rather ambiguous mandate of "equality" must be drawn from the Amendment's legislative history[133] and the existing law of equal protection.

Interpretation of the amendment

The absolute approach

The language of the ERA may be interpreted in three different ways: (1) that any sexual classification must rest on some "rational" basis; (2) that any such classification must be justified by some compelling state interest; or (3) that no state interest, no matter how compelling, can justify a sexual classification.

As noted above,[134] the first two interpretations are tests the courts now apply under the Fourteenth Amendment. The third view, first fully articulated by Professor Thomas Emerson and three law students in their article, *The Equal Rights Amendment: A Constitutional Basis for Equal Rights for*

"The Sexual Segregation of American Prisons" by R. R. Arditi et al. *Yale Law Journal*, 82 (May 1973): 1253–1268. Reprinted by permission of The Yale Law Journal Company and Fred B. Rothman & Company. (The original footnote numbers of the source are retained.)

Women,[135] holds that the law must deal with the individual attributes of the particular person, rather than make any broad sexual classifications. Differentiation on account of sex is thus totally precluded, regardless of whether it is "reasonable," beneficial, or justified by "compelling reasons."[136]

The ERA's legislative history clearly indicates that Congress adopted this third, absolute interpretation. The "rational basis" test was repeatedly rejected as providing an inadequate check on sexual discrimination.[137] Furthermore, as Senator Ervin explained, it would be nonsensical for Congress to propose an amendment to accomplish that which was already the law under the Fourteenth Amendment.[138]

Similarly, while Congress never explicitly rejected the "compelling state interest" test,[139] it did so implicitly through its clear support for the absolute interpretation.[140] The Senate Report captured the essence of the absolute interpretation when it declared that no sexual classification would be permitted under the ERA.[141] The Report also incorporated the "Separate Views" of fourteen members of the House Judiciary Committee,[142] which stated that:

> The basic premise of [the proposed Amendment] in its original form is a simple one. As stated by Professor Thomas Emerson . . . the original text is based on the fundamental proposition that sex should not be a factor in determining the legal rights of women or of men.[143]

The Senate Report characterized these "Separate Views" as stating "concisely and accurately the understanding of the Amendment. . . ."[144] A further indication of the intent of Congress to pass an "absolute" amendment[145] may be found in the repeated refusal of both houses to amend the ERA to add any qualifying or limiting language.[146]

Exceptions

Two of the ERA's leading opponents also went to great lengths to stress the "absolute" nature of the Amendment. Senator Ervin rejected any possibility of a "flexible" interpretation and claimed that the ERA would make men and women identical legal beings.[147] Professor Paul Freund similarly characterized the Amendment as a "yardstick of absolute equality."[148] However, these fears go beyond the intent of Congress; certain exceptions are, in fact, accommodated by the ERA.

Unique physical characteristics

Under Professor Emerson's interpretation, the Amendment would not prohibit legislation dealing with physical characteristics unique to one sex.[149] He explains that such legislation is permitted because it does not deny equal rights to the other sex. This exception is, however, limited to physical characteristics and does not extend to psychological differences, since the latter cannot be said with any assurance to be truly unique to one sex.[150] Moreover, the exception is to be strictly limited to situations where the legislation is directly and narrowly related to the characteristic in question.[151]

Congress clearly intended to include this exception in its interpretation of the ERA. The Senate Report expressly stated that the Amendment would not prohibit reasonable classifications based on characteristics unique to one sex,[152] and Congresswoman Griffiths emphasized in her testimony that such a characteristic must be physical.[153]

Collateral constitutional rights

Professor Emerson's interpretation also recognizes that the ERA must be harmonized with other provisions of the Constitution.[154] Two existing constitutional rights are of special significance to the operation of prisons: the right of privacy and the prohibition against cruel and unusual punishment.

Despite claims to the contrary by opponents of the ERA,[155] Congress clearly passed the Amendment in the belief that it would be balanced against the right of privacy, and that as a result the sleeping and toilet facilities of public institutions could continue to be sexually segregated.[156] This conclusion is by no means self-evident, since no court has yet found a right of sexual privacy with regard to such facilities, much less extended such a right to prisoners. Nevertheless, the right of an inmate to disrobe and perform personal functions out of the presence of inmates of the opposite sex is probably inferable from the reasoning of earlier privacy and prisoners' rights cases, at least where no legitimate security or rehabilitative interests dictate to the contrary.[157]

Although there is no discussion of the Eighth Amendment[158] in the legislative history of the ERA, that constitutional right cannot be overlooked in an analysis of the rights of prison inmates. The courts have held that prisoners have an Eighth Amendment right to be free from physical abuse at the hands of both state officials[159] and fellow prisoners.[160] The latter right stems from the affirmative duty of prison officials to minimize violence among inmates.[161] Such constitutional principles must also be accommodated within the framework of the ERA.

Problems of application

Would "separate but equal" treatment be permitted under the ERA?

In *Brown v. Board of Education*,[162] the Supreme Court invalidated the doctrine of "separate but equal" in the racial context on the grounds that separate, by its very nature, could not be equal. As noted above, however, the Court has not yet made the same determination concerning sexual segregation; nevertheless, the ERA would appear to compel such a result.[163]

The framework developed by Professor Emerson simply does not accommodate a "separate but equal" approach, since that doctrine, just as in the case of race, could be used to keep one sex in a subordinate position.[164] Although there has not been extensive study in the area, the existing evidence does tend to show that sexually separate facilities are rarely equal.[165]

Although most of the debate before Congress concerning sexual segregation dealt with schools,[166] there is evidence that Congress contemplated and, by its refusal to revise the ERA, intended that the Amendment would require sexual integration of all public institutions, including prisons.[167] The constitutional exceptions described above would not bar such integration: Privacy does not require the segregation of entire institutions,[168] and the right to be secure from physical abuse can also be accommodated, as has been required in the racial context,[169] in far less drastic ways.

Equalization up or down?

Having established that integrated facilities would be required by the ERA, the question becomes whether the conditions of the integrated facilities would reflect an equalization up to or down from the best of the present institutions. As a matter of constitutional law, the courts, when dealing with an underinclusive discriminatory law or practice, can select either remedy. As Justice Harlan explained,

> Where a statute is defective because of underinclusion there exist two remedial alternatives: a court may either declare it a nullity and order that its benefits not extend to the class that the legislature intended to benefit, or it may extend the coverage of the statute to include those who are aggrieved by exclusion.[170]

Under the ERA, Congress clearly intended that benefits be extended whenever possible. The Senate Report states that "those laws which provide a meaningful protection would be expanded to include both men and women."[171] A similar procedure has already been required in the areas of employment discrimination[172] and the equalization of other personal benefits.[173]

In the prison context, however, a problem arises from the great numerical disparity between male and female inmates. If men are found to be receiving special benefits or better treatment, it seems rather clear that both theoretically and practically the proper remedy would be to extend those benefits to *all* inmates, including the relatively few women, in the new coeducational institutions. But the converse situation is somewhat more difficult: An extension of benefits now enjoyed by the female inmate population to the far larger male population might well put an enormous economic burden on the states,[174] and it seems unlikely that the courts would mandate such a remedy. Yet since the ERA would require a program of equalization—whether it be up or down—the states and the courts would probably have to compromise in adapting the old male prisons to the needs of coeducation, equalizing up where feasible and down where necessary. The "better" female institutions would, of course, still be available, to be used perhaps as minimum security facilities for inmates of both sexes.

The sexually integrated institution

Thus, ratification of the ERA would require sexually integrated prisons which incorporate, wherever feasible, the best aspects of the previously segregated institutions. Such a system would dictate changes in many aspects of prison life and administration.

Obviously, those treatment differences which result from economies of scale[175] would be eliminated automatically by the integration of the institutions. For example, men and women would have equal access to the medical facilities and religious programs provided at a particular institution.[176] The problem of remoteness would be similarly eliminated: While a given facility might still be remotely situated, the men and women sent there would be equally disadvantaged. Many other problems would not, however, be solved by the simple act of integration.

The classification process

Where a state maintains only one institution for all male offenders and none for its female felons,[177] the process of integration would be relatively straightforward: All offenders would be housed in that one institution. However, in those states where different institutions are presently set aside for different categories of male offenders, the classification process would have to be revised to accommodate women on an equal basis.[178] The ERA would require that the classification standards employed be objective and sexually neutral in both application and effect.[179]

Because of the vastly greater number of men sentenced to confinement,[180] the application of a sexually-neutral classification scheme would raise certain problems. There is some danger that application of such a sexually neutral scheme would result in grossly *unequal* treatment for some women. For example, in a particular state system, a female inmate might find herself one of only two or three women in an "integrated" population with hundreds of men.[181] Such gross numerical disparity may run afoul of the Eighth Amendment prohibition against cruel and unusual punishment,[182] the inmate's right of privacy,[183] and her right to equal protection of the laws.[184] Balancing these rights in urgent situations, the courts might allow a woman to choose not to be confined in a particular institution. Incarcerating at least five or ten women in each institution should, however, provide sufficient same-sex companionship without significantly hindering the process of integration.

The physical environment

In terms of physical facilities and the general prison environment, most women now receive better treatment than their male counterparts.[185] The ERA would eliminate this differential by subjecting both men and women to the same physical surroundings in sexually integrated institutions. Ideally, the equalization would be up to the level presently enjoyed by the women. But in most states, this would require either renovation of almost all existing male institutions or the construction of all new facilities designed to meet the high standards now found in most female prisons. Again, if the state faces an economic roadblock to equalizing up, the ERA would tolerate equalization down to a lower, more economically feasible level.[186]

As discussed above, sexual integration of the nation's correctional institutions need not result in heterosexual cohabitation, since the constitutional right to individual privacy[187] would probably require the authorities to provide sexually separate facilities for disrobing, sleeping, and performing personal functions.[188] Although the degree to which these facilities would have to be separated in order to meet constitutional requirements is not precisely defined, a state would probably be permitted to look to "societal mores" in interpreting the right of privacy in public institutions.[189]

Rehabilitation

Under the ERA, the current disparity in both the quantity and quality of rehabilitative programs available to men and women[190] would have to be eliminated. Since the ERA also requires the integration of institutions, however, such equalization should create no significant economic costs. The Amendment would not require that every institution in a state offer identical rehabilitative programs, but rather only that both sexes within any given institution be provided equal access to all programs within that institution.[191] Assignments to prison industries and other work details would also have to be made on a sexually neutral basis.[192]

Conclusion

Patterns of sexual discrimination exist throughout the prison systems of the United States. Every state exhibits differences related to both scale and sexual stereotypes in the treatment of its male and female offenders. The discrimination involved in differential treatment varies considerably, but substantial discrimination against both men and women is widespread.

The Fourteenth Amendment has had little impact on the elimination of these patterns of sexual discrimination, and does not seem likely to bring about significant reform. But ratification of the proposed Equal Rights Amendment should require that, within certain constitutional limitations, the nation's prisons be integrated so as to insure equality of treatment for both men and women inmates.

Notes

132. The House approved the ERA by a vote of 354–23. H.J. Res. 208, 92d Cong., 1st Sess., 117 Cong. Rec. H 9392 (daily ed. Oct. 12, 1971). The Senate approved it by a vote of 84–8. S.J. Res. 122, 92d Cong., 2d Sess., 118 Cong. Rec. S 4612 (daily ed. March 22, 1972). For a summary of the pre-1971 legislative history of the Amendment, see S. Rep. No. 92-689, 92d Cong., 1st Sess. 4–6 (1972) [hereinafter cited as S. Rep. No. 92-689].

   The Amendment has now been submitted to the states which have seven years to ratify. H.J. Res. 208, 92d Cong., 1st Sess., 117 Cong. Rec. H 9392 (daily ed. Oct. 12, 1971). By March 1, 1973, twenty-eight of the required thirty-eight states had ratified the Amendment. Then, on March 15, 1973, Nebraska withdrew its approval, while Connecticut, which had previously rejected the Amendment, voted to ratify. N.Y. Times, March 16, 1973, at 1, col. 8. The effect of these two turnabouts is not entirely clear. The Supreme Court has followed a policy of non-intervention in the ratification process, declaring that the issue of vote changes is a "political question" for Congress and the Secretary of State. *See* Coleman v. Miller, 307 U.S. 433 (1939). Although a number of recent cases have narrowed the political question doctrine, they have cited *Coleman* with approval. *See* Powell v. McCormack, 395 U.S. 486, 518 (1969); Baker v. Carr, 369 U.S. 186, 214 (1961).

Congress has only been faced once with crucial changes in both directions. During ratification of the Fourteenth Amendment, Ohio and New Jersey first ratified and then withdrew their consent; North and South Carolina switched from rejection to ratification. The Secretary of State submitted the problem to Congress, which chose to include *all four* states among the twenty-eight affirmative votes required for ratification. *See* Coleman v. Miller, *supra,* at 448–49. Subsequent action by Congress and the Executive reinforces the view that only ratification is final. *See* Coleman v. Miller, *supra,* at 436 (Kansas' change to an affirmative vote on the proposed child labor amendment was accepted); at 449 n.25 (New York's withdrawal of its ratification of the Fifteenth Amendment was rejected); W. LIVINGSTON, FEDERALISM AND CONSTITUTIONAL CHANGE 230 (1956) (Arkansas' switch to ratification of the Sixteenth Amendment and similar changes by Texas and Idaho with regard to the Twenty-second Amendment were all accepted by Congress).

This interpretation has also been supported by the commentators on the theory that, because Article V of the Constitution speaks only of "ratification," only the affirmative decision to ratify has any binding effect. As a result, a negative vote can always be changed, but ratification is final and not subject to recission. *See* J. JAMESON, ON CONSTITUTIONAL CONVENTIONS: THEIR HISTORY, POWERS, AND MODES OF PROCEEDING §§ 576-86 (1887); W. WILLOUGHBY, THE CONSTITUTIONAL LAW OF THE UNITED STATES § 329a (1910).

133. *See, e.g.,* Hurd v. Hodge, 334 U.S. 24, 32–33 (1948); Shelley v. Kraemer, 334 U.S. 1, 23 (1948); Slaughter House Cases, 83 U.S. 36 (1873). *But see Hearings Before Subcom. 4 of the House Comm. on the Judiciary,* 92d Cong., 1st Sess. 75–76 (1971) [hereinafter cited as *House Hearings*] (remarks of Senator Ervin); 118 CONG. REC. S 4377 (daily ed. March 21, 1972) (remarks of Senator Stennis).

134. *See* pp. 1244–48 *supra.*

135. Brown, Emerson, Falk & Freedman, *The Equal Rights Amendment: A Constitutional Basis for Equal Rights for Women,* 80 YALE L.J. 871 (1971).

   Congresswoman Martha Griffiths, sponsor of the Amendment in the House, sent a copy of the article to all members of the House, noting, "It will help you understand the purposes and effects of the Equal Rights Amendment. . . . The article explains how the ERA will work in most areas of the law." *See* 118 CONG. REC. S 4250 (daily ed. March 20, 1972). Senator Ervin also characterized the article as "important legislative history." *Id.* at S 4264.

136. *House Hearings, supra* note 133, at 401 (testimony of Professor Emerson). *See also* Emerson, *In Support of the Equal Rights Amendment,* 6 HARV. CIV. RTS.-CIV. LIB. L. REV. 225 (1971).

137. *See* 118 CONG. REC. S 4263 (daily ed. March 20, 1972) (statement of Professor Paul Freund); Bayh, *The Need for the Equal Rights Amendment,* 48 NOTRE DAME LAWYER 80 (1972).

138. *House Hearings, supra* note 133, at 82–83 (testimony of Senator Ervin). Professor Paul Freund made a similar observation more than a quarter century ago, interpreting an earlier version of the ERA. *See Hearings on S.J. Res. 61 Before a Subcom. of the Senate Comm. on the Judiciary,* 79th Cong., 1st Sess. 78–80 (1945). Professor

Freund's analysis was recirculated by opponents of the Amendment. *See* 118 Cong. Rec. S 4263 (daily ed. March 20, 1972).

139. The House indirectly rejected this standard: The "compelling state interest" test was embodied in the Wiggins Amendment, *see* H.R. Rep. No. 92-359, 92d Cong., 2d Sess. 4 (1971) [hereinafter cited as H.R. Rep. No. 92-359], which was rejected by the House. 118 Cong. Rec. H 9390 (daily ed. Oct. 12, 1971). *See* note 142 *infra.*

140. Even if the "compelling state interest" test were used to implement the ERA, the practical effect would not differ significantly from use of the absolute rule. A state interest has only once been found sufficiently "compelling" to justify a classification along the lines of race or national origin, and then only in the context of national security in time of war. *See* Korematsu v. United States, 323 U.S. 214 (1944).

141. "The existence of a characteristic found more often in one sex than the other does not justify legal treatment of all members of the sex different [sic] from all members of the other sex. The same is true of the functions performed by individuals. The circumstance, that in our present society members of one sex are more likely to be engaged in a particular type of activity than members of the other sex, does not authorize the Government to fix legal rights or obligations on the basis of membership in one sex. The law may operate by grouping individuals in terms of existing characteristics or functions but not through a vast overclassification of sex." S. Rep. No. 92-689, *supra* note 132, at 11–12.

142. The House Judiciary Committee amended the original joint resolution on June 22, 1971, by adding the Wiggins Amendment: "This article shall not impair the validity of any law of the United States which exempts a person from compulsory military service or any other law of the United States which reasonably promotes the health and safety of the people." *See* H.R. Rep. No. 92-359, *supra* note 139, at 5. Separate views to the subsequent Committee report were filed by fourteen representatives; minority views were filed by three. On October 12, 1971, the House rejected the Wiggins Amendment and approved the resolution in its original form, as advocated by the authors of the "separate views." *See* 118 Cong. Rec. H 9390 (daily ed. Oct. 12, 1971).

143. Separate views of fourteen members of the House Judiciary Committee, H.R. Rep. No. 92-359, *supra* note 139, at 6. *See also* note 135 *supra.*

144. S. Rep. No. 92-689, *supra* note 132, at 11.

145. An absolute interpretation would perhaps be unquestioned were it not for comments by Congresswoman Martha Griffiths, a key Amendment supporter. Her position was that the purpose of the Amendment is to write women into the Fourteenth Amendment. *Hearings on S.J. Res. 61 and S.J. Res. 231, Before The Sen. Comm. on the Judiciary,* 91st Cong., 2d Sess. 225 (1970) [hereinafter cited as *Senate Hearings*]. *House Hearings, supra* note 133, at 51. During the Committee hearings in the House, she had the following exchange with Congressman Wiggins:

> MR. WIGGINS. I think it is important that we sort of nail down the breadth of this word "Equality." As I understand it from the amendment, it is not absolute but will admit of rational exception.
> MRS. GRIFFITHS: That is right.

House Hearings, supra note 133, at 46.

However, Congresswoman Griffiths' concept of rational exceptions may not in fact be inconsistent with the absolute approach: She may have been referring to rational *exceptions* from the absolute equality called for by the Amendment, not "rational classifications" as that term is understood in traditional equal protection law. The two exceptions she listed were unique physical characteristics and privacy, *see House Hearings, supra* note 133, at 46, which are the same ones Professor Emerson would incorporate into the ERA. *See* pp. 1257–61 *infra.*

146. Unlike the House Committee, which had adopted the Wiggins Amendment, *see* note 142 *supra,* the Senate Judiciary Committee rejected six proposed amendments prior to reporting favorably the joint resolution. *See* S. REP. No. 92-689, *supra* note 132. Senator Ervin then offered the following qualifying amendments from the floor:

> This article shall not apply to any law prohibiting sexual activity between persons of the same sex or the marriage of persons of the same sex.

118 CONG. REC. S 4372–74 (daily ed. March 21, 1972) (withdrawn by Senator Ervin).

> This article shall not impair, however, the validity of any laws of the United States or any State which exempts women from compulsory military service.

118 CONG. REC. S 4374–94 (daily ed. March 21, 1972) (rejected 73–18).

> This article shall not impair the validity, however, of any laws of the United States or any State which exempt women from service in combat units of the Armed Forces.

118 CONG. REC. S 4395–4409 (daily ed. March 21, 1972) (rejected 71–18), reintroduced and again rejected, 118 CONG. REC. S 4409–28 (daily ed. March 21, 1972) (75–11).

> This article shall not impair the validity, however, of any laws of the United States or any State which extend protections or exemptions to women.

118 CONG. REC. S 4531–37 (daily ed. March 22, 1972) (rejected 77–14).

> This article shall not impair the validity, however, of any laws of the United States or any State which impose upon fathers the responsibility for support of their children.

118 CONG. REC. S 4545–51 (daily ed. March 22, 1972) (rejected 71–17).

> This article shall not impair the validity, however, of any laws of the United States or any State which secure privacy to men or women, or boys or girls.

118 CONG. REC. S 4543–45 (daily ed. March 22, 1972) (rejected 79–11). This last amendment was voted down not because Congress wanted to limit the right of privacy but because it believed that privacy could be balanced against the ERA as originally worded. *See House Hearings, supra* note 133, at 403 (testimony of Professor Emerson); 118 CONG. REC. S 4544–45 (daily ed. March 22, 1972) (remarks of Senators Bayh and Cook). *See* note 157 *infra* on the accuracy of this belief.

147. *House Hearings, supra* note 133, at 82–83.

148. *See* 118 CONG. REC. S 4263 (daily ed. March 20, 1972).

149. Brown, Emerson, Falk & Freedman, *supra* note 135, at 893. *See also House Hearings, supra* note 133, at 402, where Professor Emerson explained:

> [T]he equal rights amendment does not preclude legislation, or other official action, which relates to a physical characteristic unique to one sex. . . . Such legislation does not . . . deny equal rights to the other sex. So long as the characteristic is found in all women and no men, or all men and no women, the law does not violate the basic principle of the equal rights amendment, for it raises no problem of ignoring individual characteristics in favor of a prevailing group characteristic or an average.

Professor Emerson cites the following as laws falling within the exception: laws concerning wet nurses and sperm donors; laws establishing medical leave for childbearing (but not for childrearing, since both men and women are physically capable of rearing children); laws punishing forcible rape; and laws relating to the determination of fatherhood. Brown, Emerson, Falk & Freedman, *supra* note 135, at 894.

150. Brown, Emerson, Falk & Freedman, *supra* note 135, at 893.

151. Professor Emerson suggests six factors to be weighed in determining whether such relationship exists: (1) the proportion of men or women who actually possess the characteristic; (2) the relationship between the characteristic and the problem; (3) the proportion of the problem attributable to the unique physical characteristic; (4) the proportion of the problem eliminated by the solution; (5) the availability of less drastic alternatives; (6) the importance of the problem ostensibly being solved, as compared with the costs of the least drastic solution. *Id.* at 894–96.

152. The Report explains:

> The legal principle underlying the equal rights amendment (H.J. Res. 208) is that the law must deal with the individual attributes of the particular person and not with stereotypes of over-classification based on sex. However, the original resolution does not require that women must be treated in all respects the same as men. "Equality" does not mean "sameness." As a result, the original resolution would not prohibit reasonable classifications based on characteristics that are unique to one sex.

> S. REP. No. 92-689, *supra* note 132, at 12.

153. *House Hearings, supra* note 133, at 40. The concept of "unique physical characteristic" is not new to the law. An analogous concept is found in the Civil Rights Act of 1964, 42 U.S.C. §§ 2000e to 2000e-15 (1970). Title VII of that Act outlaws sexual discrimination in employment, but is qualified "in those certain instances where religion, sex, or national origin is a bona fide occupational qualification reasonably necessary to the normal operation of that particular business enterprise." Section 703 (e), 42 U.S.C. § 2000e-2(e) (1970).

The precise meaning of "bona fide occupational qualification" with regards to sex has not yet been determined. The Equal Employment Opportunity Commission has adopted a narrow construction, saying that preference in employment to one sex is permissible only "[w]here it is necessary for the purpose of authenticity or genuineness," as in the case of actors or actresses. 29 C.F.R. § 1604.1(a)(2) (1972).

154. *See* Emerson, *In Support of the Equal Rights Amendment*, 6 HARV. CIV. RTS.-CIV. LIB. L. REV. 225, 231 (1970). Senator Ervin argued that a constitutional amendment invalidates other constitutional provisions if such provisions are inconsistent with the more recent amendment. S. REP. No. 92-689, *supra* note 132, at 46 (Minority Views of Senator Ervin). The Senator's view may well be correct, but his further conclusion that the ERA cannot be reconciled with the right of privacy is untenable. The language of the Amendment itself is extremely vague, and certainly does not expressly amend or repeal the privacy right. *See* pp. 1253–54 *supra*. The courts would therefore have to look to legislative history to determine whether the ERA *as interpreted* is in conflict with the right of privacy; they would find that the majority of Congress intended that the Amendment not deprive any person of his right to privacy. *See* note 156 *infra*.

155. Senator Ervin's position is explained in his Senate Minority Report:

> I believe that the absolute nature of the Equal Rights Amendment will, without a doubt, cause all laws and state-sanctioned practices which in any way differentiate between men and women to be held unconstitutional. Thus, all laws which separate men and women, such as separate schools, restrooms, dormitories,

prisons, and others will be stricken. . . . The proponents of the ERA mention that the Constitutional right to privacy will protect and keep separate items such as public restrooms; however, this assertion overlooks the basic fact of constitutional law construction: The most recent constitutional amendment takes precedence over all other sections of the Constitution with which it is inconsistent. Thus, if the ERA is to be construed absolutely, as its proponents say, then there can be no exception for elements of publicly imposed sexual segregation on the basis of privacy between men and women.

S. Rep. No. 92–689, *supra* note 132, at 45–46.

Professor Freund took a similar position. He testified before the Senate Judiciary Committee that the strict model of racial equality would require that there be no segregation of the sexes in prisons, reform schools, public restrooms, and other public facilities. *See Senate Hearings, supra* note 145, at 74. *See also* Freund, *The Equal Rights Amendment Is Not the Way,* 6 Harv. Civ. Rts.-Civ. Lib. L. Rev. 234–40 (1971).

156. The Senate Report states that the "constitutional right of privacy established by the Supreme Court in Griswold v. Connecticut" would permit a separation of the sexes with respect to such places as public toilets and the sleeping quarters of public institutions, even after passage of the Amendment. S. Rep. No. 92–689, *supra* note 132, at 12. The proponents of the ERA also noted the privacy exception throughout the hearings and floor debate. *See, e.g.,* 118 Cong. Rec. S 4394 (daily ed. March 21, 1972) (remarks of Senator Gurney); *Senate Hearings, supra* note 145, at 97 (remarks of Senator Cook); *House Hearings, supra* note 133, at 40 (remarks of Congresswoman Griffiths), 86–87 (remarks of Congressman Mikva); 118 Cong. Rec. H 9386 (daily ed. Oct. 12, 1971) (remarks of Congressman Ashley).

In addition to this constitutional right to privacy, the Senate Report also refers to the "traditional power of the state to regulate cohabitation and sexual activity by unmarried persons." S. Rep. No. 92–689, *supra* note 132, at 12. This power, according to the Report, would permit the state to segregate the sexes with respect to such facilities as sleeping quarters at coeducational colleges, prison dormitories and military barracks. However, except for a few cryptic references during the House Hearings, *see, e.g., House Hearings, supra* note 133, at 289–90, 305, there is no other mention of the doctrine in the legislative history. The legal basis for the doctrine, the general police power, is, of course, as pervasive as any of the reserved powers of the states, but it is not of constitutional dimension. Consistent interpretation of the ERA requires that no state interest, not even under the police power, be allowed to justify a law or regulation containing a sex-based classification.

157. Congress based this perceived right of sexual privacy on the Supreme Court's decision in Griswold v. Connecticut, 381 U.S. 479 (1965). *See* note 156 *supra.* The Court has since expanded and clarified the right of privacy, *see* Roe v. Wade, 93 Sup. Ct. 705 (1973); Eisenstadt v. Baird, 405 U.S. 438 (1972), but it has not yet been called on to determine whether that right encompasses a prisoner's unwillingness to disrobe or shower in the presence of the opposite sex. The Ninth Circuit, however, has indicated that the *un*incarcerated person has such a right. In Ford v. Story, 324 F.2d 450 (9th Cir. 1963), in which a police officer photographed the nude body of a rape victim over her objection and then circulated the photographs among the stationhouse personnel, that court said:

We cannot conceive of a more basic subject of privacy than the naked body. The desire to shield one's unclothed figured [sic] from view of strangers, and particularly strangers of the opposite sex, is impelled by elementary self-respect and personal dignity.

Id. at 455. On the nexus between the right of privacy and basic human dignity, see Bloustein, *Privacy as an Aspect of Human Dignity: An Answer to Dean Prosser,* 39 N.Y.U. L. REV. 962 (1964); Singer, *Privacy, Autonomy, and Dignity in the Prison: A Preliminary Inquiry Concerning Constitutional Aspects of the Degradation Process in Our Prisons,* in 1 PRACTISING LAW INSTITUTE, PRISONER'S RIGHTS 147 (1972).

Of course, prisons are not noted for the degree to which they protect the dignity and self-respect of their inmates. *See* Singer, *supra,* at 149–51. However, elements of personal freedom which are protected by the Constitution can only be denied to prisoners if they conflict with compelling security or other penal interests. *See* Barnett v. Rodgers, 410 F.2d 995, 1003 (D.C. Cir. 1969) and cases cited in the last paragraph of note 89 *supra;* 1 PRACTISING LAW INSTITUTE, PRISONER'S RIGHTS 117 (1972); Tucker, *Establishing the Rule of Law in Prisons: A Manual for Prisoners' Rights Litigation,* 23 STAN. L. REV. 473, 508–09 (1971). Moreover, constitutional rights may only be abridged if there exist no less drastic means of satisfying such penal interests. *See* Barnett v. Rodgers, *supra,* at 1003; PRACTISING LAW INSTITUTE, *supra,* at 117.

These principles have led one commentator to conclude that a wide variety of current prison practices violate the inmate's constitutional right of privacy. *See* Singer, *supra.* Whether or not the courts accept this position, they would probably recognize that no significant prison interest would be served by the sexual integration of institutional living quarters. On the contrary, security and rehabilitation would probably demand, and the states would probably so require on their own, the same segregation dictated by the right of privacy. *See* pp. 1249–50 *supra;* Barnett v. Rodgers, *supra,* at 1002: "Treatment that degrades the inmate, invades his privacy, and frustrates the ability to choose pursuits through which he can manifest himself and gain self-respect erodes the very foundations upon which he can prepare for a socially useful life."

Congress therefore could have reasonably found that prisoners retain a right to disrobe and perform personal functions out of the presence of inmates of the opposite sex, and that this right would require the segregation of living quarters in otherwise integrated institutions. However, even if the courts, as final arbiters of constitutional interpretation, accept this conclusion, they will find little guidance in the legislative history concerning the manner in which privacy and the ERA would interact in particular situations. On the degree to which living quarters would have to be separated, *see* note 189 *infra.*

Concerning the persons affected by the right of privacy, it is interesting to note that the male institution at San Quentin now employs two female guards, whose duties have thus far been limited to the gun towers, visiting rooms, and gates. Telephone conversation with Lee E. DeBord, Information Officer, California State Prison at San Quentin, March 30, 1973. Even this limited use of female guards, who *may* be called on to conduct skin searches and oversee showers, is being challenged in court by a male inmate. N.Y. Times, March 30, 1973, at 33, col. 8. It seems clear that certain treatment personnel, such as physicians and perhaps even counselors, must be allowed greater "intimacy" with the prisoner than would be afforded a fellow inmate. Custody officers appear to fall somewhere between these two extremes on a continuum of permissible "invasions." In each case, the court should balance the degree of humiliation (loss of dignity and thus privacy) involved, the prison's interest in causing that humiliation, and the feasibility of the less drastic method of having same-sex staff conduct the "invasion" at issue.

158. U.S. CONST. amend. VIII.
159. Wiltsie v. California Dept. of Corrections, 406 F.2d 515 (9th Cir. 1968) (beating with fists and billy clubs); Jackson v. Bishop, 404 F.2d 571 (8th Cir. 1968), *modifying* 268 F. Supp. 804 (E.D. Ark. 1967) (whipping with strap).

160. Kish v. County of Milwaukee, 441 F.2d 901 (7th Cir. 1971); Gates v. Collier, 349 F. Supp. 881 (N.D. Miss. 1972); Holt v. Sarver, 309 F. Supp. 362 (E.D. Ark. 1970), *aff'd*, 442 F.2d 304 (8th Cir. 1971). It should be noted that both *Kish* and *Holt* dealt in part with claims of homosexual rape, a problem analogous to that of sexual assault in integrated institutions.

161. In Gates v. Collier, 349 F. Supp. 881 (N.D. Miss. 1972), a federal district court held that a wide range of practices and conditions at the Mississippi State Penitentiary constituted a deprivation of Eighth Amendment rights. The court held that the inmates had been subjected to cruel and unusual punishment because of the failure of penitentiary officials to provide adequate protection against physical assaults, abuses, indignities, and cruelties by other inmates, by placing excessive numbers of inmates in barracks without adequate classification or supervision, and by assigning custodial responsibility to incompetent and untrained inmates. *Accord*, Holt v. Sarver, 309 F. Supp. 362 (E.D. Ark. 1970), *aff'd*, 442 F.2d 304 (8th Cir. 1971).

162. 347 U.S. 483 (1954).

163. A "freedom of choice" arrangement cannot be so easily rejected. In the context of school segregation, the Supreme Court refused to accept a freedom of choice plan, but only because in the instant case such plans had failed to "effectuate conversion of a state-imposed dual system to a unitary, nonracial system." Green v. County School Board, 391 U.S. 430, 440–41 (1968). Arguably, a state would not be discriminating against either sex if it maintained three equally desirable institutions— one for men, one for women, and one mixed—and gave each inmate the choice of incarceration in an integrated or a segregated institution.

Such an arrangement would, however, be both doctrinally and practically unacceptable. While the Court in *Green* conceded the theoretical legality of "freedom of choice" plans, it was referring to a system in which each pupil could select among *all* institutions in the district. The designation of one institution as "male" and another as "female" must be seen as inherently inimical to the "unitary" system envisioned in *Green*, and would also appear to be a sexual classification at odds with the basic principle of the ERA. Furthermore, the single-sex prisons would have to be equally desirable to afford each sex an "equal" choice, and the integrated prison would have to be at least as desirable to insure that the state was not covertly encouraging segregation. The cost of maintaining such "equal" institutions would undoubtedly deter all but the largest states, which would also probably be deterred by the degree to which such a tripartite system would limit the geographic and rehabilitative classification of inmates.

164. Brown, Emerson, Falk & Freedman, *supra* note 135, at 902–03.

165. *See* pp. 1231–43 *supra*. An analysis of coordinate "brother-sister" colleges reveals similar findings. *See* C. Jencks & D. Reisman, The Academic Revolution 305 (1968). *See also House Hearings, supra* note 133, at 272 (remarks of Dr. Bernice Sandler).

166. Congresswoman Martha Griffiths totally rejected the notion of "separate but equal" in this context. *House Hearings, supra* note 133, at 47.

167. Congressman Edwards questioned then Assistant Attorney General Rehnquist as to whether the various correctional institutions throughout the country would have to be integrated if the ERA were enacted. Mr. Rehnquist replied that the requirement of integration would be "a very permissible interpretation." *House Hearings, supra* note 133, at 3220. In a subsequent letter to Congressman Edwards, Mr. Rehnquist qualified his testimony by explaining that the question could not be fully answered with any certainty:

[A]t a minimum it would appear permissible under the proposed amendment to separate men and women to the extent necessary to prevent further crimes, such as rape and prostitution, as male prisoners are now to some degree separated to prevent homosexual assaults. It has been further suggested by supporters of the amendment that separation would be permissible to the extent necessary to protect a competing right of privacy. To what extent recognition of the necessity of some degree of separation of some prisoners could be generalized to permit separation of all prisoners or maintenance of separate systems is, we believe, uncertain.

Letter reprinted in *House Hearings, supra* note 133, at 329.

Professor Philip Kurland, an opponent of the ERA, testified that the Amendment would make it unconstitutional for the federal government or state governments to maintain separate prisons for men and women and separate reformatories for boys and girls. *See Senate Hearings, supra* note 145, at 99. However, Professor Kurland also noted that there are some, albeit old fashioned, notions of privacy that might properly justify a policy of "separate but equal" facilities. *See* 118 CONG. REC. S 4570 (daily ed. March 22, 1972).

Congressman Edwards noted that the Director of the U.S. Bureau of Prisons responded very affirmatively to a question concerning the possible integration of prisons under the Amendment. The Director felt that the prisons should be integrated now— "for good penology, good corrections and decent living. . . ." *House Hearings, supra* note 133, at 306.

168. *House Hearings, supra* note 133, at 402 (testimony of Professor Emerson). *See* note 189 *infra.*
169. *See* note 115 *supra.*
170. Welsh v. United States, 398 U.S. 333, 361 (1970) (concurring) (footnote omitted). *See also* Skinner v. Oklahoma, 316 U.S. 535, 543 (1943); Iowa–Des Moines Nat'l Bank v. Bennett, 284 U.S. 239, 247 (1931).
171. S. REP. NO. 92-689, *supra* note 132, at 15–16. Congresswoman Griffiths also argued that many laws which treat men and women differently would not be invalidated, but would be expanded so as to include the previously disadvantaged sex:

> Under the equal rights amendment courts would follow this established procedure of invalidating only that part of a statute which offends the Constitution, while allowing the statute to stand as modified. . . . Minimum wage laws which cover only women would be expanded to apply also to men.

House Hearings, supra note 133, at 40–41.
172. *See, e.g.,* Potlatch Forests, Inc. v. Hays, 318 F. Supp. 1368 (E.D. Ark. 1970), involving a state statute requiring overtime pay for women. When the male workers sued for equal treatment, Potlatch sought to have the state law nullified. The court ruled instead that the overtime benefits must be extended to men. *See also* Bowe v. Colgate-Palmolive Co., 416 F.2d 711 (7th Cir. 1969).
173. *See, e.g.,* Levy v. Louisiana, 391 U.S. 68 (1968) (wrongful death benefits extended to previously excluded illegitimate children); Sweatt v. Painter, 339 U.S. 629 (1950) and McLaurin v. Oklahoma State Regents, 339 U.S. 637 (1950) (access to institutions of higher education extended to include previously excluded classes). *See generally* L. KANOWITZ, WOMEN AND THE LAW: THE UNFINISHED REVOLUTION (1969).
174. As noted above, *see* note 113 *supra,* annual state budgets may not really reflect the magnitude of this burden, since they do not reveal the capital expenditure differential which originally went into providing women with "campus" facilities while creating fortresses for the incarceration of men. If the states were required to provide men as well as women with private rooms and other amenities in facilities which still meet perceived security needs, the cost might well be insuperable.

175. *See* pp. 1231–37 & note 174 *supra.*
176. The enormous costs involved in providing medical facilities would probably make it impractical for the state governments to equalize medical treatment in all institutions up to the highest level which is now available anywhere in the system. But if a particular institution were too small to support an elaborate medical facility, there would be no sex-based inequality. Rather, the men and women in it would be equally deprived.
177. *See* notes 11 and 22 *supra.*
178. A sexual integration plan which merely allocated women proportionately throughout the system would be unacceptable. Under the ERA, men and women would have to be treated equally; the classification standards which exist for men would have to be applied to women as well.
179. For example, acceptable standards would include nature of crime, length of sentence, region of the state, and age. Psychological factors could also be taken into account, so long as they were determined on the basis of demonstrably objective, sex-neutral tests administered to the *individual* inmate. The use of subjective judgments or stereotyped classifications concerning an entire sex group would be unacceptable because of the danger of reintroducing sex-based classifications into the system. For example, female inmates as a group are frequently characterized as "less violent," "less dangerous," and "less prone to escape" than their male counterparts. *See, e.g.,* Wark v. State, 266 A.2d 62 (Supp. Jud. Ct. Me. 1970), *cert. denied,* 400 U.S. 952 (1970). A classification scheme based on such generalizations could conceivably result in classification of all females as "minimum security" risks without reference to their individual characteristics. Under the ERA, the only legitimate question would be whether each *individual* woman belonged in minimum security. The ERA would thus mandate what modern penology requires—individual classification. *See generally* O. GIBBONS, CHANGING THE LAW-BREAKER (1965).
180. *See* note 5 *supra.*
181. The state of Hawaii, for example, had only four women and approximately 260 men sentenced to confinement as of the summer of 1972. Interview with Lykke, *supra* note 13.
182. Deprivation of same-sex companionship during the entire period of incarceration and of *all* companionship during those periods in which privacy considerations demand sexual segregation, *see* p. 1266 *infra,* might be held to be a violation of the Eighth Amendment, since it would be arbitrarily imposed on female inmates because of their sex. *Cf.* Furman v. Georgia, 408 U.S. 238 (1972); Trop v. Dulles, 356 U.S. 86 (1958).
183. *See* p. 1259 *supra.*
184. Within a sexually integrated institution, women would represent not merely a minority group, but a minority which had been set apart for certain purposes, *e.g.,* sleeping and showering. This differentiation might give rise to special needs, *see* note 182 *supra,* the recognition of which would be justified in order to guarantee the "equal treatment" of this minority group. Racial minorities with needs arising from their particular religious beliefs have been granted similar special treatment. *See, e.g.,* Barnett v. Rodgers, 410 F.2d 995 (D.C. Cir. 1969) (prison administration must have "compelling justifications" for denying to Black Muslims meals that comport with their dietary creed).
185. *See* pp. 1237–38 *supra.*
186. *See* p. 1263 *supra.*
187. *See* notes 156–57 *supra.*
188. Because privacy is an *individual* right, difficulties might arise should some inmates wish to waive it. Congress did not adequately address the problem of waiver under

the ERA; the only specific discussion of the matter was a dialogue between Congressman Wiggins and Professor Emerson during the House Hearings. *See House Hearings, supra* note 133, at 403–05. However, Congress undoubtedly did not intend to sanction heterosexual cohabitation and had assumed that the privacy exception would cover it. *See* note 156 *supra*.

In practice, that assumption would probably be borne out. First, even an effective waiver would not necessarily result in cohabitation. There is, of course, no right to cohabit with the opposite sex. Rather, waiver would at most force the state to assign the sleeping quarters of those who waive on a random basis. Moreover, it is possible that rights such as privacy which must be enforced through a state administrative mechanism cannot be waived on an individual basis. Arguably, this justification for barring waiver is particularly compelling in the prison context, because of the degree to which administrative decisions are tied to security needs and the difficulty of determining the voluntariness of a waiver in a coercive prison atmosphere.

If waiver should be permitted, sex offenders would not be permitted to opt for cohabitation with the opposite sex, since the state's decision to segregate in that instance is based on the offense and not on any sexual classification.

189. Brown, Emerson, Falk & Freedman, *supra* note 135, at 902. *See also House Hearings, supra* note 133, at 46 (remarks of Congressman Wiggins). Although the use of societal mores to define the new privacy right has never been expressly approved by the Court, both Justice Goldberg, concurring in *Griswold,* and Justice Stewart, concurring in *Roe,* noted the changing traditions and concepts of society in developing the constitutional right of privacy from, respectively, the Ninth and Fourteenth Amendments. *See* Griswold v. Connecticut, 381 U.S. 479, 493 (1965); Roe v. Wade, 93 S. Ct. 705, 735 (1973). It thus does not seem unreasonable to conclude that Congress and ultimately the courts, in giving content to that right, will look in part to current social mores.

In prisons, separate cells or sleeping units for the sexes would seem to be a necessity under prevailing social mores. Whether or not these separate units would have to be physically remote from those of the other sex would probably be an appropriate inquiry for the legislature or prison administration. However, the ultimate decision on such questions of privacy would be constitutional ones reviewable by the courts. *See House Hearings, supra* note 133, at 403 (testimony of Professor Emerson).

The institutions which are presently sexually integrated provide some indication of the existing mores in this area. For example, the Pennsylvania State Prison at Muncy, formerly all female, now houses a few men. According to the warden, the only facilities which remain segregated are the sleeping, shower, and toilet facilities. The prison is of the cottage type and the men reside in their own cottage. *Survey, supra* note 2. A similar arrangement has been adopted at the Fort Worth federal facility, N.Y. Times, July 8, 1972, at 27, col. 1, and the newly integrated institution at Framingham, Massachusetts, Hartford Courant, April 12, 1973, at 7, col. 2.

190. *See* pp. 1241–43 *supra*.

191. Physical integration of the institutions would not necessarily guarantee equal access. For example, the Mississippi State Penitentiary at Parchman is physically integrated to the extent that men and women are housed in the same geographic area. However, the women are not permitted to participate in the variety of vocational programs that are available to the men. Interview with Sgt. David Jones, Mississippi State Penitentiary, Aug. 23, 1972, on file with the *Yale Law Journal.*

192. The relatively small number of women in each state's prison system should not pose a serious problem in this process of equalization. Even the present all-male

institutions usually offer a variety of female-stereotyped programs and industries, *see* Appendices II and III, so women who preferred such activities would probably still find them available in the sexually integrated facilities. In addition, a deliberate attempt by prison administrators to disproportionately satisfy male preferences and slight female preferences would constitute an impermissible sex-based classification. *See* Jackson v. Godwin, 400 F.2d 529 (5th Cir. 1968) (prison officials, in selecting appropriate reading material for inmates, could not arbitrarily screen out the preferences of black prisoners).

28 Women and the Correctional Process

Linda R. Singer

Of the approximately 16,000 adult women incarcerated on any one day in the United States, about 800 are inmates of the two federal reformatories for women. State institutions house 6,000, and roughly 8,000 are held in the more than 3,500 local jails scattered throughout the country. Women serving sentences in state institutions are housed in separate institutions in 28 states (including Puerto Rico and the District of Columbia Women's Detention Center). Twenty-four state facilities for women are under the control of the wardens of male prisons in other states.[24]

Because women are required to be housed separately from men in every state,[25] women's cell blocks often become jails within a jail. In small, generally rural jails, this enforced segregation may result in the solitary confinement of women and young girls.[26] Even in jails where some work or exercise facilities are available, women frequently are excluded from them in order to prevent any contact with the more numerous male populations.

Although systematic studies of women in prison are rare, the sociologists who have examined these institutions agree that women's experiences in them is anything but positive. The one common experience of all prisoners relates to homosexuality.[27]

Because of their relatively small numbers and the failure to construct a variety of facilities for them, young women and old women, whose crimes may range from disorderly conduct to murder, are all incarcerated together in the same institutions. Despite all indications that the women in prisons are poor, under-educated and without the vocational skills necessary to make

"Women and the Correctional Process" by Linda R. Singer. *American Criminal Law Review*, 11 (Winter 1973): 300–308. Permission to reprint has been obtained from the American Bar Association which holds the copyright privileges for the *Review* published quarterly by the Association's Section of Criminal Justice. The original footnote numbers of the source are retained.

them self-supporting,[28] county jails generally have no organized educational, vocational, or counselling programs,[29] and even in state prisons and institutions for juveniles, idleness prevails. Although juveniles frequently are sent to institutions because they are truant from school, their institutional janitorial jobs often are given priority over their education.[30]

The reasons given by officials for the lack of programming range from the small number of women as compared to men, and the consequently high cost per prisoner of introducing expensive training, to the frank confession that because most women prisoners present little threat to society, the priority for spending limited budgets must be given to the males. In those institutions where vocational training programs have been established for women or girls, they are limited almost uniformly to areas good only for training housewives or menial domestic workers.[31]

Regulations

The rules that regulate inmates' conduct appear even stricter at prisons for women than at those for men, although women's prisons generally are not maximum security institutions. In a complaint[32] recently filed on behalf of female prisoners in the District of Columbia, many of whom are in a pre-trial status and have not been convicted of any crime, the prisoners allege that regulations concerning exercise, visiting, receipt of publications and censorship of mail are more rigid than those at District of Columbia institutions for men. Sometimes the greater restrictions can be explained by a lack of staff, as where women are locked in their cells for the night as early as 4:30 P.M. because there are too few staff members to guard them. Another possible explanation is the feeling frequently expressed by institutional officials that because most women offenders have been screened out of the system, those that finally are imprisoned are the very worst and must be governed strictly. Although women prisoners constantly are admonished by institutional staffs to act as "ladies," the conditions in which they are kept, ranging from the general lack of privacy to truly barbaric conditions of solitary confinement, are anything but lady-like.

Nor have institutions for women made any special provisions for pregnant women or for women with children.[33] Estimates of the number of women prisoners who are mothers range from a majority several years ago in California[34] to 70 percent in the federal system[35] to 80 percent in Pennsylvania[36] and 86 percent in the District of Columbia.[37] Despite these figures county jails frequently prohibit visits by children entirely. Even where visits are allowed, as in the District of Columbia Detention Center, mothers must see their children through glass and are not permitted to touch them. Information concerning contraceptive devices is not provided to inmates, nor are pregnant women permitted abortions; yet women whose children are born in prison often are pressured to give them up for adoption.[38] No American prisons have child-care facilities or permit infants to remain with their mothers.

Possibilities for legal challenge

In a rapidly growing body of law, prisoners are being given legal rights which they never before possessed.[39] This general body of correctional law, outside the scope of this limited article, probably offers the most hopeful possibility for women as well as for men in prison. Yet women have been plaintiffs in a surprisingly small proportion of the recent law suits. Most of the issues to be raised on behalf of the rights of women prisoners are the same as those that must be raised on behalf of men.[40] However, there are a few possibilities for specialized litigation where women are discriminated against by the criminal justice system solely because of their sex.

Equal protection

Where women are excluded from training programs, work release, halfway houses or furloughs (commonly because of the fear of pregnancy), or subjected to more rigid regulations than male prisoners, the most obvious avenue of legal challenge is the equal protection clause. Under the recent Supreme Court Ruling in *Reed v. Reed,*[41] differentiation on the basis of sex in treatment by the state must pass only the test of having "a rational relationship to a state objective."[42] Even under this lenient test many of the differences in treatment of male and female prisoners would have to fall. Furthermore, there is little question that if the twenty-seventh amendment[43] is finally ratified, a far more stringent standard will be applied and classification by sex will be subjected to stricter judicial scrutiny.[44]

In only one case have women prisoners successfully challenged their exclusion from a correctional program as a denial of equal protection. In *Dawson v. Carberry,*[45] female jail inmates in San Francisco sued in federal district court to gain participation in a work-furlough program, from which women had been categorically excluded. Jail officials defended the suit by claiming that they lacked the resources to build special facilities for women comparable to the work-furlough center they had built for men, and that the smaller numbers of female prisoners made special arrangements for them infeasible.[46] Consequently, they had made a rational classification, which could not be disturbed by a federal court.[47]

The judge who heard the case never issued a final decision. Instead, he recessed the proceedings for three months to enable officials to establish a work-furlough program for women. However, his comments during the course of the hearing that the exclusion of women from the program is "almost blatantly unconstitutional"[48] and "an outright area of sex discrimination"[49] clearly indicate that he considered such action to be a violation of the equal protection clause of the Constitution.

Attempts to gain admission for women to education and training programs may also encounter the argument that since there as yet has been established no general "right to treatment" for prisoners,[50] women cannot complain of their exclusion from the few programs that do exist. In one case, a three-judge federal court rejected an argument by Georgia prisoners that since some prisons in the state had rehabilitative programs, the others should as well:

Humane efforts to rehabilitate should not be discouraged by holding that every prisoner must be treated exactly alike in this respect . . . to order the maximum for each and every person confined, as ordered by plaintiffs here, would be financially prohibitive for this state and could result in a reduction of rehabilitative efforts rather than an implementation.[51]

On the other hand, even where prisoners are not constitutionally required to be admitted to particular programs, the Supreme Court has ruled that a state must afford due process protections to those from whom certain benefits, such as parole, are taken away.[52] The abolition of the constitutional distinction between "rights" and "privileges"[53] probably means that even where the state is not required to provide programs for prisoners, once it does, it may not exclude whole classes of prisoners from participation on the basis of their sex.

Title VII

Where employment or training for jobs is involved, Title VII of the Civil Rights Act of 1964, which prohibits employment discrimination on the basis of race, religion, national origin or sex, may prove to be a more specific remedy than constitutional litigation. Female prisoners are not given access to the same employment or training opportunities as male prisoners. Furthermore, the higher pay and statutory good-time associated with working in prison industries are denied to women, since there generally are no industries in women's prisons. This differentiation would seem to present a clear case of employment discrimination under Title VII.

The threshold question that still must be answered, however, is whether prisoners are "employees" under the Act. The courts have not yet been presented with the question. However, a recent opinion letter from the General Counsel of the Equal Employment Opportunities Commission stated that prisoners appear to be covered by the Act.[54]

In a recent case,[55] a prisoner was awarded back pay when a court found that his loss of wages due to a transfer from one job to another was the result of racial discrimination. The issue of the definition of prisoners as employees was not raised. Another recent case has held that prisoners who work for private employers under a contract with the prison are not employees of the company and hence not entitled to the benefits of the Fair Labor Standards Act.[56] However, the case did not deal with the question of whether the prisoners were employees of the prison. The question currently is being raised in Michigan[57] and New York[58] in the context of administrative hearings to determine whether prisoners are public employees and hence entitled to the benefits of unionization under state public employment relations acts.[59]

Once a woman is released from prison, she faces triple discrimination: as an ex-convict, as a woman, and frequently as a black. Title VII specifically prohibits discrimination against her for the latter reasons. Whether it prohibits discrimination against her because of her criminal record is still to be determined.

In *Gregory v. Litton Systems, Inc.,*[60] a federal district court ruled that a refusal to hire people with arrest records had a disproportional effect on minority groups and hence was racially discriminatory. Since the conviction rate, as well as the arrest rate of minority groups, is disproportionate to their numbers in the population, it is possible that this rationale will be extended to apply to ex-offenders. The Minneapolis, Minnesota Civil Rights Department recently announced that any discharge or refusal to hire or promote by the city on the basis of a conviction record would prima facie be considered a case of racial discrimination.[61] A charge raising this issue with regard to the hiring practices of the local telephone company recently was filed with the EEOC in the District of Columbia.

Beyond equal protection

It would be tragically short-sighted if legal efforts on behalf of women in the criminal justice system were restricted to demands for equal protection with men. In recent years it has become increasingly clear that the entire system of imprisonment is bankrupt and should be replaced. In the long run the legal rights and the human dignity of women cannot be protected as long as they are locked away in prisons.

In the interim, steps must be taken to ensure that the most egregious violations are curtailed. Because many of the class actions filed on behalf of male prisoners are brought on an institution-by-institution basis, their benefits are not extended to women, who are frequently housed in separate institutions and receive even less attention from the legal profession than male inmates. Legislative or administrative remedies as well as litigation will be necessary to reform. One possibility lies in the development of administrative grievance procedures for prisoners, probationers and parolees[62] or in the formation of prisoners' unions.[63]

Efforts to protect the legal rights of women who are in prison must be coupled with efforts to develop alternatives to the present system. It has been pointed out by a few observers that the system of imprisonment for females should be easier to tear down and replace than that for males, since there are far fewer women and they generally are considered non-violent.[64] Community centers, where women can receive needed services, and where some who are thought to require short-term custody can live with their children, are one answer. Such centers currently are being developed in Pennsylvania as a result of studies by women's volunteer groups. Similar centers are being sought through litigation in the District of Columbia.[65] Women residing in these centers can work to support themselves and their dependents, as well as to make restitution to any victims of their crimes. Such innovations as work release are impossible when women are housed in isolated institutions far from population centers. Yet the movement to establish halfway houses, which has grown rapidly lately, has barely touched the lives of women prisoners. For example, while the Federal Bureau of Prisons operates eight halfway houses for men, it has none for women.

In addition to a move to impel public authorities to replace jails and prisons with community centers, it will remain important to divert as many women as possible from the official system entirely. This would not be a particularly radical departure from present practice, since it will be remembered that most women are screened out of the official system anyway. What diversion requires is the development of services for the poor, who are processed through the criminal justice system instead of being afforded medical, educational, legal and vocational services in the community. One hopeful sign is the growing number of women's volunteer groups that are beginning to work with prisoners. The Pennsylvania Program for Women and Girls operates a "satellite center," staffed primarily by ex-offenders, that serves female probationers and parolees. Until the movement to remove as many people as possible from our prisons is accelerated, other efforts are doomed to be stop-gap measures.

Notes

24. Figures provided by the U.S. Dep't of Labor, Women's Bureau, Washington, D.C.
25. This requirement is statutory in six states. *See* MASS. GEN. LAWS ANN. ch. 268, § 29 (1970); N.H. REV. STAT. ANN. ch. 622, § 33 (1971); N.M. STAT. ANN. § 14 (1953); N.D. CODE ANN. § 26 (1960), OR. REV. STAT. § 140 (1971); S.D. COMP. LAWS ANN. § 70 (1967).
26. *Cf.* Davis v. Lindsay, 321 F. Supp. 1134 (S.D.N.Y. 1970).
27. A study at the California Institution for Women in Frontera, California estimated that 50 percent of the inmates were sexually involved at least once during their term of imprisonment. According to the Indiana University Institute for Sex Research, 19 percent of the outside community had homosexual experience. *See* D. WARD & G. KASSENBAUM, WOMEN'S PRISON: SEX & SOCIAL STRUCTURE 92–94 (1965). The inmates who were interviewed agreed that 90 percent or more of the women homosexually involved at Frontera had their first affair in prison. *Id.* at 97. Prison homosexuality at Frontera is seen as a temporary but major adaptation to prison life. It is considered a response to restrictions on personal freedom and separation from family and friends. *Id.* at 1.

    At the Federal Reformatory for Women in Alderson, West Virginia, correctional officers estimated that between 50 percent and 75 percent of the 639 inmates were involved in homosexual relationships. *See* R. GIALLOMBARDO, SOCIETY OF WOMEN: A STUDY OF A WOMEN'S PRISON 151 (1966). There too homosexuality was considered an adjustment to prison life. Inmates seek to create a substitute world to resist the destructive effects of imprisonment. *Id.* at 136–140.

    At both institutions, it was apparent that all homosexual relationships were established on a voluntary basis. There was no evidence of the physical coercion that exists in the male prisons. *Id.* at 141.
28. *See, e.g.,* AMERICAN ASSOCIATION OF UNIVERSITY WOMEN, *supra* note 13; U.S. Dep't of Labor Women's Bureau, Brief Summary of Survey of Job Interests at Alderson, West Virginia, and Terminal Island, California (mimeographed and undated); Statement of Elizabeth Koontz, *supra* note 11, at 6–7 [hereinafter cited as U.S. Dep't of Labor Women's Bureau].
29. THE AMERICAN ASSOCIATION OF UNIVERSITY WOMEN, *supra* note 13.
30. *See* L. FORER, "NO ONE WILL LISSEN": HOW OUR LEGAL SYSTEM BRUTALIZES THE YOUTHFUL POOR, Chapter 7 (1970).
31. In the District of Columbia

    Data Processing is the only vocational training for girls at Cedar Knoll (a juvenile institution), and no students under the age of 16 are admitted to the course. Boys, on the other hand, have access to training in printing, gardening, auto mechanics, furniture repair, upholstery, shoe repair, building trades, and electronics. The girls may only participate in non-credit classes in cooking, sewing, and cosmetology.

District of Columbia Commission on the Status of Women, Female Offenders in the District of Columbia 16 (1962). *See also* Complaint in Garnes v. Taylor, Civil No. 159-72 (D.D.C., filed Jan. 25, 1972).

In New York City institutional emphasis is placed on appearance and grooming. In the dismal House of Detention, the highlight of the year is a fashion show of clothes inmates sewed themselves. *See* Goldman, *Women's Crimes,* 22 Juvenile Court Journal 33, 34 (1971).

32. Garnes v. Taylor, Civil No. 159-72 (D.D.C., filed Jan. 25, 1972).
33. *See* Off Our Backs, A Women's News Journal, April 1972 at 5.
34. S. Zalba, Women Prisoners and Their Families 115 (1964).
35. U.S. Dep't of Labor Women's Bureau, *supra* note 28.
36. American Association of University Women, *supra* note 13.
37. Barrus, Slavin, McArthur & Adams, *supra* note 12. In addition a recent survey of inmates of the Women's Detention Center by the District of Columbia Public Defenders Service estimated that close to 6,000 children in the District of Columbia are affected each year by the imprisonment of their mothers.
38. G. Konopka, The Adolescent Girl in Conflict 22–23 (1966); Goldman, *Women's Crimes,* 22 Juvenile Court Journal 33, 34 (1971).
39. *See* R. Singer, Prisoner's Legal Rights: A Bibliography of Cases and Articles (1971) (published by Criminal Law Bulletin); Bibliography, 11 Am. Crim. L. Rev. 217 (1972).
40. *See, e.g.,* Garnes v. Taylor, Civil No. 159-72 (D.D.C., filed January 25, 1972).
41. 92 S. Ct. 251 (1971).
42. *Id.* at 254.
43. H.R.J. Res. 208, 92d Cong., 2d Sess. (1972) providing:

Section 1. Equality of rights under the law shall not be denied or abridged by the United States or by any State on account of sex.
Sec. 2. The Congress shall have the power to enforce, by appropriate legislation, the provisions of this article.
Sec. 3. This amendment shall take effect two years after the date of ratification.

44. *Cf.* Loving v. Virginia, 388 U.S. 1 (1967); McLaughlin v. Florida, 379 U.S. 184 (1965). The stringent equal protection test requires that legislative classifications be supported by a compelling state interest. *See* Shapiro v. Thompson, 394 U.S. 618 (1969).
45. No. C-71-1916 (N.D. Cal., filed September, 1971).
46. It would appear that financial hardship is not a defense to sex discrimination in prisons. In Shapiro v. Thompson, 394 U.S. 618, 633 (1969), the Court stated:

We recognize that a state has a valid interest in preserving the fiscal integrity of its programs. It may attempt to limit its expenditures, whether for public assistance, public education, or any other program. But a state may not accomplish such a purpose by invidious distinctions between classes of citizens. . . .

See also Seidenberg v. McSorley's Old Ale House, 317 F. Supp. 593, 606 (1970) (tavern could not refuse women accommodations on the basis of inadequate sanitary facilities where only its past policy of discrimination had prevented it from making expenditures for such facilities); Equal Employment Opportunity: Sex Discrimination § 1604.2(B)(4), 401 FEP 17, 29–30 (where special facilities for employees are required by state law for each sex, "provisions of these benefits to one sex only will be a violation.").

47. Record at 9–10, 14.
48. Record at 13.
49. Record at 14. Additionally, the judge stated that:

    The basic premise upon which women are excluded is the fact that there are not any facilities for handling them in terms of this program. . . . I don't think that the Constitutional principles [sic] is dependent upon its difficulty of administration. It's a principle really of just fair play.

    Id. at 6.
    See also Kirstein v. Rector and Visitors of the University of Virginia, 309 F. Supp. 184 (E.D. Va. 1970) (exclusion of women from a state university found contrary to the fourteenth amendment where the exclusion denied benefits available only at the university).
50. Although there may be no constitutional right to treatment for prisoners, *see, e.g.,* Holt v. Sarver, 309 F. Supp. 362, 379 (E.D. Ark. 1970), there frequently is a statutory right to treatment for juveniles and youthful offenders, *e.g., In the Matter of* Savoy, unpublished opinion by Harold H. Greene, Chief Judge of the Superior Court of the District of Columbia, October 13, 1970.
51. Wilson v. Kelley, 294 F. Supp. 1005, 1012–13 (N.D. Ga. 1968), *aff'd per curiam,* 393 U.S. 266 (1969).
52. Morrisey v. Brewer, 92 S. Ct. 2593 (1972); *cf.* Goldberg v. Kelley, 397 U.S. 254 (1969).
53. *See, e.g.,* Board of Regents v. Roth, 92 S. Ct. 2701, 2706, (1972); Morrissey v. Brewer, 92 S. Ct. 2593 (1972); Graham v. Richardson, 403 U.S. 365, 374 (1971); Bell v. Burson, 402 U.S. 535, 539 (1971); Goldberg v. Kelly, 397 U.S. 254, 252 (1970); Shapiro v. Thompson, 394 U.S. 618, 627 n.6 (1969); Pickering v. Board of Education, 391 U.S. 563, 568 (1968); Sherbert v. Verner, 374 U.S. 398, 404 (1963).
54. Letter from General Counsel's Office, Equal Employment Opportunities Commission to David J. Berman, Center for Correctional Justice, Washington, D.C., Nov. 20, 1972.
55. United States *ex rel.* Motley v. Rundle, 340 F. Supp. 807 (E.D. Pa. 1972).
56. Sims v. Parke-Davis, 334 F. Supp. 774 (E.D. Mich. 1971).
57. *In the Matter of* Prisoners' Labor Union at Marquette, No. C72 E-81 (Mich. Employment Relations Comm., filed Sept. 1972).
58. *In the Matter of* Prisoner's Labor Union at Greenhaven, No. C-0794 (N.Y. Public Employment Relations Bd., filed February 22, 1972).
59. *See, e.g.,* MICH. COMP. LAWS ANN. § 423.201 (1967).
60. 316 F. Supp. 401 (C.D. Cal. 1970).
61. *See* AMERICAN BAR ASSOCIATION, NATIONAL CLEARINGHOUSE OFFENDER EMPLOYMENT RESTRICTIONS: OFFENDER EMPLOYMENT REVIEW (1972).
62. *See generally* Singer, McArthur and Schuman, *The Center for Correctional Justice: An Answer to Prisoner's Grievances?,* THE PRISON JOURNAL, Fall-Winter 1971.
63. *See* Burnham v. Oswald, Civ. No. 1971-132 (W.D.N.Y., May 16, 1972).
64. *See* Reckless & Kay, *supra* note 7. Velimesis, *Criminal Justice for the Female Offender,* JOURNAL OF THE AMERICAN ASSOCIATION OF UNIVERSITY WOMEN, October, 1969, at 13–16.
65. Garnes v. Taylor, Civil No. 159-72 (D.D.C., filed Jan. 25, 1972). Ironically, while the suit was pending, plans were underway to add a fourth floor to the Women's Detention Center, agreed by all to be an outmoded and inadequate facility, and scheduled for demolition in 1976 as part of an urban renewal project. The plaintiffs' motion for an injunction to prevent the building of the fourth floor was denied by the Court.

29 Competing Goals, Heterogeneity, and Classification

Rose Giallombardo

Prison administrators hardly begin with blank canvas and primary colors, even with the first offender. With the recidivist, however, there is good reason to suppose that the staff must face the additional task of peeling off layers of values and attitudes assimilated in other prison worlds as well as antisocial attitudes and values internalized in civil society.

Some writers argue that experiences in jail, training school, and the like are not identical to the prison experience, and therefore they maintain that such information should not be included in tabulating statistics for recidivism. I think this practice may be grossly misleading, however, because evidence suggests that the banishment of the individual from society into a correctional institution—whatever rubric it claims—is sufficient to bring about certain attitudes and values inimical toward society.[1] The experience of incarceration in jails, training schools, and the like exposes the individual to an inmate culture which is not unlike that found in the prison.[2]

For the purposes of the study, therefore, recidivism was defined as any prior commitment. Inmates whose records indicated that they had previously been incarcerated in other reformatories, prisons, jails, workhouses, and girls' correctional or training schools were all classified as recidivists. In these terms, an inmate who had served a thirty-day jail sentence was classified as a recidivist. According to this definition, on a selected day the records revealed that 52.1 percent had been previously jailed or imprisoned. A breakdown of the number of prior commitments appears in Table 1. Of the 312 first offenders, 60.6 percent were white, 38.1 percent were Negro, and 1.3 percent were Mongoloid. Of the total population, 15.3 percent were recidivists of the Alderson prison. Approximately half of the inmate population, in other words, had been previously incarcerated.

Table 1 **Number and percentage distribution of the prior commitment history of inmates by race**

NUMBER OF COMMITMENTS	NEGRO		WHITE		MONGOLOID		TOTAL	%
	No.	%	No.	%	No.	%		
None	119	42.5	189	51.5	4	66.7	312	47.8
One	66	23.6	90	24.5	1	16.7	157	24.0
Two	39	13.9	45	12.3	——	——	84	12.9
Three	16	5.7	23	6.3	——	——	39	5.9
Four	15	5.4	12	3.3	——	——	27	4.1
Five or more	25	8.9	8	2.2	1	16.7	34	5.2
Total	280	100.0	367	99.1	6	100.1	653	99.9

Because recidivists constitute potent socializing agents, one of the fundamental problems which must be faced squarely by the prison administrator is whether to isolate them from the first offenders. The first offenders at the Alderson prison were scattered throughout the cottages and followed the same program as the other prisoners. Given the competing goals of the prison, it follows that to separate such a large group of inmates would pose serious administrative problems. For example, inmates assigned to work in food service are *ipso facto* assigned to live in a food service cottage regardless of age, personal characteristics, or prior criminality.

Recidivists are important because they bring with them the values they have assimilated in other institutions, tend to reinforce the values in interaction with other recidivists, and socialize first offenders to these values. Secondly, the dispersal of inmates throughout the prison system facilitates the induction of the first offenders into the inmate culture and social system. Thus, the possibility of positive identification with staff members and values is sharply reduced.

The question of whether prisoners should be isolated from one another no longer arises in connection with criminal offenses as far as classification of prisoners is concerned. A sharp distinction is made between male prisoners who are considered violent and dangerous regardless of the offense, and are said to require the bastille-type prison, and those who may be safely housed in minimum and medium security institutions. As explained previously, whatever distinctions are made in the case of the female adult prisoner, females must be accommodated within the same institution. Maximum security units exist within a single institution, but they are few in number. Yet we do not find the same sharp distinctions made for the female prisoner in terms of passivity and aggression. This lack of distinction is not a result of the range of female criminality being sharply limited. On the contrary, the data in Table 2 reveal that the criminality of the Alderson inmate population includes a broad range of federal offenses.

Despite the broad range of offenses committed by the inmates, the distinctions based on violence (and, on an informal level, on criminal offense) usually made in the male prison by staff and inmates alike are rarely made in the case of the female inmate.

A few inmates were defined as unfit to mix with the general Alderson

Table 2 **Offenses of inmates classified according to type of crime**

Type of Crime	Number	Percent
Bank robbery	12	1.8
Embezzlement	12	1.8
False impersonation	5	.8
White slave traffic	5	.8
Forgery	128	19.6
Narcotics	193	29.6
Kidnapping	4	.6
Income tax evasion	2	.3
Immigration violators	4	.6
Fraud	24	3.7
Liquor law violators	15	2.3
Larceny	204	31.2
Counterfeiting, possession or passing of counter- feit materials with intent to defraud	5	.8
D. C. cases	3	.5
Government reservation and territorial cases	12	1.8
Conspiracy	15	2.3
Miscellaneous	10	1.5
Total	653	100.0

population and were housed in the maximum security cottages, mainly because they were perceived to be behavior problems. The behavior problems were a function of incarceration, and the inmates in question were often referred to as "troublemakers" and "psychotics." (All nonprofessional personnel in the prison tended to label all inmates defined as "troublemakers" as "psychotic.") Refusal to work, for example, would be just and sufficient reason to move an inmate to a maximum security unit. It is worth noting, however, that the two maximum security cottages were filled to capacity by other inmates who chose to live there mainly because they found living with a smaller group of inmates to be less hectic; it was clear that they did not require the closer supervision and greater restriction on freedom that living in these quarters entailed. In addition, under some circumstances an inmate may find it necessary to make a "Sonya"-like Siberian trek to be with a homosexual lover. There are, in other words, several reasons why an inmate may be housed, by choice or otherwise, in a maximum security unit.

The fundamental difference between the male and female prisons in this respect may be explained partially by the fact that there is a *principle of reduction* which operates in the case of the female prisoner—from the point of view of both the inmates and the staff. In the first place, cultural prescriptions of the female prisoner make a concerted effort to reduce all female offenders, on the basis of their common criminality, to the same generalized status of equality, *criminal*, in order to neutralize the generalized popular culture pertaining to women and thus to lay the groundwork for intensive interaction among the inmates in the prison.

On the staff level a similar reduction process operates due to the persistence of the societal-cultural definition of the nature of the female criminal. It will be recalled that historically society has looked upon the female criminal as a

Table 3 **Current and commitment age distribution of
inmate population**

Age	CURRENT AGE Number	COMMITMENT AGE Number
15–19	29	53
20–24	121	132
25–29	114	129
30–34	132	114
35–39	103	89
40–44	63	67
45–49	38	27
50–54	23	16
55–59	15	13
60–64	9	7
65–69	5	6
70+	1	——
Total	653	653

misguided, sinful, pathetic creature in need of protection and as a passive rather than an aggressive individual. And the Alderson staff tends to look upon the inmates as generally lacking in moral fibre—as being "weak," "like children,"[3] as well as "selfish." This basal reduction eliminates the necessity to make sharp differentiations among inmates and makes it possible to handle them in large groups by the use of standardized routines.

For example, in the matter of differentiation, no distinctions are made by the Alderson officials on the basis of age, although there was great disparity in the ages of the inmates. As Table 3 indicates, the commitment age ranged from fifteen to sixty-seven years, with a mean of 32.2 and a median of 30.5.

The current ages of the prisoners ranged from sixteen to seventy. The mean age was 34.4 and the median was 30.8. Ultimately, of course, whether or not age is made a criterion for separating prisoners depends upon the goals of the organization. An organization committed to balancing custodial and maintenance goals against a broad scheme of differentiation which would disrupt the equilibrium of these units will be guided by convenience to the organization rather than by treatment needs indicated in the individual case.

In this context, it may be pointed out that the official in charge of classification proceedings always had a list of job "vacancies" which "had" to be filled. In other words, the function for which this structural device was created is aborted or compromised because the maintenance requirements of the organization are accorded priority. We observed earlier a similar process occurring in connection with the disposition of inmate rule infractions. In general, when convenience is the criterion used for assignment, a compromise with the treatment objective is made. In this regard, the former occupations of the inmates are particularly vulnerable to exploitation by the formal organization precisely because this experience fits so nicely the goals of the existing structure.

Although most of the information concerning occupational status obtained from the female prisoners at the time of entry is verified by a social history form filled out either by relatives, former employers, or is verified by information on presentence reports, these data must nevertheless be interpreted with extreme caution. In the first place, the stated occupational status of an inmate does not necessarily mean current occupation immediately prior to incarceration. For many inmates, as for other women in the labor force in the United States, employment is frequently intermittent to help supplement family income. At other times, an occupation is assumed prior to marriage, as a result of divorce, or because of separation. The information in Table 4, then, is an indication of the kinds of work experience which each inmate has had in the past. As might be expected, most of the inmates are represented in occupations closely allied with homemaking roles, as these have been historically filled by women. Approximately one-third of all inmates had worked in such service occupations as waitresses, hospital attendants, and beauticians. Of this group, 26.7 percent were waitresses. Eleven percent were engaged as domestic laborers and about the same number were engaged as factory operatives. The twelve women listed as owners of small business included proprietors of cafes, bars, restaurants, taverns, and grocery stores.

It is apparent that the former occupational experience of the inmates in the labor market, or their former roles as homemakers lend themselves very effectively to the efficient attainment of the prison's goal of economic self-sufficiency. . . . The bulk of the inmates are assigned to tasks concerned with various forms of sewing, cooking, and cleaning. The organization of the prison around these major functions stems historically from the theory that women should be trained in the prison primarily as mothers and homemakers. As a consequence, vocational and other "educational" treatment programs were in turn generally coordinated about the necessary occupations of the prison. Vocational "training" in the female prison actually meant training in one of the maintenance functions of the institution; thus women, upon release, could work as service workers such as domestics and waitresses, or in the needle trades. Such occupations, as well as laundry work, were available to released inmates.

The Alderson prison was built along the pattern adopted by the best state institutions of the day, where it is said to have been demonstrated that homelike units and smaller kitchens provided opportunity for training in cooking, house decorations, table service, and all phases of homemaking. Consequently, formal instructions tended to supplement and illustrate the basic training in the cottages. This was consistent with the prevailing goal of the prison, namely, to train inmates for roles as mothers and homemakers; but this training goal was never allowed to interfere with what were considered to be the necessary occupations of the prison.

Society has been slow to change the vocational preparation of female prisoners, and the emphasis on kitchen and needle arts has persisted. A vocational program in the prison, however, is justifiable to the extent that the training may be used by the inmate in earning an adequate livelihood upon release. More than likely, vocational *knowledge* rather than work "skills" and "good work habits" derived from prison labor will gain increasing importance in the future; evidence strongly suggests that the majority of female inmates must seek some form of employment when released. The marital status of the

Table 4 **Occupational status of inmate population reported at time of entry**

OCCUPATION REPORTED	NUMBER	PERCENT
None	45	6.9
Housewife	55	8.4
Domestic laborer	72	11.0
Waitress and other phases of restaurant work	174	26.7
Hospital attendant	31	4.7
Beautician	11	1.7
Factory operator	66	10.1
Laundry worker	18	2.8
Seasonal farm laborer	10	1.5
Clerical worker	72	11.0
Salesclerk	25	3.8
Prostitute	15	2.3
Teacher	3	.5
Seamstress	6	.9
Elevator operator	9	1.4
Bank teller or executive	7	1.1
Owner—small business	12	1.8
Manager—small business	3	.5
Entertainer	6	.9
Florist's helper	2	.3
Telephone operator	2	.3
Stock room clerk	4	.6
Insurance sales	1	.2
Organist	1	.2
Interpreter	1	.2
Cab driver	1	.2
Garage worker	1	.2
Total	653	100.0

inmates indicated that 27.1 percent were single; 31.5 percent were married; 20.7 percent were separated; 16.4 percent were divorced; and slightly over 4 percent were widows. Even many of the married women will find it necessary to seek employment upon release.

It is interesting to note that the most recent figures on female labor in the United States seem to point in the direction of increasing concentration of women in the clerical field in the future. Although the occupations of women varied widely in the 1960 census, the largest concentrations were in the clerical field, which comprised about 7 million women. (The three other major categories comprised service workers such as waitresses, beauticians, and hospital attendants; and professional and technical employees such as teachers, nurses, accountants and librarians. These groupings number between 3 and 3.75 million each.)[4] The underrepresentation of inmates in the clerical field is due to their low level of educational attainment. It has been reported that the median full-time income of women who had graduated from elementary school but had not completed high school was $950 in 1961.[5] A major problem which confronts the prison administrator, of course, is the realistic planning of vocational knowledge, that is, knowledge which the inmate can actually put to use in earning a livelihood upon release. Although it is true that the labor market for women is changing in the United States, the stigma of a prison sentence would perhaps exclude employment in clerical jobs for released inmates.

But without the integration of extensive community resources, it seems to me that the task of integrating meaningful treatment functions in the prison will always be seriously hampered. For example, think what it would mean to provide individualized educational treatment for inmates. As shown in Table 5, approximately half of the inmate population, or 325 inmates, had eight years' schooling or less. There is no marked discrepancy in educational achievement between the Negro and white races: 49.6 percent of the Negro inmates attended grade school; 50.1 percent of the white inmates attended grade school. A higher portion of the Negroes attended high school: 47.9 percent as compared with 44 percent of the white inmates. Of these two groups, however, a higher proportion of the white inmates graduated from both grammar and high school. For example, 17.5 percent of the Negroes completed grammar school, whereas 21.5 percent of the whites completed eight grades. Similarly, 7.9 percent of the Negro inmate population completed high school, but 13.6 percent of the white group graduated from high school.

The question is frequently raised as to whether prisoners have the mental capacity to benefit from formal educational treatment facilities. If by "intelligent" is meant whatever it is that intelligence tests measure, then a break-

Table 5 **Educational level of inmates by race as shown on classification records**

HIGHEST GRADE COMPLETED	NEGRO Number	WHITE Number	MONGOLOID Number	TOTAL
Grammar school				
None	—	6	—	6
One year	—	—	—	—
Two years	3	1	—	4
Three years	8	5	—	13
Four years	7	8	—	15
Five years	13	17	1	31
Six years	31	28	2	61
Seven years	25	40	1	66
Eight years	49	79	1	129
High school				
One year	55	46	—	101
Two years	34	46	1	81
Three years	26	20	—	46
Four years	22	50	—	72
College				
One year	1	13	—	14
Two years	3	3	—	6
Three years	—	—	—	—
Four years	2	4	—	6
Graduate school				
One year	1	1	—	2
Total	280	367	6	653

Table 6 **IQ score breakdown of inmate population by race**

CATEGORY	WHITE	%	NEGRO	%	MONGOLOID	%	TOTAL	%
Superior	20	5.4	4	1.4	——	——	24	3.7
High average	63	17.2	15	5.4	——	——	78	11.9
Average	188	51.2	126	45.0	4	66.7	318	48.7
Low average	59	16.1	64	22.9	——	——	123	18.8
Inferior	18	4.9	65	23.2	2	33.3	85	13.0
Not tested*	19	5.2	6	2.1	——	——	25	3.8
Total	367	100.0	280	100.0	6	100.0	653	99.9

* This constitutes an error of omission; it should not be thought that these inmates were illiterate.

down of the actual full scale I.Q. scores as revealed by tests administered in the prison indicates that the inmates do not differ appreciably from the general population.

As Table 6 indicates, 13 percent of the inmate population scored below a score of 70, which is generally accepted as defective mental status. Negroes scored considerably lower in the extreme categories; but 51.2 percent of the white population and 45 percent of the Negro group fall into the average category. Approximately 50 percent of the total inmate population fall into this grouping. Combining the average and low average groups, the breakdown is 67.3 percent white and 67.9 percent Negro. For our purposes, the significant point is that according to the prison records, 13 percent of the inmate population may be classified as defective.[6] In other words, the problem lies not so much in the ability of the inmates but, rather, in *what* and *how* to teach, and what relative emphasis to place on social and academic education for treatment.

The problem of implementing broad treatment functions in the prison setting is, without doubt, complex. The inmates vary in previous education from a handful of college graduates to others who can speak little or no English, their ages range from fifteen to seventy, and they enter the prison on any day of the year.

In addition, the length of the sentences for the crimes varies widely—the range is from three months to life. The mean sentence without consideration for parole is 54 months. The complete distribution appears in Table 7.

In this heterogeneous and shifting population, then, the prison must organize a "school" presumably suited to the individual needs of the inmates and at the same time adapted into the necessary maintenance work of the prison.

As the societal goal for the prison progressively shifts from punishment to rehabilitation, the conflicting purposes stand out more sharply. The competing goals of the prison induce pressures toward goal displacement. Displacement of goals has been evidenced in the function of the classification process for the prison routine of the inmates as a consequence of overconcern with organizational stability.

It is apparent that criteria such as history of recidivism, educational attainment, length of sentence, and personal characteristics such as drug addiction do not fit neatly into the organizational scheme when assignment to work, quarters, and treatment activities must be based on convenience to the

Table 7 **Length of sentences for inmate population**

SENTENCE	NUMBER	PERCENT
1 year or less	46	7.0
1 year, 1 day to 3 years	271	41.5
3 years, 1 day to 5 years	174	26.6
5 years, 1 day to 10 years	132	20.1
10 years, 1 day to 15 years	18	2.8
More than 15 years	11	1.7
Observation and study	1	.2
	653	99.9

institution. For this reason, although such information as age, education, and former occupation is carefully noted on classification reports, it is not made an integral part of the classification process.

The lack of meaningful differentiation of individual characteristics makes it possible to perceive inmates as more alike than different and, thus, to handle them *en masse* with standardized routines.

We saw in Chapter 5 that in order to maintain the equilibrium of the system, treatment structures were modified or converted to other uses. Similarly, the mechanism of classification, however nobly its purpose is stated in official publications, serves as an administrative device to balance institutional manpower needs in the prison. Because of the competing goals of the prison and the priority placed upon maintenance and custodial needs of the institution, classification requires extensive compromise with these structures.

Notes

1. See especially Sheldon and Eleanor Glueck, *Five Hundred Criminal Careers*, New York: Alfred A. Knopf, 1930. The authors followed the careers of delinquent graduates from one correctional school and found that over 75 percent of them subsequently engaged in criminal or delinquent behavior. More recently, it has been reported that 15 percent of admissions during the year 1956 had been at the same institution at one time or another and were returned either for commitment of a new offense or parole violation; see Children's Bureau, *Statistics on Public Institutions for Delinquent Children*, 1956, Washington, D.C.: U.S. Department of Health, Education, and Welfare, 1956, p. 1. See also the follow-up analysis of community adjustment and deviant outcomes of the Hollymeade group by Howard W. Polsky, *Cottage Six*, New York: Russell Sage Foundation, 1962, pp. 183–185.
2. See the brilliant analysis by Howard W. Polsky, *ibid*. For an example of the adult prison, see Donald Clemmer, *The Prison Community, op. cit.*, especially pp. 298–315. More recently, Wheeler's findings indicate that conformity to conventional norms varies depending upon the stage of the inmate's career. It was observed that conformity to conventional norms was higher at the beginning and at the end of imprisonment than in the middle. However, despite the U-shaped pattern of change, there was a tendency for inmates to move away from conformity to conventional norms with each increment of prison experience. Thus, first offenders and recidivists exhibit the same pattern, but the recidivists exhibit lower conformity than the first offenders. Stanton Wheeler, "Social Organization in a Correctional Community,"

Unpublished Ph.D. Dissertation, University of Washington, 1958. See also Stanton Wheeler, "Socialization in Correctional Communities," *American Sociological Review*, Vol. 26, October 1961, pp. 696–712.

3. See Erving Goffman, "On the Characteristics of Total Institutions: Staff-Inmate Relations," in Donald R. Cressey, Editor, *The Prison, Studies in Institutional Organization and Change*, New York: Holt, Rinehart and Winston, Inc., 1961, p. 78.

4. *American Women*, Report of the President's Commission on the Status of Women, 1963; Washington, D.C.: U.S. Government Printing Office, 1963, p. 28.

5. *Ibid.*, p. 70.

6. For the reader interested in crime statistics, the 85 inmates classified as defectives were convicted of the following crimes: 1 case of false impersonation; 27 cases of forgery; 22 cases in connection with narcotics; 1 case of fraud; 2 cases in violation of the liquor law; 29 cases of larceny (postal theft accounts for 22 of the larceny cases); and 3 cases of murder.

30 The Concrete Womb: "Gettin' In"

Kathryn Watterson Burkhart

Rules and regulations—maximum (for untried and unsentenced inmates)

This institute is a branch of the Los Angeles County Jail. It is known as the Sybil Brand Institute for Women.

Time schedules

Maximum

4:40 A.M.—Rising Time
5:00 A.M.—Breakfast
10:00 A.M.—Lunch
3:30 P.M.—Dinner
8:45 P.M.—Everyone in own bed area
9:00 P.M.—Lights out

Conduct rules

Bed areas

Bed assignments are made ONLY by an officer. Do not change your bed without permission from the officer. There are to be NO more than three inmates in a bed area or cell at the same time. Only two inmates are permitted on one bed at a time, and both are to be sitting up, with feet on the floor. When lying down on your bed, your shoes must be off. Do not hang towels, clothing or laundry in such a way that officers cannot see. Do not hang anything on the bars in cellblocks.

From *Women in Prison* by Kathryn Watterson Burkhart. Doubleday & Company, Inc., New York, 1973. Pp. 142–151, 107–113, 164–168. Copyright © 1973 by Kathryn Watterson Burkhart. Reprinted by permission of Doubleday & Company, Inc.

Bathroom areas

Except for toilet facilities, not to be used prior to lights on. Personal under-clothing is not to be washed in the wash basins. Dorm or cellblock trusties ONLY to wash and dry all personals including tennis shoes for entire area in Day Room. Showers are to be used only as scheduled. You must shower every day.

Smoking

In Dorms smoking is permitted in bed area ONLY. In cellblocks smoking is permitted inside a cell ONLY. You must not smoke in the cellblock corridors. Ashtrays must be kept empty and clean, and remain on the shelf of the locker or writing table. Never place on beds. Never smoke while lying down.

Talking

There is NO talking after lights out, during count, or when going from housing area to meals, work areas, visitation or Infirmary. There is no loitering outside of housing area. Inmates must walk by twos and close together in meal lines and when going to or from work areas. No talking is permitted in lines.

Red lines

In Dorms a red line is painted on the floor at the grilled gate. In cellblocks it is painted on the floor between the showers and the first cell. Anytime a line is formed to leave the housing area, the formation is to begin behind this red line. If you are called from your housing area by an officer wait behind the red line until the door has been opened and the officer has instructed you to step out.

Count

Count is regularly taken after lights out. However, it may be called at any time. When count is called over the public address system, inmates in Dorms are to go to their own bed areas, inmates in Cellblocks are to go inside their own cells. When the officer enters the officer's station inmates are to line up at the foot of their beds in Dorms and in front of their cell in cellblocks. Do not lean against the walls, beds, or bars. There is absolutely no talking while count is being taken. Remain standing until excused by the officer. Inmates in work areas will line up as designated by the officer, according to housing area. No movement out of dorms, cellblocks, or work areas until count is verified.

Meal lines

Meal Lines are called over the public address system. You must go to meals. There is no talking in meal lines or in the Dining Room.

Personal contact

No personal contact is permitted. This includes playing, wrestling, massaging, plucking eyebrows, etc.

Borrowing, lending, and exchanging

You are not permitted to give, exchange, borrow or loan ANY personal items such as clothing, shoes, commissary, money, etc.

Disciplinary actions

The BEST way to avoid disciplinary actions is to follow the Jail Rules and do as instructed by the officer. If you feel an order is unfair, the best policy is to do as told at the time and then write a request to see the Classification Board.

Identification bands

Identification bands are not to be removed and if showing signs of wear or if cannot be read, report to your officer at once.

Property slips

Property slips are to be kept on your person at all times.

Clothing and linens

Undergarments

Each inmate may have a maximum of five (5) sets of underclothing (bra, panties, slip). All personal items must be marked with your initials. Pettipants and girdles are counted as panties.

Street clothing

You are permitted to receive one exchange of street clothing during your incarceration. If you receive a clothing exchange, the original clothing must be returned with visitor. No exchanges will be accepted on Saturdays, Sundays, or Holidays and may be made only between 8:00 A.M. and 4:00 P.M. and between 6:00 P.M. and 9:00 P.M. during the week. No socks are to be brought in.

Needlework

Permitted in reasonable quantities in Dorms only. You may work on one (1) needlework project at a time—knitting, crocheting, or embroidery. Visitors may bring you five (5) skeins of yarn at a time or enough thread to complete one embroidery or crocheting project.

You may knit or crochet the following items: sweaters, stoles, afghans, baby clothes, socks or hats. You may *not* knit or crochet pants, skirts, long coat sweaters, dresses or shorts. Visitors may bring you only those pattern books, plastic needles or crochet hooks to complete one project.

Completed articles must be turned in to the Officer (along with your authorization or sales slip) to be placed in your property.

If you wish to release articles to a visitor, you must inform the officer when you turn in your completed article. Excess yarn, thread, needles, and pattern books should be turned in at the time the article is completed.

You must retain your authorization or sales slip with your needlework at all times, or articles will be confiscated. You may not knit for another, nor may another inmate knit for you.

Appearance—cleanliness—neatness

Cells and dormitories

Each inmate is required to keep her own cell or bed area and surrounding area neat and clean at all times. This includes your assigned share of showers and general cleaning of Dorm or Cellblock.

Lockers

Only cup and ashtray on outside locker shelf in Dorms. There are to be no liners on the inside locker shelves. Locker contents must be orderly and not excessive. Any amount over Five (5) of each cosmetic item is considered excessive and will NOT be returned to you. Dresses, etc. to be hung on rack inside locker. Do NOT hang anything on doors of locker.

Beds

Must be made prior to breakfast and kept neat during the day.

Floors and walls

Nothing is to be left on the floor during the night except one (1) pair of shoes or thongs per person. Do NOT deface or paste pictures on walls or lockers. No blankets or pillows on floor.

Trash

All trash which will burn is to be placed in the trash can. There are to be NO individual trash receptacles (boxes, paper bags, etc.) in bed areas or lockers. Soiled napkins must be wrapped securely in newspaper and placed in trash cans. Glass and metal are to be turned in to the officer.

Personal appearance

Each inmate is required to keep herself neat and clean at all times. You must be fully dressed and presentable when leaving your housing area for any reason; do NOT walk around in stocking feet or barefooted.

Showers

Shower is to be taken daily. You are allowed ten (10) minutes to shower. No showers one-half hour prior to any meal line or after lights out.

Hair

Beauty Shop schedules are posted in individual housing areas.

Hair preparation orders

Inmates may order permanents and/or have hair dye (only to maintain present color or return to natural color). Write a request to Special Services Sergeant for permission. Only one (1) request filled during month. The orders will be taken on the first Wednesday of the month. You must have sufficient money at time of order. No refunds will be made if you are released before dye is received.

Headscarves or pin curls

Headscarves or pin curls are not permitted from 7:00 A.M. to 5:30 P.M. unless special permission is granted.

Nightcaps

May be worn after 5:30 P.M. only if hair is in curlers. May be worn from bedtime to 7:00 A.M. whether or not hair is in curlers. Are to be worn above eyebrows.

Money

Ways you may receive money

Visitors may leave any amount at time of visit, to be deposited to your account. Visitors may leave up to $5.00 at time of visit, with the officer in the visiting room—to be given directly to you.

Mail

Cash received in the mail will be deposited to your account. A notation on the front of the envelope will show the amount. Checks and Money Orders will be placed in your property.

Checks and money orders

Cashier's checks and bank or postal money orders for amounts under fifty dollars ($50) are automatically cashed when received and the money deposited to your account. If it is over fifty dollars ($50) it is placed in your property. Personal checks are NOT accepted. If anyone has mailed these in, they will be placed in your property.

Money receipts

You will receive a money receipt for any cash deposited to your account by visitors, deposited to account through mail, or after checks and money orders have been cashed.

Withdrawal of money from account

Money withdrawal slips will be issued in the housing area on Tuesday evenings. You may not draw more than eight dollars ($8.00) from your account per week. Slips will be processed and money issued to you the following Saturday morning. Special request for money withdrawal should be sent to Inmate Personnel Sergeant. You are not allowed to have more than $12.00 in your possession at any time. Bills of larger denomination than $5.00 will be confiscated.

Commissary—county line

Commissary rules

You may not buy commissary for another inmate, nor can another inmate buy commissary for you. If you are going out to court, you should give your commissary order (sealed in an envelope with money) to your officer in the morning.

Regular commissary

Regular Commissary shopping daily except Saturdays, Sundays and holidays. Commissary Wagon will be in your housing area each weekday morning. A list is posted in the areas showing what can be purchased and the cost. If you wish to shop you must have a list written on a piece of paper including what you want to buy, how many, and the cost of each item. All inmates wishing to shop are to line up when the Commissary Wagon arrives. There is no talking while in the line. You must have a ditty bag.

Cosmetic commissary

Cosmetic Commissary shopping on Wednesdays only. No shopping on holidays. Commissary envelopes are available for cosmetic shopping and must be filled out prior to breakfast and deposited in the Commissary Box enroute to the Dining Room. The purchase is bagged and stapled closed. Any money to be returned will be placed in bag for return to inmate. Purchases will be distributed by the Sales Clerk and should be opened in the presence of the officer.

County line (Fridays)

If you have no money on deposit and are not receiving any from visitors, you may write a County Line Request for necessary supplies. Make this request each week that supplies are needed. Note MUST be in the mail box by Wednesday and County Line is delivered on Friday.

Visiting—mail

Visiting

Visiting hours are daily from 10:00 A.M. to 2:30 P.M. Monday through Saturday and holidays, and from 12:30 P.M. to 2:00 P.M. on Sunday. You are allowed two (2) visits per week. Each visit is limited to twenty (20) minutes. No children under eighteen (18) years of age will be permitted to visit. Ex-inmates are not allowed to visit. Visitors cannot visit more than one (1) inmate.

General information about mail

All mail is inspected. Letters may not contain institutional gossip or information about other inmates. Inmates without privileges may not send or receive personal mail. Mail pertaining to case is permitted. Incoming mail will be delivered when privileges are restored. There is no written communication permitted between inmates. No packages will be permitted.

Special permission

Must be obtained by writing a Request Slip for permission to: Correspond in a foreign language; send enclosures (except Sunday Church Bulletin); or send letters without inspection stamp or return address.

Outgoing mail

Each letter is limited to four (4) pages written on one side only. Do NOT write in margins. Top first page must have your NAME, BOOKING NUMBER and HOUSING AREA. The envelope must have the following return address:

NAME (as booked), BOOKING NUMBER
BOX 54320 Sybil Brand Institute for Women
Los Angeles, CA 90054

Leave envelope unsealed and drop in mail box on way to Dining Room. Letters will be returned to inmates if they are not prepared in accordance with those rules.

Photographs

You may receive small photographs through the mail, but may have no more than five (5) in your possession. Excess will be confiscated. You may not trade photographs and your name and booking number must be written on the back.

· · ·

Women Riot, Attack Guards at Jail Here

A band of women inmates stormed the Philadelphia House of Correction dispensary, apparently in search of drugs, touching off the second of two disturbances here Sunday.

No one was injured in the first melee, which erupted about 9 A.M. in the G-2 cellblock and took about 30 minutes to quell.

But four male guards, a matron, and an inmate were injured in the second disturbance, which broke out shortly after 11 A.M. It involved 50 women—half of the 92 held in the prison—who wielded broomsticks, kitchen utensils, and legs pulled from chairs. . . .

—from the Philadelphia *Inquirer*
Page 1-A, February 19, 1973

Whenever you have exaggerated repression, you have exaggerated response. A spring wound too tightly will recoil with extra force. A child who has no natural, direct outlet for his anger will throw a temper tantrum. A people who have been held down too long and denied alternatives will explode in anger— over a police brutality incident in the ghetto, over a prison guard insulting an inmate in a crowded cafeteria. We call the response "riot."

A woman abused by her man continually over a long period of time will "riot" just as "unexpectedly," and the relationship often ends in violence or death. Parents "lose" their children to drugs or hatred over a seemingly small incident, sometimes only casually related to the process of oppression the child has experienced for years. The overwhelming nature of disasters can often cause delayed reactions which the individual may not even associate with the accident or disaster. After a death, a hurricane, a horrible train crash, a tornado or flood, people often protect themselves unconsciously from the terrifying experience by mentally putting it away and not thinking about it. When the response finally does come forth, it can be devastating.

It seems that going to prison, in and of itself, is an emotional and mental disaster. Further, the judgments and punishment that continue once imprisoned create terrible repression. The response, the outlet, is manifested in broken windows, senseless fights. Sometimes a "riot." Although the occasional news we hear about prison rebellions would give the impression that only male prisoners stage uprisings, women also rebel. They strike, they negotiate, they boycott. At California Institution for Women alone, one fifth of the population successfully escaped in 1971, one or two at a time. The same pressures that lead women to escape often result in riots. And sometimes the incident that sparks response seems minuscule. But the reaction is one that has been pent up from day-in-and-day-out pressures, coercion and anxiety.

It may be sparked by the fact that a woman's father died and the administrative staff delayed its decision on her pleas to go home to his funeral— despite the fact that her prison friends were willing to pool their funds to pay her expenses of a guard-escort and transportation and she was collapsing with grief. This ignited a "riot" in the administrative building at Muncy, Pennsylvania, when women who went to protest were confronted by locked doors, male guards and maintenance men.

It may be the fact that two women were very ill but were unable to get medical attention from prison authorities. This sparked the so-called "riot" and break into the dispensary at the House of Correction in Philadelphia, after legitimate avenues for help were exhausted.

A minor riot can happen because a woman with hepatitis is not getting medical attention. This happened at Bedford Hills in New York. "Full investigations" can be launched, but they rarely focus on the pent-up frustration of no change after agonizing conditions have been ignored by "proper channels" even when women have gone about expressing their grievances in a reasonable way.

"What people fail to realize is that being locked up at all is punishment enough," said Barbara Collins, now out on parole after four years in a state prison. "They think you come to prison to be punished—and so you're punished in all kinds of ways while you're there.

"But there are times you can get pushed too far—and you just can't keep your mouth shut. You can't lose your pride one more time without giving up some part of yourself, and that's the only thing you have. . . ."

Like our society at large, prisons seem crisis prone. The response to disruptions is a microcosm of the American Way, where we condone or ignore the violence of racism, poverty and imprisonment—but condemn the violence of resistance or reaction to it.

We denounce violence and riots, but we fail to equate daily violence perpetrated in more subtle ways. Women at the House of Correction "hurt" four male guards and a matron. But how closely do we consider that seventy-seven out of the ninety-two women there were *awaiting* trial? Further, how adequate are the social welfare services in providing for the children of these women? And what are their feelings and experiences as confined people, helpless mothers?

When we witness any violent outburst, we seem to forget that this kind of predicament doesn't happen in a vacuum, that it is a response. To examine the crisis alone is myopic and sensational. We must probe more deeply for the real causes—otherwise we continue blindly and blandly to place Band-Aids on cancerous sores.

The origin of every outburst in prison is woven into the day-to-day fabric of prison life. First of all, women being punished for violating society's standards by being incarcerated enter a new social order with its own regulations and status quo. The order dictates a picayune system of discipline, where crime and punishment revolve around behavior issues which could never be "taken to court" in the larger society. Central to the system is the fact that prisoners have privileges, not rights. A sign in the dining room of the women's House of Correction in Chicago, Illinois, expresses the core focus of prisoner "rights":

Words were made to be spoken
Voices were made to be used

If you speak lightly, and also politely,
This privilege will not be abused.

In prison speaking can become a privilege, not a right. Visitors are a privilege. The smallest things we take for granted on the outside become a matter of rewards to be allowed or withheld: showers, mail, laughing out loud, touching, walking slowly, running, dancing, smoking, eating. Even the quantity of sugar or milk in coffee is of consequence.

"I went to get sugar for my oatmeal," Marlene Riffert says. "I took a spoonful and then the matron came up and took my bowl away and threw the cereal in the garbage. I was so shocked, I didn't say anything, I just looked at her. She said, 'You know you already used sugar in your coffee.' I was given three nights' early bed." Marlene had violated a sacrosanct rule at the House of Correction in Philadelphia: she attempted to use sugar in her coffee *and* on her cereal at breakfast. Her option was one or the other, not both.

Marlene told this story when she was testifying about conditions at the House of Correction for a Philadelphia court. Inmates from three male institutions and the women's section of the House had filed a class action suing the city for violation of the Fourteenth Amendment—cruel and unusual punishment.[1]

She sat dwarfed in the witness box and explained her history: she ran away from home at age sixteen, was declared "incorrigible" by the state and locked up at the House of Correction. That was 1962. She was there again in 1963, 1970 and 1971. She is in detention this time for possession of narcotics. Her voice is small and shaky as she talks about her unresolved drug problem, her husband at Graterford prison and their two-year-old son. She says she is testifying because she thinks "things should change" for the women who will follow her into the jail.

She tells the judge that when she finishes her testimony and goes back to the jail, she is scheduled to go into solitary confinement for another infraction of rules at breakfast. "Men work back in the kitchen," she says. "They're from over on the men's side. . . . I was on the line getting my food. Well, the men were bringing the food in from the outside and the door opened and I looked at one of the men. I didn't wave or call him or nothing. I just looked at him. When I got to the end of the line the matron said, 'Marlene, you're going to get lockup when you get back from court.' I said, 'What for? For looking at the men?' She said, 'Yes.'"

Bizarre as it may seem, this kind of infraction is not uncommon in institutions that hold both men and women in separate sections of the same jail. At Cook County Jail in Chicago, which warden Winston E. Moore describes as "one of the best-run jails in the country," women are put in lockup for talking through the window in sign language to men in other sections of the massive jail complex. Passing "kites" [notes] is an automatic lockup.

More rarely prisoners are disciplined for "talking on the wall" to the men on the floors below them. By getting down on the floor and putting your ear to the wall, you can hear voices from the other floors through the air vents. Men and women signal each other with specified numbers of knocks on the wall and sometimes carry on long, intimate conversations throughout the day and night. Since it's almost impossible to stop the conversations, inmates and guards have established a truce; matrons usually tolerate such an exchange as long as they don't personally witness it. Women shout, "Respect" when a matron's coming, and conversations cease as the women stand at attention for the matron passing their cells. ("The time goes fast when you're down on that cold floor talking on the wall," Toni says. "You get tired of talking to women all the time. Man, on Saturday nights those walls be steamin'.")

The only opportunity male and female prisoners have to see one another close up at Cook County Jail is when they go to co-ed concerts Winston Moore has instituted since he became warden. Lou Rawls, Joan Baez, Dick Gregory and several other artists have performed at Cook County in the last three years. On these occasions, the women are ushered to the front of the prison yard and seated. Then the male inmates file in and sit down. Women inmates are not allowed to turn their heads, wave, nod or look at the men. After the performance, the women walk out single file. "Heads forwards, girls." Any woman who looks to the right or left, acknowledges someone with her eyes or turns around is banned from future concerts and subject to lockup. ("They seem to think we're going to take our clothes off and lay right down," one inmate said. "They treat us like we're a bunch of nymphomaniacs—not just normal women who like to look at a man every now and then. The whole thing is in their heads. It doesn't have shit to do with what's really going on. . . .")

"Women here are locked in for 'silent insolence' if they raise their eyebrows at an officer or refuse to answer a stupid question," said a caseworker at one prison. "They are never allowed to let go except when they're watching television or having a dance. Even then they're told to keep it down. Sometimes I feel as if I were living in the middle of a nightmare; I don't know how long I'll be able to take it. I've been here one year—and it's the incredible intelligence and sensitivity of the women that's made me stay this long. They need someone to talk to. But I'm just overwhelmed by the needs they have—and my inability to meet them.

"There's no way the unexpected can be incorporated into the living situation here. Custody depends on a known and strict schedule so that the unexpected cannot happen and harm 'security.' No matter what rhetoric they have here about treatment and rehabilitation, any disruption of the schedule or the routine is a security risk. And any woman who does anything she is not supposed to do—even like talk while she's eating—means that she's a 'security risk' and must be locked up or disciplined."

In many county jails, there is no pretense of a disciplinary hearing for women sentenced to solitary jail within a jail. The women are just locked up, period. If there is a disciplinary hearing, it comes sometimes four or five days after the punishment. When women at the Detroit House of Correction refused to work in protest to humiliating search procedures and abhorrent prison conditions, in June 1971, participating strikers were locked in their rooms for several days, some up to two weeks. Before they had been locked up, they sent letters out to the mayor, city council and prison board listing their grievances. In answer to a city investigation of the incidents that followed, the then superintendent, W. H. Bannon, said that "each girl was interviewed to get the facts on how this started." He admitted they were locked in their rooms before they were interviewed, but maintained that "after a period of six or seven days we released each of them without any punishment whatsoever."

In state prisons, disciplinary hearings are more common—but if I were to describe how they seem to a stranger, I would call them "pretend trials"— with the concept of "proving" guilt only make-believe. Although the disciplinary hearings are often called "tribunals, behavior clinics or adjustment hearings," the process is not impartial, nor is guilt or innocence the issue. Guilt is an *a priori* assumption. As one administrator bluntly put it: *"The process used for determining punishment* [my emphasis] includes a hearing with a senior correctional officer, a senior counselor, the warden and a psychologist when he can attend.

"Theoretically a woman can have an attorney present if she wishes, but think of it logically. With court processes so slow and lawyers with so many clients, how many would even consider taking time to come here for a disciplinary hearing? And even if a woman could get a lawyer—how would she pay him?

"A woman can speak on her own behalf and try to convince us she's telling the truth, but *we know what really happened"* [my emphasis].

Inmates say the process is one-sided from the get-go. A matron or guard does a "write-up" or a "blue-slip" which is a summons to come to court. Sometimes offenders are put into solitary before court. If not they usually receive no prior written notice until they are called to behavior clinic or the hearing. The woman is not allowed to call witnesses in her behalf. And the board is not required to give a decision based on evidence.

"It's your word against hers," said one woman who had been in solitary confinement for a week when I met her. "She's always going to win because they're her people, they're going to listen to her. You're just a number or a blank space in their minds. You go in and sit in front of that board and you know you don't have a chance in heaven to get out of going to solitary.

"I got nine days here because Miss Brown in Central Food Service said I refused to drop a pan and clean the grill. She was just upset about her husband being sick and she was taking it out on me. She told me to quit what I was doing and I said 'Just let me finish this pan first.' She just went off on me— started hollering about my 'insolence' and then she wrote me up. Of course she blew it up in front of the Behavior Clinic. They asked me to step into the hall, and about two minutes later I came back in and heard my sentence. Then the guards brought me up here."

Getting "locked up" is a common occurrence for women prisoners, as it is with men. They are all familiar with the "bing," "hole," or "strip cell." These cells are drearily the same in every jail I've visited—windowless and bare. Some have one thin, dirty and bloodstained mattress on the floor. Some have no mattress. Some jails provide blankets for the women confined, some do not. In some quarters, women locked in solitary are allowed to wear prison shifts—in others they are allowed to wear only their underwear or are stripped naked. Toilets are most often flushed from the outside, and women complain that on occasion sadistic matrons play games with flushing the toilets—either flushing them repeatedly until they overflow or not flushing them at all for a day or more at a time. ("If the toilet backs up, there's nothing you can do about it but live with the stench.") Food is passed into the room two or three times a day between the bottom of the dusty door and the unwashed floor, as are sanitary napkins if the woman is menstruating.

"You can't even take a shower or comb your hair. Sometimes they'll remember to pass a comb into you, or toilet paper, but sometimes they forget. And you can imagine what it feels like to use a dirty Kotex. Last winter I was in solitary for six weeks and they'd leave windows open and I'd just freeze on that floor. . . ."

A joke among women is the names used for solitary confinement. What was originally called "the hole" changes to "solitary" / "max" "administrative segregation" / "punitive segregation" / "isolation" / "the quiet room" / "security cell" / "control center" / "reflection" / "behavior center" or, currently, among the satirists, "loss of privilege module." At Cook County Jail, Lieutenant Dorothy Zeno explained, "We don't call this the hole or confinement, we call it the Blue Room." [It was painted blue.]

Although the euphemisms may be more tolerable titles for outsiders or administrators, the reality for prisoners in max is unchanging. Often women say they are afraid they will lose their minds or whatever sense they might have of who they are, where they are. Women sent to solitary who are experiencing severe emotional difficulties are sometimes driven to hurting themselves by trying to slash their wrists with any sharp object they can find (such as a piece of metal from the window) or burning the mattress if they can get matches. Often they are kept even longer in solitary for having tried to hurt themselves. Some administrators say they have no other means of coping with such problems.

"You lose track of time, you start feeling crazy, even though you know you're not there for anything," one woman said. "It's hard enough if you're strong or you can direct your anger on the people who deserve it for putting you there. But some women are sick to start with and just plain need help. When you put them in there, they're going to go crazy. I'll never forget one night listening to an eighteen-year-old girl just crying and screaming. She kept saying, 'Please somebody talk to me. Please just talk to me. I think I'm losing my mind. Oh, God, help me.' Any one of us would have gladly gone down and talked to her, but we was locked up, too. It just made me cry to hear her. And you know the matrons weren't going to talk to her. Those two be sitting down there saying to each other, 'She'll get used to it. She gotta learn sometime.'"

Becky Careway, at Ohio Reformatory, said, "I guess it used to be a whole lot worse in here. Miss Riley, the warden before Miss Wheeler, would shave your head bald for walking on the grass and put you in maximum security for no less than six months."

Becky said she had been in max several times for short periods of time. Once for refusing an order from the matron while working in the kitchen and another time for stealing supplies from the storeroom. "They didn't have no evidence on me. My room was clean. But I went to max anyway. I usually go peacefully. But one night the matron, who's a drunk, told me I hadn't swept the floor good enough, and it was swept good enough. Besides, she had just been drinking and she was all loud and sloppy. I told her, 'Bitch, call the guards, 'cause you ain't taking me nowhere.' The motherfucker . . . if I didn't have two more years before parole, I would have liked to slam into her. She called the guards, though, and I went with them."

A constant source of tension for women is discretion in enforcing rules and handing out punishment. "You never get away from it—it's always different strokes for different folks." When two women behave in the same way and only one is punished, others naturally are incensed at the injustice. Often women involved in the same incident are dealt with in different ways, even when the basic infractions are just plain silly.

Sharon Wiggins, sentenced to life at the State Correctional Institution for Women at Muncy, Pennsylvania, for instance, was charged with possession of fifty cents—which is "contraband" on "campus." All official monetary exchanges are transacted on paper.

"I was sitting on the steps in front of Sproul Cottage, and Mrs. Spaulding and three guards and three maintenance men drove up and told us to come into the building. They didn't say what they wanted. She stripped us and searched us. She made me pull down my Kotex to look. She found fifty cents on me, so she wrote me up. The male guards and maintenance men were there in case we refused to be searched. But we didn't.

"I was charged with possession of fifty cents, but on the behavior sheet, she wrote that she had searched us for narcotics and implied she knew we had it on us, but she didn't find it. At the time we asked her to take us down for urinalysis after she looked at our arms. We didn't have any narcotics and hadn't used any—so we wanted a urinalysis. She said she didn't have the authority. We asked if she had the authority to search us, she could give us the urinalysis instead and that would be less humiliating—plus it would prove whether we were taking drugs or not.

"But we didn't have a chance to prove ourselves. When they searched me, they said they would have to have a hearing on the fifty cents, but they didn't say nothing about searching for dope. They just wrote it on the behavior sheet and read it out loud at the hearing.

"I spoke in my own defense at the hearing. I was guilty of fifty cents but I said it was not right to write stuff about drugs on my record when she flatly refused to give us a urinalysis which I thought was my right. After the hearing I waited five minutes in the hall and when I went back in they told me what I had. I was locked in my room for three nights from 6 P.M. to 6:30 A.M. for the fifty cents. There's no way to appeal. None of the other three who were stripped and searched were charged with anything because they didn't have nothing on them."

Many prisoners have told me that addicts are discriminated against; at other times I have been told that Chicano women, black women or white women are the ones who are more apt to be "written up" or "called on the carpet" for rule infractions.

Occasionally I heard racial antagonisms from both black and white women. "They're always complaining about how they get the raw end of everything," one white woman said, referring to black women. "But I'm a living testimony to the fact that whites get fucked over just as bad. You can't tell me any different. If you ask me, they got more privileges than I ever had. I get tired of all their bellyaching. I got some black friends, but they're not into that bag all the time. If you lived here, you'd know what I mean. I just get tired of hearing black this and black that and black, black, black. . . ."

"We don't get shit around here," a black woman said. "Don't tell me no white girl has to do time like I have to do time. They get the best and they still be carrying that white thing around on their shoulders, signifying and strutting—like ain't I somethin. . . . You'll see it, they get away with all kinds of shit we get locked for."

Although some racial hostilities give vent to "disciplinary problems," most of the women in the prisons I visited maintain that tensions are created by the staff and staff policies, not by the women themselves. They say staff tactics are used to "divide and rule."

. . .

The other significant point is that the writer said, "The cooperation of some six hundred women did not come until they were pushed so far up the wall by the staff they had no choice. . . ." For prisoners to rebel or to take collective action at extreme jeopardy to themselves is the exception, not the rule. Every day in prison, there's non-co-operation, "malingering" and disdain for the structure, resentment of authority. But this differs from conscious political attempts to overthrow the criminal justice system or the prison structure itself. A lot of people in this country theorize that if we were ever threatened with totalitarian government, people would fight back relentlessly, would take up arms and lay their lives on the line. In theory this sounds fine, but in actuality a totalitarian society co-opts the majority of people it controls. It has its system of rewards, incentives, punishments and coercion—just like the society of prison.

Prisoners develop independent standards of personal satisfaction and fair treatment within the prison system that controls their lives. Only those willing to risk death, the future or indefinite solitary confinement will consistently revolt in an open manner. No one in the "Free World" should doubt that they would behave much differently under the same totalitarian system. Many analogies could be made to our everyday lives, but I will leave that for others.

The writer also noted that women who "intimated they would not cooperate were told in vague terms what their station within the prison would be if they didn't [co-operate in the strike]. . . ." Inmate loyalty is part of the expectation of the prison code. But as we have seen before, staff policies, administrative prejudices and an individual system of rewards and punishments, from "extra privileges" to "honor status" to parole considerations, serve to break down solidarity and unity on a day-to-day level. The result is the individual woman's need to create personal strategies for accommodation and survival that will still meet the basic requirements of the code. And in such rule-clad, total surroundings, survival becomes the most important thing to every woman.

It is also true that at times peer pressure can be stifling, adding to the status quo of tensions within the prison. James Ward, a young black correctional counselor at CIW, for instance, said he had been "ineffective" in one cottage, despite his belief that the prison was desperately in need of change.

"I felt my approach was pretty much rejected," he said. "I assumed the women would appreciate a new concept and as a result I made a lot of mistakes in dealing with this population at its own level.

"One thing that hurt me more than anything else was I felt that some of the women would like to do what I'd suggest. . . . But the culture is so strong that if they're accepting the staff, the person is automatically interpreted as rejecting her peers and culture.

"It's hard to work with a group that's rejecting you outright or sitting silently while others do—or to have women come into the office afterwards and tell you what they really feel but not say it in front of the group. Some of the women would be one person in the group and another in my office. This was hard for me to accept."

Whatever the consequences, the "code" remains intact. And in the prison structure, it seems a necessity for survival.

It is amazing there are as many petitions, grievances and revolts as there are—considering pressures on individuals to stay in line. It is indicative of the conditions prisoners live in that they rebel in spite of the personal consequences they face.

But inmates are becoming increasingly aware of their rights. Administrators say they're getting "more militant." Women and men in prisons all over the country are beginning to question more and more *why* they are in prison.

As a result of massive civil rights and anti-war actions in the last sixteen years, prisoners otherwise isolated have been exposed to the politics of college-educated people and intellectuals sentenced to prison, as well as white, brown and black militants. These middle-class newcomers, including those sentenced for narcotics offenses, are shocked by the blatant violations of their rights inside prisons. Their families and supporters have been outraged by the physical conditions and mental anguish. These people have shed new light on many conditions that long-time prisoners previously saw as a way of life, "normal" for prison.

Increasing numbers of prisoners are beginning to look at the entire system from a new perspective. They are seeing it from the outrage of the liberal middle class. The pieces begin to fit together and they are beginning to see themselves as the victims of class and race oppression. They are also looking beyond the immediate conditions to the system in broader terms—realizing that anyone, for instance, who expressed their intentions to be politically involved upon release, would probably be denied a parole. And that a person who is to be considered *rehabilitated* must present an attitude of repentance and conformity to prison norms.

A demonstration at the Federal Reformatory for Women in Alderson, West Virginia, beginning September 14, 1971, reflected the increasing awareness and sophistication of demands affecting the entire system. Following the deaths of prisoners and guards at Attica, the women held a memorial service for their slain brothers. Following the service and a march around prison grounds, which was approved by the administration, some of the women gathered to sleep in the prison yard. Earlier in the summer 300 women had signed a petition urging clarification and reform of parole procedures. It was part of a petition campaign in many federal prisons. Nothing had been done about it and there had been a growing dissatisfaction with the lack of results.

About 130 black, white and Latin women then occupied the old garment factory on the prison grounds and drew up forty-two demands to present to the administration. Representatives from various "cottages" sat in on the sessions and after the first day, some 500 women out of the 600 inmate population stopped work and school for four days to support the demands. Prison officials, along with a lawyer from the Federal Bureau of Prisons, agreed to a number of the demands but said that many of the others were "out of their jurisdiction." They told the grievance committee the demands agreed to would need to be rewritten in "legal language" and then would be implemented. The women said they would wait to see how the agreements were written up.

On Saturday, September 18, male guards wearing gas masks and carrying sticks were called into the prison. The women left the building to avoid a violent confrontation. Prison officials announced the incident was over and that agreements about grievances had been negotiated successfully.

But women in various cottages were still talking about continuing the work stoppage until the demands were implemented. On Monday, September 20, about forty guards from neighboring correctional institutions again came on "campus" with gas masks and sticks. A Greyhound bus was parked nearby. One of the men called out names of prisoners through a bullhorn and sixty-six women were ordered without warning to board the bus. When some resisted they were maced and dragged aboard. The women were transferred to the Federal Youth Center at Ashland, Kentucky. About ten days later, fifty-nine were flown to the federal penitentiary at Seagoville, Texas, and the others were returned to Alderson. Their families and lawyers were not informed of the move.

Some of the women from Alderson said they'd like to know what programs could have been set up at Alderson with the money the Federal Bureau of Prisons used to finance the flight to Texas alone.

The women's demands related directly to the prison itself, including the establishment of a work-release program, an open mail policy, more case-workers, sufficient diet planning (pork-free, bland, salt, etc.), more complete commissary stock and lower prices. They asked for a complete law library, as well as medical examinations as prerequisite for job assignments, and sufficient reasons for severe disciplinary punishment. Also related to institutional life were demands for the freedom to choose cottages, and washers and dryers in all the cottages.

The chief focus of the demands, however, was on the larger, total system. They asked for contracts for halfway houses and that Congress appropriate enough funds to enable educational rehabilitation programs to function properly. They noted that the budget for educational facilities had been cut from $18,000 to $11,000. They also demanded that funds be appropriated for emergency furloughs—such as critical illnesses, family deaths, childbirth, etc.

Much of their concern was directed at the parole system. They, along with federal prisoners in Danbury, Connecticut, and Springfield, Missouri, demanded changes in the operation and effect of the U.S. Parole Board:

1. The Parole Board should recognize that prison is destructive of our personalities, our humanity, and our ability to cope well with society. Since this effect is contrary to the Bureau of Prisons' expressed aim of "rehabilitation," the board should adopt the policy of speedy release for all prisoners.
2. The Parole Board should be required to give reasons for its decisions.
3. Parole Answers for both hearings and write-ins should be given within two weeks. [Alderson inmates said it takes six to eight weeks or longer to hear from President Nixon's board. Under the Johnson administration, women said it took two to three weeks.]
4. A person should have access to all the material in the file that the Parole Board uses to judge her case.
5. There should be no parole restrictions that interfere with a person's freedom of association, freedom of travel, and freedom to participate in legal, political and social activities. Parole should not be revoked without a positive conviction on a new charge.
6. People released on mandatory release rather than parole should not be under restrictions.
7. There should be a party beyond the Parole Board to whom parole or mandatory release revocations and Parole Board decisions can be appealed.
8. The Bureau of Prisons should insure that there is institutional cooperation for prisoners who want help with their release plans (jobs, furloughs, contacting potential employers and community resources, etc.).
9. Lawyers should be made available to represent or advise people before and during their parole hearings, when this service is requested.

There has still been no real response from the U.S. Parole Board. Women are still kept waiting in the isolated hills of West Virginia from eight to twelve weeks following their interviews before they hear whether they'll be granted or denied parole.

Ninety-eight per cent of them will eventually get out—whether it's on parole or at the termination of their maximum sentence. Ninety-eight per cent of all prisoners are eventually released. Will their voices be heard before they hit the street? And will anyone listen then?

Note

1. *Bryant vs. Hendrick,* 444 Pa. 83, 1971. The court found conditions at the three jails to constitute cruel and unusual punishment. The city is appealing the decision.

31 Recidivism Among Women Parolees: A Long-Term Survey

Carol Spencer and John E. Berocochea

Summary

This analysis of long-term parole outcome among California's women parolees outlines the extent and costs of recidivism, describes the characteristics of women returned to prison, compares the California women's return rates to those in other jurisdictions, and attempts to identify factors associated with recidivism among women.

Subjects

The subjects were 660 women released for the first time from the California Institution for Women in 1960 and 1961. In general terms, two-thirds of these women were White and in their early thirties. They scored as low-normal and at the junior high school level on intelligence and educational achievement tests. Approximately two-thirds of this group had served prior commitments, and one-third reported heroin use. Most were insufficient funds check writers or narcotics offenders. At the end of eight years, 40 percent had been returned to prison at least once.

These characteristics varied among ethnic groups, with White women showing higher educational and intelligence test scores, less narcotics use, fewer pre-prison misdemeanor convictions, and fewer returns to prison after release.

Comparison of the study group with women released in 1962 through 1964 showed that the only significant differences in characteristics were related to the channeling of narcotics offenders to the newly opened California Rehabilitation Center and an increase in White parolees. It was concluded that

From *Recidivism Among Women Parolees: A Long-Term Survey* by Carol Spencer and John E. Berocochea. Report Number 47, July 1972. California Research Division, Department of Corrections.

there was no reason to reject the assumption that the study group is fairly representative of other groups of parolees.

Return rates and correctional costs

When parole outcome is examined in terms of status of subjects eight years after release and the intervening events, recidivism appears as a major problem overwhelmingly caused by repeated returns of a comparatively small number of parolees who appear to be identified before release as a special problem group.

Status of subjects

Eight years after their first release from prison, two-thirds of the women had been discharged, and one-third was still under CDC jurisdiction—ten percent in prison, 11 percent on active parole and seven percent at large.

Returns to prison

Approximately 60 percent of the women had not been returned to prison, 20 percent had been returned once only, and 20 percent from two to seven times. Assaultive offenders were the most successful parolees, with only 15 percent returned.

Time served and costs

From their first entry into prison to eight years after first release, the 626[1] women had spent a total of 4,178 years under CDC jurisdiction for a total cost, estimated at current rates, of $7,929,307. The average cost per offender rose from $8,688 for women with no returns to prison to $30,101 for one woman returned seven times. Returns to prison increased the original incarceration time and costs by 44 percent. Multiple returns to prison of 20 percent of the women accounted for 72 percent of the total readmission time and costs.

Multiple returnees

Returnees and non-returnees differed in early prison experience. Women who were returned to prison served more time during their original incarcerations, and those who eventually became multiple returnees were brought back after their first release twice as quickly as women who were returned once only.

The probability of returning to prison rose with each reincarceration; 40 percent of the women were returned after their first release and 65 percent after their third release.

Parolee characteristics and parole outcome

The variations in early prison and parole experience found among those who eventually varied in parole outcome suggest that the different groups may be identified as having different patterns of characteristics, which evoke differential correctional treatment. Consequently, characteristics of parolees with different kinds of parole outcomes were compared. Kinds of parole outcome considered were returns with new commitments (WNC), returns for parole rule violation only (TFT), and no return to prison.

Frequency of new commitments and TFT returns

Thirteen percent of the study group were returned to prison with new commitments, accounting for one-third of the total readmission time served and 20 percent of the total number of readmissions. On the other hand, 25 percent of the study group with returns for parole rule violation only accounted for two-thirds of the total readmission time and 80 percent of the readmissions. The recidivism rate is thus overwhelmingly the result of the women being returned for parole rule violations, rather than the commission of new felonies which result in new commitments to prison.

Characteristics of women with new commitments

Only one of the 70 assaultive offenders in the study group returned with a new commitment. Among other offense types new commitments occurred with equal probability.

The extent of prior commitments was the only factor consistently and significantly associated with new commitments. Narcotics use tended to be related to new commitments among women with relatively limited prior records, suggesting that narcotics may be a factor in tipping the scales toward further delinquency among these women.

Ethnic groups did not vary in proportions returned with new commitments but tended to differ in the kinds of women so returned. Among narcotics users originally convicted of narcotics offenses, more White than Black women were returned with new commitments, while among non-users originally convicted of property offenses more Black than White women were returned by the courts. Economic need as a motivation for new offenses may be more prevalent among Black than among White women.

Characteristics of women with TFT returns

In contrast to new commitments, TFT returns were significantly associated with all characteristics examined except offense type, where apparent differences were found to be a function of narcotics use. Returned more frequently for parole rule violations were parolees with a history of narcotics use and prior commitments, average and below average educational and intelligence test scores, and minority group membership.

Most strongly associated with TFT returns were narcotics use and prior commitment record. When the effects of prior commitments were examined separately among users and non-users, technical return rates were found to rise progressively from 12 percent among non-users with no prior commitments to 61 percent among users with high prior commitments.

Persistent ethnic differences in TFT returns, apparent when groups were equated on narcotics use and offense type, were found largely among narcotics users with prior commitments. The data indicate that when Black women do not use narcotics and have no or relatively few prior commitments, they are returned TFT no more frequently than their White counterparts. However, as prior records and narcotics use become more extensive, more Black women are returned, and they are returned more frequently than White parolees with the same narcotics and commitment records. Similarly, Black women committed for assaultive offenses are more likely to be returned TFT than are White women.

Parolee characteristics and correctional decisions

The findings posed the question of the relative roles of parolee delinquency and parolee characteristics as determinants of correctional decisions. Accordingly, the relationship of parolee characteristics to the decision to discharge was analyzed for women whose parole behavior was free from delinquency serious enough to warrant return to prison. Among these women, length of time on parole before discharge was found to be associated with parolee characteristics in the same manner as number of TFT returns. Non-narcotics users were discharged sooner than narcotics users, and within those groups, women with no prior commitments were discharged sooner than those with prior commitment records. In groups equated for narcotics use and prior commitments, White women were discharged sooner than Black women. Nearly all of the women with above-average intelligence and educational test scores were White, non-narcotics users, and they were discharged sooner than other White non-users with lower educational and intelligence test scores. The findings strongly indicate that parolee characteristics as well as parolee delinquency do act as determinants of correctional decisions.

Reliability of findings

Comparisons between the study group and women released for the first time from 1962 to 1964 showed no appreciable difference in the relationship of prison returns to narcotics use and prior commitments, indicating that this relationship is stable and that the findings of the study are representative of other parolees.

Some comparisons of return rates of men and women

Up to this point the study has demonstrated that the great majority of returns to prison and the larger portion of the associated costs are accounted for by TFT returns, which are the results of decisions made by the Department of Corrections and the Women's Board of Terms and Parole. Since these decisions are crucial to the problem of recidivism and apparently subject to sources of variation other than criminal behavior of the parolee, they were further evaluated by comparing them to decisions in other parole jurisdictions. Such comparisons should show how agency response affects recidivism rates and also whether recidivism among California's women is high or low in relation to that among other groups of parolees.

The California experience

Comparison of return rates for men and women released in California from 1960 to 1968 showed that: the return with new commitment rates for women was consistently lower than that for men; that after the second or third year on parole the women's TFT return rate was consistently higher than that of men; and that the difference in TFT return rates increased sharply in 1965.

The increase in differences in TFT's between men and women coincided with administrative changes brought about by the inauguration of a Work Unit Program for men but not women parolees.

The implication that the reduction in returns of men parolees to prison was a result of administrative policy is supported by previous experimental studies where the parole agent's recommendations in hypothetical cases were found to vary in accordance with his perception of how the cases would be viewed by his supervisor. Subsequent replication of the experiment found that the percentage of recommendations for return to prison in the hypothetical cases was much lower after the Work Unit Program was initiated.

The ratio of TFT's to new commitments among California parolees released from 1960 to 1965 showed that a woman is two to three times more likely than is a man to be returned to prison TFT rather than with a new commitment. If the new commitment rate is less subject to administrative manipulation than is the TFT rate, then the new commitment is the more rigorous measure of criminal involvement. By this criterion, women are less criminally involved but are returned to prison by the correctional agency more often than are men.

The nationwide experience

According to the Uniform Parole Reports System of the National Probation and Parole Institute, 11 percent of 1,931 women parolees released nationwide in 1967 and 1968 were returned to prison TFT within one year after release, compared to 19 percent of California's women parolees. The nationwide TFT rates showed little differences between men and women parolees, but more men than women were returned with new commitments.

California and the nation

The TFT rate for women in California is high in comparison to that of women in other jurisdictions; high in comparison to men in California in recent years, due to changes in administrative behavior brought about by the introduction of the Work Unit Program for men; and high in relation to the rate of return by new court commitments.

The argument that women would be expected to be returned to prison more frequently than men because the criminal justice system is more lenient toward women and sends to prison only those heavily committed to criminal behavior was tested. This argument was found to be inconsistent with study findings demonstrating that the rate for women is higher only in California; that fewer women than men return to prison with new felony convictions; and that marked differences between men and women in return rates appeared with a change in administrative policy when the men's Work Unit Program was introduced.

Since 1965 the women's TFT rate was found to average about ten percentage points higher than that for men. In relation to the number of WNC returns, the women's TFT rate was found to be more than twice as high as could be expected. It was concluded that the women's TFT return rate is relatively high and that the difference in recidivism among men and women is brought about by differences in administrative practice. More data are needed before some definite conclusions can be reached, including an analysis of the reasons for return for both men and women and, perhaps, an experimental study of the relationship of reduced TFT returns for women to eventual parole outcome.

Conclusions

The percentage of women returned to prison for parole rule violation in California is high. It is almost double the average for the rest of the nation; higher than found among California's male parolees; and high in relation to rate of return of women with new court commitments. The process is costly, boosting the total prison and parole operating expenses to nearly $8 million for the 626 women in the study group during the period studied. Returns to prison increased the original costs of incarceration by 44 percent. A disproportionately large portion of this cost resulted from the repeated returning to prison for parole rule violation of a comparatively small percentage of women. Parolees who were returned by the courts with new commitments accounted for a minor part of the recidivism.

The TFT return to prison is ordered by the Women's Board of Terms and Parole in consultation with the parole agent when violation of parole rules is judged to be symptomatic of deteriorating parole adjustment which could lead to new delinquency. Thus, the recidivism rate is seen as a product of two interacting factors, the behavior of the parolee and the response of the agency to her behavior.

Comparisons of variations in responses to parolees by agencies in several jurisdictions clearly show the impact of agency decisions on return-to-prison rates. One example was found in the experience of the men's Work Unit Program, where TFT rates were reduced when agents were encouraged by the administration to seek alternatives to prison returns. Under this system new commitments did not increase. The relationship of parolee behavior to recidivism is more obscure. Criminal behavior among women parolees, as reflected in new commitment rates, was found to be fairly constant, bearing no relationship to the marked variations in TFT rates between California and the rest of the nation or within California over time. Women were shown to be less committed to crime than men, but in California their TFT rate was higher than that of men parolees.

While parolee criminal involvement could not be related to variations in recidivism rates, a strong relationship was found between parolee characteristics and TFT rates. Women with identifiable sets of characteristics were accorded differential correctional treatment. Those with lower educational and intelligence test scores, records of more extensive prior commitments and narcotics use, and Black women were returned more frequently TFT than other kinds of parolees. They served longer original sentences, and those who eventually became multiple returnees were returned from first parole twice as quickly as those returned once only. When not returned they served more time on parole before discharge. Among White, non-narcotics users, women with average and lower intelligence and educational test scores were returned TFT more frequently than other parolees; while among narcotics users with prior commitments, Black women were returned TFT with greater frequency than were White women. Apparently these women were perceived by the agency as more delinquency-prone, posing a greater threat to society and needing more extensive correctional attention than were other parolees. Yet, women who were returned by the courts for committing new offenses exhibited only one of these characteristics, a more extensive prior commitment record. Decisions for TFT returns were thus found to be associated with parolee characteristics which were not also associated with offenses resulting in new court commitments. The obvious implication is that differences in the recidivism rates of sub-groups of California's women parolees are results of agency response to parolee characteristics not necessarily related to criminal behavior.

Emerging from the study was no evidence that lengthy incarceration or return trips to prison result in rehabilitation. Women with the shortest prison terms were the most successful on parole. The probability of reincarceration was found to increase with each succeeding incarceration. While 40 percent of the women under CDC jurisdiction were returned to prison at least once, only two percent of those discharged from that jurisdiction were subsequently returned by the courts.

Return to prison for violation of parole rules is a device freely employed in California as a delinquency-prevention measure to deter new offenses, yet in the rest of the nation where TFT return rates for women are much lower than in California, women parolees are returned by the courts with new commitments no more frequently than are California's women parolees.

These considerations touch on only a part of the total problem of recidivism among women, and much more information is needed before definite conclusions can be reached. An obvious need is an analysis of the reasons for TFT returns and the extent of the delinquency involved. The high TFT rate among women with a history of narcotics use suggests that narcotics may be the major factor in prison returns. More definitive would be a study of the effects of an experimental reduction of TFT returns especially in regard to new commitment rates. Among men parolees the Work Unit Program reduced TFT returns without increasing new commitments. Since women are less inclined than men to new criminality, a similar experimental program among women would seem to stand an even greater chance of success.

Among women returned with new commitments, the study identified two special problem areas which might profitably be explored further. One was the possible economic motivation for new offenses seen in Black women, where among non-addict property offenders twice as many Black as White women were returned by the courts. Do Black women have fewer economic resources than White women? An evaluation of the economic status of women on parole, with the possibilities of coordination of various community resources including job placement services, may be indicated.

A second problem was seen among women with relatively few prior commitments where narcotics use appeared to be associated with new court commitments. Among other parolees, narcotics users did not return with new commitments more frequently than non-narcotics users. One interpretation might be that women with limited prior commitments have reached a vulnerable turning point in their criminal careers and are in need of special support on parole.

Note

1. Omitted are 34 women who were deceased or absconded parole shortly after release.

32 The Parole System: How Women Fare

Rita James Simon

In the last few years the National Council on Crime and Delinquency Research Center at Davis, Calif. has published an annual newsletter in which parole outcomes for the country as a whole are described. Fifty-five agencies from all the States, except Alaska, are represented, although not all States report on all of their parolees. The newsletter describes parole outcomes for men and women by the type of offense for which they were committed, their history of drug and alcohol use, and their prior prison sentences.

For 1970, all States listed 100 percent of their parolees in the newsletter, with the following exceptions: Alabama, Indiana, Maryland, Pennsylvania, and Wisconsin—25 percent each; Michigan—18 percent; New York and Ohio—10 percent.

The percentage of men and women offenders who were paroled in 1968–70, by homogeneous offense categories, and the percentage of women as opposed to men who were paroled for all offenses combined in each of the 3 years are presented in table 7.1. Note first that the percentages of women who have been paroled for those years are only slightly larger than the percentage of inmates who are women in Federal and State prisons (about 5 percent) in those years. Preferential treatment for women does not appear to be a significant factor at the parole hearing stage of the criminal justice system.

When we examine the percentages of men and women who were paroled (within the same offense category), we find three offenses for which there are both big differences and a sufficient number of women to make the comparisons worthwhile. Men who were convicted of homicide, forgery and fraud, and violation of narcotic drug laws were less likely to be paroled than were women convicted of those offenses. For the 13 other offense categories listed, there are no marked or consistent differences between men and women. Among the men, those who were convicted of burglary were most likely to

From *The Contemporary Woman and Crime* by Rita James Simon. National Institute of Mental Health, Washington, D.C., 1975. Pp. 77–83.

Table 7.1 **Percentage of offenders paroled by sex and type of offense, 1968–70**

	1968		1969		1970	
	Male	Female	Male	Female	Male	Female
OFFENSE CATEGORY	N = 24,786	N = 1,720	N = 25,563	N = 1,669	N = 25,602	N = 1,710
Homicide	7	13	7	14	7	14
Manslaughter	2	4	2	4	1	3
Armed robbery	11	3	11	4	11	5
Unarmed robbery	3	2	4	1	4	2
Aggravated assault	6	5	5	6	6	5
Forcible rape	2	0	2	0	2	0
Statutory rape	1	1	1	0	1	0
All other sex offenses	3	1	3	2	2	1
Burglary	29	7	30	6	29	8
Theft or larceny	9	11	9	12	10	11
Vehicle theft	5	2	5	1	5	1
Forgery & fraud	10	26	9	27	9	27
Other fraud	1	2	1	2	1	1
Drug law violations	4	12	5	13	5	15
Alcohol law violations						
All others	7	12	6	7	6	7
Percent females paroled	7		6		7	

Source: Data for 1968–70 from *Uniform Parole Reports.* Davis, Calif.: National Council on Crime and Delinquency Research Center.

be paroled; among the women, it was those who were convicted of fraud and forgery.

These findings appear curious in light of the fact that offenders in these categories have been among those who have been the least successful parolees. But, it is also true that among male prisoners, burglars comprise the largest single category, except for drug offenders (California data); and for women prisoners, those convicted of forgery and fraud comprise the largest category, except for drug offenders. The decision to parole then must also be affected by the various proportions of prisoners who have been convicted of different types of offenses.

Note that in table 6.4 (p. 317) the ratio of women who were sentenced to prison for forgery and fraud compared to those sentenced for homicide is 2.5:1, and the ratio of women paroled from the forgery and fraud category compared with those from homicide is 2:1. Among the men who were sentenced to prison in California for burglary and homicide, the ratio is 2.8:1 in favor of burglary. Among those selected for parole the ratio is 4.2:1 in favor of burglary.

Thus, numbers alone are not likely to explain the parole decisions favoring male inmates who have been convicted of burglary. But for women, the size of the available pool of inmates may be a more important factor in determining which inmates are likely to be paroled. For both men and women, drug offenders appeared to be treated as special cases, whose chances of being paroled were much less than their proportions in the total prison population would have indicated.

In table 7.2, the percentage of parolees who maintained a successful parole career for 1 year, by type of offense for which they were originally committed is shown. (For example, among the almost 1,500 men who had been sentenced for homicide and were paroled in 1968, 88 percent maintained a successful parole for 1 year.) Note first, that the overall percentages of women who maintained successful paroles for at least 1 year are higher than they are for men—75 compared with 72 percent in 1968, 76 compared with 74 percent in 1969, and 77 compared with 70 percent in 1970.

Within most offense categories, save for violations of drug laws, a higher proportion of the women are continued on parole after 1 year than are the men.

The biggest and most consistent differences between men and women parolees occurred in the forgery and fraud and the drug violation categories. In forgery and fraud convictions, paroled women were more successful in staying out of prison than men, and in drug violations they were less successful.

When we compared the likelihood of men with that of women with drug histories gaining successful parole hearings (see table below), we found that

Percentage of men and women paroled with history of drug usage

Year	Men	Women
	12	32
1968	(23,746)	(1,644)
	15	34
1969	(25,472)	(1,668)
	18	37
1970	(25,582)	(1,710)

Table 7.2 **Percentage of offenders continued on parole for 1 year by sex and type of offense, 1968–70**[1]

OFFENSE CATEGORY	1968 Male (N = 20,855)	1968 Female (N = 1,575)	1969 Male (N = 21,654)	1969 Female (N = 1,563)	1970 Male (N = 21,845)	1970 Female (N = 1,609)
Homicide	88	91	89	93	87	92
Manslaughter	87	88	89	93	89	93
Armed robbery	74	70	75	71	78	82
Aggravated assault	76	82	80	77	79	78
Burglary	70	71	71	71	73	72
Theft or larceny	72	74	72	76	73	74
Forgery & fraud	64	73	66	71	65	74
Drug law violations	73	66	78	68	80	68
All others	74	68	73	69	75	76
All offenses	72	75	74	76	70	77

Source: Data for 1968–70 from *Uniform Parole Reports*. Davis, Calif.: National Council on Crime and Delinquency Research Center.

[1] Includes parolees not continued on parole.

more than twice the percentage of women who were paroled had such histories as did men.

But women with drug histories turned out to be the poorer parole risks: they were less likely to remain out of prison than were women who had no history of drug usage or than men who also had histories of drug usage (see table 7.3).

A history of drug usage is a better predictor of successful parole for women than it is for men (see table 7.3). When there is no history of drug usage, a higher proportion of women maintain successful paroles for at least 1 year.

We also compared the successful paroles of men and women by their histories of prior commitments. As shown by the percentages in table 7.4, men and women who had no previous prison terms prior to their parole were much more likely to have successful paroles than were parolees who had at least one prior commitment. There was no difference between the men and women who had no prior commitments as to the proportion who stayed out for at least 1 year. But having served time on at least one prior occasion reduced the likelihood (more than it did for men) that women would maintain successful paroles. A smaller proportion of the women with prior commitments remained out of prison than did men with prior commitments.

One explanation for this phenomenon may be that men are more rigorously screened than are women at the time of the parole hearing. Women are released in part because of their roles in the larger society; but men must demonstrate that they have been rehabilitated and can support themselves. Another explanation may be that parole officers expect women to adhere to higher standards of behavior than they do men, and therefore, women's paroles are likely to be terminated for behavior that would result only in a reprimand for men. Behaving properly and in conformity with society's standards is expected of the female more than it is of the male.

To summarize, the proportion of women who were paroled in 1968–70, about 7 percent, was only slightly higher than the proportion of women inmates in Federal and State institutions, about 5 percent. Once paroled, women seem to fare slightly better than men in being able to remain out of

Table 7.3 **Percentage of offenders continued on parole by sex and history of drug use, 1968–70**

YEAR AND SEX	HISTORY OF DRUG USE		NO HISTORY OF DRUG USE	
	Number	Percent	Number	Percent
1968:				
Male	2,961	64	20,785	74
Female	526	60	1,118	81
1969:				
Male	3,891	66	21,581	75
Female	573	61	1,095	83
1970:				
Male	4,688	70	20,894	76
Female	639	65	1,071	85

Source: Data for 1968–70 from *Uniform Parole Reports*. Davis, Calif.: National Council on Crime and Delinquency Research Center.

Table 7.4 **Percentage of parolees continued on parole by sex and prior prison term, 1968–70**

YEAR AND SEX	NO PRIOR PRISON TERM		1 PRIOR PRISON TERM		2 OR MORE PRISON TERMS	
	Number	Percent	Number	Percent	Number	Percent
1968:						
Male	15,160	77	4,578	68	2,087	64
Female	1,311	78	228	60	105	50
1969:						
Male	16,395	78	4,881	71	4,287	64
Female	1,366	78	221	66	82	60
1970:						
Male	17,062	79	4,519	72	4,021	65
Female	1,401	79	215	68	94	67

Source: Data for 1968–70 from *Uniform Parole Reports*. Davis, Calif.: National Council on Crime and Delinquency Research Center.

prison. There are two categories that are exceptions for women: those with a history of drug use and those with a history of prior commitments. Women in both of these categories have less successful paroles than do men. Whether it is because society places higher standards on them or because they break the rules of their parole more frequently than do men cannot be discerned from these data.

Part five
Women offenders: A cross-cultural perspective

At the fifth United Nations Congress on the Prevention of Crime and the Treatment of Offenders, the legislative bodies of the United Nations were told that:

> Among the more notable changes in forms and dimensions of criminality were recent changes in female criminality in various countries. Because there were no accurate and internationally comparable data on female criminality, there was agreement on the need for considerably more research and more internationally comparable research data before any universally valid conclusions could be reached and planning initiated.
>
> The available evidence indicated that in a number of nonsocialist developed countries the female crime rate had increased much faster than the male crime rate during the past decade, and changed police practices alone could not account for this. However, the opposite phenomenon had occurred in other countries under similar conditions. There seemed to be agreement that participation of women in the development of their countries was not a criminogenic factor. In some countries, on the other hand, an increase in female crime rates could perhaps be attributed to lack of opportunities to participate fully in socio-economic life.[1]

In response to this mandate for more information, the Secretariat included a number of questions pertaining to the incidence of female criminality throughout the world in its general questionnaire to all member states of the United Nations. The survey was designed to monitor world crime trends and crime prevention policies from 1970 to 1975. As of the publication date of this book, over sixty governments had responded, forty-five of them including data on female criminality.[2] Over half these countries reported an increase of both male and female criminality. Seven countries reported a rise in female criminality with either stable, downward, or erratic trends in male criminality. The trend figures show that in 1970 one crime in ten was committed by a female offender, while in 1975, it was one in eight. This increase is accounted for by both a decrease in the male offender rate and an increase in the female offender rate.

The selections in Part Five report on the participation of women in crime in countries with various kinds of political and economic development. One interesting question they raise is whether there are similarities in the changing criminal involvement of women across countries. A second and related question is whether there is any correspondence between patterns of criminal involvement and kinds, or stages, of socioeconomic and political development. The Simon and Sharma article reports data showing that percentages of women involved in crime are generally higher in the United States and in Western European countries than in the less economically developed countries of Asia, Africa, and the Caribbean. The distribution of crimes shows that the United States and the Western European countries continue to rank high in larceny and fraud categories, a result consistent with the hypothesis that as women enjoy increasing social and economic opportunities, and move into commercial and white-collar positions, they also engage increasingly in property and economic offenses.

There are special problems with cross-cultural study, however, which make comparative statistics, even of the type reported by Simon and Sharma, difficult to assess. Research requires familiarity with notions of what is criminal in different justice systems and understanding of the reasons why women may or may not engage in crime in different cultural contexts. It also requires taking into account the biases of different reporting procedures. Thus, reports of an increasing arrest rate for women in the United States and decreasing or fluctuating rates in Israel and Japan, as given in the Simon and Sharma selection, may lead to puzzling questions. Simon and Sharma ask if their findings about Japan, where "labor force participation is inversely and erratically related to criminal participation among women," raise questions only about that country, or whether they suggest that female status indicators are only spuriously related to female crime patterns more generally.

If it is difficult to obtain data in more bureaucratic, information-conscious countries like the United States, the problems are compounded elsewhere. The Lopez-Rey excerpt, which reports male predominance in crime internationally and considers the recent slow female increase, refers to the difficulty of obtaining even rudimentary male-female classifications in certain countries. In India, for example, Lopez-Rey finds that only scattered information about female crime among juvenile offenders is collected. In the United Arab Republic, police data are not available, and judicial statistics make no reference to female offenders. In the UAR, as in many countries, the most reliable and available data are prison statistics. The very nature of such limited sources biases what can be known and requires perhaps more inventive thinking than might otherwise be needed on the part of people who work in this field.

The historical experience of research on women in crime cited in Part One of this volume suggested the distortions that can occur when classifications are assigned to prison populations in attempts to determine retrospectively why some women commit crimes. It also spoke of the ways in which ideas, in a field where there are so few, can gain and maintain prominence for relatively long times. The dangers of mislabeling across cultural boundaries are in this light especially to be noted.

Cross-cultural study seems to involve not only the piecing together by researchers of what little evidence is available but also an awareness on their part of the basic parameters of social and economic change and the concomitant change in the roles and statuses of women. Researchers must then relate this awareness to the possibilities for involvement in crime and to the particular cultural norms that may encourage or discourage such involvement on the part of women. Something of this process is attempted in the Adler selection, which analyzes trends in the increasing participation of women in crime in different countries. Adler finds that in countries where women enjoy a high degree of equality with men, there have been steady increases in female crime. This situation contrasts with that in countries where the social gap between the sexes remains great. Yet developing countries are not immune to the phenomenon of rising female crime. Adler considers the special problems of women moving from rural to urban life, hypothesizing that the accompanying stress may encourage women to engage in more crime. But in the absence of sufficient findings to support that thesis, she reasons that cultural controls in some countries, for some time at least, may operate to limit criminal activity. The Adler selection, like those by Simon and Sharma and Lopez-Rey, runs into problems of lack of data and limits of reasoning, yet it suggests, as do the others, that the difficulties may be as important as they are perplexing.

Notes

1. Fifth United Nations Congress on the Prevention of Crime and the Treatment of Offenders, Department of Economic and Social Affairs, New York, United Nations, 1976.

2.
Female Crime Trends (1970–1975)

Up	Mauritius	Federal Republic	*Erratic*
Argentina	Morocco	of Germany	Costa Rica
Australia	New Zealand	Greece	Denmark
Bahamas	Norway	Jamaica	Kuwait
Bahrain	Oman	San Marino	Malaysia
Canada	Pakistan	Switzerland	Poland
Chile	Peru	Syria	Quatar
Ecuador	Spain		Yugoslavia
El Salvador	United Kingdom	*Down*	
Finland	United States of America	Algeria	
Guyana		Cyprus	
Indonesia	*Stable*	Iraq	
Italy		Ireland	
Japan	Austria	Trinidad and Tobago	
Maldives	Barbados	Turkey	

33 Women and Crime: Does the American Experience Generalize?

Rita James Simon and Navin Sharma

On the occasion of the Hamlyn Lectures at Sheffield University, in 1963, Lady Barbara Wootton observed:

> It is perhaps rather curious that no serious attempt has yet been made to explain the remarkable facts of the sex ratio in detected criminality; for the scale of the sex differential far outranks all the other tracts (except that of age in the case of indictable offenses) which have been supposed to distinguish the delinquent from the nondelinquent population. It seems to be one of those facts which escape notice by virtue of its very conspicuousness. It is surely, to say the least, very odd that half the population should be apparently immune to the criminogenic factors which lead to the downfall of so significant a proportion of the other half. Equally odd is it, too, that although the criminological experience of different countries varies considerably, nevertheless the sex differential remains.[1]

A lot has happened in the fifteen years since Lady Wootton made these remarks. Indeed, in the 1970s, women have come to symbolize what blacks and the civil rights movement symbolized for American society in the early 1960s, and what students and the New Left symbolized in the late 1960s. Women have organized themselves into a social movement that has demanded better jobs, broader opportunities, a bigger chunk of the political pie, and greater visibility in educational, religious, and social institutions. They have demanded changes in the law, and an amendment to the Constitution that would guarantee them equality in all spheres of public life.

Greater visibility and participation in criminal activities on the part of women may be one of the unintended by-products of the women's movement.

Source: Original contribution.

Not only has the movement provided a rhetoric that has emphasized similarities between the sexes, and an image of the female that legitimates her desire to compete with men in business, political, and educational worlds, but it has also been effective in getting women to move from the kitchen or the typing pool to the executive suite or the lecture hall. Once women have started thinking about these issues, moving to implement those thoughts, and working at changing their images and lifestyles, it should not be surprising that some would seek short cuts to monetary success and independence through deviant careers.

The FBI arrest statistics, which are compiled on a regular basis and have been published every year since the early 1930s, indicate that there has been an increase in women's participation in crime. As figures in Table 1 (p. 395) describe, women's involvement in crime, especially in serious crime, has been on the increase since 1958. But the biggest increases have occurred in the past decade. The figures in Table 1 also show that the increases have been mostly in property rather than violent offenses.

The popular impression that in recent years women have been committing crimes of violence at a much higher rate than they have in the past is disputed by the statistics in Table 1. In fact, the increase in the proportion of arrests of women for serious crimes is due almost wholly to the increase in property offenses. Indeed, the percentage of women arrested for crimes of violence shows neither an upward nor a downward trend. Thus, the news item that, in 1970, four out of the ten fugitives most wanted by the FBI were women must be juxtaposed against those statistics, which tell quite a different story.

The percentages for property offenses, however, show that big changes have occurred. In 1974, 1 in 4.8 persons arrested was a woman. Not only has there been a consistent increase in the percentage of women who have been arrested for property offenses, the biggest increases have occurred in the period starting with 1967. This last finding is congruent with our major hypothesis—that women's participation in selective crimes will increase both as their employment opportunities expand and as their interests, desires, and definitions of self shift from a more traditional to a more liberated view. The crimes that are considered most salient for this hypothesis are various types of property, financial, and white-collar offenses.

Table 2 (p. 396) describes women's participation in specific offense categories that are included in the index of serious offenses (type 1 offenses). Note that among all six offenses, only one shows a marked increase over time. After 1960, the proportion of women who have been charged with larceny or theft in any given year is much greater than is the proportion in any of the other offense categories, property as well as violent. It is interesting to note that until about 1960 the percentage of women who were arrested for homicide and aggravated assault was similar to those arrested for larceny, but in 1974 the percentage in the larceny category doubled the 1960 percentage; whereas from 1960 on, the percentages have remained roughly the same for the homicide and aggravated assault offenses.

In addition to larceny, the following figures indicate that in the past decade there has been a big increase in the percentage of women arrested for embezzlement and fraud, and forgery. In 1974, approximately 1 in 3.5 persons arrested for forgery was a woman, and 1 in 3 arrests for embezzlement and fraud involved a woman.

Year	Embezzlement and fraud	Forgery and counterfeiting
1953	18.3	14.0
1954	14.4	13.4
1955	15.6	15.2
1956	15.5	16.6
1957	14.4	14.8
1958	14.3	15.1
1959	14.9	16.2
1960	15.7	16.8
1961	15.7	17.5
1962	17.6	18.1
1963	18.3	18.7
1964	19.5	19.3
1965	20.7	19.2
1966	21.8	20.9
1967	23.4	21.4
1968	24.4	22.3
1969	26.3	23.2
1970	27.8	24.4
1971	27.4	24.8
1972	29.7	25.4
1973	31.2	26.7
1974	32.6	28.6

What all these statistics indicate is that the proportion of women who were arrested in 1974 was greater than the proportion arrested one or two decades earlier, and that the increase has been caused almost entirely by women's greater participation in larceny, embezzlement, fraud, forgery, and counterfeiting. The increases were especially marked for the period from 1967 to 1974. None of the other offenses showed as big a shift as did these property and white-collar types of offenses. If the average rate of change that occurred between 1967 and 1974 continues, female arrest rates for larceny, embezzlement, and fraud will be commensurate to women's representation in the society, or, in other words, roughly equal to male arrest rates. There are no other offenses among those contained in the uniform crime reports, save prostitution, in which females are so highly represented. And among women arrested for all crimes every year, the proportion arrested for prostitution is on the decline.

Can the American experience be generalized? Are more women in other parts of the world committing more crimes than they had been, and is there a pattern to the types of crimes they are committing that is similar to the American pattern? Comparison of female arrest statistics in the United States with female arrest data collected by the International Police Organization for twenty-five countries in 1963, 1968, 1970, and 1972 shows that the United States has moved from twelfth place in 1963 to ninth place in 1968 and 1970 to fifth place in 1972.[2] The data also show that the percentage of women involved in crime is generally high in Western European societies, compared with the less economically developed countries of Asia, Africa, and the Caribbean, which show considerable variation among themselves. For example, the percentage of females arrested among arrestees for all crimes for the four time periods looked like this:

Percentage of females arrested

West Indies	20.90	Luxembourg	16.38
Finland	6.66	Jamaica	15.46
Austria	13.75	France	14.25
Japan	9.69	Netherlands	10.25
Fiji	2.67	Tunisia	13.06
Israel	11.71	Scotland	11.53
New Zealand	20.56	Hong Kong	2.76
Thailand	17.38	Tanzania	6.85
Korea	10.51	England and Wales	13.61
Canada	9.77	Cyprus	6.38
Monaco	7.00	Malawi	4.27
West Germany	16.66	United States	13.66
Brunei	2.02		

For property and financial crimes such as larceny and fraud, the United States ranks second and first, respectively. Countries that rank directly above and below are those of Western Europe, such as West Germany, Austria, France, and the Netherlands. For crimes of violence and drugs, American women rank fifth and are surrounded by a more heterogeneous collection of countries, including the West Indies, Korea, West Germany, England-Wales, Scotland, and Canada. The positions of the United States and the countries of Western Europe in the larceny and fraud rankings are consistent with the hypothesis that in those societies in which women are more likely to be employed in commercial and white-collar positions and to enjoy legal and social rights they are also more likely to engage in property and economic types of crimes.

Table 3 provides a summary of the trend for overall female arrests as well as for the major crime categories. The numbers indicate the average rate of change in female participation from 1963 to 1972. They also show that there is no consistent pattern in the overall crime rates or for most of the specific crime categories. Only for acts involving larceny does there appear to be a consistently upward trend among the more industrialized and commercial countries.

Still pursuing a comparative framework, we want to cite some findings based on an earlier work in which we examined the relationship between female crime rates and selective indicators of women's status in the United States, Israel, and Japan. We think that Israel and Japan provide useful and interesting bases of comparison with the United States because of their social,

Table 1 **Percentage of females arrested for all crimes, for all serious crimes, and for serious violent and property crimes: 1953–1974[1]**

YEAR	ALL CRIMES	SERIOUS CRIMES[2]	VIOLENT CRIMES	PROPERTY CRIMES
1953	10.84	9.40	11.93	8.46
1954	10.97	8.89	11.60	8.18
1955	11.00	9.12	12.03	9.12
1956	10.91	9.06	13.51	8.04
1957	10.63	9.29	13.06	8.51
1958	10.61	9.73	11.96	9.26
1959	10.68	10.54	12.73	10.07
1960	11.04	10.95	11.77	10.76
1961	11.26	11.47	11.61	11.44
1962	11.47	12.38	11.51	12.57
1963	11.68	12.65	11.56	12.87
1964	11.93	13.54	11.64	13.92
1965	12.12	14.37	11.41	14.99
1966	12.33	14.80	11.32	15.58
1967	12.67	15.03	10.79	16.00
1968	13.08	15.04	10.33	16.11
1969	13.82	16.58	10.63	17.96
1970	14.58	18.04	10.50	19.71
1971	15.07	18.34	10.91	20.06
1972	15.27	19.25	11.01	21.35
1973	15.3	18.7	10.2	21.1
1974	16.1	19.0	10.2	21.2
Average rate of change, 1953–1974	+0.25	+0.46	−0.08	+0.44
Average rate of change, 1958–1974	+0.34	+0.58	−0.08	+0.58
Average rate of change, 1967–1974	+0.49	+0.57	−0.08	+0.74

Source: Data for 1953–1974 from *Uniform Crime Reports.* Washington, D.C.: U.S. Department of Justice, Federal Bureau of Investigation.

1. Arrest data for cities with populations 2,500 and above.

2. Serious crimes, according to the *Uniform Crime Reports* published by the FBI, are criminal homicide (murder, nonnegligent manslaughter, and manslaughter by negligence), forcible rape, robbery, aggravated assault, burglary, larceny, and auto theft. We have omitted forcible rape from our calculations because women are never charged with such an offense.

economic, and cultural characteristics. Japan represents a non-Western (in a religious and cultural as well as geographical sense) society that has undergone rapid industrialization. It is today a modern, highly urbanized society. Israel is less developed economically but shares with the United States many of the cultural and religious values of Western civilization. Both Israel and Japan have in common the fact that after World War II they underwent profound changes in their national identities and in their socioeconomic and demographic characteristics.

When we compared arrest statistics from the three countries, we found that the arrest rate per 100,000 women in the United States for all crimes has shown a marked increase over the years, but that in Japan it was lower in

Table 2 **Females arrested as a percentage of all arrests for various type 1 offenses, 1953–1974**

YEAR	CRIMINAL HOMICIDE	ROBBERY	AGGRAVATED ASSAULT	BURGLARY	LARCENY-THEFT	AUTO THEFT
1953	14.1	4.3	15.9	2.0	13.9	2.6
1954	14.2	4.2	15.9	2.2	13.0	2.5
1955	14.2	4.2	16.0	2.3	13.3	2.6
1956	14.8	4.3	17.6	2.3	12.6	2.5
1957	14.7	3.9	17.5	2.0	13.2	2.7
1958	16.4	4.5	15.7	2.4	14.3	3.2
1959	16.8	4.6	16.4	2.7	15.4	3.2
1960	16.1	4.6	15.3	2.8	16.8	3.6
1961	15.9	4.9	15.2	3.2	18.0	3.7
1962	17.2	5.1	14.7	3.6	19.6	3.9
1963	15.9	4.9	14.9	3.3	20.1	3.7
1964	16.6	5.3	14.4	3.7	21.4	4.3
1965	16.3	5.3	14.4	3.8	23.2	4.2
1966	15.9	5.1	14.0	3.8	24.0	4.1
1967	15.4	5.2	13.6	4.1	24.8	4.3
1968	15.4	5.5	13.1	4.1	25.2	4.9
1969	14.8	6.3	13.2	4.3	27.2	5.1
1970	14.8	6.2	13.3	4.6	29.0	5.0
1971	16.0	6.4	13.9	4.8	29.1	6.0
1972	15.6	6.6	13.9	5.1	30.8	5.7
1973	15.1	6.8	13.2	5.4	31.5	6.0
1974	14.6	6.8	13.4	5.4	30.7	6.5
Average rate of change, 1953–1974	+0.02	+0.12	−0.12	+0.16	+0.80	+0.19
Average rate of change, 1958–1974	−0.11	+0.14	−0.14	+0.19	+1.02	+0.24
Average rate of change, 1967–1974	−0.11	+0.23	−0.03	+0.19	+0.84	+0.31

Source: Data for 1953–1974 from *Uniform Crime Reports.* Washington, D.C.: U.S. Department of Justice, Federal Bureau of Investigation.

Note: Rape has been omitted.

Table 3 **Average rate of change of female percentages among arrests, 1963–1972**

Country	All Crimes	Murder	Major Larceny	Minor Larceny	Fraud and Forgery	Drugs
Finland[1]	-0.08	+1.00	-0.21	+0.39	-0.09	—
Austria	-0.08	-0.50	-0.16	+0.72	-0.39	+0.52
Japan	+1.09	+0.57	+0.15	+0.37	-0.51	-1.74
Israel	-0.08	-0.32	-0.08	+0.38	+0.51	-0.02
New Zealand[1]	+4.19	-0.20	+0.38	+1.90	+0.04	+1.35
Canada[1]	+1.20	+0.03	+0.15	+0.78	+0.56	-2.46
Monaco	-0.01	—	—	+0.49	-2.24	—
West Germany	+0.19	-0.64	-0.06	+1.48	+1.53	-0.87
Luxembourg	-0.83	+1.96	-0.01	-0.03	+0.55	-2.95
France	+0.44	-0.40	-0.01	+0.27	+0.65	+0.67
Netherlands	-0.13	-0.85	+0.08	+0.37	-0.18	-0.29[2]
Scotland	+0.15	-0.73	+0.08	+0.22	-0.11	—
Hong Kong	-0.11	-0.19	-0.23	-0.09	-0.35	-0.11
England and Wales	-0.03	+0.23	+0.04	+0.11	-0.36	—
West Indies	-2.04	+2.00	—	+0.70	+7.00	—
Thailand[1]	+1.38	-1.10	-0.82	—	-0.08	-0.17
Korea	-0.01	-1.06	-0.31	-0.29	+0.41	+0.68
Brunei[1]	-0.04	—	—	—	—	—
Jamaica[1]	+0.30	-1.67	+2.36	+0.37	+2.17	+1.51
Tunisia	+0.05	-2.64	+0.37	-0.25	+0.40	-0.11
Tanzania[1]	+0.15	+1.32	+0.19	+0.02	+0.17	—
Cyprus	-0.16	—	+0.16	-0.30	-0.11	—
Malawi	-0.03[1]	-0.20	+0.27	+0.01	+0.42	+0.54
Fiji	-0.09	+0.57	-0.03	-0.01	+0.55	+0.08

Note: Blanks in the table indicate that figures were not available for a long enough period to compute rates.

1. Based on figures from 1963 to 1970.
2. Based on figures from 1968 to 1972.

1972 than it was in 1953, and in Israel it seemed to fluctuate in a cyclical manner. Only in the United States did we find that the arrest rate for women had been going up. We found no evidence in any of the three societies that females were increasing their participation in violent offenses. In 1960, 14 percent of all violent crimes in Israel involved women, and in 1974, 12 percent involved women. In Japan in 1953, 2 percent of all those arrested for violent offenses were women, and in 1972, the percentage was also 2.[3] For property offenses, we found that Japan's trend was similar to that observed in the United States, namely, that between 1953 and 1972, the percentage of those arrested increased from 9 to 23.[4] In Israel, on the other hand, the percentage arrested for property offenses in 1960 was 7.8, and in 1974 it was 6.6. Both countries also have a designation for economic offenses that in Japan includes forgery, embezzlement, and fraud. In Israel, it includes fraud and embezzlement. For the United States we combined the crimes of fraud, embezzlement, forgery, and counterfeiting and designated them economic offenses. When we then compared female crime rates for those offenses in the three countries, we found that only in the United States was there a big increase: from 16 percent in 1953 to 32 percent in 1975. In Japan, there was a slight downward trend, from 7.6 percent in 1953 to 6.8 percent in 1972. In Israel in 1960, the percentage was 6.6, and in 1970 it was 7.

At the beginning, we suggested that American trends in female criminality are consistent with the changing role of women in American society and with an ethos that lessens the strength of traditional constraints on criminal behavior among women. We said that as women become liberated from hearth and home and become more involved in full-time jobs, they are more likely to engage in criminal activities. In particular, increased female criminal activity should be expected to occur first in those crimes that women either have increased opportunity or increased propensity to commit because of the objective conditions of their lives. Thus, as more women participate in a milieu in which they either decide to be economically self-sufficient or are forced to provide for themselves, we would expect to see a greater number of women committing economic and property types of offenses.

Two specific phenomena that would suggest an increased propensity for women to commit larceny and white-collar offenses would be larger proportions of females in the labor force and larger proportions of females as heads of households. As many more women are employed and are the sole means of support for themselves and for others, both their opportunities and their motives for committing serious property crime are likely to increase. Greater female participation in new and competitive occupational roles may also cause women to internalize a new set of values that places fewer constraints on criminal behavior than did their traditional role expectations. These changes may also explain why women are more likely to commit property offenses than violent offenses.

Typically, women's participation in violent criminal acts has arisen from the frustrations, the subservience, and the degradation that have characterized the traditional female role. Case histories of women who kill reveal one pattern that dominates all others. When women can no longer contain their frustrations and their anger, they express themselves by doing away with the cause of their condition, which most often is a man, sometimes a child, or an unborn baby. But as women's educational and employment opportunities expand, their subjection to traditional female roles decreases (as witnessed by the presence of more liberalized divorce laws and greater opportunities for legal abortion), their feelings of being victimized and exploited cease to be directed at a particular individual (or individuals), and their motivation to kill becomes muted.

A brief look at the proportion of women in the labor force on a full-time basis in the three countries shows that in the United States in 1972, women constituted 38 percent of the labor force as compared with 33 percent in 1960. In Israel, 27.4 percent of the labor force was female in 1972, compared with 25.6 percent in 1960. In Japan in 1972, women constituted 38.3 percent of the employed labor force, compared with 40.6 percent in 1960. Only in the United States, then, has there been a big increase in the proportion of women in the labor force on a full-time basis. In Israel, there has been an upward trend, but not a steep one, and closer inspection reveals that the increase occurred only among unmarried women. In Japan, there has been a decrease in the proportion of women employed in the labor force.

From necessarily limited sources of data, we compared the relationship between labor force status and economic independence with selected crime categories. We obtained time-series data on the proportion of females employed in selected occupations (those that seemed roughly comparable across the three countries) and correlated them with the arrest statistics. In addition, for the United States, we obtained the number of female heads of families as a percentage of all heads of families and the number of single female heads of households as a percentage of all single heads of households.

In the United States, the representation of women in the labor force (measured as a percentage of the total labor force) seems to be closely associated with the representation of women in crime. For all crimes together, the correlation coefficient is .92; for property crimes it is .97; for economic offenses it is .95; and for violent crime it is .70. The same pattern of relationship was found when we correlated these same crimes with the number of female heads of families and female single heads of households. By contrast, in Japan, labor force participation is inversely and erratically related to criminal participation among women. For all crimes, the correlation coefficient is −.90; for violent crimes it is −.33; for property offenses it is −.92; and for economic offenses it is −.38. A similar pattern emerges in Israel (for violent crimes the correlation coefficient is −.33; for property offenses it is −.56; and for economic crimes it is −.25) except that the overall crime rate for women does seem to be positively related to labor force participation.[5]

Of the three countries, the United States is the only one thus far to experience a movement for women's liberation that has attracted widespread support (at least among middle-class women). The rhetoric and the political agenda of that movement are concerned most directly with expanding women's occupational opportunities, enhancing their sociopolitical status, and making them more visible in institutions, organizations, and movements that hitherto ignored them or discriminated against them. The fact that in such a society, during such a period, there should be both a significant increase in full-time labor force participation and an increase in property and economic crimes on the part of women seems consistent and predictable.

The fact that such activities are not occurring in Israel also appears consistent and logical, since women's participation in the labor force has not increased, nor has there been much support for a women's liberation movement.

The fact that a movement for women's liberation has not developed in Japan on a large scale, and the fact that there has not been an increase in the proportion of women employed outside the home on a full-time basis, but that there has been a big increase in women's participation in property offenses makes the Japanese case more puzzling and less consistent than the American and Israeli ones. The case of Japan also raises the question of the nature of the relationship between female status indicators and changing patterns of female criminality. Could it be that female status indicators are only spuriously related to female crime patterns in the United States? Or could it be that different forces are at work in different countries? We need to reassess notions of the relationship between industrialization, modernization, and crime, in view of the fact that crime rates for both men and women in Japan are declining. Perhaps also the question of definitions of different types of crime in countries needs to be studied more closely, although we have tried to minimize the differences in classification in this analysis.

At this stage, more detailed information is needed from different types of societies on female labor force participation and other socioeconomic indicators that may be related to overall female crime rates and to types of criminal activities. Such data from a variety of countries representing different cultural and religious values, levels of economic development, and types of social institutions would also help to separate specific national trends from more general trends in women's roles in crime.

Notes

1. Lady Barbara Wootton, "A Magistrate in Search of the Causes of Crimes," *Crime and Criminal Law*, 1963, pp. 6–8.
2. We must emphasize, as do the editors of this book, the limitations of data from *International Crime Statistics*. The statistics cannot take into account differences in legal definitions of offenses from one nation to another; nor can it be assumed that the data from each country are equally reliable. For this reason, cross-country comparisons of simple arrest rates are questionable. However, broad comparisons of trends over time for various countries can be meaningful. *See* International Police Organization (Interpol), *International Crime Statistics, 1965–66*, pp. 11–13.
3. Violent crimes in Japan include homicide, robbery, bodily injury. In Israel they include murder, manslaughter, robbery, bodily harm.
4. Property offenses in Japan include only theft. In Israel, property offenses include theft, burglary, property damage, and receiving or possessing stolen property.
5. While the positive association between labor force participation and violent crime participation in the United States seems contrary to our hypothesis, when we analyze the relationship of specific crimes in this category, we find negative correlations between labor force participation and murder and aggravated assault, and positive relations with robbery and manslaughter. Since robbery involves economic motives, this finding lends further weight to our hypothesis, along with the two negative correlations for murder and aggravated assault.

34 The Expansion and Distribution of Crime
Manuel Lopez-Rey

Demographic data show that in the vast majority of countries the population is almost equally divided between male and female; the most significant exception is the U.S.S.R., where women still outnumber men by several millions. But the participation of men in crime far exceeds that of women. The excess varies according to the different stage at which crime is dealt with; as a rule, it rises from police to court and from court to prison statistics. Unfortunately, police data are not always available, hence the more frequent use of judicial and prison data. For brevity, as far as male-female ratios are concerned round figures are used.

In England 'and Wales in 1957 and 1967 the male-female ratio of persons cautioned by the police for indictable offences was 6 and 4 to 1 respectively. The average per 100,000 of the corresponding population was 81 and 124 male to 13 and 32 female respectively. In 1957 females over 8 years of age outnumbered males of the same age by 1,700,000, and in 1967 females over 10 years of age outnumbered the males by 1,200,000. In the same years the male-female ratio of persons found guilty in all courts was 8 and 6 to 1 respectively. However, the ratio varies when specific indictable offences are considered. In offences against the person, the male-female ratio in 1957 and 1967 was 19 and 17 to 1; in sexual offences, 103 and 132 to 1; receiving, frauds and false pretences, 6 and 7 to 1; breaking and entering, 43 and 40 to 1; and 5 to 1 in both years in the case of larceny. On the other hand, there are some specific offences in which females found guilty usually outnumber males. Such is the case with infanticide, cruelty to children, abandoning children under 2 years of age, procuring abortion, concealment of birth, larceny from shops and stalls and brothel-keeping. As a curious contrast, men far exceed women in cruelty to animals and, what is more significant, in malicious wounding, causing death by dangerous driving, as well as in reckless or dangerous driving. As for prisoners under sentence, Borstals and detention centres included, the male-female ratio, with some reservations owing to the different presentation of data, was in both years virtually the same, 25 to 1.

In the Federal Republic of Germany in the period 1963–67 the average male-female ratio in adult crime dealt with by the police was 7 to 1. The male-female ratio in 1965 for persons convicted by courts was 8 to 1. In the prison population at the end of 1966 and 1967 the male-female ratio was virtually the same, 23 to 1. In France in 1965 the ratio among persons found guilty by the courts was 10 to 1. The ratio for the prison population in 1966 and 1967 was 23 and 25 to 1 respectively. In Belgium the average male-female ratio of persons found guilty in the period 1956–65 was 5 to 1. In the prison population the male-female ratio in August 1967 and August 1968 was 17 and 20 to 1 respectively. In Spain the ratio among those brought to trial before the courts in 1965 was 10 to 1; with some fluctuations, it has been the same since 1954. If anything, there is a slight downward trend in the last few years. For sentenced persons, the male-female ratio in 1965 was 16 to 1. In 1966 and 1967 the male-female ratio of sentenced prisoners in the prison population was 20 and 22 to 1, and of prisoners awaiting trial 22 and 28 to 1 respectively. In Italy in 1965 the male-female ratio of sentenced persons was 5 to 1, and in the prison population 18 to 1. In Switzerland the male-female ratio of persons found guilty of criminal offences in 1966 was 6 to 1. In Norway in 1966 among persons charged by the police it was 10 to 1, for persons found guilty by the courts in the period 1963–65 it was 11 to 1. In Yugoslavia in 1964 among sentenced adults and juvenile offenders it was 3 and 10 to 1 respectively.

In the United States in 1967 male arrests outnumbered female arrests by 7 to 1, but the latter rose by 7 per cent while male arrests rose only 4 per cent. Females were arrested in 14 per cent of murder, robbery, aggravated assault, burglary, larceny and automobile theft. Their involvement was primarily for larceny, which accounted for more than 1 of every 6 female arrests; they accounted for 21 per cent of the forgery, 23 per cent of the fraud and 19 per cent of the embezzlement arrests. Long-term trends between 1960 and 1967 reveal that arrests for females under 18 years of age rose 71 per cent for automobile theft and 76 per cent for burglary. While the arrests of young males greatly outnumbered those of females during this same period, nevertheless the percentage increases in both these offences were not so pronounced: 53 per cent for automobile theft and 40 per cent for burglary. In the case of aggravated assault, arrests of males outnumbered those of females by almost 7 to 1. Nationwide the ratio of arrests for murder was more than 5 males to 1 female. Owing to the large number of illegal police arrests in the United States, statistical data on arrests are subject to caution, but they are significant enough to conclude that there is an obvious gap between male and female crime. In Canada in 1966 the male-female ratio of persons charged by the police was 10 to 1 in the case of adults and 7 to 1 among juveniles. If only criminal code offences are considered, the ratio is 9 and 8 to 1 respectively. For persons found guilty by the courts, the ratio was nearly 8 to 1 in 1965. In Japan female crime has fluctuated considerably since 1964; the increase in the last few years is mainly due to negligent homicide and bodily injury in traffic accidents. The rate of criminal code offenders per 1,000 female population in 1966 was 1·4, while that of males in the last 20 years has fluctuated between 15 and 21. Admittedly, females are in general more leniently treated than males. In 1965, 70 per cent of females sentenced to imprisonment were given suspended sentences, against 50 per cent of males; those sent to prison in 1966 constituted only 3 per cent of the whole prison population. In Argentina in 1965 the male-female ratio of sentenced offenders was 15 to 1.

In most developing countries the male-female ratio is difficult to establish, either because statistics are not available or are unreliable, or, if available, they are quite often not classified by sex, partly because of the relatively small number of female offenders. This is the case with India, where only scattered information about female crime among juvenile offenders is available. Police data on female crime are not available in the United Arab Republic, and judicial statistics, although very useful, make no reference to female offenders. In this and other countries the most reliable—although not the most significant—data are prison statistics. The information gathered by the writer from official sources is good enough to give an idea of the extent of female crime. In the United Arab Republic in 1965 the ratio among sentenced prisoners was 9 to 1, and for those awaiting trial 12 to 1. In Jordan in the same year the prison male-female ratio was 45 to 1, and in Iran in 1966 among sentenced prisoners it was 40 to 1. No information was available on those awaiting trial.

The small proportion of female crime has often been denied. For years there has been a criminological fashion well represented by Otto Pollak's *The Criminality of Women* (1950), according to which female crime is masked as a result of a combination of factors, such as tolerance, lenience and women's ability to avoid detection. The expression *cherchez la femme* is still used to convey the idea that, if not as material authors, women are the hidden principals in the vast majority of crimes committed by men. It is said that, since women are participating more than ever in activities originally the preserve of men, eventually female crime will equal male crime. Undoubtedly there is some truth in all this; but the fact remains that even in well-developed countries where women participate in almost every aspect of life, their participation in crime is still small.

In order to be understood, the study of female crime requires the consideration of the following aspects: the real status of women in each country; the role of sex; the analysis of female crime and the bio-psychological characteristics of women and men. Here I shall content myself with some remarks which, owing to the interdependent character of the questions involved, may overlap in some respects:

Female crime

In dealing with female crime, a distinction should be made between its extent and its forms. It is obvious that the growing participation of women in activities previously monopolized by men and in social life in general has increased the volume of female crime, although it has never equalled male crime—first, because male crime also increases and, secondly, because the traditional female role prevents it. The data already produced for England and Wales demonstrates this. More specifically, the remarkable survey, *Studies of Female Offenders* (Home Office Research Unit, 1967), shows that, although there are some fluctuations, female crime is increasing steadily. In some cases, the analysis of data tends to support the thesis that this increase is due more to the socio-economic vulnerability of women than to anything else. This is particularly noticeable in the groups over 40 years of age. Of course, other factors must be taken into account, but in all probability that vulnerability is the most significant. In France a study conducted years ago and made available to the writer by Interpol shows that during the years 1955 and 1965 crime, including police and gendarmerie data, has steadily increased, but the increase among males is greater than among females. As for female juvenile offenders, a remarkable study conducted by the Centre of Research of Vaucresson shows that between 1953 and 1966 the volume of juvenile delinquency remained in the region of 4,000 every year.

It is true that police and courts are sometimes more lenient to women than to men, but the margins are too wide to be explained away so simply. It is probably true that it is more difficult to detect women in minor offences, such as small thefts and larceny from shops and stalls and some forms of fraud, but not in the case of serious offences, which, after all, are more important. What prevents detection in many cases is the smallness of the illegal appropriation, which is not reported because it is covered by insurance. The same happens with men in cases of larceny from houses and factories and from automatic machines and meters, as well as in frauds by agents, in which they far exceed women. Leniency by the police is only exercised in minor offences, and the same applies to men, although perhaps to a lesser extent. The leniency of the courts does not affect the number of offences known, but the greater use they make of suspended sentences, probation, fines and short-term imprisonment in favour of women.

The forms of crime traditionally assigned to women are abortion, infanticide, abandonment of infants, prostitution, theft and frauds. In developing countries, insults and defamation are also frequent. In the same way as the expression *cherchez la femme* is used to explain some male criminal offences, *cherchez l'homme* may explain many cases of abortion, infanticide and abandonment. Actually, in some cases the abortion has been envisaged in advance by both man and woman, and if not the male partner often provides the address or the money or both to procure the abortion. The fact that abortion has to be performed on women, and often by themselves or by another woman in the less-privileged groups, does not make it a typical female offence. Moreover, in some countries doctors, seldom women, specialize in abortion, whether in the country of residence of the women or in another where legislation is more tolerant or progressive. It is not true that abortion is difficult to detect; more often than not a number of persons know about it, but are reluctant to say anything, even in countries where religious beliefs are very much against it. Unless socio-economic reasons are admitted as a ground for abortion, the present legalization will reduce but not eradicate illegal abortion; it continues in both Sweden and Japan.

Only countries, such as the United States, which are still not parties to the United Nations Convention of 1950 regard prostitutes as criminal offenders. Since prostitution is a crime *à deux*, it is difficult to understand why only the woman is punished. The practice introduced in New York City some years ago of prosecuting men as well as women and the small number of men prosecuted shows how strong the crescive rules are. In brothel-keeping women usually outnumber men, but are in turn outnumbered in the traffic in persons and the exploitation of prostitution. In this respect, financing prostitution, one of the main activities of organized crime, is almost exclusively a male undertaking. In 1967, according to the *Uniform Crime Reports*, the percentage of women in commercialized vice and prostitution was 77. The amalgamation of both offences so clearly separated by the above-mentioned Convention gives a distorted picture of reality. In fact, in the United States commercialized vice is mostly a male preserve. In Britain the Street Offences Act, 1959, makes a 'common prostitute' of any woman who loiters in a street after a warning by a policeman. As has been said, the Act has merely 'swept under the carpet' something that should have been faced up to. By creating this curious type of offence, the crescive rules, which in most cases favour males, won a victory on behalf of what is commonly known as public morality. In 1967, 2,422 women were found guilty as 'common prostitutes' at the magistrates courts, but only 10 men for aiding, etc., offences by prostitutes. Needless to say, the less-privileged, fortunate or intelligent prostitutes constitute the majority of the short-termers sent to prison. This I was able to ascertain during my visit to Holloway in 1968. The frauds committed by women are increasing, but as a rule are far less serious than those committed by men.

Although not a typical female offence, cruelty to children is more frequent among women than among men, and this in spite of the more tender character assigned to maternal instincts. Whether the greater number of women offenders is due to personal characteristics of the mother involved, socio-economic conditions, that the child was unwanted or is difficult, or that there are too many cannot be discussed here. In all probability, each case involves a series of factors the action of which cannot easily be prevented without long assistance, supervision, etc. What is obvious is that generally the cases are more frequent among the less-privileged classes. Statistically their number is small, but in all probability the dark figure runs into the thousands even in developed countries. This touches the question whether, if known, criminal sanctions should be applied to those who ill-treat children. The answer is not easy, since the term 'battered children' is sometimes loosely interpreted. If by 'battering' is understood more than bruises, it is obvious that a criminal offence has been committed. The reasoning put forward that family life is highly emotional, that criminal law can destroy instead of rebuilding a child's family relationship—already destroyed in many cases—that guilt is difficult to prove, etc., cannot be entertained, first, because in one way or another many criminal offences imply the same if not greater emotional involvement, secondly, because criminal law is supposed to protect anyone, particularly the defenceless person brutally attacked, thirdly, because the hypothetical rebuilding will be difficult to achieve or merely temporary, and, finally, because the effectiveness of criminal law may not protect a child as it should while protecting many others who are victims of brutal parents. In this respect, whatever is said to the contrary, criminal law, like any other sort of regulation, has a preventive effect which, although not absolute, acts in many cases. Moreover, the condition of parent carries no privilege. The solution would be that as soon as battered children are detected, they should be taken away by the social services and criminal proceedings instituted later. I do not see any benefit for the child to keep him terrorized with the parents while these are convinced that they should be nice to him and the conditions generating the battering, some of them not easy to solve or requiring a long time, are remedied. The thesis that family environment is better than any other or that certain homes may be rebuilt should be revised, not for the benefit of criminal law or of the family, but of the individual, particularly when it is a child.

35 The Interaction Between Women's Emancipation and Female Criminality: A Cross-Cultural Perspective

Freda Adler

Keep strict watch over a headstrong daughter, lest, when she finds liberty, she use it to her hurt.

Ecclesiasticus, XXVI, 10

Traditionally, the perpetration of crime has been regarded as a male prerogative. Consistent with their restricted social roles, women had been relegated to the status of second-class criminals whose presence in the crime statistics was tolerated only in the categories of prostitution, shoplifting, and an occasional husband-poisoning. But the "second sex" has risen. This rise was accompanied by a fall in the double standard. Women have entered all categories of the crime statistics. It took a general social movement sweeping the world with egalitarian forces to provide women with the opportunity for a more equal footing in the criminal hierarchy. And it appears that women have used this opportunity.

Throughout history men have attempted to solve the mystery of the female, dealing with her as if she were a foreign species which did not have like needs for security and status. The real mystery would seem to revolve more appropriately around the issues of why and how this unawareness of basic motivations has persisted and why men have chosen to exaggerate the natural differences and to perpetuate century old myths. By post hoc–propter hoc reasoning dissimilar observed behaviors led to the untested conclusion that women must have inherently different motivations and goals. This reasoning forms mental sets which are difficult to extirpate because it safeguards the dominant structure of the male hierarchy, it shapes a perceptual-conceptual framework which tends to impose boundaries on observations and conjecture to premolded ideas, and, in addition, it serves as a security mechanism for

"The Interaction Between Women's Emancipation and Female Criminality: A Cross-Cultural Perspective" by Freda Adler. *International Journal of Criminology and Penology* (1977): 101–112.

those in the disadvantaged group. These ancient notions may have elevated the status of men but they were injurious to the women who accepted them for the most part without question.

But changes are taking place. Economic, political, medical, and technological advances have released women from unwanted pregnancies, unfettered them from kitchens and baby carriages, equipped them with male occupational skills, and equalized their strength with weapons. Women are now found amongst the ranks of admirals and sea-going sailors, heads of state and stevedores; there are female sky marshals and detectives; they can be seen driving tractor-trailer trucks and flying commercial airplanes; they have campaigned for and won powerful political positions all over the world, and they have even begun to enter the ranks of scholars and philosophers who create and test theories about women.

Indeed, these transitions are merely harbingers of what may become a massive world wide movement. Indicators of change are already identifiable in countries with widely divergent cultures and ideologies. In Brazil, for instance, the world's largest Roman Catholic country, where in August 1974, the requests for separation almost equaled the number of marriages, women are mounting pressures against divorce laws. In Cairo women are beginning to use baby-sitters and are even considering males for this traditionally female role.[1] In 1967 the press reported that, "although only a little over four years ago, Afghan women rarely set foot inside a mosque because, as many men said, 'their presence would interfere with sober prayer.' ... today ... that is all changed."[2] Korean farmers are replacing dowries with college education for their daughters, in Japan women have traded in their place three steps behind the male, for a place beside him, and in Saudi Arabia veiled female university students are now permitted to work with their male instructors (albeit, as yet, via closed circuit T.V.). In Papua New Guinea, where married women risk prison sentences for having affairs while men escape penalties, there are plans to reform adultery laws. In an Arab country an old male chauvinist folk tale with a new feminist twist became a popular opener of the 1975 theater season.[3]

There is a darker side, however, to this movement for equality. Just as women are clamoring for and attaining opportunities in the legitimate fields, some among them are prying their way into the arena of major crime by succeeding at illegitimate endeavors which traditionally have been "for men only." When we consider that the barriers which once protected male prerogatives are breaking down and socially defined gender roles are looking increasingly alike, it should come as no surprise that once women are armed with male opportunities they would endeavour to gain status, criminal as well as civil. The fact that woman is advancing so aptly into male positions strongly suggests that the old order rested much more on male cultural domination than on female genetic destiny. While historically it has been, in fact, a man's world, it does not follow that modern man is biologically more dominant than the modern female. Since culture is the final determinant of which characteristics are labelled dominant, it can certainly be argued that the universal dominance of the male may well have grown more from the institutionalization of man's superior physical strength than from innate feminine submissiveness.

Of those parameters that do distinguish the sexes some have been linked with the overrepresentation of men in the criminal justice system: size, strength, aggression and dominance. While the first two are biological givens, the latter are primarily learned. However, even in non-technological societies, where size and strength were often the final arbiters of social interaction, modern advances, especially the wide distribution of machines, electronic devices and firearms, reduced the significance of these attributes. But machinery and technology are not the only equalizers. As women gain entrance into the professional, occupational and social world, with all of its liabilities and assets, they are also subjected to the same temptations, stresses and frustrations to which men have fallen prey historically. That the social and emotional concomitants of immersion into the heretofore male world are just as powerful as the technological equalizers is dramatically evidenced by the steadily changing criminal behaviors of women throughout the world.

Newspapers in many countries are increasingly informing the public about a changing breed of feminine offender. Although universally, males continue to commit the greater number of offenses, women are beginning to emulate their patterns in both forms and dimensions of criminality, and world wide statistics are indicative of these trends. In the United States, for example, the total arrest rate among females has been rising nearly four times faster than that of males.[4] During the time span between 1960 to 1975, the number of women arrested for robbery rose by 380% while the male figures rose 214%. Similar differences are found in fraud (up 488% for women, 91% for men), larceny (up 465% for women, 130% for men), and burglary (up 298% for women, 117% for men). There has not yet been a comparatively accelerated increase in female arrests for murder and aggravated assaults. This may indicate that female offenders, like their male counterparts, are primarily concerned with bettering their financial positions. On the other hand, the fact that there has been a dramatic increase in female arrest rates for possession of deadly weapons does not augur well for the future numbers of women involved in violent offenses.

Data from other nations concur with the American experience that as the social and economic disparity between the sexes decreases, there is a correlative increase in female criminality.[5] In Western Europe and Australia, for instance, where women enjoy a high degree of equality with men, there has been a rise in the female crime rate. Conversely, the male-female crime rate disparities are most pronounced in countries such as Fiji and Malawi where the social gap between the sexes as yet remains greater.[6] It would, thus, appear that the closer the social standing of sexes vis-a-vis each other, the more similar is their crime rate.[7] Although at this point little cross-cultural data are available to confirm the size of the worldwide female criminality trend, most of the scant statistical evidence demonstrates that the increasing crime rate is a universal phenomenon. Japan's White Paper on Crime, for instance, presents data showing that during the period between 1962 and 1972, the number of female non-traffic Penal Code offenders investigated by the police has increased 1.13 times, contrasted to a decrease 0.78 times for males.[8] Consequently, the percentage of females in the total number of offenders has increased from 9.8% in 1962 to 13.6% in 1972. During this period female arrests for gambling have risen 2.08 times, followed by robbery 1.40 times, larceny 1.30 times, indecency 1.28 times, homicide 1.20 times, extortion 1.10 times and arson 1.08 times. The rates of increase of female arrests for robbery, larceny, homicide and extortion are even more dramatic when compared with decreased figures for men. Table 1 shows the percentage of females in the total number of non-traffic Penal Code offenders investigated by the police. The consistency of the increase is quite apparent.

Similarly, in England and Wales, the number of women convicted in all courts of indictable offenses excluding dangerous driving causing bodily injury or death, has increased 1.87 times between 1961 and 1971 compared with 1.71 times for males.[9] Consequently, the percentage of females in the total number of persons convicted has risen from 13.5% in 1961 to 14.5% in 1971. Rates of increase during this time period show that convictions for indecency have increased 6.0 times, followed by arson 4.56 times, robbery 2.88 times, extortion 2.86 times, stolen property 2.82 times, fraud 2.65 times and homicide 1.53 times.

In the Federal Republic of Germany, the number of female Penal Code offenders investigated by the police (including both felony and misdemeanor, but excluding traffic offenses and the violation of the National Defense Act) has risen 1.33 times between 1963 and 1970, compared with 1.18 times for males.[10] The percentage of females in the total number of offenders has increased from 15.4% in 1963 to 17.1% in 1970. During that time the number of investigated females charged with robbery and robbery-like extortion increased 2.85 times, followed by larceny 2.08 times, arson 1.75 times, murder and homicide 1.42 times and aggravated injury 1.05 times. The rates of increase in robbery and robbery-like extortion, larceny and arson were greater than for males. It is quite apparent that although absolute numbers remain relatively small, slow, steady increases are occurring and, what is even more dramatic, these trends are greatest in property offenses such as larceny, serious offenses against the person such as homicide, and property/personal offenses, such as robbery and extortion, offenses historically considered "masculine."

Canadian statistics point to similar trends. They show that in 1969 women constituted 14% of the total number of persons charged with indictable offenses. In that same year, 6% of all violent crimes against the person were committed by women.[11] However, in 1960 7% of the persons charged with indictable offenses were women and 5% of the violent offenses were committed by them.[12] Except for a small peak during the war years, followed by a decrease after the war, the female crime rate in New Zealand (see Table 2) remained relatively low and constant between 1937 and 1953. After 1953, the rate increased steadily. Total charges preferred against females in the Magistrates' Courts during the period 1937 to 1965 indicate this rise.[13]

In 1971 more than 7000 persons were punished for crime (excluding misdemeanors) in Norway.[14] Approximately 700 were women. A contemporary diagram of female crime in that country would reflect the fact that women today participate in all areas of life and not just those directly connected with

Table 1 **Percentage of females in the total number of offenders in Japan**

YEAR	PERCENTAGE OF TOTAL
1962	9.8
1968	11.6
1969	11.9
1970	12.5
1971	13.3
1972	13.6

their family, kinship, or neighborhood as in the past. Dating back to the initial Norwegian statistics of 1860, and until 1958, never had females accounted for more than 4% of the criminal population. But at that time an upward trend began. Presently, women account for about 10% of the total crime census. Interestingly, during the entire period, theft and other crimes for material gains represented the majority of female crime.

Brazilian data show that although females have consistently accounted for 4 or 5% of the total arrests between 1957 and 1971, in terms of absolute

Table 2

YEAR	TOTAL CHARGES	CHARGES PER 100,000 FEMALES
1937	2800	358
1938	3000	379
1939	3000	374
1940	2600	319
1941	2500	303
1942	3300	394
1943	2900	343
1944	3200	373
1945	2900	334
1946	2700	306
1947	2400	267
1948	2800	306
1949	2900	311
1950	2900	305
1951	3000	309
1952	3700	373
1953	4600	452
1954	3800	365
1955	4300	405
1956	5300	488
1957	5700	514
1958	6800	599
1959	6600	569
1960	7700	651
1961	8900	737
1962	9900	800
1963	11000	869
1964	14000	1083
1965	14500	1101

numbers of offenses, among females there has been an 89% increase (from 1310 to 2479), whereas among males the percentage increase was 43% (from 32,139 to 46,268).[15] For women perpetrators, offenses against the person remain low, morals offenses (e.g. prostitution) remain high, abortion, drug addiction and terrorism are increasing, and other crimes, including organized crime, continue to have a low incidence.[16] In many other countries, the increases also are not as pronounced, but nevertheless are observable in the statistics. In Finland, for example, where females have accounted for approximately 5% of all prosecuted persons every year since 1950, in terms of absolute numbers, female prosecutions have increased 55%, males 53%.[17]

Developing countries are not immune to the phenomenon of rising female crime. According to the 1973 statistics from the Central Bureau of Correctional Services of the Government of India there was a 1.2% increase in the male compared to a 46% increase in the female convict population between 1961 and 1965[18] (see Table 3). A trend analysis suggests the consistency of the rise[19] (see Table 4). In like fashion, other developing countries are just beginning to feel the effects of female emancipation. In the East African nations, for instance, where women had been traditionally relegated to low status positions, changing conditions are opening new opportunities, new challenges, and new problems. It is in the urban areas where women are finding growing advantages in politics, freedom of choice in marriage, legal rights, education and employment. These females are experiencing a twofold problem. They are undergoing difficult adaptation: (a) from rural life with its subsistence economy, home education and extended family group to urban existence where the swift pace leaves many behind; and (b) from the security inherent in traditional female roles to the lifestyle of a newly liberated woman. For many who find the compounded stress too arduous, an easy way up or a quick way out is sought and either route leads to deviant behavior. Recent reports from this sector are already indicating that the "drop-out" rate of East African girls is becoming a very serious problem.[20]

The long range Polish data do not appear to support our hypothesis. However, if we consider that Polish women entered the labor force *en masse* a quarter century earlier than Western European or American women, it becomes clear that the Polish experience is consonant with the theory of this paper. The Polish female crime rate increased significantly during the years— following World War II—when Polish women were first fully integrated into the socio-economic maelstrom of Polish life (see Table 5). Interestingly

Table 3 **Sex-wise classification of convicts and undertrials in India**

Year	Male		Female	
	Convicts	Undertrials	Convicts	Undertrials
1961	354 584	484 328	11 000	12 158
1965	359 106	526 922	16 010	17 625
Percentage increase over 1961	1.2	9.0	46	45

Table 4 **Indian prison population: percentage increase over 1961**

	Convicts		Undertrials	
Year	Male	Female	Male	Female
1962	0.0	6.3	0.1	2.1
1963	4.1	3.6	1.9	4.6
1964	10.1	21.4	11.6	31.8
1965	1.2	46.0	8.9	45.0

enough, the subsequent decrease of the female crime rate may give rise to the hypothesis that normative controls (e.g. church and state) may have continued to operate, for within a decade, Polish female criminality had dropped to below pre–World War II levels. Could it be that emancipation transcended the traditional normative controls only temporarily? Could it be that there is a major difference between vocational liberation and psychological liberation? These questions as yet remain unanswered.

Up to this point we have been discussing adult female criminality. By definition the adult arrest rate is indicative of the present state of crime. But it is the statistics for juveniles under eighteen which give us an indication of future trends in rates of adult criminality. Historically, the female delinquency rate has trailed far behind the male rate. Since the end of World War II this has changed radically for many countries. Unprecedented social forces must have been at work to produce this development. The Uniform Crime Reports of the United States show that not only does the female delinquency rate outstrip the male delinquency rate by far but, in most categories, it outstrips even the adult female crime rate.[21] This amounts to saying that we will have more crime among tomorrow's female adults than we have among today's and that the gap between male and female adult crime rates will narrow even further (Table 6).

A recent German study indicates similar trends in that country.[22] Hidden delinquency research conducted in 1969 and replicated in 1974 shows that in the former year there were 9.1 offenses per boy and 5.4 per girl while in the latter year this changed to 14.3 per boy and 8.1 per girl. In terms of percentage increase, there was an increase for boys of 74%, and for girls, of 80%. The offenses showing the greatest increase for girls are drinking alcohol in public, disorderly behavior, auto theft and shoplifting.

Table 5 **Percent of total convictions in Poland**

Year	Male	Female
1932	83.3	16.7
1951	74.1	25.9
1960	79.6	20.4
1962	81.7	18.3
1966	85.2	14.3
1968	87.1	12.9
1972	88.6	11.4

Table 6 **Arrest percentage change (1960–75)***

CRIME	MALE		FEMALE	
	Under 18	Over 18	Under 18	Over 18
Criminal homicide:				
(a) murder and non-negligent manslaughter	205.7	138.2	275	105.7
(b) manslaughter by negligence	30.2	−20.2	333.3	−4.8
Aggravated assault	217.1	130.6	438	118.8
Robbery	361.3	214.3	646.8	380.5
Burglary	132	116.9	327.5	288.8
Larceny-theft	117.7	129.6	457.3	464.6
Auto theft	19.5	35.6	140.3	163.2

* Data from Uniform Crime Reports, 1975.

Comparable statistics for England and Wales point out that between 1960 and 1970, the rate of girls 17 to 20 found guilty in the courts doubled, while the rate for boys increased by less than half[23] (Table 7). It is no longer uncommon for these youngsters to participate in burglaries, auto theft and even extortion rings which prey upon schoolmates. What is more, they are even beginning to challenge the all-male domain of gang activity. Either as equal participants with males or as rivals in their own all-girl gangs, they are beginning to terrorize the streets as boys have done for generations. In London, for instance, Scotland Yard is expressing alarm over these new female gangs, presently numbering in the dozens, who rove the streets at night attacking old ladies with switchblades and razors.

Of the hundreds of studies of the various aspects of juvenile delinquency[24] the deviancy of girls has been the subject of only a few. Those who have focused on female delinquency have generally emphasized the demographic and behavioral aspects of sexual proclivities.[25] In other words, more concentration has been placed on transgressions from the female sex role expectation than from the criminal code. Hidden delinquency studies among high school students, however, reveal a considerable amount of female delinquency of the kind that is ordinarily expected from boys,[26] and it appears to be correlated with unisexual role expectations. Since delinquent activity is patterned after non-delinquent behavior, there is reason to anticipate that as the latter sex roles merge, so will the former.[27]

Because juvenile delinquency was, until recently, almost exclusively a male activity to which girls made an unimportant contribution, major theorists have sought explanations for delinquency in the study of male psychology.

Table 7 **Persons found guilty**

	GIRLS			BOYS		
	1960	1970	% Increase	1960	1970	% Increase
Number	6767	15 623		138 728	235 262	
Rate per 100,000	589	1666	98	12 116	17 235	42

However, because social forces play a more decisive role in shaping behavior than biological forces,[28] the factors advanced to explain male delinquency should apply equally well to females. The greater freedom enjoyed by males in every social stratum provided them with easier access to peer groups, while girls were usually limited to the family circle. Interestingly, many of the factors which theorists[29] have advanced as causative of male delinquency—confusing early models, a sharp role shift at puberty, and peer reinforcement of aggression—apply as well to the modern girl. She is increasingly disaffected by restraints inherent in her mother's homemaking role; she is prodded into entering fields formerly barred to females, and changing social mores grant her access to increasingly aggressive peer groups. Furthermore, they are observing patterns of sex role convergence in their parents which provide undifferentiated models of behavior. Both in the way parents act and in their expectations of their adolescent boys and girls there is a pressure toward gender uniformity in attitudes, values and practices.[30] This assimilation of sex roles often amounts to an obscuring of boundaries which have traditionally subdued and safeguarded girls.

One of the most frequently cited cultural influences upon delinquency is economic. The relationship between growing affluence and delinquency rates has been the subject of reports from many countries, including Japan, Argentina, Sweden, the Netherlands, England and U.S.S.R.[31] There are, however, existing societies which have no concept of delinquency.[32] This is so because they have no traditional period of adolescence, no period of uncertainty of the future, aimlessness, boredom or lack of parental control. In folk communities, like the traditional Eskimo village, certain tribes of India, some barrios of Mexico, the minimal problems of bad boys and contrary girls are handled informally at the family level. For other villages, those in the transitory period between folk and urban standards, contact with developed cultures has disseminated new notions to some of the youngsters, control by the elders is no longer acceptable and a new phase in the life cycle—social adolescence—that time of rebellious and impulsive behavior, is spawned. In several ways, that period of social adolescence is most traumatic for the teenage girls reared in developing countries. For them it is a transition within a transition. Not only must they learn to become women in an urbanized structure, but they must also cope with the uncertainties of the female's position in that structure. Adolescence becomes a span of psychological limbo fraught with attempts to use role models who themselves are in a tenuous position. With technological advances reducing the number of unskilled jobs and cultural changes redefining a woman's place, never before have so many young females had so much incentive to desert traditional roles and so few opportunities to find new ones. A rise in delinquency under such turbulent conditions is predictable.

The activities of another group of young women, the politicized females, are likewise increasing and becoming more violent. Recently, there was a fervor created throughout the United States when kidnapped newspaper heiress Patricia Hearst became an enthusiastic member of a political clique which called itself the Symbionese Liberation Army. What was remarkable about this episode was not so much the revolutionary activities—since the sixties Americans had watched student strikes, riots and urban guerrilla warfare—

but the fact that women had organized and staged it. No longer satisfied with their traditional limitation to the typewriter, the mimeograph machine, and the coffee-maker, they are increasingly taking a more active role in the turbulent confrontations. So aggressive did their activities become that on 28 December 1968 the females of the United States reached a criminal landmark when the first one of them was admitted to the infamous Federal Bureau of Investigation "Ten Most Wanted" list.[33] Since that time the inclusion of women for murder, robbery, kidnapping and violent revolutionary acts has become quite common. West Germany, too, has had world-wide newspaper coverage of its new breed of urban guerrilla—the female terrorist. Ten of the sixteen persons accused of being leading figures in the Baader-Meinholf gang and twenty-two of the 52 alleged terrorists who have been captured are female.[34]

In other parts of the globe women took active roles in the Entebbe highjacking incident, the bombing of a Stockholm embassy, and the Vienna kidnapping of ministers from the Organization of Petroleum Exporting Countries. In sum, there was a time when inhuman hurricanes had female names. Today the human storms include Ulrike Meinholf, Emily Harris, and Leila Khaled.

Summary

What I have depicted is a slow, but increasing social revolution in which females are lessening the distance, legitimate and illegitimate, which has separated them from men. As the gap narrows, the more similar they look and behave. To be sure there are inherent differences between men and women, but changing behavioral patterns demonstrate that women are first human, then female. Their needs and abilities are similar to those of men. Their opportunities have been different. Women's needs have not changed, but their opportunities are increasing,[35] producing new forms and dimensions of behavior whose full richness and variety have not yet been realized and whose final configuration will have universal effects.[36] Now that they have tapped into the springs of socio-political life, we are finding out that females are not as adverse as men tried to make them believe they were to taking undue advantage of their new positions.

Notes

1. Ralph Slovenko, Are Women More Law Abiding Than Men?, *Police* 1964 (July-August).
2. *Washington Post*, 31 March 1967.
3. *New York Times*, 7 October 1975.
4. Crime in the United States, *Uniform Crime Reports*, U.S. Department of Justice, Washington, D.C., U.S. Government Printing Office, 1975, p. 183.
5. E. H. Sutherland & D. R. Cressey, *Principles of Criminology*. Philadelphia, J. B. Lippincott Co., 1966 (originally published 1924), p. 139.
6. International Criminal Police Organization (INTERPOL) Statistics, 1970.

7. See H. von Hentig, *The Criminality of the Colored Woman.* University of Colorado Studies, Series C. I. No. 3. 1942.
8. Summary of the White Paper on Crime, the Research and Training Institute of the Ministry of Justice, Government of Japan, 1973.
9. Home Office, Criminal Statistics, England and Wales, 1961, 1971.
10. Polizeiliche Kriminalstatistik, Deutsche Bundesrepublik, 1963, 1970.
11. Statistics Canada, Statistics on Criminal and Other Offenses, 1969 (Catalogue 85-201) Ottawa: Information Canada, 1973, Table 2. Note: figures do not include Alberta and Quebec.
12. Dominion Bureau Statistics, Statistics of Criminal and Other Offenses, 1960 (Catalogue 85-201) Ottawa: Queen's Printer, 1962, Table 2 and 5.
13. Crime in New Zealand, New Zealand Department of Justice, Wellington, New Zealand, R. E. Owen, 1968.
14. Verbal communication with Dr. Niles Christie.
15. Anúario Estatístico do Brazil, Institute Brasileiro de Estatística, Fundacão Instituto Brasileiro de Geografia and Estatistica, 1954–1973.
16. Written Communication with Dr. Ayush Amar, Member of the Penitentiary Council of the State of São Paolo.
17. Statistics, Crimes Known to the Police, Helsinki, Finland, 1970.
18. Neera Kuckreja Sohoni, Women Prisoners, *The Indian Journal of Social Work* 1974 (July) **35**, 2, p. 137–148.
19. *Ibid.*
20. The Status and Role of Women in East Africa, Social Welfare Services in Africa, United Nations, New York, June, 1967, p. 10.
21. *Uniform Crime Reports, op. cit.*, p. 183.
22. Gerd Ferdinand Kirchhoff, "Self Reported Delinquency: Methodological Notes and Findings of a Replication Study," paper presented at the meeting of the American Society of Criminology in Tucson, Arizona, 1976.
23. Girl Offenders Aged 17 to 20 Years, A Home Office Research Unit Report, London. Her Majesty's Stationery Office, 1972.
24. For an overview of the subject see, David Matza, *Becoming Deviant.* Englewood Cliffs, New Jersey, Prentice-Hall, 1969.
25. See, for example, Clyde B. Vedder and Dora B. Somerville, *The Delinquent Girl*, Springfield, Ill.: Charles C. Thomas, 1970.
26. Nancy Barton Wise, "Juvenile Delinquency Among Middle Class Girls" in *Middle-Class Juvenile Delinquency*, Edmund W. Vaz (ed.). New York, Harper and Row, 1967, p. 187.
27. *Ibid.*, p. 188.
28. See Margaret Mead, *Sex and Temperament in Three Primitive Societies.* New York, William Morrow and Co., 1963 (originally published in 1935).
29. T. Parsons, Certain Primary Sources and Patterns of Aggression in the Social Structure of the Western World, *Psychiatry* 1947 (May), **10**, 168–81; Parsons, Age and Sex in the Social Structure of the United States, *American Sociological Review*, 1942 (October) **7**, 604–16.
30. Wise, *op. cit.*, p. 181.
31. *Japan*—Jackson Toby, Affluence and Adolescent Crime, In the President's Commission on Law Enforcement and Administration of Justice, Task Force on Juvenile Delinquency: *Task Force Report: Juvenile Delinquency and Youth Crime*, Washington, D.C.: U.S. Government Printing Office, 1967.
      Argentina—Lois B. DeFleur, *Delinquency in Argentina*, Pullman, Washington: Washington State University Press, 1970.
      Sweden—Toby, *op. cit.*

418 *A cross-cultural perspective*

    Netherlands—J. E. Baur, The Trend of Juvenile Offenses in the Netherlands and the United States, *Journal of Criminal Law, Criminology, and Police Science* 1964 **55**, 359–369.

    U.S.S.R. Ibid.

32. Ruth S. Cavan & Jordan T. Cavan, *Delinquency and Crime: Cross-Cultural Perspective*, Philadelphia, Lippincott Co., 1968.
33. "Ten Most Wanted Fugitives Program," United States Department of Justice, Federal Bureau of Investigation, Washington, D.C., December 28, 1968.
34. *Los Angeles Times*, 18 November 1976.
35. For an excellent discussion of the relationship between the changing social and economic status of women and its relationship to property offenses see Rita J. Simon, *Women and Crime*, Lexington, Lexington Books, 1975.
36. Freda Adler, *Sisters in Crime*, New York, McGraw Hill, 1975.

Index